SCHOLASTIC JOURNALISM

Tenth Edition

im to take the class as a stud

only to observe. He quickly a

reaks that rule.

HiLite What do you make

om atmosphere at Capesi

K: They offer film classes

hy can't we have film classe

e classes they take, we'd b

A: Well, all the characte

here's the ditz and the joc

alistic. In your classes you

here are the gangsters?

K: I think if there were n

now they'd make it really

ey were, like on "Saved by

R: In (Capeside) high s

ems to be drama people an

re no gangsters, no skaters.

o perfect. Their football fu

ss, even more so than Carr

SCHOLASTIC JOURNALISM

Tenth Edition

IOWA STATE UNIVERSITY PRESS/AMES

TOM E. ROLNICKI

C. DOW TATE

SHERRI TAYLOR

Tom (Thomas) E. Rolnicki has served as executive director of the National Scholastic Press Association and the Associated Collegiate Press at the University of Minnesota since 1980. He is also executive director of the groups' periodicals, *Trends in High School Media* and *Trends in College Media*. He has spoken at scholastic journalism conferences and workshops throughout the United States and in Canada, Germany, South Korea, Japan, Croatia and the Czech Republic and has received the Carl Towley and Medal of Merit awards from the Journalism Education Association and the Gold Key from the Columbia Scholastic Press Association.

C. Dow Tate is a journalism teacher at Hillcrest High School in Dallas, Texas, and the director of the Dallas County School Gloria Shield All-American Publications Workshop in Dallas. He is also a member of the Texas University Interscholastic League advisory board and the Texas A&M–Commerce University Journalism and Graphic Arts Department advisory board. His students' publications have earned the nation's highest honors, including the National Scholastic Press Association's National Pacemaker and the Columbia Scholastic Press Association's Gold Crown. Tate has been named the Dow Jones Newspaper Fund's National High School Journalism Teacher of the Year as well as the Texas Max R. Haddick Teacher of the Year.

Sherri Taylor teaches graphic design in the Visual and Interactive Communications Department of the S.I. Newhouse School of Public Communications at Syracuse University in Syracuse, New York. She is the director of the Empire State School Press Association for New York schools and directs the School Press Institute, a summer journalism workshop for scholastic journalists. She was formerly an award-winning publications adviser and journalism teacher in Irving, Texas. She was inducted into the Scholastic Journalism Hall of Fame at the University of Oklahoma and received the Gold Key award from the Columbia Scholastic Press Association and the Pioneer Award from the National Scholastic Press Association.

© 2001 Iowa State University Press
All rights reserved

Iowa State University Press
2121 South State Avenue, Ames, Iowa 50014

Orders: 1-800-862-6657
Office: 1-515-292-0140
Fax: 1-515-292-3348
Web site: www.isupress.com

Authorization to photocopy items for internal or personal use, or the internal or personal use of specific clients, is granted by Iowa State University Press, provided that the base fee of $.10 per copy is paid directly to the Copyright Clearance Center, 222 Rosewood Drive, Danvers, MA 01923. For those organizations that have been granted a photocopy license by CCC, a separate system of payments has been arranged. The fee code for users of the Transactional Reporting Service is 0-8138-2753-1 (paperback) and 0-8138-2751-5 (cloth)/ 2001 $.10.

♾ Printed on acid-free paper in the United States of America

Tenth edition, 2001

First edition *Scholastic Journalism* copyrighted 1950 and carried through four printings. Revised from *Exercises in Journalism*, first copyrighted 1939 and continued through nine printings.
Second edition, 1957 (cloth/pbk)
Third edition, 1962 (cloth/pbk)
Fourth edition, 1968 (cloth/pbk)
Fifth edition, 1972 (cloth/pbk)
Sixth edition, 1978 (cloth/pbk)
Seventh edition, 1984 (cloth/pbk)
Eighth edition, 1990 (cloth/pbk)
Ninth edition, 1996 (cloth/pbk)

Rolnicki, Tom E.
    Scholastic journalism / Tom E. Rolnicki, C. Dow Tate, Sherri Taylor.—10th ed.
        p. cm.
    Includes bibliographical references and index.
    ISBN 0-8138-2751-5 (cloth: alk. paper)—ISBN 0-8138-2753-1 (paperback: alk. paper) 1. Journalism, School. 2. Journalism. I. Tate, C. Dow. II. Taylor, Sherri. III. Title.

LB3621 .E52 2001
373.18'97—dc21   2001016927

The last digit is the print number: 10 9 8 7 6 5 4 3 2 1

Contents

PREFACE

After 10 years of personal training with a coach, a student at your school qualifies for the summer Olympics. She is a diver and has already won several national titles. As a reporter for your high school print and online newspaper, you write a story about her achievements. Your story will be read by hundreds of students at your school and others. The day the paper is published, your story is big news. Tomorrow, another person, another event is in the spotlight, and another reporter's work is praised. That's the fleeting nature of most journalism, but knowing that you were first to tell a story to the world is still satisfying.

Journalism is the first draft of history. High school journalists, whether they are reporting for their school newspaper, yearbook, magazine, broadcast news program or web site, are covering stories today that later may be significant milestones of the history of our nation and world community. This realization can inspire some to excel, to do their best, and others to shy away without trying.

High school journalism is serious business, full of excitement and potential. It's for those who understand its importance, accept its challenges and push its boundaries beyond the traditional forms of print and broadcast into new mediums made possible through telecommunications, the Internet and computers.

High school journalism is all about today and tomorrow, all about the application of new media, new technology and all the skills developed through the centuries to inform, entertain and persuade others.

If there ever was a time to champion high school journalism as a training ground and an essential part of a core curriculum and praise its merits, it is today in this new century. Although it has barely begun, the 21st century is already characterized as the age of information. How we disseminate information and how we use it is at the center of our lives, and journalists are in the forefront of those who are directing the communications revolution.

This revolution, which began in the 1980s with the launch of desktop publishing, is evident in our high school newsrooms. There is not much difference in the kind of technology used to report and produce news at many high schools and at *The New York Times*. And, in some respects, there is little difference between the content of a high school newspaper or online news site than what is published in a commercial newspaper or other nonstudent media.

A big story today is likely to be reported by student journalists whether it happens in the school's community or thousands of miles away. With the Internet as a tool, the world is now a beat for many high school journalists. War in a foreign country, deadly violence in a school in another state, or pending legislation in Congress are all potential stories for the student reporter. By adding a student or local angle, these national and world stories are now common in high school media.

Canadian media philosopher Marshall McLuhan's "global village" is a reality for student journalists. Telecommunications has made Croatia as close as the Carolinas for students in Virginia.

The results of this access to the world, to primary sources and a wealth of information so vast it would be impossible to read it all in a lifetime, is great reporting and diverse coverage that benefits the readers. Student journalists are more professional, more concerned about accuracy and fairness than ever before.

Most long-term observers of high school student media agree that student journalism is better than ever. For the first time in 2000, a high school student won a Dupont award for excellence in broadcast journalism. He reported, on National Public Radio and in his school paper, the effects of the war in Kosovo on a high school girl who lived there. He found his source on the Internet.

If anyone is surprised by the professionalism of student media today and the exemplary work done by students who contribute to it in many ways, verbally and visually, they shouldn't be. "Journalism kids do better," according to leading high school journalism researchers, including Jack Dvorak, a journalism professor at Indiana University, and others. On the Advanced Placement English Language and Composition Examination, students who had taken a special intensive journalism writing course scored higher six consecutive years in the 1990s than students who had taken honors or Advanced Placement English and no journalism. By this measure and many others, journalism "kids" excel in academics and apply what they learn in journalism to other pursuits.

Journalism students aren't necessarily brighter than their peers who don't take a journalism writing course or don't participate in student media; journalism students are often just better prepared to assimilate information and communicate verbally. These essential life skills help them immeasurably in whatever they do.

Many of the most respected and accomplished journalists of the late 20th century—some still work in media today—began their careers as student journalists. They include Allen Neuharth, founder of *USA Today*; Bernard Shaw, CNN; Dave Barry, nationally syndicated humor columnist; Abigail Van Buren, "Dear Abby"; Katie Couric, NBC *Today Show*; Robert L. Bartley, editor, *Wall Street Journal*; and Walter Cronkite, retired anchor, *CBS News*. They, and so many others, attribute their success in part to the encouragement and satisfaction they got working on student media. Considering their successes later, journalism "kids" do do better.

Even though the tools journalists use today are different than they used 20 years ago and any one student who has these tools can be reporter, designer, photographer, editor and publisher of his or her own news medium, there is still great value in traditional and new student media published or produced at school. Group learning and teamwork, which are part of a successful student media program, foster leadership and responsibility. An adviser can nurture a fledgling journalist who one day may become a network news anchor, editor of *The New York Times*, or winner of a Pulitzer Prize.

Journalism teachers and media advisers who are preparing today's journalism students—the "kids" who do better—to become astute media consumers and tomorrow's media leaders need some help with this important job. For more than 50 years, this textbook has answered that need.

Scholastic Journalism meets the needs of teachers and advisers who are looking for a comprehensive textbook for beginning and advanced journalism classes and a resource for student newspaper and yearbook production. With its emphasis on reporting and writing, it is also useful for new media—Internet news sites—and broadcast news programs. The chapters on ethics and law are increasingly essential for everyone, including the adviser. The many examples of exemplary student work—long a distinguishing characteristic of this text—inspire students to meet and exceed the standards set by their peers.

The authors are committed to diversity, fairness and equality. Examples of student work feature a multicultural population. References within chapters, such as Chapter 12, "Using Journalism Style," include points on diversity. Student media are encouraged to welcome all students of all population groups into their ranks, for diversity contributes to excellence. Paraphrasing what Professor Dvorak said, journalism kids of all colors, religions, ethnic origins, sexual orientations and social backgrounds "do better." All educators and the authors of this textbook want all "kids" to succeed.

Scholastic Journalism's authors are indebted to the students, advisers and others who shared their work and their helpful advice so a new generation of students could continue the tradition of student-published media in secondary schools. It's a tradition of excellence that is one of the most practical, beneficial and personally rewarding activities and courses of study within the school. Thank you Professor Dvorak and colleagues for proving what many already suspected.

Now, armed with this textbook, students must live up to this accolade and keep doing better as they report the first drafts of history in this new century.

ACKNOWLEDGMENTS

We'd like to thank a long list of teachers, colleagues, friends and corporations who helped us in the preparation of the tenth edition. Their support, insight and help in providing permission to use material from their newspapers and yearbooks have been invaluable in producing this textbook.

Robert Adamson, Ridley High School, Folsom, Pa.

Logan Aimone, Wenatchee High School, Wenatchee, Wash.

Martha Akers, Loudoun Valley High School, Purcellville, Va.

Jim Allen, Lancaster High School, Lancaster, Calif.

Bev Arnold, Jostens, Minneapolis, Minn.

Dan Austin, Casa Roble High School, Orangevale, Calif.

Judy Babb, (formerly) Highland Parok High School, Highland Park, Texas

Austin Bah, Tamalpais High School, Mill Valley, Calif.

Susan Baird, Bellevue East High School, Bellevue, Neb.

Brother Stephen V. Balletto, Chaminade High School, Mineola, N.Y.

Sue Barr, South Eugene High School, Eugene, Ore.

Janelle Bates, Woodrow Wilson High School, Dallas, Texas

Marjorie Bell, Bakersfield High School, Bakersfield, Calif.

Robert and Penny Belsher, Ferris, Texas

Lew Bernes, Birmingham High School, Van Nuys, Calif.

Laurie Bielong, Belleville Township High School, Belleville, Ill.

Don Bott, Amos Alonzo Stagg High School, Stockton, Calif.

Jackie Boucher, Essex Junction High School, Essex Junction, Vt.

John Bowen, Lakewood High School, Lakewood, Ohio

Jan Bowman, Walt Whitman High School, Bethesda, Md.

Diane Boyle, Parkway Central High School, Chesterfield, Mo.

Wayne Brasler, University High School, Chicago, Ill.

Pam Carlquist, Park City High School, Park City, Utah

Meg Carnes, Robert E. Lee High School, Springfield, Va.

Rebecca Castillo, Columbia Scholastic Press Association, New York, N.Y.

Claude Catapano, Horace Mann School, Riverdale, N.Y.

Gary Clites, Northern High School, Owings, Md.

Charles Cooper, National Press Photographers Association, Durham, N.C.

Ron Cueba, Overfelt High School, San Jose, Calif.

Jeff Currie, Oak Park and River Forest High School, Oak Park, Ill.

Kathy Daly, Overland High School, Aurora, Colo.

Albert DeLuca, James Madison University, Harrisonburg, Va.

Kay Dillard, Abilene High School, Abilene, Texas
Drake University, Des Moines, Iowa
Jon Paul Dumont, Indiana University, Bloomington, Ind.
Terry Durnell, Lee's Summit North High School, Lee's Summit, Mo.
Jennifer Dusenberry, Dallas, Texas
Lori Eastman, (formerly) Arvada High School, Arvada, Colo.
Ray Elliott, University High School, Urbana, Ill.
Paul Ender, (formerly) Independence High School, San Jose, Calif.
Brenda Feldman, Coral Gables High School, Coral Gables, Fla.
Karen Flowers, Irmo High School, Columbia, S.C.
Bob Frischmann, Hazelwood Central High School, Florissant, Mo.
Katherine Gazella, St. Petersburg Times, St. Petersurg, Fla.
Mark Goodman, Student Press Law Center, Washington, D.C.
Brenda Gorsuch, West Henderson High School, Hendersonville, N.C.
Peggy Gregory, Greenway High School, Phoenix, Ariz.
H.L. Hall, (formerly) Kirkwood High School, Kirkwood, Mo.
Jack Harkrider, L.C. Anderson High School, Austin, Tex.
Nancy Hastings, Munster High School, Munster, Ind.
Bobby Hawthorne, University Interscholastic League, Austin, Texas
Alan Heider, Minneapolis, Minn.
Brother Peter Heiskell, Chaminade High School, Mineola, N.Y.
Andrea Henderson, Torrey Pines High School, San Diego, Calif.
Dr. J. Henery, Wooster High School, Wooster, Ohio
Diane Herder, Laingsburg High School, Laingsburg, Mich.
Herff Jones Yearbooks, Montgomery, Ala.
Betty Herman, Putnam City North High School, Oklahoma City, Okla.
HighWired.com
Patricia Hinman, Robinson Middle School, Fairfax, Va.
hj magazine, Syracuse Newspapers, Syracuse, N.Y.
Dean Hume, Lakota East High School, Liberty Township, Ohio
Mark Johnston, City High School, Iowa City, Iowa
Jim Jordan, Del Campo High School, Fair Oaks, Calif.
Paul Kandell, Lowell High School, San Francisco, Calif.
Linda Kane, Naperville Central High School, Naperville, Ill.
Crystal Kazmierski, Arrowhead Christian Academy, Redlands, Calif.
Marilyn Kelsey, Bloomington High School, Bloomington, Ind.
Jack Kennedy, City High School, Iowa City, Iowa
Linda Kennedy, Hinsdale Central High School, Hinsdale, Ill.
Jason King, Kansas City Star, Kansas City, Mo.

David Knight, Lancaster, S.C.

Mitchell Koh, Crossroads School, Santa Monica, Calif.

Nancy Kruh, Dallas Morning News, Dallas, Texas

Deanne Kunz, Westlake High School, Austin, Texas

Pete LeBlanc, Center High School, Antelope, Calif.

Patricia Ladue, McClintock High School, Tempe, Ariz.

Gary Lundgren, Jostens, Minneapolis, Minn.

Steven Lyle, West High School, Davenport, Iowa

Chris McDonald, Viking Shield, Spring Valley High School, Columbia, S.C.

Jim McGonnell, Findlay High School, Findlay, Ohio

Susan Massy, Shawnee Mission Northwest High School, Shawnee, Kan.

John Mathwin, Montgomery Blair High School, Silver Spring, Md.

Steve Matson, Charles Wright Academy, Tacoma, Wash.

Faye Milner, Lincoln High School, Tallahassee, Fla.

Cathy Molstad, Wausau, Wis.

Pat Monroe, Burges High School, El Paso, Texas

Peggy Morton, Stephen F. Austin High School, Austin, Texas

Mark Murray, (formerly) Lamar High School, Arlington, Texas

Kathy Neumeyer, Harvard-Westlake School, North Hollywood, Calif.

Newspaper Career Guide, Newspaper Association of America, Vienna, Va.

Erik Olson, Laguna Creek High School, Elk Grove, Calif.

Janet Owens, Gresham High School, Gresham, Ore.

Jane Pak, Dallas, Texas

Joe Pfeiff, Mountain Ridge High School, Glendale, Ariz.

Marci Pieper, Clayton High School, Clayton, Mo.

Pizza Hut, Inc., Dallas, Texas

David Porreca, University High School, Urbana, Ill.

Mary Pulliam, Duncanville High School, Duncanville, Texas

Betsy Pollard Rau, H.H. Dow High School, Midland, Mich.

Carol Richtsmeier, DeSoto High School, DeSoto, Texas

Tim Roberts, San Dieguito High School Academy, Encinitas, Calif.

James Rogers, Ferris, Texas

Polly Rolnicki, Wausau, Wis.

Kathy Rossi, John W. North High School, Riverside, Calif.

John Scott, Thomas Downey High School, Modesto, Calif.

Natalie Sekicky, Shaker Heights High School, Shaker Heights, Ohio

Susan Sloan, McLean High School, McLean, Va.

Paul Spadoni, Peninsula High School, Gig Harbor, Wash.

Howard Spanogle, Asheville, N.C.

Dot Stegman, Kapaun Mt. Carmel High School, Wichita, Kan.

Heather Stockdell, Southport High School, Indianapolis, Ind.

Edmund Sullivan, Columbia Scholastic Press Association, New York, N.Y.

Katharine Swan, Lowell High School, San Francisco, Calif.

C. Dow Tate, Hillcrest High School, Dallas, Texas

Lee Terkelsen, Golden West High School, Visalia, Calif.

Barbara Thill, Lyon's Township High School, LaGrange, Ill.

David Thurston, Allen High School, Allen, Texas

TLP Advertising, Dallas, Texas

Bernadette Tucker, Redwood High School, Visalia, Calif.

Tina Turbeville, Crossroads School, Santa Monica, Calif.

Randy Vonderheid, Interscholastic League Press Conference, Austin, Texas

Harvey Wehner, Live Oak High School, Morgan Hill, Calif.

Alan Weintraut, Annandale High School, Annandale, Va.

David Weisenburger, Gahanna Lincoln High School, Gahanna, Ohio

Lorraine Wellenstein, Schurr High School, Montebello, Calif.

Tony Willis, Carmel High School, Carmel, Ind.

Scott Winter, (formerly) Albert Lea High School, Albert Lea, Minn.

Kristie Yellico, (formerly) Arvada High School, Arvada, Colo.

Clay Zigler, Rockwood Summit High School, Fenton, Mo.

Kathleen D. Zwiebel, Tide Lines, Pottsville Area High School, Pottsville, Pa.

Cover Photo Credits

Tim Carroll, Allen High School, Allen, Texas

Steve Doan, Hazelwood Central High School, Florissant, Mo.

Aviva Grinnell, Hillcrest High School, Dallas, Texas

Josh Kaufman, Birmingham High School, Van Nuys, Calif.

Matt Slocum, Duncanville High School, High School, Duncanville, Texas

A TRIBUTE

For more than 50 years Earl English and Clarence Hach trained tens of thousands of students to become journalists through nine editions of *Scholastic Journalism*. The book became a "best-seller" and the standard for all others that followed it. Its half-century of success is a tribute to their dedication, wisdom and love of student journalism. With each new edition, their desire to improve the book and keep it current was unfailing. The book achieved the status as the best of its kind, and this pleased both of them greatly. They always were the consummate teachers. Clarence led the English and journalism programs at Evanston Township High School (Illinois) for many years, and Earl served as the dean of the School of Journalism at the University of Missouri, Columbia, for decades. Clarence died in 1998, and Earl died in 2000. The 10th edition of *Scholastic Journalism* is dedicated to them.

lds that know wha
ure talking about. I
ds on who you're
g to.

don't think they're
ing too intelligently
ere is no immaturity

Go to our school o
ok at how I act some
I mean, we're all re
mmature. They are
ng around and are
Walk down our ha
ng. (The people on t
. The maturity leve

previous episode, th
on was denied entry
g course because he
eacher has bent the r
o take the class as a sn
to observe. He quickl
that rule.

e. What do you ma
atmosphere at Cape
hey offer film class
an't we have film cla
asses they take, we'd
Well, all the charac
's the ditz and the j
ic. In your classes yo
are the gangsters?

think if there were
they'd make it reall
vere, like on "Saved
In (Capeside) high
to be drama people a
gangsters, no skate
rfect. Their football
ven more so than C

(Josh Jackson) conti
his English teacher, M
chool tutorial. This fl
ssing rapidly into a p

SCHOLASTIC JOURNALISM

Tenth Edition

Understanding News

The president of the United States played golf yesterday. You played golf yesterday too. Today, your city newspaper has a picture of the president playing golf on an inside news page; there is no picture of you on the golf course, even though you got a hole-in-one on the ninth, and the president, reportedly, rarely breaks 100 on 18 holes. Why wasn't your achievement reported?

The difference has to do with what news is and what it isn't. Understanding news is fundamental to writing for a news medium, be it a newspaper, magazine, yearbook, broadcast station or Internet site. It is important because it enables a reporter to sort and prioritize information and help readers distinguish between what is relevant—what they need to know—and what is less important, even though readers may be interested in the subject. This understanding of news is also useful to reporters so they can make all stories appealing to readers. Faced with busy readers who can get their news from print, broadcast and Internet sources, a reporter who knows what news is will likely write better than one who doesn't. Delivering information fast and first are two goals of most news organizations today, but the consumer will rely upon and trust that source that delivers it with accuracy and relevance.

The president made news by golfing and you didn't simply because he is the president and you aren't. That's called *prominence*, and it's just one of the many aspects of the definition of news to be explored here.

A DEFINITION OF NEWS

The president as a golfer and why he made news is easily understood, but this is only one part of a more complex definition of news. News, by definition, isn't an orderly, exact list of "it's always this, but never that." Circumstances and nuances can change almost anything into news.

To arrive at an understanding of news, the following points are important to know:

1. News must be factual, yet not all facts are news.

2. News may be opinion, especially that of a prominent person or an authority on a particular subject.

3. News is primarily about people, what they say and do.

4. News is not necessarily a report of a recent event.

5. What is important news to one community or school may be unimportant or have little or no news value in another community or school.

6. What is news in one community or school may be news in every community or school.

7. What is news today is often not news tomorrow.

8. What is news for one person may not be news for another.

9. Two factors necessary to news, interest and importance, are not always synonymous.

Of these nine points, numbers 4 and 9 may need further explanation.

The full text of a news story need not be about a recent occurrence. Often only the first paragraph and one or several follow-up paragraphs contain the facts or opinions that make an old story news again. An event that happened months or even years ago may be news if it has just been disclosed. In the midst of a political campaign, for example, often something in a candidate's past is revealed. Events that have not yet happened may be news.

Interest and importance are not always synonymous because the most important news story is not often the most interesting or compelling one. For example, two stories appear on page 1: the school board announces the building of a new gymnasium for the school and the school's athletic director is being sued for sexual harassment by one of the school's coaches. If you didn't know about either event before the stories were published, which one would you read first? Which would be more interesting to you? Which would be more important and have a greater impact on you? If you think the sexual harassment suit is more interesting than building a new gym, but you think the new gym will have a greater impact on your life, then this illustrates the conflict between important and interesting regarding news value. There are many variables, and personal preference is one of them.

Occasionally a story that receives the most display in a newspaper or time on television or radio is often not very important to most readers or listeners. However, editors decided to devote extensive space or time to the story because it has one or more unique characteristics, sometimes involving a conflict. For example, a story about the rescue of a mountain climber stranded on Mount Everest may not be important to the majority of readers or viewers, but it is interesting to many because of the man against nature conflict that is a big part of the story. When planning their lead or most prominently displayed stories, editors for all media will consider both importance and interest and then choose stories with both elements for the prime, lead-off positions.

HARD NEWS AND SOFT NEWS

News can further be defined as either hard or soft; the difference, to the news consumer, is sometimes obvious and sometimes not.

Hard news has significance for relatively large numbers of readers, listeners and viewers about *timely* events that have just happened or are about to happen in government, politics, foreign affairs, education, labor, religion, courts, financial markets and the like.

Soft news is usually less important because it entertains, though it may also inform, of course, and is often less timely than hard news. It includes human interest and feature stories that may often relate to hard news. It appeals more to emotions than the intellect and the desire to be informed.

For example, the announcement by a software company of its plans to issue public stock is a hard news story. A companion story about the person who started this same software company and her collection of motorcycles is soft news.

Hard news, despite its importance, usually attracts fewer readers, listeners or viewers because it unfortunately is less interesting to many or is often more difficult to understand than soft news, particularly if one has not been following a continuous story every day. Though reporters always "fill in" some essential background, readers need to think about the information presented to comprehend its significance. As a result, much straight reporting of facts for hard news has given way to interpretive reporting in which the reporter explains the significance of facts and gives the background necessary for people to understand what they read, hear or see. Often, this type of story is written by an experienced reporter who is an expert, for example, in foreign affairs or in science. This interpretation, which sometimes borders on informed opinion, usually carries the writer's byline.

In radio and television, this type of interpreted news will be presented by a commentator or by a specialist in the type of news such as in politics. Many reporters and commentators become well-known, and their bylines are sought by readers, listeners and viewers who wish to hear or read stories by certain news analysts or specialists. Today there are special television and radio shows and Internet sites devoted exclusively to discussions of news events. *Meet the Press*, *Crossfire* and *Washington Week in Review* are just a few of the many broadcast and cable television shows that feature journalists analyzing the news. These shows are comparable to the editorial pages in print newspapers and appeal to those who wish to be well informed and hope to learn different points of view.

Most large newspapers have reporters whose expertise lies in the reason that make news—government, foreign affairs, law, education, science, finance, religion, entertainment and the like. Smaller papers depend on the Associated Press, Reuters, United Press International or a syndicate, such as the Tribune Media Services, for example, for nonlocal stories of significance. Many large radio and television stations and some Internet news and magazine sites have reporters expert in certain fields, such as state government. Reporters are stationed in the state capitol during legislative sessions. Smaller broadcast stations depend on nationally syndicated experts whose services, particularly news or features on health, entertainment and money matters, are purchased by the station. The television and cable news networks have their own specialists.

Many stories combine hard and soft news elements. Hard news about personal conflict may trigger an emotional response from the reader, listener or viewer. Skillful writers will often highlight a human angle to a story about an important subject—softening the hard news—with the hope of attracting a wider audience. For example, a news story about Congress lowering federal income tax rates will usually be written predominately as hard news, but some soft news elements, such as a description of how the change affects typical persons with specific incomes, will be prominently featured, humanizing an important but mostly uninteresting story. The human or personal angle will often be the lead or one of the follow-up paragraphs. By doing this, the writer indirectly tells readers why this story is important or relevant to them. Writers also try to add a local element to a national or international story for the same reason—to connect the important story to some aspect of the local reader's, viewer's or listener's experience.

CONNECTING FACTS, INTERESTS AND THE AUDIENCE

The basis for all news is fact, and there is a dependent relationship between fact and audience (reader, viewer, listener), fact and interest, and interest and audience. Essentially, the job of a reporter is to make facts interesting to a particular audience. Therefore a reporter for a school news medium should write all stories for those particular readers. A story would be written somewhat differently for a school newspaper than for a city paper. The audiences for each, though they may overlap some, are mostly different.

News, which must be factual, is based on actual occurrences, situations, thoughts and ideas. Yet, as already written, not all facts are news.

News must also be interesting, but not all facts are interesting to everyone. The degree and breadth of interest will vary. One story may have a high degree of interest for only a small number of people. Another story will have some interest for a great many. Still another story will have great interest for large numbers. This story, especially if it is also very important, will be the number 1 story and given the lead position on page 1 of the paper or will be the first story read on a news broadcast.

The death of Diana, Princess of Wales, in 1997 led to unprecedented international news coverage. Her death was clearly an example of a story of great interest, but not necessarily of great importance, to a large number of people worldwide. Though tragic and a personal loss to many, her death had little consequence for most people in the world. A hard news story with many elements of soft news, it was interesting to many because of her fame and prominence and the circumstances of her death. The war in Kosovo in 1999, though of great importance, was not of great interest to many unless their fellow citizens were somehow affected by the war. It was a hard news story, and reporters sought to add more interest to the facts by including personal accounts from the war's victims.

Editors realize that their papers, web sites or broadcast news programs should have broad appeal even for a target audience. They select a mixture of stories of varying degrees of interest and importance in the hope of reaching every audience member with at least one story of particular importance to that person. Simply, newspapers and news programs have something for everybody. Smart editors know the demographics of their audience and publish content to meet its needs and wants.

NEWS IS DIFFERENT FROM OTHER FORMS OF WRITING

News must be accurate. Factual accuracy means that

every statement, name and date, age and address, and quotation is a verifiable fact. This unwavering commitment to accuracy is essential to a news medium's credibility and a journalist's personal integrity.

Accuracy means correctness not only of specific detail but also of general impression—the way the details are put together and the emphasis given. It is very easy to distort the importance of a particular fact by giving it major importance when in reality it is a minor detail. It is also easy to "play down" an important fact. A reporter's judgment is always involved. That's why complete objectivity really does not exist. That is also one reason readers should think as they read.

Accuracy is difficult to achieve because of the myriad facts that go into a story, the speed involved in modern journalism, and the many people who help to produce the finished story—the copyreader, the editors and the anchorpersons in radio and television whose vocal inflections may even distort the facts. Use of the Internet as a news medium, with its speed and global reach, makes the conflict between the time needed for checking for accuracy and the ability to get the news out quickly even greater than ever before. Every news medium wants to be the first to break a story, but does it do this at the expense of accuracy? That is debated today by many media critics.

Reporters must work painstakingly to achieve accuracy. They must check *every* note, particularly such specific details as names, dates, ages, times and addresses. Nothing must be taken for granted, even a name pronounced smith. Is it Smith, Smithe, Smythe? Or is it Schmidt, Smeeth or even Psmythe? Is Friday, April 26—the night of the National Honor Society induction—really Friday, or is the 26th Saturday?

Reporters must learn to question sources carefully. Informants sometimes misinform, rarely intentionally. School reporters often do not ask enough questions to get all the facts necessary to write an accurate story, especially if they don't understand their assignment and have not thought it through before conducting the interview. A reporter needs to "talk out" a story with the assignment editor and ask pertinent questions to develop the main idea or focus for the story. Only then will a reporter be able to ask intelligent questions to fill in the details pertaining to the main idea or focus.

For beginners, it is helpful if a reporter writes the main idea of the story in sentence form before going on the interview. The "bottom line" is that a reporter must understand clearly what a story is about before preparing for the interview. One of the weaknesses of the student press is that student reporters often rely on their informants to tell them the story rather than ask enough questions during interviews to "dig" it out.

News is balanced. Balance in a news story is a matter of emphasis and completeness. It is a reporter's giving each fact its proper emphasis, putting it into its proper relationship to every other fact and establishing its relative importance to the main idea or focus of the story.

A sports reporter could have every statement in a story correct, but if only the action of his or her school team was covered, the reporter would be guilty of imbalance and incompleteness. A reporter who covered a teacher strike by only talking to striking teachers and not the school board would be equally guilty.

News is usually considered balanced and complete when a reporter informs readers, listeners or viewers of all important details of a news event in proper relationship. Balance and completeness do not mean reporting every little detail. Rather, balance is the selection of *significant* details as a result of informed judgment. The purpose of balance is to give a reader, listener or viewer a fair understanding of an event, not a detailed account of every fact.

Balance is related to objectivity to some degree. Since a reporter is not in reality completely objective, it is important, especially for controversial subjects, for the reporter to at least consider information and opinions from sources who may be opposed to the mainstream or majority viewpoint. At the same time, a reporter has to use common sense and dismiss the views or statements of "crackpots" or fringe elements whose positions are implausible and too extreme. For example, a story about a racial conflict at school would not have to include the opinions of a white supremacist or neo-Nazi group just for "balance" if no such group was involved in the racial incident being reported.

News is as objective as it can possibly be. News is the factual report of an event, not the event as a prejudiced person might see it or as the reporter or assignment editor might wish it to be seen. For the reporter and editor, staying out of a story means relying on the most knowledgeable sources for all pertinent information (Fig. 1.1).

A reporter should report news as impartially and honestly as possible. That's always a worthy goal.

Because the world is so complex, people often cannot understand all factual stories unless facts are interpreted and evaluated against background information. This situation has led to an offshoot of news, interpretative reporting or, as it is also called, news analysis. Sometimes giving background information may mean reporting opinions or facts at variance with those given by a source.

Objectivity, an essential principle of news practice, is often difficult to achieve. A reporter's own opinions and emotions can easily interfere with factual presentation in stories about which strong biases are held. Being aware not only of prejudices but also of responsibilities will help. If a reporter is too close to the story (knows the sources intimately or has expressed strong opinions about some aspect of it), it might be better to reassign the story to another reporter to avoid any questions of bias.

News is concise and clear. For a newspaper most hard news stories follow the inverted pyramid form (see Chap. 3) and are written concisely and simply so that the meaning is clear to an average reader. There are other forms, however, that may fit the story better, such as beginning with the inverted pyramid form and, after the lead and follow-up paragraphs, changing to a chronological or storytelling form for the rest of the story. This combination of forms is often used for covering sports. Other forms used for most features, sports and interview stories are discussed in later chapters.

Although newswriting is concise—every word counts—it is still lively, with strong and colorful verbs. Subjects are complete and specific, opinion is attributed to the source and direct quotes rise above ordinary comments and vague information. With a writer's best efforts, newswriting can be as creative and descriptive as any other form of writing.

Usually, news is recent. Timeliness is of the greatest importance in this era of fast

Fig. 1.1. For this story, the reporter interviewed sources who were relevant authorities and close to the students involved in the incident. *Lance*, Robert E. Lee High School, Springfield, Va.

JOE MEIBURGER

ATTENDANCE NIGHTMARE Senior skip day, combined with students sick with the flu and failure of a computer system, created problems for secretary Kathy Leger.

One out of four absent on skip day

JOE MEIBURGER
Editor-in-Chief

Nearly one out of every four seniors was absent from school on an unofficial senior skip day last Monday.

Principal Donald E. Thurston declined comment until he had a chance to discuss the issue with senior class officers.

Attendance secretary Kathy Leger said the attendance office took over seven pages of entries from parents calling in to excuse their child's absence from school. The attendance office had taken a higher-than-average five pages of absences the Friday before and the Tuesday after the skip day. On a normal day, the office takes only two or three. Leger said seven pages was "abnormally high."

"The flu going around was a big problem on Friday," Leger said, "but the number of excused absences went up on Monday."

Leger suggested the administration require a doctor's note from all students whose parents called them in sick on future unofficial skip days.

Approximately 24 percent of the senior class was absent, 15 percent with the absence excused by a parent. Four percent were listed as tardy.

Senior class president Chrissy Smarr said the skip day may have been publicized by a student writing "senior skip day" on the calendar in senior hall. Although Smarr said she "whited out" the message, it was rewritten over the whiteout later.

Smarr said students who skipped made "pretty bad choices."

"It was a really irresponsible thing to do. Seniors are supposed to set an example for the underclassmen. I know skipping may be a tradition, but you don't really get a lot out of it," Smarr said.

Committee proposes school calendars for next two years

By LUCAS TATE
copy editor

Two new calendars have been proposed by the Calendar Committee for the 1999-2000 and 2000-2001 school years, and they will to go to vote on Jan. 26.

The first calendar, expected to be popular with high school parents, offers an Aug. 16 start date, and semester exams before holiday break. The second, pushed by elementary interests, starts on Aug. 30, when the temperatures have dropped slightly.

Both calendars have been changed to move spring break away from Easter and into March. However, students will still have Good Friday off.

This time, the vote will determine the district calendar for two years. The change has been one entirely born of logistics, according to assistant principal Karen Meyer.

"It's time consuming," Meyer said. "[Voting for only one year] just doesn't seem logical anymore."

The committee wants to be clear that the amount of school days has not been changed from the standard 175.

January's vote will be at the school of each family's youngest pupil. Parents are encouraged to come vote that night.

The board is expected to approve the vote's recommendation, but it does not have to.

"This is what the committee recommends," Meyer said. "It is not set in brick solid stone."

Fig. 1.2. Current facts and a "what will happen next?" angle combine to make this story relevant. *Ridge Review,* Mountain Ridge High School, Glendale, Ariz.

communication. Other facts being equal, a news editor will choose one story over another because of its timeliness.

Timeliness does not necessarily mean that all the events or facts of a news story are current. It may mean only that the story is appropriate at the time it is printed or broadcast. For example, a story about the last time an American president visited Russia may appear in connection with the announcement of the current president's trip to Russia. Recentness alone does not determine the timeliness of every news story.

Because school papers are not published daily and rarely published weekly, timeliness is a factor very different from that for a daily or weekly paper. For a paper published monthly, *current* may be a better word than *timely* as a factor for news. Journalists for these infrequent publications can also capitalize on timeliness from a different perspective by writing the advance story about what is going to happen soon (Fig. 1.2). News sites on the Internet, with the capability to change content within minutes, can take full advantage of timeliness as a key factor in writing news that is important to readers.

A NUMBER OF NEWS ELEMENTS MAKE FACTS INTERESTING

Immediacy or *timeliness* is the most essential element of most news. A reporter usually emphasizes the newest angle. For daily papers and broadcast and online news, the words *yesterday, last night, today* and *tomorrow* characterize most stories. Occasionally a story will concern events that happened in the past. In this case, the reporter tries to seek a "today" angle to the previous event. For example, on Nov. 9, 1999, the 10th anniversary of the fall of the Berlin Wall made the news pages of many newspapers, was aired on many news broadcasts and was published on Internet news sites. The *news angle* was the anniversary. Most stories were presented in a form other than the inverted pyramid and included a summary of the changes that have occurred in Germany and former communist countries in Europe since the wall was torn down.

Another example:

The old angle
West High girls' basketball center Lori Harris hurt her right knee Saturday while skiing at Alpine Village.

The team's trainer said that Harris is recovering quickly but may not be able to play in Friday's game.

Harris is the only player injured.

The new angle

Girls' basketball center Lori Harris will not play in tonight's game between West High and conference rival East High because of a knee injury she sustained last Saturday when she fell while skiing at Alpine Village.

All other members of the team are in good physical condition according to Coach Dave Adams.

The team trainer said that Harris is recovering quickly from her skiing accident.

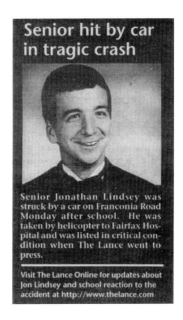

Senior hit by car in tragic crash

Senior Jonathan Lindsey was struck by a car on Franconia Road Monday after school. He was taken by helicopter to Fairfax Hospital and was listed in critical condition when The Lance went to press.

Visit The Lance Online for updates about Jon Lindsey and school reaction to the accident at http://www.thelance.com

Fig. 1.3. Late-breaking news can be added to a school paper in the form of a news brief, and a link can be included to a story with up-to-date information on the paper's Internet site. *Lance,* Robert E. Lee High School, Springfield, Va.

The most significant difference between these two stories is that the second one begins with the most recent development, Harris' inability to play during tonight's game. Leading off with this angle keeps the story more timely, more immediate. Six days after it happened, her injury is no longer "news," but the consequences of it are.

Editors need to seek ways of keeping school print, online and broadcast news *timely* and therefore interesting. This is especially important for printed publications, which have deadlines a week or longer before the publication date (Fig. 1.3). Online and radio and television broadcast sites have the ability to update, edit and delete stories quickly, sometimes within minutes before they are uploaded on the Internet or broadcast.

For printed newspapers, hardly any stories are breaking or spot news because of early deadlines. Consequently, many school papers publish background and analysis pieces about major news events (Fig. 1.4). Many of these takes are more in-depth, with many sources and sidebar, or companion, stories clustered together. These in-depth stories have a broader time implication than the yesterday, today or tomorrow angles of many news stories. Despite the restriction of early deadlines, news stories can still be written, but the latest development or consequence should be in the lead. The advance news story, writing about what is soon to happen, is also a way for print papers to be vital and interesting.

If the principal resigns on Nov. 1 and the public was informed, you cannot expect readers of your school newspaper to be as interested in that fact on Nov. 13, when the next issue of your paper is published. The governor visits your school and speaks at an all-school assembly on Nov. 3. A speech coverage story, reporting the highlights of the governor's talk, would be a good, timely news story if the paper came out one or a few days after the event. However, the Nov. 13 publication date makes the speech story less vital than it seemed the day after it occurred. The *timeliness* or *immediacy* aspect of the news is mostly gone.

In addition to solving this print news problem with more advance, background, analysis and in-depth stories, a reporter can develop a "nose for news," which can also be a solution to potentially "tired" news.

If the reporter has a nose for news, he or she will find out something about the principal's resignation or future plans that hasn't already been reported. (See Fig. 1.5.) The governor's talk may be tied to pending legislation or a trend in national

LITERACY: Students improve reading skills, make large gains in new class

SPECIAL EDUCATION
special report

rachel larsen
NEWS EDITOR

This is the second article in a three-part series. Next month we will be covering the Special Day and Severely Handicapped students and the vocational skills they are learning in the BOSS Center and the Campus Cafe. There are more than 4000 special-education students in SUSD, more than 300 of whom are enrolled at this campus.

When sophomore Steven Abujen first entered the special-education reading class this year, he couldn't pick up a newspaper and understand it.

The reading program, now in its second year, is geared to help Abujen and students like him to be able to read and comprehend what they have read.

With approximately 90 million adults reading at the two lowest levels of literacy, according to a 1992 national survey, this class appears overdue.

"I got by with it," Abujen said, speaking of his previous reading ability. He recalled several instances when he did not know the meaning of a particular word on an assignment. "I would get a little upset," he said. "I would go up and ask the teacher what it meant."

Reading and history teacher Camilla Wolak says that students can be very clever with the way they prevent their peers from discovering their problem.

Sophomore Pheany Hong, who has been in the reading class since the second semester of last year, explained how she hid her reading problem.

"I would just tell my friends, 'If you help me with my reading, I'll help you with something else,'" she said.

Robert Lichter, special-education department chair and one of the program's teachers, remembers when the program started.

"There was this one kid that would sit there and look at the pictures in his low rider magazine. Now he's reading the articles."

To be eligible to take the course students must score a 3.9 or below on the Woodcock Johnson test. This score indicates that the individual is reading below fourth-grade level.

But Lichter said this is not the only factor. Attendance and behavior are also taken into account during this selection process.

Attendance in the reading class is the best that she has ever seen, Wolak said.

"They (students) drag themselves here just for the reading program," she added.

These students have fallen behind their peers for various reasons. Some have a learning disability and others merely weren't taught effectively.

Wolak says that many students suffered because of the switch made from teaching phonics to the concept of whole language teaching in the 1980's. Gov. Gray Davis is now working to revert back to the use of phonics in the classroom.

The whole language approach teaches students to read by recognizing whole words whereas the reliance on phonics requires that students identify words by breaking them down into syllables.

Through decoding and a system called "corrective reading," students are learning how to use phonics to understand the meaning of words that were once beyond their comprehension.

But Lichter says, even with a more effective teaching method, dealing wth someone who is struggling to learn how to read is similar to dealing with an alcoholic.

"They have to admit, 'I don't read very well and I want to read,'" Lichter said. "If you know you can't, we can help you."

Abujen says that the reading class will benefit him in the future when entering college. Another aspect of the program that Abujen likes is that the class is voluntary.

"I could easily get out of this class if I didn't want to be in it tomorrow," he added.

Behavior problems have also been few. Only one student has been removed from the class.

The class engages the students the entire period in group activities. Students seldom, if ever, work on their own. Students and teachers agree that the program is progressing.

"The kids have a real bond," Lichter said. "Maybe the bond is that they all have the same goal."

Reading gains

- 35 students are currently enrolled in the reading program
- teachers instruct the students in the reading classes
- Already, significant improvements have been made

The average student in the reading program improved 2.6 grade levels during the course of one year. The following are the progress reports of six individuals in the reading class.

	student 1	student 2	student 3	student 4	student 5	student 6

politics. The talk may have led to students becoming involved in some community action program, or it may be part of a re-election campaign. Anything the reporter finds out about these stories that hasn't already been reported will be *new* (*timely*) to readers—and therefore news. Many news stories have the potential for an update or further reporting if the reporter persists.

During a public school board meeting and in a letter to parents, the school announces that it will change its class schedule effective next year. Students are also given a letter with the announcement during a homeroom period. Therefore a straight news story in the school paper reporting the same details would have little interest and would not be timely. A background story, however, relating the reasons for the change, the history of the present class and time structure, an account of how the new schedule works at schools already using it, and student and faculty opinions about the change would be a timely and interesting update of the original announcement.

Proximity or *nearness* refers not only to geographic nearness but also to interest nearness, sometimes called *impact*. In other words, what effect will the story have on its readers, listeners or viewers? What will it mean to readers? Impact can come from many interesting quotations from sources interviewed for the story. For example, a story about the change in the dress code, with direct and indirect quotes from proponents and opponents, can be more interesting to readers, more compelling than even a spot news story announcing the adoption of the dress code. Often interpretation or explanation is part of the news story announcing the most important fact, the reason for the story.

Usually a reader is more interested in an event geographically near than in one far away. School readers are usually more interested in events of their own school than in those of a neighboring one. Yet an incident in Kosovo during the 1999 war between NATO and Yugoslavia involving e-mail sent between a teenager in Kosovo and one in California may not have been near geographically but may have been of great interest to students at almost every school in the United States. This is *interest nearness*, or *impact*.

The naming of a graduate of a school to the president's cabinet or the Baseball Hall of Fame is news to the school's paper and online and broadcast sites; it is also an example of interest nearness. A graduate winning the mayoral election in the same town the school is located in is an example of geographic nearness.

A reporter emphasizes a local or school angle of a story whenever possible (Fig. 1.6). For example, when President Clinton signed into law the National Service Program, which allows students to do public service work in exchange for tuition and living allowances, many school papers had stories that interested many students. The stories were a way of making facts about a federal government program interesting to high school readers. They "drove the story home." They added *impact*.

Stories in school print, broadcast and online media are usually restricted to school activities and classroom academics; the activities and opinions of students, faculty and other school personnel; and those community, state, national and international events and issues that concern readers and in which they should be interested. Some of these stories did not originate on the school's campus, but some readers may have a connection to the event or social issue, and students and others are talking about it on campus. These off-campus, student interest stories have recently been reported in the high school press: abortion, nutrition, sexuality, road

Fig. 1.4. The newsworthiness of this story is not tied to an event that occurred on a specific date. It's timely in a broader sense, relating to a situation that has occurred for some time. *Stagg Line,* Amos Alonzo Stagg High School, Stockton, Calif.

Armstrong to retire, plans move to Hawaii

by Jessica Silver-Greenberg

If you need to find Mrs. Armstrong next year, you should check out the senior tennis circuit in Hawaii. You may find her playing a match on the sun-speckled courts of Waikiki. For at the conclusion of the school year, Emmy Lou Armstrong, assistant head of upper school and employee of the school for 23 years, will retire and move to Hawaii.

Armstrong had been debating the move over the summer and made the final decision over winter break. "I decided this was the time to go," Armstrong said.

Since her first visit in 1950, Armstrong has always harbored a deep love for Hawaii, and promised herself that one day she would live there. Both her granddaughter and her daughter live in Hawaii and Armstrong visits about three times a year.

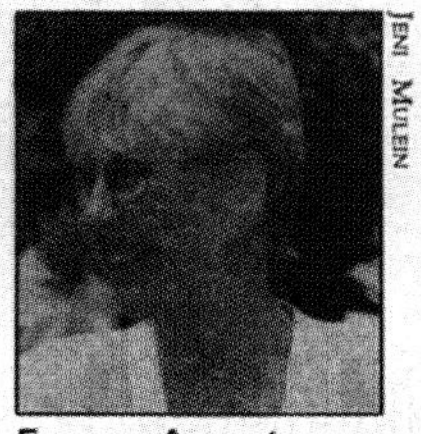

"I am just going to kick back and chill out for a long while," Armstrong said.

It is an opportunity for Armstrong to finally pursue her aspiration of playing on the senior tennis circuit.

"That is what I have wanted to do for a long time," she said. "I haven't

Emmy Armstrong

been able to because they start on Thursdays and I work."

Although she is excited about her future in Hawaii, Armstrong laments having to leave the students.

"It was really scary making the decision because I love it here so much," Armstrong said.

If she misses teaching while residing in Hawaii, Armstrong plans on substituting at local high schools. She hopes to maintain the close relationships she has developed with students and faculty members over the years.

Fig. 1.5. Despite infrequent publication, school newspapers can still break news even if some facts are already known. In this story, the retirement of the school official is likely known, but what she will do once she retires probably is not widely known. *Chronicle,* Harvard-Westlake High School, North Hollywood, Calif.

rage, gun violence, alternative medicines, breast cancer, censorship of the Internet and legal restrictions on personal freedoms. The key to getting students to read stories like these is accurate reporting, the use of expert sources and lively writing, always with a student angle. Interesting displays, with graphics and photography or other art, will likely increase readership.

Consequence is another important element of news. It pertains to the breadth of appeal—to *importance*—and to the effect a story will have on readers. In other words, *impact.*

A story that affects every student in the school—one on a change in graduation requirements—will have more interest than one affecting only members of one class—the destination for the senior class trip. Since the audience for the medium is usually wider than one class, the reporter should emphasize the angle of the story that will interest most readers, listeners or viewers. Sometimes the reporter will need to interpret the significance of a story. For example, will a change in the school's graduation requirements affect seniors, or will the changes affect only incoming freshmen? The reporter considers all possible reader questions and then tries to find the most knowledgeable authorities to give the answers.

Consequences that affect a person's well-being will make the news story more important to readers. How many people will be affected and how badly are considered by the reporter when the story is developed and by the editor when determining how much display the story gets in print and online media or how much time it gets on a news broadcast. Sometimes the *impact* is good—every student gets one more vacation day during spring break this year.

Prominence, as a news element, includes persons, places, things and situations known to the public by reason of wealth, social position, achievement or previous positive or negative publicity.

Generally, names make news. Reporters should always include as many names as possible in their stories. The more well-known a particular name, place, event or situation, the more interest the story will have. The president's golf game, discussed

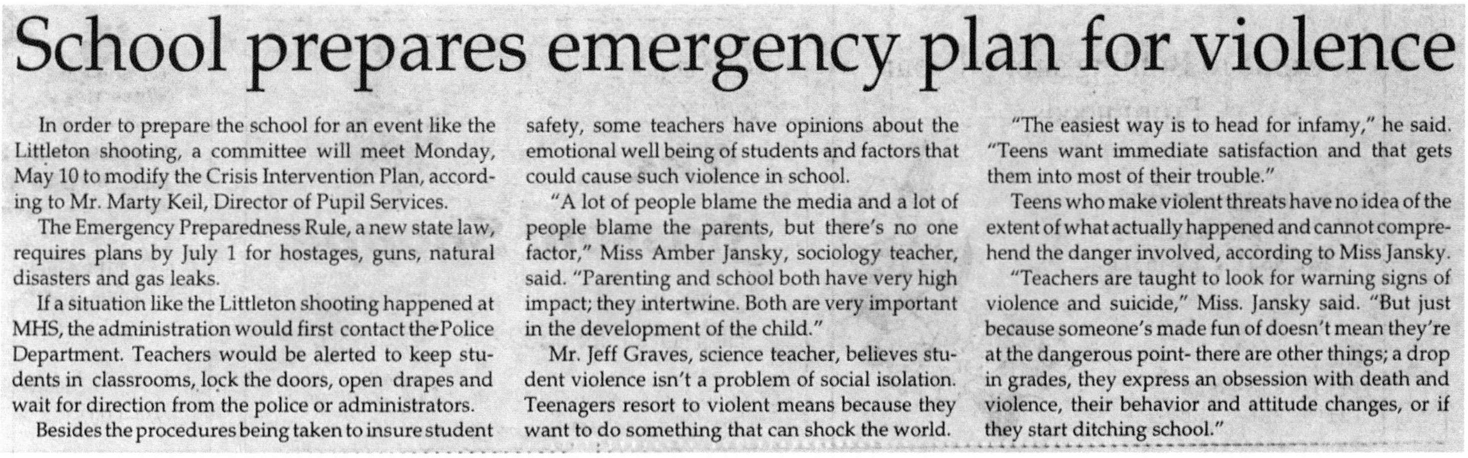

School prepares emergency plan for violence

In order to prepare the school for an event like the Littleton shooting, a committee will meet Monday, May 10 to modify the Crisis Intervention Plan, according to Mr. Marty Keil, Director of Pupil Services.

The Emergency Preparedness Rule, a new state law, requires plans by July 1 for hostages, guns, natural disasters and gas leaks.

If a situation like the Littleton shooting happened at MHS, the administration would first contact the Police Department. Teachers would be alerted to keep students in classrooms, lock the doors, open drapes and wait for direction from the police or administrators.

Besides the procedures being taken to insure student safety, some teachers have opinions about the emotional well being of students and factors that could cause such violence in school.

"A lot of people blame the media and a lot of people blame the parents, but there's no one factor," Miss Amber Jansky, sociology teacher, said. "Parenting and school both have very high impact; they intertwine. Both are very important in the development of the child."

Mr. Jeff Graves, science teacher, believes student violence isn't a problem of social isolation. Teenagers resort to violent means because they want to do something that can shock the world.

"The easiest way is to head for infamy," he said. "Teens want immediate satisfaction and that gets them into most of their trouble."

Teens who make violent threats have no idea of the extent of what actually happened and cannot comprehend the danger involved, according to Miss Jansky.

"Teachers are taught to look for warning signs of violence and suicide," Miss. Jansky said. "But just because someone's made fun of doesn't mean they're at the dangerous point- there are other things; a drop in grades, they express an obsession with death and violence, their behavior and attitude changes, or if they start ditching school."

at the beginning of this chapter, is news because the president of the United States is a prominent person. Princess Diana's death made news worldwide because of her prominence rather than because of the circumstances that caused her death.

At a high school, the principal and other top administrators, teachers and student leaders and those students who excel in some endeavor are prominent, and what they do may be more newsworthy because of their status. The principal's resignation makes page 1 in the school newspaper and leads on the school's broadcast news show; a teacher's resignation will likely not get the same treatment because the teacher is not as prominent as the principal. A star athlete gets a football scholarship to a Big Ten university; another student, not an athlete, gets a scholarship based on academic achievement to the same Big Ten university. The athlete's scholarship and decision to attend the university is usually news, and the nonathlete student's scholarship achievement may only be included in a composite story, a list of who received scholarships and where they are going to college. Again, prominence makes the difference.

Drama adds vitality and color to a news story and is another ingredient of news. A reporter always tries to find picturesque background and dramatic action. Often the more picturesque and dramatic a story, the more appealing it is to the audience. However, since this is news, all the colorful details and dramatic action are true.

Mystery, suspense, comedy, the unusual and even the bizarre are the chief elements of drama. If the facts of a story have one or several of these elements, the reporter should develop the story to take full advantage of them. The storytelling method of development would seem the best way to relate the facts to the reader. Yet relating dramatic facts in the storytelling form isn't all a reporter can do to attract readers. Reporting the story as a human experience—someone's personal story—will usually enhance the story even more.

Three hikers in Yosemite National Park are lost for four days during a blizzard. The park rangers and others search around-the-clock and eventually find all three alive, cold and hungry, huddled in a makeshift shelter. To keep awake and prevent themselves from freezing to death, they played trivia games. This story has suspense, a colorful setting, possible dire consequences and even some humor. It can best be reported as a personal survival story, through the eyes of one or all three hikers, with all the suspense that chronological storytelling can facilitate.

Fig. 1.6. A story that emphasizes the local angle of a new state law has impact. *Crier,* Munster High School, Munster, Ind.

Oddity, or *unusualness,* almost always helps to make facts interesting. The greater the degree of unusualness in a story, the greater its value as news. A first-time or last-time event often is more interesting to the audience. One-of-a-kind or rarely happening events are news. Solar and lunar eclipses are news. The last baseball game in old Detroit Municipal Stadium was news in 1999, at least in Michigan, and the outcome of the game didn't matter as much as the fact that it was the last game ever to be played there. The end of the century, end of the millennium on Dec. 31, 1999, also was a significant story because of its unusualness. The first baby born each year in many cities becomes a news story. The birth of a Panda bear in a zoo in North America is news because Pandas are rare outside of their native China.

Some stories depend almost entirely on this element. The persons involved are not prominent, the impact on others is negligible, and timeliness is only important in some cases such as the birth of the first baby born in the new millennium in a city. Yet readers, listeners and viewers usually love these kinds of human interest stories.

Conflict is one of the most basic and important news elements. It is the news element that appears most frequently in news media. An examination of the front page of a daily paper or the content of a radio or television news program will illustrate this point.

Conflict is inherent in all sports stories; all news of war, crime, violence and domestic disputes; much news of government bodies such as city councils, state legislatures and Congress; and all stories involving differences of opinion.

Much news of conflict involves other news values, such as drama and oddity, and therefore has emotional impact, a factor that appeals to many people and sometimes causes media to overplay this news element.

Conflicts can be both physical and mental. Even stories of one person's ideas versus another's are colored by this important ingredient. The more prominent the opponents, the bigger the news.

Conflicts can involve human versus human, human versus animal, human versus nature, human versus environment, human versus space or animal versus animal. For example, a story about the first all-women expedition, led by Ann Bancroft, to the North Pole, is a story primarily about human versus nature. Because it involved a "first," it also had the oddity element. Another conflict story example would be a space shuttle launch, human versus space.

If a reporter really understands news and the elements that it contains and knows who the audience is and what its interests are, the reporter can sometimes inject conflict into a story and therefore make it a story of wide appeal. It involves how the facts are presented, how the story is told. For example, a school newspaper story about the resignation of a principal could be told in several ways, usually as a prominence story but also, perhaps, as a conflict story, if facts reveal that the principal's ideas or work was opposed by a school board member, the superintendent of schools or the teachers' union. In this sense, a reporter can be creative and not rely solely on facts given out in a statement or press release. The reporter digs deeper to see if there is some conflict, some more facts. That's why a reporter really needs to understand a story well before going on an interview.

Sex, an integral force in human life, is the news value in stories of romance, marriage, divorce and other relationships. The treatment of sex varies widely, particularly in different types of print, broadcast and online media. For print and other media with visual components to news, photography and video have helped media to focus attention on sex and sometimes exploit it. School media journalists should be aware of their community standards and audience ages when sex is an element in a story. Sex can be reported maturely in an informative and nonsensational way.

Emotions and *instincts* as news elements involve the desire for food, clothing and shelter; the universal interest in children and animals; and the elements of fear, jealousy, sympathy, love and generosity.

The public likes stories that appeal to its emotions. For example, the international group Habitat for Humanity, which builds houses for the poor in various countries, is news. The elements of generosity, sympathy and even prominence (President Jimmy Carter is actively involved with this group) are key to these stories. Each year, broadcast news media report from food shelters and facilities that feed the homeless at Thanksgiving. These stories appeal to viewers' emotions. Stories about asteroids striking earth appeal to peoples' fears, and stories about births in zoos appeal to people's love of animals, especially young or helpless ones.

For high school media, stories with emotions and instincts as ingredients include those about student or faculty deaths or serious illnesses, food drives, charity events, community volunteerism, new fashions and fads, students who have pets, animal shelters, organ transplants and organ donations, homelessness and lottery winners, among others.

Stories with emotional elements are generally the most widely read in print media and watched or listened to on broadcast news and public affairs programs. Editors who realize this high audience potential will assign several emotionally involving stories for each edition of the paper or news program. A yearbook, which is an ideal medium for feature writing, will also benefit from a large number of stories that are emotions and instincts based.

Progress, another news element, involves any significant change for the betterment of humanity. It may refer to achievements in a research laboratory, a business, a legislative body, and other concerns from the multinational to one-person homes.

Progress may refer to advances in the treatment of breast cancer or HIV/AIDS; cleaning toxic waste sites; multinational space stations and exploration; acceptance of alternative medicines by the mainstream public; and growth of global communications, among other wide interest topics. Progress, as a key news element, may also refer to schoolwide stories such as the physical expansion of the school, changes in the school's graduation requirements, or adding new courses to the curriculum.

TEN ELEMENTS OF NEWS

1. Immediacy or timeliness
2. Proximity or nearness
3. Consequence or impact
4. Prominence
5. Drama
6. Oddity or unusualness
7. Conflict
8. Sex
9. Emotions and instincts
10. Progress

JOURNALISTS MODIFY THE IMPORTANCE OF NEWS ELEMENTS IN PRACTICE

Why one newspaper, online site or broadcast station reports a story differently than another, or whether it

publishes it all, depends, in part, on the policy of the news medium regarding news and its elements. The policy may increase or diminish the importance of a story or kill it entirely.

The political and religious beliefs of the news medium's owner or management may alter news value. A story on abortion or gay civil rights would probably get different treatment and display in a Catholic newspaper than it would in a nonsectarian metropolitan daily. Even in a nonsectarian newspaper, whether or how a story is reported can be influenced by the political, religious or other biases of the publisher and the top editors.

The attitude of the news medium toward labor, agriculture, gun control or particular racial, ethnic or sexual orientation groups may change news value. For example, a story on the number of blacks in Congress or in federal judgeships would likely be reported differently in the *Chicago Defender*, a newspaper read primarily by blacks, than it would in one of the other Chicago dailies. A story about farm subsidies might receive more display in the *Star Tribune* (Minneapolis) than in the *Baltimore Sun*.

Demographics, a scientifically done profile that tells many aspects of a target audience such as its education level, racial and ethnic mix, family income and median age, among others, determines largely what is news for most newspapers, magazines, online news sites and broadcast stations. Media owners want to know who their audience is and as much about how it lives and uses media as possible. This information not only relates to coverage but also to potential advertising income.

Although demographic studies aren't important for high school news media, it is helpful for editors to know generally the ethnic, racial, religious and sexual orientation of their audience so they can report stories of importance to these groups. This population profile should be done at the beginning of the school year for it to be useful in long-range planning.

Special interest groups, such as racial, labor, religious, sexual orientation and others, often have their own community or national newspapers, magazines, web sites and broadcast programs and networks. On cable, there is the Black Entertainment Television Network, the *Christian Science Monitor* is a popular newspaper with religious ties and *Today's Education* is a magazine representing the work and views of the National Education Association, a labor union.

A news source aligned with a particular political party or other special interest groups may also publish news and commentary in opposition to its own positions. Nationally syndicated columnists representing a wide range of backgrounds and opinions are often published in newspapers or included on public affairs news shows to diversify the content of the medium.

School media may want to achieve the same diversity by inviting guest commentators who represent minority groups within the school to write for the school print media or speak on broadcast shows. Additionally, editors and advisers should try to recruit minority students to join the staff. Staff diversity will usually broaden coverage and better serve a diverse school population.

The amount of space given to a story in a print or online medium or the amount of time on radio or television determines whether a story is told briefly or in detail. An online news site mostly prints brief to medium length stories; the medium itself—the computer monitor and method of accessing stories—is more suited to shorter rather than longer stories. Broadcasters have the benefit, as do online media, of adding content quickly. They can break into regular programming at any time with a news bulletin.

Timing often alters the value of a story. All news must be judged in competition with the news available at the moment it is to be published or aired. All other stories, for example, "took back seats" on the day Princess Diana died in 1997. Had Princess Diana not died on that August day, some other story would have been number one.

Previous publication or broadcast of a story changes its value. A story published in an early edition of a paper or broadcast will rarely receive the same attention later. Other events will likely have preempted its importance. At the very least, a paper, online news site or broadcast station will update the story, reporting the newest or more timely angle.

With the ability of online and broadcast media to publish and air stories within minutes of when they happen, print media today, especially newspapers, have to compensate for their inability to break much news to the public. Few newspapers today will publish an "extra" edition when a major story breaks. Rather, the papers focus more on the "why" and "how" of news, since the "who," "what," "when" and "where" are often known already by the public. Newspapers will publish more news analysis and background stories. They will also concentrate more on local news, which may be easier to break to the public.

School print media have the same lag time problem as their commercial counterparts. School newspapers, which publish monthly or less frequently, can also emphasize the "why" and "how" of a news story, as well as publish advance stories. *Timeliness* is mostly lost for school papers as a news value, with the exception of the advance story. News is either packaged as news briefs or presented as a news-feature, with other news elements, such as emotions or prominence, as the focus.

Print media can compensate in another way for their inability to compete with other media on *timeliness*. A newspaper can create a companion web site on the Internet and refer readers to its electronic version for updates, breaking news and other materials cut from the print version or created especially for the online version.

Censorship can also change news value, especially during war or national crisis for non–student media. Sometimes stories are not published or broadcast for years later. Reports involving the CIA and FBI, even of American involvement in the Persian Gulf War and the bombing of U.S. embassies in Africa in 1998, are examples of government censorship. Often, private papers of prominent persons, including presidents, are not made available to the public and the press until after their deaths or even years longer.

Censorship can take other, less direct forms, including an absence of presidential press conferences in order to keep a president from answering questions about events or decisions. Occasionally a news medium may ignore a story, even a rather explosive one. Some of these permanently or temporarily censored stories are ones with sex and prominence as news values.

Although there is a Freedom of Information Act, which allows the public and the press access to most government information, sometimes government officials hamper the press and others from finding this information. The press, as one of its functions, is the watchdog on government. In that capacity, it sometimes finds itself in an adversarial position with regard to government. This can also interfere with the free flow of information.

DEVELOP A SENSE FOR NEWS

Students who want to be journalists should develop a "nose for news," a sixth sense. They should develop a curiosity about people, what they do and what makes them act as they do. Student journalists should have the ability to recognize a newsworthy event. Understanding the news elements already explained will help a student journalist develop an instinctive nose for news, which many of the best professional journalists have.

A reporter for a newspaper, yearbook, web site or broadcast program should begin to think of everything that happens that is of interest to students, whether at school or in the community, as a possible story. Reporters should tell their editor about all possible ideas. If they interest both the reporter and editor, they probably will interest others.

EXERCISES

1. Bring copies of your city's (or nearby city's) daily newspaper for five consecutive days to class. Examine page 1, especially the lead or top story for each day. Which of the elements of news can be found in each page 1 story?

2. Record one of the broadcast network's evening television newscasts. Show the recording in class, list all the stories and identify the elements of news in each story.

3. Analyze a news story on page 1 of a daily newspaper. Identify any opinion that is in the story. Is the opinion expressed by the reporter who wrote the story, or is it attributed to someone else whom the reporter quoted, indirectly or directly?

4. As a class, list five major news events from the past 10 years. For example, the 1999 war in Kosovo could be one. Discuss how each of these events could again be a page 1 newspaper story or be reported on a broadcast news show.

5. Get two or more newspapers from different cities that were published on the same day. Examine page 1 to see what stories are covered. If there are different stories on page 1, how do you account for the differences? Which of the elements of news could have been considered by the editors that might explain the differences?

6. As a class, list all of the events that occurred during the past week at your school. Which ones are newsworthy and why? Rank the events from the most to least newsworthy.

7. Consider the idea that what is news for one person isn't news for another. As the publisher of a news medium, how could you provide news that would interest each subscriber? The news medium can be print, broadcast, online or other.

8. Why are these elements of news seemingly so interesting to so many people: prominence, sex and oddity? Do stories with mainly these elements in them deserve to be reported? Cite some examples from recent newspapers or broadcasts. Is coverage of these stories overshadowing coverage of other stories that have other elements of news in them?

Gathering News

Sitting in a newsroom in Phoenix, a reporter writes a story about the discovery of dinosaur bones in Africa's Sahara desert. At Chicago's O'Hare International Airport, another reporter, using a laptop computer, is filing a story to a newspaper in Atlanta about the just-announced selection of new inductees into the Rock and Roll Hall of Fame in Cleveland. In Dallas, a 16-year-old reporter completes a story on school shootings nationwide for the high school newspaper. While in Eugene, Ore., another teen reporter files a story on a proposed dress code for the school.

In 24 hours, this slice of journalism life is repeated by hundreds of thousands of journalists worldwide, including thousands reporting for high school media. There never is a "no news" day, and the work done by reporters for print, broadcast and online media never stops. With global telecommunications and massive amounts of information available to all reporters, regardless of age, a reporter has more sources available than ever before. Distance, cost, time and politics are no longer barriers for most reporters, even high school students. During the 1999 war in Kosovo, a high school broadcast journalist in California reported the war in a unique way through his e-mail source, another teenager, in Kosovo. It is possible today to have the world as a news beat without ever leaving home.

For those who work in news media, there are three core considerations:

1. What is the story?

2. Where do I find the facts?

3. How do I report it?

With so much information available, a journalist has to distinguish what is news and worth reporting and what isn't. What is the story? In Chapter 1 of this textbook, news is defined as information that has one or more of these elements: immediacy or timeliness; proximity or nearness; consequence or impact; prominence; drama; oddity or unusualness; conflict; sex; emotions and instincts; and progress. A reporter looks at information with these elements in mind. If this information has at least one, but usually many, of these elements, it is newsworthy and may even be selected for publication. Not all news is published in every news medium because of space and time limitations.

PRIMARY VERSUS SECONDARY SOURCES

What often separates a good story from a better one is the quality of the sources used by the reporter, both in gathering the facts and in what is later published. To use the best possible sources is the goal, but sometimes a reporter, who can't always be on the scene or has limited time, has to settle for less. But less doesn't mean inferior or insufficient.

Fig. 2.1. News beats, such as the school's district administrative office (school budget story), cocurricular groups (Science Bowl), a community/state business philanthropy (Bank of America recognitions) and the principal's office (new wireless system), can be a regular source of timely and significant news stories. *Blue and White,* Bakersfield High School, Bakersfield, Calif.

Two kinds of information sources are tapped by journalists, primary and secondary sources. Primary sources are eyewitnesses to an event or are the creators of an original work—a physical or intellectual property. Primary source information can be in print or other recorded form. A secondary source is a person who has some knowledge but didn't get it through personal involvement or is a published work that cites the words of others, words that have already been published in a primary source. Published work isn't restricted to print on paper, but includes tape, film and electronic files.

Journalists often get their information from both primary and secondary sources. Access and time may limit a reporter, but lack of either or both does not necessarily harm a story. Even though an eyewitness to a devastating flood in Texas lives 1,000 miles from a reporter, that reporter can conduct a phone interview with the eyewitness, who is a primary source of information. Even though a reporter has less than 10 hours to write a long story about the hurricane damage in North Carolina and the reporter lives 1,000 miles away and is writing for a Michigan newspaper, the reporter can get plenty of facts on previous hurricanes that damaged North Carolina from various Internet databases. This retrieval of background or secondary source information takes minutes.

The quality of the primary and secondary sources is also a factor. Credibility and degree of involvement of eyewitnesses are worth considering. Are they the most expert persons available? Were they actively involved in the event being reported or did they just observe it from the sidelines? Is their age or some physical characteristic a factor? There are many ways to categorize and rank the potential credibility of the primary source, and the reporter will have to choose the best available source based on his or her judgment. Ideas, opinions and other intellectual property can be good primary sources if they are cited from the original works.

Other primary sources for news media include leaders and spokespersons for organizations, associations, political and social causes and government agencies, among others. Often, these persons are contacted regularly to get facts for a story and comments. These primary sources are sometimes part of a beat system (see below).

Some secondary information sources, such as the weekly newsmagazines *Time* and *Newsweek*, are cited by young journalists as sources of information for stories. Although these magazines are well written and credible, they are not the best secondary sources or the only sources easily available to students. Generally, student journalists should not get their story facts from or quote an expert's opinion published in newsmagazines or other popular culture periodicals. It's better to go to more scholarly sources. For example, a student reporter who is writing a story on teens and HIV infection rates can get information from a scholarly journal, such as the *New England Journal of Medicine*, or directly from in-person interviews or bulletins from the Center for Disease Control in Atlanta. For this reporter's story, these primary sources are better than the secondary sources *Time* and *Newsweek*.

A BEAT SYSTEM AND HOW IT WORKS

Not all news stories come knocking on the newsroom door. Reporters have to find them, and that's done through a systematic and routine procedure called the *beat system* (Fig. 2.1).

A beat system is a plan to cover routinely all potential news sources in a specific area. Each contact or information source is called a beat. For high school news media, beats can include these:

- Each academic department and its chair

- Each extracurricular or cocurricular activity, its faculty sponsor and its student leader

- The athletic department and its director

- The student activities department and its director

- The school principal

- The school's superintendent and district office

- The school board chair

- The guidance and counseling office

- The discipline office and director

- Student government officers

- Drama director

- Vocal and instrument music directors

- Cafeteria or food service director

- School transportation director

- School maintenance director

- Directors of any special, in-school programs such as for student mothers and their children

- Athletic conference office or director

- State education department office (public information and legislative affairs)

- City government youth liaison office; youth recreation; youth employment

- City organizations with youth outreach programs such as the Urban League

Beats can also be topical and not specially tied to a location or spokesperson. These kinds of beats require the reporter to make multiple contacts, perhaps in many distant locations. Some of these beats are

- The environment

- Popular music

- Fine arts

- Juvenile justice

- Presidential politics

- Travel

- Medicine, health, nutrition

- Money and finance

- Religion

- The Internet

- Law

- Fashion

All of these, and others, have student angles and are often of great interest to teen readers. High school reporters who cover these beats usually need a local or school tie-in to increase the relevance and potential im-

Fig. 2.2. An international story is localized by an extensive interview with a student who formerly lived in the war zone. It is an exemplary way to report a story originating thousands of miles away and of interest to students. The Internet can also be used to interview primary sources for a story like this one. *Southport High School Journal,* Southport High School, Indianapolis, Ind.

pact of the story. For example, a travel story could focus on popular destinations for students during spring break. A story with a religion base could be about student missionaries or students who do church-related volunteer work.

These beats and others that may be unique to a community can be regular sources of information and possibly news for high school media. For example, a call or visit to the athletic director could lead to information about an upcoming sports banquet or changes in the composition of the athletic conference; a call or visit with the school's food service director could lead to information about menu changes or statistics on food costs or wastage; a call or visit to the city's youth liaison office could lead to information about a summer employment program for teens; a call or visit with the school board office could lead to an advance copy of the agenda for the next meeting; and a call or visit to the state education department office could lead to information about a newly proposed, statewide testing program for all high school juniors.

To make a beat system work, one reporter should be assigned to each beat. If the staff is small, a reporter could cover more than one beat. Several weeks before each deadline and just before the content is finalized for the next edition of the paper or other news outlet, the reporter should phone or visit the beat's spokesperson and ask for any new information. Although the reporter is not conducting an interview, he or she should probe for as much information as possible, especially if it's a follow-up on a tip. The reporter should try to develop a cordial relationship with the spokesperson so information is given readily and completely.

A good reporter will get some information from a beat every time a contact is made. As the source or spokesperson gets to know the reporter, it is likely he or she will start collecting information to save for the reporter.

With the nearly universal use of e-mail, a beat reporter can check with the source more frequently and even more quickly in some cases than with a phone call. However, personal contact is important too. Relying only on e-mail could preclude the special rapport that often develops between two persons when they meet in person or talk on the phone. A mix of phone calls, personal visits and e-mails could be a workable goal. Good rapport between a reporter and regular source can be invaluable when a story is being developed that requires more than the usual amount of information.

When the news staff gathers to plan an issue of the newspapers or the next broadcast news program, each beat reporter can share story leads received from the beat spokesperson. Then the editors can decide if the information has enough news value to warrant a story.

A reporter who enjoys a particular beat, one that has a nonschool counterpart such as city government, nurtures sources and learns as much as possible about the subjects and contacts related to the beat, can begin a life-long career extending from high school journalism through the world of commercial media (Fig. 2.2).

OTHER CONTACTS AND INFORMATION SOURCES

Although beats are good for story tips, information and primary source interviews, there are other sources for news tips and information.

A master calendar of all school activities is likely kept in the school's office. At the beginning of the school year, the news staff should get a copy of this calendar. Each month, or even weekly, it should be updated. The calendar, or "datebook" as

THE SOUTHPORT HIGH SCHOOL
Journal

A student publication for the faculty, staff and students of Southport High School and the community.

Volume 76 ■ Number 15

■ **BREAKING NEWS** ■

Kosovo update: Early this week, air strikes continued. On Wednesday, the Serbs sealed their border, stopping the flow of refugees and leaving them unsure of their fate.

Thought for the **"DAY**

"It's all right letting yourself go, as long as you can get yourself back."
—Mick Jagger

FRIDAY, APRIL 9, 1999

NEWS

Going to Mexico

Three students are traveling to San Luis Potosíto to study Mexican culture. For seven weeks, they will stay with native families.

DIVERSIONS

Your parents had them and now you do

Many teachers have been teaching at Southport for many years. See if you can recognize them from old pictures.

SPORTS

Boy earns volleyball letter

The boys volleyball team members finally have the opportunity to earn an athletic letter for their efforts.

FEATURE

What is love

Love has different meanings for different people. Read about some of the things love can be and about what girls and guys look for in relationships.

Contrasts *photo spotlight*

On assignment downtown, this reflection of the Indianapolis Capitol Building was captured. Modern and antique contrast here to demonstrate the architecture that is commonplace near the circle. *Photo by Alex Craig.*

COVER Kosovo crisis hits home

Cory Schouten, features editor, interviews Ranko Radlovic, junior, who is a Serb and a former resident of Yugoslavia. *Photo by Alex Craig.*

CORY SCHOUTEN
FEATURES EDITOR

For nearly three weeks now, bombs have rained on targets in Yugoslavia and the province of Kosovo. The bombs, part of a North American Treaty Organization (NATO) campaign, have targeted the capability of Serbs and president Slobodan Milosevic to commit atrocities and 'ethnically cleanse' Albanians in the Serbian province of Kosovo.

For many students, who knew nothing about the region until the crisis began, the problem is a distant, yet important concern for the country.

It's a fair guess that when Mr. Terry Wright turned on CNN for his fourth block class the Friday before spring break, many of his students' minds were on tropical destinations and a week of relaxation. But at least one student, Ranko Radlovic, a seventeen year old junior, was paying close attention and having a hard time taking in all that was happening in his homeland. The country he now calls home was attacking his former home, where he's still in contact with friends and family.

"I came to school. I was physically here, but wasn't mentally," Radlovic said.

"One thing I noticed in class was his concern," Wright said. "On the first day of the bombing we were in the classroom, I saw his concern getting wider, but I think he handled it the way a mature, young person should handle it."

"I can live wherever I want and I'm still going to be Serbian. I can't change my past just because I'm living here," Radlovic said.

Radlovic and his family have lived in the United States for ten months. He started school here at the beginning of this semester. Wright says that he is a good student who has a good understanding of European history and is intellectually talented.

> "My friend said they just pray to God that [the U.S.] sends army troops over there, because they're ready to fight."
> — Ranko Radlovic, junior

"I'm totally against what [the U.S.] is doing against my people," Radlovic said.

He believes that the U.S. and western countries have been inconsistent about their Balkan policies. They were not concerned about Serbian refugees in Bosnia, why should they be concerned now, he argues. He says that what Yugoslavia does doesn't have an affect on any other country and that they don't represent any threat to Europe.

"We want to keep what's ours," he said. Radlovic says that the same thing happening now happened to the Serbs five years ago, and Serbs also lost their homes. "We give [the ethnic Albanians] autonomy (the right of self government) and all they want to talk about is independence of Kosovo," Radlovic said.

Radlovic hates that NATO is using air strikes. "Air strikes are long and can't produce anything. They just make Milosevic stronger," he said. "The air strikes make the people mad and they feel that they need to deal with the Albanians. They are going to attack the Albanians until the air strikes stop."

"My friend said they just pray to God that [the U.S.] sends army troops over there, because they're ready to fight."

see **Kosovo** pg. 5

Radlovic, who lived 30 miles north of Belgrade, and his family are concerned about their former country and the family and friends they left behind. *Photo by Alex Craig.*

it is sometimes called, should be reviewed as each issue of the school newspaper, each broadcast news program and each update of an online news site is being planned. Since the reporting of future events—what will happen—is vital for monthly newspapers, it may even be useful to look more than one month ahead. Events scheduled on the calendar can be reviewed as potential stories.

The school's handbook is another useful reference for student journalists. An up-to-date version is necessary. It can provide background and may be cited as a source for a variety of stories such as ones about dress code, tardy and absence policies, and emergency building evacuation, among other topics. Since policies may be updated after a new school year has begun, it is important to verify the contents with school officials if information from the handbook is being cited in a story. The handbook can also be reviewed for possible opinion columns, editorials or other stories that examine school rules that may be ignored or not enforced.

A current student, faculty and staff directory is also useful to identify and locate sources. Although the directory may be reliable, a student journalist would be wise to double-check spellings of names with a phone directory to avoid errors, which may be embarrassing or even result in legal problems. The school may maintain its directory online. A directory published at the start of the school year may not be inclusive of all students and others as the year progresses; the newsroom should ask for an updated version periodically. There may be some privacy issues about the identification of sources: names and class affiliation are acceptable; home addresses are mostly unnecessary and are not published.

Bulletins from the school administrative, counseling, activities and other offices will likely be sources of news. These are often posted in the main or guidance office or in a public area. All student media should request a mailbox in the main office and request copies of these bulletins when they are distributed to the faculty and others.

Minutes from school board meetings, press releases and bulletins from the school's district office should also be reviewed by student journalists for possible story ideas and sources. With the exception of personnel records, these documents are open to the public and should be available to students.

Other resources that may be helpful to student journalists include, either in print, online or in CD-ROM form: telephone and city directories, zip code directory, encyclopedias, world almanac, biographical dictionary, various government databases and other books useful for copyediting.

School and city libraries have several other useful resources, especially to find background facts for a story. These are the indexes of magazine articles and include the *Readers' Guide to Periodical Literature* and the *Education Index.*

Press releases and bulletins from colleges, universities, technical schools, the armed forces, scholarship-granting agencies, U.S. government agencies, businesses (computer hardware and software and telecommunications are especially relevant), charities (volunteer opportunities) and other sources can also be leads for news and feature stories. Student journalists should usually not publish these releases without some verification of the information, editing and localizing the angle with some original interviews. A new lead should also be written. Press releases are often slanted to put the business or sponsor in the most favorable light. Consequently, journalists should be wary of accepting the content without some scrutiny. The journalist should ask: Is there legitimate news value in this information?

Back issues of the school newspaper and yearbook and tapes of previous

NEWS NOTES

Environmental Club focuses on recycling

Recycling of paper will be a new focus of Environmental Club. Members recently contacted teachers to make sure that those willing to have paper bins in their classrooms will be provided with one.

Aluminum recycling will be done in barrels recently purchased and placed outside of the school buildings at various locations of the campus. The bins inside of classrooms were often unsanitary and viewed as eyesores.

"One of our goals is to keep the campus clean," Environmental Club co-adviser Carol Alex said.

Due to misuse of the containers, D&M Recycling moved the bins from the parking lot below the auditorium.

"People were dumping all kinds of things there," Alex said.

The Environmental Club has asked teachers to have students in their classes empty the classroom bins in a large paper recycling container outside the 600 building. Club members will assist in emptying the classroom bins if a teacher requests it.

By narrowing their focus, club members hope to improve their efficiency.

"We'd rather do a little bit well," Environmental Club co-adviser Karen Peck said, "than trying to do too much and doing it poorly."

The club is in the process of placing aluminum recycling containers around the campus. The bins will be emptied regularly by the community organization C.A.L. (Citizens Against Litter).

The Environmental Club is encouraging cooperation in using the new containers properly.

SIMONE TORREGGIANI

Classrooms updated with new technology

The Science and Math Departments are getting a technological boost from Peninsula School District.

The Science department recently acquired specialized devices called Calculator Based Labs (CBL's). The tools can interface with newly purchased TI-83 calculators to preform certain tasks including measuring temperatures and pressure. This information can then be graphed and displayed on the calculators.

"I really like it," Thorson said. "It's a lot of initial work, but it's the way that science needs to progress."

The new equipment was supplied with hopes of integrating more technology into the classroom.

"We're driving a Volkswagen when the rest of the world is driving a Cadillac," Thorson said.

The CBL's cost a 180 dollar, while the new calculators were $90 (retail value). The expense of the tools allows only so many to be bought at one time. Spencer, however, believes that there are set backs in these devices.

"It (technology) gives a lot of power in the classrooms," Spencer said. "Students sometimes tend to rely too heavily on it though."

New tools similar to the CBL's are helping the district catch up with the upgraded technology of other schools. Twelve additional computers were purchased and recently added to the yearbook/newspaper class.

"They're so fast and so cool," sophomore Dawn Hasbrook said. "They help you get work done a lot quicker."

BILL BUCHANAN

Newspaper finalist in national contests

The Peninsula Outlook has been nominated a Pacemaker finalist by the National Scholastic Press Association. The Outlook website, The Outlook Online, has also earned an award in the Best of the Web contest.

The Outlook's placement in the two contest will be announced Nov. 21 at NSPA's fall convention in Washington DC. Nine students will attend the convention, where they will participate in contests and attend workshops presented by media professionals.

The Pacemaker competition, sometimes referred to as the Pulitzer Prize of high school journalism, is based on four issues of the newspaper published during the 1997-98 school year. Tom Merry, now a student at the University of Washington, was editor, and senior Michael Sherman, current co-editor, was managing editor. Paul Spadoni and Deborah Anderson are the newspaper's advisers.

CHRISTINE LEE AND KATRINA MIKITIK

Sean Bonsell photo

TAKING OUT THE TRASH — Environmental club member, senior Brooke Westmoerland, recycles paper products outside the 600s hall. Citizens against litter have taken charge of emptying the bins for the world recycling effort.

Teams to collaborate for dance Halloween night

A Halloween night dance, thrown by the Peninsula and Gig Harbor High School basketball teams is intended to benefit both teams.

"We wanted to get the two schools together," said GHHS parent volunteer and coordinator Marlyn Jensen, "so we thought, why not have both the schools at the dance and promote the basketball teams too?"

The Halloween dance will be held at GHHS on Oct. 31 from 8 to 11 p.m., and tickets can be bought at lunch for $5, with or without ASB card.

Not only will this dance support basketball, it will hopefully bring together students from the different schools.

The Halloween dance is going to have a '50s theme. Door prizes will be donated by parents and businesses. There will also be an award for the best Elvis impression. Despite the theme, the music will be diverse.

"The reason we wanted the '50s motif instead of masks is so that we can check who's coming in," Jensen said.

Also, there will be a tribute to Jeff Lane, who played on the PHS basketball team before he passed away last year.

"We're hoping this is going to become a tradition, and the beginning of bringing the schools together," Jensen said. "I think it's just going to be an exciting, wonderful night."

JOAN SIMON

High test scores on AP test give college credit

Of the 13 students who took the A.P. tests in English, math and U.S. History last year, 11 students passed with scores three or higher, receiving college credit.

Five students took the English test, and four passed both the language and literature parts. One section of the test was taken by three students who all passed with a score of at least three.

"Overall our scores were very high," counselor Dave Reichel said, "and we are very enthused about it."

One student passed the math test with the rare score of five points, the highest grade possible.

"I'm very pleased for the students when they pass," math teacher Stephanie Spencer said, "especially with the top mark. The test is very difficult and it requires a great deal of preparation."

Out of four participants, three passed the U.S. History test.

"The College Board has conducted studies that show an AP grade of three is comparable to a college course grade of B or a C, depending upon the institution the student attends," Reichel said. "Each college decides which A.P. exam it will accept for credit or advanced placement and most accept a grade of three or higher."

Students could not take as many A.P. classes as they wanted to last year because some classes were held concurrently. Class sizes were small and not every student signed up for the A.P. tests. The number this year is expected to be larger because the schedule conflict was fixed.

"For any college-bound student," Reichel said, "I encourage them to take A.P. classes if they can."

ANNA-MARIA KÜHNAST

PHS drama department Performs 'The Crucible'

The Peninsula Drama Department performed "The Crucible" last week for students and the community. "The Crucible," written by Arthur Miller, is based on the events that took place during the McCarthy era.

"The Crucible" was written in the 1950s, when McCarthyism was prevalent. Miller's story was created to depict the witch-hunt of Communism during this time.

"The Crucible is a serious drama with serious acting," senior Rory Adams said.

"The Crucible" received fair community support, with over 250 people in attendance on Oct. 17, the only public show performed.

"It's a historic story of what happened and could happen again," junior Erin Jensen said. "It shows what the human nature can do when left unguarded."

SHANA HEISER

Senior artists beginning development on mural

Senior mural plans are in gear. The artists have had a slow start because of the problem of lack of time to meet. Senior meetings during Seahawk hour have been the major conflict.

Claire Carlson, Naomi Howe, Amber Lacheney, Wendy Reynolds, Rory Stevens and Chris Waldron were chosen to be on the committee.

Each student will come up with an idea that is influenced by a particular artist, and they will vote on which one to use.

"The senior mural emulates and represents their class," art teacher Christine Hill said.

The senior mural is a time honored tradition.

"It's cool that next year, and the year after that and the year after that will see what the seniors thought reflected the class of '99," Waldron said.

ASIA WRIGHT

broadcast news shows can be valuable sources of information for a reporter. Many stories are updates of some event or issue reported earlier. Other stories can be better reported if some relevant background—what happened in the past to lead up to this new development?—is included. If the story is essentially about a school-related event, then the most comprehensive account should have been published in a previous edition of the paper or news broadcast. Back issues of the school paper, a set of back volumes of the school yearbook and a tape library of former broadcasts should remain in the staff newsroom for this research purpose. Some papers are storing their back issues on CD-ROMs; an electronic library is easily accessible and takes less storage space than print.

THE INTERVIEW

The most important and common way for a reporter to get information is through an interview with a person, called the "source." Facts can be found in previously published documents, available in print and online form, but almost every story needs one or more primary sources. Fact-based reporting is more credible, professional and important to readers if there is evidence of first-hand reporting. If the reporter did not witness the event, then did he or she talk to those who did? This is an important reader expectation, and journalists need to satisfy it for the reader.

An interview can be as informal as asking someone in a crowd one question or a series of questions on the phone or through e-mail. Or an interview can be formal, with an agreed upon time and place and much advance research work by the reporter. Many stories combine every possible approach.

Student journalists must realize that writing a news or other journalism story is not like writing a term paper or essay for another class, where secondary source information sources may be all that is necessary to complete an assignment. For journalists, the secondary sources, though important, only provide background or some of the necessary information for a story.

Before any interview, other than spontaneously asking someone at the scene of an event a question or two, the reporter needs to do some research and even prepare questions. Exploration of any story begins at a news staff meeting when the story is assigned. The assignment editor, reporter and others brainstorm for potential information sources, including personal inter-

views, and angles for development of the story. Even a story that may be slotted as a "news brief"—restricted to one or a few paragraphs—will likely mean the reporter has to talk with at least one source. Longer stories, with many facts and different angles to develop, will usually lead the reporter to multiple sources and several personal interviews (Fig. 2.3).

Once the story has been discussed and especially if the reporter knows little or nothing about the subject, the reporter needs to research at least the basic, established facts, if any exist. This research will help the reporter frame the questions that will be asked during the interviews. The research will also help during the writing stage following the interviews. In addition to researching the subject, a reporter may also find it useful to research the person being interviewed, especially if he or she is noteworthy and is connected in more than a circumstantial way to the subject.

Depending upon the complexity of the subject and the anticipated depth of the interview, the reporter prepares a list of questions following the initial research of the subject and the interviewee. Doing this does not mark the reporter as a beginner; veteran journalists often do this to help ensure a successful interview.

Prepared questions help a reporter conduct a complete interview. Fear and nervousness could cause a reporter to forget some or all of the questions. If they are written, it is less likely that this will happen; it also means the reporter will only have to write the source's responses.

The prepared list should begin with one or several easy questions that help establish a comfortable, trusting rapport between the reporter and the source. Even before the first question is asked, it is acceptable and often beneficial for a very brief amount of "small talk" to happen. The reporter could comment on the weather or note something interesting about the location or some items in the room. These openers or icebreakers often help the interviewee feel at ease. However, some powerful, tightly scheduled persons want to get right to the point of the interview. The reporter needs to be flexible. The reporter also needs to be in control of the interview: If the source wanders off the topic and the new information isn't newsworthy, the reporter needs to bring the source back to the topic at the first opportunity.

Often, the interviewee expects the reporter to know the basics of the subject and will be displeased if time is "wasted" with background questions.

Interview questions often relate to the basic reader

questions, the "5 *W*'s and *H*"—what, who, where, when, why and how. Although all six of these basic questions should give the reporter facts, it is the "why" and "how" that need to be emphasized during the interview. Answers to these will more likely give quotable material and a more interesting insight of the topic. As a reporter writes the prepared questions, the "5 *W*'s and *H*" should all be considered.

Questions that could result in a yes, no, maybe or "I don't know" response should be rewritten to potentially get a more complete answer with concrete details:

Poor

Will the benefit dance raise money for the school's athletic budget?

Better

What programs will benefit financially from the money raised at the dance?

The first question will likely get a yes or no response. The reporter should know the answer to this before the interview takes place. The second question will likely get concrete details. The first question would be acceptable if a "What programs will benefit?" follow-up question was asked.

To avoid sounding stiff and too formal, a reporter should not actually read the questions word for word. Rather, the reporter can glance at the prepared questions, note some key words and then casually ask it while looking at the source rather than at a piece of paper. As a reporter does more interviews, this becomes easier to do.

During the course of the interview, the reporter, even while taking notes, must have passing eye contact with the source and listen carefully to the responses. Listening is something reporters have to do well. A reporter should not try to impress a source with how much he or she knows; the purpose of the interview is to find out what the source knows.

Even though a reporter has prepared questions, the need to ask new questions to follow up an unexpected, unclear or incomplete comment made by the source is always possible. Veteran reporters say that some of their best stories have come from unexpected or new information that came up during routine questioning. Reporters need to be ready to deviate from their prepared list of questions and pursue a new area; the reporters can return to the original list later.

For accuracy, a reporter needs to take notes during an interview. If the source agrees, the interview can be taped or digitally recorded. Doing both may be desirable. The notes will help the reporter write the story more quickly than can be done if only a tape recorder is used. The recording will be especially helpful for the accuracy of direct quotes. Many reporters develop their own note-taking shorthand. They may leave out the articles "a," "an" and "the," spell words without vowels or abbreviate long words—whatever helps them take notes efficiently and quickly. Immediately following an interview, a reporter should review the notes to complete sentences and add missing details. The story should be written as soon as possible after all interviews have been completed.

The time to verify facts and opinions given during an interview is during the interview. If something is unclear or incomplete, if statistics are too complex or given too quickly by the source, or if the opinion given is unusual or potentially controversial, the reporter should repeat the fact or statistic or read the statement back to the source and ask if it is correct. It is also acceptable to follow up an interview with a phone call to verify information and statements. It is not professional to show a completed story to a source for approval before publication. If a source retracts a statement—denies making it originally—that contradiction could be used as part of the story. It is important for reporters to take accurate notes and to save these notes and any recordings for some time following publication of the story.

Tips for conducting a successful interview:

- Research the subject and the source (interviewee).

- Make an appointment.

- Prepare a list of questions.

- Create some shortcuts for note taking, including abbreviations.

- Bring a pocket-size recorder; make sure it has fresh batteries and it works.

- Bring a notebook—something with a hard surface so you can write on your lap—and two pens (one may run out of ink).

- Wear clean, suitable clothes. Shower and wear deodorant but don't wear cologne or perfume (distracting and possibly offensive).

- Arrive on time or a few minutes early. If you are going to be unavoidably late, phone and give an estimated time of arrival.

- Introduce yourself as a reporter (always) and give the name of your news medium.

- Smile and say something friendly to break the ice. Don't sit until you've been invited to sit or ask where you may sit.

- If you brought a recorder, ask permission to record the interview.

- Turn on the recorder, open your notebook, make eye contact with the source and begin.

- Ask one or two easy questions, ones that aren't threatening to the source.

- Ask the tougher questions. Make eye contact.

- Ask follow-up questions to get examples or explanations: "Could you give me an example?" "Could you explain that?" These are not on your prepared questions list, but they need to be asked.

- Follow up unanticipated responses or new information with new, spontaneous questions. Quickly add these new questions (using some shorthand) to your questions list in your notebook.

- Ask the source to repeat any facts, statistics you don't understand or information you missed because the source was talking too quickly. Check the spellings of names given by the source in his or her responses.

- Ask the source if you can repeat something he or she said if you think it is unusual or controversial or if you want to quote it in your story. You want to get it right.

- Ask your last question.

- Ask the source if she or he has anything else to say.

- Quickly check your list of prepared questions to verify that you asked all of them. This is especially important if the source wandered off the topic.

- If you agreed upon a time limit for the interview, try to respect that agreement or ask if you could have a few more minutes.

- Quickly note the setting and any incidentals in the location that could add color to the story or reveal something more about the source. This observation could lead to a new question or two.

- Thank the source. Make eye contact and smile.

- Give the source your phone number or e-mail address and ask the source to call you if he or she has anything more to say.

- Turn off your recorder and take your notebook and recorder with you.

Some sources are reluctant to talk or are shy. Public officials have a duty to talk to the media; private persons don't have to. By looking professional and being polite and considerate, a reporter will likely put the uncomfortable source at ease. Brief small talk also helps. When an interview appointment is made, ask the source when it would be best for him or her to be interviewed; that will also reduce some tension. Being punctual will also help. Sometimes some charm or a compliment can disarm an unfriendly source. Tough questions—ones that may reflect negatively on the source—should be asked carefully and in a respectful tone of voice. If the source does not answer, the tough question could be rephrased and asked again. Probably the question should not be pursued if no answer is given after two attempts. In the story, the reporter can write that the source "declined" to comment on whatever the subject was; writing "refused" to comment is harsh and has a different connotation than "decline."

Reporters should be especially careful when they interview a source who is involved in a personal tragedy. Media, especially broadcast, have a tendency to be intrusive during large-scale disasters and small but violent accidents. A reporter should respect the wishes of the immediate survivors and the dignity of the dead as much as possible and still report the event. By being courteous, showing appreciation for the dire circumstances and asking questions politely and gently, a reporter may get access more easily to information from survivors and others close to the event than reporters who are uncaring and confrontational.

Phone and in-person interviews are somewhat alike. In a phone interview, a reporter will not be able to include details about the person's appearance, mannerisms or surroundings. However, phone interviews save time and are a common way all reporters get information and comments. Phone interviews can be taped, but in many states it is illegal to tape people over the phone without their permission. It may be just as important, depending upon the availability of the source, to make an advance appointment for a phone interview. As in every interview situation, the reporter identifies himself or herself by name and as a reporter for a specific news medium. Phone interviews are usually not long; interviews for long stories, especially personality profiles, are best done in person.

Interviews can also be conducted by e-mail on the Internet. In some ways they are like phone interviews; usually you are not observing the source and are unable to note physical details. However, the e-mail interview has advantages: Responses are already written, thus eliminating note taking, and the responses can be made at a time when it is convenient for the source. The e-mail responses may also be more carefully written and so more coherent than answers given in person or over the phone. This can be good and troublesome. Responses may have more substance, but they also may be less conversational, more formal. Readers may not find the resulting interview story as "human" as one that followed an in-person interview.

An e-mail interview can be followed up with a phone call to the source to verify important facts and unusual or controversial comments. A reporter may want to verify that the person who responded to the e-mail was really the source; some e-mail names and addresses are cryptic.

Reporters can assume that an interview is "on the record" (for publication) as long they identify themselves as a reporter. Sometimes a source will say that something is "off the record" (not for publication). The reporter has to decide whether to accept this change. There is no rule all journalists follow. However, if a reporter agrees to listen to something that is off the record, then the reporter should clearly understand exactly when the interview is back on the record. When a source is talking on the record, everything that is said can be quoted directly or indirectly and attributed by name to the source. However, just because there is an assumption that the interview is on the record doesn't mean that the reporter is obligated to use all of the facts and comments given by the source during the interview.

INFORMATION ON THE INTERNET

The Internet links reporters to information stored in computers throughout the world. What used to take reporters hours and days to find at libraries and through phone calls now takes minutes to find on the Internet,

even using a palm-size, wireless computer. The blessing: speed and a wealth of information. The curse: too much information, perhaps.

No one can deny that the vast amount of information now available to anyone, including reporters, has enriched stories published in print or online and broadcast. More and better statistics from databases representing a wide variety of public and private agencies have added more depth to stories. Student media haven't been left out of the boom either. A reporter for the *Lowell* at Lowell High School in San Francisco has equal access to the same information sought by a reporter for the *San Francisco Chronicle*. The Internet is the great equalizer.

The Internet is also popular as a communications link between people, and for journalists, between a reporter and a source. Fast and inexpensive interviews can be conducted over the Internet. A student reporter in Twin Falls, Idaho, can e-mail a source in Washington, D.C., and ask questions about federal legislation to allow prayer in public schools. The *Shakerite*, of Shaker Heights High School in Ohio, uses the Internet to report what's happening at other high schools throughout the nation (Fig. 2.4).

While reporters have increasingly used the Internet as a tool for reporting, they haven't abandoned the other methods of gathering information. Reporters still conduct in-person and telephone interviews and still consult print resources for information. The Internet has added to a reporter's "bag of tricks" and not decreased it.

To take advantage of all the information available on the Internet, a reporter needs to know where to look, what specific web addresses have the kind of information useful for certain stories. Many journalists who work for commercial media have access to a subscription database, such as Nexus Lexus. For a price, a journalist can find specific data easily. Few student journalists have access to these commercial database sites.

If specific web addresses are not known, reporters and almost everyone else who uses the Internet will use a "search engine" (a web site with an electronic researcher) that finds information. With so much information stored in computers, apparently no one search engine can find all of it. Many people use more than one engine to search for data. Two of the more popular search engines are Alta Vista and Yahoo.

Each search engine lists some of the many web sites on the Internet. A "robot" for the engine searches the

Internet for web sites that fit its criteria and then adds these site addresses to its ever-expanding site database or list.

To do a search using one of the Internet's search engines, it's wise for a reporter to save time—there could be millions of references—and do the following:

1. If the search engine offers any shortcuts in its menu, the reporter should try them. This can save time, especially if the search is wide and could yield hundreds of leads.

2. Choose the keyword or keywords carefully. Be precise and include the alternate ways to refer to something or someone.

3. Even though a search engine presents a list of addresses in some hierarchical form, it's wise to review the entire list. A reporter who has a good sense of what news is, and what facts may be important, will likely be a better judge than the search engine engineer.

4. Review the site addresses given in the search. Addresses that end in "gov" (government) may be the best sites to go to first if the reporter is looking for a senator's voting record or population data. Addresses ending in "org" (organization) are for associations or other groups. An "edu" ending is for an educational institution such as a university, and one that ends in "com" is for a commercial venture. Depending upon what kind of information the reporter is searching for, an examination of the sites' addresses can steer him or her to the best sources, although all sites could be reviewed if the reporter has enough time. Web address endings include:

- **gov** (federal, state and local government departments, agencies and officials)

- **edu** (colleges, universities, high schools and other educational institutions)

- **mil** (U.S. military sites)

- **org** (nonprofit organizations and associations)

- **int** (international organizations)

- **com** (commercial)

- **net** (networking organizations)

If the reporter doesn't already know the web addresses, selection of the keyword for the search is one of the most important steps toward using the Internet successfully in news gathering. For example, if a student reporter is assigned a story on gun violence in schools, he or she may want to include, as background, shootings in schools in the United States. Using Alta Vista as a search engine, the keywords "gun violence schools" are entered for the search. The results are a list of more than 3 million addresses, too many for anyone to look at. In a second search, the words "in the USA" are added to the keywords; the search yields 2.6 million, still far too many.

Changing the keywords to "statistics on shooting in American schools in 1999" brings 6.7 million addresses; it seems millions of web sites include some content on the topics of guns, violence and schools. The reporter only wants information about students who shoot others in schools in the United States, not every site in the United States that mentions any or all of these keywords.

Alta Vista, as do other search engines, offers some help to narrow this abundance of information. If the + (plus) symbol is typed before a word in a keyword search, the search will yield a narrower field: only sites that actually use those words. Placing quotation marks around the key words means that the search will only give sites that have those exact words in that order, another useful shortcut. With a new keyword search, "+statistics on +shootings in +American schools in +1999," entered, the yield is about 3,000 addresses. This is more manageable, but still too many for a busy reporter to check.

This illustrates the potential frustration of using a search engine for reporting and the importance of keyword(s) selection when a search engine is used. The choice of precise words and the use of the engine's tools (the + and quotation marks) will save time.

The student reporter who is writing about gun violence in schools could get statistics for this story from a U.S. government web site such as the site for the Federal Bureau of Investigation at www.fbi.gov or the Bureau of Alcohol, Tobacco and Firearms at www.atf.treas.gov/. However, many of the sites found during the Alta Vista search could provide some unique information for a story, and some of these should be searched too.

Journalists should be careful about the selection of facts from web sites. Some, such as the government ones, are more likely to have accurate facts than those hosted by private persons. Several addresses could be searched to compare facts, and other traditional sources could be used to verify the accuracy of web site information. Not everything on the web is true or usable for a reporter.

Some of the most useful web sites for reporters, including students who localize national and international stories, include these:

www.splc.org/ltr_sample.html

Maintained by the Student Press Law Center, this site provides a sample letter for students to use to request public records from government bodies, with appropriate language for each state.

www.census.gov/stat_abstract

Maintained by the Census Bureau, this site will help journalists get a wide range of statistics on various economic and social aspects of the U.S. population.

www.thomas.loc.gov

Named after Thomas Jefferson, this site contains a wealth of information on Congress, including the full text of House and Senate legislation, the *Congressional Record* and *Congressional Record Index*, voting records of members of Congress, e-mail addresses of senators and representatives, the text of the U.S. Constitution and more.

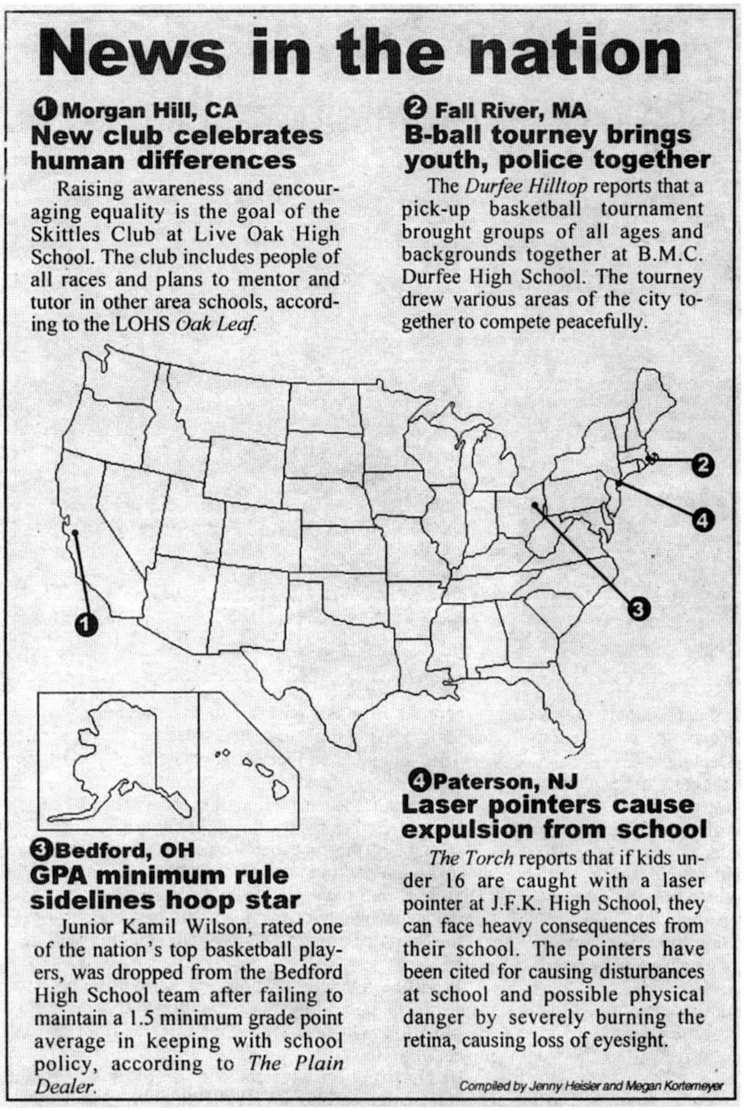

www.ncbi.nlm.nih.gov/PubMed

Maintained by the National Library of Medicine at the National Institute of Health, this site is almost a one-stop shop for medical information. It has stored in its database information from more than 4,000 medical journals.

www.nytimes.com

The New York Times online is a good resource for background information on all national and international events.

www.cnn.com

This is a source for the latest developments in news, sports, weather and the financial markets, and useful for background information, especially on current events.

News in the nation

❶ Morgan Hill, CA
New club celebrates human differences
Raising awareness and encouraging equality is the goal of the Skittles Club at Live Oak High School. The club includes people of all races and plans to mentor and tutor in other area schools, according to the LOHS *Oak Leaf.*

❷ Fall River, MA
B-ball tourney brings youth, police together
The *Durfee Hilltop* reports that a pick-up basketball tournament brought groups of all ages and backgrounds together at B.M.C. Durfee High School. The tourney drew various areas of the city together to compete peacefully.

❸ Bedford, OH
GPA minimum rule sidelines hoop star
Junior Kamil Wilson, rated one of the nation's top basketball players, was dropped from the Bedford High School team after failing to maintain a 1.5 minimum grade point average in keeping with school policy, according to *The Plain Dealer.*

❹ Paterson, NJ
Laser pointers cause expulsion from school
The Torch reports that if kids under 16 are caught with a laser pointer at J.F.K. High School, they can face heavy consequences from their school. The pointers have been cited for causing disturbances at school and possible physical danger by severely burning the retina, causing loss of eyesight.

Compiled by Jenny Heisler and Megan Kortemeyer

Fig. 2.4. School news Internet sites and student newspapers on the Web are often good and easily accessed sources for coverage of news from other schools throughout the United States and in other countries. Previously, schools had to exchange papers through the mail. *Shakerite,* Shaker Heights High School, Shaker Heights, Ohio

www.historychannel.com

Television's History Channel provides a web site component, which is a useful resource for background on stories with a historical link.

www.ncaa.org

Maintained by the National Collegiate Athletic Association, this site can be used for information for sports stories dealing with college athletics and eligibility standards.

www.espn.go.com

Sports reporters who write about major league, collegiate and other sports can get information at this site.

www.billboard.com

Reporters who cover music can get the latest information on everything from concert schedules to top selling records. The site also includes an archive of past "Top Ten" music charts. It is helpful for those who review popular music.

www.imdb.com

The Internet Movie Database has information on nearly 200,000 movies and information on movie directors, actors and various facts about the production of each film. It is helpful for those who review movies.

www.tc.cc.va.us/writcent/gh

Maintained by Tidewater Community College in Virginia, this site is a grammar and writing "hotline."

www.nilesonline.com/data

A journalist maintains this site as a journalist's guide to finding information on the Internet.

www.nicar.org

Maintained by the National Institute for Computer-Assisted Reporting, this site can help reporters find information for stories.

These and many other web sites, many with specific information that would be helpful to beat reporters and columnists, can be either starting points for a reporter or checked at anytime during the reporting and writing stages for a wealth of reasons. Since the Internet adds sites constantly, it is essential for a reporter to periodically update his or her list of web contacts. For example, if a student reporter is writing a story about the impact logging of a nearby virgin forest would have on the area, including the parents of many fellow students, the web sites of several special interest, environmental groups could be read. The reporter could also visit the web sites of area federal and state legislators to find out their positions on the issue. The web sites of the local and state capital newspapers could be read for background information from previously reported stories.

Student reporters should bookmark the web sites for their local and state capital newspapers, state and local governments and their own schools; these can be valuable resources for current and archival information for stories with local and state links.

Web sites maintained by scholastic press groups, including the National Scholastic Press Association, Journalism Education Association, Columbia Scholastic Press Association and Quill and Scroll, may also have information that could assist a reporter.

Reporters can subscribe to electronic mailing lists from a wide range of special interest groups, government bodies and others. All the information sent is likely not completely reliable; as always, a reporter should verify any information received this way with other sources. However, an electronic mailing list can be another valuable source. To locate the list most useful for any story or beat, a reporter can go to this web site and search by keyword for the most appropriate ones to subscribe to: **www.reference.com**. Before searching this site, the reporter should select "Mailing List Directory" from the menu.

Newsgroups are sites on the Internet where persons with similar interests can gather electronically and enter messages about related topics. Newsgroups operate on the Internet's Usenet system. This can be useful for a reporter to find sources and experts, gather background information, pose questions and generally gauge the current interest and opinions on issues. Newsgroups are unlike mailing lists in one important way: Once a person subscribes to a mailing list, messages are automatically sent to the subscriber's electronic mailbox; to participate in a newsgroup, the person has to actively go to the site on the Internet to read the posted messages and add any new ones.

Newsgroups are organized on the Internet into seven categories:

- **Comp**, computers and computer science
- **News**, Usenet and Internet issues
- **Rec**, recreational activities and hobbies
- **Sci**, sciences
- **Soc**, social issues and socializing
- **Talk**, debate and controversial topics
- **Misc**, a variety of miscellaneous topics that do not fit clearly into the other categories

To help a reporter find the most appropriate newsgroup to join and monitor, there are several search engines: **www.reference.com**, **www.liszt.com** and **www.cyberfiber.com**, among others. Not all search engines find the same sites, so several should be checked.

Another useful site for searching newsgroups by topics or keywords in messages posted on these electronic bulletin boards is **www.dejanews.com**. More than two years' worth of postings can be searched from more than 50,000 newsgroups through this site. Searches can be by topic, writer and e-mail address. The **dejanews** site can save time for reporters who don't want to monitor a newsgroup for a long time but only want a quick look at what's being posted on the group's bulletin board.

EXERCISES

1. Plan a beat system for your school newspaper. List 12 or more different sources of information, departments or offices in your school, a contact person or spokesperson for that beat, and the contact's phone number and e-mail address.

2. Prepare a beat system for six specific interest groups outside of the school, such as MADD (Mothers Against Drunk Driving), travel or intercollegiate sports. List a contact or spokesperson for each group and that person's phone number and e-mail address.

3. Prepare a list of six things you should not do during an in-person interview. Share your list with the class and discuss, as a class, the "dos and don'ts"

of an interview. Do two short mock interviews in class, with one demonstrating several mistakes and the other done correctly.

4. As a class, select a popular topic, one that is "in the news," such as assisted suicides or the legalization of marijuana for the treatment of illnesses. Each person in the class should randomly select another person in the class to interview about the topic. Each student should write five prepared questions and then conduct an interview. Follow-up and new questions should be encouraged. Each student will be an interviewer and interviewee.

5. Each student should select one person within the school or in the community who is a leader or spokesperson for a department, special interest group, organization or other agency to interview either in person or on the phone. Acting as a news staff, the class should discuss each "story" and suggest angles and sources of background information to help the "reporter" prepare questions. Following this "news staff meeting," each student should prepare for the interview by researching the person and topic, writing advance questions and calling the person for an appointment. The student should conduct the interview. Afterward, the student should submit to the teacher for evaluation the advance questions, the responses received during the interview and any new or follow-up questions and responses (a transcript of the interview). Later, following the completion of Chapter 4, "Writing the News Story," the student could write a story based on this interview.

6. Using print or online resources, students should find these facts: (1) the name of the 36th president of the United States; (2) the population of France; (3) the highest-grossing film of 1999 and amount; (4) the NBA (basketball) team with the most championship titles; (5) the names of three special interest groups that focus on the environment; (6) the spelling of the name of the president of South Africa; (7) the number of time zones on earth; (8) how the Roman Catholic pope is selected; (9) all the countries bordering Hungary; (10) stock mar-

ket abbreviations for Microsoft, General Electric and Sony; (11) the meaning of the abbreviation GMT; (12) three possible or alternate spellings for the surname Anderson.

7. List 10 web sites that have information on pregnancy rates among unmarried teens in the United States in the last five years.

8. List three newsgroups that posted messages within the last two years about anorexia.

9. Develop a strategic search for information on teenage suicides in the United States for a story you could write for your school newspaper. List as many resources as you can, including several persons you could interview either in person, on the telephone or through e-mail and 10 or more print and online sources of information.

10. Review the web sites of these two organizations and write a brief summary of what they do and what they offer on their web sites: Center for Investigative Reporting and National Institute for Computer-Assisted Reporting.

Writing News Leads

Chapter

3

Except for the barely audible drone of the computer and someone talking on a mobile phone in another cubicle, the newsroom is silent. A reporter sits in front of a glowing monitor, impatient keyboard and restless mouse. An empty window waits, offering a wealth of choices on its menu. It's a window of opportunity for the reporter, who is about to begin writing. Newly on the job and armed with copious notes, the reporter momentarily wonders where to begin.

Begin at the beginning: Write the lead—that's what the reporter wants to do. It's the logical place to start. And like all good stories, this one needs to begin with the right words and a tantalizing hook that will, it is hoped, attract some readers or listeners. The reporter knows that there are thousands of other stories that will be written today, and all of them will be waiting for an audience. As the reporter writes, the audience is getting busier and more distracted than ever.

Given the nearly universal complaint today—too many choices, not enough time—it's no wonder that print media are in fierce competition with broadcast and electronic media for readers, listeners and viewers. For print media to compete successfully with other, more immediate information services, they have to package their content in a visually appealing way. When it comes to packaging writing, it means beginning a story with something that will grab the reader's attention due to its relevance or unique personal appeal. A reporter must rise to this challenge with each story.

A headline, accompanying photo or other art can bring a reader to the story, but there will have to be some carefully chosen words to make the reader continue into the body of the story and even reach the story's end. These first words—typically less than 40—form the lead (pronounced *leed*) of the story. Many veteran news writers think the lead is the most important element of a news story. At the very least it is pivotal in the goal of achieving high readership of a story.

Simply, if you want someone to read your story, write a great beginning.

In daily newspapers, most timely and featured news stories are written in the traditional news form, the inverted pyramid. Facts are presented in decreasing order of importance. The inverted pyramid wasn't always the form of choice for the daily press: The narrative form—often called "storytelling"—was popular through the mid–19th century. During the Civil War, news bulletins from the battlefronts, with timely updates on the war's progress, were received at newspaper offices and printed at the top of the story. The "older" news fell a few notches lower in the story.

Eventually, prioritizing the facts from the latest information and often the most important to the less timely information and often least important became the common practice. The beginning or lead for the inverted pyramid story was almost always a brief summary of the most up-to-date and important facts. The news summary lead remains a popular choice today for those who write for the daily press.

High school print media, especially newspapers, are mostly published month-

One Story, Six Possible Leads

The *who* beginning:

Los Angeles Board of Education members agreed today to extend the current school year for some one million area public school students until July 20. The 15 additional school days were added to make up for the time when schools were closed due to the October earthquake.

The *what* beginning:

The current school year will be extended until July 20 as the result of a vote today by the Los Angeles Board of Education. Some one million area public school students will have to spend 15 more days in school due to the school closure following last October's earthquake.

The *where* beginning:

In Los Angeles today, the Board of Education extended the current school year until July 20 for some one million area public school students. The 15 additional school days were added to make up for the time when schools were closed due to the October earthquake.

The *when* beginning:

Today, the Los Angeles School Board extended the current school year until July 20 for some one million area public school students. The 15 additional school days were added to make up for the time when schools were closed due to the October earthquake.

The *why* beginning:

To make up for the time when schools were closed due to last October's earthquake, the Los Angeles Board of Education agreed today to extend the cur-

ly; some are published weekly. This frequency factor, compared with dailies, means the inverted pyramid, with its characteristic news summary lead, has limited value. There are few breaking news stories in the school newspaper and perhaps none in the yearbook. School news web sites may break news if they update content frequently. If school newspapers use the news summary lead and a traditional inverted pyramid form for stories that already happened a week or more before the paper is published, they risk low readership. The central issue: Who wants to read old news, especially if it hasn't been updated? However, the inverted pyramid, with its signature news summary lead, is a useful form for advance stories in the school paper and, in a modified form, for most other stories.

Here is a story in inverted pyramid form with a news summary lead.

SGA members hold votes on School Council

Two seniors hold voting seats on the School Council, Lee's largest governing body.

SGA president Patricia Lopez and SGA member Alison Douglass attend weekly council meetings after school and vote equally with other members.

Lopez said all council members encourage the students to give their input because they often have ideas different from adult members.

"They have one way of thinking, and we have another," Lopez said.

According to Council Chair Mike Cooley, both students see things from a student's angle that adult members may not see.

"They give us a student perspective on issues around the school," Cooley said. "We often ask for their opinions and are given insight we wouldn't have."

Cooley said they were instrumental in approving student surveys, a duty of the School Council. One survey had been approved by all adult members, but when read by both students, neither understood it. The council then asked for changes to be made.

"If the students didn't understand it, what's the sense of putting it out?" Cooley said.

Although both students have been present for discussions such as B lunch, MU, the school plan and a time-out room policy, the only issue the School Council has formally voted on this year has been the teacher of the year. Government teacher Adrienne Green was selected.

The School Council is a school governing body, comprised of 13 faculty members, one parent and two students, the SGA president and another student selected from the SGA class.

The School Council makes decisions on issues such as the three-year school plan, which will be submitted to Area 1 before Dec. 21.

Lance
Robert E. Lee High School
Springfield, Va.

In the above story, the most important information—two students serve on an important, decision-making council—is in the lead, the first paragraph of the story. The next most important information—the names of these two students—is in paragraph two. Usually, the first thing a reader wants to know is "what happened?" The next natural question is "who was involved?" The first two, brief paragraphs in this story answer both of these questions. The other paragraphs in this story answer other, less important questions and further describe what happened through the "voices" of those who are involved.

THE NEWS SUMMARY LEAD

Also called a "direct" or "hard news lead," the news summary lead gets readers immediately to the main point of the article. A well-written news summary lead gives structure to the rest of the story.

To write an effective news summary lead, the reporter needs to review all the facts and opinions gathered for a story. Six important reader questions must be answered in each news story:

1. *What* happened? *What* will happen next?

2. *Who* was involved?

3. *Where* did it happen?

4. *When* did it happen?

5. *Why* did it happen?

6. *How* did it happen?

The news writer may even organize his or her notes in an informal outline form, writing these questions and then answering them. Once the writer is satisfied with the answers, the news summary lead will be easy to write.

Usually, the *what* and *who* are the most important of these six questions. With this in mind, the writer can begin with either the *what* (what happened?) or the *who* (who was involved?) answers. If the person or persons involved are prominent—well-known—then the *who* can begin the lead.

Here is a news summary lead that begins with *what* will happen for an advance story.

> **A meeting is to be held with administrators and parents today to discuss the switch from selling Coke to Pepsi on campus. The transition was made in compliance with a contract change that took effect this year.**

Stagg Line
Amos Alonzo Stagg High School
Stockton, Calif.

rent school year to July 20 for some one million area public school students. Fifteen more days were added to the school calendar.

The *how* beginning:

By a vote today, the Los Angeles Board of Education extended the current school year to July 20 for some one million area public school students. The 15 additional days were added to make up for the time when schools were closed due to the October earthquake.

All of these leads are acceptable, but some are better than others. The *what* and the *why* are direct and begin with more important facts. The *who* and the *how* are somewhat important; the *when* and *where* are not very important.

The main *what* fact in this lead is "a meeting." There are other *what* facts in the second sentence, including "Coke," "Pepsi" and "contract." The *who* facts, which follow the *what*, are "administrators" and "parents."

In this lead and follow-up paragraph, a *who* fact begins the story.

> Area students now have the opportunity to receive high school credit by using the Internet.
>
> The program offering the credit is called Virtual High School. It allows students to choose from more than 105 semester and year-long classes.

> *Lakewood Times*
> Lakewood High School
> Lakewood, Ohio

The *who* in this lead, "area students," is general. The *what*, "an opportunity," is also not specific. The follow-up paragraph expands the *what* and provides more details. This is a common way to develop an inverted pyramid story with a news summary lead. This lead is also an example of the effectiveness of a simple, declarative sentence in newswriting. The subject ("students") is first, followed by the verb ("have") and then the receiver or object of the action ("opportunity"). Newswriting should be conversational in most cases.

Another news summary lead that begins with the *who* fact and expands on it with more details also answers nearly all of the essential reader questions.

> One of the most recognizable figures in women's basketball, Los Angeles Sparks center Lisa Leslie, will speak at the annual Women's History Assembly March 8. Leslie, a three-time collegiate All-American, Olympic gold medalist and WNBA all-star will be the first speaker in the school's history to highlight the increasing contributions of women in athletics.

> *Chronicle*
> Harvard-Westlake School
> North Hollywood, Calif.

Many facts can be included in a news summary lead without it becoming too long, awkward to read and ineffective. In the following example, the *what* question is answered first, but the other reader questions are also answered.

> A policy designed to control all forms of school sponsored expression will be presented at the Peninsula School Board meeting Thursday, April 22, for possible implementation.

> *Peninsula Outlook*
> Peninsula High School
> Gig Harbor, Wash.

News summary leads can begin with any of the other reader questions: *where, when, why* and *how*. An example of a lead that begins with the *where* angle:

> Nevada is getting its first taste of the impact of charter schools with the opening of the I Can Do Anything High School in Washoe County. Charter schools offer alternatives to traditional schools, although they are funded through the public school system.

> *Excalibur*
> Robert McQueen High School
> Reno, Nev.

Beginning with the *where*, the location of what happened, is sometimes the best choice to open a story. Proximity or nearness is one of the key news elements. Localizing a story will make the facts at least seem more relevant to readers.

An example of a lead that opens with the *when* angle and a follow-up paragraph that shows effective parallel construction:

> April 20, the nation watched in horror as students in Littleton, Colorado, fled their blood-stained Columbine High School.
>
> April 21, two incidents at LHS involving threats prompted school officials to in-

tervene, although principal Vince Barra said the Littleton incident was not the reason.

Lakewood Times
Lakewood High School
Lakewood, Ohio

An example of a lead that begins with the *why* angle, this is also called beginning with an **infinitive** ("To look …"):

To look for suggestions to improve the outlook of the community, a public meeting May 10 at Naperville North High School will discuss the results of the Search Institute Profiles of Student Life.

Central Times
Naperville Central High School
Naperville, Ill.

An example of a lead that opens with the *how* angle, this is also called beginning with a **present participle** ("Rejecting …"):

Rejecting an appeal to a school's expanded drug testing program, the Supreme Court ruled last month that schools have the power to extend drug-tests to all students involved in extracurricular activities.

Falconer
Torrey Pines High School
Encinitas, Calif.

The infinitive and present participle lead openers are called **subordinate clauses.** Although a subordinate clause delays briefly the subject-verb-object flow of the declarative sentence form, it is acceptable for news writers to use them. In addition to the infinitive and present participle openers, there are others writers can use.

Begin with a **prepositional phrase:** a group of words beginning with a preposition and not containing a subject and a verb.

After two years of discussion, the banning of book bags will become a school policy effective at the beginning of next school year.

Blue and Gold
Findlay High School
Findlay, Ohio

Begin with a **gerund:** the *ing* form of noun becomes the subject.

Flying planes has always been David Ashamalla's ('99) dream. Last year, Ashamalla competed in aviation at the Skills USA competition, another step towards becoming a pilot.

Lion
Lyons Township High School North Campus
LaGrange, Ill.

Begin with a **temporal** clause: a period of time is an important fact.

After months of anticipation and the loss of half of the teacher's parking lot, construction on the new library, theater and other bond improvements officially began Wednesday, March 31.

Edition
L.C. Anderson High School
Austin, Texas

Begin with a **conditional** clause: express speculative interest or a condition. If *this* happens, then *that* will happen.

If the Board of Education's planned budget is approved by the Dare County Board of Commissioners, a debt of approximately $19,000 created by the athletic department will finally be eliminated.

According to Mary Ann Bohannon, finance officer for MHS, the debt has been accumulating for the past several years.

Sound to Sea
Manteo High School
Manteo, N.C.

Begin with a **concessive** clause, a subordinate clause that begins with *though* or *although* and expresses either circumstances that make a result unusual or difficulties overcome.

> **Although former principal Jim Blanche left West to be superintendent of schools, some will probably be seeing his face around the halls of West between now and the end of the year.**
>
> **Except this time he might be a substitute teacher.**

Beak 'n Eye
West High School
Davenport, Iowa

A well-written news summary lead does not have to answer all of the reader's questions—*what, who, where, when, why* and *how*—in the first sentence or even the first paragraph. A second sentence in the lead paragraph or a follow-up paragraph can include facts that answer all or most of the remaining ones. Although *when* and *where* lead openers can be effective as the above examples illustrate, they are usually less important and less interesting than the *what, who, why* and *how* openers. To begin with a date that has no significance is usually a weak start. Writers should think about all the facts and select the most important one for the lead opener. This is sometimes called the **feature fact**. Knowledge of the elements of news, found in Chapter 1 of this book, is helpful in determining the feature fact.

Although reporters should not write according to a formula or follow too closely restrictive guidelines on structure, a good news lead is often about 35 words or one or two sentences. Certainly, good leads of one word to more than 35 words have been written, including some for the best, prize-winning stories in journalism history. However, short sentences and paragraphs are easier for persons to read.

A news lead often cites the source of the news. This gives the story and the newspaper credibility.

Here is an example of a news lead with the source of the facts cited.

> **Stony Point High School has been completed three-fourths of the way and is set to be finished July 1, according to Ruben Whitney, campus principal.**

Spitfire
Round Rock High School
Round Rock, Texas

In this example, the source of the facts is given in the second paragraph.

> **The computer lab has been upgraded by the addition of 28 new IBM compatible computers.**
>
> **Technology Committee Chairman Al Bell said that the PC lab will help prepare students to use both IBM and Macintosh computers.**

Blue and Gold
Findlay High School
Findlay, Ohio

It is necessary to not only identify the news source by name but by title too. For the facts to be believable to readers, the rank or authority position of the source is considered: The higher the source is in rank, the more credible the facts are likely to be or at least perceived to be by the reader. Citing only one source, no matter the rank of that source, is risky if the facts are being disputed or if the source's opinion is mixed in with the facts.

When citing a source, use the past tense verb "said" and add a time reference, such as "last week," "today," "recently" or a specific date. The time reference will help make the lead more complete.

If a student is cited as a source, the student's year in school is given after the name. For example: Alan Heider, '03, or Alan Heider, junior. A teacher cited should be identified with his or her subject or department. For example: Ann Tiffany, English, or Ann Tiffany, counselor.

If opinion is included in the lead, then the opinion is attributed to a source, a person. This is done to increase story objectivity and credibility.

Here's a lead that includes opinion attributed to a source.

A number one ranking for the boys' soccer team has evaporated under a recent rash of injuries, said coach Randy Freeman.

Smoky Hills Express
Smoky Hills High School
Aurora, Colo.

The attribution is needed in this lead because the potential inability to compete for the number one ranking is speculation, someone's opinion. The most credible or believable person to speculate would be the coach. The sports writer could not make this statement since he or she needs to remain objective. A writer's opinions are left out of the news or sports story.

Reporters who write for papers that publish infrequently need to also consider timeliness of the facts as they write their news summary lead. Leads can be revised at press time if a new development has occurred. The reporter may have to actively seek more information and interview again the story's sources to get an update.

Here's an example of a news lead with an updated *who* and *what* angle.

The administration has decided not to take action against the senior class even though 24 percent of the class was absent on an unofficial senior skip day Jan. 25.

Lance
Robert E Lee High School
Springfield, Va.

This story was published in *The Lance* one month after the senior skip day. Since a month had passed since the skip day, the reporter made a wise decision to feature the latest development in the story's lead.

The news summary lead is frequently used because hurried readers who may not have time to read an entire story can still get the most important information by reading the story's headline and the first few paragraphs. Some who favor its use also say that it is logical when telling someone about an event to tell the most important facts first; others disagree and think methodically building a story from a set-the-scene introduction

to its most important facts at the end is better.

Today, newspapers use both forms. Another advantage of the news summary lead and inverted pyramid form is that if an editor or page designer needs to cut a story to fit a layout, it may be easier to trim the final paragraph or two, since the lead and immediate follow-up paragraphs have the most important facts and the final paragraphs have the least important facts.

Writing a headline for an inverted pyramid story with a news summary lead may be easier since the main facts are presented in the opening paragraphs; the headline writer does not have to read the complete story to select the key words that accurately represent the key facts in the story.

As more people get their breaking or hard news as bulletins or short reports on television, radio or the Internet, the need for the traditional news summary lead for an inverted pyramid story decreases. News-features, news background and analysis stories have increased in newspapers as a consequence, either pushing out hard news or turning those hard news stories into news briefs. For newspaper writers, the new content means fewer news summary leads and more creative choices. As already discussed in this book, the school newspaper is even more likely than a commercial daily to begin more of its stories with modified news summary leads, including many novelty or feature approaches.

THE MODIFIED NEWS LEAD AND THE NUT GRAPH

In the face of competition from other media, newspapers—those published daily and less frequently—have tried to make news and other information more interesting and relevant to readers to give them a good reason to keep buying and reading newspapers. Newspaper reporters have varied the form of their work, including writing more creative story leads. These leads are often less direct and less "formulaic" than the traditional news summary lead. Some journalists call these soft or indirect news leads.

The most obvious way to modify a news summary lead is to use only the feature fact or perhaps two of the *what, who, where, when, why* and *how* in the lead. By delaying some of the answers to these essential reader questions, the sentences can be short, and the writer can create a "hook" to catch or entice the reader to continue into the body of the story.

Sometimes the writer simply modifies the news

summary lead by dividing the essential facts into two paragraphs, delaying complete disclosure of the main facts.

Here is a modified news summary lead.

> After taking her junior year off from the tennis team, Kari Olsen (12) is back as the number one singles player on the varsity team.
>
> She took the year off to concentrate on her own individual game and earn herself a twelfth place ranking in Southern California.
>
> Since returning, she has helped the Falcons to another CIF team title.

Falconer
Torrey Pines High School
Encinitas, Calif.

In the first paragraph, the *who* and *what* are introduced. In the follow-up paragraph, the reader learns *why*, *how* and, generally, *where* and *when*. Together, they complete the news summary.

Another example of a modified lead shows a creative flair.

> With last year's state championship still fresh in its mind, the boys' volleyball team began its season hungry for a second helping.
>
> After losing seven seniors to graduation last year, the team enters the season unranked. But after several early victories, the boys earned a number 7 ranking from the *Chicago Tribune*.

Central Times
Naperville Central High School
Naperville, Ill.

Many writers use a brief anecdote as the first paragraph, or some suspended or delayed interest statement. The follow-up paragraph then is a more conventional summary of the main fact of the story. It answers the most important of the reader's questions. This follow-up is called the **nut graph**. It gets its name from a com-

parison of a nut to a news story. The nut, the follow-up paragraph, contains the hard news, the feature fact. *Graph* is simply an abbreviation of "paragraph." Another term for nut graph is **focus graph**.

In this example of a story that begins with an anecdotal lead and follows with a nut graph, the opening paragraph refers to prominent persons and places to create a memory flashback.

> Growing up playing football in the backyards, going to Memorial Stadium, or listening to Kent Pavelka on the radio or Keith Jackson on ABC, many dreamed of wearing that red "N" on their helmets or being the next Tommie Frazier or Ricky Williams. As people get older, however, those dreams start to fade away.
>
> On Feb. 3, that dream became a reality for four Southeast football players as seniors Chris Loos, Ty Gifford, Sean Blue and Brandt Bacus all signed to play football for either Division I or II schools next fall.

Clarion
Southeast High School
Lincoln, Neb.

The first paragraph is soft and indirect, and the follow-up, the nut graph, is direct and summarizes the facts.

Another example of a story with a suspended interest lead and a follow-up nut graph has some shock value.

> Justine Yeung always wanted a cat. She is now the proud owner of a dark male named Chimichanga. Unfortunately, Chimichanga is skinned and in a garbage can, and junior Yeung is preparing to remove its musculature.
>
> These nightmarish scenes may offend the weak of heart, but in Ms. Rama's anatomy class, they have become the order of the day as the latest shipment of cat cadavers have arrived for dissection.

Day Times
Detroit Country Day School
Beverly Hills, Mich.

The nut graph answers other readers' questions: So what? Why should I read this story? If the anecdotal lead is used, it is important for writers and editors to remember to write a nut graph, even one that is one sentence long.

THE VIGNETTE LEAD

Commercial newspapers, such as the *Wall Street Journal*, have relied increasingly upon a form of the storytelling method of story development for story leads. As already mentioned, these leads are followed by a nut graph, which includes the feature fact and one or more of the other main facts of the story.

The **vignette lead**, as these brief anecdotes are called, often is used for reports on social, economic, political, environmental and other major issues to bring the stories to the human or personal level. Readers seem to relate to these "big" stories more easily if they begin with a personal story. A vignette is a brief descriptive sketch or story.

Vignette leads are longer than anecdotal–nut graph leads. A vignette may be many paragraphs long, but eventually the writer returns to a more conventional newswriting form to present the hard news facts and opinions in the story. The writer may return to the vignette later in the story, including in the ending. Usually the result, the final story, is a combination of two methods of development, (1) narrative or storytelling and (2) inverted pyramid.

Some stories are so broad—drug abuse—or so complicated—the federal budget—that use of the vignette is the first and only effective choice to begin the story. Since the reader may be asking "so what?" about all stories, the vignette may provide the most direct response when the stories are broad based.

Here is an example of a vignette.

> Senior Josh Bartlett gets home from school around 4 p.m. He squeezes in half an hour of homework—some sociology or maybe a little econ. At 7 p.m., after a workout, a shower and a quick dinner, he is ready to hit the books again, this time for advanced chemistry or calculus.

> "On a normal night I can do probably about three hours," he said.

> After he has finished his school assignments, Bartlett also has to prepare for a mock trial, model UN and an upcoming engineering competition. If he works straight through, he can be done by 10:30 p.m., but more often he shoots to finish at 11 and be in bed by 11:30. He rarely makes it.

> Bartlett is one of thousands of students in the United States being smothered by homework. According to researchers at the University of Michigan, kids are doing more school work than ever before and at much younger ages. In 1981, grade school students spent 84 minutes a week on homework. In 1997, that figure was up to 134 minutes per week. In 1997, junior high students were pounding out upward of three and a half hours of homework per week, compared to only two hours in 1981.

Update
Herbert Henry Dow High School
Midland, Mich.

In the above story, the four-paragraph vignette leads into a fact-filled, hard news paragraph. The subject of the story, teens and homework, is, for the high school press, a significant, far-reaching story. Although the topic affects every student, the vignette brings it immediately to the personal level—one person's story is everyone's story. What *The Update* reporter has given readers is a short, descriptive sketch, complete with a direct quote, which paints a compelling picture.

To end the homework story, the writer brings the reader back to the vignette:

> Meanwhile Bartlett is finally ready for bed. On an average night he gets about six hours of sleep. The recommended amount is eight. But everything is done. His assignments are completed and his books are packed away.

> "Besides sleep and relaxing," he said, "I've managed to fit everything in."

Tips for Writing the News Lead

•Ask yourself, "What do I want to tell my readers?" Can you write your answer in one or two sentences? Try it. This is a way to keep you focused on the purpose of the story.

•Organize your notes to answer the six basic reader questions: **what, who, where, when, why** and **how?**

•Decide which of the six reader questions is most important. Think about the elements of news from Chapter 1 of this textbook. Your choice is called the **feature fact**—the fact you are going to feature first in your lead. There can be several facts of equal importance in a news lead.

•Begin writing your lead in sentence form with the feature fact first. Then add a few more facts, a few more answers to the remaining reader questions to complete the sentence. Keep the sentence short.

•Use specific nouns and complete names. Use colorful, lively verbs. Adjectives and adverbs add opinion. Attribute opinion to the source.

•If the lead has some unusual or especially important facts, name the source of this information in your lead.

•A second sentence in the first paragraph can amplify or expand the facts given in the first sentence or answer more of the reader questions.

•If the lead paragraph is in-

Another example of a vignette opening is for a story about a major social issue, family time and meals.

> Every morning Ray Gautschy '01 eats breakfast before going to school. This alone is an impressive feat for many teenagers, but Gautschy doesn't stop there. He actually sits down to eat with his entire family.
>
> "We've been doing it forever," Gautschy said of his family's breakfast ritual. "We try to eat dinner together every night, too."
>
> Gautschy's family proves to be the exception rather than the rule, as many teens say they never eat together.

> *Lion*
> Lyons Township High School North Campus
> LaGrange, Ill.

The remainder of this story about the demise of at-home family meals is built around comments from other students and a sociology teacher who serves as the "expert" source.

Another short vignette introduces a story about programs for teen mothers.

> Senior Amanda Williams sat calmly in her chair among playing children, holding her sleeping son, 10-month-old Daniel.
>
> "I didn't know what I was living for before I had him," Williams said.
>
> She was at the Mommy and Me meeting held every Thursday at Lakewood Hospital. The program gives teen parents a chance to talk with other teen parents.

> *Lakewood Times*
> Lakewood High School
> Lakewood, Ohio

Long or short, vignettes are a useful tool for news, sports and feature writers. They are also effective for broadcast features. Writers should always find real persons to sketch, to help set the scenes for the presentation of fact, figures and opinions that follow. Fabrication—making up a vignette—is unethical and unacceptable. (See Chap. 22.)

OTHER CHOICES FOR LEADS

In addition to the news summary, modified summary and vignette leads, the news writer has some other choices to consider as the lead is written.

Facts, opinions and other information gathered by the reporter for the story are considered when the story is written; not every lead type is suitable for every story. What a lead is called isn't important, especially to readers. What counts most is the creativity of a writer to see the possibilities in the facts and always anticipate reader interest.

A **descriptive**, or **background**, lead describes the story's setting or gives details leading up to the story itself. It can also include dialogue. Although it delays the introduction of the feature fact or answers to reader questions (*what, who, where, when, why* and *how*), it can be effective for a story setting that is unusual or contribute to the core news elements.

Here is an example of a descriptive lead.

> Hundreds of thousands of televisions were tuned into the Weather Channel as the announcer spoke of destructive winds and massive waves. Awaiting the next update and hoping for a change in course, vacationers and residents alike wondered if they should leave.
>
> On Aug. 25 they got their answer.

Sound to Sea
Manteo High School
Manteo, N.C.

In this descriptive lead, dialogue is used to set the scene.

> "Pssst! Have you heard the news?"
>
> "She did WHAT?"
>
> "So and So told me that he said ..."
>
> Sounds like the typical chatter of GLHS students as they switch classes each day. But these conversations, full of details that change as quickly as a child's game of telephone, will be brought to the stage Nov. 13 and 14 as the GLHS Theatre Department present *Rumors,* a farce by Neil Simon.

Lion's Roar
Gahanna Lincoln High School
Gahanna, Ohio

A **direct address** lead temporarily speaks directly to the reader by using the second person pronouns "you" and "your." After the lead, the body of the story is then written in third person. It is informal and is intended to involve the reader in the story.

Here is an example of a direct address lead.

> You may have seen Justin Lopez roaming through the halls and wondered "Should this guy be in college?" It turns out that this 6'6", 235 lb. giant is a sophomore.

direct or delays the feature fact, write a **nut graph** as the follow-up to the lead to tell the reader the feature fact.

• If you have written your lead in the S-V-O (subject-verb-object) sentence form and think it is effective, then continue developing the rest of the story. If you think the lead you have written will not attract many readers to your story, try one of the lead variations listed in this chapter.

• Review your lead once your story is done. If you began with the *when* angle as your feature fact ("This year ...;" "On Feb. 23, ..."), you might want to reconsider and rewrite it. Usually, the *when* fact, though often important, is not the most interesting way to begin a story. Would the *who, what* or *why* facts be better?

• Update your lead to include the latest development if your story is written a week or more before it is published. Keep your news as timely as possible.

Horizon
Westwood High School
Austin, Texas

Another direct address lead:

Minutes before your vocabulary quiz, cheat sheets are being passed around the room from student to student. Do you take one? Many of your peers feel you shouldn't.

Highlights
Coral Gables High School
Coral Gables, Fla.

Direct quotation leads are used infrequently, and only if the direct quote is brief. Sometimes a partial direct quote may be effective. A long direct quote slows readers and may inhibit comprehension of the facts.

Here is a direct quotation lead in question form. It can also be considered a descriptive lead, as it sets the scene and delays the feature fact.

"When I say Colombia, what do you think of?" Pilar Gonzalez asks an intent group of Uni students.

"Soccer," ventures one. There are a few giggles.

"That's right, what else?" Drugs and coffee are added to the list. Gonzalez is a speaker from the Colombia Support Network, here to speak with the Spanish Club.

Gargoyle
University High School
Urbana, Ill.

Another infrequently used opener is the **question** lead. It can be effective if the question is the crux of the story. More than one or two question leads in one issue of the school newspaper is not recommended.

Here is an example of a question lead.

What happens to all of that recycling? Blue bins have been placed in classrooms, and sometimes students remember to put their used paper in them, but when they fill up, what happens to all that stuff?

A-Blast
Annandale High School
Annandale, Va.

There are several kinds of **comparison** or **contrast** leads. A widely used one is a **time comparison** (then and now; yesterday and today). Two other ones are **size comparison** (macro to micro; global to home) and **cultural comparison** (Asian to European; liberal to conservative).

Here is an example of a time comparison lead.

From the time she was a little girl, Sarah Harvey ('99) has loved flying in commercial jets. A year and a half ago, on her 16th birthday, Harvey sat in the cockpit of a Cessna 150 and began flying herself.

Academy Times
Charles Wright Academy
Tacoma, Wash.

Here is another time comparison lead, one with a cultural twist.

Two-stepping and line dancing have slid out of physical education class. Now when students put their badminton rackets and basketball shoes aside, it is to do Tae-Bo.

Falcon's Cry
Jordan High School
Durham, N.C.

Here is a size comparison lead, going from a global to a home setting.

While the media may focus on the battles in Kosovo, another war is being waged right here at OHS. It is the struggle between the fireants and the termites in US Government teacher Dale Reichard's classroom.

Lion's Tale
Oviedo High School
Oviedo, Fla.

This size comparison lead goes from a universe of "all" to a much smaller one of "eight."

Unlike the rest of their classmates, eight seniors will not be attending college this fall. They are taking a year off to pursue special interests, volunteer, travel or do an internship.

Gargoyle
University High School
Urbana, Ill.

Novelty, or **oddity**, leads are a catch-all category. They are creative leads that likely succeed at attracting readers simply because they are different. They may be humorous or startling or make an allusion to some other existing writing.

Here are two novelty leads.

Most high school students have been told not to play with matches, but not all of them listened.

The five fires in February alone that scorched the Jordan bathrooms brought attention to a problem of trash can and paper dispenser fires that is neither new nor easily solved.

Falcon's Cry
Jordan High School
Durham, N.C.

It's a strange twist on an old classic.

The Disney-fied version presents a sweet blond in a dress and apron, but Thursday night at 7:30 the curtain goes up on The Charles Wright Players pro-

duction of *Alice in Wonderland* ... in an insane asylum.

Academy Times
Charles Wright Academy
Tacoma, Wash.

All of these lead variations can also be effective to begin feature and other kinds of stories in school newspapers, yearbooks and online news Web sites.

EXERCISES

1. Select a news story from page 1 of your city newspaper. Identify the "five *W*'s and *H*" in the first two paragraphs. Which one of these begins the story? Why do you think the reporter chose that one to begin the story?

2. Read the leads (opening paragraphs) for all the stories on page 1 of your city newspaper. Identify the kind of lead. Is there one kind that is used more than others? Do any of the leads include a nut graph? How long are the paragraphs in a story of your choice (number of sentences and words)?

3. Select one news story on page 1 of your city paper that has a news summary lead. Identify which one of the "five *W*'s and *H*" that begins the story. Rewrite the lead five times, with a different one of the five *W*'s and *H* as the opener. Which one, including the original, do you think emphasizes the most important angle or feature? Which one features the most timely angle? Which one is the least important and why?

4. Select one news story from anywhere in your city paper that has a news summary lead and rewrite the lead using either a descriptive, comparison or contrast, question or direct address lead.

5. Look through all stories in your city newspaper and find an example of a story with a vignette lead and one with a modified news summary lead, which has

a nut graph. Do you think these leads are effective and why?

6. Clip one lead from your city paper that begins with one of these types of clauses: infinitive, present participle, preposition, gerund and conditional.

7. Interview one of your classmates about either his or her hobbies or recreational interests. After reviewing your notes, select what you think is the most interesting or newsworthy fact or comment and write a one-sentence news summary lead for your story based upon that fact. Then, with the same fact, write another lead that is either a modified news summary lead or some other type presented in this chapter. Which one do you like better? Which one will likely appeal to more readers and why?

8. Analyze one issue of your school's newspaper or a section of your school's yearbook. Identify the kinds of leads written for all or most of the stories. If a variety of types are used, why might this be a good strategy?

9. Find one story that was reported in a print newspaper and also online on a news web site. Which is longer? Compare their leads. What are some similarities and differences between the two versions of the same story? Does the method of publication—print versus online—affect the telling of the story? Which medium do you prefer to get your news from and why?

Writing the News Story

"Hope of finding the three climbers missing for four days on Mount Rainier is fading."

Who are these climbers? Why is finding them so difficult? Who is giving up hope of finding them? These are just a few of the questions someone might have after reading this bulletin or news summary.

Even in a fast-paced, computer-driven world, where headline-style news is delivered within an instant to almost anyone, there remains the need for the fully developed news story. In the "information age," the need to be informed defines success. For every person who wants only the headlines and the one-paragraph summaries, there is someone else who needs all the facts. Journalists provide all three—the headline, the summary and the full story. Where the full story is published is secondary today; it can be read or heard almost anywhere on a variety of media. The print newspaper remains a primary outlet, but journalists can write for the new media—the Internet for example—as well.

A journalist who understands the purpose of news and masters the art of newswriting will be prepared to work in both traditional and new media. No matter what type of reporting and writing is eventually done by a journalist, learning how to write a news story is fundamental.

Writing the news story is another step in the news dissemination process. First comes learning about what news is and what it isn't (Chap. 1). Then, the news reporter gathers all the information for the story (Chap. 2). Following the fact-finding stage, the reporter organizes his or her notes and writes the beginning of the story or the lead, which to many is the critical part of the story (Chap. 3). After the lead, the rest of the story, the body and the conclusion, is written. The result is a fully developed story, not just a one-paragraph summary.

The missing climbers on Mount Rainier in the hypothetical story above will be more than anonymous persons if the bulletin is developed into a fully developed news story. All or most of the reader's questions will be answered as the writer goes beyond the headline and the summary to tell the rest of the story. And it's likely someone will want to read it from beginning to end.

THE INVERTED PYRAMID FORM

Writing a news summary lead is the first step in writing a fully developed, inverted pyramid news story. The inverted pyramid form presents facts in descending order, from most important to least important. The most important facts, based on news values and selected by the reporter, are given in the opening, the first and sometimes the second paragraph. All of the succeeding paragraphs expand the lead by supporting it, explaining it or making it specific. Often some of the important reader questions, the five *W*'s and *H* (*what, who, where, when, why* and *how*), are put into a second paragraph to keep the first paragraph as short as possible. Many hard

The Lowell

Lowell High School San Francisco Unified School District

Red Edition

Friday
March 12
1999

Volume 191, Number 2

Penny prom

Backpage prepares you for that special night without putting a dent in your wallet.
Page 20

Oxygen overload?

Style investigates new oxygen-based health and beauty products.
Page 10

INSIDE

★ Meeting your favorite stars may not be all it's cracked up to be.
Columns, Page 17

★ Enlightening experiences change the lives of a student and a teacher.
Profiles, Page 9

| Campus P. 8 | Sports P. 11-16 |
| Opinion P. 18-19 | |

DRIVING FOR VICTORY

CHARLIE BECKERMAN

Driving home. Senior forward Nathan Pratt dribbles past a Marshall defender in a March 3 AAA quarterfinal match. Although Lowell beat Marshall 41-27, the Cardinals lost to Lincoln in the finals by a score of 36-37. For the full story of the basketball season, see Sports on Page 11.

Latino, black acceptances drop sharply

By Sarah Pearce

IN THE WAKE of a federal court ruling last month, the San Francisco Unified School District has accepted a smaller number than in past years of African-American and Latino students for Lowell's incoming class for the third year in a row.

At the same time, the numbers of Chinese and "Other White" students has grown significantly.

African-American students make up less than 1.97 percent (17 of 864) of eighth graders accepted as incoming Lowell freshmen, down from 5.6 percent (44 of 789) last year, according to the district's Educational Placement Center, which handles

See DECREE on Page 6

District bracing for budget cutbacks

By Gregory Krimer and Adrienne Sneed

A $12.7-MILLION budget deficit projected for the San Francisco Unified School District could shave off the mandatory seventh class for next year's freshmen and affect students in other ways, according to principal Paul Cheng.

"Freshmen would be required to take six classes [next year], and would not be able to take a seventh," Cheng said.

Other areas that the deficit may have an impact on include the eighth period in middle schools and Advanced Placement prep periods in high schools.

Ninth-grade resource cen-

See BUDGET on Page 4

Journalism programs rapidly deteriorating.
See Page 7

Cafeteria staff still selling expired food

▣ District had promised to get rid of outdated products

By Charrylenne Soriano

ONE MONTH AFTER cafeteria workers promised not to sell expired food to students, recent purchases of expired milk and carrots on campus are raising further questions about food safety.

The renewed focus on food-handling procedures comes after the cafeteria staff sold milk that expired Feb. 9 to English teacher Elizabeth Rogers on Feb. 18, and sold carrots with a Feb. 14 expiration date to freshman Jenny Chan carrots on March 2.

Rogers said that she now worries about the sanitary condition of the food and its effects on students.

"My main concern is the health of the children," Rogers said. "It [the expired foods] made me very concerned about what the students are getting in San Francisco. What if they got spoiled, rotten food? What happens if a small child eats it?"

Chan also is disappointed after buying expired foods and said she finds it difficult to depend on the cafeteria staff as much as she did before the incident.

"I trusted the cafeteria enough, thinking that they would not serve spoiled food, but it turned out I cannot trust them with sanitation," Chan said. "Now I have to look at all the items I eat from the cafeteria."

The incidents have caused some uneasiness among students and faculty.

"I think that it [the selling of outdated food] is scary," freshman Janet Chung said. "I think the caf-

See CAFETERIA on Page 2

Grant compromise reached

By James Lee

AFTER A MONTH of heated debate regarding a possible one-year postponement of a $771,300 Digital High School grant, the administration has come up with a compromise which seems to satisfy everybody involved.

According to Sam Dederian, program director of the district's educational technology team, the school will postpone the DHS grant application eight months instead of the 12-month delay the administration advocated at a series of meetings last month.

A slip in the timeline for building the new science-academic wing triggered the DHS crisis because the new wing and the construction of a new school-wide computer network — a prerequisite to a $125,000 follow up grant — are bound within a single contract, according to assistant principal John Mahoney.

With the wing postponed, the network would also be delayed, preventing the school from constructing the network in time to qualify for the subsequent grant.

But last week the administration received word from Luster Construction Management, the company overseeing the creation of the wing and accompanying campus renovations, that construction of the network could start earlier than that of the new wing.

In a memorandum to the administration,

Sam Dederian, technology director

See DHS on Page 2

Parents save coach's job

KATE LAZARUS

Swim coach Art Octavio shares a laugh with sophomore swimmer Maria Poggio during Friday's meet against Washington at Rossi Pool. Octavio almost lost his job mid-season, but thanks to support from swim team members' parents, he retained his position. For the complete story, see Page 6.

IN THE NEWS NEXT WEEK

COSTUME COMMOTION

Don't be weak next week — show off school spirit by participating in Theme Week, sponsored by the Spirit Committee. Model red and white apparel Monday on Lowell Day; on Tuesday, hook up with a buddy and dress identically for Twin Day; on Wednesday, get into St. Patrick's Day spirit by donning green; on Thursday, dress in your jammies for P.J. Day; to end the week on Friday, zoom back to the past by sporting retro attire on Flashback Day. The Spirit Committee will vote on the best-dressed person each day and will award winners with theme-appropriate prizes. A Tower Records gift certificate will go to the top all-week dresser.

news stories will have a two-paragraph lead.

Before and after writing the story's lead, the reporter studies all of his or her notes carefully to see the story as a whole, perhaps grouping the separate notes under topics that are the related areas of the interview and from other sources during the fact-finding stage. Some reporters may find it helpful to actually answer the basic reader questions—*what, who, where, when, why* and *how*—before the lead and the body of the story are written. This helps the reporter order the information from most to least important. It can also help in organizing all of the details and elaborations of the basic facts. As they organize their notes, reporters can actually put numbers—1, 2, 3, etc.—opposite the facts to indicate decreasing order of importance.

Here's a news story that presents facts in descending order of importance, or in the inverted pyramid form.

Library provides Internet access

Through the Montebello Unified School District Network (MUSD Net), students will have access to the Internet for educational purposes.

"The majority of students don't have access at home so this is a great way for them to get up-to-date information," said Principal Terrance Devney.

Students can log on through the computers in the library by signing in at the desk with their IDs and stating a valid reason to use the Internet.

Assistance will be available in the library for Internet users. "We all need to be trained because there is more to the Internet than looking up sites," said Librarian Randie Hayward.

The District Internet Consent and Waiver Form for Students will be issued to students next week. Once the forms are returned to the Student Store, students will receive Internet stickers that will be applied to their IDs.

"It is a tremendous tool for students," said Assistant Principal Russ Davis. Students can lose this privilege if they break any of the network access rules. The MUSD Net can be only used for purposes consistent with their approved curriculum and not for commercial profit services. Those who use the network illegally or improperly will lose their privileges.

"Every teacher will have the responsibility to supervise the use of the Internet in the classroom," said Davis.

The Board of Education Policy and Administrative Regulations addresses disciplinary actions for vandalism of computer equipment, unauthorized access to information, computer piracy, hacking and any tampering with hardware or software. Students will be liable for damage or information loss. According to the policy, students may not use the network to annoy, harass or offend people.

Fig. 4.1. Significant news, including stories on school funding and enrollment trends, marks this paper as professional and valuable. *Lowell,* Lowell High School, San Francisco, Calif.

"Internet misuse is serious because the district could be liable," said Hayward.

According to Davis, classrooms and offices have or will have Internet access. MUSD Net links to various MUSD schools and offices. Students can also connect with businesses, major universities, national libraries and other schools and students around the world.

Spartan Scroll
Schurr High School
Montebello, Calif.

Writing a focus statement that states, in a sentence or two, what the story is about is not only helpful in writing a summary lead but it can also keep the writer on track as the rest of the story is developed.

For example, a possible focus statement for the *Spartan Scroll* news story about new Internet access for students within the school could be: "Students will get access to the Internet for the first time at school if they have permission from their parents or guardian." This one sentence summarizes the main point of the story and gives it direction for development. The reporter will then answer the reader questions—*what, who, where, when, why* and *how*—in a more journalistic style.

Some professional reporters write their leads last, but for a beginning reporter it is advisable to at least write a draft lead, a lead that can be edited, polished or even completely rewritten later. Even a draft lead will help the reporter stay focused on the essential facts of the story. Eventually, every reporter will do what works best; it's part of a reporter's style.

School papers that publish infrequently should consider the timeliness of all stories. A summary lead for an inverted pyramid story could feature the most recent development or an expected future development: What can the reader expect to see happen next?

The lead for the *Spartan Scroll* story on Internet access opens with the answer to *how* and continues with the *who* and *what*. The lead reads: "Through the Montebello Unified School District Network (MUSD Net), students will have access to the Internet for educational purposes." This brief, direct one-sentence summary lead tells the reader first *how* something will happen ("Through the Montebello Unified School District Network"), then tells *who* it will happen to ("stu-

dents"), and finally *what* will happen ("will have access to the Internet").

After the lead is written, the remaining facts should be reviewed again. If some of the five *W*'s and *H* have been omitted in the lead, they will need to be included in the body of the story. Additional details about the person or persons involved and more details about what happened will need to be considered and possibly added to the story. This is called "fleshing out" or expanding upon the summary facts in the lead. Opinions of those who are involved in the story are included with the facts to help explain and humanize the story. These opinions and explanations are either indirect or direct quotes.

The second paragraph of the *Spartan Scroll* story answers another one of the five *W*'s and *H* reader questions, the *why*. The second paragraph reads: "'The majority of students don't have access at home so this is a great way for them to get up-to-date information,' said Principal Terrance Devney." The principal is quoted directly. Short direct quotes are preferable to multisentence ones in a news story.

The third paragraph in the *Spartan Scroll* story expands the *how* fact and tells the reader *where* it will happen. "Students can log on through the computers in the library by signing in at the desk with their IDs and stating a valid reason to use the Internet."

Subsequent paragraphs—of various lengths but all brief—expand the story with more details. Various persons involved provide explanations and give their opinions. By including them in the story, the reporter adds a human element, which should increase reader interest. A story that is only a list of facts without attributed comments and explanations from those involved is not very interesting to most readers. All opinions are attributed to someone specific. The reader knows who said what. Some comments are quoted directly ("'Every teacher will have the responsibility to supervise the use of the Internet in the classroom,' said Davis"), and others are indirect quotes ("According to Davis, classrooms and offices have or will have Internet access"). The reporter got facts from multiple sources for the story.

The last paragraph, about the wide range of Internet connections students can now make from school, has the least important facts and could be cut from the story. This is characteristic of the inverted pyramid form. However, when writing, the reporter should not assume that the last paragraph of his or her story will be cut; facts or opinions of interest to readers should be included even though they aren't as important as the ones placed higher in the story.

The reporter who wrote the *Spartan Scroll* story used personal judgment in ranking the facts from most to least important. Every reporter does this. Later, in the copy-editing stage, another person will read the story and determine, among other things, if the facts are presented in a logical and relevant order. If the copy editor thinks they aren't, the lead or more may be rewritten for better emphasis or to highlight the most recent development in the story. Beginning writers may consult with an editor during the writing stage about emphasis and order.

Despite the notion that an editor could cut the last paragraph of an inverted pyramid story and the story wouldn't suffer, in recent years editors and reporter have resisted this practice. Now, they put more emphasis on the story ending. This change is also the result of editors' attempts to hold readers throughout the story. To do this, reporters sometimes save an especially interesting quote or fact until the end, or they answer a question posed at the beginning of the story that remains unanswered until the last paragraph. This deviation from the inverted pyramid form shows the ongoing evolution of journalistic writing, especially for newspapers.

Paragraphs in a news story are short, with usually one main fact or one person's opinions or explanation in a paragraph. Another main fact and another person's comment will be in a new paragraph. To avoid a monotonous pattern, the number of sentences in a paragraph should vary from paragraph to paragraph. Most paragraphs in a news story will have one to three sentences. Sometimes a reporter will write a series of one-sentence paragraphs for emphasis, but generally this is not done. However, this is a guideline not a rule; structure is secondary to content, but structure is still somewhat important. Because of the typically narrow column width in a newspaper, a paragraph with more than four sentences will look long and complex and may discourage readers from starting or finishing even an interesting story.

CONTINUITY

Paragraphs and sentences should follow one another smoothly. If they do, the story will have continuity, or achieve coherence. If a story coheres, it sticks together, making the development easy to follow. Besides putting related information together, continuity, or coherence, is achieved in the following ways.

PRONOUNS

In a news story, the writer uses third-person pronouns (*she, he, they,* etc.). First-person pronouns (*I, me, my, we, us,* etc.) and second-person (*you, your*) are only used (1) when they are in a direct quote or in an indirect, paraphrased quote, both attributed to a source, or (2) in a question or direct address lead (Chap. 3).

Sentences and paragraphs can be linked through the use of pronouns as well as demonstrative adjectives *this* and *that* and to refer to nouns in preceding sentences.

> Beginning next fall, teachers will have Internet access in their classrooms. ***This*** will allow ***them*** to tap into resources available worldwide within minutes.

REPETITION OF A KEY WORD FROM THE PRECEDING PARAGRAPH OR SENTENCE

> In an attempt to boost its sagging treasury, the ***Student Council*** announced last week the sale of school mascot phone cards.

> About $2 of the $10 retail cost of the card will go directly to the ***Student Council***. According to Carlos Raimerez, ***council*** treasurer, card sales will begin in mid-January and could raise as much as $500 in profits the first month.

In the first two paragraphs of this hypothetical story, the key term "Student Council" is repeated, and the shorter version, "council," is also used.

USE OF A SYNONYM REFERRING TO A KEY WORD IN THE PRECEDING PARAGRAPH

> Two members of the ***class of '01*** were named to the ***All-State Marching Band*** following their appearance in a day-long competition in Madison last Saturday.

> ***Senior*** band members Pam Tiffany and Robert Wilson received superior ratings in the tuba category to receive the ***statewide honor***.

The synonym for "class of '01," given in the first

paragraph, is "senior," which opens the second paragraph and otherwise identifies the two students by class. "All-State Marching Band," first paragraph, and "statewide honor," second paragraph, are also synonyms.

ELABORATION OF DETAILS IN LOGICAL SEQUENCE OR ORDER OF IMPORTANCE

> New graduation requirements will affect the class of '03 if a proposal before the Medford School Board is passed at next week's meeting.

> The changes include the addition of a second year of Spanish, reducing the physical education minimum to two years and eliminating World Literature as a required course.

The first paragraph introduces the fact that graduation requirements could change. The second paragraph elaborates on this, specifying the changes.

TRANSITIONAL WORDS

Special words and phrases can be used to tie paragraphs together and develop story continuity. These are called "transitions," and they point out the sequence of thought and help the reader move from paragraph to paragraph.

These transitional words show time: *then, now, shortly thereafter, meanwhile, afterward, later, soon, all this time, formerly, previously, at last, finally, following.*

> With a ten-foot bonfire lighting the night sky, the annual Homecoming festivities began for some one thousand students and others at Parade Stadium last Friday night.

> *Later,* during the half-time ceremonies of the football game, the glowing embers provided a backdrop for the crowning of Rita Mach, senior, as homecoming queen.

The transitional word, *later,* is used to begin the second paragraph to show progression of time and to link the two paragraphs. (Use of the word "embers" in the second paragraph is also a link to "bonfire" in the lead.)

These transitional words and phrases show emphasis: *similarly, furthermore, in addition to, especially, moreover.*

> Lighted candles flickered in the breeze as 35 juniors and seniors were initiated into the National Honor Society May 13.

> *In addition to* achieving high grade point averages, the new society inductees were recognized for their community service and participation in school activities.

The transition from the first to second paragraph is with the phrase *In addition to.*

These transitional words and phrases show contrast or change in viewpoint: *however, but, nevertheless, also, of course, instead, in another way, otherwise, in addition, in general, seriously, in a lighter view.*

> Girls rule! At least they do on the honor roll for first semester. Girls outnumber boys 3 to 2 on the list, which was released last week.

> *However,* the news isn't all bad for the boys. The number of boys who made the list rose by 12 percent.

The transitional word *however* is used to show contrast between (1) the statement and facts in the lead and (2) the fact in the follow-up paragraph.

These transitions show place: *here, there, near, opposite, beyond, adjacent to.*

> Twelve students from West spent their spring vacation building a house in San Antonio with the Habitat for Humanity program.

> The house, *near* the Alamo, was built in four days by the students and three supervising carpenters from the city.

The transition *near* is used to locate the site within

the city of San Antonio. ("City" in the second paragraph refers to "San Antonio" in the first paragraph, an example of using a synonym to refer to a key word in the preceding paragraph.)

THE MODIFIED INVERTED PYRAMID

Occasionally, a news story takes a short step back into time to recap a past event that is related to the topic of the present story. This is often within the paragraph following the lead.

Bond project finally breaks ground

After months of anticipation and the loss of half of the teacher's parking lot, construction on the new library, theater and other bond improvements officially began Wednesday, March 31.

Two years ago, schools voted on what changes were to be made on their campuses with money from the bonds. In addition to the construction of new buildings, changes such as the expansion of the band hall, girl's dressing room, and the renovation of select classrooms are scheduled to take place at Anderson.

"(After the changes) we will have one of the finest high school campuses in the country," principal Dr. David Kernwein said. The changes are scheduled to take approximately 15 months, so the new buildings will be accessible to students at the end of next year. Though construction at other AISD schools has been running behind their expected schedules, construction field manager Craig Johnson said, "Even if we slide off a week or two, we have methods to make up the time."

Most of the construction will be done during normal working hours (7:30 a.m. to 3:30 p.m.), with interior work being done after school and on the weekends. The majority of the exterior work on the new buildings will take place over the summer. Kernwein does not expect construction to distract students.

"We have had contract work going on all year," Kernwein said. "They know how to do it." Though construction has blocked off much of the north parking lot, after the building is finished, Kernwein expects to lose only 15 spaces.

"I don't think it is right that we aren't allowed to park in the teacher parking lot after we have paid for a spot," sophomore Natalie Hopkins said.

The groundbreaking ceremony provided photo opportunities, such as Kernwein in an Anderson hard hat sitting in a tractor surrounded by students. Kernwein also introduced many of the people involved in the construction.

WSM architect Craig Estes took on the project not only for business reasons, but also because he had two daughters graduate from Anderson.

In addition to the changes included in the bonds, Anderson will get a new track around the football field over the summer. This project, funded by the district, is expected to be completed by July.

Edition
L.C Anderson High School
Austin, Texas

Without disrupting the flow of this story, the second paragraph recaps what had happened earlier. This story also includes some examples of good transitions, including using the synonym "changes" for the noun construction "bond improvements" and the use of "In addition to the changes" to link the previous facts to the final ones. Paragraphs are short, and new paragraphs are used for most new quotes, including the indirect quote or paraphrase of the response from the WSM architect Craig Estes. The final paragraph also deviates from the inverted pyramid form by presenting some new information, facts that shouldn't be cut from the story.

C O R A L   G A B L E S   S E N I O R   H I G H

highlights

450 Bird Road
Coral Gables, FL 33146

Volume 39 Issue 8
May 5, 1999

Non-Profit
Org.
U.S. Postage
PAID
Miami, FL
Permit No.
3790

Inside . . .

School Board votes to close campuses
Phase-in will end off-campus lunch

BY DEIRDRE CONNER
AND BIANCA PENALOZA

It's one of the rites of passage for Cavaliers - with the respect garnered as an upperclassman comes the privilege of going off campus for lunch.

However, in a vote on Apr. 15, School Board members voted unanimously to close all high school campuses for lunch by the year 2001. Principals were given discretion as to whether the closing would be immediate or phased in. Here at Gables, the closing will be phased in, making this year's freshmen, the class of 2002, never to get a taste of lunch off campus.

"I chose to phase it in to give students time to adjust," Alex Martinez, principal, said.

Next year, no changes will be made in allowing juniors and seniors out to lunch. In the 2000-01 school year, only the seniors will be allowed out. By the '01-'02 school year, the campus will be completely closed for lunch. Superintendent of Schools Roger Cuevas must submit a plan for each school to the Board by June 21.

Many see the Board vote as a reaction to the March 19 shooting death of a Miami High ninth grader while visiting her friends during lunch. At the Board meeting where the issue was discussed, around 60 senior citizens showed up carrying signs supporting the closing of the campuses.

Some said they were supporting board member Demetrio Perez, who proposed to close all the campuses at the start of next school year.

"Personally speaking, I think it was fantastic to have freshmen and sophomores work their way up to going out to lunch," Martinez said. "But the School Board has a good reason . . . they've been dealing with issues like narcotics use and violence. I really support the decision."

Some question whether the closing of campuses for lunch is an effective way to prevent these problems.

"The Board is a political body and what sounds like good policy is what they're going to do," said Daniel Blackmon, history teacher.

Earlier in the year, Superintendent of Schools Roger Cuevas told Board members that it was not logistically and fiscally possible to prepare all the cafeterias and build additional lunch shelters in time.

Many students agree, although here the closing will be phased out.

"How are they going to have facilities to support freshmen, sophomores, juniors and seniors in four years?" Faye Ibars, freshman, said.

Martinez promises to have more on-site vendors, such as McDonald's, Burger King, and Subway, and a covered area for lunch will be made available for rainy days.

"You're going to spend half your lunch period in line," freshman Aniah Arias said.

Others question the funding that will be necessary to make closed-campus lunch a possiblity.

Some schools may require construction, others more money to bring in more vendors, most will need extra custodians and security guards. In all, the estimated cost of the plan for the whole county is $6.3 million.

"I think there are better things for [the

Photo by Jorge Arauz

FINGER-LICKING GOOD: Eating lunch in an overcrowded cafeteria requires a great deal of skills. Sophomore Gerry Guerra can't understand why his friend is smiling—he's too busy trying to get a french fry in his mouth without bumping his elbow against the guy next to him.

School Board] to spend money on," said Blackmon.

Local businesses that often depend on student lunch business are also upset by the vote.

Restaurants such as the Cajun Grill, Burger King, Miami Heroes and McDonald's all are frequented by students for lunch.

"From what we've seen here students have been very responsible," Stephen Yeung, manager of the Cajun Grill, said. "We've had no problems, and they are a large part of our business."

Not everyone, however, is unhappy with the School Board decision, though. Lula Bogein, who has been working for 13 years at a lunch kiosk here believes that students should stay in school for lunch.

"With all the trouble waiting for kids," she said, "they've got no business outside during school hours."

Youth Summit on Ethics targets behavior

BY WHITNEY WARD

Minutes before your vocabulary quiz, cheat sheets are being passed around the room from student to student. Do you take one? Many of your peers feel you shouldn't.

Students put together a youth summit, or a convention, to teach students the importance of ethics and morals. It was led by co-chairmen Ursula Prado, from Hialeah-Miami Lakes High, and Alan Rosenthal, attorney and representative of Greater Miami Chamber of Commerce, along with the help of the Rotary Club and Interact members.

"Our main purpose was to create a convention and get students to question themselves 'Is this really the way I want to live?' and to create a change," Prado, junior, said.

Several representatives from across the county have been meeting every Saturday

since January to organize the summit on ethics, including several from Coral Gables High: Talia Turnball, Katie Bishopric, and teacher Debbie Cole. Together they have begun Integrity Rocks.

Apr. 20 a group of about 500 students from across the county united at the Hyatt Regency, in downtown Miami, to discuss ethics in athletics, drugs and alcohol, culture and religion, relationships, and education.

"Anytime you have a lot of people working together for a good cause, I think it helps somebody,"Cole, Interact sponsor, said.

The summit began with welcoming speeches by co-chairmen Rosenthal and Prado, as

> *My hope is that students will take a long look at their behavior...* **"**
>
> ROLFE CARAWAN

well as a performance by the Gables' Cavalier singers. Motivational speaker Rolfe Carawan of Seattle, Washington, was the guest speaker. He spoke of the importance of integrity and ethics. He added his personal life experiences, as well as humor, to keep the students interested and listening.

"My hope is that students will take a long look at their behavior and adopt a lifestyle that will give them a great opportunity to succeed while eliminating as many negative consequences as possible," Carawan, keynote speaker, said.

This was followed by breakout sessions. Each student attended a specific session to discuss ethics in certain aspects of life.

The sessions were held by

different schools: Hialeah-Miami Lakes, Sunset, School of Advanced Studies, St. Brendan, and Coral Gables. The sessions consisted of skits, speeches, discussions, and other fun activities.

"I think it went well and I enjoyed it. Hopefully it will have an impact," Tim Palmer, junior at Hialeah-Miami Lakes, said.

Schools across Dade, Broward, and Monroe counties will continue to spread the knowledge they have learned.

Various schools have been holding activities that help show students what needs to be done.

Students here received 'Integrity Rocks' stickers to wear, and discussions were held in social studies classes.

"The turnout here today sends a very large message," Rosenthal said, "What they [students] are saying loudly and clearly is integrity rocks."

ATTRIBUTION AND QUOTES

Attributing the source of facts and opinion in a news story—telling the reader where the information came from and who said what—is an essential aspect of establishing person's professionalism and the medium's impartiality and credibility. Readers need to know that the reporter got his or her facts from the best possible sources and the opinions expressed and explanations given are not the reporter's own opinions.

By telling the reader the source of the facts, the reporter is also allowing the reader to make a judgment about the facts. The need to separate, in a news story, fact from opinion is also crucial. The reader deserves to know whose opinions are being expressed. A news story is not the place for a reporter to express his or her opinion, even a seemingly innocuous one such as: "Homecoming was a success." That may be true, but in a news story, the reporter has to tell the reader who thought the event was a success: "Homecoming was a success," Lisa Washington, senior class president, said. A reporter has an opportunity to express his or her opinion only in a signed opinion column or in an unsigned editorial.

Unattributed and attributed opinion in a news story is called **editorializing.** Reporters and editors who find unattributed opinion, even a single somewhat harmless adjective or adverb, should delete it from the story. For example, it may seem harmless to use the adjective "beautiful" in front of the noun "decorations" when writing a story about prom, but unless someone the reporter has interviewed said the decorations were beautiful, the adjective has to be deleted.

Sometimes opinion can be attributed to a general source if the assessment is generally accepted by most if not everyone who would read the story. For example: "Homecoming was a success, according to many who attended the parade, game and dance." The reporter has attributed the opinion, "success," to no one in particular, but to many persons. This can ethically only be done if the reporter actually asked a number of persons who participated in these Homecoming activities and the majority of them said they like or enjoyed the events, had a good time or called it a success.

Not every fact in a story needs to be attributed if the facts are all from the same source. Once the attribution of facts is made near the beginning of the story, the reader will likely assume the following facts are from the same source. However, additional attributions to the same source can be a good linking or transitional device. Some facts are general knowledge and also do not have to be attributed. Sometimes it will be obvious to readers that the facts are firsthand knowledge because the reporter witnessed the event. A reporter should use common sense in deciding which facts need attribution and which ones don't.

The preferred verb for the attribution of all direct and indirect quotes is *said.* Occasionally, the present tense *says* can be used. *Says* is a good choice when the quote, direct or indirect, is something a person repeatedly says or is a "signature" or "trademark" statement, identified with the person.

Direct quote with *said* in attribution:

"Violence will stop in school when students learn to respect their classmates who may be a different color or have a different religion, ethnic background or sexual orientation," school psychologist Marian Anderson **said**.

Fig. 4.2. Student newspapers report events originating on- and off-campus. These stories on page 1 have a student tie-in to make them relevant for the paper's target readers. *Highlights*, Coral Gables High School, Coral Gables, Fla.

Indirect quote (paraphrase) with *said* in attribution:

Violence will stop in schools when students respect each other and ignore differences based on color, religion, ethnicity and sexual orientation Marian Anderson, school psychologist *said*.

Use of verbs other than *said* in quote attributions is limited and often not recommended. *Stated* is very formal and should only be used if someone in authority issues a formal statement, either in person or on paper. Another possibility, *remarked*, is also formal.

News writers should not worry that frequent use of *said* is too repetitive or shows lack of creativity. Repeated use of *said* will likely not be noticed by readers, and this is the desired effect in most cases.

Opinions and facts should be quoted directly if the information is unusual and if the opinion is colorful and especially if it is controversial. Ordinary facts and "expected" opinions and explanations can be paraphrased (or left as they were said) and then attributed without quotation marks as indirect quotes. Learning what to quote directly and what to paraphrase comes with experience. If a reporter does quote someone directly—with quotation marks—the exact words must be used and in the intended context. An indirect quote—no quotation marks—is safer, but it still needs to be accurate.

Long quotes—more than one sentence—often interfere in the smooth flow of the story and can confuse readers. Short quotes, one sentence or even a phrase or word, are often more effective than long ones.

When deciding to quote someone directly or to paraphrase what was said, the reporter should ask: What would this direct quote contribute to my story? If the words are unique, controversial, colorful, poignant or in some other way memorable, then they should be quoted directly. If they are ordinary, then they shouldn't be.

Yet a story can be more interesting to readers if it has one or more direct quotes. During the interview stage, a reporter should ask questions that will possibly elicit quotable responses. If the initial interviews are finished and the reporter, as he or she is writing the story, has nothing worthy of a direct quote, the source could be asked additional questions; these new responses could provide memorable comments for a direct quote.

Effective news stories are often built around both facts and reactions to facts or opinions. A story with a fact, fact, fact flow, paragraph after paragraph, without the addition of a reaction or explanation provided by a source is usually not as interesting to readers or as effective. Most events need explanation for reader comprehension and relevance. As someone is reading a list of facts, he or she may ask: What does this mean and why should I care about it? A story with a pattern of fact, fact, quote, fact, quote, for example, may be more satisfying and effective than only a successive list of facts.

The following news story can be examined regarding its structure, transitions, use of direct and indirect quotes and attribution.

Program raises hopes for higher standards

With hopes of raising academic standards in all classes, the International Baccalaureate (IB) program is making a start here.

The IB program, coordinated by social studies teacher Carol Daiberl, consists of high level classes in not only core subjects such as English, math, social studies and science, but also in fine arts.

Although pieces of the program may be offered in various classes next year, the program won't officially start until Gresham is designated an "IB school."

To do this is a long process, according to Assistant Principal Paul Boly.

"We're in the application phase now," Boly said. The next step is for a representative of IB North America to come visit the school and community to "gauge the depth of the community's commitment to IB." This is expected to happen sometime between January and spring break.

The IB classes, which will be available to juniors and seniors, will officially be offered when current freshmen are juniors.

Boly hopes that at least one IB class will appeal to every student. "I'd like to see many of our kids as juniors and seniors take one or more of our classes," he said.

According to Jay Morris, one of the 16 teachers being trained to teach the curriculum of the IB program, IB has been a success for other schools and is expected to have a very positive effect here.

Boly also has high expectations for the program.

"(IB) is a very positive program," he said. "It helps students focus on academic achievement."

Morris thinks the IB program not only will benefit students while they are in high school, but also prepare them for the future.

"It's definitely going to help college-bound students," he said.

Both Morris and Boly also believe that besides helping students academically, IB will also act as a "magnet," attracting students from Barlow, where the program will not be offered. According to Boly, Gresham was chosen over Barlow to house the program since it is centrally located and has a smaller student population.

"Barlow will do a wonderful job preparing ninth and tenth graders," Boly said.

Boly also thinks the positive attitude of teachers such as Morris, combined with the high quality academic program here, will add to the effectiveness of the program.

"Students at Gresham High School are every bit as capable as students all over the world," Boly said.

Gresham Argus
Gresham High School
Gresham, Ore.

The *Argus* story represents many points about good news writing. Structurally, all the paragraphs are short, with no paragraph containing quotes from more than one person. There is a mix of indirect, direct and even partial direct quotes. "Said" is used most often for attribution. Three sources of information are cited, with two of them, misters Boly and Morris, cited more than once. Transitions between paragraphs are smooth, and there is good narrative explanation following most quotes. The story is a modified inverted pyramid, with a moderately interesting quote saved for the last paragraph. After reading this story, it is apparent that the facts and opinions were collected from several interviews.

A common mistake made by some beginning writers—trying to write the questions asked during an interview into the story—is not in the *Argus* story. The transitions and summaries between direct and indirect quotes make the reporter's questions apparent and unnecessary.

Wrong
When asked what she thought of the new graduation requirements, Rita Mach, principal, said they are an important step toward preparing students for a changing world.

Right
Principal Rita Mach said the new graduation requirements are an important step toward preparing students for a changing world.

Some reporters modify the inverted pyramid significantly by telling the story in a chronological way following the lead. The opening may be a news summary lead or a variation, possibly including a nut graph (Chap. 3). The lead usually features the most recent development, the most timely information. Following the lead, the story is then developed, with facts and attributed opinions, in a time sequence rather than most to least important.

The **time sequence** or **chronological news story form** is sometimes called **storytelling**. This form seems suited to certain kinds of topics. Some possibilities include accidents and natural disasters; anniversary commemorations and historical timelines; construction and renovation projects; competitions; and other stories with a step-by-step sequence. The sequential information should be interesting to readers; otherwise the traditional—most to least important facts—inverted pyramid form should be used.

BECOMING A BETTER NEWS WRITER

Although newswriting is meant to be direct and simple, good newswriting doesn't lack color, emotional appeal and occasionally drama. The topic may have inherent qualities that automatically attract readers, but even what would seem to be mundane can be reported with clarity and color. No story is too short to not merit a reporter's best writing.

Accuracy and fairness are the foundation of good newswriting. A good reporter checks facts and balances the story to provide a true account of what happened. This becomes second nature. But there is more to being a successful reporter than dedication to these two principles. What often separates a good reporter from a great one is how they use words.

To become a better news writer, the following points should be considered.

Begin each paragraph with a **significant** or **interesting fact** and use interesting, specific words. Avoid, if possible, beginning sentences with *It is, It was, It will be, There is, There are, There was* or *There were.*

> *Weak*
> There will be a college fair next Tuesday in the gym.
>
> *Better*
> A college fair will be held in the gym next Tuesday.

Sentences with the subject-verb-object order are direct and desirable for newswriting. However, sometimes a clause can precede the subject to emphasize some interesting or significant fact (opening the *why* or *how* of the five *W*'s and *H*).

> *Good*
> Parking permits will be sold to students beginning next week.
>
> *Better*
> To raise money for the Student Council, parking permits will be sold to students beginning next week.

Familiar, conversational words are usually better for newswriting than less common words found in scholarly work. Even greatly respected newspapers such as *The New York Times* and the *Wall Street Journal* report with simple, direct words.

Possible	conflagration
Better	fire
Possible	concept
Better	idea
Possible	proliferation
Better	spread
Possible	initiate
Better	begin
Possible	utilize
Better	use
Possible	finalize
Better	end
Possible	peruse
Better	read
Possible	endeavor
Better	try

"Say what you have to say as simply and concisely as possible and stop" is good advice to a news writer. However, **tight writing** is sometimes difficult and requires practice. By using one word for several and eliminating repetition of different words with the same meaning, a reporter can write more clearly and directly. Writers should always avoid wordy and unclear sentences.

Wordy	reached an agreement
Better	agreed
Wordy	submitted her resignation
Better	resigned
Wordy	held a meeting
Better	met
Wordy	put in an appearance
Better	appeared

Wordy	take into consideration
Better	considered

Redundant	end result
Better	end or result
Redundant	new record
Better	new or record
Redundant	close proximity
Better	close or proximity
Redundant	general public
Better	public
Redundant	true facts
Better	facts
Redundant	original founder
Better	founder

Wordy	The drama club won the one-act play contest that it entered last Saturday.
Better	The drama club won the one-act play contest last Saturday.

Wordy	The program for the spring band concert will include a Sousa March.
Better	The band's spring concert will include a Sousa march.

Wordy	Bob Schmidt, who is a member of the social studies department faculty, was named Teacher of the Year.
Better	Social Studies teacher Bob Schmidt was named Teacher of the Year.

Vigorous, **exact verbs** that suggest action and precisely state it will often improve a story. However, verbs should be familiar ones, ones used in everyday conversation. Most people don't use verbs such as sauntered,

sped or ambled, even though they are fine words to have in one's vocabulary. When choosing a verb, the writer should ask: Is this something I would say or is it something I would hear? If not, consider another choice.

Active-voice verbs are often a better choice than passive-voice verbs for news stories. They are more direct. However, sometimes the passive-voice is the only workable choice. For example, when a story begins with the *who* element of the five W's and H, the passive voice is often the only choice, as in: "Joe DeLuca was elected president of the Student Council."

Passive
The football *was kicked* by George Taylor 40 yards through the goal posts.

Active
George Taylor *kicked* the football 40 yards through the goal posts.

Passive
Salt Lake City *was selected* as the site of the 2002 Winter Olympics.

Active
The Olympic committee *selected* Salt Lake City as the site of the 2002 winter games.

Concrete nouns will add more color to a story. They are precise and readily identified objects. Stories are often enriched with details. However, it is not necessary, and it can be annoying to cite brand names if they are mentioned too often or if they aren't necessary.

General	dog
Concrete	dachshund
General	book
Concrete	world atlas
General	food
Concrete	bagel
General	injury
Concrete	broken wrist
General	blue
Concrete	azure

Clichés and popular slang have limited value in a news story. If they are included in responses from sources, then they may be used in direct and indirect quotes. It is possible that a cliché or some slang could be included in an effective story lead, in an ending or within the body of the story, but it is unlikely that it would be more effective than original phrases and sentences from the news writer.

Some clichés are worse than others. For example, really tired ones to avoid include *breath of fresh air, leave no stone unturned, bite the dust, calm before the storm, proud parents, leap of faith, Mother Nature, Old Man Winter, storm of protest, true colors, heart of gold, Grim Reaper, light at the end of the tunnel* and *drop in the bucket,* among many others.

Occasionally a cliché can be a good choice, but only if it specifically applies. For example, a story about an antique or junk store could use the cliché "white elephant" if the store actually sold one.

Using a cliché or even a quote from a well-known book, song or other genre is really a question of opinion. Some journalists like to use them occasionally because they say readers identify with the cliché. They say a cliché is like "comfort food" (another cliché) for the mind. A story with more than one cliché is suspect. Writers who use them too often may be considered lazy by readers and their professional peers.

If a cliché is used in a story, it should not be put in quotation marks.

Language evolves. Each year, lexicographers (those who write dictionaries) add new words to dictionaries. These words are created by others who invent words to fit objects, actions, emotions or ideas. If enough people use the new word, it becomes part of the spoken language. Many new words were created for the information age of the 1990s: *web, cell phone, chat room, e-mail* and *e-commerce,* among others. Journalists should use new words carefully and slowly. Newly coined words and jargon may not be understood by the general population. Newsrooms, including those in high schools, should buy a new dictionary and journalism stylebook every two years or sooner.

Slang or street language, especially coarse or sexually suggestive words, even though they may be in a dictionary, are usually not used by journalists—with some exceptions. For example, if a source is quoted directly or indirectly, slang or vulgar words may be necessary to publish for accuracy and fairness.

CHECKLIST FOR WRITING A GOOD NEWS STORY

• Do I have all the facts?

• Did I verify these facts with my sources?

• Have I checked the spelling of all names and are all persons identified?

• Have I certified all the dates with a calendar. Is May 13 a Friday as it is written?

• If a news summary lead is written, does it feature the most timely and important facts?

• If a soft or feature lead is written, is it followed by a nut or focus graph?

• Is the lead short?

• Are too many of the five W's and H in the first sentence? Should the lead be two sentences or two short paragraphs?

• Are the opening words interesting, good choices?

• Does the lead flow smoothly to the next paragraph?

• Do all paragraphs follow one another in logical order, with good transitions from one paragraph to the next?

• Are the paragraphs short? Do the paragraphs vary in length?

• Does each paragraph begin (the first few words) with significant or interesting facts worded in an interesting, specific way?

• Is the writing objective, with no editorializing?

• Is the story concise? Can any words be deleted or can any sentence be tighter?

• Is the story unified? Does it develop the focus statement?

• Have I included a mix of direct and indirect quotes from my sources?

• Are all direct and indirect quotes attributed? Is the attributive verb *said* used?

• Are my word choices simple, conversational and specific?

• Does the last paragraph have some fact or quote that

is worth reading?

- Have I checked my story for all spelling, punctuation, subject-verb agreement and other possible style and grammatical errors?

- Am I satisfied with my story? Am I proud to have the story appear under my byline?

- Have I saved my notes? The accuracy of facts and quotes may have to be verified after the story is published.

EXERCISES

1. Clip a news story from your city newspaper that has a summary lead and has inverted pyramid story development. Write a one- or two-sentence focus statement for this story. Do you think the writer followed the focus statement throughout the story? Do you agree with the order, most important to least important listing of the facts? Could the last paragraph be cut from the story without losing anything interesting or important?

2. As a class, select one major news story from the past year. List as many facts as you can about the event without concern about order or importance. Next, relist these facts from most important to least important. Discuss why one fact may be more or less important than another fact. Separately, each student should write a summary lead for this story.

3. Before class, the teacher should select and photocopy one or more news stories from the city newspaper. Then, the original story should be cut into single paragraphs. During class, ask students to reassemble the story according to how they think it appeared in the paper. Compare their restructuring of the story to the original story as it was published.

4. To reinforce the need for attribution for direct and indirect quotes, and attributive verbs, the teacher should give each student a photocopy of the same news story from the city paper. Each student should circle each attribution. As a class, discuss the use of direct and indirect quotes in the story.

5. To reinforce the importance of transitions and the smooth flow of a story, the teacher should give each student a photocopy of the same news story from the city paper. Each student should circle the transitional words and phrases used to promote the flow of the story from one paragraph to the next.

6. To reinforce the need for objectivity in a news story, the student should clip one news story and one signed opinion column or unsigned editorial from the city paper. In about 250 words, the student should compare the two pieces and show how one is objective (the news story) and the other is subjective/the writer's opinions (the column). The student can note other differences too.

7. As a class, list different events at the school and in the community scheduled for one week. Discuss who sources of information would likely be for each event. Assign one or two students to write a news story—either an advance story or a recap after the event—for each of these events. The story should be about 250–500 words and contain direct and indirect quotes from two or more sources. The story should conform to all newswriting guidelines and style. It should be written as if it was to be published in the school's newspaper.

8. Write a 250–500 word news story about one event you participated in during the last six months. The event could be school- or nonschool-related. It should be written in the third person, not first person. The inverted pyramid or a modified inverted pyramid (chronological) form should be used. It should conform to all news story guidelines and style. For example, a student who participated in a school play may want to write a news story about the play and cite him- or herself as the source. Remember: This is a news story, not an opinion column.

Writing Specialty Stories

Take a walk through the bookstore and notice the array of specialty magazines—everything from *Newsweek* to *Teen Star Hairstyles* to *Natural Health*. The cable television explosion brought hundreds more specialty shows. Newspapers have followed suit in creating more specialized beats in areas such as health and science. High school publications are covering an equally wide array of specialty stories.

HEALTH WRITING

For years, acne was the primary health concern of teens. The pimples haven't disappeared, but in the last decade, teens and school publications increasingly began taking an educated look at a wider variety of health issues—both physical and mental. Depression, AIDS and anorexia, among many others, have become teen health issues. A look at the causes, cures and stresses of health-related issues is now an important part of a publication's role of helping high school students understand their world (Fig. 5.1). Some of the stories covered by high school publications were

- Chemical dependency treatment centers and how they try to help adolescents overcome their addictions to everything from marijuana to heroin to inhalants

- A student's fight with brain cancer

- Biological brain differences in males and females. The story covers how boys and girls handle their emotions differently with examples such as what a kiss means and why guys won't cry.

- The physical strains and hazards of wearing a heavy backpack

- The nutritional values and calories in school lunches

- Tips on preventing sunburning and skin cancer

- How students cope with attention deficit disorder

- The mental trauma of living in an abusive relationship. The story not only showed vividly how abusive relationships can be among boyfriends and girlfriends but also dealt with solutions for how to get out of the relationship and how to help a friend get out of the relationship.

- An anecdotal piece on how students cope with burnout

Health-related issues must be communicated with the utmost care because so much of the public's health knowledge comes from what it reads in newspapers and

Treatment center fights addiction

by Sarah Rorvick

He rolls out of bed to find it is broad daylight. The time is irrelevant to him. He reaches over to the night stand to find another joint and a lighter waiting for him. He gets high and nothing really matters anymore. Grabbing a magazine off the floor, he opens it up not to read, but only to look like he is actually doing something. Productivity is no longer part of his lifestyle. He is on his tenth job this year and he should be at work right now. He doesn't remember or care though because he is an addict.

"Addiction begins when the use becomes a problem in a person's life and they still continue to use," Shirley Behrends, adolescent chemical dependency counselor at Fountain Lake Treatment Center, said. "When it starts to cross the line where it is more important than anything else it becomes a problem."

The Fountain Lake Treatment Center has admitted patients between the ages of 13 and 80 for addictions to chemicals ranging from alcohol and marijuana to cocaine, heroin and inhalants. Patients come either on their own will, at the urging of their family and friends, but most commonly it is a combination of both, along with legal issues and school or work.

"Patients are admitted due to a variety of reasons ranging from family, the law, school and lawyers," Mary Tubbs, certified chemical dependency counselor reciprocal at Fountain Lake Treatment Center, said. "They often receive ultimatums and then choose to come."

Most commonly patients initially react by denying their addiction. Tubbs says admitting to having a problem is the hardest step for people to conquer. She says once the realization of the situation hits those that admit they have a problem, depression becomes a

Success Rate

Fountain Lake Treatment Center follows up on its former patients for two years after their release. The percentages below are those who have stayed clean.

alcohol	65%
marijuana	45%
heroin	15%
inhalants	60%
cocaine	40%

Source: Clinical Director Garth Barker

strong emotion in many.

"We see lots of depression, lots of depression," Tubbs said. "If they are not on chemicals they see their losses."

Opening a patient's eyes to losses through sobriety does not necessarily work in all cases. Tubbs said she sees people come through saying all the right things and nodding their heads when they should only because they have to. Behrends believes many patients find it difficult to deal with the present. She says many can only see treatment means alcohol and drugs can never be a part of their lives again and that seems too difficult.

"They look at the future and see that they can never drink again instead

of dealing with the present," Behrends said. "They cannot think of the now and take it day by day. When they do that they will make progress."

Behrends says the success rate for adolescents is lower than that of adults because they don't want to cooperate.

"Adolescents are more defiant," Behrends said. "They don't see the consequences and believe they are invincible."

Counselors take a different approach to treating adolescents. Instead of focusing on their own problems right away, counselors show the problems addictions have created in other people's lives.

"Many kids are very perceptive of other people," Behrends said. "They can see the problems in their lives and it is less personal."

John McGinnis was a patient 12 years ago for marijuana addiction. He had used for 10 years, beginning at the age of 13. McGinnis says he experimented with marijuana out of curiosity and naivete but as he continued to use, it became a daily affair. By about age 16 he was smoking marijuana five to six times a day. When he was 19 his parents urged him to go through treatment. It did not work for him though.

"Treatment was unsuccessful because I wanted it to be unsuccessful," McGinnis said. "I just nodded my head like I understood but thought what they were saying was crazy."

He finished treatment and went back to the same lifestyle as before treatment. He said by age 22 he hit bottom.

"I felt like I was selling my soul," McGinnis said. "I really didn't want to live anymore. I wanted to quit (smoking marijuana) because I knew what it was doing to me."

He says he would wake up each morning with the intent of staying clean that day but by the afternoon he

would be high. McGinnis decided to admit himself to the treatment center. Treatment was a painful and reflective time for him that allowed him to see his life and losses.

"When you have to look at the whole picture it is very disturbing," McGinnis said. "To see that a simple choice at 13 created all the insanity was very powerful."

Overwhelming sadness, fear, depression and anger at himself are the feelings McGinnis says he remembers when he was first admitted. During this time he realized all of the opportunities, goals and dreams he lost.

"It seemed so hopeless to get a life back," McGinnis said.

McGinnis says seeing what he lost motivated him to take what he had and move forward with his life. Group therapy was also a vital part of his treatment. The other patients in group became his lifeline and kept him from quitting when he went through tough times.

"(The patients) feel like you're the worst people in the world and together you realize you can get through it," McGinnis said.

This time treatment worked for

Fountain Street and the surrounding area are common sights for patients through the windows of Fountain Lake Treatment Center. During the first days of treatment patients are not allowed outdoors and this view is their only connection to the outside.

McGinnis. Eight years ago McGinnis began working as a chemical dependency counselor at Fountain Lake Treatment Center. Within the last few months he has changed jobs and began working as a chemical dependency counselor for Addiction Recovery Technology incorporated. He has stayed straight and sober for the past 12 years.

"If I have any strength from this, it is because I am determined," McGinnis said.

Fig. 5.1. Health feature. *Ahlahasa,* Albert Lea High School, Albert Lea, Minn.

magazines rather than from what it learns from physicians or textbooks. A reporter who is inaccurate is like a doctor who gives bad advice.

The biggest pitfall for young health writers is writing about something they don't understand. Going into a world of medical jargon and complicated concepts can lead to writing such as this:

> Advil relieves pain. Body aches are caused when cells release a substance called prostaglandins, Dr. Foster said. Prostaglandins cause muscle stimulation which causes inflammation in the muscle. Advil is a nonsteroidal, anti-inflamma-

tory drug. It goes to the cells that produce the prostaglandins and inhibits prostaglandins and inhibits prostaglandin synthesis and decreases muscle stimulation.

The writer later admitted he didn't understand what he was writing about. In trying to do a story about how pain medicine actually works, he succeeded only in confusing the reader.

Which leads us to this:

Science Writing rule No. 1: Never try to explain something that you don't understand. Don't be shy about asking your sources to explain something again, if you don't get it the first time. And don't cop out by quoting the scientist's unhelpful explanation. If your scientist source is not a good explainer, ask him or her to refer you to somebody else, maybe one who teaches the field. Once you think you understand something, check yourself by saying it back to the scientist in your own words.

Boyce Rensberger
A Field Guide for Science Writers

Understanding the topic before interviewing will help you understand the doctor or scientist and in turn help you explain the story to the reader. Read books, medical pamphlets or magazine articles on the subject first. For subjects such as sleep deprivation or the athletic enhancement drug creatine, reading background material will provide knowledge of the specialized language and research. But do not use a lot of secondhand material in the reporting of the story. Health writing depends on interviews with local physicians, psychologists or students coping with the subject to make it relevant and real to the readers. Use interviews with first-hand sources to make sure you accurately understand the information. Do not avoid asking questions, even ones covering information you have already read about.

No question is dumb if the answer is necessary to help you understand something. There's a difference between not being prepared for an interview and feeling embarrassed about asking a question that you think may sound stupid or silly. Don't pretend to know more than you do in hopes of impressing a source. You need to know the information in order to write an accurate story.

The most important tool a journalist has is the ability to ask questions. Answers always raise more questions and you should keep asking them until you understand the subject.

Ronald Kotulak
A Field Guide for Science Writers

The point can't be emphasized enough: Know what you are writing about before you write about it.

The following tips from professional science writers in *A Field Guide for Science Writers* should help the beginning health writer communicate complicated subjects to the average student.

1. Do echo interviews.

   Mentioned earlier, the practice calls on the reporter to repeat the key information in his or her own words to the scientist to see if the interpretation is correct. The reporter gets an immediate check on how well he or she is grasping the material. For example, the reporter would listen to an answer and then say, "So my understanding of how Ritalin affects a teenager is …"

2. Get the face behind the statistic or the issue, but make sure the personal story has relevance.

   Showing the reader a student who daydreams during a physics lecture, doesn't do his or her homework but makes an A on the test can help clarify a clinical psychologist's definition of a gifted person. The reporter must understand that the reader can relate to a story of an individual better than to a statistic or a medical description. A story on asthma should include a statistic on the number of people with asthma as well as a description of the challenges of the ailment. But a story on a student's effort to control his breathing disorder while playing baseball gives life to the story.

A reporter should not assume that a student is an example of the larger story but should seek a professional's confirmation that this is the case. Just because a reporter finds a student who seems tired all the time does not mean he or she has found a person who suffers from chronic fatigue syndrome. Confirm the diagnosis with a doctor.

3. Analogies, anecdotes, examples and metaphors are very effective in helping people understand any new ideas and concepts.

Giving the reader specifics he or she can relate to is important to clearly communicate complex information. Here, the writer makes a comparison to clarify the dangers of a relatively unknown herbal cigarette.

> **However, cloves include 60–70 percent tobacco and twice as much nicotine as the average Marlboro.**

In this next example, the author explains how small the chances are of contracting tuberculosis at a school where there is an infected student. Rather than making the vague statement that "the chances are rare," the writer follows up with this specific quote.

> **"You have to breathe the same air as a person with TB in a small area," Dr. Goodman said. "You might contract TB if you lived in the same home as [an infected person] but classrooms are so large that it would be unlikely to catch it because that is a small amount of bacteria in a huge amount of air."**

ACADEMIC WRITING

If a discussion between a mother and her 15-year-old daughter were the public's best source for academic coverage, there would be no reason to have this section.

> **"So what did you learn at school today?"**
> **"Oh nothing."**

The answer is an easy escape from having to talk to your mother, but it is an exaggeration. Academics are a huge part of the school experience that should not be ignored in the high school publication. As a high school writer, your ability to see and cover what's going on in classrooms is critical. The publication can help students learn more about their education and make them more responsible for their own learning. Coverage can bring up curriculum issues that need to be debated so the public makes sure the students are getting a strong education.

Coverage should include

- Changes in graduation requirements and standardized testing

- Updates on student body progress—failure rates, testing rankings

- Creative or interesting assignments or projects in the classroom

- Curriculum issues such as the elimination of a class on jewelry making or the addition of the study of religion

- Education issues such as the introduction of block/alternative scheduling or the lengthening of the school year

Here are a few examples of academic stories covered in high school publications.

- A feature on the ways grades are weighted—honors classes, advanced placement classes and the like—combined with interviews of faculty and students

- A feature on mainstreaming in which less able students are in classes with those of average or better than average ability

- A feature story on the techniques teachers use to make academic classes interesting

- A news-feature story on the science class's project to study the school's garbage to show what it throws away

- A story on the impact the state's tougher graduation plans are having on electives

- A feature story on the school's creation of a two-day camp where students and teachers participated in team-building activities to bridge a communication gap (Fig. 5.2)

Camp Outlook
Bridging the social gap

By Ryan Mason
Associate Editor

He walked blindfolded up the ladder and smiled nervously as the group leader told him to fall backward off the platform. He crossed his arms over his chest and fell back, flat as a board. Just when it seemed like he was going to hit the ground, his group caught him.

The trust jump is just one team-building activity in the Challenging Outdoor Personal Experience (COPE) course at Camp Outlook. But, the parts of the excursion that take up the most time are the five, one-and-a-half-hour long Communication Training groups.

Camp Outlook is a two-day excursion where about 60 students and 15 staff members travel to Clare's Camp Rotary to get to know each other better.

"We want to have students understand that regardless of where we come from in life, people share the same problems," co-chairperson of Camp Outlook, Laurie Stevens, said.

Students gain an understanding of teachers by interacting with them.

"Everyone calls each other by first names, even teachers," Stevens said. "Students see teachers in a whole new light and teachers see students in a whole new light."

Students enjoy getting to know their teachers and are able to see where they are coming from, which allows them to understand how they work in class.

"I got closer to most of my teachers," junior Katie Johnson said.

The selection committee has to pick a diverse group from all different social groups so people get to know others whom they wouldn't normally get to know.

"I really liked meeting and hanging out with people I've never hung out with or never would have seen before," sophomore April Sloggett said.

But according to co-chairperson of the selection committee, Social Studies teacher Ric Shahin, the committee works very hard to get a good representation of the school, and even if they do a good job, it won't please everyone.

"If everyone is happy, then we'd be taking 200 kids. As long as nobody's completely unhappy, we (the selection committee) probably did it right," Shahin said.

The selection committee is made up of ten staff members who get together as many times as needed to make the final decision on campers.

"We look for students who have

A moment ot Camp Outlook

Photo by Mitch Early

Mrs. Lee leads a group of Camp Outlookers in a sharing circle, where they introduce and talk about themselves.

leadership potential, either positive or negative; it's not a goody-two-shoes kind of thing," Shahin said. "Also a balance between male and female and grade level, and to make sure that they fairly represent the student body."

The process starts out with nominations. Nomination forms go out in parent newsletters and are also in the main office. The completed forms then go to the committee.

"The committee sits down and narrows the list by looking for balance," Shahin said. "People speak in favor of certain students as we go name-by-name down the list. We take each person and judge by their attitude, personality and leadership skills whether or not they would fit into the balance we're trying to make."

Students are many times nominated more than once. Although, teachers can't nominate more than five students.

"The number of nominations or who the nomination is from won't affect the outcome of the decision," Stevens said.

Fewer seniors are selected to go because the idea of the camp is to teach students leadership skills. Underclassman will have more time to share this knowledge with the student body.

"Only 12 seniors were taken because they only have six months left to apply what they've learned," Stevens said.

Staff members must also be chosen by the committee. Teachers and other staff let the committee know that they are interested and then the committee chooses based on the same criteria used to choose students.

"We base it on departments and personality, (again) trying to find that balance," Shahin said.

Other things go in to Camp Outlook besides the selection process.

Student Union helps out financially each year by donating profits from the magazine drive. The rest of the money is earned through fund raisers headed by committee member Dorothy Horan.

"We work on the Charger Family Barbecue and girls' basketball concessions among others to raise money for the trip. We work with staff to make sure people go work at those events," Horan said.

Most of the money raised goes to Camp Rotary for lodging, and toward the use of their COPES course.

"Money goes to food, snacks and T-shirts for all participants," Horan said. "We get grants from organizations around town and also other donations. All in all, it costs around four thousand dollars."

Staff members who are involved in the process of getting ready for Camp Outlook get into it, and appreciate the response from students.

"It is the best thing I've done, from an academic point of view," Stevens said. "It has made me a better staff person and parent, and has opened up my eyes as to why kids think the way they do."

Students feel the same way, too. They all feel that it is a very worthwhile experience and are very glad they were able to go.

"It was awesome. The Communication Training groups made you closer to people in particular, but the free time just pulled it all together. Everyone should go," Johnson said.

Unfortunately, not everyone can go. But, the idea is to take a few people from every group. That way, the camp's ideas touch everyone eventually.

"It's a pet project of mine," Stevens said. "I put hundreds of hours into it, and I wish that there was a way that the whole school could go. That would be the ideal."

Fig. 5.2.
Academic feature. *Update,* Herbert Henry Dow High School, Midland, Mich.

classes a little...
Crowded?

Students and teachers alike are suffering from increased class sizes

TIMELINE

- Measure 5 shifted financial burden to the state legislature.

- Between 1989 and 1995, 4J certified staff dropped 13.6%.

- In 1996, the state instituted a policy which gave equal government funding to all districts.

- In 1990-91, South's enrollment was at 1,662 and its full-time staff positions were 74.38.

- This year's enrollment reached 1,772 students. Full-time staff positions are 62.5.

Source: Department of Human Resources

❑ Class sizes are affected by a variety of factors. Increased enrollment and a dwindling budget are some reasons you may find yourself elbow to elbow in class.

Annie Zosel-Johnson
Expression Assistant

Is your Physics class a little snug? AP Government a bit too cozy?

Overpopulated classes have become typical at South. Although class sizes have been gradually increasing for the past 10 years, both teachers and students feel classes this year have reached an uncomfortable level.

"I don't feel like I can connect with my students, see how people are doing, just check in," says math teacher LeAnn Thompson. "That individual attention is really lost in a large class; even having a few extra people makes a huge difference." According to the Math Department, every Pre-Calculus class exceeds 40 students.

"For the people who grasp concepts quickly a large class is all right," says senior Elle Selko, "but for people who need extra prodding, a large class can be really overwhelming. It's impossible to keep a steady pace that suits everyone."

"Having such a huge history class really changes discussions," says IB candidate Stacey Kepler. "Not so many people can participate and be involved, and it's really hard to get to know your teachers and classmates. It's also ridiculously difficult to get the classes you want. People aren't getting the education they deserve."

"It seems everyone can agree on the problem," says Principal Jerry Henderson. "The solution's a bit more complex."

According to Henderson, a variety of factors increase class sizes. The reduction in staff and increase in enrollment are the most significant factors.

According to The Human Resource Department, in 1990 South's enrollment was 1,662 and 74.38 staff positions were filled. This year South's student body tolls 1,772 and there are 62.5 staff positions.

Henderson also mentioned how numbers shift because South's staff voted to teach five out of eight periods, instead of the average six out of eight. "Our staff wanted to be available during students free periods for one-on-one attention; the backlash is a 1/6 increase in classes," notes Henderson.

Another compounding element is South's abundance of AP courses and alternative pro-

Photo: Jason Thelen

CROWDED: Seniors Helen Yu, Stacey Kepler and Nick Klonoski crowd into thier IHS class. During some periods, students have to sit on the windowsills and heaters because there aren't enough seats.

grams, such as IHS and French Immersion. According to Henderson, AP classes are either singletons (offered once a day) or doubletons (offered twice a day).

For example, a student in morning IHS must decide between AP Spanish and AP Chemistry because each is offered twice, once in the morning and during sixth period.

The major reason for large AP classes and other junior and senior courses is also because the administration strives to keep underclassmen and lower level classes significantly smaller.

"We really want to maintain small classes for developing studies and for younger students who tend to need more personal attention," says Henderson. "Therefore, higher level students are directly affected."

These complexities have been caused by the reduction of school funding. Ever since Measure 5 was passed in 1990, school funding has been steadily dwindling.

Measure 5 was a proposed tax relief, installed in a five-year reduction plan.

Measure 47 was created to clean up Measure 5 by shifting the financial burden to the state legislature. Since 1991, funding has been derived from income tax instead of local property tax.

The repercussions have been severe. The Human Resources Department noted that be-

tween 1989-1995, 4J staff was cut by 18.7 percent.

According to Henderson, in 1990 the legislator also cancelled local equity tax return because of the inequalities it created within school districts. The bill allowed community members to give up to 5 percent of their equity taxes to local schools.

"School districts were growing very unevenly, says Henderson. "The ones located in wealthier communities were constantly improving, while schools in lower economic ones drooped. It was necssary, but hit us hard.

To equalize funding, Measure 5 made everyone come down; we had to come down further, it really effected us. For the first time ever South was being funded like average, and still is."

So is there light at the end of the tunnel? Gov. John Kitzhaber recently unveiled his three-point ballot initiative to improve state funding for schools.

He plans to ask voters in 2000 to approve a "rainy-day" fund, which would provide state subsidies to property-poor school districts that approve local tax increases, and change the Oregon constitution to guarantee school funding at a level that allows students academic standards imposed by the legislator.

"Everything's on the drawing board right now," says Henderson. "I don't see huge funding increases right around the corner. Therefore, we're going to have to start becoming more creative and focus our energy within the school to make the schedule more flexible and accommodating with the resources we have."

> *"Having such a huge history class really changes the discussions. Fewer people can participate. People aren't getting the education they deserve."*
> **Stacey Kepler**
> senior

Fig. 5.3. Academic news feature. *Axe*, South Eugene High School, Eugene, Ore.

Fig. 5.4. Academic story (p. 72). *Northwest Passage*, Shawnee Mission Northwest High School, Shawnee, Kan.

Fig. 5.5. Death story (p. 73). *Little Hawk*, City High School, Iowa City, Iowa

- An informative feature on girls-only classes and whether girls participate more and learn better in these classes

- A how-to piece on college application essays told through interviews with college admissions officers and high school alums

- A feature story on how to work effectively in group projects

- An in-depth story on alternative education possibilities. The story looked at the state's consideration of a voucher program, the district's opposition to the program and litigation over voucher systems in other states. The newspaper compared public with private schools and covered the experience of home-schooled students.

- A feature story on a physical science class trip in a hot air balloon to study Charles' Law and Archimedes Principle

- A news story on the causes and impact of increased class sizes (Fig. 5.3)

All of these stories are appropriate in school newspapers. How well they are read, of course, depends on how well they were investigated, written and displayed. Most, of course, are not hard news stories dependent on a spot news peg (a timely, newsworthy event or element), although academic stories are often related to a recent event such as a school board meeting or a topic of high reader interest such as grades.

Stories of interesting classroom activities, such as a business law mock trial, should not be neglected. Sometimes a class has speakers whose comments would have interest beyond the classroom. Occasionally a field trip can be developed into an interesting story (Fig. 5.4).

Yearbook academic sections or spreads should highlight interesting activities and issues of the year. Typically features, the yearbook academic stories should highlight interesting class assignments, teachers and educational issues. But they should do so through vivid storytelling that revives the reader's memories of the wobbly desk in science class and that faint whiff of formaldehyde.

Keep the student in mind when covering academics. If the story's about changes in science curriculum, make sure to get examples to show the student reader how the classes will be different. Don't just republish the dry text of the district's mandates. If the story's about new

science lab computers, get anecdotes from students who felt like real surgeons using the virtual operating room software in anatomy and physiology class. Don't just tell the reader how many computers the district is installing and "how excited" the science teachers are.

DEATH COVERAGE

In the middle of all the emotion of a death, a student publication must maintain a sense of objectivity. Guidelines or a policy set up before such an event happens may outline tough ethical questions for tough circumstances. Guidelines should cover what news-judging criteria to use in deciding whether to do an obituary, a straight news story or a eulogy-like news-feature. Considerations are the deceased's impact on students and the school, the nature of death and often the time of death in relation to the deadline.

Yearbooks should be wary of dedicating books to a student who has died during the year. The practice can lead to fairness questions if another student dies after the final deadline, the student has moved away or a new student dies in a car accident. One yearbook staff simply places a gray bar across the student's name in the class section with the date of birth and death placed underneath. Others cover the death as a story and base coverage on news value. Allow family or friends to purchase an ad to increase coverage if they want.

News or feature death coverage should be free of editorialization. Any expressions of sympathy from the writer or staff should be reserved for the opinion section. A reporter should avoid euphemisms such as "passed away" and "Death's call." Simply use "died," unless as a religious-affiliated school the publication uses another term.

Accuracy of facts is always important, but in an obituary it is even more so. Common facts included in an obituary are full name (make sure of correct spelling), identification, age, date of death, cause of death, biographical details, survivors, date, time and place of funeral, and memorials. These facts appear in a news-feature story along with more anecdotes and quotes surrounding the student's or teacher's life. Those quotes come from family, friends, teachers or the minister who presided.

In the news-feature coverage from the *Little Hawk* (Fig. 5.5), the writer combines accurate storytelling of how Katie's parents saw her and how they were impacted by her death. The writer includes the oddity of

In the Flesh

Biology II and Anatomy students get a look at a real autopsy at a local morgue

BY SAMANTHA THOMPSON
Staff Writer

As they walk into the room the students shiver at the temperature. After all, this room is 10 degrees colder than most. It's a large room with muted colors and is surprisingly homey... compared to what most students were expecting.

One wall is covered with sinks, presumably to wash the bodies out. There is a large vacuum hose also.

The students in Al Frisby's Biology II and anatomy classes are in the Jackson County Examiner's office to watch human autopsies.

Frisby began offering the program about eight years ago when he started calling professionals he knew in the area. He then set up times for his students to come in and observe the professionals in their daily routine.

"A lot of students want to go into a medical field and this gives them the opportunity to see what it's like before they invest the time and money," Frisby said.

The program has grown so much that he is able to set up visits to a private doctor's practice, four different surgeons, three veterinarians, two physical therapists, three hospital operating rooms and an electron microscope specialist.

For the past two years, students have worked with Dr. Sam Gulino. Gulino decided to allow students to come watch him perform autopies because he wanted students to understand what his career really is about.

"Most people don't understand the true service we provide," Gulino said. "As long as people have a true interest in the field and not just a morbid fascination, we like to have them come in."

Gulino was hoping that students would realize from the experience that the information they are learning from the textbook they will use later in life.

"When I was in school, I took physics and I thought I would never use what I learned," Gulino said. "It's amazing what I use everyday whether it involves car crashes or people falling out of buildings."

To be eligible for this program students simply have to be in one of the two classes, Biology II or Anatomy, and be on code six.

McGowen was a member of the first group to observe Gulino performing six autopsies. Though McGowen doesn't want to go into the medical profession in the future, she does plan to become a biologist. She thought the experience would be educational.

"I thought it would be neat to see what an actual human body looked like, and to see what the organs really looked like," McGowen said.

QuickLook

How did students have this opportunity?

The morgue is not open to public viewing, but students got the chance to view an autopsy because of a special arrangement Al Frisby made for SMNW.

Juniors Kiley McGowen and Jennifer Parrott take a first look at the body and reac to the copse.

Junior Jennifer Parrot, senior Elizabeth Marvel and junior Andrey Hicks react when viewing the first cut through the skin of the body of a woman's corpse.

McGowen was nervous that seeing the dead bodies would make her sick, but said that she did pretty well considering that one cadaver had its eyes open and another was beginning to turn green.

"It was really cool," McGowen said. "I was expecting it to be really medical, but it was just a room."

McGowen said that the experience was very strange and unusual. The room was very cold and she just couldn't get over how fake the bodies looked. Though she said that the outside looked like wax, she was positive the inside was real.

"They take out the organs and weigh them and find out the cause of death," McGowen said. "Then they put them in a bag and put them back into the guy, that was weird."

McGowen thought her time was well spent and that the whole experience was very interesting.

"I'd like to go back, I just can't see why anyone would want to do that as a profession," McGowen said.

Junior Andrey Hicks also attended the autopsy. Hicks, who is currently planning to go into the medical field as a pediatric cardiologist, thought the experience would be valuable. He discovered that he could handle at least a small part of being a doctor.

"I was reassured that I wasn going to faint if I saw blood or some one died," Hicks said. "It was inter esting to see the inside of the body. I really looked a lot like the inside of cat's body."

There were some interestin moments in the morgue; the wors part of viewing the autopsy fo Hicks was when he saw the corps that was turning green. He found th most interesting part of the autops to be when the pathologist cut th frontal lobe of the brain. In mos cases, the brain is not cut open dur ing an autopsy, but the deceased hac fallen and hit his head prior to death, so the pathologist had to ru tests on the brain.

"It gave me a better understand ing on a part of my field," Hick said, "I got to see the gray and white matter of the brain. It just gives yo a better understanding when you se it first hand."

Even if these students are no planning to become medical exam iners, the experience is something they won't forget soon.

"(Going to the morgue) was a one time thing. A medical examiner is definitely not the career choice fo me," Hicks said.

Katherine Marie Tully
March 27, 1981- March 16, 1999

A memorial has been set up in Katie's name at the Humane Society. "She loved animals so much," Marge said. "We'd call her St. Francis. The Humane Society was most befitting for a memorial."

Musical remembrances

Both Katie's mother and father requested songs for Katie's funeral. The following are excerpts from those songs, along with explanations as to why the parents chose them.

Song: Bridge Over Troubled Water
Written by: Paul Simon
Explanation: "Once we were coming back from vacation and it was on the radio," Jim said. "Katie was up in the front with me and I started crying. She asked me why I was crying. I said, 'This has always been my song for you.'"
Excerpt:

I'll take your part
When darkness comes
And pain is all around
Like a bridge over troubled water
I will lay me down
Like a bridge over troubled water
I will lay me down

Sail on Silver Girl,
Sail on by
Your time has come to shine
All your dreams are on their way

See how they shine
If you need a friend
I'm sailing right behind
Like a bridge over troubled water
I will lay me down
Like a bridge over troubled water
I will lay me down

Song: My Heart Will Go On
Written by: James Horner and Will Jennings
Explanation: "We laughed about how Katie would be pissed [that we played this song at her funeral]," Marge said. "But the words are so meaningful."
Excerpt:

Love can touch us one time
And last for a lifetime
And never let go till we're one
Love was when I loved you
One true time I hold to
In my life we'll always go on

Near, far, wherever you are
I believe that the heart goes on
Once more you open the door
And you're here in my heart
And my heart will go on and on

There is some love that will not go away
You're here, there's nothing I fear
And I know my heart will go on
We'll stay forever this way
You are safe in my heart
And my heart will go on and on

Gift of Love

Friends and family remember the life of Katie Tully

There is a stark difference between the room former junior Katie Tully lived in at her mother's home and the room she lived in at her father's home.

Decked in Marilyn Manson posters, the room in her father's house represents what her dad calls "the beginning of the teenage rebellion."

On the other hand, the music box collection, Winnie the Pooh stuffed animals, and pair of sparkling red *Wizard of Oz* Dorothy shoes at her room in her mother's house is what her mother describes as Katie's "not being afraid to be a child."

"Katie led a few different lives," Jim Tully, Katie's dad, explained. "She needed to be coddled, but at the same time, she needed to be independent."

Katie's mother, Marge, believes Katie's range of interests was what made her so special. "Katie is an exercise in contradictions," Marge said. "She loved classical music, classical ballet, and she loved reading Shakespeare. Yet she also loved Marilyn Manson and *The Exorcist*. I guess you could say she was a well-rounded person."

A fatal illness

Katie died on March 16 from complications of an Influenza A illness. Just over 24 hours before, she began to feel ill while at her mother's house. Later in the day, she started vomiting.

When Katie left for her dad's house, she was still feeling ill. She stayed in bed all day and went to sleep early. Around midnight, she came out into the living room. "I was reading when she wandered out here," Jim said. "I asked her if she was doing okay and she said, 'Yeah.' I said 'Love you.' And she said 'Love you.'"

Katie went back to bed. Around 1 a.m., Jim heard a crash. "I thought it was probably the cat that had knocked something over," Jim said. "I went into Katie's room and I found her lying next to the bed. She wasn't breathing."

Jim checked for a pulse after putting Katie back on the bed. He felt nothing. He got Katie's brother, Mark '98, from downstairs and brought Katie into the living room. While Mark called 911, Jim started CPR. Once the paramedics arrived, Jim called Katie's mother, Marge. "I flew over to the house," Marge said. "I didn't stop for anything."

Jim watched as the paramedics started to work on Katie. "One of the paramedics asked me when the last time was that I saw my daughter alive," Jim said. "That wasn't what I wanted to hear."

Katie was brought to Mercy Hospital in an ambulance, where a team of nurses and doctors continued the CPR. "I was still hoping something miraculous would happen," Jim said. "But there was no spark left to kindle."

When it was apparent CPR wasn't going to bring Katie back, she was pronounced dead around 1:30 a.m. "The entire staff was haunted," Marge said. "They couldn't believe they couldn't save a 17-year-old girl from the flu."

The Influenza A had filled Katie's lower lungs. She was unable to get oxygen and her heart gave out. For Jim, realizing he did everything he could still isn't enough. "I have such regret," Jim said. "I tried to do CPR. It was the one time she really needed me. I kept thinking 'This cannot be happening.' But it did."

For Marge, the reality of Katie's death still hasn't hit. "It's impossible to believe that she's gone," Marge said. "Every time the phone rings, I think it's going to be Katie on the other end."

Learning to cope

For three days after Katie's death, Jim could not sleep. "I couldn't picture her face," he said. "When I finally did see her face, I could only picture her dead. Then one night, I said 'I love you Katie.' Right away I could picture her face. It had changed. Her eyes sparkled. I don't know if Katie needed to hear it one more time or I needed to say it, but now I can see her face whenever I want. She has a big smile."

Jim often tells Katie he loves her when he's feeling depressed. "It gets to a point where the loss is like waves and it's like you're drowning," Jim said. "But I can ameliorate the pain by saying 'I love you.'"

Since Katie's death, Marge has found comfort in living with Katie's attitude. "It's up to us to carry on her legacy," Marge said. "We need to look beyond the outward appearances to see what's on the inside. That's what important."

Katie's 18th birthday was March 27, 11 days after her death. On her birthday, her family took her ashes to Dubuque, where they were spread by her grandmother's grave. "Katie was always really close to her grandma," Jim said. "She would always visit her at the nursing home and play euchre with her. Katie was really devastated when she died. We joke that she's up in heaven with grandma playing euchre."

While Katie never did see her 18th birthday, she did receive one birthday present. The Friday before she died, she came home from a Korn concert with a few friends. Her mom had been shopping that day and a bag with her birthday present fell over and an embroidered pillow fell out of the bag. It was a Mary Engelbreit pillow and it said, "Princess of Quite a Lot."

"We had Mary Engelbreit coffee mugs that we used to drink out of together in the morning," Marge said. "I was the Queen of Everything and Katie was the Princess of Quite a Lot. When the pillow fell out of the bag, Katie knew it was for her. I'm so glad I was able to give her one present for her 18th birthday."

Marge still plans on buying Katie one last gift. She was going to buy a Dorothy music box for Katie to add to her collection. "I'm still going to buy her the music box, because "there's no place like home" and Katie's home now."

Katie with Mickey Hankes at Mickey's wedding. Katie met Mickey working at a dinosaur exhibit. As a present for being in the wedding, Mickey gave Katie a pair of drop earrings and a pendant. Katie was buried wearing those earrings and pendant. Katie's mother says it was one of Katie's proudest moments.

Radiating love

Katie's cheerful disposition is something her friends will never forget. "Katie was always smiling," Laura Morgan '00, said. "She was always so happy. She really had a lovable personality."

One of Katie's greatest traits was her indiscriminate love of people. "Katie's ability to love people was never affected by their behavior. She had a basic trust in human nature," Jim said. "Katie loved better than anyone I ever knew."

Marge and Jim share a great pain in the loss of Katie's affection. "She was never afraid to show affection—the hug and the kiss whenever she left or came back from a weekend at her mother's," Jim said. "That's what I miss the most—the hugs and the 'I love you Dad.' There are times when it's almost a physical hurt."

The last words Katie said to both her mother and father were "I love you."

"I'm glad that was the last thing I said to her," Marge said. "But what's really important is that we said it all the time. It wasn't just the last time."

Katie will be remembered by her friends as a conscientious person. "If Katie didn't agree with you, she wasn't afraid to tell you," said Elisabeth Arnold '00. "Her attitude toward things is what I remember most about her. She always stood up for what she believed in."

Marge believes Katie's sense of right and wrong was one of her best qualities. She recalled a story from when Katie was in kindergarten. "A couple of kids were making fun of a black student in her class," Marge said. "She told them they were wrong and marched down to the principal's office and told him the kids' names."

When Marge picked Katie up after school, Katie was still upset. "She told me, 'It doesn't matter if he's short or tall, fat or skinny, black or white. It's in here that matters.' And she pointed to her heart. She knew that when she was five years old. How many adults know that?"

The circle of life

At one point during the CPR, one of Katie's doctors had to leave because another one of his patients was giving birth. "At the same time Katie was pronounced dead, a baby was pronounced alive," Marge said. "That brings me some amount of comfort."

Before Katie died, she told her cousin that she wanted to have all of her organs donated. "Before they even bothered getting out the forms, I knew what to say," Marge said. "I told them to use anything they could."

Marge has found yet another way for Katie to go on living. Because she died in the spring, many of the flowers the family received are perennials. Marge plans on making a memory garden of all the flowers. "Katie always loved flowers," Marge said. "And this way, we can remember her each year by something she loved."

For Jim, accepting Katie's death is something he knows he'll have to face every day. "The minister [at the funeral] was pretty positive, talking about life everlasting," he said. "But there are times when that all seems pretty far away. It's like the poet wrote, 'All thousands of golden tomorrows that won't be quite so bright' because she's gone."

Sitting in Katie's room with all of her stuffed animals, books, and music boxes, Marge can feel Katie's presence. "Inside there's a certain peace," Marge said. "I can't explain it. But I know she's home."

by Britta Schnoor

A tribute to Katie

Life for Katie from the time she was born was not easy. Even the simplest things for you and me were stuggles for Katie. Her first hour, her first day, her first week, her first month, her first year, and her first step. Yes, the doctor said she would "probably never walk." But she did.

Her eyes were so bad as a young child. She had numerous surgeries to attempt to correct her vision. She struggled to see, but she learned to *read*, and *read*, and *read*, and *read*. School was extremely difficult for Katie, but she always succeeded.

In all of her struggles and her challenges in life, Katie never complained. I sat and asked myself how could a child be so confident, there can only be one answer, "Katie experienced true love."

Katie's parents, Jim and Marge gave her the gift of unconditional love. With their love, encouragement, and continual gift of self-esteem, they brought Katie to use, to love and, yes, to learn from.

Not only can we learn from Katie's attitude of not giving up, there's nothing we can't do if we just accept things the way they are and deal with struggles the best we can, without complaining.

by Keith Hunt, uncle

Board considers freshmen wing

Vanessa VanAtta
Reporter

A new addition to the high school has been proposed to the board of education, and may be voted on at Monday's meeting.

"The new wing would include 16 new classrooms, eight on each floor (two of which would be science rooms) and two rest rooms. It will be built where the modular classrooms are sitting right now.

"The three corner classrooms on each floor will have operational walls which could be removed for open lectures ," Board of Education Member Marty Rothey said.

There are a variety of reasons the new addition is needed.

"We have taken existing rooms and made them computer labs, open enrollment is also increasing the number of students at the high school," Rothey said.

According to the enrollment report, the high school population has increased by 111 students in one year.

The new addition will be a freshmen wing, but will not segregate them from the rest of the school.

"They (the freshmen) are getting the best of both worlds. They are not totally separate, they will be connected to the building and will not have all of their classes in the new wing," Principal Dr. Kathleen Crates said.

Though students will not spend all their time in the new wing, they may feel segregated.

"The new wing would relieve a lot of congestion in the halls and would allow the new freshmen to get to know each other better. It's a really good idea because the high school is crowded," Sophomore Kristy Coppes said.

Now that the new wing has been discussed, the board of education is searching for a way to finance the addition.

"At the last meeting (Superintendent) Mr. (Robert) Lotz discussed different ways of paying for the new wing. We want to lease a purchase with a bank (take out a loan). Now we are waiting on comments from the public," Rothey said.

Fig. 5.6. Advance meeting story. *Blue and Gold*, Findlay High School, Findlay, Ohio

the facts surrounding her death.

While asking those questions, especially of family, is often awkward for reporters, Chip Scanlan, Director of Writing Programs for Poynter Institute, has suggestions. Scanlan said that he rang the doorbell of a victim's home to talk to the father.

> I said, without thinking, that I was a reporter and that I was very sorry to intrude at this time, "But I just didn't want you to pick up the paper Sunday and say "Couldn't they at least have asked if we wanted to say anything." It was as if I had said, "Open Sesame." Within moments, we were standing in their daughter's room. On the bed was an unopened package that had come in the mail that day. It was a set of pots and pans for her hope chest. That single detail still haunts me and I think really conveyed what the victim and those who loved her lost. In that way, I think I was able to honor the legitimate journalistic reasons without greatly re-victimizing the family.

Following is a hard news story on the death of a student, an excellent example of straight objective reporting.

> Steve Mitchell, a senior, died early Wednesday morning, October 8, of a gunshot wound he had received two days earlier.
>
> Mitchell, who was 17 years old and lived at 1416 Park St., had been shot in the head when he and three other youths "were fooling around with a gun" in a house at 1700 Marshall St., according to a police report.
>
> The other three youths said the shooting was accidental, according to the report, but police did make an arrest in the case. Arrested was a 17-year-old youth, also a Central High student, who resides at the 1700 Marshall St. address.
>
> Police said the shooting happened at 3 p.m. Monday, October 6.
>
> *Tiger*
> Little Rock Central High School
> Little Rock, Ark.

This story appeared in the *Tiger* two days after the young man's death. It is strictly a news story. Had the story not been published until the following week, it probably would have been a news-feature, one perhaps with a feature lead since the spot news would have been common knowledge. The reporter could have researched the story to find significant facts of the young man's life. Outstanding or interesting activities he engaged in, achievements, anecdotes and recollections of friends and teachers can make for a good feature story. Details of the funeral service; comments from the minister, priest or rabbi; and other human interest details can be part of the story as well.

ADVANCE STORIES

Giving readers advance notice of a meeting or an assembly is an important role of the high school publication. Not all the news has already happened. Give the readers information about events that they can enjoy or participate in. The advance story is simply a story published prior to an event.

The advance story can be a news or a feature story. The reporter can use an inverted pyramid lead or a feature lead. The impact or an interesting aspect of the event makes up the lead. While in either form the time, day and place are not the first things to mention, they are covered early in the story.

THE ADVANCE MEETING STORY

Students often have opinions about issues such as a proposed change in the dress code or use of $5,000 raised by the senior class. The high school publication must play a role in helping students understand how and where to voice those opinions. An advance meeting story informs the readers of all sides of an issue so they can play an enlightened role in the democratic process (Fig. 5.6).

The reporter should find out the primary purpose of the meeting or the issue on the agenda that has the most impact on readers. If a series of events will take place at a meeting or a number of decisions will be made, the reporter will select the most important as a possible feature.

The basics included in an advance meeting story are (1) the purpose of the meeting, (2) the time and place (these are especially important in an advance story—double-check to be sure you are right), (3) the name of the organization, (4) the persons who will lead or par-

ticipate, (5) any background information about the speaker or speakers, (6) the kind of meeting, (7) the feature angle.

Avoid wordy, dull beginnings, such as "There will be a meeting of ..."; "The purpose of the meeting will be ..."; "At 3:30 this afternoon the club will ..." Also avoid saying, "Everybody is invited." It's assumed that the meeting is open to the public if the story reports the time and date. If the meeting is closed to the public, tell readers so.

FOLLOW-UP STORY

A follow-up story is simply a news or news-feature story that reports on an event after it has taken place. The time delay from the event to the date of publication dictates the way the story is covered. The city council's passage of a teen curfew three weeks before a publication's deadline makes the straight news lead obsolete. A lead summarizing the unanimous approval of an 11 p.m. curfew for those under 17 probably doesn't tell readers much new. Instead the reporter searching for a story angle may look for the newest information, such as a petition circulating to change the curfew to 1 a.m. The news-feature angle of the impact the curfew is having on students who work late hours or those who have been ticketed or detained by police for curfew violations makes for a more interesting story.

News staffs, however, need to be alert to events that should be covered. A teachers' strike, for example, would be covered by the local newspaper, radio, or television in the community as a hard news story, yet there are a number of stories available for the school paper. One might be how days missed are to be made up, another how graduation would be affected if the strike is a prolonged one, and still another how students and parents feel about the strike. There are many other news-features, feature stories, even editorials that the school paper could provide on this event. A number of issues can probably be covered in one follow-up story that simply refers to the existing strike.

Sometimes, of course, the strike can be over before the newspaper comes out. Should the newspaper then ignore the event as though it had never happened? In that case even the results of the strike would have been covered in other media. The important principle for a school newspaper staff is not to publish "old news" but to handle events in different ways so that there will be

District's Y2K compliance questioned

■ School district prepares for millenium computer dangers, which threaten grade reporting systems

BY JOHN HEATH
Assistant Editor

Underachieving students in AISD hoping the advent of the Millennium Bug would delay or destroy district grade reporting systems be warned——AISD officials report that all essential systems are Y2K compliant.

As late as mid-November, some district personnel were concerned that a few crucial computer systems in AISD would not be able to handle problems associated with the Millennium Bug (Y2K). During a Nov. 22 board meeting, technology staff informed board members that the district's grade and attendance systems were not Y2K compliant.

According to AISD Director of Management Information Systems Bonnie Pearson, however, all critical systems in the school district have been checked and approved for Y2K compliance. The AISD technology staff has been working on preparing the school district's 16,000 computers and servers, plus 22 mainframe systems for Y2K since November, 1998. They have currently spent $1.6 million of the $1.8 million originally allocated for Y2K, though Pearson expects all of the money will be spent in the end.

"[Y2K readiness] has been a very intense project," Pearson said. "We've had a lot of paid staff working on the problem for a long time."

However, not all of the systems Anderson Registrar Karen Brannan uses for reporting credits are ready for Y2K. According to Brannan, her computer system will not allow credit reports for the year 2000, which has the potential to logjam mid-year student grade reports. District person-

nel are working on the problem. However, as of Dec. 6, the system was still not compliant.

"Right now, I'm on hold," Brannan said. "[The student reports are] the big thing for me right now."

Apparently, though, all systems should be ready in time.

The Year 2000 Bug is a computer glitch expected to cause problems as computers make the transition between Dec. 31, 1999, and Jan. 1, 2000. The problem stems from the modern computer's origin in the 1960s, when computer programmers programmed only the last two digits of a year to save precious—and expensive—memory.

Even though memory gradually became more advanced and inexpensive, programmers continued to program just the last two digits of the date. Hence, many experts believe that computers will read "Jan. 1, 2000" as "Jan. 1, 1900." The experts are, however, divided on the severity of the Y2K problem: some believe it will cause little more than minor inconveniences, others are warning citizens to prepare for a doomsday occurrence.

To prepare for Y2K, AISD first had to check all of its workstations and mainframe components and determine the critical systems.

The biggest test for the district came this weekend as technology staff performed a simulation with the mainframe, which contains all critical district systems. They rolled the mainframe forward to Jan. 1, 2000, to ensure that their preparations have been successful.

"[Preparing for Y2K] been a long, hard road," Pearson said.◆

> *"We've had a lot of paid staff working on the problem for a long time."*
>
> **Bonnie Pearson**

Fig. 5.7.
Follow-up story.
Edition,
Anderson High
School, Austin,
Texas

reader interest: news-features, feature stories and sometimes in-depth reporting. See the Chapters 4, 6 and 9 for those types of stories.

WRITING FOLLOW-UP STORIES

Leads in a follow-up story should be timely or significant information. The information can be delivered in a summary inverted pyramid style or in a feature style.

The key is giving readers something they don't already know (Fig. 5.7).

If the school band wins an area contest, the story should cover how the win makes it eligible for the state contest in two weeks, or it should cover the band's 1 a.m. practice the night before the contest. When the deadline comes two days if not two weeks after the contest, the band's win has already been on school announcements and has spread by word of mouth.

Follow the lead with the tie-in, or the nut graph—one or more paragraphs briefly summarizing what has gone before. The tie-in, or nut graph, enables the reader who has not followed the story to this time to understand what it is all about. It also helps the reader who has followed the story to identify it.

Follow the tie-in, or nut graph, with facts to explain or build on the lead. The structure of this part may be chronological or narrative or an inverted pyramid style, depending on the story.

The following story is a hard news story because the newspaper from which it was taken is a weekly with an all-night print shop. Therefore, a story happening Thursday evening could easily be in Friday's newspaper.

The tie-in paragraph, or nut graph, is the second paragraph, with background information that had already appeared in the newspaper the week before.

The remaining four paragraphs are in the order of decreasing importance. Notice that the final paragraph doesn't end abruptly with the least significant fact; it cites a significant quote from the local sponsor of the contest.

Andy Kende became the top science student in the United States when he won the Westinghouse Science Talent Search Tuesday night in Washington, D.C.

Originally one of 3,161 entrants, Andy went to Washington last Friday as one of 40 finalists to compete for the na-

tion's top science award. Each entrant submitted a project demonstrating ability to do scientific research and took a comprehensive examination.

Andy won a $20,000 scholarship. Gretchen Warvel, a New York City high school girl, won second place and a $15,000 scholarship.

According to Mr. Sailsbury, biology teacher who supervised Andy's project, "Andy definitely has what it takes to excel in science, for he performed his project with the ease and skill with which a trained housewife boils water."

Andy's winning thesis and project was on "Grignard Reagents Synthesizing Organic Compounds." Andy discovered 18 new reagents not published in science literature before.

Summing up what he believes is Andy's most significant characteristic, Mr. Sailsbury said, "He is simply one of those unusual people who are highly motivated. He really can't think of any reasons why he shouldn't do almost everything."

Note particularly how the tie-in paragraph, or nut graph, gives the reader the necessary background that preceded this story and relates it to the preceding stories.

Because Andy had not yet returned from Washington, D.C., when the story had to be written, the story is a hard news story that appeared in a weekly paper. If Andy had returned before the story was written and even more time had elapsed before its publication, how might you have handled the story? What would you have included that is not in this story?

The following is another type of follow-up story, one that shows staff initiative. Some reporters would think that because there is not to be a spring honors assembly there would be no story. The writer of the following dug into the reasons for the decision not to have an assembly and followed up with an interesting story.

U-High's annual spring honors assembly is no more. Both the Student Legislative Coordinating Council (SLCC) and

Above: Erica Devine '00, Claire Galluzzo '00, Liz Hill '99, Kyle Petrie '02, and Matt Brems '99, pose with Dith Pran. **Right:** Dith Pran speaks at the 2nd annual UI International Day.

Above photo courtesy of Helen Finken, right, Brett Roseman, The Daily Iowan

The mission of a survivor

Cambodian holocaust survivor, journalist, and speaker, discusses life's journey at UI

As important officials were fleeing Phnom Penh, Cambodia, directly after the Vietnam war, Dith Pran and four fellow journalists were getting assembled for the story of their lifetime. It was April, 1975, and the Khmer Rogue, a nationalist communist party, was about to take control of the Cambodian government.

"First they were your friend, they helped out in Vietnam, they told you to fight for Cambodia," Pran said of the Khmer Rouge. "Then in just a few hours they turned into monsters, killed their own people, and took over."

Surviving the takeover

During the coup, Pran witnessed the murders of many high-ranking government officials who had protested the takeover. Persuading the Khmer Rogue that his colleagues were neutral French journalists, Pran saved their lives by taking them to the French Embassy in Phnom Penh.

Watching in horror as many of his friends and family members were killed, Pran posed as a taxi driver to save his life. "The Khmer Rouge was killing all of the intellectuals," Pran said. "They knew that the educated ones wouldn't let the power abuse the people." Being a Cambodian, Pran was sent to a forced labor camp to spend four years enduring starvation and torture.

At the camps, intense work days were usually 14 hours long with a break for just one bowl of soup. Prisoners were forced to search in forests for food, eating things like rodents and insects to stay alive. "Some people here [in America] might say, 'I can't eat rat or scorpion or cricket.' People in my camp said 'Oh! Where is cricket?'"

Leaders of the labor camps tortured and murdered workers. These heinous acts are portrayed in the movie, "The Killing Fields,"

which Pran worked together with the writers and directors to make as historically accurate as possible. Though the movie showed many graphic scenes, the extent of the destruction and horror actually caused was immeasurable. "For an American to understand how we lived over there is impossible. It is the exact opposite of how you [Americans] live your lives each day. We lived in constant pain and fear of death."

After four long years in the labor camp, Pran fled and made a successful escape to Thailand. He was then reunited with the English journalists whose lives he had saved four years before. Along with the help of American officials, Pran came directly to America. He then vowed to begin to educate the world of the atrocities committed by the Khmer Rouge. "While I was there [in the labor camp], I prayed a lot, I prayed that if I survived, I would never stop talking. Too many people died there for me to be quiet."

Human Rights Awareness

To celebrate the 50th anniversary of the Declaration of the Human Rights, UI hosted Dith Pran, the first person to tell the world of the Cambodian holocaust. The victim and survivor of the genocide and a correspondent for *The New York Times* gave a lecture to over 800 people on Oct. 27. The next day, he was the honored speaker at the University's 2nd annual International Day Workshop.

Students from Iowa City schools took part in the seminar, learning about and discussing the need for more human rights activism. "Though learning about the Cambodian holocaust was horrifying, Pran put the necessity for awareness of it in perspective," Claire Galluzzo '99, one of the students who attended the workshop, said. "If more people know about what happened, the likelihood of something like

that occuring again will be smaller."

Along with 17 other visiting professors and teachers, Pran spent the day speaking about his many experiences lobbying for human rights. Pran is the founder of the Dith Pran Holocaust Awareness Project, and was also appointed the Goodwill Ambassador by the UN High Commissioner and has received four doctorate degrees.

"Just a look at Dith Pran and one could never fathom the suffering his small stature has gone through. His voice reaffirmed his wise expression, and as he spoke, I begin to realize exactly why he says what he does," social studies teacher, Helen Finken said of her encounter with Pran. "He was truly inspirational."

Pran now travels the world speaking on behalf of the Awareness Project and the book he compiled with the help of his wife last year. *Children of Cambodia's Killing Fields: Memoirs by Survivors* is a gathering of 29 essays written by the young survivors of the genocide.

"The reason that I gave the spotlight to the children is because when I leave this world I will need someone to go forward with my project. I will need someone to tell the next generation and the generation after that so this will never happen again."

by Liz Hill

Fig. 5.8. Speech story. *Little Hawk,* City High School, Iowa City, Iowa

Principal Margaret Fallers felt the program should not be continued, citing last year's restless and unsympathetic audience.

"It was nice for the recipients but not for the student body," SLCC President Erwin Chemerinsky observed.

"It was organized," Mrs. Fallers said.

She is, however, seeking an alternative to the assembly because she feels "it is suitable for a school to recognize a special service given to the school."

The Senior Service Award and similar citations in past years announced at the assembly probably will be given this year, Mrs. Fallers said, though she is not certain when and where.

Awards have disappeared not only from the school calendar but also from the first floor trophy cases which formerly housed athletic, debate, journalism, language and math awards. They now house displays of student work and exhibits arranged by the library staff.

Advisers of activities which have received several awards this year generally do not feel an assembly or trophies are necessary to honor recipients.

"Only debaters understand debate awards," Debate Coach Earl Bell said. He feels recognition of excellence is important, and provides incentive but would like to see useful books and briefcases replace trophies as awards.

Music Teacher Gisela Goettling said she enters her students in contests so they can gain experience, not to win awards. She feels an honor itself is relatively unimportant.

Publications Adviser Wayne Brasler said, "Awards play an important role in high school journalism because they single out the excellent from the vast amount published.

"I'm against the school publicizing awards through assemblies and trophy displays, however. The number of awards an activity receives can be a misleading indication of its merit. Take drama, for example. Because of its teamwork nature the students and teachers involved have felt awards would do more harm than good. So you don't hear about awards to drama, yet it's probably the outstanding activity in the school."

Karen Uhlenhuth
U-High Midway
University High School
Chicago, Ill.

When the follow-up story is about a meeting, give the reader the point of the meeting and its meaning in the lead. Avoid beginning with time or place unless either is extremely unusual. Avoid a lead like this: "The Academic Decathlon team met Monday." Time, place and group name are included in the story, but not in the opening words.

SPEECH STORIES

The speech story is not as prevalent in high school publications as it is in professional publications. Still, the speech story should be written when someone knowledgeable speaks to a group about a timely and relevant issue (Fig. 5.8). A gubernatorial candidate speaks to a teacher's group. A Holocaust survivor talks to a history class. Both could have insightful points to make or interesting stories to tell that readers would like to hear.

Preparing to cover a speech varies based on the background of the person speaking. The reporter should gather information about the person's background. The gubernatorial candidate will have a resumé, background information provided by his campaign staff, stories on past speeches and possibly a copy of the upcoming speech. The Holocaust survivor may have some of these things, but more than likely, the reporter will have to depend upon the history teacher for background. In either case, the reporter should know as much as possible about the speech topic, whether it is private school vouchers or a comparison of Eastern European ethnic cleansing of the 1990s with the Holocaust of the 1940s.

The reporter needs to make sure of the time, day

Fig. 5.9. Civic journalism. *Stinger,* Irmo High School, Columbia, S.C.

and place of the speech so that he or she can arrive early to cover it. Even if the reporter has a copy of the speech, being there to hear what exactly the speaker says is a necessity since some speakers change drafts at the last minute. Being in a position to hear the speaker clearly and to take plenty of notes is important.

Here's where the skills discussed in Chapter 2 take over. The reporter will not have to take down every word but must have a good ear for news value. Identifying the primary focus and main points is important but may be difficult if the speaker rambles. The quotes the reporter will want to write down will be the ones that mean the most to the audience, the most descriptive ones or the most insightful ones. Remember that direct quotes mean you record the speaker's exact words. Listening before writing will help.

Other considerations for assessing what to quote directly are

- Listen for statements that emphasize a speaker's main points. Summarize others in your own words.

- Note references to your school or community. Often such statements, although perhaps of no great importance as far as the speech is concerned, do have considerable reader interest.

- Listen for references to topics of current interest to readers.

- Watch audience reaction carefully. What an audience applauds or jeers may make a good quotation.

Once the speech is over, have follow-up questions ready to ask. The questions should be for the speaker and for the audience. Ask follow-ups to points he or she made during the speech. Clarify any possible misunderstandings from the speech. Get the speaker's reaction to how the speech went or to the audience's reaction. Check the audience's reaction yourself. Once all reporting is done, read over notes as quickly as possible to make sure they are clear and understandable. Fill in missing information while the speech is still fresh.

The writing process begins with organizing the material around the primary focus of the speech. The lead will typically come from an interesting summarizing point or anecdote of the speaker. The lead can take a summary or feature approach. Give the reader something interesting about the speech in the lead. The basic information answering the five W's and H should always be high in the story.

> Thomas Meier ('97) had just graduated from high school, had just won the World Championships for close-up magic as "probably the youngest person ever to do that" and was planning to attend the University of Southern California on a full scholarship. Despite this recognition, Meier suffered from deep depression. By incorporating Buddhist thought into his life, he was able to find personal happiness.
>
> Meier shared his experience with students Nov. 2 in Chalmers East. He began his talk with a card trick, dazzling the audience with his magical talent as well as his heartfelt messages.

Find out what all your night-time thoughts really mean. Dreams are on page 7.

Centerspread

Not sure about what to do over Spring Break? Pages 8 and 9 offer a few ideas.

Take a look inside the huddle at Adrienne Suffridge on page 16.

the Stinger

36 years as the student voice of Irmo High School

6671 St. Andrews Rd. Columbia SC 29212 • Vol. 36 Issue 8 • March 26, 1999

Irmo's diverse environment

Racial diversity: Dialogue begins with focus group

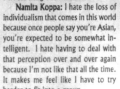

Senior Erin Beasley

Senior Sheena Campbell

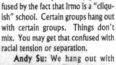
Sophomore Ashley Gentil

Senior Namita Koppa

Freshman Miggie Lopez

Teacher John McMillan

Senior Alice Milligan

Junior Robin Otterbacher

Junior Andy Su

Freshman Meghan Walker

Senior Jonathan Wallace

Senior Kofi Whitney

Kofi Whitney: You may get confused by the fact that Irmo is a "cliquish" school. Certain groups hang out with certain groups. Things don't mix. You may get that confused with racial tension or separation.

Andy Su: We hang out with people we are like. That's only natural.

Miggie Lopez: I remember when I first moved here people automatically assumed that I would hang out with black people, but I started leaning more toward band people and white people. Everyone was like "What's up with that?" Since I was Hispanic, all the black people assumed I would hang out with them.

Namita Koppa: I hate the loss of individualism that comes in this world because once people say you're Asian, you're expected to be somewhat intelligent. I hate having to deal with that perception over and over again because I'm not like that all the time. It makes me feel like I have to try harder to fit into a group.

Changing race relations

Meghan Walker: When we were younger we didn't really notice races, but as you get older you start to see that maybe a lot of people think you're not the same.

Whitney: There are people in my classes now who treat me totally different than they treat everyone else because of my color. I just figure that's people and that's how people are going to be.

Erin Beasley: People look down on you if you're a black person and you hang around with a lot of white people. They call you a sellout.

Su: You feel, for example, if you're Asian you need to fit in by hanging around with other Asians. You begin to look for people to identify with otherwise you feel like you'll lose your identity.

Interaction between races

Sheena Campbell: If I see someone with a unique skin color or look, then I ask them what they have in them because I'm curious. I don't want to offend anyone. I'm just interested.

Su: I think about 75 percent of my friends met me that way. It all depends on how they ask.

Robin Otterbacher: It's also an icebreaker to ask someone where they're from. A lot of times it's a good way to start a conversation.

Teachers

Gentil: Some teachers definitely look at me differently because I date black guys.

Campbell: Also, with teachers I feel like I have to prove myself and work harder to get over the stereotype of the black person who sits in the back of the room and cuts up, curses, or raps to themselves. I feel like I have to work harder than anyone else to prove I'm intelligent.

Su: I think if any of my teachers feel that way, they do a pretty good job of hiding it.

Gentil: It seems like a lot of teachers hide it, but you still know what they're thinking. It's more noticeable when you work more closely with a teacher. It's not like a teacher does something to you, but more of a feeling you get when you're around them.

Role of parents

Alice Milligan: A lot of people at this school just don't know better because that's the way they were raised by their parents. You can't really hold that against them. That's just how they've been taught.

Wallace: I don't arrive with my set of beliefs because they were passed down to me through my parents or through my culture. I resent that people automatically assume that I think a certain way.

John McMillan: Racism is a learned behavior. You pick it up from your parents or whoever. I believe initially your parents have a big factor in either eradicating it or perpetuating it. If they're walking around using casual racial slurs, you guys pick that up. Parents have to get involved and help alleviate the situation.

Mixing of races

Campbell: America is a lot like a salad bowl now. There are a lot of different groups but they don't mix together.

Wallace: That (salad bowl theory) is so sad. It shows a lack of brotherhood.

McMillan: It's not sad. Everyone's still together but expressing their own flavor and learning from one another. That's the whole concept behind the salad bowl theory.

Solution

Whitney: The only way things are going to change is for people to start being independent and not caring so much about what others think. I think here at Irmo that is going to take some time.

Wallace: If we generalize people as humans, rather than black or white, then we all have come from the same origin.

Koppa: This school has already tried to address this problem and has already failed with things like the Uni-Team, but I think they did try to promote some sort of social equality. You can have people like that trying over and over again but the main problem is larger than that.

Whitney: I don't think they've failed. It's just not going to happen overnight.

McMillan: Whenever you bring people, animals or what have you from different backgrounds or cultures, there's never going to be complete and ultimate unity and harmony. It's just about giving everyone an awareness, making them racially sensitive and eradicating little comments like "Indian Giver." This is something that can seem so innocent but could be really offensive to someone who is an Indian. Communication and making race a casual word are good starting points. You're going to have a lot of different races coming to Irmo. This (focus group) is a start though - talking about it and addressing it.

Whitney: Talking about it will help, but we've got to have other approaches. Here at Irmo we want quick results, but time will change things.

Editor's note: A Publications Board discussion about a letter that was to run in the February Stinger revealed a growing concern about the racial and cultural atmosphere at Irmo. In order to begin some dialogue among the diverse groups, the Stinger staff asked for input from students and faculty. Following are excerpts from a focus group meeting March 12.

See survey results, page 2; photo collage, page 3; staff editorial, page 10.

Nancy Pak
Chronicle
Harvard-Westlake High School
North Hollywood, Calif.

Notice how the author suggests the oddity of the speaker's story in the lead through specifics from the speaker's life and speech. Then the reporter inserts the basic information in the second paragraph.

A summary of the speaker's main conclusions, especially when he or she calls for change, can make a good lead.

Here the basic information is blended into the opening two paragraphs.

> **A complete reorganization of the school's guidance services is the number one need of Georgetown High School, Dr. Jan Gray, superintendent of the Georgetown schools, informed the PTA at its annual meeting last Friday.**
>
> **In an address at the PTA's annual business meeting in the auditorium, Dr. Gray …**

While rarely is a direct quote strong enough to open the lead, an indirect quotation stressing a significant or interesting point can make for a solid lead.

> **While America has the most open and un-suppressed news media in the world, the First Amendment rights guaranteeing freedom of the press to scholastic journalism are being violated.**
>
> **Mr. Peter Jennings, renowned ABC anchor, issued this warning and charged continuing censorship of student journalists in an exclusive Trump interview this week.**

In your lead, avoid stating the simple fact that a person spoke:

> **District superintendent Nick Belsher spoke to the National Honor Society Friday.**

The reader's response is "who cares," and then he or she is off to the next story.

Typically, organize the body of the story in order of decreasing importance. The points do not have to be presented as they were in the person's speech. However, make sure not to distort the meaning of the speech if you change the order of the points. Clearly connect the points together and to the primary focus of the speech.

A few more tips to speech story writing are

- Be careful not to distort the speaker's meaning by taking quotations out of context.

- Normally, do not quote grammatical errors, awkward sentences, slips of the tongue or dialect unless there is some significant reason to do so. Rephrase these statements in your own words. If there is a reason to use a grammatical error or slip of the tongue, use *sic* in brackets [*sic*] or parentheses if brackets are not available. In Latin *sic* means "thus" or "exactly as stated." This device can weary your readers; don't overuse it.

- Avoid letting your own opinions and prejudices color your report.

CIVIC OR PUBLIC JOURNALISM

Print and broadcast media not only cover the community but are a part of it. In the same way, high school journalists are also members of the student body, and they have a stake in the well-being of their school. Understanding this connection is at the center of a movement known as "civic journalism" or "public journalism."

Civic or public journalists believe it's not enough to report on a problem. They also must work to stir public conversation and problem-solving. When covering conflict, public journalists work "to frame" issues in ways to promote understanding and compromise, rather than hostility and intolerance. They also don't limit their work to the opinion page; they figure out ways to encourage attention and involvement in every section of the newspaper.

If, for example, a school is besieged with a high number of fights, public journalists not only would cover the incidents but would also explore the motivating factors, report on efforts at other schools to decrease similar violence, perhaps even convene a representative group of students to discuss possible solutions and then cover the get-together. When the district is faced with hiring a new principal, civic journalists would canvass

To leave or not to leave...

Open campus lunch hot topic

by
CARLA CHAVEZ &
CARA SIMPSON
news | writers

For freshmen and upperclassmen alike, open campus is a legend. However, the majority of the student body, 93% would like open campus lunch according to a recent *Battery* survey.

"I think people should get to choose whether they want to eat at school or home," one junior said.

Arcelia Morales, freshman, thinks that students could prove through a temporary run that they could handle open-campus lunches.

"It will give us a chance to show we are responsible," she said.

Still 6% would keep things the way they are

"Open campus (lunch) is too risky to the students. There's a great risk that something may happen and the school officials wouldn't know about it to notify the parents," Jason Tepe, senior, said.

Even though many would like to see open campus lunches, not all want to share the privilege. More than half think that freshmen shouldn't be allowed to leave campus without parent consent.

"Freshmen could be intimidated into doing things they do not want to do or should not do by upperclassmen," Ashely Kent, junior, said.

However some feel freshmen should be able to leave, regardless of parent consent

"Freshmen should be allowed to leave campus with upperclassmen because we're all in high school. If they're not mature enough to know who not to go with, then they shouldn't be in high school," one junior male said.

Clay Walker agrees that it is time for parents to allow their children more freedom.

"It is high school and parents should understand their kids are growing up," he said.

Even a freshman said that it is not such a good idea for freshman to be able to leave with upperclassmen without parent consent.

"The school would be responsible if anything happened off campus." Gina Guesner, freshman, said.

Restricting open campus lunches to certain people should be a factor, says 45% of the students.

"We should restrict open campus lunches to seniors (as a privilege). Eventually everybody would get it," one senior girl said.

Arcelia Morales thinks that if a student has more than average absences, they should be restricted to campus and not receive the privilege.

"They've already had their turn by skipping. We deserve a chance," Arcelia Morales, freshman, said.

Grades, attendance, and tardies should be part of a policy according to 25%.

"Many people instead of eating will go drink or get high," Elizabeth Salinas, freshman said.

Right at 60% would be willing to extend the school day to change to open campus.

"I would rather stay longer and have a better lunch," Danielle Valdez, sophomore, said.

Others would not be willing to extend the school day. Extra curricular activities already keep many students at school late into the day.

"I don't get out of school till 6:00 already due to athletics practice." J.P. Gonzales, junior, said.

Ms. Melody Roper, associate principal, said that the school board, staff, and parents would not support open-campus, much less even take it seriously.

"The school would not be liable for students behavior when they are off campus. If a freshman left with a senior for open-campus, and they got in an accident, the senior would be liable." Ms. Melody Roper, said.

Fig. 5.10. Poll story. *Battery,* Abilene High School, Abilene, Texas

students, teachers, parents and other members of the community, seeking each group's shared and conflicting perspectives on what qualities a new principal should have. When the school board calls a bond election—a topic that may seem like a snore on the surface—civic journalists would show how the vote has a direct impact on the lives of students and why they should care. In Figure 5.9, the *Stinger* staff reacted to a letter to the editor by creating a focus group of students to discuss the racial and cultural concerns facing the school. The staff also ran an editorial and poll results on the issue.

Civic or public journalists, by the way, do not consider this practice a special genre of journalism. In fact, they see it as journalism fulfilling its highest calling to public service.

POLL STORY

After a series of school shootings in the late 1990s, a *New York Times* poll showed that 87 percent of teenagers still felt at least "somewhat safe" in their schools. Were students so naïve that they believed this wouldn't happen in their school? Were they so resilient that they refused to be frightened by these well-publicized incidents?

We are naturally curious as to whether others think as we do. The poll story or a story based on a survey of the school population is a good way to assess the pulse of the community (Fig. 5.10).

In news and in-depth stories, high school writers often want to write "Many students believe ..." after talking to only two or three students. The only accurate way to assess if "many" believe a certain way is to do a poll story. The poll story is useful in connection with elections. Student poll stories often cover issues such as dress code changes and open campus decisions and entertainment choices, such as most popular TV show.

Accuracy in the polling procedure should be a consideration. A poll of 10 people can be very misleading when there are 300 people in the school. While a poll distributed to two classes may seem sufficient, if both classes are honors classes, the results may be skewed.

SELECTING RESPONDENTS

The group to be surveyed must be carefully defined. For example, if the survey is aimed at students who are eligible to vote in a forthcoming national election, age must be considered. If, however, the question involves lengthening the school day or awarding school letters on sweaters to students who participated in all extracurricular activities, then many more students need to be polled. Since it is not possible to interview everybody, a sample must be selected to represent the large group. Major pollsters such as Gallup have specific guidelines to make sure polls are scientific and report a specific margin of error. The goal in sampling is to give every member of the group an equal chance of being selected. A listing of all members in a directory or a school roster from the data clerk makes this much easier.

Researchers recommend polling at least 10 percent or 50 individuals, whichever is more. To make the poll somewhat accurate, choose every tenth name in a school list, for example. No name should be substituted. If the poll is for only one grade level, then again every tenth name should be used, or if there are not enough students in that grade, then perhaps every ninth or eighth name should be used. But it is important not to choose students arbitrarily. Distribution during English classes that include the varying demographics of the school is another suggestion. Make sure the sample has percentages that represent all grade levels, sexes, socio-economic groups and races.

Sampling error, or degree of confidence of the accuracy of the poll, defines the difference between those actually interviewed and the opinions of the entire group. The larger the sample the greater the confidence that the observed difference is real and not an accident. In the case of close percentages, such as the 45–55 division, determine if this is a real difference before making an arbitrary statement about the findings.

Choosing and phrasing questions can be the tricky part. Just because the writer phrased them with one meaning in mind does not mean the poll taker will interpret the question the same way. For example, one school asked teachers "Do you feel safer in the school now than you did five years ago?" Yes and no were the answer choices. The student pollster interpreted a teacher's no answer to mean that the teacher felt unsafe. However, some teachers answered no because they felt the same as they did five years ago. They felt safe then, and they feel safe now.

The best way to make sure questions are clear is to pretest the survey. Choose a variety of different people outside the journalism room to pretest the survey. After they take the survey, ask them what they thought each question meant and why they answered the way they did. Avoid asking the question "So did you understand everything?" Few people would readily admit they did not for fear of looking stupid.

The questions used in the survey can each have a different function.

- Filter questions eliminate those who are not in a position to respond meaningfully. For example, attitudes toward the cafeteria food may not be meaningful from someone who does not patronize the cafeteria.

- Background questions give information to help interpret the results of polling. For example, those who plan to go to college may give different responses to the ideal marriage age from those who do not.

- Closed questions are answered with a yes or no. While they offer easy statistical results, an open-ended question or multiple-choice question may follow to give more depth to the poll taker's opinion.

- Open-ended questions seek answers to what is thought about issues and events. The questions encourage detailed answers, and while they may elicit rich quotes for a survey story, they may be difficult to summarize with other findings.

- A multiple-choice or -range question will give the pollster easier results to tabulate but may not offer as much insight into the poll taker's thoughts as the open-ended question. Examples of the answers to this type of question are "strongly agree" to "somewhat agree" all the way to "strongly disagree." Add "don't know" and "no opinion" answers when they are relevant.

A poll can be conducted over the phone or by distributing the poll to classes. Design must be a consideration for distributed polls. A survey should have a headline to identify the poll topic. Make sure the questions are separated enough for readability. Make sure the questions are short. Too many questions will decrease the chance that the poll taker will complete the poll.

The poll story itself should offer some insight into the results. One paragraph may highlight the statistical finding that 55 percent disagree with a proposed change from a block schedule back to a seven-period day. The quote in the next paragraph may illustrate a sophomore's frustration that the change would not allow him

to have enough classes to get in journalism and athletics. An anecdote may be included, but a follow-up interview with a poll taker may be necessary to fill in the holes of his or her story. The reporter needs to make sure that the focus of the story accurately matches the poll results. A 12 percent result of students who didn't feel safe in the school should not be the primary story focus since it does not accurately reflect the school opinion. The number of people selected and how they were selected, the questions they were asked and the margin of error should all be included in the story.

A survey can also be useful in

- Locating people to interview. If a reporter is doing a yearbook feature on people who take self-defense classes, a poll can help the reporter reach out beyond his or her small group of friends to increase the diversity of people represented in the story.

- Assessing who is reading the publication and what they are reading.

- Assessing the buying habits and power of the publication's readership. Information about how much money students make and spend as well as what they spend it on and where they spend it can be useful for an ad salesperson.

- Brightening up the design of the publication by putting the results into an information graphic.

EXERCISES

1. Clip and mount a health story from a major daily newspaper. Make a list of the specific terms or medical-related phrases that are used. What did the writer do to make them clear to the public? Was each of the phrases made clear? What could the writer have done to make the story clearer?

2. Invite the school nurse to discuss a teen health issue. Prepare questions to ensure that you understand the issue well enough to write a story. Work on questions that will elicit clear explanations, examples and anecdotes.

3. Discuss and list three of the top health issues facing students at your school. Develop a list of three sto-

ry ideas for each. Pick one and write a story for your school publication.

4. Ask members of each classification (freshman through senior) to describe the three most creative or interesting assignments from their other classes. Pick the most interesting and write a story on it.

5. Discuss the three biggest academic concerns or issues for students at your school. In small groups, discuss what story ideas could come from those three issues. Pick a story, develop a list of sources for the story, and write the questions for the sources.

6. Write your own obituary.

7. Clip and mount an example of a well-written advance story and a well-written follow-up story from your school or daily newspaper. Opposite each make a list of the good story qualities that it illustrates.

8. Ask a member of a speech class to present a speech before your journalism class. Before the talk obtain the person's name and qualifications. (The teacher may make up some qualifications to fit the type of speech the person will give.) Take notes and write a good draft. Pair up with another member of the journalism class and read each other's story. Discuss the answers to these questions with your partner: Is the lead appropriate for the story? Does the body of the story adequately support and expand the lead? Why does or doesn't the story create a unified and accurate impression of the speech? Rewrite an improved draft of the story.

9. Cover a speech at one of your assemblies or a public meeting in your community. Write the story and submit your notes and the finished story to your instructor.

10. In class, discuss several controversial school issues that may lend themselves to a poll or survey. Divide into small groups, with the group's size depending upon the number of issues that seem pertinent. Each group should discuss one issue, develop a questionnaire, pretest the questions and revise them before use. Using an appropriate school directory to decide upon the number of students (and/or teachers) to be polled to give valid results, each group should conduct its poll. Results of the poll should be shared by the group; members of each group will write their individual stories. Stories should be discussed within the group. Perhaps some of these stories can be used in the school paper.

Some topics may not be school issues but may be topics of real interest to students: the relationship of high school students to fast food restaurants, diet foods, bulimia and the need "not to look fat"; the concern for a healthy body—depression, carbon monoxide levels in the blood, heart rate, blood pressure, cholesterol level, nutrition and general fitness; the problem of drug use, especially steroids in bodybuilding and athletic performance; part-time jobs and their ramifications; the school community—a world of minorities and multicultural interests; political correctness issues; sexual harassment; SAT or PSAT scores (or if your state has state exams, what are the results for your school?).

Writing Feature Stories

The news story reports that 10 percent of the senior class did not pass the standardized graduation exam. The feature story tells how Brent hid his failure notice in the bottom of his dresser to keep his parents from finding out that he will be the first of their eight children who won't graduate.

The news story reports the shooting of 15-year-old freshman Mike Bodine outside the Dairy Queen. The feature story covers ways teens cope with death.

The feature story can show the excuses students give for not doing homework or the pain students go through when a childhood pet dies. Neither of the two stories is necessarily timely, but both have human interest.

While a feature may be timely and informative, the story's primary role is to bring an issue or a person to life. The feature story's goal can also be to entertain and appeal to the emotions. If connected to a timely event, the feature story puts it in a bigger perspective, helping explain the event's impact through anecdotes and examples. The best feature story is accurate storytelling that makes the reader understand and feel. Be careful, as a feature writer, not to get so caught up in making the reader feel that you create scenes or images that are not true. Feature writing is not fiction.

This chapter outlines a few types of feature stories. Concentrate on what makes for accurate and interesting storytelling. Let the story types serve as ways to help brainstorm ideas. Notice how many different types of stories are in the feature category.

A monthly high school publication may sacrifice timeliness, but it has the opportunity to give the reader more of the story.

Today even daily newspapers print more features and feature news because they know that radio, TV and web sites may provide readers more up-to-date coverage.

For the yearbook, the feature story is the staple form of copy.

THE FEATURE STORY IDEA

The feature story comes in all forms. The stories are as serious as date rape and gun safety. The feature story can be as informative as stories on steps to buying a car or the investigation of fire hazards of a crowded gymnasium. Or the feature can be as entertaining as a story on the impact that childhood toys make on a person or a sophomore's tales from her summer as a roadie on a concert tour.

Tying all these stories together are the ideas that

- They are factual, requiring reporting and interviewing.

- They are not filled with the writer's opinion.

- They have a beginning, middle and end.

- The organization is as varied as the story ideas. However, the inverted pyramid form, which is typically used in straight news stories, is rarely used in features.

As with all quality stories, coming up with a quality idea is the first step.

The feature idea comes from a keen sense of awareness of life around you. Talking to the kid in the Star Wars T-shirt who sits on the steps outside the cafeteria leads to a story on extremely shy teens. Listening to an announcement for the deadline to turn in National Honor Society community service hours leads to a story about juniors who tutor the kindergartners at the neighboring elementary school. Reading a news story on a bus accident in Paradise, Texas, prompts a story on bus safety, whether a publication's 10 miles or 2,000 miles away.

Timeliness factors into a feature story. A story describing the ways teens cope with death can be printed at any time of the year because many students can relate to the subject. However, when such a story is covered after the death of two students, the story will have a more powerful impact on the reader. Writing about a teacher who acts out one-man plays in front of the class or dances to old English tunes to teach literature may be worth a feature story. Doing the story when the teacher has been named the school's teacher of the year gives the reader one more reason to read the story. Even if this teacher has been performing in the classroom like this for 10 years, his story warrants coverage in a yearbook academic spread when he's been given the award that year.

Listed below are a number of feature ideas and angles covered in high school publications. Look for relevant story angles at your school.

- Factors in a teenage relationship. With interviews of teen couples, parents and psychologists, the story looks at what holds relationships together and tears them apart, covering everything from college to parents to pregnancy.

- A month after two boys slashed the throat, ears and legs of a Westside High School senior leaving him to die, a story on the victim's recovery. The story covers his physical therapy and the mental trauma since the assault.

- Fake IDs. The story covers students' increased use of fake identification cards, complete with a student poll. Covering online fake identification card companies and do-it-yourself computer programs offers a fresh angle to an old story. Interviews with police, bouncers and club owners on the impact of the use of fake IDs rounds out a balanced story.

- With the tobacco industry facing increased government regulation, a story on the increased use and possible health hazards of herbal cigarettes

- What happens to teens when they get fired? The story includes a discussion of how to keep a job.

- JROTC boot camps. A sights and sounds piece on the grueling obstacle courses and drills of cadets going through military service training

- A how-to story on creating a job resumé

- High school stress—what causes it? How harmful can it be? A discussion of how to relieve the stress

- The life of a 16-year-old living on his own. The story covers his struggle to pay bills with a monthly social security check without any chance to save money for college. His loneliness after his mother and grandmother died is also a part of the story.

- An informative feature on freshman initiation. The story delves into whether initiation is harassment or harmless tradition.

- A where-are–they-now piece on those alumni voted "Most Likely to Succeed"

- How honest are we? The story looks at people's thoughts and stories on stealing, lying and cheating. The package includes a sidebar on how the staff "lost" a wallet with $3 and an ID to see whether the wallet would be returned or not.

- A feature on a group of students at school who design their own clothes

- A story of a girl who was sexually abused by her father and how she coped

- A symposium feature with a group of male and female students discussing dating rules

THE FEATURE-WRITING PROCESS

Once a reporter collects the information for the story, the organization and writing process begins. Short reader attention spans and increasing amounts of information challenge the reporter to write a strong enough lead to get and keep the reader's interest.

The feature lead is not a summary of the story. The feature lead is often an example, an anecdote or a statement that sets the tone for the story. The vignette, descriptive, contrast or oddity leads discussed in Chapter 3 can apply when writing a feature story. When the reporter has completed interviews and observation, he should choose the lead by asking:

- What about this story did I react the most to?

- What anecdote would I go back and tell a friend about?

- What did I see that made me say, "That's what this story is all about"?

Typically, features will have a nut paragraph or focus paragraph following the lead. This nut, wrap or focus paragraph ties the lead into the focus of the story. The nut paragraph helps the reader understand the main point of the story and gives the reader a sense of why he or she is reading this story. A feature tied to a news event will establish the timeliness in the nut graph. For example, the bus safety feature will have mention of the recent accident in the nut graph.

Read these opening paragraphs of high school stories and see if you get a sense of what the story is about.

In fifth grade, life made sense to John Brzozowski. He played soccer on Saturdays, attended church on Sundays and did his homework on weekdays. For one assignment, John wrote: "If I could get Santa to grant two wishes ... 1) Get rid of all pollution. 2) Get rid of all the drug dealers and tell everyone that drugs kill."

Somewhere down the road, however, his mother Linda said her middle child got lost. On a rainy day, Brzozowski was found dying in his car of a suspected heroin or cocaine overdose, ending a six year battle with drugs.

Melissa Borden
DeSoto Eagle Eye
DeSoto High School
DeSoto, Texas

In the simple opening sentence, the author alludes to the fact that at some point life is no longer going to make sense for John Brzozowski. Then she paints a picture of a normal child who is very aware of a problem. The idea that a child so aware of the dangers could find himself in his own six-year battle with drugs hooks the reader. The wrap graph in this one is subtle. It's the second paragraph. The reader knows that the story is about a kid becoming lost in a drug scene for six years. The reader has a focus and is now ready to read the rest of the story.

Another type of feature lead is the startling statement lead. The opening line is a stunning statement that sets the tone. The second sentence is the wrap graph. See if you can understand why.

Nothing says "I hate you, Mom" more than a stainless steel bar through your tongue. While most parents look at body piercing as a form of rebellion against them, pierced students tend to say that piercings are a form of expression.

Michael Weisman
Valkrie
Woodbridge High School
Woodbridge, Va.

While question leads are rare, this next one offers vivid images, especially to the reader who knows the area.

Gastonia—city of redneck farmhands with limited vocabularies, wads of chewing tobacco and Dale Earnhardt T-shirts cruising down Franklin in lowriders? Undeniably, Gastonia is viewed differently by different people. However, a large number of both Gastonia residents and "them that ain't from 'round here" see the town as farm community populated by pick-up trucks with shotguns on the dashboard and rebel flags in the windows. On the other hand, others see it as an emerging suburb of Charlotte—one with smalltown charm yet lacking all big city headaches.

John Woody
Wavelengths
Ashbrook High School
Gastonia, N.C.

In the following leads, answer the following questions: What is the tone of the lead? Do you think it fits the story? How did the reporter get the lead? What are the best details in the lead?

> She knows she is facing an 8 percent chance of dying. She understands it could affect her ability to have children someday. She realizes there will be a large scar on the side of her waist.
>
> Yet despite the realities, senior Miriam Flores is ready and willing to donate one of her kidneys to her father.

Alice-Anne Lewis
Gopher Gazette
Gresham High School
Gresham, Ore.

> In downtown Charlotte last summer, local passers-by had to do double-takes to make sure sophomore Oriana Johnson was not dead.
>
> During breaks on the set of *The Rage: Carrie 2,* Johnson and her fellow extras would sometimes have a little fun and go outside in their fake blood-soaked costumes. "Some people would pretend they were dead," she said. "There were all these cars that almost got in accidents. People just stopped to watch us. This one man got out and asked 'Do you want me to call the police?'"

Becky Dingsor
Falcon's Cry
Jordan High School
Durham, N.C.

> The automatic doors opened and a student with heavy pockets entered Nelson's Food. He took a few short steps to the customer service desk and requested three tickets to the "Blackhawk" concert. The total was $68.25 or 273 quarters. Senior Dave Anderson unloaded 300 quarters onto the counter.
>
> Anderson, along with senior David Hoffman, is the owner of the Sweet Tooth Candy Company, which provides the 25-cent candy machines found in the eight classrooms and the library of Albert Lea High School. This enterprise began with only one machine and has now evolved into their major source of income. The profit of the machines is Anderson's and Hoffman's spending money.
>
> "We love being able to make ourselves money, and not have to have a boss pay us," Hoffman said.

Chrissy Thompson
Ahlahasa
Albert Lea High School
Albert Lea, Minn.

Feature stories can be organized in any form and written at any length. Writers often use a fiction device such as suspense, surprise, dialogue, description, narration and climax in the development of the body if the device is appropriate to the topic.

The entire goal is to keep the story and the reader moving. Organize the story so the reader can logically and smoothly move from point to point or anecdote to anecdote.

The organization possibilities are as varied as the feature story types. The feature story can be told chronologically. Or just as a movie sometimes has flashbacks, feature stories can move around in time, as long as the reader follows. If the writer is using suspense, the storytelling will build, teasing the reader with bits of information while keeping the reader interested—a most challenging task. Feature writers should organize and outline their structure before they write.

ELEMENTS OF FEATURE WRITING

Observation or firsthand reporting can help you create an accurate and descriptive written scene. Taking notes firsthand is easier than trying to get a subject to recreate the scene verbally. Good feature writing is *not* done over the phone. Reporting is best done when a reporter gets out of the journalism room, visits the subject of the story and uses all five senses to describe what he or she observes.

You're assigned a story on agriculture students and their life at the barn. As a good reporter, you will want to go to the barn and spend part of the day with agricultural students.

What can you observe with your five senses?

Sight
A 1,000-pound Hereford steer that lumbers toward his owner's blue Dodge Ram pickup.

Feel or Touch
The slick mud in the animal pens gripping your rubber boots.

Smell
The sour stench of fresh manure mixed with the syrupy sweet hint of feed molasses.

Sound
The yelped "Whoop"s and "HI-ya"s of the boys herding the Angus bull.

Taste
The sweet chocolate taste of Yoohoo, pulled from the old-time drink machine, that the freshmen drink as they sit waiting for their parents to pick them up.

An interviewer talking to young agricultural students would have been challenged to ask enough follow-up questions to gather such detail. An observer can

manage those details by developing a keen eye as well as an understanding of what observation is relevant to telling the story. A good reporter will make note of a great many more details than he or she will actually use. The story focus dictates the mass of details the reporter observes.

The following are the elements of a good storytelling feature.

PRECISE WRITING

Observation and reporting is best when it is precise. Precise writing means choosing an accurate and specific word. How important is precise writing? Let's say the writer simply states: "The dog jumped up on the boy." Replace "dog" with the more precise Saint Bernard, and the scene dramatically changes. Or if the reporter writes: "The officer ran past the gate when the dog turned on him." Rewriting the sentence with more precise nouns and verbs changes the scene. "The officer sprinted past the gate when the Chihuahua turned on him." Precise nouns and verbs help make good feature writing.

If the reporter has to use an adjective, it should be a specific one. It's better to write "the teacher put on his cashmere sweater" than "the teacher put on his nice sweater."

DETAILS

Details are the small, specific facts that help make a larger point or impression. The reporter must choose details that add to the overall focus of the story. For example, the use of the cashmere sweater in the example above would be good detail use if the story is about a teacher who won the lottery but still teaches. The cashmere sweater helps to show how the teacher's life changed. The detail becomes needless if the story is about the heater in the school breaking down.

PACE

A reader needs variety. Variety can be achieved through pace. Pace is the rhythm created by word choice, sentence length and construction, and paragraph lengths. A good pace keeps the reader moving through the story. Read the story aloud to hear the rhythm and pace. If you have to take a breath in the middle of a long sen-

Fig. 6.1. "Into the arms of love" by Katherine Gazella. *St. Petersburg Times,* copyright 1999.

tence or the writing slows, go back and work on pacing. If all the sentences begin the same way, go back and change sentence construction.

Good pace can also help the reader feel the emotion of the moment through varied structures. For example, a series of three short sentences can help recreate the anxiety of a situation. Another way to vary pace is by writing a well-crafted longer sentence, then following it with a short sentence. The use of other writing elements discussed in this chapter such as details and dialogue can alter pace.

EXAMPLES

Examples are specific and typical cases or samples. The basic premise in feature writing is "Show Don't Tell." Don't leave the reader guessing or filling in blanks left by vague words. A beginning writer might tell the reader that "it's different being home-schooled." But in the following lead, Sadie Grabill from Harrisonville, Md., writes:

> Her freshman year of high school, it took Katharine Steinmetz ten seconds to get to school. It was a matter of getting from her bed to her kitchen table.

The reader now understands at least one way that Steinmetz's life is different from most students—an example to which teenagers can relate.

DIALOGUE

A device borrowed from fiction, dialogue is the use of quotes and conversation. Dialogue is useful if the sentences say more than the writer can put into his or her own words. The dialogue must be specific and relevant. The quotes can reveal the character of the speaker. You must have a keen ear or use a tape recorder to capture and use long segments of dialogue. Quotes must be exact. Be wary of dialects. If you choose to try to capture that dialect in writing, be fair and balanced. You may hear the accent of someone from another state or country, but you must be a good reporter to hear the accent of people who speak as you do.

VOICE

In Roy Peter Clark and Don Fry's book *Coaching Writers: Editors and Reporters Working Together,* voice is described this way:

> Writers often talk about "finding their voice." Readers and editors may talk about how a story "sounds." All are describing the same phenomenon: the illusion that a single writer is talking directly to a single reader from the page. This effect derives from the natural relationship between the writer's speech and prose and from artifice and rhetorical invention. All writing, even newswriting, has a voice, although the voice may be described as objective, dispassionate or neutral.

Interview with Katherine Gazella of the *St. Petersburg Times*

I was taken back by the wonderful job you did observing for the piece. What was your observation process for this story?

Gazella: I actually was in a really good position on this story because it happened to be the one girl's birthday party and her mother invited me to come to the party, so it was just a matter of writing down all these great details that were there. They played this music that I had to go around and ask the kids who the artists were and what the songs were. I felt old at this thing. ... The party itself was such a great forum because they had a disco ball and they had all these wonderful details. So for me it was just writing all these things down and later on deciding which ones I had room to use. There were a lot of great things that I just didn't have room for.

How important do you think observation is in your writing?

Gazella: I think it's key. I think it's the most important thing. I wanted to be at as many places I could with them in the short time that I had between the time that it was assigned to me and the time that I had to turn it in. It turned out that there were some great opportunities for that. But I think you just have to walk around and do things with people that they normally would be doing. One of the things that people will often say to me, and I said it in this story I believe too, is that they had to make time with me, to spend time with me. I said, "Don't do anything other than you would normally be doing." I just wanted to see them in their normal setting. Just what they're normally like when they get in and out of the car and go to basketball games together and go out on a date.

How do you put them at ease like that?

Gazella: They were amazing—these two kids in particular. With other kids it has been more difficult, but with them they liked the idea of having a reporter with them, and they were popular at school, so they were used to having attention. Their other friends at school were kind of jealous that they had the reporter. They kind of liked it because it was sort of a status thing for them. They were just really sweet about it too. They were both very nice kids. They were very talkative and pleasant. In that case I didn't have to do that much. The harder thing with this project was getting the parents to be at ease with it. In fact, I had set it up with a different teenage couple, but one of the moms said, "No, I'm not comfortable with my son even having a girlfriend, and I certainly don't want it in the newspaper."

Let's talk about the piece a second here. How and why did you choose that stuffed monkey battle for your lead?

Gazella: [Laughing] It was just sort of a light-hearted scene. Every time I saw them, they were holding hands or trying to be that much closer to each other, so that was a good representation of that. Also, the scene in the car. It was so funny. I mean they were on a date, but they had the dad in the front seat, and they had this little 9-year-old brother that they had to deal with. It was just not exactly the most romantic of scenes, so it seemed perfect for the kind of a relationship that they would have at the age of 14—that they have to deal with these little kids shooting fake machine guns.

One of the things you do well in the story is you have great use of pace in your writing. When and how do you think about pace in your writing, or is that something you consider?

Gazella: I don't think about it ahead of time, but I'll try to read it out loud in my head when I'm done writing it, and I guess I listen for that. And sometimes I'll feel like I'm going "vroom" right through the story, and I'll try and slow it down a little bit if that happens.

Summarize what your typical reporting and writing process is like.

Gazella: For a story like this, try and spend at least a couple of days with the people involved just to get to know them and what their routines are like. As opposed to just interviewing them for a half hour like you might do on a daily story. When you're there, you can interview about the important things, but just to really observe what their life is like is key. I just try to write down everything I can. It's hard sometimes because they are saying something important and you are also noticing some detail about the way they walk or the kind of car that they drive. But those are just as important, if not more so, when you're writing the story than what people say. I just try to write down as much as I can and wade through it later.

For these two, it was like this gift was given to me. They were both very talky. They said a lot of funny things. A lot of things, you would expect a 13-year-old and 14-year-old to say and with the sort of syntax that they have, so the actual quotes were really great. But also the style of clothing that they wore. The way that they looked at each other and joked around with each other turned out to be really great things to write down.

What kind of rewriting and reinterviewing did you go through? Was this one of those pieces where you sat down and sort of blast-drafted the whole thing?

Gazella: For me finding the top of the story is one of the last things that I do, and I think that's atypical. So I didn't know what the top was going to be until almost the end. So first of all that came last. The scene at the birthday party, I knew that would be a separate scene, so I just sat down and wrote that. Once you have something on paper, it's sort of a relief that you have a piece of the story done. But that was so lively, so fun and so energetic that I just wrote that one and then added some other details in later like about her mom and things like that. And a lot of that came from phone calls that I made later on. [That's how I] found out how long she and Jessica's father had been divorced.

If there's an easy section to pull out like that, then I'll start with that one. There's no order beyond that, except that [I'm] trying to organize it in a way that makes sense. Some of the stuff on their date fit together with some of the history of their relationship, and so a lot of it I'll just sort of write in pieces, then figure out how to piece it together later. It's not the most organized way of going about things [laughing]. Often I'll have the last line of the story written way before I'll have the top of it written.

Is it just something that stands out at you?

Gazella: The kickers usually come to me before the top does for whatever reason. The scene in the car didn't come to me, not long before my deadline.

Voice comes from the writer's combination of pace, word choice and use of examples, dialogue and details. Voice in a feature story helps the reader capture the feel of the subject, place and time.

In this *St. Petersburg Times* story, Katherine Gazella shows what young love is all about. As you read, take note of how she wrote the story. Where does she use a variety of sentences to achieve pace? What observations are the most vivid ones? What points is she making with the details she chose? How would you describe her voice?

> SAFETY HARBOR—They sit shoulder to shoulder in the back of the white Mercury minivan, her neatly manicured right hand locked in his left. Mike throws a stuffed monkey at Jessica with his free hand; she catches it with hers and whips it back. They won't let go of each other, not even to fight.
>
> The moment is sweet but hardly intimate. In the middle seat, Mike's 9-year-old brother, D.J., and his friend Andrew cackle loudly and spray each other with imaginary machine guns. You can always count on a kid brother to destroy a romantic moment.
>
> Mike's dad is behind the wheel, good-naturedly performing his duties as chauffeur. He is driving the couple to Steak 'n Shake in Clearwater, where Mike and Jessica will sip milkshakes and Mike will steal strips of chicken from Jessica's plate and Jessica will gently stab Mike's hand with a fork. The last time they were there, they caught Mike's dad standing outside the restaurant, spying on them through the windows.
>
> Let him look. Jessica Replogle, 14, and Mike Sharkey, 13, are in love, and they don't care who sees it—which is a good thing, because they are hardly ever alone. Theirs is a roller-rink-and-Gummi-bear romance. They talk on the phone for hours. He's slender and athletic, so naturally she calls him Chubby. They celebrate an anniversary every

> month. In classes at Safety Harbor Middle School, he writes her notes that begin, "Hey, Beautiful." She wears a charm necklace, a gift from him. "Taken," says the charm. (Should they ever break up, Mike jokes, he'll give her another charm: "Available.")
>
> Jessica and Mike love being together and being in love.
>
> On this day in the minivan, they have been going out—dating each other exclusively—for precisely four months and nine days, a fact Jessica has at her exquisitely decorated fingertips. It is an endurance record for each of them.
>
> "Things are, like, perfect right now," Jessica says. How many people can say that about their relationships? But like any romance between eighth graders this one is fragile and probably fleeting. Perfect things often are. When we began working on this article, we met an eighth-grade girl from New Tampa who said oh, yes, she and her boyfriend would just love to tell us their story. But when we called to set up the interview, she made an excuse and backed out. Her mother later explained why. Ten minutes before we talked to her, the boy dumped her.
>
> Mike has no such plans; he's smitten. Still, if we want to understand where love begins, we need to watch Mike and Jessica now, in this pristine moment.
>
> At last the van arrives at Steak 'n Shake. When it stops, Mike bolts out so he can open the restaurant door for Jessica, an act of chivalry she has come to expect from him. Their love is one of the sweetest and most uncomplicated they will ever know.

The great wall of hair

> The list of perfect things in the relationship includes Mike's tucked-in shirt.
>
> It is Monday afternoon and Mike and

Jessica are in his bedroom getting ready for a date. The time they will spend here provides a clear picture of the relationship, right down to the banter about Mike's shirt.

Mike, a snazzy dresser who sometimes changes his clothes three times in a day, twists and turns in front of the bathroom mirror, looking from all angles at the plaid button-down shirt he just put on. He pulls it out of his jeans a little in front, tucks it in a little more in back, checks the mirror again.

Mike is seeking what he calls The Perfect Tuck.

"It takes him, like, an hour to do," Jessica sighs.

While she waits, she obsesses over a few details of her own appearance. She flattens her red shirt against her small waist, glosses her lips and brushes her long, middle-parted, blond-streaked hair.

Finally, Mike puts the finishing touches on the tuck of the century.

"Jessica, do I have it?" Mike asks, holding his arms up like a gymnast after a dismount.

"Nope," she says, then fixes one part of the shirt that was uneven. "There."

In some ways, Jessica and Mike are like an old married couple; they know each other's bad habits and quirks. It drives her crazy when he twitches his knee. He jabs her in the side when she says "like," which is often. And she knows that even if she tells him to wait for her call, he will grow impatient and call her first.

"And have you seen his wall of hair?" Jessica says, poking her finger into his heavily-gelled 'do. They gained this knowledge by spending a lot of time together. They meet in the hallway after fifth period when she's leaving math and he's coming out of language.

They study together after school. They attend school basketball games together—Mike as a point guard, Jessica as a cheerleader. Go, Warriors.

At night they talk on the phone for hours at a time, but none of the conversations goes too deep. They usually end these marathons with a debate: "I love you more," she'll say. "No, I love you more," and so on.

They're like an old married couple, yes, but without the lingering resentments, the deep affection, the cycles of pain and forgiveness. Their love is true but it's also lite.

And they know it. When they are out with friends, as they will be today, Jessica will playfully drape her arm around another boy's shoulders and Mike will hug other girls.

"We'll both flirt with other people," Jessica says. "I mean, we're going out. We're not dead."

Me, you—and Pooh

It is Jessica's 14th birthday, and 60—that is not a typo—of her closest friends are jammed into her living room for a party. These are the children of the mid-'80s, Generation Y. They wear hair scrunchies on their wrists and platform sneakers and low-slung Tommy Hilfiger jeans. Their names are Meghan and Tyson and Justin and Kalyn.

They're a peculiar subspecies, 14-year-olds; somehow, they're both children and adults, yet neither children nor adults. Theirs is a world of love notes passed in the hallways at school and i's dotted with hearts. It is also a world of skimpy tank tops, provocative songs, sexual exploration and sultry dancing.

You can see some of that right here, in Jessica's living room. Everywhere you look, kids are grinding their skinny hips to techno music. On a makeshift stage in the corner, other kids sing along to the music of a rented karaoke machine, appearing free of all inhibitions as they perform.

"Oooh! Me so horny," they sing.

At the same time, Winnie the Pooh and Rugrats balloons drift side to side, as if they, too, are trying to keep the beat.

One girl goes into the kitchen, her arms folded across her chest, and asks Jessica's mom to turn off the black light. One of the boys has announced that he can see her bra through her black sweater.

It's unlikely that any couple here has been dating more than a year, and chances are none will be together a year from now. And yet the songs they sing are all about grown-up romance, with all its passion and peril. On the karaoke stage, Jessica and eight other girls line up for one of the big numbers of the night.

"At first I was afraid, I was petrified," they sing.

The song is *I Will Survive,* the anthem of women's heartache and resilience. The girls belt out these words with dramatic flair, squinting to demonstrate pain, shouting loudly to portray passion. Jessica's mom, Beverly, smiles as she watches. She's 42 and surprisingly calm amid all these boisterous teenagers. Five years ago she and Jessica's father were divorced—for the second time. She doesn't want to discuss it.

On stage, Jessica and the girls are still shouting out their song. "I'm trying hard to mend the pieces of my broken heart," they sing. One girl places her right hand over her heart, which is doubtless as pink and tender as filet mignon.

"They have no idea," Beverly says.

Save the last dance for me

One of the kids keeps turning the light on and off, on and off, until finally someone tells him to stop it and the room goes dark.

"Ladies' choice!" one of the girls shouts. Most of the ladies choose to giggle and look at their shoes, too coy or bashful to ask a boy to dance. One girl pulls a girlfriend into the corner, in a whisper, asks whether she should approach the boy she likes.

But Jessica is not shy or uncertain, and just a few notes into the Aaliyah song *One in a Million* she makes her move. She walks over to Mike and playfully butts her head into his chest. He grins, folds his arms around her waist and whispers something only she can hear.

Aaliyah sings:

Your love is a one in a million.

It goes on and on and on

Several couples join them on the carpeted dance floor. Many of the girls tower over their partners, their arms slanting downward to rest on the boys' shoulders.

But this is not the case for Jessica and Mike. She is three inches shorter than he is, the perfect height for dancing in the way long favored by teenagers: Her arms clasped behind his neck, his behind her waist, leaving no airspace between them. They shuffle side to side, hugging more than dancing, careful not to step on each other's bare feet.

To have and, like, to hold

For eighth graders, Jessica and Mike have had their share of experience in love. Asked to count their past relationships, they realize they have both reached the double digits. Off the top of his head, Mike knows how many girlfriends he has had.

"Fourteen," he says after taking a sip of his chocolate milk shake at Steak 'n Shake. "Swear to God."

Jessica has to do some math. Steve was her first flame, in fifth grade. Later, there was that guy who thought they were going out but she never knew it, so she doesn't count him. Then there was the guy who was involved in the kissing accident.

"He didn't actually bite my tongue," she says. "He just scraped it."

In all, she has had 10 relationships, most of them lasting only a couple weeks. "That's my usual—two weeks," she says, then turns to Mike and grins. "You got lucky."

Her count of 10 includes the first time she and Mike hooked up, back in the sixth grade.

He asked her out—that is, asked her to go steady—over lunch in the school cafeteria. Twelve days later they had their only real date, at an after-school dance. They arrived separately and paid 50 cents each to get in.

The afternoon did not go well for Jessica, who expected Mike to slow-dance with her, or at least acknowledge her existence. He did neither.

"I was just all aggravated with him," Jessica says.

Afterward, they went with some friends to Astro Skate Center in Tarpon Springs, where he continued to neglect her. Well, there's only so much a 12-year-old woman can take. She decided she would break up with him the next day.

But Mike had made a decision of his own. Jessica and Mike were skating on opposite sides of the rink when Mike's friend Steve—Jessica's fifth-grade boyfriend—skated over to talk to her.

"He came up to me and said, 'Yo, Mike doesn't want to go out anymore,'" she says, rolling her eyes.

Yo!

Now, at Steak 'n Shake, Mike tries to defend himself. "I knew she was gonna dump me the next day, so I got to her first."

Jessica smirks. "Yeah. Whatever."

She exacted her revenge the next year, in seventh grade. She flirted with him incessantly in hopes he would become interested in her again. It worked.

"He'd ask me out and I'd say, 'Nope!'" she recounts gleefully.

Her attitude changed this year. Once, in September, they talked on the phone late into the night. Near the end of the conversation, Mike asked her if she wanted to go out with him. She said she would tell him the next day after school.

"But I had volleyball practice that night, so I had to wait an extra two hours," Mike says. "She made me wait the whole day."

Jessica the secret agent slayer

Jessica and Mike are spending a rainy afternoon in Mike's bedroom, with the door open as always. House rule. Other 14-year-old kids are having babies or doing what it takes to get them, but Jessica and Mike are in a simpler time of life, one filled with talking and wondering but not with doing, not yet.

At this moment they are surrounded by all the things that matter to a 13-year-old boy: posters of Michael Jordan, his tongue wagging, his body defying physics. On the dresser is a gift from Jessica: A Halloween photograph of the couple dressed as Sandy and Danny from *Grease*, with the words "I love you Chubby" painted on the frame. Pictures of Sarah Michelle Gellar, who plays the title character on TV's Buffy the Vampire Slayer, adorn three of Mike's walls. There's Buffy on the cover of YM magazine, Buffy on a motorcycle, Buffy with big devil horns and blacked-out teeth. The last one was altered by Jessica.

Jessica and Mike sit side by side on Mike's twin bed, playing the Nintendo 64 game GoldenEye 007, which involves secret agents. Jessica barely knows how to play, and Mike, an expert, is taking advantage of that.

"Hey, wait, which one am I?" Jessica asks. "You keep changing the controls! Am I the guy on the top or on the bottom?"

Seconds later, her secret agent dies. She was, as it turns out, the character at the top of the screen—the one that was blown to pieces by Mike's secret agent.

"No fair!" Jessica says.

They elbow each other, pout and giggle, delighting in this perfect moment when being together is all that matters. And why shouldn't they enjoy it? Someday, whether or not they stay together, things will be far more complicated for Jessica and Mike. If they're like most people, sooner or later they'll build up a little scar tissue on their hearts. It's a hard thing, getting together and staying there. Just ask Jessica's mom. And yet you see Jessica and Mike and it gives you hope, if you didn't have it already.

Yes, things will be hard. But for now, this is the way it should be: lighthearted and carefree and set to the rat-a-tat-tat soundtrack of a video game shooting match.

After a while, Jessica and Mike put on their shoes to go outside. When Mike bends over to tie his sneakers, Jessica grabs one of the controls and slaughters his unsuspecting secret agent.

Mike lets out a yelp. "Oh! No way!" he shouts.

He gently strangles her, then puts her in a headlock. She pats his stomach and says, "I'm sorry, Chubby."

And with that, all is forgiven.

Katherine Gazella
St. Petersburg Times, copyright 1999
St. Petersburg, Fla.

The feature writer used all the elements discussed earlier: precise writing, details, pace, voice, examples and dialogue—all creating a vivid feature on junior high love.

A lesser writer would have written about young love in terms of "innocent" and "going out and having fun together." The same writer might have described how "they always hold hands" or "they like to do things such as going out to eat and roller skating." Then the reader would have to work to visualize Mike and Jessica's relationship. Gazella lets the reader live this relationship.

Let's look at several particular pieces. Notice the pace of the opening paragraph. Look at how in the second sentence the author uses a semicolon to tie the two thoughts together. The connection of the two thoughts makes Jessica's reaction seem quick and instinctive. The sentence paints a picture of two people who won't let go of each other, physically or emotionally. Then after two long sentences, the third sentence is short to emphasize the point of the opening scene.

Pace is used well again in the fourth paragraph. After explaining that they caught Mike's dad spying on them through the restaurant window, Gazella follows with the short sentence "Let him look." The sentence length emphasizes the proud defiance of a junior high couple. The details and observations are photographic. What details did the author use to show the naïveté of the relationship? What verbs are particularly vivid?

What dialogue and observations in the opening scene does the author use to make the point that Mike and Jessica are like an old married couple? What effect does pace help create in the third paragraph? What specific images does Gazella capture to contrast the innocent and not-so-innocent nature of the teenagers at the dance? What point do the mother's quotes make in the story?

FEATURE STORY TYPES

The breakdown of feature story types is anything but definitive. Just let the story types serve as ways to help you brainstorm ideas.

PROFILES

Rufus Coleman's favorite color is blue, and he is into Superman underwear and the Backstreet Boys, but few people care. The profile is more than a list of facts about a person, but it is not necessarily as comprehensive as a biography. A profile captures a central focus of someone's life that others might find interesting or entertaining (Fig. 6.2). If Rufus has the largest Superman underwear collection in the state, there's your profile focus.

The personality sketch related to a news story should not be overlooked. For example, the school board has appointed a faculty member as the new principal. The story of the board's action would be news, but here is a chance for a personality interview or sketch.

Readers would be interested in knowing that the new principal has just made his first hole-in-one this spring, that he bakes luscious lemon pies, and that as a college student he was a Big 12 gymnast. Readers would also be interested in his views on education, his plans and his goals. The reporter writing this story would want to enable readers to "see" as well as "hear" the new principal.

The profile is not an encyclopedic listing of the subject's life and accomplishments. Rather, the reporter should select facts that individualize the person and suggest the type of personality he or she has. The account of what makes the subject unique should permit readers to clearly know the person. Typically there is one dominant reason the publication is doing a feature profile on the person. The reporter should collect information and details relevant to that central reason. The central reason should be in the wrap or nut paragraph of the story.

In collecting the information, the reporter should interview the subject's friends, relatives, colleagues and sometimes enemies. Reading all previous stories about the person will give the reporter a good background to work from. Good interviews with others may lead to information the reporter will look for or ask about in the interview with the subject. Another teacher's stories about the volunteer work a coach does at a homeless shelter provide good insight. An All-State actress's mother may have great anecdotes about how her daughter used to dress up the dogs and act out movies. Both interviews may lead to good leads or good body development.

The point of the profile is to bring the person to life. The reporter should reveal personality through incident and anecdote rather than through a summary of the person's life and achievements. Permit the reader to see the subject in action. The person's appearance, dialect and words; others' words about the subject; as well as his or her actions should help give the reader a clear picture of the subject.

Observation is one way for the reporter to get such description. A student leans down to just 3 inches above an English assignment to read five sentences typed so large they cover the page. Showing the reader this observation gives a better understanding of that student's challenges. The observation works better than the words "severely sight impaired."

Fig. 6.2. Brief feature profiles. *Little Hawk*, City High School, Iowa City, Iowa

people are StRAnGe
the wackier side of CHS

● **A little extra on the side**

When **Katie Frey '01**, was born, her parents and the doctor were surprised to find that she had six fingers on her right hand. Born with an extra thumb, Frey now only has a scar and a couple of tiny casts to remember that she was born with this small defect. Frey had the extra thumb until she was six months old, before having it surgically removed.

"My parents felt kind of bad because we had a lot of finger problems in our family," she said. Frey's older brother cut off some of his fingers when he stuck his hand in a lawn mower when he was two.

Katie Frey '01, gives a thumbs up.

No one really knew why she had an extra thumb, but the fact that Frey's mother was in her 40s and smoked when she was pregnant may have been the reason. The scar only hurts when something hits it, but otherwise, her thumb is normal.

Frey said, "People ask me about [the scar] all the time, and I tell them what happened and they're like, 'you're kidding!' But it's true."

● **A dentist's dream**

Megan Lineau '99, has a big mouth, literally.

Five years ago, Lienau had three jaw surgeries, and ever since, she has been able to open her mouth unusually wide. If you get a good look, her voice box is visible.

"People in my family say 'come on, Megan, show us the voice box,' to make fun of me," Lienau said.

The surgeries caused other abnormalities. A metal plate that was put on the roof of her mouth shifts back and forth when it thunders. "It feels kind of cool," she said.

Lienau has gotten a lot of attention from her strange mouth features. "One time I had a new student dentist," Lienau said.

Megan Lienau '99, opens wide.

"When he told me to open my mouth, he leaned back and said, 'I'd love to be married to you.'"

● **Ferrets and other furry friends**

While many people would run screaming after seeing a rat in their house, **Sarah Simpson '99**, is used to it.

Simpson used to breed rats, in an attempt to breed a special kind of "blue rat." She also once rescued around 100 rats after a woman who had been keeping them was arrested for not taking proper care of them.

"I placed as many as I could," Simpson said. She gave them to friends and brought them to Pet Degree, where she worked.

Although she no longer has any rats, Simpson has kept up her interest in rodents. She now owns six ferrets. The ferrets live in large cages in her house that are located in two rooms of her house.

Simpson has a "ferret playgroup," where her friends bring their ferrets over to her house.

"I like their personality," Simpson said. "They're always playful and happy."

compiled by Elizabeth Dunbar, Maria Parrott, and Will Weinstein

The description could easily become a lead for a story on how a freshman is working to overcome a visual impairment. The lead must clearly match the primary focus of the profile. The profile on a teacher who rides bulls on the weekends could begin with an anecdote about being saved by a rodeo clown but not an anecdote about an unrelated scene in her biology class.

An indirect quotation, relevant description or pertinent anecdote can make for a strong lead on a profile. Direct quotations are used less than indirect ones by experienced reporters because interviewees do not often provide strong quotations that make the point as tightly and effectively as the reporter's own careful paraphrase can. The wrap graph of a profile will clearly identify the primary reason you're doing a story about this person. The story's body will vary as it will in all features.

Here are a few tips for profile writing.

- Use only the most descriptive or entertaining words of the interviewee as direct quotations. If you can say what the interviewee said more concisely and interestingly, then you should paraphrase.

- Weave characteristic expressions, mannerisms or gestures into the story if appropriate. Avoid paragraphs in which you describe personality. Show personality by including precise descriptive details throughout the story.

- Dialect can provide wonderful development of the subject's personality. However, you must be careful to use the subject's slang and dialect consistently and honestly in the piece.

- Avoid overworking the interviewee's name by using noun substitutes that apply, such as "the noted foreign correspondent," "the author," "the former Council president," "the Heisman trophy-winner," "the well-known educator," "the editor of the local paper," "the former Olympic champion," "the new lottery millionaire."

In the following example, the writer captures the random and humorous characteristics of a teacher. While the use of first person "I" is not typical or recommended in features, this feature uses it well.

He's a terrible artist. When I walk into physics teacher Dan Harper's classroom, he's sitting alone sketching gazelles. The stick figure equivalent of several of the long-legged creatures covers his page, and he carefully pencils in the arched antlers of another.

"One of my students said I needed practice," he says, frowning at the paper with the stick gazelles.

In an effort to lighten the concepts of physics, Harper's classes have long employed the gazelle as their mascot to demonstrate linear momentum—how fast a gazelle is soaring through the air when it falls off a wall and other important measurements.

A metal ball appears in his hands from nowhere, and he begins to trace its circumference on the gazelle paper.

"What are you doing," I ask.

Fidgeting, he looks up and admits he's worried because he doesn't know what to expect from this interview. The P.A. interrupts us, informing all teachers that if they want to eat before their inservice, they have only 10 minutes until the cafeteria closes.

He mentions he's hungry and I suggest interviewing him later.

"Maybe I won't be so nervous next time," he says.

As I walk in the door for our second interview, Harper offers me his package of Oreos. I take a cookie and sit down, but he shoves the bag toward me.

"Take more or I'll eat them all," he says. "I'm trying to lose 10 pounds."

He sits across from me, and with no gazelle sketches in sight, crosses his hands and looks at me expectantly. He seems less edgy than he'd been at our last meeting, and I throw out a question about his goals.

It seems I've approached guarded territory. He sighs.

"I really hate these goal things," he says, scrunching up his face as if he's tasted rotten food. "You can write that down. I've had to think of goals during educational courses in the past. For most people they're good. But any time I think of a goal it sounds trivial. I look at it and think, 'Is that really what I want?'"

"I avoid making goals. That pretty much says a lot about me. I have a hard time completing tasks. It's not something I'd recommend for students. There are probably counselors for that."

"Intelligent. Hilarious. Random." is senior Julie Schwartz's response when I ask for a description of Harper.

"Once I was walking down the hall and I saw him skateboarding upside down on his hands," senior Elizabeth Poole said. "It's got something to do with physics—you know, perpetual motion."

He's been known to demonstrate Newton's laws by shooting plastic monkeys with a dart gun and encourage paper ball fights in the halls to teach about nuclear reactions. So what's his teaching philosophy?

"Okay, let me ramble a little," he says. "We can make the most dull thing fun if we try to. I try to make it as fun, interesting and different as possible. That involves students working with each other and being able to control their own learning. Students have to pretend they're interested in the subject when they are not."

Harper's students don't seem to do much pretending.

"He's so excited—he's even giddy—just to be teaching us. It actually excites him to put equations together," senior Chase Shryoc said. "And every lesson has a funny story from the farm."

With lessons that regularly draw incidents from Harper's cow-milking, sheep-shearing, fence-repairing days as a boy on a West Texas farm, he brings a new meaning to real-life problem solving.

"It's sort of a career by default," the 14-year veteran says of teaching. "I'm glad I decided to become a teacher but I don't know why I did."

Harper's upbringing in the "desolate desert" region of Texas ("I see more people now every day than I did in the first five years of my life") didn't call for elaborate plans for the future.

"I didn't give it any thought—I just didn't want to live out on a ranch. When you come from a poor background, you don't think about what you're going to do for college or for a career. You just do what happens to you."

While his parents hadn't graduated from high school, Harper sought to leave the farm life and headed for college. Where to?

"You should probably ask where I didn't go," he says.

After a short-lived stint at Abilene Christian University, Harper cringed at the costs of a private education compared to value and headed to UT-Permian Basin, where he earned a B.S. in biology. Up next came an Electronic Engineering Technology ("be sure to write down that technology part") degree from Texas A&M.

"People say that if you're stimulus-deprived as a child you grow up to be stupid," Harper says. "I don't believe in any of that but it affected my ability to socialize some."

"Mr. Harper doesn't talk a lot," senior Andrew Ketcham said, "but he's probably the best teacher at Westlake."

"Not only can I handle being alone—I have to be alone," Harper says. "I grew up out of the city and was alone a lot so I learned to entertain myself. I find

Volume 71 ☐ Issue 4 ☐ Woodrow Wilson High School ☐ 100 S. Glasgow Dallas, Texas 75214 ☐ January 27, 1999   25¢

Hands, eyes, memory

Volunteers interract with handicapped

Jadranka Poljak
Editor-in-Chief

Sometimes all it takes is a touch of a hand. Or maybe a simple movement of a finger to the sky. Then the eyes will flicker. Shunte's sleepy eyes might grow to the size of ripe chestnuts. Hermelinda will give a big, toothy smile. There could be an eye contact.

They are just small gestures, so often ignored by others but so sweet and precious to senior Meredith McClelland.

"That's when I get most satisfaction," she said. "Even though they are unresponsive, they can understand you. They have their ways of communicating but you've got to get to know them."

And as a regular volunteer for the special education program McClelland has come to know these students as real friends do.

"I just treat them as my friends," she said. "Prescilla is the most responsive one of them and I even gave her my phone number.

See Volunteers, p. 9

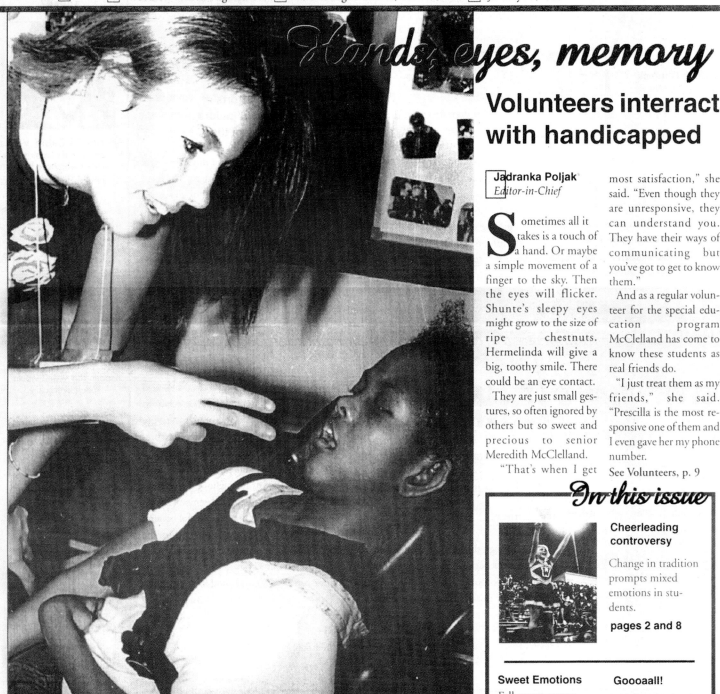

Senior Meredith McClelland, a regular volunteer for the special needs program, gets 16-year-old Shunte to follow her hand movements. Most of the students in the program lack basic mobile skills and getting any response from the can be hard, McClelland said. "Even though they are unresponsive they can understand you," she said. "They have their ways of communicating , but you've got to get to know them." ☐ *Photo by Jadranka Poljak*

In this issue

Cheerleading controversy

Change in tradition prompts mixed emotions in students.

pages 2 and 8

Sweet Emotions

Fall sports season might have ended, but the spirit of the season is preserved in pictures.
page 6

Goooaall!

Both boys and girls soccer teams start season off with wins

page 11

Fig. 6.3. Human interest feature. *Wildcat*, Woodrow Wilson High School, Dallas, Texas

Volunteers, handicapped students forge friendships

continued from p. 1

She and I talk on normal teen to teen basis. She lives with her family and she has the same feelings of 'my mom pays more attention to my brother than me.' She is just like an ordinary person to me."

But there is no doubt that their living circumstances are anything but ordinary. Most of the students are strapped to wheelchairs and lack many mobile skills. Only two live at home with their parents and the others come from the Dallas Rehabilitation Center.

"They have had a lot of abandonment," McClelland said. "Some of them live in a center and there is no telling how many nurses come in there and how many different people they see everyday."

The number is enlarged when the masses of transient volunteers who come through the program are taken into the account, she said. They are the volunteers with "no consistency," the ones who come in once to satisfy the minimum requirement set by their teacher.

Emotionally they are a lot happier. They have fun. Meredith touches them and talks to them and they love to have the affection.
-Bob Standphilly-
DPS bus driver

"You have got to come in everyday and show them you care," McClelland said. "When I first came in they were giving me the initial 'Who is this person? Are they gonna stay here?'"

And she has stayed, coming in regularly during her PALS period and other times "just dropping by to say hi." This consistence has had a profound effect on the students, Bob Standphilly, a DPS bus driver and a regular volunteer himself, said.

"Emotionally they are a lot happier," he said. "They have fun. Meredith touches them and talks to them and they love to have the affection."

The joy of rewards

It is a typical school day and McClelland is taking rounds with each student, vibrantly pushing their wheelchairs down the halls, rolling them outside for a fresh breath of air.

"I show them the nature," she says. "This is the only time they get to go outside. It is important they have as normal life as possible."

Once McClelland takes hold of the Shunte's wheelchair there seems to be a special kind of tenderness to her. Bringing her to a large window she softly whispers her name and tries to get her attention by pointing to the trees outside. At first the girl remains unresponsive, her hands and body seem rigidly twisted in the chair, but then her eyes flutter and she is following McClelland's hands, softly cooing, probably the only words she will speak the whole day.

McClelland admits relating to the 16-year-old the most, citing their age similarities among the things they have in common.

"Shunte doesn't get in [the school] a lot," she says. " She gets phenomena a lot. So when she is here it's really special. I work the best with her."

But the progress done with the other students is quite special too.

"The other day I was outside with Hermelinda, sitting down and talking to her," she says. "She stretched out her hand to hold me and she just started smiling. To acknowledge the fact that I was there she [had to have]

developed some level of security with me. I really got a sense of fulfillment."

It is this fulfillment that also drives senior Aurora Vasquez. She started volunteering after a science teacher offered extra credit for a one-hour worth of work. She says the stint just led her to "click

cramped together, softly rocking herself. "Now I just hold her hands and she pulls toward me."

It is these unforgettable moments that overshadow the somewhat depressing reality that these students are stuck with their limiting conditions.

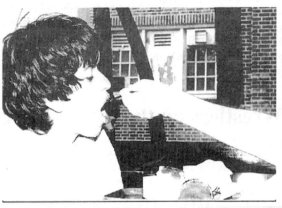

McClelland helps feed Hermelinda. Her other duties include taking the students outside for a fresh breath of air, as well as assisting in their general care. ☐ *Photo by Jadranka Poljak*

on" to the students and she's been coming "ever since."

"I remember when Carla first started walking I had to pull her towards me," she says of the 20-year-old girl. Afflicted with muscular dystrophy she spends much of her time in a corner, arms

"I can't imagine being in their position," McClelland says. "I wonder if they are hurting, what are they feeling. But this is the most I can do. I can't change their situation but I can make it easier on them."

---

things to occupy my time." We discuss bee keeping, his lifelong hobby that has assured that "people are afraid to come into my backyard." He talks about his garden and admits that he spends a good bit of his free time in the company of his television.

"I have endless projects," he says. "I built a wall this summer in my back yard."

A wall. As I ponder the usefulness of a backyard wall, he beats me to the question, sharing that he's often asked the purpose of the wall.

"I tell people it's a meditation wall, but of course I don't meditate there," he says, his voice lowering a bit as if it's a secret. "It's a small, strong wall. I just wanted a wall in my back yard."

And if there's a wall, it's possible to calculate the speed of a gazelle jumping off of it.

Corrie MacLaggan
Westlake Featherduster
Westlake High School
Austin, Texas

Notice how the reporter begins with something that establishes the physics teacher's character. Then she brings the story full circle when she refers back to her lead in her conclusion. The story is full of feature-writing elements such as dialogue, examples, voice and details. With your classmates discuss how she uses those elements. Also notice how she weaves into the story the background information on his teaching experience and his education.

HUMAN INTEREST STORY

The human interest story is a story without much news value other than offering a closer look at the oddities of life. These features appeal to the emotions with entertainment as the goal. The human interest story can be about almost anything: persons, places, animals, inanimate objects (Fig. 6.3). This type of feature can be about the track team's unofficial mascot, a rabbit who makes his home along the practice track. Or the human interest feature can be a story about how two band students discovered they were distant cousins.

Any major news event has a human interest angle. A new bridge dedication may bring to mind a story on the first person to cross the bridge. The baseball fan who stood in line 18 hours to buy the first bleacher ticket becomes the human interest angle in connection with the start of the World Series.

Keen observation and intellectual curiosity will lead to most human interest stories. Learn to think of interesting little happenings as possible stories. No doubt there are little happenings or incidents in many of your classes that could be developed into good human interest stories that would amuse your paper's readers.

Consider possible story ideas in

- Any situation or incident that makes someone smile or laugh

- Any situation or incident that arouses someone's sympathy

- Any situation or incident that is unusual

The human interest feature usually is not written in the inverted pyramid order. Many follow the narrative or chronological order or a combination. Here are a few tips for the writing of the human interest feature:

- Select only the details necessary to develop that emotion. Don't overload your story.

- Try to present your story in an original, clever way to hold reader interest.

- Write to a particular reader, not just to anyone. That technique will help to create a conversational tone.

- Avoid presenting your story in the form of a condensed summary, which will not let your reader become involved. A reader must become part of an event if the story is to be successful. Do not say someone was angry, for example. Let us see the person in an actual scene.

- Follow the lead with concrete, actual details and examples.

- Try to include some dialogue if possible. The story becomes more personal because your readers will "hear" the persons.

INFORMATIVE FEATURE STORY

Informative features give the readers information about ordinary topics that they may deal with each day, in and outside of school (Fig. 6.4). Stories about college application tips or Internet addiction are both informative features. While the topic may be timely, the story does not revolve around one central news event.

The informative feature often seems to overlap with the news-feature. The informative feature may not be as timely as a news-feature, but the informative feature may cover a recent issue. Internet addiction is certainly a relevant subject for an informative feature story. However, the same story would be a news-feature if it comes after the school board's call for parents to limit their children's Internet use.

The informative feature can be as everyday as taking care of your car or keeping a good friend. Coverage of lifestyle features is becoming more prevalent in professional and high school publications. Informative features on health, exercise and diet are part of the newspapers. Health story writing is covered more thoroughly in Chapter 5.

Some tips for informative feature stories:

- Talk to knowledgeable sources. Use in-school sources if knowledgeable but do not forget area col-

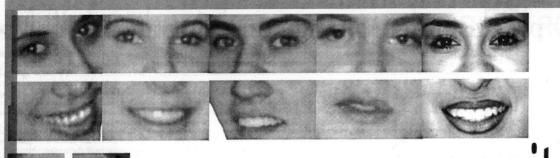

WHYopposites attract

It might be those bright blue eyes or those big, full lips that catch your eye. When looking for a date to the movies or to prom, there are reasons why you choose to go with one person and not the other.

Beauty is not just good looks

nikki**pavoggi** ———— staff reporter ————

Lying in perfect arcs across the top of his eyes with each hair in its proper place, the one feature junior Becky Cano is drawn to the most in a boy is the perfect eyebrows.

"Eyebrows are really attractive in a guy," Cano said. "I really like the way they move when a person talks, and it shows off a person's facial features. Eyebrows can be really expressive of how a person behaves."

Junior James Rodriguez said when he is at a party and sees a girl he is attracted to, the first thing he notices is the face.

"She has to have a pretty face with an outlined bone structure," Rodriguez said. "A lot of people like light eye colors like green and blue, but I like dark brown eyes on a girl. Short hair is also something that is attractive on girls."

Through the ages, society's outlook on beauty has changed. The Chinese used to bind young girls feet together at the age of five because small feet were expected. Starting with whalebone corsets to today's girdles, the idea of being petite and small waisted is relatively modern history teacher Kelly Groves said.

"It wasn't really until the 60s that the idea of a small

woman was considered attractive," Groves said. "There was a model named Twiggy who had big eyes, short hair, and a small waist. Until then, a moderate woman was found attractive."

The subject of beauty has been illustrated in lines of countless poems and gratifying songs. English teacher Sylvia Polhamus said movies and magazines have held teenage imaginations to a higher standard of their ideal person.

"Everyone has their expectations of the men and women of their dreams that they get from magazines, videos, and television," Polhamus said. "As you grow up, you find more people and find out there is no such thing as the ideal person so you have to try and get as close as possible. Who would want to be somebody's ideal anyways. It would be hard to live up to someone's idea of perfection."

Everyone has a different definition of true beauty and the saying that beauty is in the eye of the beholder follows Rodriguez's philosophy.

"Beauty is a girl who can be beautiful on the outside yet still carry herself in a confident manner to where if she wasn't physically beautiful people would still respect her and be attracted to her," Rodriguez said. "A person is attractive when they wear something that makes them seem polished and like they care about their appearance."

Dealing with homework

Fig. 6.5.

Symposium interview feature. *Northwest Passage,* Shawnee Mission Northwest High School, Shawnee, Kan.

Seven students and two teachers' discussion about daily assignments

MODERATED BY BEN LAWRENCE
Indepth Co-editor

Homework is a big concern and issue to many high school students. For many, hours of time and energy goes into projects and school work after the school day ends. This issue is faced everyday by students so, we decided to ask students and teacher their opinions about homework.

Freshman Bobby Schmuck; juniors Nick Frisby, Megan Twait and Sarah Gieseman; seniors Mike Foster, Michael Lewis-Jones and Heather Wetzel; English teacher David Mesh, and math teacher Barbara Turnbull; were all participants in a roundtable discussion. They were invited to share their thoughts and opinions about homework.

What is the purpose of homework?
MT: To make us learn outside of school.
BS: Instill the lesson plans of the day.
SG: I know it's supposed to increase your learning, but sometimes it just feels like busy work.
DM: In the professional jargon, a lot of the homework they are talking about would be called "expanding the learning." There's also preparatory homework to prepare for the next days lesson, such as when you need to know the vocabulary words that will be dis-

cussed the next day. And there's also homework that synthesizes long term ideas like book reports such as book reports or collages.

What is the majority of the type of homework you get?
NF: I think with U.S. History a lot of the homework falls under preparatory because the teacher can't lecture over everything.

Should teachers give time in class to do homework?
SG: That is something that I would like more of. That is something that causes the hours of homework. It's better to have time in class when you have the teacher right there. When you get home and you start doing it and you get confused and no one can help.

If Northwest went to block scheduling with a seminar, would you use it to do homework?
All: Yes.
MJ: If we had block scheduling, we probably wouldn't have homework.
NF: I would do all of it in class.
DM: Another supposed advantage of seminar is if you missed a test you can use that time, on a pass, to make it up, as opposed to having to come in before or after school. I've never taught with block scheduling, but I think where you would get in trouble is with the teachers that want to do one thing for the 90 minutes: lecture. I can't imagine lecturing for 50 minutes.
BT: I don't really care about block scheduling. Whatever they decide, I

The roundtable panel turns to listen to junior Sarah Gieseman's comments. Each member was given an opportunity to speak their mind.

will adapt myself to. I'll tell you where it would be very difficult: A class where the students don't want to learn, and don't want to be there.

If homework was optional, would you do it?
MJ: If I was having trouble in a subject, I would probably do it, but if I was doing well, I wouldn't do the homework.
BS: I think the subject you'd most likely do the homework in would be math.
MF: If it's something I need for college. If it was something that would help me in the long run.

How much of your grade should homework count?
NF: Not much, because the exams should show whether or not you know the material.
BS: I think homework should count more on completion rather than on correctness.

Should it be possible to get an "A" in a class without doing the homework?
DM: Another thing homework tries to do is teach responsibility and accountability. If it is pointless, then it can't do that. An "A" is a superior grade. I think to get that, you have to jump through all the hoops. From what I've heard, you guys think the test should be the most

important.
MF: If I'm being a good student and I'm getting "A's" on all the tests, then I think I deserve an "A." I have a busy schedule. I have a job and I play golf.
DM: It's not required to have a job.
MT: I know with some families, the students have to have jobs. With NHS, you have to have other activities.

Which is better, long-term or short-term assignments?
HW: It varies with the person. It depends on whether the person can manage their time. Sometimes short term is better, because you know it is due the next day.

Have you ever sacrificed your health to stay up late to finish an assignment?
HW: I used to when I was a freshman and even a little when I was a sophomore, but my junior year, and so far this year, I haven't.
MT: If it's a small assignment and it won't impact your grade, then it's not worth it.
BS: Last year, I got mono from staying up late with various activities.

Is it fair for a teacher to personalize the homework to each student?
BT: If a student can learn it with five problems and another with 20 then that's the way it should be.
HW: The other thing you need to remember is that is not fair.
BT: We are very concerned with treating everyone equally. I think it was Thomas Jefferson who said, "There is nothing more unequal than the equal education of the unequal."

The students said homework should not count as much towards their grades and the amount of 'busy work' should be reduced.

English teacher, David Mesh talks about different types of homework while senior Mike Foster listens. Mesh provided a teacher's point of view

"An "A" is a superior grade. I think to get that you have to jump through all the hoops."
David Mesh
TEACHER

"If I'm being a good student and I'm getting A's on all the tests, then I think I deserve an "A.""
Mike Foster
SENIOR

"I think homework should count more on completion than correctness"
Bobby Schmuck
FRESHMAN

"I know it's supposed to increase your learning, but sometimes it just feels like 'busy work.'"
Sarah Gieseman
JUNIOR

lege professors, businesspeople or professionals.

- Avoid using secondhand sources such as encyclopedias or books, other than as background for interviews.

- Use student quotes and anecdotes to bring life to the areas explained by professionals or knowledgeable sources.

- Be accurate. A reporter needs to make sure he or she understands the topic before informing the public.

OTHER TYPES OF FEATURES

A *community feature story,* usually of the informative type, relates the school to parts of the community with ties to students. Many of today's school newspapers have features on aspects of the juvenile court, the police department, the voter registration bureau, the emergency department of a hospital, the hospital itself (for example, care of drug addicts), mental health clinics, local colleges and universities, even nursing homes and other homes for the aged. If used, all these subjects must have a slant of interest to school readers.

Interpretative features explain various aspects of school, such as art exhibits, new courses, changes in graduation requirements, school financial problems, and the like. Art displays, for example, often need interpretation to help viewers understand the artist. Exhibits of work in home economics and industrial arts departments also lend themselves to interesting features that interpret the functions of the departments. The whys and wherefores of new courses and changes in graduation requirements will interest readers if they are handled informatively and are well-written. A behind-the-scenes look at the school's financial structure can help readers understand where school money comes from and perhaps why the school is in financial trouble. Some school newspapers have published interesting statistical features on the cost of operating a school for one day, one week and one year. Interesting graphics could accompany such stories.

Historical feature stories are stories that bring the past to life. Historical coverage is usually tied to a timely event. For example, the school's fiftieth, seventy-fifth, or one hundredth commencement would lend itself to a comparison and contrast feature, complete with pictures if records and files are available. Old yearbooks are often an excellent source for historical information.

The *symposium interview features* are written panel discussions on timely topics of interest to school readers (Fig. 6.5). Some examples are opinions on the counseling system, information kept on student records, merit pay for teachers, graduation requirements, the value of foreign languages, low enrollment in certain courses, censorship or prior review by administrators for school newspapers, or nonschool topics such as drugs, child abuse, divorce, police brutality, runaway teenagers, racial problems, or classification of movies as PG, R, or X. Background on the panelists should be included with the story.

There are many other types of feature stories—really beyond classification because types are limited only by the ingenuity and resourcefulness of a staff. One of the best ways to get ideas is to study exchange newspapers, particularly those that have been cited for imaginative feature coverage.

EXERCISES

1. Clip and mount on 81/2 x 11-inch paper five different types of feature stories from school and daily newspapers. Label each. Beneath each type explain in detail what makes it a feature rather than a straight news story and what some of its best characteristics are.

2. Use the following categories to list possible feature story ideas.

   a. List five topics for informative features. Indicate possible sources for each story. Try to have several that are related to timely events.

   b. List five persons who would be excellent subjects for personality sketches or profiles. Opposite each indicate the reasons why each would make an interesting story.

3. Read and evaluate five different leads from the daily newspaper. Rank them. Which one does the best job of grabbing your attention? Why? Why did the

writer choose the lead?

4. In small groups create a list of 10 things that interest students. Now develop at least two feature stories for each item on the list. Consider all types of features: profile, informative, human interest, community, interpretive historical and symposium review.

5. Find a major news story in a daily newspaper that has affected high school students. Create a list of possible feature story ideas based on the news story.

6. Interview a classmate on one of these experiences and write a feature story.

   a. First or worst date

   b. Scariest accident you've been in

   c. The time your parent embarrassed you the most

   d. Best holiday memory

   e. Best or worst job experience

7. Pick a subject, such as the preparations for a Student Council bake sale or the school mascot at a basketball game, and observe. Use all your senses. Write down as much information as you can. Be precise and accurate. Based on your observations, decide what your focus would be for a story and circle the relevant details or dialogue to go with that focus.

8. Write a feature story from the following information.

The Student Council sponsor Amanda Webb is in her first year of teaching. She attended Eastfield Community College and then transferred to University of North Texas. Five years ago at Eastfield a friend of a friend asked her if she would like to join the rodeo club. The friend's friend was the club president.

She started going to the practice arena to learn how to ride a horse. She started riding with rodeo team members. Then one day, the president asked her to try chute dogging, a form of steer wrestling. She became the first female to steer wrestle for Eastfield. She still competes in rodeos on weekends. She's won several competitions that have earned her $420 in prize money, T-shirts and ribbons. Each competition during the rodeo season, she earns points for the grand prize, which is a belt buckle. She's never won a buckle. To pay for riding time, she has worked at the ranch repairing barbed wire fences, painting barns and repairing the rodeo arena's concession stand.

Quotes from an Amanda Webb interview

"I guess I've always wanted to do it. Ever since I was a little girl I've wanted to own horses. It's hard to explain; this is just something I love to do. The first time I went to the ranch, I rode a 20-year-old horse named Honey. He only walked in circles. I got bored pretty quickly. I was moved up to a horse named Star, and I would walk, trot and lope in circles with it. I was trying to teach the horse rein control. Walking in circles is good practice. I had to work at the ranch to get more riding time. Whatever it takes to be around the sport, I'll do. You can't be afraid of getting a little dirty. I've gotten manure in my hair so many times, I can't even count."

(on chute dogging): "It's actually easier for me than it is for some guys because of my size. I'm small enough to get up under the bigger steers, and I can use leverage to swing those big son-of-a-guns down. I'll battle one after the other. I'm not afraid of them. I've never been afraid of much. When I was 4 or 5, my mom said I'd walk right up to a barking Doberman."

"Anything a guy could do, I wanted to do. Anyway, it's the big ones (steers) that are easy. The little ones are the ones that will charge after you."

"The money and the scholarships don't mean anything. You compete for the buckle. It's all about the buckle."

Details

Webb is also the art teacher. She grew up in the city. She's 22. She's 5-foot 1 and 100 pounds. She wears cowboy boots with dresses to school. The average weight of a steer she wrestles is 600 pounds. She has a scrapbook with her ribbons in it. The scrapbook is decorated with cowhide drawings, cutout horses and cowboy hats made from construction paper. Her favorite song is Garth Brooks' song "Rodeo."

She has to drive 45 minutes to get to the rodeo arena.

In the chute dogging event, the competitor starts in the chute with the bull. The competitor grabs hold of the steer's horns. The gate opens. The steer is prodded with an electric device so that it runs out onto the floor of the arena. The wrestler's goal is to pull the steer off all four feet. The person who does so in the fastest time wins. Average time is five seconds.

9. Write a feature for the newspaper from the following information.

A group of Key Club members are helping teach kindergarten students. The students are from Virginia Bodine Elementary School. The Key Club is an all-boys club from the junior and senior class. The main activity the members participate in is reading to a class of 16 kindergartners. They go to Miss Kate Mider's class every Wednesday. Key Club sponsor Mary Tuttle said she has had 21 students who participate. She said four students volunteer to read more regularly than the others. Those who read regularly are Junior James Rogers, Senior Sam Jones, Junior Alan Ricks and Senior Alex Johnson. Some of the books that Key Club members have read are *Green Eggs and Ham, Fox and Socks, The Foot Book, The Armadillo from Amarillo, Chicka Chicka Boom Boom* and *The Very Hungry Caterpillar.*

Quotes

Sponsor Mary Tuttle

"I have two children. I thought of doing this after James (Rogers) came over this summer for a meeting and started reading a book to my youngest. He was great, and she loved him. So I called Kate and asked what she thought of the idea. She loved it, so we started about the second week of school. It's great for everyone. The kids will sit and listen to every word. These boys are role models for these kids. Afterwards, they want to talk to them. I saw little Kemble showing his football cards to James the other day. Then he wanted to talk about his dog. They hang on these boys' legs and climb all over them.

"I think it builds self-esteem for my Key Club kids because they see how much others care about them."

Kindergarten teacher Kate Mider

"These boys are great. When they started, they were a little timid. Then they got into it. My kids' favorite is *Green Eggs and Ham*. James decided one day he'd dress up to read it. He wore a long red and white hat and a red bow tie.

"He's quite an actor. He's created different voices for Sam-I-am and for the guy he's chasing around. He's great at bringing the book to life.

"Then there's Sam. Here's this guy who's 6-8 and about 230 pounds lying stretched out on the floor reading *The Very Hungry Caterpillar*. He may be three times their size, but he really relates to these kids. He gets down on their level, literally and figuratively."

Junior James Rogers

"I just remember how my mom used to act out all the books when I was little. I had this Dr. Seuss outfit that I wore for Halloween, so I thought the kids would get a kick out of it. Then I bought these toy eggs and ham and painted them green. We just have a good time. I was surprised that they'd really sit and listen to me. Their eyes get so big when you read to them. I could really see myself as a teacher. It's just neat to think I could help them want to read. They just hang on every word even though they've heard the same book at least five times. Now I'm really getting to know some of the kids. Every time I go, Kemble and I have to talk about football cards. I don't have any brothers or sisters, so it's pretty cool to kind of have a little brother."

Senior Sam Jones

"At first, I was like, naw man. Then I did it once, and it was cool. The first time I did it, I stood up and read. They had to crane their necks to look up to me. So next time I laid down on the floor with them. I think they liked that. It put me on their level. They'll even climb on my back when I read.

"I go home and read to my brother now. I'll finish my homework, then I'll sit him on the couch with me, and we'll read. He's only three, but Miss Mider said I should point at the words as I read them and he'll learn to read that way.

"James is crazy, but he has great voices for the characters. I get to read *The Polar Express* next week, so I'm going to wear my big coat and hat."

Kindergartner Kemble White

"I like when they come to read. They're funny. I like it when James dresses up. He's crazy."

Details

Miss Mider has been teaching two years.

Senior Sam Jones is a starting center for the basketball team.

Junior James Rogers is the president of the Key Club. His mother is a teacher at Martin Luther King Jr. Junior High School.

Key Club sponsor Mary Tuttle also teaches English I. Her two children are Heather, 5, and Thomas, 7.

Miss Mider's room is decorated like a rain forest, with lots of green leaves stapled to the ceiling and plants of all kinds sitting around the room. She decorated it like this because she's teaching about wild animals. She lays out blue gym mats for the kids to sit on during the reading time.

The first book that James read to the Tuttle children was Dr. Seuss' *Fox and Socks*.

Sportswriting

His clip-on tie barely covered the fourth button on his shirt. Still, the large figure known only as "Coach" standing before the young reporter was rather intimidating. Coach leaned across the desk and pounded his fist on the reporter's spiral notebook, emphasizing each word. "You can quote me on this. We ... are ... going ... to ... give ... it ... one hundred ... ten ... percent."

Hearing the conviction in the coach's voice, the reporter just knew he had a zinger quote.

Suckered. Just like that, another cliché lives on in scholastic journalism sports reporting.

The ultimate goal in sportswriting is to give the reader a fresh approach to the struggles and the pain of the people who slip on a mesh uniform and strive to be better than the other team.

If the reporter does a two-minute interview where the only question is "How did you feel about the game?" then he or she can plan on coaches and players turning on the tape recorder in their brain to spit out all the clichés they've heard since they played Little League. "I think if we just play our game, we'll be okay." "We had better come to play today." If the reporter stops there, he or she doesn't have much of a story.

In developing a story that goes beyond the trite angles of the last 10 years to capture the real spirit of the game, a sports reporter can

- Read magazine and newspaper stories about the sport and the team to understand what is trite or overdone.

- Spend time talking to coaches and players before the season starts and before game days. In a more relaxed setting, the reporter will find out what kind of a game the coach expects and what parts of the game his or her team is working on during four-hour practices.

- Know that sports are not only play-by-play recaps and statistics; sports stories are about people.

- Understand that sports stories should ask *why*. Why was the team more motivated in the second half? Why has the softball team started hitting home runs in the last three games?

- Look beyond the action on the field for stories. See the stories of relationships off the field that lead to results on the field.

- Understand that playing and winning are not the only stories. A lacrosse team that hopes to win its first game in two years can be a fascinating story of perseverance.

- See that sports has become more than the game. In professional newspapers, as players' unions wage contract battles, business writing finds its way into the sports section. In high school newspapers, as football players face pressures of using performance-enhancing drugs and dealing with college recruiters, hard newswriting finds its way among the game stories.

A good sports reporter must be a student of the game. A reporter must

- Know sports well: rules, strategy, team and player records and the like. Become as well-informed as possible by reading up on the sport, including rulebooks, and talking to coaches, players and managers. Don't rely on your prior knowledge.

- Follow team and participatory sports during practice. It is not enough to secure information secondhand from coaches, players or spectators.

- Work at detecting the strengths and weaknesses of a team or an individual.

- Know coaches and players as well as possible and interview them.

- Refrain from attending games or meets as a cheering spectator. The writer has the responsibility of interpreting difficult plays and decisions to fans too excited to notice exactly what happens.

- Observe accurately.

- Be able to take notes quickly without losing the sequence of play.

- Be fair and unbiased, even though you have a favorite team or individual.

- Support all opinions with facts. Although a sportswriter has more freedom than any other news writer, he or she must not make comments without supporting them, even in byline stories.

- Be informal and as original as possible.

WRITING THE SPORTS STORY

Developing a clear focus is important in writing a good sports story. Sometimes the focus is assigned by the editor and sometimes the writer develops the idea on his or her own. Either way, the focus must be specific. Too many editors say, "Go write a story about lacrosse."

Instead, the idea should be based on specific research. The lacrosse team's 10-game winning streak and the pressure it faces from entering the playoffs undefeated will make for a much more motivated writer because he or she has a clear focus.

Later in this chapter, we cover five different sports story types. Within each type, there are examples of story ideas—not just general story topics. But in each of the five types of sports stories, the use of statistics and sports terminology is unique and a constant writing consideration. Both deserve some special discussion.

THE DIFFERENCE BETWEEN SPORTS SLANG AND SPORTS LANGUAGE

The drama of sports should speak for itself. Slang terms, hyperbole and forced language only distract from the event being reported. Instead of writing "The 145-pound blazer rumbled through the giant gridders of the goal line for sweet six," simply focus on a good factual description: "Senior running back Robert Belsher leapt over from the one-yard line for the game-tying touchdown."

So how does a sports reporter know the difference between sports jargon and standard specialized language of the sport? The sports stylebook of the University of Missouri's teaching newspaper, the *Columbia Missourian,* offers this advice.

> If a word or phrase is so obviously silly that nobody would say it, don't write it. Nobody says "grid mentor" when he or she actually means "football coach" or "cage tiff" when he or she means "basketball game."

> Try for interesting or colorful angles in your leads. But do not cram too many images into one lead or story. It can make things confusing for your readers. Adjectives and adverbs crowd stories and leads. Stick to good verbs and genuine description where possible. Use slang sparingly.

> A sportswriter should use the specialized writing of the sport that the average reader understands without getting too technical. You're not expected to explain what a jumper is in basketball but

you might want a simpler explanation for "swing backside on a low post pick."

Sports Clichés

This list is just the beginning of trite quotes and phrases that a sports reporter should avoid using. Just because a coach or player said these things does not mean you have to use them.

- "We have to play as a team."

- "We have a lot of potential."

- "I think we're going all the way to state."

- "We're going to have to take it one game at a time."

- "We've got our backs against the wall."

- "The best defense is a good offense."

- "It's a rebuilding year for us."

- "These guys played with a lot of heart."

- "We need to get back on track."

- "The ball just didn't bounce our way tonight."

Developing a Sports Story with Statistics

Sports are about people; statistics and records are just measures of people. Still, statistics are an important way to develop a sports story—just don't get carried away.

Rather than say the running back "had a good day," show the reader that he "ran for a season-high 220 yards and two touchdowns." The reader now understands how good the player's performance was. The sportswriter needs to know that numbers are relative, meaning the writer often needs to put the statistics in perspective. If the goalie had 28 saves, an average reader may not know how good that is. The writer may then have to tell the reader that her save total is the second-highest total in the district.

Perspective is also important in discussing the team's record. If a team's 10–2 for the season, the reader needs to know that the two losses came to the third- and fourth-ranked teams in the state.

When using sports stats, also

- Avoid long lists of scores. More than three numbers in a sentence or a paragraph is typically too many.

- Choose only those stats that warrant highlighting or that develop the focus of your story. Use other relevant statistics in an accompanying sidebar, agate or sports briefs section.

- Double-check accuracy. See that scores add up. Question numbers that don't sound logical or reasonable.

Game Story Reporting

Whether looking for a feature angle or deciding the information in a straight news story, consider this list for information to focus on or include

- Significance of the event. For example, is the league title at stake?
- Probable lineups and comments on changes in lineups
- Records of the teams or individual competitors during the current season
- Analysis of comparative scoring records of teams
- Tradition and rivalry. How do the teams stand in won-lost figures in the series? Here is where the use of a graphic would be desirable.
- Weather conditions. How will possible changes affect the outcome?
- Systems of play or strategies used by teams or individuals
- Condition of players, physical and mental
- District, state or national rankings
- Individual angles, such as star players
- Coaches' statements
- Who is favored and the odds, if available
- Other specifics: crowd, cheering-section antics, new uniforms, appearance or condition of playing field

STATE in '98

Panthers to face Judson for 5-A Division I title

By DUSTIN FINLEY
Staff writer

Whatever It Takes.

Coach Bob Alpert used this motto to motivate his football team when they reported to the first day of practice. Now, four months and 14 games later the Panthers have made school history by doing whatever it takes to earn a spot in the Texas Bowl.

One more victory would give the school its first football state championship.

"The best is yet to come," quarterback Jeremy Hurd said. "We've lost games , but we've learned from our mistakes."

The Panthers will face Converse Judson, arguably their toughest opponent all season, tomorrow at noon in the Houston Astrodome. Judson (14-0) is going for its sixth state title, and the Rockets have been in the title game six times this decade.

"We have to raise the notch each week," Coach Alpert said. "That is the way you have to play to win football games."

Defensive back Grayson Jackson cites team unity as the reason behind their success.

"With Killeen Ellison, we were the underdogs. Nobody expected us to win, but we believed in ourselves, which brought us closer and brought us here," he said.

With Hurd leading the way with five straight games in which he has rushed for over 100 yards, the Panther running game appears to be peaking at the right time.

The Panthers gained 406 yards on the ground in the 31-7 semifinal win over Houston Jersey Village last Saturday. Hurd carried the ball 14 times

(See Whatever It Takes, page 4)

Crushing victory
Jersey Village runner William Kennard finds the going tough when he gets hit head on by Nick Howard while Kione Franklin grabs him from behind. After making adjustments in the first quarter, the Panther defense swarmed the ball carrier on every play to stop the Falcons and earn a berth in the state title game. (Photo by Matt Slocum)

Fig. 7.1. Advance story.
Panther Prints, Duncanville High School, Duncanville, Texas

- Gather statistics from old newspaper archives and yearbooks. Some coaches keep files on school records or old scorebooks.

- Package statistics not used in a story. Sidebars and separate coverage are discussed later.

TYPES OF SPORTS STORIES

ADVANCE STORY

"How do you think the team is going to do tonight?"

The girls' soccer team could be 0–11 or playing for the school's first state championship ever, and people would ask the same question. This kind of public curiosity helps explain why there are 10 hours of pregame coverage for the Super Bowl.

IT TAKES

(Continued from page 1)

for 173 yards, Terrence Dean ran 23 times for 168 yards, Eric Richardson 8 times for 57 yards and Brandon Kajihiro twice for 24 yards.

"All we can do is give our best and do our best. That's all we can really do," Hurd said.

Now the Panthers (11-3) must measure the running offense against Judson, which edged Aldine Eisenhower 29-22 in the other semi-final. Eisenhower had averaged nearly 300 yards a game rushing, but got only 139 against the Rockets.

Eisenhower drove to the Judson 8 in the last five minutes. The Eagles had a first-and-goal, but three incomplete passes and a four yard loss ended the threat.

The Panthers rolled to an easy victory over Jersey Village. The offense needed just three minutes to get on the board first, and then they never looked back.

"It feels great," Coach Alpert said about advancing to the state finals. However, he said the Panthers don't

---

Texas Bowl

5-A Division I
State Championship
Duncanville Panthers
vs.
Converse Judson
Rockets

Houston Astrodome
Kickoff 12:07 p.m.
TV- Fox Sports 59
Radio 1190 AM

---

want to just make it to the title game, they want to win it all.

The Panther offense isn't the only part of the game that has improved. In the regional final game, the defense held Permian to just 183 yards, when they had been averaging 417 yards per game. They also held them to just 14 points when they were used to scoring an average of 37 points per game. The final score was 24-14.

"That's the kind of defense that wins games in the playoffs," Coach Alpert said.

The players knew the defense had to shut down the Permian offense.

"We wanted to stop their big guy, which was our main focus," senior Kevin Young said. "We knew that if we shut them down then we would have a pretty good chance to win."

The defense held state ranked running back Koefie Powell, who had 1600 yards for the regular season, to just 18 yards rushing and receiver Roy Williams to 34 yards when he had 1,500 going into the game.

There was only one worry on Coach Alpert's mind— special teams. Permian scored following a long kick-off return, and they recovered an onside kick that led to another "Mojo" touchdown.

"I thought that was a bad call on the onside kick, but we still have to play better on special teams," Coach Alpert said. "There is absolutely no room for error at this point in the season."

The advance story satisfies public curiosity and gives insight into the upcoming game, providing as many specifics as possible (Fig. 7.1). It should always answer the five *W*'s and *H*.

The high school advance story can also mirror professional sports journalism where the advance story is often told within a feature story. The advance feature story chooses one specific aspect of the upcoming game to highlight. The story is told through strong quotes, description and anecdotes. For example, the advance story may be about the possibility of a coach getting his 300th win. Another advance story may focus on how the team will replace three injured star players. The game's significance and key matchups can be primary feature focus. In a feature format, the basic five *W*'s and *H* will appear in the wrap or nut graph of the story that comes right after the lead.

Because of infrequent publication schedules and early deadlines, the advance story provides certain challenges for school newspapers. When story ideas are being passed out, the sports editor or writer must think ahead to the date of publication and have a sense of how critical the game will be and how to cover it.

Games played after the deadline date but before the publication date can often change the meaning of the game that is the subject of the advance story. In this case, the sports reporter should inform the readers of the impact last week's game could have on tonight's game.

Interviewing for the advance story may require coaches and players from competing teams to look ahead to a game in three weeks. Coaches may be reluc-

A season to smile about

Talented volleyball team is poised to take state

The members of the CHS volleyball team sure smile a lot as they play against Fort Madison. They smile during the time-outs, smile as they effortlessly keep the ball alive, and smile as they spike the ball brutally into the poor defenders. They even smile when their opponents finally score a side out.

Maybe the Little Hawks were just a little too relaxed during their regional final; one player used the word "poopy" to describe their performance. But that's what happens when you just happen to be the best team in the state. And the best volleyball team in CHS history.

They have a lot to smile about. It's been a dream season, starting last year when the seven juniors led the team to its first state tournament appearance in 21 years, placing 3rd overall. In fact it's been a dream season ever since the girls, now all seniors, started their careers in the South East Junior High gym, having undefeated records even that early. This year, they have a 41-1-1 record going into the state tournament.

There are many reasons why this team is successful. The five years the girls have played together, from summer through winter, is part of the explanation. The team is so well melded that the girls don't have to communicate much on the court—although they do—because they know where everyone is going to be.

Ingredients for success

All the girls are varsity letter winners in other sports, but they keep coming back to play volleyball. Even track superstar Teesa Price, who is used to the individual spotlight in track and originally wanted to play football in junior high, can fit into the mold easily. She said, "In track you get more personal recognition, but I like volleyball because not just one player can win the game."

Or even two players. Stacy Moss and Kelli Chesnut, at first glance, are the obvious choices as team captains. They both have the most experience and they make a dynamic duo; Moss is the best setter in the state, and Chesnut holds the school career record for kills. However, the seniors decided to break tradition thi year by not choosing two captains, but instead, naming themselves all as captains. The girls are all on such an even level, both in terms of friendship and experience, that it would be awkward if only two were named as leaders. "We didn't feel that it was fair to say any one of us was more of a leader," Karla Hirokawa said. "We all lead at different times and in different ways."

"There's no hostility on the team," Chesnut claims. "People are like, 'Oh man, after all these seasons aren't you ready to kill each other?' And I think, 'Not really.'" Chesnut's words are hard to believe when watching some of the games in practice that can consist of the girls violently smacking serves at each other or pushing their teammates over in order to win. Protests of "you cheated! You cheated!" are frequent among the competitive group. For most of the practice, though, the players tend to smile and laugh a lot for members of a team that's supposed to be feeling the pressure of being the top-ranked team.

But that's the plan of the new head coach, Diane Delozier. After coach Bond Shymansky left abruptly, Delozier had to make a decision within days. She had been set on coaching freshmen like she did last year, but decided to take charge of the varsity squad. "I've always been on the outside as an assistant coach," she said. "I saw it as a challenge and a way of growing." Her 10 years of experience as a gym teacher show as she devises new games and activities, like step aerobics, to keep her team's interest and competitiveness alive.

For a player like Stacy Moss who has been doing drills for almost a decade, Delozier's creativity is a blessing. There were times at summer camps that Moss's fingers would be bleeding from setting up so many balls, but she would still continue to set the next day with sore fingers. Her persistence has paid off. Volleyball is not the most graceful of sports, especially when players have to perform awkward moves to save a sloppy pass, but Moss makes the Little Hawk offense look smooth with her precise passing, earning her the title of best setter in the state for two years.

Winning attitude

Delozier will not only be remembered as the coach that led the volleyball team to its best season, but maybe also as the nicest coach in history. During the nail-biting playoff match against West High, her calm and supportive manner helped the nervous City players as they struggled through the emotional game. "Even if we're playing badly, she never gets mad at us. She always stays positive and we respond to positive reinforcement better," Megan Recker said.

The most negative comment Delozier made that had to do with the West game was during the next day as the girls and coaches pored over congratulation cards and newspaper articles. She was upset that an article portrayed her as boasting by omitting all the praise she had for West High. "My players are supposed to be humble," she complained.

Despite its lofty perch, the team knows

> "We didn't feel that it was fair to say any one of us was more of a leader. We all lead at different times and in different ways."
> *Karla Hirokawa '99*

---

tant to think ahead of the next night's game. Clarifying the release date of the story may help calm fears that players will overlook their present opponent.

TREND STORY

In the month since the last issue came out, the football team has lost 66–0, 74–28 and—in the homecoming game—49–0. For three weeks, the area daily newspaper has run scores, and in the halls students have talked about the disappointment.

To relive every single scoring play of each of those games in the next issue would be repetitive, if not downright torturous. A trend story is not a rehash of the plays from each game. Instead a trend story covers the highlighted trends in the course of a team's play since the last issue (Fig. 7.2).

In a trend story the big question high school sports reporters may ask is what's gone on over the last month and why?

In the football season mentioned above, interviews with players and coaches may be highlighted in a story on the verbal abuse the players are taking for their lack of offense. You may talk to defense players who are angry because they have spent three-fourths of the game on the field. Anecdotes of players being booed by band members may be part of the story. Talking to coaches about how dejected they have become after the seven turnovers in the last three games allows you to work in statistics and show just how bad the situation has become.

Because high school newspapers rarely come out weekly or even bi-weekly, the trend story has become the primary sports coverage as the alternative to the game story (see below). Rather than include a list of the team wins of the last 10 basketball games since issue 6 was published, the story may look at the team's increasing use of the three-pointer to win six of the last seven games.

The trend story, along with the sports feature (discussed later), is the preferred format for a yearbook story.

The trend story covers a highlighted trend of a team since the time of the last publication. Even professional newspapers, which face competing television

Fig. 7.2. Trend story. *Little Hawk,* City High School, Iowa City, Iowa

coverage including several all-sports networks, are moving away from straight game summary stories in their next-day coverage and toward more analysis and players' stories.

Covering a high school game two weeks after it has happened is like getting Tickle Me Elmo the Christmas after it was hot. By the time you get it, it is nice, but you've seen it, your friends have all talked about it and everyone has moved on to other things. In some student newspapers, by the time the newspaper story comes out on the football team's 66–7 romp, it's baseball season.

Add information on the upcoming game to the trend story—including the impact the last month's games could have on the next game—and the advance/trend story is born (Fig. 7.3). If the girls' team is playing for the state championship the day after the publication comes out, the audience will want to learn about how it won the last five playoff matches, but readers may want to know first what to expect in the next day's title matches.

- Include the information on the coming event as the first part of the story and the information on the past event as the last part of the story.

- Devote more space to the coming event than to the past event, for future news is usually more interesting to readers than news of past events.

- Condense into the space available as many of the highlights of the past event as you can.

- Follow the advance story tips

photo by Britta Schnoor

humility. Recker, for instance, played on the "B2" team in junior high before moving her way up to becoming the best server in the City High record books. Emily Rowat, in particular, is used to being in the shadow of her teammates, despite playing a solid game all season long. In the low points of the West game, her steadiness never wavered and she received much of the praise after the game. But she still doesn't mind being out of the spotlight. "I like not having to worry," she said. "I just like to play my best, but I appreciate it if maybe people come up to me and say 'Wow, you did a really good job last night.'"

Poised for victory

It's the Friday after the victory against Fort Madison, and a week before state. The Little Hawks took it easy for a couple of days, but today it's time to get back on track: conditioning, drilling, and scrimmaging are on the agenda. The players play brilliantly, maybe even better than at their blowout of Fort Madison. Passersby regularly pause in awe when Tanya Hammes goes up to the net to smash a spike. Standing a head or three above the rest of her teammates, Hammes has the most impressive physical presence. It doesn't require much of a jump for her to send a thundering kill down and to get the crowd roaring "Big T."

Her height is even more emphasized when the team's shortest player, Karla Hirokawa, hi-fives Hammes to sub in for her. If Moss and Chesnut are the perfect match, then Hirokawa and Hammes are the odd couple. Hirokawa doesn't receive as many booming cheers as Hammes does, but she can silence an opposing crowd just the same when she dives and saves a seemingly lost ball. She doesn't mind playing behind the big hitters on her team. "You get to do the fun stuff like diving," she said jokingly. "I'm close to the ground so it doesn't hurt me as much."

Stacy Moss isn't practicing because of a slight back injury, but she uses this as a chance to tell stories about the team, like the time when Recker gave Price a literally real "sponge" cake. Or when Shymansky made the girls run so hard they cried. She rolls around red-faced and laughing, barely able to tell of the junior high days, when the girls covered their faces with their hands to avoid getting hit by the ball and merely fell to their knees when diving. It's difficult to believe her stories, watching the players scrimmage against each other. They can hit tremendous spikes and long dives with ease, and they never cower from the ball.

Practice ends with a session of visualization. The girls sit down on the mats of the musty wrestling room, the walls of which are adorned with slogans like "Train like a madman." Right now, though, the lights are shut off and the girls are told to close their eyes and inhale deeply. Delozier tells them to imagine the Friday of the state tournament. They see themselves stepping off of the bus and entering the arena. They imagine hearing the wild fans and seeing the opposing team warm up. They see themselves perform every move and hit perfectly and confidently, and see the final game score 3-1, City High. "OK, come back to reality," she says as the players open their eyes dreamily. "No," she quickly corrects herself. "That was reality."

by Dan Nguyen

Good luck at State!

The Volleyball team will be leaving at 9 a.m. today for the tournament at the Five Seasons Center in Cedar Rapids. The first match will be against Oskaloosa at 1 p.m.

Excelling in all sports

This year's volleyball team holds many school records in many sports:

Teesa Price
4 sport letter winner
Track: 4x100 (48.83s), 4x400 (1:43.46), long jump (17'10.5), 100 hurdles (14.10), 400 low hurdles (1:03.05)

Megan Recker
Volleyball: season serving percentage (.98)

Emily Rowat
Tennis: Best singles record in the state of Iowa

Tanya Hammes
Basketball: Game, season, and career record in blocks

Kelli Chesnut
Volleyball: Season kill rating: .416
Track: 4x400

Karla Hirokawa
Softball: Total hits in a season: 73

Stacy Moss
Golf: Best district (1st) and regional place (2nd)
Hole in ones (1)
Volleyball: School record: Game, season, career number of sets.

compiled by Dan Nguyen

Ready for battle

Pantherettes face Lady Tigers in battle for district championship

By JENNI HEINRITZ and WALTER SIMS

Staff writers

The "Big Game" is tonight: Duncanville Pantherettes (20-7) vs. the Mansfield Tigers (28-0) at 6:30 p.m. in the Sandra Meadows gym. The district championship is on the line.

"Mansfield's time is coming, when they visit our house," senior Moe Ferrell said about tonight's re-match.

In their first district game, the Lady Tigers ended the Pantherettes' 16 year, 202 district game win streak. Mansfield's gym was packed with students, teachers, administrators, fans, and a surplus of sportswriters. The game was a struggle for the Pantherettes, who lost 33-57.

Tonight, the Pantherettes' 33 year district title string is on the line.

But, there is some encouraging news to uplift the Pantherettes. Junior Jamie Coleman is back, showing her quick skills on the court by scoring 11 points against Arlington Tuesday night.

During the first game of district play, Coleman broke her thumb. "I kept thinking, I can't be out again," she said.

As a warm-up to tonight's game, the girls brought home a 19 point win over the Arlington Colts Tuesday night. High scorer was sophomore Amy Mueller with 13 points.

Even with the tough district schedule the girls have claimed wins over Lamar 42-39, Sam Houston 46-38, and Bowie 61-58.

The team has been successful in shutting down those school's "star" players, leading to the wins, senior Brianna Brown said.

With the strong rivalry between Duncanville and DeSoto, the girls faced a challenging game. In a packed Eagle gym, the game was set at a very fast pace with constant pressure from both teams. It was one of the most physical match-ups this season.

Pantherettes vs. Lady Tigers

Record: 19-7	Record: 28-0
Rank: #4 in area	Rank: #1 in area
Team statistical leaders:	Team statistical leaders:
Brianna Brown- 10.3 points, 7.5 rebounds per game	Kaira White- 12.5 points per game
Moe Ferrell- 6.3 rebounds per game	Tori Wilson- 9.8 points, 7.9 rebounds per game
Jamie Coleman- 2.8 assists, 3.0 steals per game	Robyn Miller- 7.0 rebounds per game

Due to the though competition, the game went into double overtime before the Pantherettes pulled out a 71-67 victory. Unfortunately for the girls, during the first overtime Junior Michelle Hames went down for the season with a torn ACL during an aggressive play to keep the ball within court boundaries.

Following the girls game, the Panthers will face the Tigers in what is expected to be fast paced action.

Ranked 13th in the nation, the varsity Panthers have been on a roll since bringing home the consolation championship at the Slam Dunk on the Beach Tournament in Delaware.

Their last loss was in the first game of the tournament when they played the number two team in the nation. They are 5-0 in district play.

Coach Phil McNeely says that he expects the players to play hard every game and their goal is to win every game.

"Since the beginning of the season, the team has gotten better," he said. "They are executing better and playing smarter."

Coach McNeely expects his players to be leaders.

"I expect the players to be the best person they can be off the court, get their grades, and play hard on the court," he said. "As far as me being the coach, I feel the same way about myself as I do about the players. I expect to be a leader, work hard, and be committed to the team."

Though the coach has seen improvements, players cite areas where they need to improve.

"The stronger effort we give in the second half, we need in the first," senior David Sykes said.

When the Panthers head into each game they have a mindset of confidence and are usually well prepared. According to Coach McNeely, that team has developed nicely.

In a compettitive district, every game is extremely important to the Panthers.

Senior Ryan Randle is enjoying the team chemistry.

"I feel great at this point of the season," he said. "Everyone is working together and playing better. My ultamate goal is to win state. We will win state this year.

Senior Hassan Conteh says that the team is having a good season, but it can do better.

"We can make our defense better and raise our intensity," he said. "We also can come together as a team a little bit more."

Coach McNeely says the team's strength is their experience and the only weakness are a few inconsistencies here and there.

"The problem of inconsistency is worked on every day," he said. "We want to keep everything at the same level and have no ups and downs.

Coach McNeely says the players work each day to improve..

"We talk about our problems everyday, and it is more mental than anything."

Fig. 7.3. Advance and trend combination story. *Panther Prints,* Duncanville High School, Duncanville, Texas

Hockey fans on thin ice...

Fans' behavior results in three arrests

Webster Groves Police arrested one KHS student and two '97 graduates during the annual Turkey Day hockey game, Nov. 27, at the Webster Groves Community Center. Principal Franklin McCallie said he quit attending hockey games because of fan rowdiness like the Nov. 27 incident.

According to Sergeant Al Rudolph, a Webster Groves policeman, the incident began when an officer repeatedly asked Jeff Whitmore, senior, to put on his shirt.

"I was part of a group of boys spelling Kirkwood on their chests to promote school spirit," Whitmore said.

Whitmore said he exited the game with one minute remaining, and an officer arrested him as he was in the process of putting on his shirt. According to Rudolph, the police arrested him on counts of peace disturbance, resisting arrest and assaulting an officer.

Following Whitmore's arrest, Kirkwood fans outside the building began yelling vulgar insults at the officers, insults which Larry Eberle, KHS parent, recorded on video tape. Police reacted to the fans' taunting and arrested the two graduates.

Dale Curtis, Webster Groves chief of police, told the *Call* that police had arrested David Kochera, '97 grad, on counts of peace disturbance, intervening with arrest, resisting arrest and assaulting an officer.

According to an article in the Dec. 6 *Webster-Kirkwood Times*, an officer struggled with Kochera and then allegedly placed Kochera in a headlock. In response, Kochera allegedly brought the officer to the ground, when a second officer entered the scene and allegedly hit Kochera three times with a baton.

"When someone is resisting arrest, the law gives the right and obligation to the officer to overcome an individual's resistance," Rudolph said.

Rudolph said police arrested a third individual, whom he refused to name, because he violated the law by intervening with Whitmore's arrest, for disturbing the peace and for trying to escape custody.

Eberle said he captured the incident on videotape but that the tape "was not very clear. It was extremely dark and the camera was turned off briefly a few times during the incident. In my opinion, however, the incident could have been avoided

by the police if they had taken it easy. The police seemed like they were looking for trouble."

McCallie said the fans' rowdy manner sometimes occurs because of the involvement of alcohol.

"When drinking is involved, fans lose control, and they lose perspective of what to do. Then they refuse to obey authority," he said. "To my understanding, alcohol was involved at the hockey game, Nov. 27."

Kirkwood and Webster Groves faced off again, Dec. 8, at Queeny Park.

Three Webster students, according to a report in the *St. Louis Post Dispatch*, Dec. 10, harassed the Kirkwood goalie at that game. Officer Paul Neske said he asked the boys to stop cursing the goalie.

The boys then proceeded to throw trash onto the ice. The *Post* report said that after being removed from the game, the boys continued to yell insults, argue with Queeny Park rangers and kick over trash cans.

According to Neske, the boys "smelled like breweries."

McCallie also said the rowdiness at hockey games occurs because of the overall atmosphere and lack of sportsmanship.

"Unlike most other high school sporting events," McCallie said, "it is common to hear opposing fans yell at each other and at the players. At athletic events, fans should not yell at opposing teams. They should encourage and support their team."

McCallie said he has no authority during hockey games because the Missouri State High School Activities Association does not sanction it. However, he said he does have an obligation as a Kirkwood citizen to work with those involved to eliminate the rowdiness.

He believes the solution lies with the hockey board, and he said the board could ask for his help in containing the fans.

The problem may not go away, even after Kirkwood builds its new ice rink because of limited seating.

The *Post* article said Scott Stream, who leads the group which planned the rink, indicated it will hold 350- 400, so when Kirkwood hosts the game with Webster, it will be at Queeny Park, because there will not be enough seats for the fans at the Kirkwood facility.

Amy Bild

Fig. 7.4. Sports news story. *Kirkwood Call*, Kirkwood High School, Kirkwood, Mo.

when writing about the upcoming game; then use the trend notes to cover the earlier games.

- Do not include a running or chronological account. That structure is suitable only for newspapers that can be more timely than most school newspapers can be or for the very special event in which there would be interest despite the late follow-up.

SPORTS NEWS STORY

Sports are a business at the professional level and have become so at the collegiate level. While some may see the high school level as unspoiled territory, issues have crept into the secondary sports scene.

Student athletes face questions surrounding recruiter tactics, NCAA eligibility, performance-enhancing drug use and sports funding. These issues have taken newspaper sports coverage outside the realm of sports as "just a game." Figure 7.4 shows strong news coverage of fans arrested at a school hockey match.

The sports news story follows the inverted pyramid style and the other suggestions in Chapter 2 on newswriting. Make sure to consider balance, objectivity and libel and ethics in writing sports news as you would for other newswriting.

GAME STORY

Only when the high school publication gets a very late deadline on a significant game or event is the game story used. The game story offers the significant details, game summary and highlights, and player and coach analysis on a timely basis (Fig. 7.5). But the game story is not a play-by-play recap. Anyone covering a high school game will most likely have to keep game statistics. Coaches may provide stats but not quickly enough for deadline purposes. Anyone having to write a game story needs to understand the sport well enough to keep statistics. For example, if a quarterback is sacked for a 10-yard loss, the yards are deducted from rushing yards even though he was trying to pass.

A good sports reporter writing a game story will look for key statistics, trends or moments to weave the story around. A key statistic is often a poignant fact in the lead. A senior's three-run homer that changed the momentum and started a 10-run inning may be a worthy moment to be the primary story focus.

The story is typically written in inverted pyramid structure. The lead can follow the variety of leads offered in Chapter 3 and does not have to be a summary lead. If the sportswriter chooses a non–summary style lead, then the team names, score and primary significance of the game should come in the wrap graph. In whatever form, game story leads should begin with something significant about the game or match.

> **Despite slogging through mud and puddles of water, which added precious seconds to times and made the course slick, the cross country team's overall performances Oct. 16 produced the best City League finish in 15 years.**
>
> Lisa Burgess
> *Paladin*
> Kapaun Mt. Carmel High School
> Wichita, Kan.

> **The 1999 state wrestling tournament was coming to a close, but Kapaun Mt. Carmel fans and wrestlers were not ready to leave. Junior Ryan Frazier swung coach Tim Dryden around on the mat, freshman Dough Hoover held up three fingers for the fans to see and the KMC audience was still on its feet chanting "Frazier, Frazier." The Crusaders had just gained its third state champion of the night.**
>
> **In state competition Feb. 26–27 at the Kansas Coliseum all eight wrestlers made it to the second day; three advanced to the finals.**
>
> Elaine Meyer
> *Paladin*
> Kapaun Mt. Carmel High School
> Wichita, Kan.

Since the game story is not a play-by-play rehash, the story does not have to be organized chronologically. Give the reader interesting and game-changing moments first. Weave in postgame quotes from players and coaches. The quotes can give the reader insight into a second-half strategy or a record-breaking day. Then move on to less important moments or points.

Possible information for a game story:

- Significance of the outcome. Was a championship at stake? Do the standings of the teams change?

- Spectacular plays. Tell about the last-minute fumble, the triple that won the game or the jumper from mid-court.

- Comparison of the teams. How did their weights and heights compare? In what part of the game did the winners excel? What were the losers' weaknesses? Make sure to support analysis with facts or coach and player quotes.

- Individual performances. Who were the game's top performers and how good were their performances? Did the pitcher throw 92-mile-per-hour fastballs and give up only one hit, or did the right halfback run for 230 yards and score on four runs of more than 30 yards?

- Weather conditions. Did mud, sunshine, heat, cold or wind make a difference?

SPORTS FEATURE STORY

The head basketball coach who coaches his three nephews and the volleyball player who plays despite the challenge of a prosthetic leg are both good sports feature story subjects. The sports feature is a story behind or beyond the game. Based primarily on human interest and oddity, the sports feature idea comes from being aware of the stories on and off the field (Fig. 7.6). For example, in science class, football players discuss wanting to make a big hit to earn the "black mask" award. A good sports reporter might find an interesting story in the mask and what players are doing to get it or a story on incentives coaches use. In the cafeteria, soccer players mention how great it will be to see the coach get her 200th win. A story on the coach and her career highlights may be timely for the next issue.

While newspaper sports features do not have to be timely, running them while the sport is in-season will make for higher reader interest. If the story is tied to a news peg, such as the expectation of the coach's 200th win, that fact should be in the wrap graph.

The types of sports features are as varied as the types of feature stories discussed in Chapter 6.

Some examples of sports feature stories that have appeared in high school publications include

- A player profile on a 6-foot 8-inch basketball forward who, despite having played the game for only four years, has been named to the All-State team and is being recruited by Division I colleges

- A human interest feature story on the increase of female weightlifters who are trying to stay in shape and prepare for their track events

- A news-feature story on the increasing number of students who are paying to have personal trainers for advice, motivation and health information

- A human interest feature story on a school's and area's top golfer who, after seeing his game break down in his last two tournaments, walked away from the game

- A human interest feature story on a group of students who coach Little League teams. The story covers why these student coaches are working with younger kids and how the coaches' advice is helping players on and off the field

- An informative feature on the latest sport of Tae-Bo

Billo succeeds in racing debut, Blunt takes sixth after collapsing
by Jamie Albertine

In his first organized race ever, senior Andrew Billo won the Maryland State Mountain Biking Championship at Greenbriar State Park in the junior beginner race class division April 25.

Billo toured the 13-mile course, which consisted of two 6.5-mile laps, in 1:45:00 to take first in his division. His time put him 10 minutes behind the fastest racer of the day and placed him fifth overall out of 100 racers.

"It was a very technical course," Billo said. "The trails were very rocky and steep, but I had a strong showing for my first race."

Billo said he has been training since the beginning of February, biking for an hour-and-a-half to two hours on area streets everyday. "I usually try to work some big hills into my routine, traveling down Massachusetts Avenue to the National Cathedral and back, which has four or five really tough hills along the way," he said.

Senior Bertrand Blunt competed in the sport junior class of the same race; however, after riding in second for 17.5 miles of the 18-mile race, and with only a quarter of a mile of uphill climb left, he collapsed on the side of the trail. He got back up 15 minutes later and went on to finish sixth.

"I bonked, which basically means you're doing fine and then all of the sudden you can't ride and you can't move," Blunt said. "It was almost as though I was beyond exhaustion."

Blunt, a veteran to the sport, attributed his exhaustion to lack of physical preparation. "I had just finished training with the crew team and I hadn't been riding much, so I think that I just wasn't in good shape to race."

Billo and Blunt will both continue to train for upcoming competitions in the Subaru Atlantic Mountain Biking Series' eight-race spring schedule. They will go on to compete in the "Mother's Day Mauler" at Patapsco Valley State Park May 9 and in the "Crack the Nut Race" held at Walnut Creek Park in Charlottesville, Virginia May 16.

Fig. 7.5. Game story. *Black and White*, Walt Whitman High School, Bethesda, Md.

Ultimate flies high at City High

Sean Voight '01, demonstrates his ultimate skills. Voight is part of team Carousel Motors, which is currently undefeated.

A league of their own

The disc hits the ground. Nate Davis '01, stops dead in his tracks, and whirls around, running full tilt in the opposite direction. He calls to his teammate, who picks up the Frisbee and throws it in his direction. As Davis lunges for the frisbee, another player, a large member of the other team, does also. In the collision that follows, both players fall to the ground.

According to the Ultimate Players Association, there are certain rules that one should obey when playing Ultimate Frisbee. One such rule reads as follows: "It is the responsibility of all players to avoid contact in any way possible. Violent impact with legitimately positioned opponents constitutes harmful endangerment, a foul, and must be strictly avoided."

But according to Dan Nguyen '99, chairman of the Student Senate Intramural Ultimate Frisbee league, the captains of both teams determine a lot of the rules.

"Ultimate is sort of an honors game. The players make their own calls how they want to. If the game is a little bit physical, that's okay. Pushes tend to even out."

For the second year in a row, the ultimate league has encountered no shortage of interest. There are 16 teams, each with eight to ten players.

Each team begins by playing four games. The top eight teams and the bottom eight teams from these initial games will each participate in their own tournament. The top eight teams will be decided mostly by record, though Nguyen will make the final decision. "The schedules should determine the true top eight teams," Nguyen said. "But if one team beats three teams with poor records, it shouldn't be in the winners' bracket."

The champion team from the winners' bracket will represent CHS in the unofficial state championship, to be held on May 16 at CHS. Teams from West, Regina, and other schools from Cedar Rapids and Des Moines will take part in the state championship.

Some schools, including West High, are running leagues similar to the one at CHS to determine their representative. West High senior Chuck Riggs is one of the organizers of the league. According to Riggs, West has eight teams that play two games every Sunday. Midway through the season, the top four teams will have a round robin to decide the representative for the state championship.

The state tournament will be strict, with referees watching the games to make calls. Nguyen hopes to get some of the players from the UI ultimate team to ref at the state tournament.

After all is said and done, one high school team will be crowned the unofficial ultimate champions of Iowa. Riggs is excited with the idea of a state championship. "It's going to be exciting to participate in this tournament."

by Sean Thompson

Ultimate challenge

1. Each team plays four games in the regula... season.
2. The top eight teams from the regular seaso... play for the chance to represent CHS in the sta... championship.
3. Schools from around eastern Iowa meet... Iowa City to take part in the state championshi...

Teams to watch

Carousel Motors
Key players: Sean Voigt '01, Dave Weingei... '01, Conor Hanick '01, Duncan Monserud '99.
"We have more depth than other teams," sa... Sean Voigt '01, team captain of Carousel Mo... tors. "All we have to do is play with intensi... because we already have the skills to win."
Who they have beaten: En Fuego 12-2

Nuns in a Knocking Shop
Key players: Ross Cram '99, Rob Lindenboo... '99, Sam Rapson '99.
"Our major advantage is our height, plus we ha... five long distance runners," Ross Cram '9... said. "We plan to finish in the top three and w... should be able to beat more athletic teams be... cause of our experience."
Who they have beaten: QA 12-6, Old Scho... All-Stars 12-2

The Shameless Honkey Tonk Association
Key Players: Quee Phou '00, Zach Evans '9... Hugh John Barry '99.
"If we can get everyone to show up then we w... definitely mop up," said Hugh John Barry '9... "But we will have to rely on our athleticis... because we don't have a whole lot of exper... ence."
Who they have beaten: Drinking Buddies 5-...

all information compiled b...
Brett Green, Adam Yack, an...
Claire Lutgendo...

Ultimate rules!

✔ A regulation field is 70 by 40 yards with endzones 25 yards deep
✔ Each team has seven players
✔ Points are awarded when a pass is completed into your team's goal.
✔ A player has 10 seconds to throw the disc. The thrower may only pivot from one foot.
✔ Defenders may not double team the thrower.
✔ When a pass is dropped, blocked, intercepted or thrown out of bounds, the defense immediately takes possession.
✔ No physical contact between the players at any point. If any contact occurs, a foul will be called. Players act as officals. If the player the foul is called on disagrees with the call, the play is re-done.
✔ 175 grams is the regulation weight for a tournament frisbee.

Throw like a pro

Backhand
This is the basic throw that even the most novice of players can master. Just reach across your body and throw the disc parallel to the ground. This is the most versatile of throws and it gives you the most distance.

Difficulty: (out of 5)

Forehand
When you are being guarded closely, this may be your best choice. To do this move, reach to the side and flick your wrist. Warning, you must keep your forearm stiff upon the release.

Saucer
The saucer is a variation of the forehand throw. This throw is a floater so make sure your receiver is ready to run. To perform this move, use the same technique as you did for the forehand but your release should be at shoulder level.

Hammer
When you want to throw the d... over your opponent's head,... is the move to do. Grip the d... with your fist and throw it p... pendicular to the ground. If d... correctly, the disc will travel v... quickly and will level itsel... mid-flight.

The organization of the sports feature story is as varied as that of other feature stories; however, the inverted pyramid form is rarely used. Just like other strong feature stories, the sports feature is told through strong use of quotes, observations and details.

Refer to Chapter 6 for tips on feature writing.

Strong reporting is critical in sportswriting. In Figure 7.7, the reporters interviewed college coaches, parents, athletes and counselors for an insightful look at college recruiting.

FEATURE LEADS FOR SPORTS STORIES

If you're not writing the straight-news game story lead, a variety of feature lead types as discussed in Chapter 3 can be used. Read and assess the following high school sports leads.

> Pointing to the slender substitute teacher standing awkwardly among a group of teenagers, physical education instructor Linda Wolf asks one of her students ... "Do you think you could beat him at hoops?"
>
> The student cautiously eyes his 6'4" opponent. Upon seeing the patches of white hair fringing his face, he states in a clear, confident voice, "Yeah, like this old man could beat me."
>
> The odd pair steps onto the basketball court, the giant towering over the dwarf. The boy tries dribbling around his opponent's long legs, but to no avail. Finally, the man's arms reach out and snatch the ball. In one fluid movement, the man turns and shoots. Swish. "Give me the ball," he says as he returns to the top of the key. The boy, momentarily taken aback, plans to steal the ball back. However, instead of dribbling, the man simply jumps and cocks his arms, aiming the ball for the basket. Swish. "Give me the ball," he says again, the first sign of a grin cracking his face. The boy never gets the ball back. The old man wins, ten to nothing. Wolf forgot to warn the boy that Sam Jones, his substitute teacher, is a basketball legend.

Jennifer Song
Silver Chips
Montgomery Blair High School
Silver Spring, Md.

> If there's one man who knows how to dodge an oncoming tree at 40 mph, it's Peter Durham. If there's one man who knows the pain of an all-too-firm bicycle seat, it's Peter Durham. If there's one man who knows his bike's body better than his girlfriend's, it's Peter Durham.

Michael Jordan
Bagpipe
Highland Park High School
Dallas, Texas

Fig. 7.6. Sports feature story. *Little Hawk,* City High School, Iowa City, Iowa

Packaged Coverage

Complete coverage of all sports and all levels—varsity, JV and freshmen—should be the goal of each publication. In a newspaper, sports briefs or tidbit sections can help cover all the teams without long stories with long lists. The packaged coverage can include game scores with highlighted player performances, district standings, key matchups and area or state rankings, among many things (Fig. 7.8). The creation of this type of coverage can be fun and varied. A list of scores from the last 20 years may accompany a preview story about a rival school. A graphic showing the team's game-winning scoring play can give the sports junkie something fun to study. Using a type size that is smaller than the body copy for the lists of scores or district standings can help save space and help the page editor pack more into the section. In the yearbook, the scoreboard should serve as a history of the year's game scores. Packaging all-district team members, statistical leaders and quotes with the scoreboard can give the reader even more of the year's highlights.

Student athletes explore intercollegiate athletics, confront intricacies of

College Recruiting

by Sara Hunninghake
sports editor
Erika Sauerwein
asst. sports editor

Out of 75 students surveyed at Kapaun Mt. Carmel, 69 percent said they wanted to play sports in college. Of that percentage, 60 percent said they wanted to play Division I.

"We had a great [baseball] season last year by winning City League," junior Neil Schmitz said. "I love to play, and I definitely want to play in college, but I don't know exactly how to go about doing that."

According to the 1998-99 *NCAA Guide for the College-Bound Student-Athlete*, less than three percent of college seniors will play one year in professional basketball.

The odds of a high school football player making it to the professional level at all are about 6,000 to 1; the odds for a high school basketball player, 10,000 to 1.

The Process

"There's all these myths about the whole recruiting process and about how all of these people are going to knock on your door and the phone is going to be ringing off the hook," said Kelly Norlin, regional director of College Prospects of America. "But, that just doesn't happen to the average athlete."

All athletes have to go through the recruiting process. Most people believe it begins in the sophomore or junior year.

"The process really starts when you step into the high school doors," said Mark Potter, head men's basketball coach at Newman University. "I can't emphasize how important it is not to sluff off in freshman and sophomore classes when, down the road, it could really pay off for you."

How to Prepare

Students planning on playing Division I or II athletics must be certified by the NCAA Initial-Eligibility Clearinghouse.

Head counselor Liana Torkelson said this form, and taking the ACT, should be done by the spring of junior year.

Coaches recommend students write letters to colleges letting them know they are interested in the

Photo Illustration by Kelly Ely

program. Other ways for an athlete to get his or her name out is by making a video, visiting schools and going to high-performance camps.

Norlin emphasizes the importance of club play.

"Club teams have the opportunity to travel and compete against some of the top level competitors in the country, whereas high school teams are limited to what is in the league," he said. "The overall talent pool is greater."

Coaches visit showcase tournaments and regional and national tournaments.

"If you want to play basketball in college, AAU would be the way to go," said senior Mike Mileusnic, who plays for Team Kansas, a club basketball team. "When my team went to Orlando, I saw Roy Williams and the Duke coach there. I saw them everywhere."

Recruiting Services

Another way to be noticed is through recruiting services. Beginning Aug. 1, Norlin introduced a franchise of CPOA in Wichita. Currently three KMC athletes have signed with the program.

"Sometimes a lot of the schools locally may not

have a position or any money available this season, so if you miss out, the window shuts after you sign," Norlin said.

"Across the country, there are several schools that are looking for student athletes, but they just don't find out about them because they don't have the time or money."

Norlin said CPOA is beneficial because it sends out a profile of the athlete to approximately 500 colleges that meet his or her needs.

In addition to this, CPOA offers high-quality videotape enhancement, financial aid counseling and unlimited personal guidance. The cost of the service ranges from $200-$1,000.

"I had done a lot of looking on the Internet at schools that have volleyball programs," said Rita Schierer, mother of senior Erin Schierer, who is using CPOA. "Out of doing that, some responded, but there were lots that didn't.

"We felt it would get her more exposure to more schools because [CPOA]

Three teams, one field and a lot of complications.

In the next two years, the new Flower Mound Jaguars will be sharing Max Goldsmith Stadium with LHS and MHS. In 1999, the Jaguars will only have JV, sophomore and freshman teams. The year 2000 is a whole different story.

Robert Green
Marquee
Marcus High School
Flower Mound, Texas

AMBITION:SUCCESS:

CENTRAL HOCKEY'S WORK ETHIC:?

A)Triumph

B)Victory

C)State Contender

D)All of the above.

The correct answer is D. It does not take an English major to figure out that hard work results in success. This year, Central's hard work is paying off.

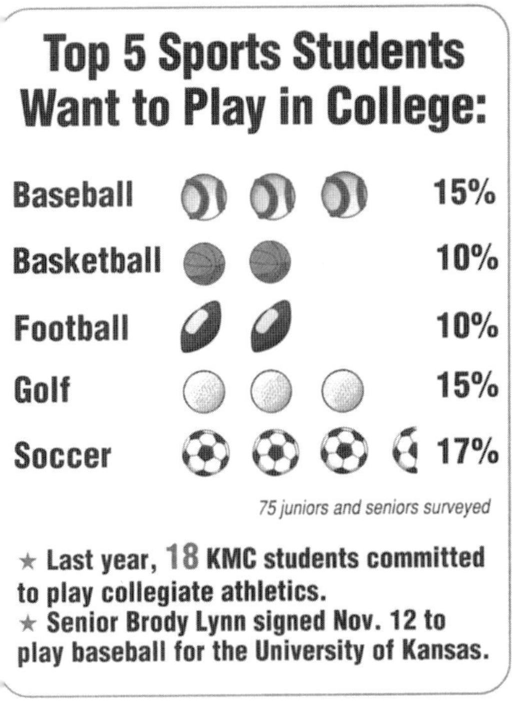

Top 5 Sports Students Want to Play in College:

Baseball	🏐 🏐 🏐	**15%**
Basketball	🏀 🏀	**10%**
Football	🏈 🏈	**10%**
Golf	⚪ ⚪ ⚪	**15%**
Soccer	⚽ ⚽ ⚽ ◖	**17%**

75 juniors and seniors surveyed

★ Last year, **18** KMC students committed to play collegiate athletics.
★ Senior Brody Lynn signed Nov. 12 to play baseball for the University of Kansas.

will do the mailings. It will supplement what we've done on our part."

CPOA's Role

Norlin stresses CPOA's role in recruiting.

"We don't guarantee scholarships, because if we did, then we would be an agent, and that is actually a major violation of NCAA rules," he said. "We just guarantee to people that we get them maximum exposure. Ultimately, the student's strengths and abilities will determine how much they get either academically or athletically."

Even though CPOA has had a 90 percent success rate, college coaches are hesitant to recommend it.

"If you were to check my mail today, I would have a stack of millions of form letters," said Bill Shillings, head men's soccer coach at Friends University. "I usually just throw them away."

Gary Oborny, the coach of the Wichita Fly-

ers, an elite club volleyball team, said an athlete's attitude and work ethic will attract coaches.

"You can save yourself a lot of work that isn't fun by doing work in practice and on the court that is fun," he said.

Athletic Commitments

When considering athletics in college, students must not underestimate the commitments. Major college programs practice anywhere from 15-20 hours per week with weight training and conditioning and a study hall.

"You would make more money and have more time with a part-time job than you would if you played soccer in college," Shillings said.

1998 graduate Brian Perkins plays Division I soccer at Drake University.

"Playing soccer has taken major time management. I barely have free time," Perkins said. "We have weights twice a week before class and then we have practice for two hours. We shower and eat as a team, and then I have study tables from 7:30 to 9:30.

"During the winter, we will be having individual workouts and weights and we practice and play a few

> *My advice is to communicate with coaches early on and to be yourself. Coaches judge your personality, especially your academics. They recruit the entire person.*
> **Brian Perkins**
> **1998 graduate**

games in the spring. During the summer, the coaches want us to train with semi-pro teams.

"My advice is to communicate with coaches early on and to be your-

self. Coaches judge your personality, especially your academics. They recruit the entire person."

Athletic Responsibilites

Torkelson warns students of the impact athletics can have on grades.

"The student needs to think that college sports can be a detriment to the GPA," she said. "Unless the student is highly organized and intelligent, academics can suffer while a student is on the road playing."

Oborny said athletes need to be responsible for their decisions.

"One of the biggest things is making mature decisions," he said. "The big focus needs to be why you're there. One, you're there to get an education, and two, if it's via the route of sports, then your next responsibility needs to be your athletic life."

Sam Zvibleman
Parkway Central Corral
Parkway Central High School
Chesterfield, Mo.

Fig. 7.7. Sports feature story. *Paladin*, Kapaun Mt. Carmel High School, Wichita, Kan.

As the varsity football locker room clears after practice, senior Eric Parks see his helmet next to the three index cards taped to the back of his locker. The first card reads, "first team All-State kicker and punter," and, "All-American selection." The second card reads, "straight As" and "be a respected member by classmates."

The last card, filled with scriptures from the Bible, seems to stand out from the rest in his mind. It reads: "I can do all things

The FranklinTimes **SPORTS** Page 11

Busted and Broken
Injuries cut through Tiger defense, special teams

by Joe Leporis

After closing last year's season 4-2 in district and unable to reach the playoffs, Hillcrest is ranked 19th in *The Dallas Morning News* area poll one spot in front of South Oak Cliff.

Team members prepared over the summer by lifting weights and playing 7 On 7 in hopes of being better prepared for district.

Even after losing graduating seniors running back Terrace Watkins and defensive lineman David Sullivan both varsity coaches and players

feel that this year they will have a strong defense. Defensive and special teams drills such as fumble recoveries and strip drills are being practiced to increase the number of turnovers.

After starting quarterback Dupree Scovell was injured, sophomore Ryan Gilbert took Scovell's spot. Gilbert led the team to a 4-4 record and the coaching staff is confident that Gilbert will be more successful this year, Johnson said.

Junior Sterling Storey is going to be vital to special teams because he is handling kickoffs, field goals and punts. Storey was 10 for 10 of extra

points last year and practiced over the summer by kicking 60 to 70 balls a day and by playing soccer.

"Sterling is definitely one of the best kickers in Dallas," Coach Johnson said. "He practiced with a bag of balls over the summer, stayed in shape by playing soccer, and hit the weights."

The Panthers are going to play in a blitz style defense with five linemen and two linebackers. Coach Johnson said that the attack style defense puts more pressure on the secondary, but thinks that the rush can pressure the quarterback.

THE TICKER

THEY SAID IT

"Teams get more excited when they play us. You always have to dogfight."
- Senior Gino DiGuardi, captain of the Men's Soccer team, on the amount of close tough games the team has played this season.

"We should have scored even more points."
- Sophomore quarterback Antwaan Robinson, after JV Football's 42-14 win over Central High.

"We just couldn't match their intensity in the first half. In didn't matter what coach said in the locker room, we were going to lose."
- Senior guard Lauren Adams, after the Varsity Women's Basketball team lost to Canisuis North.

PLAYER OF THE MONTH

Joseph Johnson
Running Back
Freshman Football

Even after losing graduating seniors running back Terrace Watkins and defensive lineman David Sullivan both varsity coaches and players feel that this year they will have a strong defense. Defensive and special teams drills such as fumble recoveries and strip drills are being practiced to increase the number of turnovers.

After starting quarterback Dupree Scovell was injured, sophomore Ryan Gilbert took Scovell's spot. Gilbert led the team to a 4-4 record.

BEST LINE:
October 24 at Jefferson
23 rushes, 140 yards, 2 TDs

Gilbert led the team to a 4-4 record and the coaching staff is confident that Gilbert.
photo by Jon Ulster

OTHER TOP PERFORMERS

Alicia Smith-Wagner
Junior, Midfield, Women's Lacrosse
vs Newton, October 12
5 goals, 5 assists

Ben Morales
Sophomore, Center, JV Men's Basketball
vs Jefferson, October 16
23 points, 18 rebounds, 6 blocks, 2 steals

Kristi Sanderson
First team, Women's Golf
DrPepper Tournament, October 14-15
Course record 16 under par

INJURY REPORT

Freshman Tom Sanderson
Guard, Freshman Basketball
torn ACL, out for season

Junior Susan Tedsci
Pole Vault, Women's Track and Field
sprained ankle, out for district meet

TEAM UPDATES

JV Football
After giving up 3 punt returns for touchdowns in the first 4 games, the team will shake up its special teams unit. Younger players will get more starts.

JV Mens Basketball
The team is off to its best start ever, winning 3 of 4. Coach Stulten Smith hopes to continue that success into district play, which starts in less than a week.

JV Womens Basketball
When the Varsity squad graduated 7 seniors last year, the JV knew they were going to have a shortage of players. "We've had to give them all our players," Coach Jim said.

BY THE NUMBERS

6 Number of offensive rebounds for the Varsity Mens Basketball team Oct 12 vs Jefferson

30 Wins by the Freshman Football team over the last 3 years

114 Number of goals allowed by the Women's Lacrosse team in 10 games

SPOTLIGHT GAME

Mens Lacrosse at Evansville
5:45 pm, Tuesday at Wilkie Stadium
With both teams tied for second going to into the last game of the season, the winner will make the playoffs and the loser will go home.
"We're going to have to do something we 've had trouble doing all year, knock some guys out," head coach Will Penn said.

DISTRICT STANDINGS

VARSITY FOOTBALL		FRESHMAN FOOTBALL		VARSITY MENS BASKETBALL		VARSITY WOMENS BASKETBALL		MENS LACROSSE		MENS SWMMING/DVNG		MENS TRACK&FIELD	
JEFFERSON	13-0	JEFFERSON	13-0	JEFFERSON	13-0	JEFFERSON	13-0	JEFFERSON	13-0	JEFFERSON	13-0	JEFFERSON	13-0
NEWTON	11-2	NEWTON	11-2	NEWTON	11-2	NEWTON	11-2	NEWTON	11-2	NEWTON	11-2	NEWTON	11-2
FRANKLIN	8-3	FRANKLIN	8-3	FRANKLIN	8-3	FRANKLIN	8-3	FRANKLIN	8-3	FRANKLIN	8-3	FRANKLIN	8-3
MISS COM.	3-9	MISS COM.	3-9	MISS COM.	3-9	MISS COM.	3-9	MISS COM.	3-9	MISS COM.	3-9	MISS COM.	3-9
ROOSEVELT	9-3	ROOSEVELT	9-3	ROOSEVELT	9-3	ROOSEVELT	9-3	ROOSEVELT	9-3	ROOSEVELT	9-3	ROOSEVELT	9-3
EVANSVILLE	7-5	EVANSVILLE	7-5	EVANSVILLE	7-5	EVANSVILLE	7-5	EVANSVILLE	7-5	EVANSVILLE	7-5	EVANSVILLE	7-5
NORTH	1-8	NORTH	1-8	NORTH	1-8	NORTH	1-8	NORTH	1-8	NORTH	1-8	NORTH	1-8

JUNIOR VARSITY FOOTBALL		VARSITY MENS BASKETBALL		FRESHMAN MENS BASKETBALL		JV WOMENS BASKETBALL		WOMENS LACROSSE		WOMENS SWMMING/DVNG		WOMENS TRACK&FIELD	
NORTH	13-0	NORTH	13-0	NORTH	13-0	NORTH	13-0	NORTH	13-0	JEFFERSON	13-0	JEFFERSON	13-0
FRANKLIN	10-2	FRANKLIN	10-2	FRANKLIN	10-2	FRANKLIN	10-2	FRANKLIN	10-2	NEWTON	11-2	NEWTON	11-2
ROOSEVELT	9-3	ROOSEVELT	9-3	ROOSEVELT	9-3	ROOSEVELT	9-3	ROOSEVELT	9-3	FRANKLIN	8-3	FRANKLIN	8-3
JEFFERSON	5-4	JEFFERSON	5-4	JEFFERSON	5-4	JEFFERSON	5-4	JEFFERSON	5-4	MISS COM.	3-9	MISS COM.	3-9
MISS COM.	2-7	MISS COM.	2-7	MISS COM.	2-7	MISS COM.	2-7	MISS COM.	2-7	ROOSEVELT	9-3	ROOSEVELT	9-3
EVANSVILLE	2-8	EVANSVILLE	2-8	EVANSVILLE	2-8	EVANSVILLE	2-8	EVANSVILLE	2-8	EVANSVILLE	7-5	EVANSVILLE	7-5
NEWTON	0-11	NEWTON	0-11	NEWTON	0-11	NEWTON	0-11	NEWTON	0-11	NORTH	1-8	NORTH	1-8

Fig. 7.8. Sports package design.

Designing A Sports Briefs Package

Since more sports news occurs than can be covered with full stories, a box of news briefs and statistics can greatly expand a newspaper's coverage. When packaging sports briefs keep these tips in mind:

Create a set style. Save time by designing the package once and using variations of the layout for the rest of the year.

Space is the enemy. Avoid wasteful elements, like bullets and extra white space. Most often type effects, like bold and italic, can replace these.

Mix up the sports. If not every sport can be covered, keep a good mix of freshman, JV, Varsity, Men's and Women's news bites.

Use agate. Agate type is small text used for stats and standings. By shrinking a sans serif to as small as 6-7 points and expanding the horizontal width to 110 percent, the paper can save a lot of space. An example:

JOHNSON 6-12, 2 HRs, 8 RBIs, 6 RUN

Set features. Come up with 8-15 different pre-designed features and mix and match them each publication.
Some ideas include:
Player of the month, top performers, division standings, quote box, injury report, team updates, interesting numbers, marquee matchups, next week's big game, strategy highlight

through Jesus Christ who gives me strength." Philippians 4:13. It is these scriptures and goals that guide Parks and allow his faith to carry over into all aspects of his life.

Ranked as the second best kicker in the state in a coaches' poll, Parks has received over 100 recruiting letters before his senior year. He now receives two to three letters a day from top programs at universities such as Nebraska, Illinois and Iowa State. Through all his achievements, Parks has always looked back to the Lord for spiritual guidance.

Brendan Fitzgibbons
Hillcrest Hurricane
Hillcrest High School
Dallas, Texas

As you can see in these leads, good reporting and storytelling is at the heart of every sports story. The lessons in the chapters on news and feature writing apply in sportswriting. This chapter covers the differences that come with covering sports. Review Chapters 1–4 and 6 to improve your sportswriting.

Many young sports fans see being a high school sports reporter as an ideal spot on the publication staff. While the young sports fan's command of the sport is helpful, becoming a good sports reporter requires work to get beyond the clichés of the game to the drama and storytelling inherent in sports.

EXERCISES

1. From daily newspapers or sports magazines, clip and mount 10 examples of good sports story leads.
   Make note of what information the writer used in the lead. Was it a particular play? A particular trend? An anecdote? Or something else? Why do you think the writer chose that focus for the lead? Was the lead written in straight news or feature style? Why did the writer choose that style?

2. Watch one of your favorite professional sports teams over a two-week period. Make note of the team trends you could cover.

3. Make a list of 10 cliché quotes or phrases from your high school or daily publication.

4. Clip, mount and label 10 descriptive sports quotes from your school or daily newspaper or a sports magazine. Explain why the quotes are good ones.

5. Clip, mount and label 10 examples of sports statistics that were used in stories. For each, explain why you think the writer chose the statistic he or she used in the story.

6. Write an advance story from the following information. Your story will run the day before the game.

The Bristol High School Bandits are playing the Ten Mile Creek High School Bullfrogs in a boys' basketball game.

The game will be for the regional championship. Your school is Bristol. Bristol is 23–8 so far. Ten Mile Creek is 26–1. The teams have played each other two times this season. Ten Mile Creek is the defending state champion.

Ten Mile Creek's only loss was to the Hawthorne Bearcats, 88–86. Bristol beat the Hawthorne Bearcats 64–58.

Key players for the Bristol Bandits

Clayton Hunter—position: point guard; statistical averages: 14 points per game average, 8 assists per game average; height: 5 feet 10 inches.

Johnny Miller—position: center; statistical averages: 22 points per game (best in the district), 12 rebounds per game; height: 6 feet 7 inches.

Donald Lampier—position: forward; statistical averages: 10 points per game, 9 rebounds per game; height: 6 feet 3 inches.

Key players for Ten Mile Creek Bullfrogs

Geoff Mitchell—position: forward; statistical averages: 16 points per game, 10 rebounds per game; height: 6 feet 6 inches.

James Robertson—position: center; statistical averages: 28 points per game (second best in the state), 12 rebounds per game; height: 6 feet 10 inches.

Game 1: Finals of the Spring Creek Tournament, score 85–83

Highlights: Bullfrogs' Robertson scores 35, including the last 8 points of the game. Robertson hits game-winning shot with two seconds left. Bandits' Miller scores 15 points and has 5 shots blocked. Bandits' leading scorer is Hunter with 30, including 6 three-pointers.

Game 2: Finals of the Lake Bardwell Tournament, score 72–70

Highlights: Bullfrogs' Robertson scores 24 including the game-winning shot with five seconds left. Robertson also blocks 6 shots—all of them Miller's. Bandits' Miller scores 8 points. Bandits' leading scorer is Hunter with 23, including 4 three-pointers.

Coaches' quotes

Bandits' head coach Buck Cargal (lifetime coaching record 299–71)

"We just have to go out and play much harder. We've been really close in two big tournaments, but this one's bigger. This could be Bristol's best chance to win a state title, and as you've seen, we're just a bucket or two away from that. We must get Robertson in foul trouble or keep him from getting second shots. You thought Godzilla was big. You thought King Kong was tough. I mean I saw *Halloween* when I was 10, and nothing is scarier than this kid on the court. He has dominated our team in both of the past two games. We will double-team to see if the rest of their team can beat us. I told our kids 'Robertson will not keep us from winning a state championship.' I'm expecting Hunter to have another big game. Hunter's on such a streak now. I'm giving him the green light in this game. He may shoot 20 three-pointers this game."

"This game would mean a lot to me. Not just because it would mean our first trip to the state tournament but it could be my 300th win. I can't think of any better way to hit 300 than to beat last year's state champion."

Bullfrogs' head coach Mike Keeney (lifetime coaching record 112–30)

"We just have to go give it 110 percent. Bristol has a good team. They've pushed us to the limit every time we've played this year. We better show up to play. It's not going to be a cake walk."

Keeney on Robertson: "He's the most dominating kid I've ever coached. He's such a quick jumper. And when you're already 6–10, it makes him a force that can control a game. He's clearly headed to a Division I school. He has been sick with the flu all week though. We hope he's well and ready to go at game time. If I have to rest him for the first half, I'll do it. We need a healthy Robertson on the floor."

Player interviews

Clayton Hunter

"I'm pumped for the game. We just know we can win tonight. We've been so close both times. Coach has said he wants me to take the game over. I felt really good after we beat Hawthorne. Ten Mile couldn't beat them. Our losses to Ten Mile were earlier in the year. I've been shooting a lot better since then. And Johnny (Miller) has been working on making the other guy foul him. I really want to give coach his 300th win too. He takes us home. He spends his whole summer opening the gym for us. The guy deserves it."

Johnny Miller

"Nah, I ain't scared of him (Robertson). The first two times we played them, I was going up too slow. I'm much better now. I get my shot off quicker now, and I have better fakes. He'll foul out this time, and then he won't be around to make those game-winning shots. Clayton will be doing that."

"We'll be hyped for coach to get his 300th (win). Both of my brothers played for him, and they told me 'you better win this one for coach.' I want to see coach get his state championship ring, too."

Additional information

Bandits' team scoring average: 80.0 points; opponent's scoring average: 54.1 points.

Bullfrogs' team scoring average: 78.0 points; opponent's scoring average: 55.0 points.

State rankings: Bullfrogs—number 1; Bandits—number 10. The Bandits are 0–6 in the last three years against the Bullfrogs.

7. Write a yearbook sports story from the following information. The story can be a trend story with a feature angle.

You are from Hazard Hill High School. The team mascot is the Lions. The girls' fast pitch softball team finished 19–10 for the year. It was 10–4 and finished third in the district. The team went 7–0 in the second half of district, beating every team in the district. The team opened the district schedule losing its first three games. The third place finish was the team's best ever. The team earned its first playoff berth. It lost 12–6 in bi-district to the Paradise Cougars. The team lost three starters but returned seven for the next year.

Key players: Hazard Hill finished the year with three first-team All-District players, which included freshman pitcher Jennifer Dusenberry, junior catcher Katie Mitchell and senior first baseman Karen Greening.

Dusenberry was also named Newcomer of the Year. Dusenberry pitched every game. She's 4 feet 11 inches and 100 pounds. She throws 58 miles per hour. She played for the Amateur Athletic Union team last year, and the team went to the state championship. Dusenberry struck out 10 batters in the district finale against the Tucker High School Mustangs.

Mitchell averages throwing out three people per game. She has a batting average of .376. In the district finale against Tucker High School, she threw out one base runner in the 3rd inning when the Lions led 2–1. In the top of the 7th inning, she hit a home run, giving the team a 3–2 lead. Then in the bottom half of the 7th and final inning, she threw out another base runner at second and blocked the plate getting the final out. The Lions won 3–2. The win meant the Lions would go to the playoffs.

Greening finished with a .340 batting average. A team captain, she hit three game-winning home runs in the first three games of the team's district win streak.

Player and coach quotes

Head coach James Rogers

On Dusenberry: "She's so tiny you would think a big gust of wind would blow her into the outfield. And off the field she's a clown. Those two different kinds of rainbow socks she wears are her trademark. Plus she loves to talk. You can put her in the corner, and she'll talk to the wall. But that's what the other players came to like about her. On the field, though, she takes care of business. She hasn't played long enough to be flashy and flamboyant yet. She doesn't pump her fist when she strikes out someone. She's all business. She's in control. She tells everyone where to line up. If she's going to throw a fastball, she'll move the second baseman to the left and the shortstop to the right because she knows the ball will come directly to them.

"The first game she had to prove herself. We had an honorable mention all-district pitcher coming back. The girls came to me and said, 'Why is this kid up here? Why is she on varsity?' Then she struck out 10 batters, and they finally realized she belonged."

On Mitchell: "She single-handedly got us into the playoffs. What an incredible game. She's the real leader of the team. She helped make Dusenberry a part of the team when others didn't want to give her a chance. She makes plays that you don't think she can make. She seems to have a knack for knowing when runners are going to go. Then if they're trying to score, she will not give up the plate."

On the win streak: "After a poor district start, we couldn't go anywhere but up. We played good defense. We stopped making mental errors. In the first half we were throwing the ball to the wrong base, and we would step off the base before the ball even got there. We went back and started working in practice. Everyone got 100 grounders a day. Getting you used to doing the same thing over and over makes you com-

fortable in the game. When the ball's coming at you during the game, you've seen that over and over so you just do it naturally.

"It got to where me and my family would eat, sleep and drink softball. I'd wake up, get a cup of coffee and read the paper to see how the other teams did the night before. By the week of bi-district, my wife would have to leave me messages on my cell phone just to reach me."

Jennifer Dusenberry

On the playoff week: "Parents brought us balloons. People were telling us how good we were. It was cool. Then, the day of the game, we were scared. No one was saying anything. We didn't understand how much attention we were going to get. We thought we were really focused on the game, but we were really worried about what color of socks we were going to wear, how our hair was going to look."

On her play: "No one liked me at first. After I did pretty well my first game out, they started to let me be a part of the team. Karen invited me to eat breakfast with the team. After that we all got along. I'd try to do crazy stuff just to make them laugh. We had a good time. Once we knew we could have a good time and work hard in practice, we started winning."

Katie Mitchell

"Duse made the difference for us. She's a lot of fun to have on the team. She's crazy. She'll braid her hair in little knots, wear different colors of eye shadow just to get people to laugh at practice. Then when she's on the mound, she just wants to win.

"I'll never forget that game against Tucker. I just knew I had to play my best if we were going to win. When that girl came barreling down the line, I kept telling myself, 'this is for the playoffs, this is for the playoffs.' I was looking around for someone to hug after the umpire called the girl out."

Karen Greening

"I got so tired of taking ground balls at practice, but coach said it would pay off. By the time we played Tucker, we knew we weren't going to make the same stupid mistakes that cost us the first game against them. Coach just wouldn't quit on us. You can tell he loves the game. His whole family loves the game. His son would go with him to scout. He'd sit there with his crayons and chart the hitters. His wife would bake us cookies and send them to us during the winning streak. They'd have little messages on them. One would say 'Work Hard in Practice.' Another would say 'We're Thinking about You' and 'Good Luck Tonight.'"

Additional information

Tucker High School was the district champion. Two hundred people showed at the bi-district game. At most district games about 40 people showed up. The Paradise Cougars lost the next week in area competition. They finished the season 25–6.

Writing Editorials and Opinion Columns

Your community is about to hold a special election on funding an addition to your school. The proposed new construction will add more classrooms to relieve over-crowding and new athletic facilities for the expanding sports program. Voters will decide if they want to raise their taxes to pay for the addition. As the editor of your school newspaper, you think the addition is needed and hope the voters pass the tax increase. You assign a news story about the election and one about the architect's plans for the addition. To be fair and as objective as you can be since not everyone supports the tax increase, you realize that these news stories will need to present both sides of the story—those who support the plan and those who don't. But what else can you do?

To influence the voters to support the tax increase, you can use the power of the press in another way. The news stories will present the facts and sample the opinions of those who support and oppose the plan. This is an example of how the press uses its power, its ability to inform the public. Another power the press has is to persuade the public to accept something new or a change in something that al-ready exists. The opportunities for the press to use the power of persuasion are plentiful, but nowhere do they become more evident than on the paper's editorial or opinion pages.

The editor who backs the tax increase and supports the expansion of the school's facilities can write an editorial or an opinion column and maybe persuade others that they too should support the plan. The right words in a carefully con-structed argument can change the world—or, as in this case, help decide an election. Having this power, and recognizing the corresponding responsibility to use it wise-ly, is why so many journalists love their work.

Editorials are the voice of the newspaper at large and are not signed even though they are usually written by one person. Editorial writers use the first-person plural pronoun, the *we* voice. An opinion column is signed and obviously represents the thoughts of one person. Opinion columnists use the first-person singular pro-noun, the *I* voice. The journalistic "license" to use the *I* and *we* pronouns, restrict-ed to editorials and other forms of opinion writing when they refer to the writer, brings a certain authority to the piece. To the reader, these two pronouns signal a change from fact-based reporting to opinion writing. By using the *we* in editorials and the *I* in opinion columns, the writers are putting the credibility of the paper and their personal reputations on the line.

High school newspapers and other school media that publish student staff opinions should never underestimate the potential they have to influence their au-dience. For the newspaper staff, this means that topics should be chosen carefully. Historically, editorial and opinion pages aren't widely read unless the topics are

Fig. 8.1. A combination of one editorial in a traditional form (*top left*) and the "Lancer Lampoon" editorial briefs directly under it gives the editorial staff more than one opportunity to express its opinions and attempt to influence readers. *Lance*, Robert E. Lee High School, Springfield, Va.

highly controversial. That fact challenges the paper's editor: Since not all topics that deserve editorial page coverage are controversial, all content needs to attract, with good writing and enticing headlines, readers who usually spend little time with this section of the newspaper (Figs. 8.1 and 8.2).

To start, editorial writers should look at what will be reported on page 1 and the other news, feature and sports pages of the same issue of the paper. If the editors used good news judgment in selecting stories for these pages, then the topics covered are fresh, relevant and of interest to a sizable number of readers. Some of these topics may be judged important enough to comment on by the editorial writers and columnists. These stories will include opinions of experts and those associated with the events or issues covered, but the reporters' opinions are not included. But on the editorial page the journalist's opinions about these news, feature and sports stories can be published.

Sometimes the topics for opinion columns and editorials are not directly related to other content in the same paper, especially if the paper publishes more than one editorial in each issue. Regardless, the topic should still be of interest to students who are the paper's target audience. Topics worthy of editorial comment are not restricted to school-originated events. Some editorial topics in school papers in recent years that did not have a news or feature story tie-in elsewhere in the paper included these: prayer in public schools; weapons in schools; dress codes; drinking alcohol and driving; wars in the Balkans; presidential elections; community volunteer service; and hate crimes.

Editorial writers and opinion columnists who write about far-reaching or global events and issues should localize their commentary in some way, bring it home to the readers and make the readers care. To editorially support a drive to end famine in Africa is commendable, but to link it to malnutrition and poverty in the United States and suggest ways students can donate time and money to end both is better.

Because editorials are the voice of the paper and are unsigned, even though they are usually written by one person, the opinions expressed in them represent the majority of those student staff members designated as the editorial board. An editorial board discusses the topic, arrives at some majority agreement and then presents one or more arguments in favor of the position it is taking. For the high school paper, those students who are editors usually make up the editorial board.

Opinions expressed by columnists usually don't undergo the same discussion and consensus process as do staff editorials. This does not mean that a signed opinion column is not edited for style, content and legal factors such as potential libel.

TYPES OF EDITORIALS

The voice of the school newspaper is heard on the editorial and op-ed (opposite the editorial) pages. Staff editorials, unsigned, are traditionally the most prominent opinion pieces in the paper. These editorials can be written for different reasons, such as to interpret the significance of an event (the news), to criticize something that has happened, to commend someone or some group for some achievement, or to advocate change and persuade readers that the paper's viewpoint is worthwhile. Some of these editorial types, especially ones that criticize or identify a problem, will also propose one or more solutions. Knowledge of all types is important for editorial writers. The power of the press, as expressed through the editorial, can be used to commend as well as criticize. With this power comes the need to use it responsibly for the good of the community the paper serves.

ADVOCACY EDITORIAL

Editorials that interpret, explain, persuade and advocate change will usually be tied to a significant news, news-feature or sports story found within the same issue of the paper. The editorial will tell the reader why whatever happened is important. It can also explain the significance of an idea or condition. In some cases, it defines terms and issues, identifies persons and factors and provides background such as historical, cultural, geographical and pre-existing conditions, among others. The writer's attempt to persuade the reader to accept a certain interpretation or conclusion may be overt or subtle.

The editorial that interprets, explains or persuades can also examine the motives of persons related to the issue or event discussed or speculate on the consequences of various courses of action.

Through this interpretation of the news or explanation of an idea or condition, the staff is persuading the reader to agree with the staff's conclusions. The editorial can promote or advocate change. The facts are presented clearly, and the reasoning will seem logical to the reader if the editorial succeeds in its purpose. The editorial may also offer solutions and recommend a course of action. However, the overall tone of the editorial is not negative, nor is it a point-by-point criticism.

Editorials that interpret, explain and persuade are called advocacy editorials.

Here is an example of a straightforward advocacy editorial.

Longer lunch period a gift for students, staff

The quarter-long trial period of the new 45 minute lunch will be up for review in April by the administration, who will determine whether to continue this schedule for the fourth quarter.

The proposal was originally made by members of the Student Senate, and was later passed by student, staff and faculty vote.

By adding the five minutes subtracted from morning break to the lunch period on block days, the schedule has given all students a gift. Obviously, students now have more time to eat their lunches. But this extension does more. It allows students to relax and take a real break between their morning and afternoon classes.

Additionally, staff and faculty members benefit from the longer lunches, as they are under the same, often stressful, bell schedule of the students. Like students, they can utilize the extra time to eat their lunches and complete errands during lunch.

The Student Senate made a positive and reasonable request with their proposal. No instruction time is lost with the longer lunches, and students and staff are given more time to eat and gear up for their afternoon classes. The administration should vote in favor of keeping the 45 minute lunch this April.

Tamalpais News
Tamalpais High School
Mill Valley, Calif.

In the above example, the facts are presented, an assessment of the change is made, and a course of ac-

136

The Lowell
Continually published since 1898

RED EDITORIAL STAFF

EDITORS-IN-CHIEF
Stephen Feyer • Lisa Macabasco

NEWS
Kathleen Khong, Gregory Krimer,
Lily Wong, Kristen Lee,*
Wei-ying Wang*

PROFILES
Lisa Macabasco, Alice Yuen

CAMPUS
Danielle Jue, Ryan Lim

STYLE
Alexandra Sugarman, Adrienne Sneed*

SPORTS
Michael Chan, Stephen Feyer,
Josephine Ho, Sharon Ng,
Monique Abadilla,* Melanie Sun*

COLUMNS
Katherine Seat

OPINION
Danielle Broude, Anna Grabstein

BACKPAGE
Jennifer Chow, Audrie Lee
Assistant editors

REPORTERS

Natalie Alizaga   James Lee
Cara Abdo   David McBride
Diana Banh*   Matthew Mewhinney
Charlie   Sarah Pearce
  Beckerman   Anna Pignataro
Valerie Camacho*   Lily Robert-Foley
Clifford Chen*   Alejandro Romero
Kameela Din   Lin Shan*
Patrick Gong*   Charrylenne Soriano*
Alan Herzfeld*   Aldrich Tan
Chris Koehler   Tania Texidor
Ruby Kumar*   Sarah Tyler*
Jonathan Lai   Margaret Zalvidea

The Lowell on the Web assistant editors

COPY EDITOR
Stephen Feyer

PHOTOGRAPHERS
Charlie Beckerman   Lily Robert-Foley
Christine Wong

ILLUSTRATORS
Chris Koehler   Samuel Williams

COMPUTER GRAPHICS
Nick Elprin   Bram Whillock
Gabriel Gilder

The Lowell on the Web
EDITOR-IN-CHIEF
Gabriel Gilder

NEWS & SPORTS
Bram Whillock

CAMPUS
Jennifer Bestpitch

OPINION/COLUMNS
Bronnie Konecky

FEATURE
Nick Elprin

ADVERTISING DESIGN
Monique Smith

PUBLICITY DIRECTOR
Monique Smith

Internet services donated by
Global Network Services

ACCOUNTANT
Jennifer Chow

ADVERTISEMENTS
Nina Harris

FACULTY ADVISER
Paul B. Kandell

1999 CSPA Gold Crown
1998 CSPA Silver Crown
1997 CPSA Silver Crown
1996 NSPA Pacemaker
1996 CPSA Gold Crown
1995 CPSA Gold Crown
1994 CPSA Silver Crown
1993 NSPA Pacemaker

Published every four weeks
by the journalism classes of
Lowell High School
Room 251, 1101 Eucalyptus Drive
San Francisco, CA 94132
(415) 759-2730, ext. 3251
Internet: pkandell@thelowell.org

Visit The Lowell on the Web
http://www.thelowell.org

Comments on school-related issues from
students, faculty, and community members
are welcomed. Letters must be signed. Names
will be withheld if requested. We reserve the
right to edit letters before publication.

The Lowell and The Lowell on the Web strive to
inform the public and to use their opinion sections
as open forums for public debate. All unsigned
editorials are the opinion of the staff.

Printed through the assistance of
Grant Printing House,
with special thanks to Ted Fang,
Lowell Class of 1980 and
publisher of the SF Independent.

All contents copyright
Lowell High School Journalism Classes.
All rights reserved.

Editorial

Naughty Rojas finally going bye-bye

BY THE TIME A child graduates from elementary school, most people would expect him to know a few basic tenets of life: don't play with things that aren't yours, don't intentionally destroy what others need, and perhaps most of all, don't leave others to finish what you start.

But the superintendent of the San Francisco Unified School District has failed time and again to prove he can incorporate these lessons into his management of the district. We breathe a sigh of relief that Waldemar Rojas has decided to leave San Francisco for a job as Dallas' superintendent, thus ending a long, turbulent ride that has left our district in a critical fiscal condition.

The district's financial predicament and the political brouhaha that followed resulted from a line of superintendent-initiated acts and unethical policies.

In the first of these, Rojas attempted to get his budget proposal for this year past the school board with minimal questioning last summer by slyly slipping his spending plan onto a list of routine items — concealing it in a group of articles the board could approve all at once, according to the March 24, 1999, edition of the *San Francisco Chronicle*. Though the board eventually approved the plan, members first yanked it out of the list for closer examination.

In his second questionable act, Rojas' financial plan banked on a $12.7-million reimbursement from the state for desegregation costs, and included the money in this year's budget despite the fact that the money was not guaranteed. When the reimbursement didn't come, the superintendent discovered too late that he had spent money he didn't have.

But Rojas' reckless fiscal ride got bumpier. His management skills came under renewed fire after the public discovered he had funneled money from a general fund that pays for substitute teachers and summer school to buy a building that stands vacant months after its purchase, according to an April 5, 1999, article in the *San Francisco Examiner*.

Of course, summer school students, hundred of teachers and consultants, whose funding has been threatened to alleviate the financial crisis, are left wondering how to justify a trade-off between a good education and an abandoned building.

But bad policy is one issue; blatant bribery to gain support is quite another. Rojas was desperate to sell the district's lucrative property at Fifth and Market streets, the site of the San Francisco Shopping Centre, and unwisely trade a lucrative stream of rent for one sum. He asked his staff to tell principals to offer pizza to the class that could drum up the most parental support for his property idea, according to school board member Jill Wynns.

In so doing, Rojas disregarded students, and turned the school board into a defunct real estate office that bought useless structures and sold money-generating complexes, plunging itself deeper into debt.

To gain back the money, Rojas marched to Sacramento, demanding money, with the tact of a spoiled child. He hurt the district's relationship with the state by threatening to slash and burn AP classes, honors classes, extra academic periods for grades six through nine, and hundreds of jobs unless he received $12.7 million to alleviate the budget crisis he caused.

Assembly member Kevin Shelley said: "It [the district] severely hurt its credibility in Sacramento."

Although the lawmakers eventually voted to bail out San Francisco by approving the money, their parting words accused Rojas of outright mismanagement.

The bill that ensures the money will arrive must also be signed by governor Gray Davis, which is not a sure thing. Davis' Department of Finance balked at the measure, saying the state doesn't have the money to hand over to San Francisco.

Rojas' unwise financial plans neither benefited students nor improved the district's prestige in the eyes of the state.

Finally, in the middle of his district's massive financial rut, Rojas decided to say goodbye to San Francisco for good. After accepting a position as superintendent of Dallas' school district, he will be leaving our school board members to clean up the mess he made. "For the superintendent to walk away from us in a time of crisis, a crisis that is his making, is a total betrayal and is cowardly and pathetic," board member Dan Kelly said.

In doing so, Rojas has acted childishly and totally ignored the cause he allegedly represents.

The sooner Rojas is expelled, the sooner the school board can find a superintendent who has actually remembered the lessons of all our childhoods.

Blackboard image text:
I will not was te funds
I will not wo te funds
I will not v te funds
I will not te funds
I will n te funds
I will te funds
I wil te funds
te funds
e funds
0
-12,700,000
-12,700,000
DEBT

CHRIS KOEHLER

Superintendent Waldemar Rojas deserves to sit in the corner like a misbehaving child after leaving the SFUSD in a state of disrepair.

Letters to the Editor

Alumna cheerleader praises current squad

[Re: "Cheer picks up varsity status," Dec. 18, 1999] As a former Lowell cheerleader and captain, I'm super excited to hear that cheerleading has become a sport.

I'm also glad to see that since my era of cheerleading, which launched the competitive routines, has grown immensely consistently reaching national status. It's times like this when I wish high school would last forever (without homework).

Since graduating in 1984, I continued to support LHS cheerleading as a voluntary coach. I then went on to join San Francisco State's squad, but the program was not nearly as fulfilling.

I will always be an avid spirit squad supporter. I recently moved to Dallas, Texas (home of the NCAA), I'm always on the lookout for competitions (You should see the squads out here; they are massive). Any emails would definitely be very appreciated, thanks! ethanpak@yahoo.com.
— *Ethan Pak, Class of '84*

Student describes prom gone wrong

In response to your prom article from the March issue of the paper, it really got me thinking about how important my prom was going to be for me. I wanted to take my 25-year-old friend along. She is a close friend of mine, and I know if I brought a 25-year-old bombshell I would get stares and looks, and whispers. That was the idea; however, the whole thing backfired.

I was gonna go all out on Junior Prom. So when I went to get my guest form signed, the wonderful words I heard were: "She can't go."

"What!" I replied. It seems that Lowell has an age restriction on dances. Who knew? Supposedly, people 21 and over are not permitted.

"Great," I said to myself. "I'm not going to prom. This definitely sucks!"

Believing that I could not go to prom, I gave up. However, Friday night, I found myself a new 20-year-old friend. I knew I couldn't buy tickets at the door, but I was sure that some exception would be made under the circumstances.

Saturday night, 7:35. Car washed, hair done, teeth brushed, deodorant on, cologne on, tux on, basically I was looking "spiffy." When we arrived at the door of the Galleria, because of the massive lines, we were forced to wait in line for almost an hour. I was so annoyed.

Finally, I made my way to the door. There was no sympathy, and no prom.

On a final note, the restriction was unfairly applied to me. One girl brought her 12-year-old brother, and another brought a (40-year-old looking) 22-year-old, and the IDs of the people who went through the door were not always checked.

To the people who helped make this night really memorable, "Thanks a lot!"
— *Willy Dang, 0004*

NATO war a reminder of Cambodian Killing Fields

By Katherine Sear

THE REFUGEE CAMPS engendered by the war in Kosovo have awakened a ghost from my family's past.

The ghost is that of the Pol Pot regime, which was responsible for deliberately and fiendishly annihilating two million Cambodians from 1975 to 1979. So horrific was the genocide that Cambodia became known as the Killing Fields.

When the United States lost the Vietnam War in 1975, she withdrew entirely from Southeast Asia, including from Cambodia, the sideshow of the Vietnam War. But Cambodia was not merely a sideshow. She was the hidden war behind the Vietnam War.

In the past six weeks, my parents, survivors of the Cambodian holocaust, have cringed and winced at seeing pictures of the NATO bombings and of the refugee camps on the Yugoslav-Macedonian border.

The images bring back memories of praying to God that the U.S. B-52 bombings of 1972 wouldn't hit their families, and memories of being lost and afraid in the Khao-I Dang refugee camp in Thailand eight years later.

Cambodia was a nightmare. Communist Pol Pot and his Khmer Rouge fighting force purged Cambodia of traces of the old regime — eliminating family life, religion, education, art — in a word, culture. The Cambodians had to obey or die; in some cases they did both.

The Khmer Rouge broke up my father's family as they turned Cambodia into one great labor and concentration camp. The pain of simply not knowing whether his little brother is dead or alive still silences my father when the subject comes up.

Not knowing causes my father to imagine, to try to infer what probably happened. Would he imagine the worst? Should he put his brother into one of those heinous murders he saw happen to his neighbor?

In search of answers, my father went to the Tuol Sleng Genocide Museum in Phnom Penh in 1979, where photographs of men and women primarily of the elite class cover the walls. Each stare seems to ask the simple question of "Why?" At Tuol Sleng, interrogation meant execution. The Khmer Rouge snapped the photos before interrogating or torturing the prisoners. Death soon followed.

Death was probably more painless than the slow torture implemented to force each prisoner to confess to "crimes" against the new regime. Some prisoners had their fingernails pulled off or tongues electrically shocked. The mass murder at Tuol Sleng, officially known as the S-21 interrogation center, was only part of the Killing Fields.

To this day, my father wonders what exactly became of his little brother. His face wasn't on the walls of Tuol Sleng when he was there, but perhaps more death snapshots have been discovered since. The mystery continues; I hope to solve it someday so that my family can find some closure.

In Kosovo, whether it is genocide or "ethnic cleansing" is of no importance. Forget the labels and subtle distinctions. What it ultimately comes down to is barbarism and inhumanity.

This century is saturated with the heinous crimes of Mussolini, Hitler, Lenin, Stalin, Mao and Pol Pot. The list goes on, and Yugoslav president Slobodan Milosevic is the newest member of the Hall of Hate.

Each 20th century horror story is different, and we can forever dwell on the differences. But we all suffer directly or indirectly from crimes against humanity.

Our different religions, cultures, languages and backgrounds don't make these experiences any less painful. Inhumanity speaks a universal language by flagrantly inflicting hunger, fear, loss and pain.

As future citizens of the world, we must pledge to exorcise from our world the ghost of inhumanity, which has been haunting this century and uneasily lingering in the hearts of its victims and even their posterity.

SAM WILLIAMS

Yugoslav president Slobodan Milosevic's policies echo those attributed to Pol Pot during his notorious reign in Cambodia from 1975 to 1979.

Fig. 8.2. Creative and provocative art helps draw the reader to these long opinion pieces, including an unsigned editorial, a signed opinion column and reader feedback. *Lowell,* Lowell High School, San Francisco, Calif.

RAMPANT OPINION

If you have a problem, don't just sit there and complain. If you have an opinion you think everyone should hear, submit your rampant feedback in the envelope outside Room 251 or at our Web site (*www.thelowell.org*). Please sign all entries, but names will be be witheld upon request.

I wrote this short essay at the request of a dean after I was caught using my cell phone on campus. I thought the readers of the Lowell might be interested: It is necessary to follow the school guidelines to ensure safety and order amongst the natives. Paging devices, cellular/mobile phones are handy tools but are not allowed on school grounds. I understand that the school authorities do no want any form of breech of the SFUSD school codes and I will respect that authority and comply. The conversation [with the deans] extended beyond its original intent towards the operation of a motored vehicle. I do understand that driving a car or being in one during school hours is against school mandate. I will no longer drive to buy lunch during my free mods. Instead I will take up different means of transportation (eg. walking, biking, running, jogging, etc.). I fully understand that the school guidelines apply to me equally as they apply to others and if such tomfoolery persists, action by the deans shall be taken. In conclusion, I am now fully aware of what is requested of me at school and in action will take all consequences under consideration before I commit perfidious acts.

— *Daniel Baron, 0021*

"Carpe diem!" The problem at Lowell is that some students spend too much time doing their homework and not enough time seizing the day. I'm not implying that we should blow off all our responsibilities and live the day like it is the last day on Earth, but simply find time to enjoy all the little things in life that we take for granted.

— *Tiffany Leung, 0014*

When the student governments of high schools were created, oftentimes not as much time was taken to ensure those same freedoms granted by the Constitution [of the United States of America]. Within Lowell, especially during student government elections, certain means of expression are stifled. If student government is to be a training ground for democracy, how can it be so very different from our American democracy? Unlike the American government with three branches, the Lowell government has only two branches of government. I propose a third branch of Lowell government to provide for the proper, equitable representation of all opinions on campus. This third branch should be called the Student Review Board (SRB), and should be composed of nine students: one SBC appointee, four administration appointees, and four popularly elected representatives of the student body at large. Members of the board, as well as members of the SBC must be held to high levels of accountability to the student body. The SRB should act much as the judicial branch of the United States government does. It should be responsible for the review of actions of both the SBC and the faculty, when such actions affect the student body or any individual students therefrom. Students should have the right to review teachers, just as teachers have the right to review students.

— *Michael Block, 0017*

For the full text of this letter and others, visit the opinion page of The Lowell on the Web at www.thelowell.org

From the broken equipment, taped-up mats, and thin padding, many Lowell gymnasts have suffered injuries. The lack of funding for sports teams has resulted in cheap equipment and pain. The floor that we use for competition is a wrestling mat. It is so thin and hard that it sucks in all the spring of our tumbling. At the other schools that we compete against, there are spring floors that are carpeted. The other gymnasts can leap higher and prettier, tumble with more power and lift, and save their bodies from major injuries. Our wrestling mats create major back and joint injuries. I for one am a product of the damage that the wrestling mat has caused. I had to quit competing because of a reoccuring back injury due to the impact of landing on that cardboard floor. Our eight-member varsity team is now down to five. The wrestling mat is killing our team. If we don't get real gymnastic spring floors, our entire team may be plagued with injuries. We need more money!

— *Brenda Joy Huey, 0016*

Due to bad equipment, this gymnast suffers major back injuries.

SAM WILLIAMS

tion—advocating continuation of the longer lunch period—is recommended. The editorial attempts to persuade readers that the longer lunch period is a success.

In the following advocacy editorial, the staff explains a proposed program and recommends its adoption. The storytelling opening, an attempt to humanize the topic, is often a successful way to persuade readers that they have a stake in the outcome.

Service learning worthwhile project

The old man's face peeps out from surrounding layers of warm winter clothes. He slowly lifts his paper plate and humbly looks up. "More potatoes?" a smiling teenager asks.

His face breaks into a wrinkled, toothless grin. The volunteer piles on the steaming mashed potatoes, and the old man walks back to a table.

At first, the teenager was skeptical about serving at the shelter, but when he walked through the doorway, he realized this was where he needed to be. The 50 poor or homeless people who passed through his line and took seconds and even thirds of mashed potatoes made an impact on him as he realized he wasn't just giving out food; he was giving acceptance and an optimism that had been absent from their lives.

"There's nothing to do in Hendersonville!" is a common cry, but a new program that is in the works will provide meaningful activities for students. The program will also give students an opportunity to change the perception that young people are slackers. A local group is currently designing a service learning program to be offered in area schools.

Some students fear this new program could be a way to force students to volunteer. For instance, at Chapel Hill High School students must do 40 hours of community service to graduate.

But that's not what the local service learning program is about. It will give teenagers a chance to be involved and learn from their experiences, and it will be totally voluntary.

While service learning will not be required, teachers, principals and parents should definitely encourage participation. Being unselfish is not always easy, and stepping outside one's comfort zone may sometimes be required, but in the long run, service learning can teach lessons no current classes teach.

West students should not ignore the coming opportunities to learn by serving.

Wingspan
West Henderson High School
Hendersonville, N.C.

The following advocacy editorial is an example of how a major news story is interpreted in an editorial. In a persuasive argument, the staff likely hopes readers will agree with its position.

Mourning Columbine: Strong must lead in fight for understanding

We can blame it on the guns, their parents or their music. It could have been the movies, the Internet, the video games or maybe even their mental health. However, no matter who we blame, what happened at Columbine High School in Littleton, CO, was more than a human tragedy. It was a wake-up call.

By the time April 20, 1999, was over, two students—Dylan Klebold and Eric Harris—part of a group called the Trench Coat Mafia, had killed 13 people in that quiet Denver suburb just before turning the guns on themselves. We were all in shock. How could two children do this?

New security policies and procedures have been established at WHS and suddenly schools all over the country are being evacuated, locked down and closed as a result of this incident. This case has begun to be less of a tragedy and more of an epidemic. Similar incidents are going on everyday, and we don't have to go to Colorado to find them, not to a high school. Right here in Wooster, Melrose, Wayne and Layton Elementaries have all had student threats. Safety in schools is suddenly being questioned like never before.

Following the shooting, President Clinton proposed legislation that would require instant background checks for the purchase of explosives, hold parents criminally liable when their guns are used by juveniles in a crime and raise the minimum age for purchasing a handgun from 18 to 21. Critics of gun control, though, say our society is to blame for crimes like school violence, not guns.

Yet finger pointing won't cure this issue. Taking every weapon and restricting the media won't do the job either. It is up to us as human beings to take the initial step. It is up to us to put an end to the root of the violence: intolerance and prejudice. We must not be scared and judgmental but competent and accepting.

It is time for the strong to lead instead of the weak. We must take hate into our own hands instead of waiting for the law to stop it.

Jocks don't need to live in fear and trench coat wearers don't need to live in isolation and ridicule. We're all people and we all have needs. Human contact and love are necessary for a desirable existence, for we must give love in order to receive it.

If we turn our backs now, if we don't individually start to stand up for humanity, the momentum of these catastrophes will continue.

As long as the hate flows freely so will the violence.

Blade
Wooster High School
Wooster, Ohio

In the following editorial, interpretation of the news (why is this important?) is an indirect advocacy of proposed state legislation relevant to students.

HD scholarships

FREE CASH. It caught your eye, didn't it? If State Sen. Greg Server gets his way, high school students might find themselves with some of that free money for college.

Under Senate Bill 0022, students graduating from a public or private high school in Indiana with an Honors Diploma would qualify for a scholarship award in the amount of 50 percent of the educational costs at public universities in Indiana.

What does it mean? The long-established Academic Honors Diploma would serve a purpose beyond an HD denotation on a graduate's diploma. With an Honors Diploma in hand, a student could expect to receive a scholarship equal to half of the educational costs at any public university in Indiana, a reward for four years of diligent work.

Students who meet certain financial requirements may apply for a full scholarship under current standards upon completing an HD. Under Sen. Server's current proposal, however, students would be eligible for a scholarship regardless of financial conditions.

Counselor Martha Street believes that such a program as proposed by SB0022 would "definitely" encourage students to pursue an Honors Diploma. "This would be a wonderful opportunity to help deserving and hard-working students," she said. However, Street suggests that a program might be more accepted by the general public if students were required to work at least two years in Indiana after completing a degree.

Sen. Server's proposal would not only restore the Honors Diploma to its once-sought-after glory, but it would compel students to pursue their academic work more fervently. Instead of merely offering students an "HD" at the end of a diploma, it would offer diligent students a tangible benefit at the end of their high school career.

Optimist
Bloomington High School
Bloomington, Ind.

In this brief advocacy editorial, the staff makes two recommendations following an athlete's death.

On life

No one at the Lawrence North basketball game could have known what would happen that night when John Stewart collapsed and died. In the wake of this tragedy, lessons are to be learned.

Life is fragile. A visibly strong athlete with a bright future seems safe from death. However, through Stewart we are reminded that we are not guaranteed tomorrow. The great philosopher Seneca said, "Our care should be not so much to live as to live well." Make your days count.

Secondly, we should always remember that tragedy must result in change. As more information becomes available in the next few months, it will be necessary for us to draw informed conclusions concerning the current physical examination system for sports. John Stewart's death must not be remembered only as a tragedy but as a milestone for change.

Optimist
Bloomington High School
Bloomington, Ind.

Advocacy editorials must be reasonable to be effective. Overstating a point, preaching or scolding can turn readers away.

PROBLEM-SOLUTION EDITORIAL

The problem-solution editorial is another type commonly found in newspapers. Sometimes called an "editorial of criticism," this type of editorial is used when the staff wants to call attention to a problem or wishes to criticize someone's actions. Because of the need for the paper to act responsibly, facts need to be presented to back up the criticism or to explain the causes of the problem, and solutions must be offered. This three-step process is similar to the scientific method of discovery: statement of the problem, presentation of evidence and conclusion with potential solutions.

Criticism should be handled carefully. In an editorial, it's fair to criticize a person's actions if they have some impact on others; it's unfair to criticize a person's physical characteristics or purely private actions. Readers will discount allegations that aren't substantiated with proof or evidence. Because they are expressing an opinion, editorial writers have a little more freedom than news writers regarding libel. However, name-calling and offensive language will also harm the effectiveness of an editorial and the credibility of the paper. Lies and fabrications are unethical.

In the problem-solution editorial or editorial of criticism, the persuasiveness of the problem, the quality of the evidence and the practicality of the solutions will affect its success with readers. Staffs should select problems to write about that are being talked about by a sizable number of students, and ones that offer the potential for real solutions. For example, a common problem in some schools is the lack of school spirit, but it is hardly worthwhile to write about it unless the newspaper staff has some real, workable solutions to offer.

In the following problem-solution editorial, a common school problem, student parking, is addressed by the staff.

Safety of students' cars should be an issue: Cars should be more closely monitored to prevent random vandalism

It all comes down to one question: Why must we pay $5 for a parking spot when we can't be assured that our cars are safe?

Recently, in the Live Oak parking lot, there have been multiple acts of random vandalism. Cars have been keyed, things stolen and antennas destroyed; not to mention the damage on Half Road, the only alternative parking place. All this has happened while we have two very capable and attentive yard monitors, who simply have too much area to watch at once.

This year the ASB, which has always collected $45 for senior spaces, started charging $5 to park in the parking lot for the rest of the school. The money collected goes primarily to paying for the plastic decal that hangs on the rear view mirror and the rest is saved for school activities sponsored by ASB.

We would be better off using this money to fix the lighting in the parking lot, or hiring a third yard monitor to watch the parking lot or even begin fixing the overhangs. A few individuals have proven that we need to worry about vandalism at our school and that we need to do something about it.

For those of us who drive and park in the parking lot, this is a serious concern and not to be taken lightly. While sitting in class, our last worry should be about whether or not our cars are safe.

Car damage, no matter how slight, is expensive. We, as students, need to respect each other's property and each other.

Only through mutual respect and thinking about our actions will we achieve the level of tolerance and acceptance that we want and need at Live Oak.

Oak Leaf
Live Oak High School
Morgan Hill, Calif.

In the above editorial, the problem, vandalism of student cars, is clearly stated, and several solutions are offered by the staff.

The criticism given in the following problem-solution editorial is muted, illustrating the need to avoid preaching or severe scolding in an attempt to change behavior or someone's attitude.

Students need to do their part

The season of perpetual hope is nearing once again, bringing with it a flood of opportunities for giving and kindness.

Before Thanksgiving break, Food for Families had boxes set up in the halls. With the recent devastation of Hurricane Mitch, donations of food, clothing and money were taken for the victims of that disaster. And boxes are being set up for donations to Samaritan's Purse, an organization that provides a brighter Christmas for needy kids around the world.

That's all well and good, but these efforts will come to little without the support and help of the student body. For whatever reason, Uni's response has traditionally been a bit tepid.

Maybe this year it will change. Food for Families was an enormous success, and the Gargoyle hopes that present and future efforts at giving become as established as that one.

It's cheesy, yes, but give a little.

No, give a lot.

Clean out your pantry, donate your clothes, and give money to charitable organizations.

Give of your time. Free time is in short supply among Uni students so it's important to make time.

Christmas is now the holiday of getting, despite what we'd like to believe in America. Let's return to it to where the focus belongs: on giving to others.

Gargoyle
University High School
Urbana, Ill.

Here is another example of a problem-solution editorial, one that criticizes the school's strict adherence to policy. The primary subject, the reversal of the school board's decision not to allow a student to participate in graduation ceremonies despite his inability to complete his studies due to an illness, was reported extensively on the front page of the same issue of the paper in which this editorial was published.

District lets Schmidt walk for graduation

Schmidt walks.

It was at first a rallying cry, a demand by the student body for Cameron Schmidt to participate in graduation. After a student protest and media blitz, the Deer Valley School District Governing Board took a vote, and it became a statement of fact. Schmidt walks.

"Rocket Boy," David Silverstein, is returning to Desert Sky Middle School on April 26, after a vote in a closed-door session on Tuesday. He was suspended after school officials discovered a homemade rocket in his locker. The rocket, which the district considered a firearm, fell under DVUSD's zero-tolerance policy.

Tuesday night, the Governing Board buckled under pressure from students and national media, taking two votes, relenting two times. The hard line was sacrificed, but they did the right thing. The decisions were in the best interests of both the students and the district—a win-win situation for all parties. We hope that in the future, it will not take NASA astronauts and *The Today Show* for school officials to make such judgments.

These two events reflect a disturbing attitude in education. The Deer Valley District has shown a dedication to the letter of the law, the policy by which we are governed. This attitude starts at the top. The Superintendent, Dr. Gerald Cuendet, stated that policy was law in this district. It is an outlook common in district officials, administrators, and some teachers.

The job of a school district, the education of students, requires that students come first in all decisions. Educators are here to educate, and students are here to learn. Each should do this to the best of their ability, and the school district should facilitate, not disrupt, this process. When considering tough issues and making hard judgments in the future, the district must keep this in mind. Their first priority must always be people, not policy.

Ridge Review
Mountain Ridge High School
Glendale, Ariz.

COMMENDATION EDITORIAL

Commendation editorials are an important option for editorial writers. In most communities, including the school, a newspaper has status and is a power center. Because of its position, the school paper observes what is going on in the school and in the other power centers. When a person or a group does something extraordinary, the paper notices and may report that achievement in a news, feature or sports story. But it also has another choice; the paper can praise the person or group directly in an editorial. This elevates the person or group to a special level of notoriety.

Typically, these commendation editorials praise or pay tribute to someone or an organization that was performed successfully beyond the norm. Topics can include, among others, the retirement of a teacher or administrator; a state sports championship for a team or a state title for an individual athlete; the death of a student, teacher or administrator who was an inspiration to others; a successful end to a charity drive or fundraiser; the addition of new sports to the athletic program; and student community volunteer work.

If the paper publishes more than one staff editorial in each issue, it may be that one could be an editorial of commendation. If the paper publishes only one staff editorial in each issue, the decision to write an editorial of commendation should be carefully considered, and the person or group praised should be especially deserving. Persons and groups can also be commended in opinion columns.

In the commendation editorial, the reasons for the praise should be clearly stated and the impact of the achievement on others should also be included. These editorials are not usually long unless the person has achieved much or the impact is varied and complex.

An organization and a person are both praised in this commendation editorial. Why they deserve this praise and the impact of the changes they made are clearly presented.

Getting and spending: Customers profit from store's improvement in efficiency, variety

The past months have seen significant changes in the student store, all to the benefit of the students.

Most important was the addition of the barcode scanner. This makes store operation quicker and easier. Workers are no longer required to use the tedious numbering system that was previously in place, and can simply scan the item. This reduces the number of workers necessary in the store at any given time and speeds the line.

Another time-saving change is the elimination of cash. Now, instead of receiving change, students will receive credit in their store accounts, even if they don't have a standard charge account. Students will then be able to buy until the money in their account is gone.

In addition, Treasurer Cody Truscott ('00) has expanded the product line and is confident the store is well stocked enough that it will not run out of products again. The student store has made progress toward providing healthy food for students. After Spring Break, the store will begin selling fresh bagels.

We praise Truscott for improving this stu-

dent service, and thank the Student Council for appropriating the hundreds of dollars necessary for the repairs. Their progress is encouraging, and the Student Council should continue improving its most prominent student service.

Academy Times
Charles Wright Academy
Tacoma, Wash.

In this commendation editorial, the school's administration is praised for changing a policy. The editorial also explains and interprets the news behind the commendation.

Prudent change in graduation time: Religious conflict averted through change in the ceremony's time

By changing the time of the graduation ceremony from 7:30 p.m. to 8:30 p.m., the administration has clearly made the prudent and correct decision.

The decision will enable students, who otherwise would have found it impossible to attend the ceremony due to religious commitments, to be present.

This year, Central was unable to reserve its commencement on a Sunday evening. Instead, it was planned for a Saturday evening, a day that presents religious conflicts for various students.

In delaying the commencement, the administration gives all students—regardless of their religious faiths—an opportunity to participate in the memorable ceremony.

The other alternatives for the administration are limited to changing the ceremony's location and day. Both of these options are costly, impractical and unrealistic. Thus, delaying the ceremony one hour is fair and accommodating.

As principal Bill Meyer points out in a recent letter addressed to the seniors' parents, the change in time may actually help those students who want to spend more time with their families before the ceremony. Perhaps this later starting time may become a new tradition at Central.

The fact that the problem was solved immediately points to a healthy educational environment. Central's diverse student population differs from most schools in the St. Louis area. It is not likely that these other schools would have made similar accommodations. Hence, Central students gain a unique lesson in tolerance and understanding.

The way in which the administration handled the potential problem deserves commendation. They conferred with parents, teachers and students. STUCO members, who were also included in the dialogue, offered reasonable solutions to the problem. This exemplary determination to solve the problem on everyone's behalf serves as a model on solving similar school-related issues.

Parkway Central Corral
Parkway Central High School
St. Louis, Mo.

BRIEF EDITORIAL COMMENT

Brevity has its merits, and one- or two-paragraph editorials can be effective. They are mostly useful if only one point is made and little evidence or background information needs to be given. Sometimes these editorials have standing column heads, such as "Ten Second Editorials," but they are unsigned as are longer, fully developed editorials.

Here is an example of a brief editorial comment in two paragraphs:

Seniors urged to celebrate graduation in safe manner

It seems that every year around this time the news is filled with tragedies of graduating seniors getting killed due to alcohol related incidents.

The Demon Dispatch implores the members of the class of '99 not to become another statistic. Though graduation is a special moment in every teen's life, drinking is not the way to celebrate. There are plenty of ways to celebrate without endangering your life or the lives of others.

Demon Dispatch
Greenway High School
Phoenix, Ariz.

EDITORIAL SHORT

Another type of editorial, especially popular in the student press, is the editorial short or quip. It is distinguished by its length and organization. As its name indicates, it is brief, from one word to one or a few sentences. Usually, editorial shorts or quips are grouped together as a list under a standing column heading and include commendations and negative criticism.

Editorial shorts or quips are also random comments: One commendation or criticism does not necessarily relate to any other one on the list. Student papers sometimes label their shorts as "thumbs up, thumbs down," "cheers and jeers" or "rants and raves," or they apply a letter grade to each to indicate pleasure or displeasure. Many of these brief comments are not specific to school, but they are of interest to students. Sometimes they are humorous or note the changes in styles and popular culture (Fig. 8.3).

EDITORIAL CARTOON

Perhaps the most succinct form for an editorial is the editorial cartoon. In a few words or a sentence or two if the cartoon is a strip rather than a single frame, the editorial cartoonist can do what the editorial writer does—commend, criticize, interpret, persuade and entertain. Coupled with distinctive art, usually a line drawing, the cartoon is a favorite form of commentary for readers.

Cartoons can stand alone, unrelated to other topics on the editorial page, or they can be directly tied to a print editorial. By a distinctive drawing style and a voice, an artist should develop an opinion that comes through in both words and in the drawing itself. Because an editorial cartoon is opinion and the artist often uses caricature (exaggerated features), the artist has some freedom in creating something that may be humorous, satirical, ironic and even stinging. However, the art should not ridicule in an unjustifiably mean-spirited or hateful way. When a caricature is created, the exaggeration of someone should be in good taste and not unduly note someone's physical abnormality.

If editorial cartoon captions or conversation "bubbles" are hand-lettered, they should be legible. Art should be carefully drawn so the reader can quickly grasp the intended message. (See Figs. 8.4 and 8.5.)

WRITING THE EDITORIAL

For an editorial, the writer should select a topic that is tied to some story that will be published in the same issue of the paper in which the editorial will appear or has some merit and the potential for high reader interest. A local angle, even on a national or international situation, or on a widespread belief, is important to the success of the editorial. Readers will connect more quickly and in greater numbers if they see immediately that the topic has some relevance for them.

Before the editorial's opening is written, the writer should phrase the main point of the editorial in one or two sentences. By doing this, the writer will likely find it easier to keep the focus of the editorial on target. This will also help unify the editorial.

The topic needs to be thought through carefully, especially if the focus of the editorial is to negatively criticize a condition or an idea. The writer needs to fully understand the topic.

Since an editorial requires the presentation of some facts, some evidence, the writer needs to do research. Data should be gathered, and opinions should be found and considered. An Internet search can provide data and expert opinions, but the Internet is not fully reliable. A second source should always be checked to provide verification. *Fact checking for accuracy is as important for editorials as it is for news stories.* Since brief or medium-length editorials are more likely to get read and influence readers, the writer will have to ultimately be selective in the evidence that is presented. Finding local data and local opinions to help support or to refute an argument is also important, and this type of evidence may be preferable to national data and experts who live far beyond the school. An Internet search and in-person or phone contact to gather information and opinions are both recommended.

Ideally, an editorial board, made up of the editors and assistant editors of the paper, will review the topic, consider the evidence and agree on a position taken.

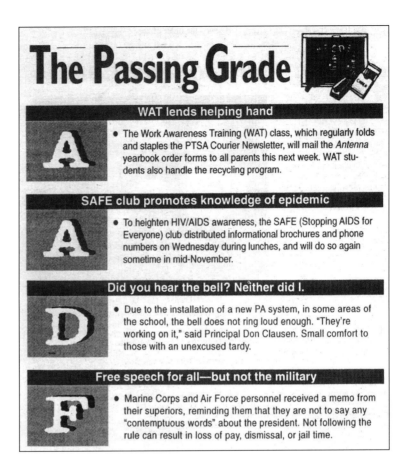

Fig. 8.3. Editorial briefs can be packaged into a visually appealing form such as this report card with its heading "The Passing Grade." *A-Blast,* Annandale High School, Annandale, Va.

Fig. 8.4. Student editorial cartoon. Alison Wong, cartoonist, *Parkway Central Corral*, Parkway Central High School, Chesterfield, Mo.

The writing is traditionally done by one person. Since many editorials argue a point, it is important for the board and writer to weigh all possible counterarguments; this will help the writer to select the best evidence to include in defense of the position the paper will take in the editorial.

If the editorial board members are divided on an editorial stand—no unanimity—the results of a board vote—in favor, not in favor—can accompany the editorial. Other options, especially for highly controversial topics, include inviting someone with an opposing viewpoint who is not a member of the paper's staff to write a guest editorial. Someone on the staff who has an opposing viewpoint could write a signed opinion column on the topic.

Most editorials are divided into three parts: (1) the introduction, (2) the body or evidence and (3) the conclusion. The opening tells the reader what the staff believes; the body tells the reader why the staff has this belief or opinion; the conclusion tells the reader what the staff thinks should be done based on the evidence presented, or it summarizes the situation without providing any solutions.

Although any type of lead presented in this textbook for writing news, feature or sports stories can be used for an editorial if it suits the topic, the exact type may depend upon the purpose of the editorial. In addition to an attractive headline, the opening sentence should also stimulate or pique reader interest.

Since the lead is the introduction, the first or second sentence should also state briefly the situation that prompted the editorial to be written. For example, a commendation editorial praising the accomplishments of a retiring drama coach could open with: "'The play's the thing,' and it has remained so for both William Shakespeare and Betty Johnson, MHS drama coach who is retiring in June after 30 years and 60 productions on the MHS stage." This opening sentence includes an often-quoted line from Shakespeare's "Hamlet" and the reason for the editorial, the retirement of a long-term teacher.

The body of the editorial is developed by presenting the facts that support the opinion or stand taken in the introduction or opening. The body can also include the opinions of experts and others who support the position taken by the newspaper staff or who refute the opinions of others on the topic. This is done clearly and concisely. Writers need to select the best facts and opinions that support the position. Too many facts and opinions will result in an overly long editorial and diminish the editorial's effectiveness.

Good, precise facts are essential in an editorial. Generalizations and clichés weaken the argument. Tell the reader where the facts come from if this seems important. Examples and comparisons and contrasts may also strengthen the supporting evidence. Sources and authorities quoted should be of the highest quality and level of expertise possible. For example, it is better to cite the U.S. Department of Education as a source for statistics on high school graduation rates rather than an article in *Time* magazine. For an editorial about teens and sexually transmitted diseases, it would be better to cite the opinions of a doctor than a receptionist in a clinic that specializes in this area of public health. Documentation of statistics and facts is important for the credibility and strength of the editorial.

The conclusion of the editorial should include one or more of these: a summary of the situation; suggestions or recommendations to solve the problem addressed or change the minds of those who have opposite viewpoints; or a new but related question or provocative statement for the reader to think about. Sometimes, an editorial can

Fig. 8.5. Student editorial cartoon. Michael Clough, cartoonist, *Blade,* Wooster High School, Wooster, Ohio

be effective if it only poses questions and doesn't provide any answers; the editorial writer wants the reader to do some soul-searching or arrive at his or her own conclusions or answers. The conclusion can also bring the reader back to the opening through repetition of key words or by fulfilling the reader's expectations raised in the opening. If a question is posed in the introduction, then the conclusion would logically provide the answer.

Whether the conclusion offers a solution, summarizes the main idea or poses more questions, it should have punch and leave the reader with something worth remembering. It can be thought provoking, challenging, affirming, clever or alarming. In the example of the commendation editorial that used a popular line from "Hamlet" to begin, another quote from Shakespeare could be used to conclude: "'All the world's a stage' for Mrs. Johnson, and her many fans will be waiting at the stage door after the final curtain call for the spring play to get her autograph this time. She's the real star of MHS theater." The quote used in this conclusion is from Shakespeare's "As You Like It."

WRITING THE OPINION COLUMN

The editorial and the opinion column have one major similarity: They are both opinion or subjective analysis. They have some important differences.

Opinions columns are signed and are the opinions (using the first-person pronoun *I*) of one person, unless the columnist chooses to include the opinions of others. Editorials are unsigned and are the opinions of the staff as a whole, even though they are written by one person. Opinion columns are less formal than most editorials; columnists have more freedom and usually more space to present their ideas.

Columns often are structured the same way as an editorial, beginning with an introduction, followed by the body and ending with a conclusion. The storytelling or chronological method of development can also be used. Rarely would the inverted pyramid style of development—most to least important information—be chosen by the writer.

Columnists often develop a style and a voice or select topics to write about that are consistently one type. Some always select topics that can be written about hu-

Checklist for Editorials

• Are the form and style appropriate to the content and purpose?

• Does it have a purpose and accomplish that purpose?

• Does it make the reader think?

• Is the writing clear, vigorous, direct and simple?

• Are conversational words used?

• Is the argument logical?

• Is the evidence clear and the best available to support the position taken?

• Are enough facts given?

• Does it sound sincere?

• Does it get to the main point quickly?

• Does it make points without preaching or talking down to the reader?

• Is the opening sentence interesting enough to attract readers?

• Are the paragraphs short?

• Is the editorial overwritten and too long?

• Does the topic relate to the school or to student interests?

• Will the headline attract readers?

• Is it written in the second person?

• Is the topic connected to a story published in the same issue?

• Does the position taken represent the majority of the paper's editors?

• Is it unsigned?

morously. Others always write about money or travel or sports. Some write about what is often called "the human condition," the triumphs and tragedies of human life. Some always champion the underdogs in society, those less fortunate than most people. There are columnists who write above the average reader's vocabulary and intellect, appealing to highly educated readers. Some write only about the English language and how we use or abuse it. There are countless possibilities for each columnist to "own" a unique or nearly so subject.

Many columnists develop a unique opening or closing line or a word or phrase that is always included. This helps distinguish the columnist from others who may be writing about similar topics and becomes a sort of trademark or signature style. High school columnists can do the same thing with their column writing. It works when it is unique and consistently used.

A column is also identified with a consistently used title, often set in a typeface and with graphics that are the same as those for other regular columns in the paper. These are sometimes called "standing heads," since they are in every issue of the paper and never change. The columnist's byline is prominently featured, and sometimes a mug shot (small face shot) of the writer is included. Column titles may or may not be indicative of the column's usual content. Titles are usually brief, and many use clever wordplay. For example, "Jock Talk" could be a sports column, since "jock" is a slang term for athlete. Or, "B-sides" could be a title for a column on alternative music: A "B" side is a slang term for the old 45 rpm record, which had two sides. The "A" side was the hit single, and the "B" side was the usually seldom-played opposite or flip side.

The following opinion column ties into a major national story about the murder of a Wyoming college student who was gay. It is an example of how a columnist can express personal opinions that may or may not be shared by others on the newspaper staff. Opinion columns are one person's voice, not the voice of the paper (the editorial is the group's voice). The columnist also cites credible and appropriate sources for some of her statistics.

Message results from Shepard's death

An unopened letter sits on my desk. I can't send it but I can't throw it away. I remember vividly the day I decided to write it. I sat at the kitchen table on a cold Thursday morning eating my breakfast and scanning the paper.

Before anything else on the front page, his image first caught my eye. He was beautiful, with dirty blond hair, piercing blue eyes and a youthful easy smile. I remember the wave of shock that overcame me as I read the headline: "Police arrest four in beating of gay student."

As I read the article, I became nauseous as images of his smashed-in head and his scarred and bleeding body flashed through my mind. He was hung crucifixion-style on the fence post where he was left to die—a display to the whole world of the overwhelming hate two men felt toward homosexuals. This beautiful, promising young man was on the verge of death because of someone else's hate.

That night I wrote him a letter. I told him to remember that the whole world was not like those two men who beat him. I said that I held him in esteem for his courage to be openly gay. I told him he was constantly in my prayers and my thoughts.

I wanted him to not give up hope; I wanted him to live.

Right before I went outside to put the letter in the mailbox that Monday morning, I heard the news on the radio. I was too late. Matthew Shepard, the beautiful boy with the dirty blond hard, piercing eyes and the easy smile had died the night before. I remember the tears of grief that I fought back that morning and during school. When I got home I cried bitterly.

I felt like I should have done something to prevent what happened. I couldn't understand how people's hate could drive them to kill. Few events in the past have affected me so strongly.

I've heard it said "Hate is a strong word," but that adage contains more truth than most people realize. Hate is the strongest emotion. It's an emotion that doesn't have to be triggered by something large because it gains momentum quickly. This emotion knocks away all morals, reason and control and can push someone so far that he would even hurt or kill for hate.

There were 7,947 hate crimes committed in the United States in 1995, according to an FBI report, and 1,016 or those incidents were based on sexual orientation. According to an Amnesty International public statement on Matthew Shepard's death, while violent crime in the United States in general has gone down, hate crimes are on the increase.

How can someone hate a group of people or person he does not know or has never even met? Sadly, hate is usually directed at people who are different from others. Whether it be a person's personality, clothes, race, religion or sexual orientation, the reason for the hatred all boils down to the fact that a person is different. Ignorance, also, causes hate. Often, when people are not familiar with others, they may not understand the other's ways. People generally fear what they do not understand and therefore hide this fear with hate.

If one were to ask those who hate homosexuals if they have homosexual friends or relatives on which to base their opinion, most would probably answer "no." Instead, many use stereotypes to justify why they hate certain people because inside they really don't know why.

The last reason why someone hates another person is rarely ever admitted but often true. Many choose to hate so that they may hide that they are surprisingly similar to the person they are hating. This hatred occurs because they fear being ostracized and, therefore, choose to hide under a shield of hate.

Why hate? It takes so much effort and energy and certainly doesn't accomplish anything positive. Hate may hurt the person at which it's aimed but in turn shows one's lack of knowledge, lack of respect and lack of confidence.

The sad fact is that our community and school are not immune to the hate that brought about Matthew Shepard's murder.

I become distraught when I walk down the steps of B building and see that someone has "I hate gays" written across his backpack. I look sadly at the words of hate angrily etched onto bathroom stalls, school walls and desk tops. I cringe at the constant animosity among the varied groups of students in our school.

Hate is hate. Insulting words have the same impact as the butt of a gun smashing in someone's head.

The letter I wrote to Matthew remains on my desk as a constant reminder of how far hate can go. Often, I pick the letter up and think about Matthew. I'm certain that he's in a better place now, but I feel guilty for not being able to prevent his death.

If only I could have been his friend. If only I could change people's minds. If only people didn't hate.

Clare Jellick
Lion's Roar
Gahanna Lincoln High School
Gahanna, Ohio

EXERCISES

1. Bring copies of your city paper to class and read the editorials. Are the topics related to news stories on page 1 or an inside news page? Classify the editorials according to type: advocacy, problem-solution or commendation.

2. List five groups or persons in your school who should be praised for some special achievement. Select one and write a short, about-200-word, commendation editorial.

3. List five concerns students have today about their lives. For example, students may be concerned about lack of privacy or violence in schools. Select one and write a short, about-250-word, advocacy editorial.

4. List five problems in your school. The problems could be with the schedule, the building, the curriculum and the athletic program, among other possibilities. Select one and write a short, about-250-word, problem-solution editorial.

5. You are invited to be an opinion columnist for your school paper. You are asked to write about life as a teenager—a wide-open field. Select a name for your column. List five topics you would like to write about. For example, you might like to comment on dating, your siblings or getting your driver's license. Select one topic and write your first column. Keep the length to about 350 words. Since this is a signed opinion column, you will write in the first person.

6. With your school, community and peers in mind, write a list of 10 editorial shorts. Half of your list should be commendations ("thumbs up"), and half should be negative criticism ("thumbs down").

7. In small groups, form editorial boards. As a group, list three topics worthy of an editorial in your school paper. Discuss the topic and determine if you can agree on the paper's official position on the topic. Someone in the group should write a summary statement (one or several sentences that states the situation and the paper's decision). When the class convenes as a whole, each group should share the results of its editorial board meeting.

8. Bring copies of a current issue of the local newspaper to class. Select a story, column or editorial that you read that you would like either to question or comment on positively or negatively. Write a short (about-150-word) letter to the editor of the paper. (Most papers publish letters from readers.) Send it and then watch to see if it is published.

In-Depth Reporting

Schoolwide cheating is rampant in some communities. School districts try to decide how to solve problems with inequitable school and learning situations. School boards constantly debate how to spend tax dollars. Violence in schools is a new national dialogue. Charter schools are beginning to affect public school enrollments and funding dollars. States try to connect school funding and performance. Students are required to pass exit exams to earn diplomas in some states.

As school communities grow more complex, opportunities for in-depth reporting present challenges for scholastic journalists in reporting for both the newspaper and yearbook.

In-depth reporting is needed when complex issues or situations are being discussed and written about. Coverage of in-depth topics may require a greater commitment of resources—both staff members and time—as well as a greater need for understanding of all sides of the issue. Teams of reporters, photographers and editors may need to be assembled to properly cover complex topics of concern to the publication's readership. Those teams may be gathering information over a course of time before they ever come together to actually write and report a story.

In-depth reporting may take many forms. It may be a single page of coverage in the newspaper, or it may be a series of articles published over a period of time. It might be published on the double truck—the center spread of the publication, where the pages are actually printed on one sheet of paper. The double truck allows different opportunities for layout. Since the pages are a single sheet of paper, headlines and visuals can be brought across the two pages to unify them. Two pages of content can also appear on facing pages without actually appearing on the double truck. Or an in-depth story may appear as a "package" of content, taking up a majority of space on a page in a specialized presentation.

In the yearbook, in-depth reporting can also take many forms. The opportunity to cover topics of significant reader interest will not only broaden the depth of the yearbook's reporting but will allow the publication to occasionally break the pace of presentation. Breaking this pace will offer opportunities for different kinds of content.

TOPICS FOR IN-DEPTH COVERAGE

Controversial, sensitive topics such as drug and alcohol abuse, sexuality and school violence have been used as topics for in-depth coverage. While these topics are relevant to teenage audiences, reporters and editors need to make sure their decisions on covering in-depth topics are appropriate for their school communities. Coverage of sensitive topics should be discussed carefully among staff members, and decisions about how these topics can be covered should be carefully decided. In some cases, neutral reporting methods may offer more sensitive ways of topic coverage. For instance, rather than using first-person accounts of student drug use or sexuality, in-

Living through torn pasts

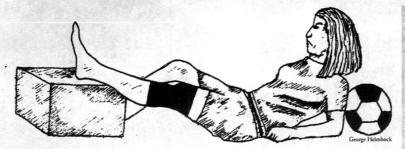

George Helmbock

Athletes overcome knee injuries, return to sports

BY NATALIE MOORE

In Week 12 alone of the National Football League (NFL), each of the 30 teams amassed at least one knee injury, totaling 70 players suffering this ailment. But this kind of impairment does not solely belong to professional athletes. Students here have proven just as susceptible, if not more, to knee problems.

Sophomore Abby Wild, who plays soccer, experienced this when she tore her right anterior cruciate ligament (ACL) last May. In the third game of a Dynamo Soccer Tournament, Wild planted her foot in one of the field's many ruts, but her body did not rotate the same direction. Wild said, "It was just weird. I heard a snap and then I couldn't stand up. (My knee) just buckled."

Wild fell victim to a rising problem in athletes — knee injuries. According to Malka Orthopedic's web site, more than 4.2 million people a year seek medical attention for a knee problem.

Without the ACL to guide the knee, the joint becomes unstable. This is why many people who have torn the ligaments cannot stand or put pressure on the knee.

Earning her Masters of Science from the University of North Carolina, Miss Sherry Molinar, AT, C (Athletic Trainer, Certified), said the ACL is the worst knee ligament to tear, but it usually is not career-ending. She said the most common injuries to that part of the body are dislocated knees and patella tendinitis. Molinar has seen one ACL tear here when soccer player and senior Stacy Martin tore hers for the second time during the soccer Sectional.

ACL injuries, though common, are not preventable. "There's not much you can do for ACL tears, especially like with what happened to (Martin.) There wasn't anything she could have done. She was in about as top physical condition as you can be in," Molinar said.

Problems here

Molinar cited a few examples as to why the occurrence of this injury in high school girls seems high. "(ACL tears are common) especially with women because of the way their hips are (not as straight as men's). High school athletes are not as strong and do not have as good of technique as older athletes," she said.

Wild said, "It was strange because it was painful at first but not excruciating pain. I was able to hop off the field. My knee wouldn't straighten, and it buckled when I put weight on it. I had to elevate (my knee) and watch my team play the rest of the day."

She was familiar with the symptoms of a ligament tear, though, as Wild said she had friends who had done the same thing to their knees.

Infamous challenge proves harmful

Surgery not only is required for athletes with torn ligaments who continue in sports but also for other problems to the knee. Senior Darcy Vannatta experienced this her freshman year at Carmel

Junior High School when she dislocated the joint after the powder puff football game. "We were up in the bleachers after the game, and I had turned real fast and slipped. My kneecap had slipped out," Vannatta said. "I was like, 'Oh my gosh, that's not right.' Just by instinct, I straightened my leg and (my kneecap) popped in."

As with many who experience injuries, Vannatta missed some of her freshman softball season. "(Since the accident) I have played varsity softball my sophomore and junior years, and I will play this year. It was the best time for it to happen since I really didn't miss anything."

Allie Heyworth, powder puff participant, soccer player and senior, fell victim at the all-female football game the spring of her junior year when she was tackling the opponent on a kickoff return. "I planted my foot, but my body didn't twist the same way," Heyworth said.

Playing against her father's wishes, Heyworth realized what happened to her left knee immediately, as she knew the symptoms of an ACL tear. "I was laying on the ground, and I looked over into the stands and just thought, 'Oh, no.' My dad was there, and I knew what had happened because (Martin) had torn (her ACL) two weeks before."

Heyworth, though she seemed to have a quick recovery of about 10 weeks, had more trouble in the beginning than her friends who had torn their ACLs, she said. After the injury occurred, Heyworth said it took her about two weeks to walk again. Soon after she began to walk, Heyworth had surgery to replace her ligament.

Having two friends going through physical therapy, senior Ashley Fritz and Martin, was helpful, Heyworth said. The three worked through Methodist Sports Medicine for their PT. "Emotionally I am a lot stronger now. Seeing that I got through this makes me realize I can overcome anything," Heyworth said. She went on to lead this year's girls' soccer team to a State title as co-captain.

Recovering, moving on

After having surgery to replace her ACL July 28, Wild said the most frustrating part is the time it takes to regain her previous ability. Wild said she still is working on her physical therapy and has reached about 80 or 90 percent of her strength. She has set her goal at 100 percent for this month when spring soccer training begins.

Vannatta had advice for people recovering from any injury. "It's discouraging at first, but you just have to keep working. (The therapy is) something that you might not want to do, but you have to overcome that."

SENIOR ALLIE HEYWORTH: SHE TORE HER ACL DURING POWDER PUFF FOOTBALL LAST SPRING

SENIOR DARCY VANNATTA: SHE DISLOCATED HER KNEECAP DURING HER FRESHMAN YEAR

SOPHOMORE ABBY WILD: SHE TORE HER ACL LAST MAY DURING A SOCCER TOURNAMENT

> *"It was just weird. I heard a snap and then I couldn't stand up. (My knee) just buckled."*
>
> SOPHOMORE ABBY WILD

Operating

Before

After

◄ *The surgery, though not always necessary in people who will not participate in athletics, is shown here. Both are pictures of HiLite staff member Rob Dro's ACL procedure Nov. 25. Above, the ligament is ruptured and curled in a ball. The ligament then is reconstructed and screwed into the knee cap and tibia. The new "ligament" is as strong as the previous one, as it comes from either the patellar or Achilles tendons or a cadaver. Below is a picture of the replaced connector. After surgery, one must continue physical therapy, usually for at least eight weeks.*

What are the knee ligaments?

Of the four knee ligaments, the anterior cruciate ligament (ACL) and the medial collateral ligament (MCL) are injured most often in sports. The posterior cruciate ligament (PCL) also frequently is torn.
Some other facts include:
* The ACL is the most commonly injured ligament in the knee.
* Over the past 15 years, ankle sprains have decreased by 86 percent and tibia fractures by 88 percent while knee ligament tears have increased by 172 percent.
* Twenty-five percent of all reported skiing injuries involve the knee.
* The ACL is a cord about the size of a person's index finger yet permits forces of up to 500 pounds to be exerted on it.
* As the largest joint in the body, the knee uses the ACL to guide the shin bone through a normal, stable range of motion.

Signs of a tear

Swelling, pain and instability in the knee comprise symptoms of an ACL tear. One may feel or hear a pop in the knee and not be able to apply pressure to the joint if a ligament is torn.
A doctor or certified trainer can do a test immediately after the accident and before the swelling sets in to see if the ligament is torn. He would stretch the knee to tell if the joint was loose. The injury can be assessed through a magnetic resonance imaging (MRI).

Immediate first aid

Ice and immobilization should be placed on the knee immediately. Miss Sherry Molinar, a certified athletic trainer who works through St.Vincent at sporting events here, said, "A lot of ice and elevation are helpful. If they go in and see it is torn, normally (doctors) will wait a week or two weeks before doing any surgery. (In that time) they can start doing some leg strengthening exercises to be more prepared for surgery."

Recovery exercises

As it takes a minimum of eight weeks with a good physical therapy program before a participant can return to more demanding sports, the rehabilitation process is one that must be completed thoroughly. A program must cover all aspects of fitness for the knee: flexibility, strength, power, coordination and specific sport drills.
* One should do many repetitions of an exercise, up to 30, several times a day. Avoid sideways stresses on the knee, and many people use exercises that allow full motion but are controlled as in deep water workouts.
* With little use of the quadricep while recovering, one must rebuild both this and the hamstring muscle with exercises like cycling, half squats, on one leg or two, a step machine and a hamstring curl machine.
Some things to avoid during physical therapy:
* Do not squat past 90 degrees, as this may stress cartilage inside the knee.
* Do not perform knee extension exercises.
* Do not do any exercises where the injured leg is planted and used as the only support.

More information

Web sites that are sources for this story:
http://www.hyperski.com/articles/apr96maitland.aclexer.htm
http://www.hyperski.com/articles/apr96maitland.aclinjuries.htm
http://www.medfacts.com/d_acl.htm
http://www.os2bbs.com/malka/acl2.htm
http://www.stoneclinic.com/aclrept.html

terviews with professionals will provide less controversial, though maybe not as interesting, ways of covering the issue. Student journalists must make sure they cover topics responsibly.

Schools continue to face the same difficulties as the community in general. However, students need to look specifically at the concerns of their individual readers as possible topics for in-depth coverage. Following the beat system already in place on most publications staffs, student journalists can start to look for areas of concern.

SCHOOL BOARDS

What the school board or the school's governing body decides affects every student at the school. Is the school considering changing graduation requirements, changing the length of the school day or year, requiring students to wear uniforms, allocating money for new facilities, debating whether to hold a bond election or tax levy for a special project? All of these topics would be of concern to student readers. Someone from the student newspaper staff should attend all school board meetings.

Beyond the local school board, the state's educational governing body will also make decisions that affect schools in your state. Many of these decisions are studied for months in advance. Monitoring the decision-making process will offer opportunities to share possible changes with readers and report their initial reactions before the changes are made. National educational trends and decisions may also be important in your school community.

ATHLETICS

Athletic programs in schools are rich areas for in-depth reporting. How does the athletic department monitor use of illegal substances such as growth hormones and steroids among athletes? Does the school have an athlete who is being heavily recruited by colleges or professional programs? Who decides how much funding is provided for sports in the school, and is it equitable among major/minor sports and men's/women's sports? Do programs share equal facilities for equal amounts of time? Is the school changing scheduling of teams and opponents that could affect competition or travel time? Be sure reporters are talking frequently to coaches and athletic directors in the school (Fig. 9.1).

CURRICULAR AREAS

Maintaining contact with the heads of curricular programs and development, school department heads and others who make decisions about academics will enable student journalists to monitor changes in curriculum that will affect students and the programs in which they participate. Other areas of curricular concern include elimination of programs, reduction of teachers and consolidation of school resources such as counseling and advising programs. Teacher concerns such as students buying essays on the Internet or rampant cheating in the school could also be examined. Do students sign an honor code? Is it uniformly enforced among students and athletes?

Fig. 9.1. An in-depth look at knee injuries suffered by students concentrates on female athletes. Due to the length of the main story, text heads are used to help provide visual relief and provide various entry points for readers. In addition to the main story, a sidebar details four aspects of the story, helping to define and provide additional information about aspects of knee injuries, including web sites that were used as resources for the story. Visual relief is provided by the illustration at the top of the story, as well as through the head shots and short summaries of the students featured in the story. In addition, a staff member's injured and repaired ligament is shown in medical pictures taken during the procedure. *HiLite,* Carmel High School, Carmel, Ind.

Oral Expressions

MARIE KHOURY '99 S

by BRANDT GASSMAN, GENNY DEPPE & KATE TRESLEY

The oral piercing trend is increasing in popularity as more people open their mouths and say "Ahhhhh" to new forms of self expression.

THE LATEST FASHION TREND TO HIT THE TWENTYSOMETHING generation is a far cry from the bell-bottoms and polyester of generations past. In fact, the American Dental Association (ADA) has put out multiple statements over the past several years warning both doctors and patients against it. The trend is oral piercing and its popularity is increasing rapidly across the country.

Alex's Story

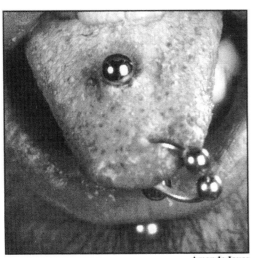

Amanda Joyce

ALEX ALAVI '00 DISPLAYS his pierced tongue.

AFTER GETTING HIS TONGUE PIERCED MORE THAN A year ago, **Alex Alavi** '00 has grown increasingly fascinated with the piercing lifestyle. "The first oral piercing I ever received was done at home...which is not something I would recommend, as it is very risky," said Alex. "Since then, I've just become fascinated with the entire atmosphere and process of piercing...like when I was a kid and seeing pictures of tribal piercing practices in Africa...it's just a process I enjoy going through."

Despite the ominous warnings from the ADA and other doctors, Alex says that the risks associated with oral piercings are often overblown. "If you pierce yourself, don't take care of a piercing, or you go to piercers who don't know what they're doing, yeah, you're asking for problems," said Alex. "The people who get infected are the ones being irresponsible about taking care of their piercings. If you are responsible about it and care for it properly, you shouldn't run in to any problems."

With seven piercings on his face alone (including two in his tongue), and a handful of others on his ears, Alex sees piercing as a form of artistic expression. "There's a release from piercing...definitely, because it's basically a form of body art," he says. Alex also says that, contrary to popular opinion, pain really isn't an issue when getting an oral piercing. "First, comparatively speaking, the tongue is one of the least painful piercings you can get compared to the septum or bridge, for example. But in general, if you go into the process completely scared out of your pants, the pain factor is naturally going to be a lot higher," said Alex.

According to Alex, his father and mother have different opinions about his piercings. "My dad doesn't really approve of my piercings," he said, "but on the other hand, my mom is completely supportive of what I'm doing, and she's an orthodontist!" Alex says that the image he conveys isn't what's important to his mother. "It doesn't matter to her how I look...she just wants me to make something of myself," he said.

Ultimately, Alex gains the most satisfaction from the release of energy that accompanies a piercing. "When I'm getting pierced, I'm so relaxed it's like I'm in another world. It's almost like a

numerous piercings.

interview with...
the piercers

THERE'S NO DOUBT THAT PIERCERS HAVE GOTTEN a bad rap in the public's eyes. Their under ground nature has sparked concern among many doctors and parents about oral piercing's standard of safety. As it turns out, the piercers are often the most knowledgeable people involved in the entire piercing process.

Aaron Wing, a four year piercing veteran working at Chicago's Tatu Tattoo, stressed the importance of finding a qualified piercer. "Make sure you go to a reputable shop -- someone you know is good or has done work on you before," Wing said. "If you feel uncomfortable or get a bad feeling from [a piercer], your first instinct is probably right."

Wing also encourages customers to follow the aftercare procedures laid out by piercers. "Basic hygiene and following a piercer's guidelines are essential to preventing problems in the future," said Wing. "When people come in with problems and you ask them how they've been taking care of their piercing, it's nowhere near what [the piercer] told them when they received it."

Because this liability is certainly a risk for piercers, many tattoo parlors, including Tatu Tattoo, require that customers sign a legal waiver before receiving any sort of modification. Most tattoo parlors also require that a piercee must be at least 18 years of age, or 16 and accompanied by an adult.

Some piercers are even more passionate about the care of customers' piercings. "When people come in to get a piercing, what I tell them is that if they don't take good care of it, I'm gonna come and find 'em!" said Chuck, the head piercer at Downers Grove's Skin Gallery. Chuck also wants customers to be more actively involved in the piercing process. "Everybody heals differently," said Chuck, "so we encourage people to do research themselves and find out more about how they're going to heal and best ways to care for [their piercing]."

According to Wing, the piercer plays a key role in educating customers about their piercings, but ultimately customers are responsible for their own care. "Pay attention to what [the piercer] is telling you," said Wing, "because in the end, you're responsible for making sure your piercing doesn't go wrong."

-Brandt Gassman

form of acupuncture...piercing gives you this huge rush and release of energy. It's truly undescribable," he said. Alex also says that he will continue to experiment with piercing as he grows older. "New techniques and new trends will be developed, and I'll want to try them...body modification will always be fascinating."

Marie's Story

ACTING MOSTLY ON IMPULSE, THREE MONTHS AGO Marie Khoury '99 decided to get her tongue pierced. In fact, impulse is the reason for most of her piercings. Marie has had her ears pierced four times in addition to her nose, belly button, tongue, eyebrow and librae (below her lower lip).

A few days after getting her tongue pierced, Marie's mother found out and was very upset. "My mom just said, 'Do you want me to throw up?'" said Marie. For a few weeks after she got her librae pierced, Marie's mom made her cover it up with a Band-Aid when they would go out of the house. "[My mom's reaction] was annoying and stupid. It's like, what did I ever do to you?" said Marie.

On the other hand, Marie's piercings have got-

> 66
> **When I'm getting pierced, I'm so relaxed it's like I'm in a different world.**
> 99
>
> *-Alex Alavi '00*

piercing
places & prices

Chicago Tattooing Comp. - $70
922 W. Belmont Ave., Chicago
(773) 528-6969

Skin Gallery - $50
1410 Ogden Ave., Downers Grove
(630) 493-1199

Tatu Tattoo - $55 to $65
prices depend on jewelry
1754 W. North Ave., Chicago
(773) 772-8288

prices include piercing and standard jewelry

see **ORAL PIERCING** *following page*

What is YOUR reaction toward people with oral piercings?

None of it is necessary, just like none of the fashions we have are necessary. Piercing is just a different [fashion] standard -- it's not right or wrong.
Brian Bers '99

Oral piercings aren't necessarily bad, but people [with oral piercings] are treated differently because they're perceived as not good.
Darcy McNutt '99

It doesn't bother me personally because an oral piercing doesn't define a person's personailty. Rather it defines their appearance.
Chris Chan '00

[A person] could have 20 lip rings and a tongue ring for all I care. As long as they don't bother me, I'm not going to do anything to bother them.
Kyle Johnson '01

-complied by Christina Chan

ORAL PIERCING

continued from previous page

ten some positive feedback at school. "Most of my friends like [my piercings]," said Marie. However, Marie has noticed that certain teachers and even a small number of students treat her differently because of her piercings. "It's irritating. It's like, why don't you open up your narrow little mind and try to get to know someone [before making a judgment]?" said Marie.

According to Marie, her tongue piercing procedure was relatively simple. Everything was sterile and the piercers wore rubber gloves. After she rinsed with mouthwash, the piercers marked Marie's tongue with a pen, and seconds later, her tongue was pierced.

Following the piercing of her librae, Marie applied Neosporin and Bacitracin on her librae for a couple of months. "If you don't take good care of [the librae] it can get really puffy and nasty," said Marie.

As for her tongue, Marie carried Listerine around with her, rinsing her mouth after every meal and drink. "[My friends] were all making fun of me for a while after I got [my tongue] done because I couldn't talk," she said. "But [the constant cleaning process] got really annoying really fast. I think I went through more than a liter of Listerine."

Marie's most severe "injury" was when she accidentally chipped the enamel on one of her teeth when biting down.

For the time being Marie has not considered getting any more facial piercings. "I think I have quite enough [piercings] as it

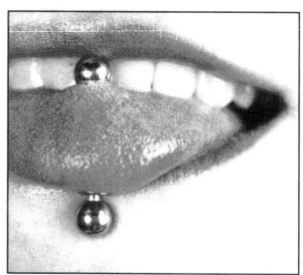
Amanda Joyce

A CLOSE UP OF DENISE DUREK'S '99 TONGUE shows the top and bottom balls of her stud.

is," said Marie. "Piercings are better than tattoos because you can take them out like when you go to work. [On the other hand] you can't be like 'Oh! I have to take off my tattoo!'"

Denise's Story

AFTER THE END OF HER SOPHOMORE YEAR at Central, **Denise Durek** '99 moved to Colorado for one year. It was here that Denise's interest in oral piercing peaked. "When I moved to Colorado, I went with my friend on her eighteenth birthday to a piercing parlor and saw what [piercing] was all about — I knew I really wanted it

even WEIRDER...tongue splitting

Tongue splitting is a process in which the tongue is split from center to tip in order to achieve a "forked tongue." The tongue can be split using multiple piercings, a deep incision in the tongue or with laser surgery -- the most favored method among doctors who perform the procedure. Some people have split their tongue by stretching their piercings and cutting between them using stitches or dental floss. Since tongue splitting is largely an unknown practice, no standard procedure for it has been established, and only a few doctors and piercers throughout the entire country will perform the procedure. A tongue split takes approximately one month for full healing, and side effects on speech and ability to eat are minimal.

Information courtesy of the *Body Modification F.A.Q.* - e-mail *bme@freeq.com* for more details

en," she said. "I was being partly rebel-
us — I wasn't enjoying life out there. I
t bored with myself. I wanted to change
y look. I wanted it so badly that I told
yself I wouldn't turn back," said Denise.

At the start of this year, Denise braved
e needle herself. "[After I gargled with
sterine], the piercers marked a spot on my
ngue with ink where they would pierce. I
d them move [the spot] back so that my
om wouldn't see it," she said.

In fact, Denise had no intentions of tell-
g her mom about her tongue piercing.
My mom didn't know until three weeks
ter I did it. She found out when she heard
e lisping," Denise said. Her mother's an-
cipated disapproval was an incentive for
enise's piercings. "Part of [the reason for
tting the tongue piercing] was to spite my
om. I went against her will — I knew she
ouldn't like it," said Denise. One of her
om's main concerns was the stereotypes
sociated with oral piercings. "[My mom]
dn't want me looked down upon," she
id.

Denise regarded the healing process to
e more painful than the piercing itself.
When I first got [the piercing], my tongue
t sore," said Denise. "I ate ice for two
eeks and lost six pounds. I don't know if
d [get another piercing]. I don't know if
d go through the pain." This discomfort
d not come cheaply either. By the time

> " When I first got it, my
> tongue got sore. I ate
> ice for two weeks and
> lost six pounds. "
>
> -Denise Durek '99

enise left the piercing parlor, she had spent
55 between the jewelry and piercing costs.
ccording to Denise, there is no set rate for
piercing. "It depends on the difficulty. Dif-
rent places have different rates. My eye-
row was cheaper than my tongue," she
id.

While vacationing in Maui this past sum-
er, Denise discovered that the top ball of
er tongue ring was missing. "I was basi-
ally freaking out. I called all the tattoo and
iercing places in the area. My mom took
ental tape and wrapped it around the
ngue ring and ball until I could get a new
ne. It was not a pleasant experience,"
enise said.

Despite her Hawaiian fiasco, Denise has
o regrets about her tongue piercing. "Now,
's who I am and that's different than who
was before. It's a fad stage of life," said
enise. "I may decide I am bored and
hange my looks again!" ■

what's up doc?
Q & A with prosthodontist, Alexander Chan

A prosthodonist is a dentist specializing in replacing missing teeth with bridges and dentures; they are sometimes refered to as cosmetic dentists.

Q: Why don't you or other doctors and dentists perform any type of oral piercing?

We only do things to enhance your appearance or body—we don't do anything to mutilate it. It's just understood throughout the medical and dental professions not to perform such procedures. It's in our Code of Ethics—oral piercing is hazardous to a patient's oral and general health.

Q: What are some of the hazards and problems associated with oral piercing?

There is always the risk of biting, swallowing or inhaling the piercing—these are all life threatening situations which can occur. You could also have an allergic reaction to the nickel or chrome which is in the jewelry. [In these reactions] the pierced site becomes swollen and usually tender with pus—it usu-

ally subsides once you remove the ring or stud.

Q: Have you ever had any patients with oral piercings? What happened?

One time I had a patient with a tongue ring. She accidentally bit on it when she was eating and fractured one of her molars. Her tooth needed a crown in order to be restored. Sometimes the fracture damages the nerve and requires root canal treatment. In even more severe cases, the tooth can't be restored. It's easy to bite on your [tongue] ring when you're eating since most people leave it in when eating.

Q: What is your advice to those who wish to have an oral piercing?

Don't get one.

IS IT REALLY WORTH IT?
Possible health complications

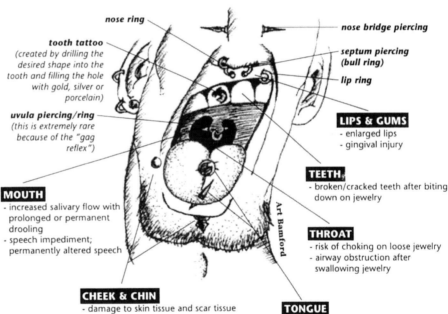

nose ring

nose bridge piercing

septum piercing (bull ring)

lip ring

tooth tattoo
(created by drilling the desired shape into the tooth and filling the hole with gold, silver or porcelain)

uvula piercing/ring
(this is extremely rare because of the "gag reflex")

LIPS & GUMS
- enlarged lips
- gingival injury

TEETH
- broken/cracked teeth after biting down on jewelry

MOUTH
- increased salivary flow with prolonged or permanent drooling
- speech impediment; permanently altered speech

THROAT
- risk of choking on loose jewelry
- airway obstruction after swallowing jewelry

Art Bamford

CHEEK & CHIN
- damage to skin tissue and scar tissue formation

TONGUE
- swelling after the piercing (as much as twice the normal size) which can interfere with breathing and make swallowing difficult
- damaged sense of taste
- blood clots which may induce life-threatening strokes

MISCELLANEOUS EFFECTS
- infection, swelling and pain
- nerve damage
- keloid scars
- contraction of hepatitis, HIV and other bacteria from unsterilized needles
- blood poisoning
- toxic shock
- allergic reactions to jewelry

Fig. 9.2. In this in-depth look at oral piercing, writers localized the story by finding students who had been pierced and who were willing to share their personal stories of the experiences in individual profiles. In addition to the main profiles, a sidebar on piercing artists, a forum of student opinion, a Q&A with a local cosmetic dentist and an information graphic on health complications from piercing amplify the coverage without repeating any information. *Devils' Advocate*, Hinsdale Central High School, Hinsdale, Ill.

What about computer resources in the school? Are filters used to censor student browsing? Are books censored from the library? Do local citizens with extreme viewpoints show up at textbook adoption time?

EXTRACURRICULAR AREAS

Changes in clubs and organizations and student activities will affect every student who participates in them. Some schools have cut funding of club activities; others have restricted student field trips and activities because of funding cuts. Schools are constantly debating whether or not religious clubs can meet or activities can be held during the school day or in school facilities. Prayer before school activities continues to be a national and local issue.

BEYOND THE SCHOOL

Community changes that affect the school should also be examined. Is the school's neighborhood changing in ways that would affect the school? Is the school located on a major street that might be dangerous to cross? Are the lights and turning lanes adequate for the numbers of cars that use them? Has the school started safety measures such as installing radar detectors or locking all entrances except the main one during the school day? The school's effect on the neighborhood should also be considered. Do students gather in stores and fast-food restaurants close to the school? Do these businesses ever restrict the number of students who can be in the store at one time? Have the businesses been in touch with the school about their concerns?

LOCALIZING NATIONAL TRENDS

Obviously, the last few years have been volatile for many schools. Changing times and trends are ripe for in-depth coverage. Offering students the opportunity to voice their concerns about these changes is a valid use of space. Publications can also offer readers forums for discussion of issues as complex as voting rights, drug and alcohol use and abuse, teen pregnancy, body piercing, stress, college acceptance and juggling the stress of school, jobs and financial commitments (Fig. 9.2).

The key to good coverage is localizing the issues—reporting them from your readers' point of view. Stories with a local angle will always be of more interest to the readers of a particular publication. Quotes from local sources will help place the story in context for the publication's readers. Discussing the relevance of the topic to the readers will also be important in helping them place it in context.

Local professional sources can also be interviewed and used as sources to help put the topic in perspective in your local community. For instance, in a story on sexually transmitted diseases in the *Crossfire*, Crossroads High School, Santa Monica, Calif., February 1999, student writers interviewed the assistant director of Teen Health Services at the Westside Women's Health Center, a local community facility, and school counselors. Interviewing local professionals helps provide information relative to the school community.

In-depth reporting should also pique readers' interests about issues that will help them understand the diversity of students in the school, with topics ranging from racial differences and sexual preferences to students who categorize themselves as alternative in the school.

Basically, good journalists listen. They observe. They hear. They bring these observations into the publications arena by discussing them at staff meetings where the exchange of information will help the staff decide how to cover them.

GETTING STARTED

Unlike traditional story reporting, in-depth will usually require far more time. Much of that time will be spent doing research in different forms, from talking to fellow students and teachers to learning and reading on the Internet or in the school or local library. Often, in-depth reporters won't even be able to start interviewing until they've done a fair amount of research so they learn and understand the topics they're writing about. If the topic is one being localized for the school publication, reading national reports will give the reporters access to information that will help form questions and lead the reporters to logical sources and resources. Reporters should be careful to only use this backgrounding information for research and to avoid repeating quotes that have already appeared in print in professional publications, even if attributed to those publications.

Once the basic research has been done, the reporters or teams can begin to understand what kind of space commitment they will need for their in-depth report. Making that decision before the research has been done may only ensure that the story isn't given enough space or is given too much space in the publication. If reporters, editors and photographers are working together, the entire team needs to sit down together to talk through the research and reporting and to decide just how much space will be needed to present the information.

Regardless of the space allocation, the publication should help the reader understand the significance of the information through its placement and layout in the publication. Identifying the story as a special report, in-depth report or other such label will help focus attention on the importance of the information (Fig. 9.3). Starting the story on the front page and continuing it inside the publication is another way of alerting the reader to the special content. This coverage is known as "jump coverage" since it jumps from one page to another. Many yearbooks have begun using jump coverage for serious issue reporting.

Fig. 9.3. In a story that received extensive national media coverage, a male teacher in this California school suffering from gender dysphoria, a disorder that caused him to change his gender to female, resulted in the newspaper staff's decision to publish a special edition of the newspaper to be distributed the first week of school. The newspaper followed an August school board meeting in which the popular teacher was placed on administrative leave with pay. Each story in the four-page edition examined some aspect of the story and included an editorial encouraging the students to fight the board's decision. *Blue and Gold*, Center High School, Antelope, Calif.

FULL-PAGE COVERAGE

In the newspaper, a full page of coverage may be all that's necessary to adequately cover a topic. Even with a full page, the reporter should be discussing the story's angles with a photographer or visual thinker so the story can be visually interesting as well as adequately reported. Well-written, detailed headlines will help the reader understand the importance of this story. Visuals will offer another layer of information that can attract the interest of the reader. With a long article, the layout should also offer some visual text relief such as text heads or drop caps at natural junctures in the story. Or pull quotes from the story can be extracted and used in the layout.

DOUBLE TRUCKS

If the story demands more space, the natural space to consider is the double truck—the center spread, as it is oftentimes referred to (Fig. 9.4). The newspaper will always have two facing pages printed on one sheet of paper that offer options for layout and presentation. Multiple visuals can be used. Information can be presented in a variety of story-telling forms to amplify the main story. This information offers the reader an opportunity to learn something presented in a different way, possibly a more visual way, than the main story. Because readers are attracted to information in different ways, these smaller, different story forms may pull the reader into the main text (see Chap. 20).

BEYOND THE DOUBLE TRUCK

When coverage demands more space, reporters should consider series reporting: stories broken into parts and presented over the course of several issues. The challenge in series reporting is to make sure the information lends itself to a series of stories and to make sure the information is logically presented in the series. Complex topics such as cheating or a series of changes planned for the school's curriculum would work for a series of reports. A visual device such as a logo helps readers identify with the story as it appears in each issue. A series would be less effective in a publication printed monthly or less frequently. Even in a bimonthly or tri-monthly publication, the series should recap the previous reports before presenting the new information so the reader remembers the context of the previous report.

SPECIAL ISSUES

In the case of a story with a strong timeliness factor, such as a tragedy or breaking news event, the staff might consider publishing a special section or a special edition if an event occurs between the publication's publishing deadlines. Marshaling the staff's resources, editors may be able to quickly bring together necessary writers and visual reporters to report and photograph the event. Cooperative publishing efforts between different schools are another possibility if events occur in school districts with multiple campuses. If the staff doesn't have the resources to obtain pictures or other visuals, obtaining copies from local media such as community newspapers is another possibility.

THE YEARBOOK

Yearbook staffs should not overlook the in-depth form for coverage either. In-depth coverage helps change the pacing of storytelling in the yearbook, offering staffs the possibility for longer stories and different reporting. Covering significant or complex issues that have occurred during the year can amplify coverage in other parts of the book. Sports sections can tackle the same kinds of issues as the newspaper or can give special coverage to teams that have won championships. Academic coverage offers possibilities for discussion of curricular changes or changes in policy and procedure. Coverage of issues that help date the year add dimension to student life sections. Many schools have been experimenting with magazine format reporting, using topic-oriented coverage for issues such as pressure, achievement or stress. Focusing on personal profiles of interesting or accomplished students is another way to add some dimension to the coverage. Significant school events during the year that attract large numbers of students are other possibilities for in-depth coverage (Fig. 9.5).

WRITING THE IN-DEPTH STORY

Rarely will traditional news story forms work successfully for the in-depth report. Reporters will need to build the story around the information and the significance of the information that has been gathered. The depth of the information gathered will make the task of organizing the information more important. Talking through the story with the other team members, other reporters or editors will help the process of writing. Writing an in-depth story will be more similar to writing a long feature story: The lead needs to grab the reader's attention and make the story's importance clear from the outset.

Note the way this lead begins on a story titled "A date with Dawson's Creek":

Everyone wants Dawson Leery.

I, on the other hand, don't fall for all of the teen melodrama in Dawson. I am more of a Jack McPhee type of girl. I would take Jack any day. And although Jack recently made his debut on the list of gay characters on prime time, nothing can hide his charming and sensitive nature that deeply appeals to me.

Who would've guessed that one day Kerr Smith, who plays Jack, would have his arm around me as I struggled to find the words to express my teen infatuation? And who would've guessed that later that night I would witness this altruistic heart-throb as he actually cleaned up his puppy's vomit from the floor?

Lauren Mitchell
Mustang
San Dieguito High School Academy
Encinitas, Calif.

Would you continue reading this story? Probably. If your interest in *Dawson's Creek* was strong enough. Maybe even if it wasn't.

Here's another one on a story about three separate summer accidents that killed former or current students of a high school in Ohio.

Attendance secretary Liz Bycynski will always remember answering the phone on July 9, 1998. From the moment she learned of her daughter's automobile accident, Bycynski knew that Kylene would not survive.

Jenny Bindel
Blue and Gold
Findlay High School, Findlay, Ohio

Because reporters will gather information for in-depth reports over a period of time, the deadline pressure of a normal story won't usually apply. This will give the reporters more flexibility in polishing the writing. In addition to an interesting lead, in-depth reporters should make sure they have interesting anecdotes and illustrations, effective transitions, tighter writing and stronger emphasis on the relevance of the topic or event to the reader. A good editor can make a big difference in improving the writing of in-depth reports to make sure the story's organization is clear and logical.

Here's more of the story on *Dawson Creek*. Note the details and anecdotes.

Fig. 9.4. A multifaceted double truck on teen smoking includes several content areas helping to break up the space but amplifying the detail and content of the story. A primary visual area, a photo illustration, also provides the space for the spread's primary headline. In a nod toward creativity, the staff used a typeface that mimics the look of a label maker to create headlines for the story. On the left, a feature on quitting smoking cold turkey provides key information and is attributed to its professional source. On the right, a statistical infographic also credits its source, cleverly using the visual of a cigarette to separate each individual piece of information. In the middle of the main story, a sidebar on quitting is placed in a narrow column in a sans serif typeface on a gray background to visually separate it from the main story. *Hillcrest Hurricane,* Hillcrest High School, Dallas, Texas

Why Aren't TEENS

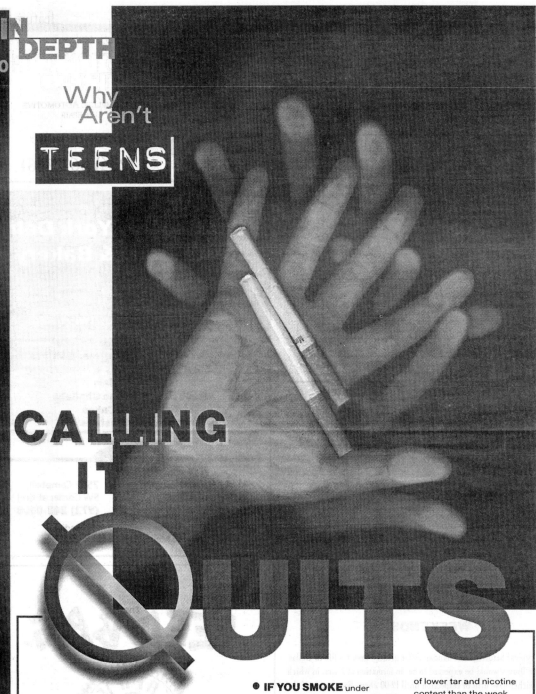

CALLING IT QUITS

Slogans such as "Smoking is a de
campaign, aren't making impacts on tee
smoking everyday, it may be possible th
lighting up. But a new movement is acting t
the 27,000 Texans who, according to the Texa

Junior Adam Kaba decided not to adhere to
found himself with a real addiction – never
smoked a pack a day for three years but

Teens are still pic

A NEW SOLU

Eight hours is all it takes
Department is reporting more
Texas, not yet operational in D
tion and cessation class for bei

Through these statewide e
ers don't quit at earlier ages a
don't work for them, Dr. Denni
who developed the program, s

The course is being praised
getting results but also for bei
ferocious stage _ fully addict
getting just 3000 Texas teens o
American Cancer Society (AC
ing for other states to adopt si

Most of the students atter
pack a day. Some had tried u
cessation never occurred. Thre
four 2–hour classes of tobacco
completely, Dr. Smith said. Al
in quitting but said they will

WANT I

The biggest obstacle for th
pose of these classes is to imp
giving up cigarettes, not bein

"We try to base our classes
when they're ready," Dr. Smith

Any smoker who recogr
whether it's really possible to
ter how much progress the ir
peer's negative additude can
class voluntarily, Dr. Smith sai

When Kaba tried to quit
because he had been smokin
mornings, all he could think a
didn't want to give in. For the
extremely inviting.

"Being around smoke whil
teased with water," Kaba said
smoking, and I knew that if I

Most adults who try to qu
lung cancer especially, psychol
factors and social consequence
in their cessation program, but
their feelings of invincibility.

IF YOU'RE READY...

Quitting cold turkey is hard, even when using the doctor recomended support system, Dr. Enrico said. But there are many tactics to calm the cravings.

- **IF CIGARETTES** give you an energy boost, try gum, modest exercise or a brisk walk. Avoid eating new foods that are high in calories.

- **WHEN YOU CRAVE** cigarettes, you must quit suddenly. Try smoking an excess of cigarettes, so the taste of cigarettes is spoiled.

- **IF YOU SMOKE** under stress at school or work, pick a date to stop smoking when you will not be in either of these two situations.

- **DON'T CARRY** your cigarettes, matches or lighter around with you. Keep them as far away from you as possible while you try to quit.

- **IF YOU LIKE** to smoke with others, make yourself smoke alone. Never smoke while watching television.

- **CHANGE YOUR** brand of cigarettes weekly so that you are always smoking a brand

- of lower tar and nicotine content than the week before.

- **IF YOU GAIN** weight because you are not smoking, wait until you get over the craving to start dieting. It's easier then.

- **AFTER YOU QUIT**, start using your lungs. Increase your activities and indulge in moderate exercise, such as short walks.

Source: Texas Department of Health's Office of Tobacco Prevention and Control

s Department of Health's newest antitobacco
oking each day. Considering 3,000 teens start
cartoons or horror stories will keep kids from
e teens don't become one of
Health, die each year from
tobacco use.
en he was 13 years old and
rmanent his habit was. He
arette in five months after
quitting cold turkey.

Kick ASH

"I started [smoking] when I was 13 just to fit in, then I was addicted. A cigarette to a smoker is like water to an athlete," Kaba said. "I was smoking one night and started hacking up stuff. I was so mad that I threw my cigarettes away."

Because Kaba's self-motivated cessation program happens too rarely for the Texas State Legislature's taste, laws stiffened once again last year with the passing of Senate Bill 55 making minors possessing tobacco as serious as possessing alcohol. But through the development of revolutionary programs, the state is helping teens quit, even if they don't want to quit.

KATHRYN DEES

p the habit, state getting more involved in when they quit

GETTING THERE

When trying to quit smoking, most psychologists suggest a system to cater to your physical and emotional needs. This includes supplements such as nicotine patches and gum. Having a support group to encourage success can be just as important, Dr. Enrico said.

FROM A PSYCHOLOGIST:

Dr. Enrico feels that possibly the most successful cessation process is a gradual one. At the smokers own pace, they choose a specific smoking time during the day, like after lunch, and give that one up. Eventually, all of the "regular" cigarettes are given up and the only thing left to deal with is the spontaneous cravings.

ALSO SUGGESTED:

The Texas Department of Health suggests to start by making a list of reasons to quit and any obstacles that could keep you from succeed-ing.
Choose a date to stop smoking for good. It's best to choose a stress-free time.
Withdrawl symptoms are the main reason people relapse. With support, you can learn to manage them.

BREAKING THE DEFENSES

The instructors are surprised to see careless teens who are able to recite specific numbers of people who die from tobacco-related diseases each year but say they won't be quitting any time soon, especially before they graduate from college.

"Teenagers are famous for believing that bad stuff won't happen to them," Dr. Enrico said. "Death and disease aren't factors in deciding to smoke. In fact, people don't usually come to terms with death until 30 [years old]."

But 20 years come a lot quicker than smokers realize, Dr. Smith said. Most of the adults who are trying to quit today were once teens who didn't care either. The mission of the course instructors is to make teens understand quitting now is easier than dying later.

It was this fear that made sophomore Kimberly Johnson° determined not to become like her mother. Kimberly began smoking with her two best friends more than two years ago. Her mother also began smoking as a high school freshman. Kimberly smoked half a pack a day became concerned with her new "smoker's cough."

Thinking she might also be losing the connection to her friends, she reluctantly decided to quit, never telling her friends. She felt that some of the best times she had with her friends was while they shared a pack of Marlboro Lights and sat in the middle of her bedroom talking.

"A lot of teens don't realize when they start smoking, that they're doing it to fit in and identify with a certain group of people," Dr. Smith said "Asking them to quit, is like asking them to give up their friends."

Kimberly felt that to keep from becoming like her mother, who tried repeatedly to quit smoking, she needed to quit now.

THE ADDICTION

The course instructors quickly realized addiction needed to be dealt with very realistically after seeing that most of the students didn't think cessation was necessary within the next few years because they would be quitting around the age of 21. Smoking was just a temporary fix for stress for most teens as the course's surveys found.

"Smoking is as addictive as heroine and cocaine. And the more you smoke, it just gets worse. Waiting to quit doesn't make it any easier," Dr. Enrico said. "The younger you are when you start, the harder it is to quit."

With each cigarette a teenager smokes now, it will lead to a more serious addiction later in life. According to the Food and Drug Administration, two cigarettes in the bloodstream of a high school senior, 10 years later will require an entire pack to fulfill the addiction.

"We don't believe everyone who comes through [the state cessation program] is going to become a nonsmoker. But we want them to think about it," Dr. Smith said "And at the end of the course, we survey them again and the age they say they'll quit drops to 19. So that means they're thinking about it." **H**

°Name changed to protect identity

Contributions to this story were made by Adrienne Brown

3000 teens smoke their first cigarette each day, equaling more than one million annually. Approximately one-third of these children smokers will die of smoking-related illnesses.

The average teen smoker starts at age 12 and becomes a daily smoker by age 18.

Of adolescents who have smokes at least 100 cigarettes in their lifetime, most of them report they would like to quit but are unable to do so.

Currently, over 43 percent of high school students use tobacco products.

The annual American death toll attributed to tobacco use is about 430,700. This is the equivalent of three jumbo jets crashing every day of the year in the United States with no survivors.

Tobacco kills Americans in the prime time of life; 27 percent of Americans who die between the ages of 35 and 64 die from tobacco-related diseases.

Among high school students, a greater number of girls smoke than boys.

If a person can make it to age 19 without picking up a smoking habit, experts say there's a 90 percent chance he'll never smoke.

LOOK.

Surrounded by young men dressed in suits and young ladies in satin dresses, Matt Clendenin (10) marched to his own beat and dressed in his Pez best. Who decided what was in or out, what was cool or what was not? You did!

P. C.H.S.?

I think something is politically correct when nothing is weird or different. Who is to say what's weird? Clayton's not what I would consider to be overly politically correct, but that's probably impossible in any high school. Why fix something that doesn't need fixing? The differences that are around everyday prepare us for the real world.
• *Ingrid Smith* (11)

Is CHS P.C.? On one hand, Clayton students

"I think we genuinely strive to be politically correct, but there are a lot of things that make us not that way. A lot of people have stereotypes about everyone and everything that people believe, including the teachers. Some of the teachers, for example, are really prejudiced against some of the students. If a student is in good standing with good grades, they get easier treatment than someone with not such good grades. Also, sometimes they walk into a classroom and expect more from students of certain races."
•*Chris Bollinger* (11)

As a member of Community Service Club, Nancy Lang (11) plays with an inner city child.

12 • Politically Correct

Fig. 9.5. In a special section toward the front of the yearbook called "Look," student editors tackled a series of timely topics in two-page spreads. The section further defined the book's overall theme: "Made You Look." The book's format turned the normal 7.75 × 10.5-inch printing size horizontal, resulting in wide, two-page spreads.

Notice how Lauren puts us there as she tells us what it's like on the set.

But then again, who would've guessed that one day I would hang out with not only Jack, but Dawson, Pacey, Joey, Jen, and Andy of the hottest teen show to hit TV? Not me. But I guessed wrong.

Walking through the halls of Capeside High, I felt comfortable. I had been there before. Every Wednesday night, I watched the same halls, and saw the same faces. But from being actually there, I found out how shy James Van Der Beek really was and the fact that Michelle Williams only wore a size-five shoe. I discovered that Joshua Jackson lugs his black lab, Shuma, with him everywhere and that Kerr Smith smells like "Cool Water" in person. And to think, it all happened in the small town of Wilmington.

The town rests on the Southeast shore of North Carolina, along the Cape Fear River. I had just stepped off a jet at the world's smallest airport, or so it seemed, and taken my first breath of the Southern evening. Our taxi cab driver explained that it was "definitely a college town," and that it could be "sleepy at times."

Outside the cab window, trees slipped beyond hills and eventually into quiet marshes and shorelines. We rolled along the historic streets of Wilmington, heading toward the water.

I was there to experience one of the hottest teen TV shows in the history of television. Its unprecedented ranking among young audiences has made its stars into demigods of the screen. I pondered actually meeting the celebrities of "Dawson's Creek" as another quiet beach cottage passed by the cab, its lit windows glowing.

I landed upon this great opportunity to meet the cast and crew of

"Dawson's Creek" and spend a day on the set with them by very good fortune. Our family is good friends with one of the cast member's family and arrangements were made for me to visit the set and spend five days on the Atlantic shore.

When I awoke the next morning, the sun was already high above the water. Wilmington had a tranquil quality of light, just as it appears on television—beautiful, warm and charming. On the other hand, it took quaint to an extreme. The same cab driver, Ski, who picked me up at the airport, also arrived to take me to the studio where they filmed "Dawson's Creek." In fact, Ski became my faithful cabby for the rest of the four days.

I was greeted at the Screengems Studio by a familiar looking PA (personal assistant) named Craig. I later learned that he was also the sassy fan who practically drooled on Rex Manning in the flick "Empire Records." Craig was responsible for checking all of the actors in and out, as well as making sure they were on set when they need-

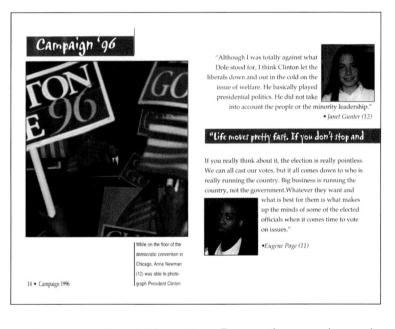

ed to be. Two huge studios loomed over my head like old trees. "This one," he pointed out, "is where we keep the houses you see on the show. Dawson's house, Jen's house, and Joey's house." As we approached the other studio, he pushed the door open.

Inside, a painting of a scenic landscape covered the walls and studio lights were pervasive. As we stepped around a series of upright wooden planks I found myself in Capeside High School. Advertisements for the dance club and the yearbook cluttered the yellow halls and a group of typical high school students gabbed around the lockers. Had it not been for the

Topics on these spreads ranged from politics to cultural diversity and helped provide context and broadened the book's historical value. *Claymo*, Clayton High School, Clayton, Mo.

SARA FLORIN
Goin' My Way?

Speed Zone Ahead

When I told my friends I resolved to drive the speed limit in 1999, a resounding, sarcastic "why?" overwhelmed my parents' approval.

Does that surprise me?

No. Not in a country where the president's approval ratings go up after he is impeached for allegedly lying under oath and obstructing justice.

American society breeds lax behavior for "minor offenses" - a broken promise, running a red light, shoplifting.

Kids and teenagers often run around with an "If I don't get caught, it doesn't matter" mentality. Sometimes, this mentality spreads to "If I get caught but it was fun anyway, it doesn't matter."

Speeding, with its minor $75 penalty, means so little to a wealthy Naperville teen. Maybe it's a wasted 14 hours at work, a weekend spent grounded or a little groveling at daddy's feet.

Believe it or not, some of us run around with the mentality I just mentioned, and immorality has actually permeated our Napervillian bubble.

But it's so easy to rationalize speeding. When put in perspective with doing heroin or committing homicide, maybe speeding isn't so bad. In fact, it isn't bad at all - so why not do it?

But that insane rationalization, made in the minds of thousands of drivers everywhere, is not my point right now.

Why do Americans feel little or no moral responsibility to themselves or anyone else?

Honesty, too, is a virtue, and that means moral excellence. Don't we have a responsibility to uphold other people's safety through something as simple as obeying the law?

I think we do, and in 600 words or less, I'd like to try to make a point without sounding like the Wicked Witch of Moralityville.

Whether your religion or your good conscience dictates it, don't lie to people.

Obviously, a situation like in Liar, Liar would be unreasonable and extreme. The line has to be drawn somewhere.

Perhaps choosing not to tell someone something is fair, but deceiving him is not.

The gray areas extend farther, though. Is it wrong to lie to kids about Santa Claus and the spectrum of tooth-exchanging fairies and egg-leaving rabbits?

Perhaps it isn't wrong, but is it necessary? Only tradition and culture would dictate it as such.

How does speeding relate to lying? It boils down to morality. Are you moral enough to drive 30 m.p.h. down West Street even when Camaro Cop isn't lurking in the gravel lot?

In my mind, morality encompasses everything from not swearing to keeping promises - wouldn't it be nice to be able to put faith in another person's word because you knew he had a high moral standard.

Yes, it would - but only in an ideal world. But even though I don't speed and preach about moral standards, I break so many other "moral codes" that it's a world I could never be part of.

So, maybe I can't convince you that driving the speed limit falls into the moral necessities category. Talk is cheap, but lies are expensive.

As far as my resolution, I've stuck to being passed and honked at (mostly by teenagers) for the sake of being able to control my actions.

And, I've noticed that instead of speeding to each stoplight and waiting for the green, I can sail through as the light changes just before I arrive - probably the speed limit's only perk. Moral or not, at least I stopped having those reoccurring nightmares about getting a ticket.

Little White Lies?

▶ Today's moral climate relies less on the "honor system" than ever before and sends a dual message. Students admit cheating on everything from homework to final exams, and a low percentage have been caught. But is cheating the only way to get ahead in one of the nation's top districts?

In a competitive atmosphere, cheating remains some students' last resort

by malini rao

Stretching her arms to lean over and snatch a quick glance at her shoe; twirling his pencil as his eyes scan his neighbor's paper; blatantly whispering answers through a secret code; students everywhere must face the dilemma of answering tough questions on their own, or weaning off of another's hard work.

Faced with a zero on the exam, suspension, or even expulsion, cheaters know the consequences of their actions. However, even though the punishments for cheating have grown in severity, cheating still occurs in high school and in the adult world.

Driven by their GPA, or parental expectations, high school students cheat because "cheating is more acceptable to make the cut," senior Dave Urlakis said. "Cheating is terribly wrong but more and more necessary [for college]."

Some students, nevertheless, have avoided cheating at Central. "[Cheating] throws off rank and curve," senior Carolyn Torson said. "People make excuses and do the little thing, [then cheat] on bigger things in life."

But cheaters can affect fellow students, not only through ranks and curves, according to junior Matt Nord. "People who cheat get better grades and may make other people cheat [to meet the competition]," he said.

Sophomore Jenny Kombs* knows that when she cheats, "it's wrong, but [I] do it to get ahead." Students cheat to get into a better college or to live up to their goals, according to Kombs.

"[Catching cheaters] is more of a prerogative of the staff member," Dean Bill Seiple said. "[But] the competition we put on [students fosters cheating]." Aware that the stakes are high, Seiple feels students "think they must be better than the next guy to get into college."

"Sometimes we send mixed messages," he said. "We teach how to efficiently study, the tricks of the trade, but then we say 'don't cross this line.'"

But cheating isn't limited to worksheets and tests in high school. Everyday at the lunch table, rumors fly about who's dishonest in a relationship.

"It's totally disrespectful," Torson said. "[In a relationship] you wouldn't want [someone to cheat on you]; you have to be honest." Nord agreed, saying, "You should be faithful to the person you're with."

"I've done it, but I'm not proud of it," Kombs said. "Morally, I feel bad, but it's just something in high school—it's not a time to be with a serious relationship." Kombs questions the necessity of staying true to a relationship when "you're not going steady."

"Things in high school are far different from real life," she said. "In real life [cheating] is a loss, but in high school [cheating] is a gain [because you meet different people]."

But although students feel that cheaters can get away with most of their behaviors in high school, many think that the real world is much more difficult.

"In the real world, it's harder to cheat or squirm your way into anything," Kombs said. "There is always a penalty."

"People get caught and must face the consequences," Torson said. Urlakis agreed, adding, "People can't try to cut corners all the time; everybody needs to play by the same rules because altering the standard makes it harder to achieve it."

Kombs added, "Adults should set the standard, show us what is right and wrong."

With soap operas demonstrating a million ways in which to cheat on a spouse, and with businesses using underhanded techniques to close deals, Kombs feels that adults in the real world should show students the correct, moral behaviors.

The advantages of cheating far outweigh the disadvantages, according to many high school students. Although there is always the possibility of getting caught, students "shortcut work and effort, making time for other things like activities and sleep," Urlakis said.

"Even though it's wrong, people do it anyway for the heck of it," Nord said. "They can't get ahead any other way." Kombs agreed, adding, "When stuff depends on it [cheating], it's hard not to, although that doesn't justify [the act]."

Although the proverb says cheaters never prosper, some students wonder if cheaters always prosper. Catching a cheater in high school is more difficult than ever thanks to high tech devices and students' ingenuity.

Teachers must depend on the integrity of the student, Seiple said. Although cheating continues in the real world, more students are able to swindle their way out of it in high school.

Only with increased supervision during test times will cheating diminish.

*Name has been changed to protect identity.

percent of students answering "yes"

STUD

H

WESTERVELT

Caught red-handed

Student shares her experience to reveal the truth about lie detectors

by laura zimmermann

"Can I come in and take a polygraph test?"

"You want to what?" the secretary on the other end of the line asked disgustedly.

"Um, I figure an interesting way to research lie-detector tests is to take one myself...," I answered half-heartedly.

A few seconds later, I hung up the phone, defeated. The Naperville Police Department has its own Camaro, but no polygraph instrument; figures. The local police call independent companies and pay them to do the "lie-detecting."

So my possible rendezvous with the famous "lie-detector" remained unfulfilled.

I share the wonder and curiosity with many regarding a machine which distinguishes truth from deception when even I sometimes have a hard time putting my finger on reality.

Despite my failed attempt to challenge the polygraph instrument, I spoke with Detective Ken Keating of the Naperville Police Department

"Generally, we avoid using it on people under the age of 16," he said. "Their physical reactions haven't stabilized yet."

Polygraph testing is, after all, a measure of three things: palm sweat, also known as galvanic skin response, blood pressure and respiratory response. In theory, when one lies in response to the polygrapher's questions, one fears getting caught. This fear sparks physiological changes which the polygraph measures.

Sounds simple to me. Control your breathing, tell yourself you'll be okay, don't fear getting caught.

However, Keating shared with me the most common outcome when suspects ask to take a polygraph (perhaps trying to beat the machine, I thought).

After the electrodes are attached to their palms, the sphygmomanometer cuff placed about their bicep, and the respiratory sensor strapped around their chest, the subject fails miserably. "We get the head drop, the deep sigh and the 'All right, I did it.'"

According to polygrapher Jerry Wohl, studies conducted in 1972 found that in 4,039 test subjects who were evaluated by a polygraph instrument, only three errors were made. According to Wohl, when feeling fear, a person's sympathetic nervous system (SNS) voluntarily takes charge of the body, increasing heart rate and dilating irises, blood vessels and lungs. Also, sweat glands kick in.

The polygraph instrument measures the level of SNS in use. The level is practically proven to sky-rocket in response to questions where lying occurs.

Some argue that polygraphs only measure general emotional arousal. Someone nervous about the test or unaccustomed to having his word questioned may fail.

In Illinois, polygraph tests showing guilt may not be used in court if the dependent pleads not guilty, according to Keating, but tests proving innocence can be used as evidence. In other words, the state believes the test can beat you, but you can't beat the test.

My teenage invincibilty factor shouts loud and clear: I could beat it. Of course, I underestimate the elusive polygraph instrument. But, who can help it when being a successful member of society seems to entail beating "lie-detectors" everyday. We all just thank our stars that the "white-lie detector" hasn't been invented...yet.

The Proof is in the Polygraph

▶ The term "polygraph" means "many writings," referring to the physiological activities which are simultaneously recorded.

▶ The two researchers responsible for the modern lie detector test are John Larson and Leonard Keeler.

▶ The test consists of three phases: the pre-test interview, the test and the post-test phase.

▶ All questions require a simple "yes" or "no" answer.

▶ To establish physical responses, the examiner develops baseline readings for questions called known truths. For example, the examiner might ask, "Are you 17 years old?"

▶ Twenty-eight states, including Illinois, prohibit use of polygraph evidence in court.

▶ Want to beat the lie detector? Take a tranquilizer before the polygraph session. Some simple countermeasures, such as stepping on a nail concealed in a shoe, can fake a strong reaction to the control questions, thus "beating" the test.

sources: FBI Educational
Internet Publications
www.polygraphplace.com

valent is cheating?

The Questions

1. Have you ever copied homework from anyone?

2. Have you ever told or asked other students what was on a quiz or test?

3. Have you ever used a cheat sheet on a quiz, test or final exam or look at another student's paper during a quiz, test or final exam?

4. Have you ever plagiarized an essay or research paper from a book or bought an essay or research paper from the Internet?

5. Have you ever helped another student by giving him homework, allowing him to copy off your test or writing an essay for him?

6. Have you ever used Cliff's notes or watched a movie to avoid reading a novel?

sted at right)

cheated, **9 percent** said they were **caught.**
he punishment was appropriate.

lso asked to choose all applicable reasons for
answers or cheating on tests. They are ranked as
pular to least popular answer):

rn the material or do the work
ter grade
to maintain current grade in class
work
material was necessary

810 students surveyed

Fig. 9.6. In this double-truck coverage of white lies, a dominant typographical headline provides entry into the main story; the headline is connected to a drawing that strongly connects to the verbal message. The use of the outline-type letters on the word "White" is another clever visual/verbal connection. The secondary, or deck, head provides good detail in its three sentences. The staff used a very comprehensive survey of 810 students as the basis for an infographic box that accompanies the story. Extracting statistics from stories and using them in visual forms is always a good idea. One sidebar column on a student who volunteered to take a polygraph test to write about it provides an interesting dimension to the content. Note how bullet points in a contrasting sans serif typeface summarize important information about polygraphs while adding to the content of the sidebar. An additional column piques readers' interest by challenging them to think of speeding without getting caught as another form of immorality in a lax society. *Central Times*, Naperville Central High School, Naperville, Ill.

cameras, sound systems, crew members and TV monitors, I would have felt right at home. Before I had a chance to settle myself into the set (it's difficult adjusting to standing in the middle of the high school that you watch on TV every Wednesday night) I heard the familiar voice of Dawson Leery coming around the corner.

James Van Der Beek, the actor who plays the idealistic Dawson, was an enigma to me. I was struck dumb. I'm not the type of person who would pass out if I met Madonna but I couldn't believe that the Dawson Leery was standing ten feet away from me.

Another important consideration is keeping multiple sources straight in the reporting. Readers need to keep straight the names and identities of the sources quoted in the story. Information can become difficult to understand if the readers can't follow the source of the quoted material or remember who that source is.

In the continuation of this story from The Findlay, Ohio, *Blue and Gold*, note how the writer keeps the multisources straight.

"The highway patrol called and said that she (Kylene) was being life-flighted but I knew in my heart she was already dead (which she was). I just prayed that she didn't suffer," Bycynski said.

Soon after hearing that her daughter had been killed, Bycynski started the process of dealing with her emotions.

"At first I prayed that she wouldn't suffer and that I would have the strength to go on. I did everything I had to do like making the funeral arrangements and then I was a basketcase, crying and upset," Bycynski said.

This summer, because of three tragic accidents resulting in the deaths of Bycynski, 1990 Graduate Ben Lunn and 1994 Graduate Andy May, many have had to find their own ways of dealing with death.

Missing pieces

Junior Elizabeth Schwartz lost her cousin, Lunn, after a skydiving accident in South Carolina this July.

"His death was surprising because he had been in the hospital after the accident, but the doctors were hopeful that he would make it. He just had a sudden backfall (in recovery) and we lost him," Schwartz said.

Lunn's former History Teacher Dan Matheny found his accident to be unbelievable.

"Ben was just a great kid. He went into the Army Rangers and his mom would be worried whenever he would make a jump (skydive) but I used to tell her that if there was anyone I'm not worried about it's Ben.

"You just felt like nothing could ever happen to Ben. When he died, I felt like a liar and a thief," Matheny said.

Schwartz, however, found aspects of Lunn's death comforting.

"I was glad that he was happy before he died and he was doing something that he loved to do right before he died. He struggled to live (during a hospital stay after the accident) but he didn't make it. It was the way God wanted it," Schwartz said.

Schwartz's family also helped each other deal with the tragedy.

"We got really close as a family after Ben's death. We're a close family anyway, but we really tried to give each other support and we all called to South Carolina to see how he was doing two or three times a day," Schwartz said.

Junior Meghann Vermillion, a friend of Kylene Bycynski, also relied on other people to deal with her grief.

"I talked with my parents and I was in her funeral (as a pallbearer) because I went to her church. Basically, I just talked with other people who knew her, especially in our church," Vermillion said.

The circumstances of Bycynski's death changed the way Vermillion dealt with it.

"Her death was different because it wasn't her fault (it was accidental). She was so young and she had so much to live for," Vermillion said. Bycynski had a similar reaction because of the circumstances surrounding her daughter's death.

"The hardest part is that her death could have been prevented. The young man driving could have slowed down, and Kylene asked him to slow down (according to the driver), but the point is that it was a preventable death," Bycynski said.

However, the anger Bycynski feels is not directed toward the driver, but rather the accident itself.

"I'm not angry at him, I'm angry at what happened. I'm angry when I see my family struggling because of what happened," Bycynski said.

Emotional impact

Watching others deal with the loss of her brother, Andy May, is also difficult for Freshman Kate May.

"It's really hard watching all of his friends, because nothing major has ever happened in their circle of friends, no one has gotten really sick or lost anyone. That's the hardest part," Kate May said.

Ironically, one of May's close friends, 1994 Graduate Arnie Niekamp, found watching May's family to be most difficult.

"It's hard to see the family and all that's expected of them during the funeral ceremonies. For a family that just lost their son to have to stand there for two hours by his coffin and talk to everyone that comes by (during the visitation) is very difficult," Niekamp said.

Putting the focus on others was indeed one of the ways Niekamp coped.

"You focus on other people that are there a lot, like the family, and try to comfort others so you don't have to worry about yourself," Niekamp said.

Now, he finds that his emotions about his friend's death are mixed.

"I don't really think about it much anymore (having moved to Arizona), which is good and bad. In some ways you don't want to let go of the sadness because it's all you really have left. After awhile there just becomes a sense of something missing," Niekamp said.

Learning to cope

Dealing with her own emotions is difficult for Kate May as well.

"It (her brother's death) is not really real yet. Some days I think about it a lot, and other days it hardly crosses my mind. When I do think about it, I try to put it behind me, like if I blink my eyes hard enough it will just go away," May said.

Matheny, May's former Forensics coach, looks for a way to ignore the accident with anger.

"I wish there was something I could point to and be against, but I can't be against accidents (like May's). I would feel better if I had something to blame or be mad at, but there is little for me to feel angry towards," Matheny said.

Reminders of May bring back the pain of his death for Matheny.

"I have to drive through the intersection where the accident happened (in Delaware, Ohio) probably 10 or 20 times a year and I can't drive through it without thinking about him, that this is where he died," Matheny said.

Bycynski finds that little things bring back emotions about her daughter's death as well.

"Now it's an emotional rollercoaster. Anything that might remind you of her, like a song or a movie, it just brings it all back," Bycynski said.

Bycynski and her family are dealing with these feelings in counseling.

"We go to counseling as a family and read books. We have also joined a type of grief counseling group. People are getting us through with lots of support from family and friends," Bycynski said.

Today, her outlook can best be summarized by the motto that sits by her desk.

"Be a living memorial to Kylene by being the best you can be, enjoying life and by making a difference."

Vermillion finds that Kylene's death has inspired her in a similar way.

"I guess her death was different because it wasn't her fault. Remembering her makes me want to just live each day to the fullest," Vermillion said.

ANONYMOUS SOURCES

When reporting controversial or sensitive topics, students may request that reporters not use their real names. Using them may prevent the student from agreeing to be interviewed for the story. Using a real name or closely identifying circumstances of a student's particular situation could cause embarrassment and ridicule. Reporters should be sensitive to the need to protect identity when the story is sensitive or controversial, but the publication should have a policy in place for dealing with anonymous sources. (See Chapter 22 for more information on this topic.) In the following story on drugs, the newspaper chose to change students' names to avoid problems when the story was published. Asterisks by the names indicated a name change.

> All hell was breaking loose in Brian's apartment. It was the day of DHS senior

*Josh's eighteenth birthday. He and *Mike, also a senior, had left Josh's parents' house to find a "real" party, leaving Josh's mom with a black forest cake to eat herself. They had made their way to the small, private party at *Brian's apartment. Upon arriving they had taken three hits of acid each. Instead of seven people in the two-room, 680 sq. ft. apartment, there were now nine—and anyone else who wanted to wish Josh a happy birthday would be arriving soon.

Heather Bell
Update
Herbert Henry Dow High School
Midland, Mich.

LAYERING INFORMATION

Beginning with the headline, readers should understand the story's intent: where the story is heading and what its details will provide. The story's lead should be interesting and relevant to the reader. Visuals, whether photographic or illustrative, should add to the information provided in the story. Alternative story forms such as sidebars, infographics, factoids, quote boxes or question/answer formats should amplify the information in the story form, rather than repeating information in the story itself. Complicated statistics or numerical information should be extracted from the story and presented in alternative story format, where this information will be more easily understood by the readers (Fig. 9.6).

THE NEED FOR ACCURACY

In-depth reporting often involves complicated and complex information. It may require the journalist to find meaning in numbers, to examine public records or to edit a lot of information that may have occurred over a course of time. Working with a good editor will ensure that information is logical and clearly and accurately presented. Numbers and dates should be checked and rechecked for accuracy of information. Complex quotes should be simplified so they are easy to understand. Running quotes—those that are too long to contain in one paragraph—should be an option. Running quotes don't use closing quotation marks until the end of the quote. Each new paragraph of quoted material begins with opening quotation marks.

In-depth reports are among the most important forms of reporting for student publications. Not only do they provide important information but they provide context and texture for the events that occur during the year.

EXERCISES

1. Make a list of possible topics for in-depth coverage in your newspaper or yearbook. Divide your list into beat areas that are currently used by student reporters or beats that could be used to generate topics. Or use the examples of possible beats discussed in this chapter, beginning with school boards.

2. During class changes, during lunch periods and using time before, during and after school for a complete week, make a list of topics that students are talking about with each other. Write down all topics, including those that would not, at first, appear to be subjects for stories in the school paper. Bring the lists back to class the next week and make lists from everyone's lists. What topics appear most often on the lists? What topics have you already covered? What topics should be further discussed?

3. Using professional newspapers or magazines, find examples of three in-depth stories. Find one that begins on the front page (or cover) and continues somewhere else. Find one story that only takes up one page (or spread). Find one story that includes one form of visual storytelling (see Chap. 20). Analyze the stories and answer the following questions:

   a. What is the news value of this story?

   b. How many sources were used in the story?

   c. What background information appears?

   d. What anecdotes and personal information are included?

e. Are the sources kept separate and logically referred to?

4. Using one of the in-depth story ideas generated in exercise 2, brainstorm for a possible headline idea and for visuals to accompany the story.

5. Using one of the in-depth story ideas generated in exercise 2, begin backgrounding the story by doing some research on the topic. Begin by consulting resources available in your library or through the Internet. Prepare a list of information resources for the topic. Next, make a list of possible local sources; use the local phone book or other local resources. Prepare a list of questions you would ask of your local resources.

6. Using an in-depth story published in your school newspaper or yearbook, or in an exchange publication, find an example of an in-depth story or account. Analyze it by answering these questions:

   a. Is the topic relevant to the school, and is that relevance clear?

   b. Has the story been localized?

   c. Does the story contain difficult statistical or numerical information that needs to be extracted from the text?

   d. How many sources were quoted? Is the source information clear and relevant?

   e. Does the story contain effective anecdotal evidence?

   f. Do you lose interest in the topic? If so, at what point and why?

   g. Does the story answer all your reader questions? If not, which questions still need to be answered?

7. Read a week's worth of copies of your local community newspaper for possible in-depth coverage ideas or go online and read five different online newspapers from different locations.

Compile a list of 10 story ideas that could be localized and used in the school newspaper. Compile a list of sources and resources.

8. Invite a couple of members of the school board and your principal to class to discuss possible changes or issues being discussed by your school board, your district and the state's educational governing body. Have an informal discussion with the school officials about coverage of these and other topics. Discuss coverage of controversial topics that affect your school or that students are talking about that you would like to see covered. What suggestions do the school officials have for covering sensitive or controversial topics?

9. Read the following story in which the student's identity was protected (see *). Do you think it was necessary for the writer to omit the identity? Are there clues provided that would make the student's identity obvious to a student reader? Is this an appropriate use of changing the identity of students?

Effects of drinking and driving spill over into adulthood: A night like any other turned into a nightmare for two teens

The sirens flashed and the ambulance came to a deadly halt. The street lights cast an eerie glow on the pavement and a young boy's body lay twisted at the curb. Shards of glass glistened and alcohol laced his breath. It could have been anyone, but on this night, it was him. It was him, and he was only 16.

"We'd done it a hundred times before but just didn't think about it. Someone tried to stop us, but we were like, whatever. We'd seen it on TV, but when you're 16, you think 'It could never happen to me.' That's the world's biggest cliché," Jeff* said.

The night ended with a bad accident and a dead friend. No one knew who was driving, and at that point no one cared.

They were just two average high school boys. Both did relatively well in school, played sports and liked girls. On the weekends, they partied.

He'd only had a few drinks and although no one was supposed to leave, both Jeff and his friend thought they could handle it. "We all put our keys in the hat, but it wasn't like we'd never done it before," he said.

Despite attempts to stop them, the two got into the silver-gray car and rolled out of the driveway. Neither was sure who should drive or which route to take. It didn't matter why they left. As they headed down the main roads and veered onto the side streets, Jeff and his friend began to take driving less seriously. In a split second the car had struck the curb, rolled viciously, and Jeff's friend lay silent, just outside his reach.

"I wish I would've known that could have happened," he said. "We just wondered where we could find our next buyer—no second thoughts."

In a single night, it was over, but the pain followed Jeff into the upcoming week and still remains with him to this day.

"The whole time they said, 'Oh no, he's going to be all right,' but they lied to me. I knew they were lying," Jeff said. "The entire time I didn't care about me. I was scared and wanted things to be okay."

Only a few hours after reaching the hospital, Jeff's friend was pronounced dead. "I knew it before they told me," he said.

The days that followed were riddled with guilt, fear and worry. How could anything like this happen to someone so young, so innocent, and with so much potential?

At school, some people were dealing well

with it while others found it difficult to grieve and even harder to cope. The hallways echoed mourning and Jeff felt sick.

"Some people were like 'What the hell is wrong with you? How could you let this happen,'" Jeff said. "And others tried to tell me it wasn't my fault. But if it wasn't my fault, whose fault was it?"

The emotional wounds were still fresh and Jeff had to face his friend's parents before he could heal.

"The hardest thing I had to do in my whole life was to tell his parents I was driving the car," he said. "They told me they were glad I told them and they were glad it wasn't me."

Though the days at school were extremely difficult to deal with, nothing could compare to the funeral Jeff had to face only a few days after the accident.

"I remember going in there to see him. That was the worst part by far. When you see the person in there and they're dead," Jeff said. "I remember the smell—I'll never forget the way he looked. Seeing him there, dead, was the worst part. You could tell there was a lot of make-up; it didn't look like him."

With the accident behind him, Jeff never did forget. "I never tried to," he said.

For years he didn't drink and was even paranoid when his parents had a glass of wine with dinner. "I've never driven drunk since," he said. "I hang out with some of the same people and they haven't learned anything from it.

"When it's not you, they still think, 'It'll never happen to me,'" he pauses. "And like I said, that's the biggest cliché ever."

Update
Herbert Henry Dow High School
Midland, Mich.

Covering Entertainment

Spending the evening parked on the couch watching two World Wrestling Federation featured stars duke it out in what many people could only describe as "acting" might not appeal to everyone. But whether students spend their money on the latest CD by their favorite artist, the newest action movie on DVD or a decent meal to impress a new date, students like to be entertained. New forms of entertainment aimed at young viewers, such as many of the programs on the WB network, continue to evolve.

Students spend their free time and weekends listening to music, going to movies, renting videos, watching television, attending plays, reading, eating out and participating in a wide array of activities that draw their interests. These activities, more than anything else that goes on in school, bond students to each other through shared interests. School publications can hardly afford to ignore entertainment if they want their coverage to appeal to student readers. Entertainment can be broadly interpreted to include everything from seasonal coverage of events such as Halloween haunted houses to coverage of the fall television lineup.

Entertainment reporting can also include coverage of lifestyle topics such as fashion and health and fitness, particularly if the publication doesn't offer a section tailored to student interests outside of school. As in other forms of reporting, entertainment writers need to make sure they are backing up their opinions with specific facts and examples.

Good entertainment sections seek to offer a broad range of entertainment coverage. Students should consider the varied forms of entertainment available to them when deciding on content and coverage. These include movies, music (live and recorded), plays and performances, television, books, restaurants, videos, games, museum exhibits and web sites. Beyond these forms, subcategories of genres exist. For instance, music falls into categories as broad as country to heavy metal. A good entertainment section seeks to cover all interests, not just those of the writers on the staff. Inviting voices into the newspaper's coverage from outside the staff will help diversify this coverage.

Entertainment in school publications takes four primary forms:

- Advance stories—those that appear in the publication before an event occurs. These stories help create interest in upcoming events and provide students with information about attending the event, purchasing tickets and what to anticipate from the event.

- Reviews—student critiques of entertainment in which student writers offer their opinions about events that have already occurred or about new releases or issues.

- Columns—personal, on-going articles that provide information about various entertainment topics, usually about narrowly focused topics.

Fig. 10.1. An advance story about a swing dance planned specifically for high school students gives readers an idea of what to expect at the dance, how much it costs to attend and the hours for dancing. The page's feature story is complemented by a calendar listing events of interest divided by categories. *Axe*, South Eugene High School, Eugene, Ore.

• Features—stories whose focus is built around particular topics or events with entertainment angles.

WRITING THE ADVANCE STORY

When events are occurring in your community or in nearby communities that appeal to students in the school, they can be covered in advance of the actual performance (Fig. 10.1). When possible, editors should assign these stories to students who are interested in the particular artists or events; these students will create stronger stories because of their greater understanding.

Advance stories about musical performances should mention new information such as the release of a new CD or hit single that often provides the basis for such events. Describing past performances will give the readers a basis for comparison between the new and previous performances.

Writers should be careful not to draw information from professional publications when writing advance stories. Writers should not quote professional publications that have had opportunities to interview the artist or the performance. Instead, the writer should concentrate on interviewing students who have seen the performer previously or who are fans of the performer and can talk with an informed voice about new releases and likely highlights of the upcoming event.

Providing extra information, such as the dates, times and locations of the performance, the cost of tickets and the availability of tickets will be useful to student readers. In suburban areas or outlying locations, maps to the performance venue can also be helpful to students interested in attending the event, particularly when held in downtown locations in large cities.

Students should be industrious in seeking to obtain copies of publicity pictures to use with the advance stories. Students can use file photos of a previous performance or could contact a local record store to get press kits or publicity photos. The Internet can also be a source for students seeking to contact record labels. It also is becoming more common for performers to "go live" in online chat rooms to answer fans' questions. Many performers are using the Internet to get in touch with their fans and create stronger interest in their latest releases. Snippets of songs from new albums are often available through audio clips on the Internet.

Often, reporters can obtain and use CD-ROM publicity information provided by the promoters' or performers' labels or movie distributors. These CDs often provide downloadable digital images and other useful publicity information. Information about television seasons and new shows is constantly available on the networks' web sites.

In large cities, it wouldn't be possible to write advance stories about every upcoming event. Editors should seek diverse coverage appealing to a wide range of student interests. Coverage can be supplemented with the publication of an ongoing calendar of listings. Publications with web sites can maintain updated calendar listings on the sites, encouraging students to visit the sites to update their knowledge of upcoming events.

WRITING THE REVIEW

Have you ever read a review and become furious over the narrow-minded point of view expressed by the writer? Few publications offer students the opportunity to read a review of something written from their point of view. Student publications can provide that voice. Not only can reviews be written by members of the publication staff but staffs should seek to include diverse points of view through the inclusion of reviews written by student readers, particularly those who are interested in a particular area of entertainment. Reaching out to students who are known for their musical knowledge or their dramatic knowledge can provide publications with strong, diverse coverage and thoughtful, informed points of view (Fig. 10.2).

Newspapers that publish infrequently must pay particular attention to how they review entertainment. Writing reviews of performances that are still fresh in the students' minds and still present in their conversations will prove to be far more effective than covering events long after they've occurred. If it isn't possible to review the entertainment in a timely manner, it may be worth using only a picture from the event with a well-written caption or using a quote collection featuring a series of short quotes from a variety of people on the highlights or disappointments of the event. Publications with web sites can offer student-written reviews of concerts and other performances as soon as they are written. This frees the pages of the printed paper to stay more current and timely.

Reviews of some forms of entertainment, such as CD and video releases, books,

Fig. 10.2. Just after the Academy Award nominees for 1999 were announced, the *Update's* "Pulse" section chose its favorites for the awards. In addition to including its own associate editor's opinion, the paper included the votes of the drama club president and a Spanish teacher. Color coding the votes of the three judges makes for a quick and fun read. Stories of general interest and timeliness in the news are more interesting to student readers when they are localized to the school community. *Update,* Herbert Henry Dow High School, Midland, Mich.

CULTURE Corner
Exploring a Cultural Gem

by Vinny
De Rosa '99

"Occupying the entire house, the Frick Collection is composed of paintings, small sculptures, and beautiful furniture."

With so many museums in New York City, deciding where to go for cultural kicks is often a daunting task. Because of this difficulty, students often decide it easier not to visit these storehouses of cultural treasures at all, thus denying themselves the opportunity to view some of man's greatest artistic achievements.

In fact, if you've never been to one of the city's myriad galleries and museums, it's really rather easy to narrow down your choices. A good place to begin your cultural experience is the Frick Gallery on Fifth Avenue and East 70th Street. It's easily accessible; manageable in size; and filled with some of the world's most important pieces of medieval, Renaissance, and seventeenth-century art.

Originally home to the wealthy Frick family, the gallery is a work of art in itself. The museum's stone walls are ornamented with intricate floral reliefs and borders which gradually lead the eye to detailed ceilings of oak. In the center of the house, a plant-filled atrium with benches and a reflecting pool offers respite to the feet, but not the eyes.

Occupying the entire house, the Frick Collection is composed of paintings, small sculptures, and beautiful furniture. Most of the Frick's spectacular ensemble of paintings can be attributed to the Dutch masters of the seventeenth-century. Rembrandt, Vermeer, and Van Dyck are only a few of the famed names found here. Also scattered throughout the collection are works by Velasquez, El Greco, Fra Filippo Lippi, and Titian, the likes of which are seldom seen outside of Europe. Students can see the original portrait of St. Thomas More (a copy of which hangs in room 235), as well as the original "Man in a Red Hat" by Titian, which was the basis for senior Karl Cragnolin's second-place entry in last year's art contest.

If the variety of Mr. Frick's collection is its most wondrous aspect, the use of light in these creative masterworks is certainly a close second. Whether by intention or accident, the Frick's collection of paintings is a lesson in illumination. The best example of this is Vermeer's "Soldier and a Girl." The plot of this painting involves a soldier and a young lady who is apparently the object of his attention. However, it is neither the sanctity nor sensuality of the characters' relationship which is of interest to observers. Rather, it is the

light pouring into the room. On a canvas smaller than one square foot, Vermeer demonstrates with complete accuracy the displacement of natural light in a room, with all of its refractions, reflections, and shadows. This, rather than the two characters, is the amazing feature of this piece.

Leaving the continent for a moment and examining several pieces by English artist Joseph Turner, we can observe this illumination in a second body of work. As an ongoing project, Turner painted several ports along the southern channel coast to depict the history of eighteenth-century shipping. Dull as that topic may seem, the observant museum-goer will recognize that the merit of these paintings lies in their skies. Like Vermeer, Turner has reached a mastery of color, allowing him to depict dawn, midday, and dusk in all of their golden glory. Such an achievement in painting makes these some of the most valued members of the gallery.

Sharing the gallery with these portents of painting is a smaller, but no less exquisite, collection of Italian sculpture. Most of these pieces are bronze castings of horses — all attributed to the ancient Roman period. Each casting demonstrates that its unknown creator possessed advanced knowledge of equestrian anatomy.

Reaching the Frick is most easily done by a train ride to Penn Station, followed by a subway ride uptown. Take the 1, 2, 3, or 9 train one stop uptown to 42nd Street/Times Square. There, transfer to the N or the R line uptown to the Fifth Avenue Station. Then walk ten blocks north along Fifth Avenue (Central Park will be on your left.) to the museum. If you find the city subway system intimidating, you can always take a taxi from Penn Station. Traveling by car is possible but ill-advised, since parking is almost non-existent uptown, and cars in Manhattan are more a hindrance than a help. You'll find the museum most pleasant between ten and noon, when crowds of tourists are small. Make sure to bring your Chaminade ID to get the $5.00 student rate.

If you're looking for an exciting adventure in art, or if you just get caught uptown in the rain, the Frick is the place for you. Although it is not as grand in size as the Met or the Modern, I give the Frick Gallery high marks on the cultural scale. Its exciting variety, superb quality, and dignified setting make this little-known museum a gem in New York's shining crown of cultural experiences. ➤

restaurants, web sites, games and museums or galleries have longer timeliness factors.

Good reviews recap basic information such as the date and location of the event and give the reader a sense of the event from the beginning paragraph. Was it fabulous? Was it a disappointment? Was the performer in rare or weak form? Reviews maintain reader interest by supporting information that is specific and detailed. Were particular songs included that might be indicative of a performer's range? Was something omitted that left the people in attendance feeling disappointed?

Reviewers should provide information about the show, as well as the performer. How did the supporting performers do? What about the staging? The quality of the sound might also be a factor in the show's evaluation.

Giving the reader a sense of the crowd size, the size of the arena or venue and the weather conditions—particularly if the event is staged at an outdoor arena—can also provide relevant information.

When reviewing dramatic productions, books and movies, writers should give the reader a sense of the plot but should be careful to avoid giving away endings, surprises or developments that could spoil the performance for the reader.

In all cases, opinions should be backed by relevant examples. Writers shouldn't be timid about being critical if they feel the performance warrants a negative review. But the writer must also make sure the examples support and justify the opinion of the performance.

In the case of certain kinds of reviews such as book, CD, video and web site, quick reviews of several diverse kinds can interest a greater number of student readers. This is another area where student opinion can be brought into the newspaper. Students ask their friends' opinions frequently about good books, videos and CDs. Reviewers should establish a simple, but relevant, rating system for various entertainment forms, similar to the ubiquitous thumbs up and down from movie reviewers Roger Ebert and the late Gene Siskel. *Vanity Fair* magazine always includes a quick read survey of three to four well-known celebrities, asking them, "What book is on your nightstand?" or "What CD are you listening to?"

At certain times of the year, homecoming, schoolwide special dances or prom time, publications could provide reviews of restaurants that students might want to frequent for a special occasion. Letting the reader know the range of entrées, the price range of the food, the ambiance and other relevant information about the dining experience (are reservations needed? how about extra money for valet parking?) can be useful and informative. Occasional reviews of new restaurants in town or in nearby communities can expand students' knowledge of opportunities close-by.

Reviews of cultural venues specific to communities near the school or those that students would drive to visit on weekends also are effective and provide a service to the newspaper's student readers (Fig. 10.3).

An excellent way to review the fall television season is through polls or surveys asking a wide variety of students for projected hits or misses of the season. Asking questions such as what someone likes about a show and who his or her favorite character is and why and providing information about the show's airtime and channel can give students information they will use.

Many students play hand-held or computer video games. Reviews of new games and options will attract the interest of these players.

At night, at home, many students spend their free time surfing the Web. A com-

Fig. 10.3. For the staff of the *Tarmac*, reviewing museums in New York City is a logical entertainment choice. In this review, the reporter articulates the qualities of the Frick Gallery. *Tarmac*, Chaminade High School, Mineola, N.Y.

puter surfer in the school might be a good voice to add to the entertainment page or section. He or she could offer students a review of popular sites and navigation tools. These sites could help students plan spring break vacations, access information for term papers or learn about colleges and programs they offer.

Students publishing in communities with museums can provide information about exhibits of local talent, traveling exhibits or special performances hosted by the museum. Touring shows and performers will be of interest to many students. Many of these performances are tied to holidays. A touring company might be performing "The Nutcracker" at Christmastime.

WRITING THE COLUMN

Just as editors with thoughtful comments add significantly to the editorial page, entertainment columnists can expand the voice of the entertainment page or section. Columnists should be chosen for their thought-provoking commentary on a wide range of entertainment issues and topics.

Columnists should avoid the pitfall of using column space for reviewing and critiquing entertainment unless that is the designated purpose for the column and only if additional, shorter reviews are provided from other student voices.

Columnists should make sure to use fresh, original material, taking advantage of the fact that their voices are unique. Quotes and information should not be borrowed from published sources or taken from the Internet without permission of the site manager. As in other forms of information, columnists should make sure to substantiate their opinions with strong, supporting statements (Fig. 10.4).

Fig. 10.4. The lack of places to hang out is the topic of an interesting, well-written and thoughtful column. *Wingspan,* West Henderson High School, Hendersonville, N.C.

Fig. 10.5. The popularity of the Pokémon Game Boys provides the basis for the coverage of four students at this school, all of whom are big players of the games. *Blue and Gold,* Center High School, Antelope, Calif.

JASON TULLY

jIve talkIn

Nothing to do can cost big bucks

One of the major problems of being a teenager is finding stuff to do with free time. This is a problem all around, but I believe it is very much so in Henderson County.

It's not so much the lack of things to do as in the lack of funds we have to do things with. For example, I have been to four or five Asheville Smoke games this season. Minor League Hockey is great; you can't go wrong watching a fight that they incorporate into a game. Yet the last three games I've been to, I've gone for free. In the beginning of the season, I paid for the tickets and went when I wanted to; now I must wait for an opportunity to go for free. Thirteen bucks, plus refreshments, can get expensive.

Movies add up fast and get boring, and though playing pool is great, $3 an hour can add up for high school students with part-time jobs. Going to Greenville can be a really fun time, yet last time I went, I wound up blowing $50. (It was worth it though.)

Teenagers like places to hang out — places to go to get away from Mommy and Daddy. Restaurants can get expensive unless you know the servers. What we need is a place like The Max on *Saved By the Bell.* Those kids spent more time there than in class. And I never saw Zach and the gang picking up the tab for their drinks.

Plus, it would be cool to have a waiter that could perform magic tricks. Even the crew from 90210 had the Peach Pit. Of course I guess that grew old since they turned it into a night club. And no one forgets Arnold's where those wild Milwaukee boys would spend their nights either watching the Fonz play pinball or picking up girls.

Hendersonville has no such place. Sure, there are hangouts, but none of them are good. And the cool things to do cost money. What we need here is a cool place where we don't have to spend much money. That's a lot to ask for. But I can ask.

scene
Movies•Music•Styles•Features•Trendsetters

◆ Theater production of "The Diary of Anne Frank" warms the audience. **PAGE 9**

◆ CHS comes together at an Online party to chat about the Internet. **PAGE 10**

◆ The once religious power beads become a new trendy fashion. **PAGE 11**

7

Dec. 17, 1999

Battle of the POKÉMON

Hosted by the Elite Four

By Nicole Searls
B&G Scene Editor

Geridos has hyperbeam, but you can't use that. Like, Gaslig's powers are awesome. Drowsy, and Eggsecute are pretty common, but Eggsecutor has stronger attacks, or basically is just a stronger Pokémon, which makes him uncommon.

While this may seem like a foreign language, it has become the talk of the town. The Pokémon fever has quickly spread throughout the country, including CHS. The hugely successful Pokémon Game Boy game was just the beginning of the Pokémon phenomenon.

Pokémon, 150 in all, have special powers that can be used to kill one another. Conflicting with their powers, there are also weaknesses, and hit points, both of which may cause your Pokémon to either win or lose. But why, may you ask, have these funny little creatures captured the interests of such a wide age group? How can the game itself be easy enough for a five year old to understand, but challenging enough for adults to play?

We found the answer from a group called "The Elite Four." Named after the video game, junior Daniel Hughes, junior Michael Hammett, senior James Thorsted, and sophomore Kenneth Rosell, are the top four officers in a group they have created to compete against themselves and other Pokémon fans.

"We are going to open this up for anyone who wants to compete," Hughes said. "Competing is a single-elimination tournament. They are one-on-one games, where the winner advances, and the loser is eliminated."

Each of the Pokémon cards has a creature that fights for you. Using the energy, and hit points, you try to kill all the other Pokémon in the 60-card deck. Each kill is worth one point and a total of six points declares the winner.

So why do these cards have such an impact on children? Because of the animated characters on

▲ **BIG BATTLE: Junior Daniel Hughes starts up a game of Pokémon after his physics test in A-3 on Dec. 13. Hughes and others often play whenever they have the chance.**

the TV show. When seen on TV, these violent creatures seem pleasant and cute, an instant grabber for younger viewers. Now with their first full motion animation movie playing now, the Pokémon craze is now bigger than ever. Kids everywhere are falling in love with these unique Pokémon.

"Watching the TV show is okay when you have the time for it," Rosell said. "But sometimes you watch the show and get confused, because the cards and the game don't have the same powers and attacks as the same guy on TV."

Just as appealing to an older crowd, the Elite

Four saw this as something challenging. Hammett, who first started playing with the cards, started after watching the TV show a couple of times last year. Because of boredom after school, he and Hughes played against each other, until they were good enough to compete in a tournament in San Diego.

"Over the summer, I started picking up some cards," Hughes said. "Once I started playing, I got really into it. There's a national league, and today I am one step below the national level."

Because the card game attracts a variety of age groups, winning is more than just luck. Kids have fun playing with characters they see on TV, while

they are subconsciously learning math, adding and subtracting hit points to win the game. For adults, winning depends on the well thought out strategies used to defeat other players.

"Over the summer, there was a tournament in Honolulu, for $15,000," Hughes said. "The final match was between a 34-year-old man, and a 10-year-old boy. The 34-year-old barely won, achieving victory by a slim one point lead. So it doesn't really matter what age you are."

Another reason the game attracts such a wide age span, is the different aspects of it. First is the actual game being played. You can also collect the cards for money, which eventually leads to money tournaments. But it doesn't stop there. There are the video games, the game boy games, the movie, and finally the cartoon itself.

Bringing this game onto campus is what the Elite Four are now trying to do. Hesitant at first because of fear that the school would put a ban on the cards, and because of disloyalty, theft and cheating, the four are now ready for taking action towards their interest in the competitions. They are doing whatever it takes to make it happen.

"Pending on the approval from Mr. Wehr, we will be taking sign-ups of people that want to compete," Hughes said. "Out of fairness, we are discouraging traders, people who trade the cards just for money value. We are promoting a fair game play. Tournaments will hopefully be held in Mr. (Vic) Tresvisanut's room. We are trying to show administrators that there are people on this campus who play fairly, and play responsibly, and we shouldn't have that right taken from us."

Rule number one: talk about *Fight Club*
Three Central students get physical over the latest male rage

What was it that originally drew you to go see this film?

R: The fighting, without a doubt. The film appeared so raw and in your face... the fighting really drew me in as a male and made me want to see it.

A: In the trailer, they had this line, "The things you own end up owning you," gave me the idea that the film was yet another attack on our value system. I had just seen *American Beauty* as well, so I was hoping that *Fight Club* would be another movie dealing with people rejecting the mainstream.

Did the movie strike you as having a much deeper significance than the previews let on?

J: I think the previews made it look like a really big action movie with Brad Pitt swinging at people. Now don't get me wrong, if that's all it was I'd probably go anyway just to see Brad Pitt getting beat up. But ultimately no preview could have really done that plot justice.

R: The previews didn't really let on anything about the plot, which for me was great because I hate going to see a film that's predictable. But I went into *Fight Club* blind, thinking I was just going to see some sort of fight flick. So the plot really struck me.

You're in the theater, sitting in your seat, the film starts. What's your immediate reaction?

J: It's not what you expect. The first 20 minutes are really intense, but you're asking yourself, where's the fighting? What's happening here?

Art Bamford

A: Honestly, I found the premise to be somewhat predictable. In the trailer they show the line, "You wanted a way to change your life, I gave it to you, and in the end you'll thank me," which reflected this idea of catharsis and rejection the film introduced in the opening scene.

R: It's like nothing you could ever have anticipated. It takes every preconceived notion you have about the film and tosses it out the window in the first few minutes.

What about the film really struck you?

R: The fact that the film drew an audience with fighting, yet the last thing the film was actually about was fighting. There was this entire subplot underneath the violence that wasn't really apparent until you got into the film.

A: I saw a major parallel between this film and *American Beauty* in that everything came together perfectly in the ending, which I loved. What was even more amazing about this film was that, at various points in the film, Ed Norton's character is not always a physical person and mental person at the same time; he switches back and forth at points. In a way, the fact that I needed to go back and see the movie again was what really struck me.

What was the most significant observation you took away from the film?

J: The most overwhelming thing was that I began to see a lot of parallels between Durden's character and someone like Hitler for example. The way Durden built an army and the dehumanizing process his followers went through both seemed to be very Hitler-esque.

A: Obviously the people in the movie needed a catharsis; they're fighting because they have no direction in their lives. What made the violence funny was that, as the director said, we're programmed to be hunters yet we live in a world of shoppers, so there's this constant internal conflict. It was a mockery of commercialized violence.

"It was the gang anarchism of *A Clockwork Orange* for the technological generation."

Aditya Chawla ("A")
senior

"It reflected my frustrations in school... what's the point of doing some of the stuff I do?"

Rob Thorsness ("R")
junior

"Men can't be as masculine as they once were, and the film captured that helpless feeling."

Jon Yochim ("J")
junior

Fig. 10.6. Instead of reviewing the movie *Fight Club,* the *Devils' Advocate* staff wrote a forum in which three male students were asked questions about the controversial and violent movie. The answers to the forum questions were edited, allowing the editors to use the best responses. To keep the responses separate, the participants' first-letter initials were placed next to their responses. *Devils' Advocate,* Hinsdale Central High School, Hinsdale, Ill.

Students with strong interests in narrow entertainment forms may be too limited for column writing. In that case, the staff should consider using a variety of columnists who could alternate writing the column. These alternating columnists could also write about a variety of entertainment forms. Opening up the column space to a guest columnist from outside the newspaper's staff could also add to the diversity of entertainment coverage. The occasional use of two columnists with opposing points of view could broaden the coverage.

WRITING THE FEATURE

As with other kinds of feature stories, the entertainment page or section offers writers opportunities to enrich the newspaper's coverage with stories of interest to a wide range of readers.

Student writers should brainstorm with fellow staff members as well as with non-staff members from throughout the school to originate fresh coverage (Figs. 10.5 and 10.6).

A drive-in theater, a popular hangout, an unusual restaurant, the history of the oldest movie theater in town or a behind-the-scenes look at a dramatic production can all provide interesting feature coverage.

Feature coverage does not have to be limited to traditional writing. Photographers can team up with writers to tell stories visually: to show performers studying their lines, building the sets, sewing costumes and learning choreography, for instance. These pictures might be a more interesting feature approach to a behind-the-scenes look at a dramatic production. The writer could add a short, well-written story to the mix to provide the details.

Expanding traditional definitions of entertainment coverage, writers should think about adding coverage of other forms of entertainment such as health and fitness training. Some of this coverage could be used in the sports section, but if that section is already taxed for space, consider the broad appeal of its addition to entertainment. After all, entertainment is what students choose to do to amuse themselves in their spare time. What students do for entertainment will continue to evolve. Entertainment writers should be looking out for ways in which they can expand their traditional coverage and tap in to emerging student interests. If students are spending their evenings in the living room watching the World Wrestling Federation on TV and then spending $30 on a ticket to see a live version of the show when it passes through town, the newspaper should be tapping into that interest. The more diverse the coverage, the better.

EXERCISES

1. Read a professional review in a popular cultural publication such as *Entertainment Weekly, Premiere, TV Guide* or *Rolling Stone.* Make note of the reviewer's use of opinions backed up by examples. Underline each opinion and its supporting example in the review. Next, note how the review begins. What other details are provided by the publication to help the reader learn more about the entertainment form being reviewed? For instance, is there an overall rating, a separate listing of a cast, a list of songs from an album or a plot summary? Are these extra details helpful to the reader?

2. Attend a local production of a play or dance group, the opening of a museum exhibit or a live concert performance. Write a review of the production. Make sure to obtain a copy of the program, if there is one, to provide you with correct spellings of names. Determine what supplemental information could be provided visually with the story. Make sure to back up your opinions with examples.

3. Gather a sampling of opinions from at least 10 students on several TV shows that they enjoy. Edit the survey information to reflect the most interesting information you obtained. How could this information be presented in the entertainment section of the newspaper? Draw a pencil sketch of how you would use the information.

4. Generate a list of entertainment story ideas using Internet resources, local magazines, newspapers and calendars. Make a list for seasonal coverage, community coverage and coverage of cultural entertainment trends such as the World Wrestling Federation or teen television programs. How could these be covered in the newspaper?

5. Prepare an advance story for an upcoming entertainment event coming to your town. Do research by reading about the event on the Internet or by reading previously written articles about the performers. Localize your story by talking to students in your school who will be attending the event. Prepare a list of questions you could ask them to help you include relevant information in your advance story. Should you supplement the advance story with an additional story containing information such as the time, date, ticket price, location and location details of the upcoming event? How could you present that?

6. Write a column about an entertainment issue about which you are concerned. Begin by doing some research about your topic as background for the writing. Interview other students in your school to get their opinions. Since you're writing a column, you can use the first-person form of writing.

7. Read this restaurant review by Laura Flamm from the *Devils' Advocate,* Hinsdale Central High School, Hinsdale, Ill.

A new twist on an old tradition

Finding a traditional Chicago pizza place—complete with dark booths and a host from the old country who doesn't take names—can be difficult in a world full of generic pizza franchises. But an excellent traditional Chicago pizza place that doesn't have a traditional pizza on the menu?

Yes, it's true. Located in the basement of an old Victorian house rumored to be a lookout post during the 1929 St. Valentine's Day Massacre, The Chicago Pizza and Oven Grinder Co. has seen plenty of business since its opening in 1972.

Though the menu is limited, the originality and quality of the food make up for any lack of variety. The baked-to-order half or one-pound pizza pot pies and calzone-like Oven Grinders follow the Mediterranean bread appetizer well without any drastic belt loosening. Throw in some tortoni for dessert, and you're set. Though this pizza place is pretty easy on the pockets (a typical meal runs anywhere from 10 to 20 dollars), watch out, young credit card-wielding patrons; this place takes only cash.

In a world of warmed over Domino's from the cafe, the Chicago Pizza and Oven Grinder Co. gives Grandma's home-made pizza pie a run for its money.

Chicago Pizza and Oven Grinder Co.

2121 North Clark Street (three blocks south of Fullerton), Chicago

773.248.2570

Open: Monday–Thursday (4 p.m.–11 p.m.), Friday (4 p.m.–12 a.m.), Saturday (12 p.m.–12 a.m.), Sunday (12 p.m.–11 p.m.).

Directions:

Take Interstate 290 (Eisenhower) to Lake Shore Drive, follow north to Fullerton exit, turn left onto Fullerton and follow west to the intersection of Clark and Fullerton, turn left onto Clark.

Now answer these questions:

a. Underline the passages in which the writer describes the atmosphere of the restaurant.

b. Did she like the restaurant's food? List specific ways in which she justified her opinion of the food in the review.

c. Did she leave anything out of the review that would have helped you decide whether or not to eat at this restaurant?

d. What are her criticisms of the restaurant?

e. How do you think this restaurant review serves the needs of her suburban Chicago's high school reading audience?

Yearbook Reporting and Writing

Elvis, Andy Warhol, the Statue of Liberty, Disneyland, Cheerios and the high school yearbook are all icons of American culture.

As an icon, a revered symbol, the high school yearbook enjoys status that exceeds that of almost any other memento of the teenage years for many. Sophisticated or not, it is eagerly anticipated before publication and cherished afterward. It has enjoyed this status for more than 100 years.

With such an endearing history, it's no surprise that the production of a yearbook is often serious business, requiring specialized training in many areas, including reporting, writing and editing. Even though the photograph remains the most enjoyed and important piece of a yearbook, the accompanying text—photo captions, stories and headlines—is a significant contributor to the effectiveness of the yearbook as a memory or history book.

THE MISSION OF THE YEARBOOK

Clear and simple, the yearbook's mission is to report the events and issues of the day and the persons involved in them. It shares most of the goals of a school newspaper, and many of the skills needed for success in one are as important for success in the other.

Reporting in a yearbook is done through words, photographs and story-related art. Since the book is published annually, the scope of its coverage extends for one 12-month period, beginning with the events that occurred and issues that were discussed since the last volume of the yearbook.

Although most of the book reports events that occurred on campus or at a school-sanctioned or -directed event off campus, some non–school-related events, issues and activities involving students are included in the yearbook. Some nonstudent and nonschool stories, such as condensed coverage of major world news, may be included to broaden the usefulness of the book as a more complete history of one year.

To be fair and inclusive, all student population groups—racial, ethnic, religious, cultural, economic, sexual orientation—are represented in the pictorial and editorial coverage. This pluralistic or multicultural approach is a conscious part of the book's balanced coverage plan. Photographers and reporters make a special effort to include students outside of their own group of friends.

Each story that is reported in the book, in words and pictures, is accurate, fair and honest. Successes and failures are reported, even though the overall tone of the book is usually upbeat. Minority viewpoints are included, and topics of concern to

Everything you ever wanted to know...

Without fail, the arrival of 9:30 a.m. brought the "Ding!" of the speaker system and the morning announcements: the daily distribution of information—club parties, parking problems, Panther praises—kept Northerners involved, aware and up to date. And as usual, there was plenty to talk about.

Kent Mathers and Ray Bohannon won the title of the state's top administrators, while Donna Hansen and Trish Winnard earned National Teacher Certification. SUN hit it big with an unopposed bid for OASC State Secretary, and the yearbook took top honors at OIPA with the best book in the state. Five Merit Semi-Finalists and four Drama All-Staters added accolades.

The hype and headlines blared loud and clear, but the what about the *rest of the story. . . ?*   (CONTINUED NEXT PAGE)

scream too Excited enthusiasm pumps up the crowd at the home football game against Lawton Sept. 25. Sophomores Crystal Kudron and Lindsay Guttery, freshman Casey White and sophomore Abbie Broughton scream Panther pride from the stands. "The best part of the game is the crowd," Broughton said. "Sometimes it's kind of mellow if we're losing, but everyone cheers and has a blast when the team's winning." Off a big win over sister school Putnam City, the varsity faced a crushing 32-0 loss to Lawton's Wolverines. PHOTO BY CASSIE GILL

Senior Khoa Lam lets loose with a bingo. Junior Tracey Ashcraft gets helping hands. Seniors Casey Hiss and Mathan Parasuram act out. (PHOTOS BY CASSIE GILL, MICHAEL DOWNES, JUSTIN GLASSON)

Fig. 11.1. "Et cetera" is the word theme for this book, and on its opening spread, it promises readers, with a bold headline, that the book includes "Everything you ever wanted to know." A word theme can be used to unify or link content throughout the book. *Panther Tracks*, Putnam City North High School, Oklahoma City, Okla.

teenagers, even if controversial, are presented in a fair, mature and tasteful way.

Like the school newspaper and magazine, the yearbook is free of libel and observes the restrictions placed on it by law and media ethics. In an attempt to be humorous, some yearbooks have published captions, photos and other content that were false, were not in good taste and even damaged a person's good name and reputation. This type of seemingly harmless but potentially harmful work is prohibited in a book that follows the standards of good journalism. A yearbook is more permanent than a newspaper, magazine or web site, and errors and libel published in a yearbook are more difficult and costly to correct.

COVERAGE PLANNING FOR EACH SECTION

Coverage—the picture and word stories—within the book's major sections reflects both traditions and new events, issues and personalities. The traditional sections— student life, academics, clubs and organizations, sports and portraits—can be presented with fresh angles. Other sections, including magazines-within-the-book, advertisements, student art and literary work, among others, can supplement the core sections.

Even the core or traditional sections can be defined in other ways as content is shuffled to present the overall story of the year in a different order or format. As long as the reader is not confused or hampered when he or she is reading the book after publication, creative ways to organize content can be successful. Some books

Fig. 11.2. Homecoming, a traditional student activity, is often reported in the student life section of a yearbook. *Trail,* Overland High School, Aurora, Colo.

have successfully organized content seasonally, month-by-month and even day-by-day. Others have organized it thematically, such as students at work, students at play and students after-hours.

THEME DEVELOPMENT

One option for the yearbook is to select and develop a word theme, a single word, phrase or sentence that serves as a hook for story and design continuity throughout the book. The word theme can be topical and linked to stories reported in the opening, closing and other sections of the yearbook (Fig. 11.1).

A word theme tied to specific events or issues related to the school community or to teenagers in general is often more effective than one that has no relevance to students or is hackneyed. Before a word theme is finalized, the yearbook staff should ask this question: Will this theme be as clever, exciting or fresh when the book is finally published as it seems now as the book is being planned? Some word themes, like product advertising slogans, become tired clichés within months if they are overly used and too popular.

If the word theme isn't obvious or is complex, its meaning or the reason why it was selected should be explained briefly near or in the opening of the book.

In addition to introducing a word theme on the book's cover and developing it initially in the opening, it can reappear on divider spreads and, occasionally, within sections before it is concluded in the brief closing section. Even the endsheets,

Fig. 11.3. In a book that reported the events of the year month-by-month, several newsworthy happenings inside the classroom during October were covered on this spread in the academics section. *Pioneer,* Kirkwood High School, Kirkwood, Mo.

which hold the book's cover onto the pages, can include some theme development. The words themselves can also be altered to add variety and relate more specifically to a section.

Word themes are not mandatory for a book to be a successful history of the year. Themes can unify coverage and help the book's marketing plan, but continuity can also be achieved in other ways, including through design. A mix of a design motif, such as a logo, and a subtle, sparingly used word theme can be a successful compromise between an extensively developed word theme and a book with none at all.

THE STUDENT LIFE SECTION

Often a catchall section, the student life portion of the yearbook contains coverage of social activities and the discussion of issues of concern to teenagers (Fig. 11.2). In addition, this section may include local, state, national and international news.

Events are reported and issues presented because they are newsworthy or have substantial human interest appeal and may be a significant part of the school's traditions.

These events, both social and academic, such as prom, homecoming, plays and musicals, concerts and graduation, that are tradition-based are usually reported in this section of the book. Although they are likely to be included every year, an angle is presented in both the editorial and pictorial coverage that is specific and newsworthy or emotionally involving.

Breaking news (coverage of events that are not yearly school traditions such as a visit to the school by a dignitary, the opening of a new addition to the school and unusual weather that disrupts the school) is often placed in this section of the book.

Summer and vacation activities, after-school work and leisure time recreation such as hobbies, dating and travel are also found in the student life section. To present an accurate and complete picture of teenagers today, coverage of off-campus, nonschool activities involving students is important.

In addition to events and activities coverage, issues important to teenagers are reported in several forms in this section. Social issues, such as sexuality, religion, drug and alcohol use and personal safety and violence, and academic concerns, such as study habits, cheating and college entrance exams, are the sources of some of the topical stories reported in student life.

Humorous features on a wide range of topics, from April Fools' Day pranks to first dates and summary reports on significant local and international news, usually with a local or school tie-in, round out the student life sections in many books. Humor should not contain any libel or innuendo that may conflict with community standards of acceptability. Reporting student reaction to world and national events is preferred to secondhand summaries of the events with no local angle.

If books from different schools are compared, differences in school traditions and the racial, ethnic and religious makeup of the student population will result in content differences within the student life sections. As the student life section is planned, the special observances and activities of the school's minority groups should be included. Even in nonminority-related stories, photographers and writers should put minority faces in candids and their opinions in word stories throughout the book.

The catchall nature of the student life section gives editors the freedom to add some new stories each year. Even though the coverage of annual events dominates this section, the first-time story will likely be popular with students and help mark the book as a unique edition.

THE ACADEMICS OR LEARNING SECTION

Learning takes places both within the classroom and in more informal settings in the school, home and other places. The academics or learning section of the yearbook presents an opportunity to present both classroom and nonclassroom education. How extensive this coverage will be will depend upon the size of the book and the extent of the school's curriculum (Fig. 11.3).

Each academic department and course considered for coverage should be examined for news value. The traditional news values—consequence, timeliness, proximity, prominence, human interest—should be considered when coverage is planned and content is judged. This question is central to editorial and pictorial coverage: What's new this year? Focusing on the answer to that question and examining its news values will help ensure fresh reporting and prevent nonspecific content with little potential reader interest.

Another approach to coverage in this section can be tried if after careful research little is found of hard news value or little has changed from the past year. The human interest angle can be pursued. The editorial content can be interview driven, with emphasis on issues or personalities. Those enrolled in a class and those teaching it can be the focus of the story rather than what's new in the course content or how it is being taught.

If all subjects are not covered in separate stories, ways to combine coverage can be tried. For example, all core curriculum courses for a grade level could be reported as one story. Or all courses that involve laboratory work or focus on workplace skills could be combined. All courses that include computer use could be linked. Another way to condense coverage of formal classroom courses would be to select, for coverage, one class for each hour or time period of a school day.

Learning that takes place outside the formal classroom has a place in the yearbook. Within the school itself, students studying alone or in groups in media centers, in libraries, in lounges, in cafeterias, or on outdoor lawns and patios can be the focus of a story. Tutoring and mentoring activities and students who take classes at colleges or other schools to supplement their regular high school courses can be covered in this section.

Feature stories with an academic angle can be included in this section too. Some suggested topics are student study habits, using the computer and the

SWEETSOUNDS

By Russell Graney and Kella Haner

1. Elyse Morel (7) whose violinist grandmother got her started, plays at the winter concert. 2. Perfecting their style, violinists rehearse during class. 3. Soloist Won Jun Lee(8) entertains the audience with *Concerto Grosso*. 4. Concentrating on his music, bass player Sean Freeman (8) sight reads a new piece. 5. Jina Kim (8) rehearses with her cello. 6. Symphonetta cellist Cassie Johnson (8) practices her scales. 7. Orchestra concert performances were important for bass players Steven Petty (7) and James Hirsch (8).

The delicately balanced harmonies of violins, violas, celli and basses could be heard outside the door to Room 401, the rehearsal room for the middle school orchestras. The advanced orchestra,

Orchestra members perform a combination of modern, classical music at concerts, competitions.

directed by Ms. Dow, provided an opportunity for experienced musicians to become competent in the performance of both classical and modern music. Mr. Knudson, the beginning orchestra

conductor, worked to make younger musicians comfortable with their first encounter in orchestra. Asked why she chose the viola, beginning orchestra member seventh grader Dana Jones explained, "All my life I've been like my sisters, so I was happy to find that I could play something other than the cello and violin." Practicing at home was stressed and weekly record sheets showed how much time students had spent.

Some of the music played this year included selections from *The Lion King*, Dvorak's *Symphony #8* and the *Concerto*

Dvorak's *Symphony #8* and the *Concerto Grosso*, featuring eighth grade soloists Won Jun Lee, Russell Graney and Michael Sullivan.

The orchestras presented three concerts this year in December, March and May. They also took part in two competitions. The District Festival in March included local schools, and the *Music in the Parks* festival in May involved middle schools from the entire Mid-Atlantic region. Following the May competition, students enjoyed the rest of the day at Busch Gardens in Williamsburg.

Sarah Rich • *8*

"I got started playing violin because my dad and older brother played before me. Also, you can be concert master if you play violin."

Jeannie Rose • *8*

"I enjoy playing theme songs from movies because the audience seems to enjoy them more."

88 Orchestra / Organizations

Organizations / Orchestra 89

Fig. 11.4. Action candids and a feature story comprise the coverage of the school's orchestra on this spread in the clubs and organizations section. *Sentry,* Robinson Middle School, Fairfax, Va.

Internet to learn, career and life skills learned from various classes, studying for exams, preparing for college entrance exams and standardized tests, favorite books read for class, favorite science lab experiments and recollections of learning in junior high and elementary school. Some books have randomly selected one student from each grade level and reported his or her class-hour by class-hour day, including lunch, with pictures and text story.

Some books include teacher and staff portraits within this section; however, a section with just teacher and staff photos is not a true academics section. Others include these faculty mug shots in a schoolwide portrait section.

THE CLUBS AND ORGANIZATIONS SECTION

The clubs and organizations section traditionally has two purposes: to document through group photos those involved in the activity and to report on the activities sponsored or undertaken by the group (Fig. 11.4). If space allows, each school-sanctioned group is covered on a separate page or spread in the book. If space limits this, coverage of groups can be combined on a single page or spread, if possible, by similar goals or activities. For example, all groups that do volunteer work in the community, all groups that perform for the public, or all groups that perform music could be clustered together.

Group photos with identification of those pictured, though important, should not dominate or represent the only presence of the group in the yearbook. Care should be taken to produce a photo with face sizes large enough so that each member can be recognized. Usually, group photos should be cropped to remove anything below the shoulders and above the tops of the heads. Large groups can be divided into two or more segments to ensure sufficient face size and recognition.

As is the case with other sections, news values are considered for the editorial and candid photo content that accompany the group photos on these pages. Reporters should ask: What's new this year? Even if the club sponsors the same events every year, there are new participants and, perhaps, new results. Candid photo content needs the same approach as copy to stimulate reader interest. Even if the space allocated to a club is less than one page, a minipackage of a group photo, one candid and captions and a brief story could be effectively integrated into a multigroup page or spread.

A feature rather than a news approach can be taken for editorial coverage. Club participants' involvement, including their reactions to club activities or goals, can become the coverage focus. Other feature approaches could be used: exploring the group's history, reporting the benefits or drawbacks of membership, focusing on post–high school, college, career or life links, and writing about time and financial commitments made by members. A single theme, perhaps linked to the book's word theme, could run throughout the section, unifying all copy for clubs. However, reporters should guard against formula writing—text that has that same type of lead and story development from page to page with only the names, dates and other specifics changing.

Some books place all group photos for organizations and sports in a separate section or in the book's index. Some books integrate the clubs section with the academics section; in many cases, the clubs have an academic tie-in. If a book has a section exclusively for group photos, some graphic or minifeature running throughout this section will unify it and add more reader interest.

As in other sections in a yearbook, even well-written copy can be monotonous if the same approach is used repeatedly within a section and throughout the entire book. A mix of news-features and human interest feature copy may prevent this from occurring.

THE SPORTS SECTION

Yearbook journalists often find the sports section to be the easiest to apply news values to content. The most obvious news value is conflict, with prominence also being likely. Largely, this section is a review of specific athletic accomplishments by team. Each contest has all or most of the characteristics that make it newsworthy. (Fig. 11.5)

One of the first decisions made by a yearbook sports editor or reporter is which contests to cover and which ones to ignore or list in a summary, composite scoreboard. Space limitations usually prohibit the reporting of all contests for any team sport. The reporter weighs the importance of each contest when selecting the ones to write about.

After the reporter selects the most significant contests, they are ranked from most to least important; the season wrap-up story will open most often with the highlights of the most important contest, a summary of the season's record or the exceptional accomplishments of one or more team members. Further story development will likely include summaries of the contests judged as less important than the "big game."

Assessments about the successes, shortcomings or failures of the team should be sought by the reporter from key team members, coaches and fans and then reported with attributions within the story. The reporter should avoid the temptation to comment on the quality of the team's performance.

Usually, an end-of-season wrap-up story that is presented chronologically fails to capture the most significant highlights or interesting facts in its opening paragraphs; reporters should avoid the chronological summary, except as a follow-up to the opening paragraphs and initial story development that present the season's most important achievements.

The sports reporter may choose to write something other than a season wrap-up story for any or all teams. If a complete season's scoreboard is published in the book, there may be no compelling need to reiterate this information. A feature story on some aspect of the team would be an appropriate substitute. Some possibilities include a comparison of the team's record for the past 10 seasons, coaching strategies, training procedures, rivalries, player superstitions, what it's like behind-the-scenes during a game, and player statistics or end-of-season awards.

In addition to either the season summary or other

Fig. 11.5. Word reporting is segmented into six stories in addition to complete captions on this sports spread. In addition to the main story, there are four first-person shorts (two from athletes, one from a coach and one from a fan) and one brief summary under "What we saw." *Aerie,* Lancaster High School, Lancaster, Calif.

feature story and a season scoreboard, editorial coverage can be augmented with other text sidebars. These are shorter than the main story and can be stand-alone quotes from players, coaches or fans, individual player statistics, a brief history of the sport, an explanation of rules, an athlete's diet or training schedule, collegiate or professional sports highlights (to make the book more of a comprehensive history of the year) or other information of interest to readers.

Photo coverage in the sports section usually includes a team group shot and candids of the team in action. It is often desirable to link the main story lead to one or more of the candid photos. Behind-the-scenes candids and a limited number of mug shots can supplement the game candids and group photo.

Some yearbooks have expanded coverage in the sports section to include personal, nonteam student sports and recreation, as well as athletic-related issues and controversies of general interest. Examples of nonteam or nonschool sports that could be reported include snowboarding, in-line skating, rodeo, cycling, climbing, hiking, weight lifting and surfing. General interest, sports-related stories could include college scholarships for athletes, the Olympics, use of supplements for muscle growth, sports injuries, eligibility requirements and sports heroes.

To a certain extent, tradition plays a role in how much space is given to each sport. Sometimes this has been seen as unfair by some readers or some athletes who think their sport deserves as much or equal coverage. It is important to provide sufficient space to girls' as well as boys' teams and to include recreational sports that are popular with a minority population group within the school, but fan interest should be considered too. The sports editor must balance the need to be fair with the realities of spectator or reader interest and real news values.

THE PORTRAIT SECTION

Since one of the book's purposes is to document those persons who were enrolled in the school for a specific time, the book's portrait section is especially important. For many years, books have done that and more, expanding coverage within the portrait section to include many human interest feature stories and other information (Fig. 11.6).

Portraits should be uniform in size within a class or division, but uniformity in poses, dress or background is optional. Since this may be the only picture of a student in the book, it is important to spell the person's name correctly and get the best possible reproduction of the photo from the camera stage to the final printing.

If a person is not pictured, do not substitute an empty space or cartoon character with any words such as "camera shy." Simply list all those not pictured in an alphabetized list at the end of the portraits for that class or division.

In addition to formal names adjacent to the portraits, some books list school activities and other data such as a brief motto. Variations in the amount of extra copy accompanying a name may disrupt the layout. An alternative is to place these activities in a separate addendum at the end of the portraits or near the close of the book. If mottoes, prophecies or other material is included, the editors should review them carefully for libel or derogatory or unsuitable words. The editor, adviser and school may all be legally responsible for everything that is published in the book, including content submitted by those pictured but not on the yearbook staff.

It is now common to include short features and candid photos on portrait pages. Usually, these features are pertinent to the class or grade level in which they appear. One popular feature is a brief personality profile or a story focusing on one aspect of a person's life such as a hobby or unusual accomplishment. Some features are on student nonschool interests such as music, movies, cars, aspirations for the future, foods and restaurants, after-school jobs and opinions on national politics and concerns "in the news." Sometimes, these features focus on students who excel academically, such as the top 10 students. No topic is potentially off limits for reporters assigned to the portrait section. Sometimes

the book's theme can suggest a series of topics for features in this section.

Candid photography in the portrait section should be varied. Since the portraits (face shots) dominate the pages, it is advisable not to use too many close-ups of faces as candids. Graphics can be used to enhance the design and to carry bits of editorial content and even the theme throughout the section.

THE SPECIAL SECTION AND SPECIAL CONTENT

Some stories don't seem to fit into any section, and some, including those once-in-a-lifetime ones, are just so important that they deserve a special section of their own. The school celebrated its centennial, the principal of 25 years retired, a graduate was elected the state's governor, a hurricane closed school for a week and damaged the building or the girls' basketball team won the state championship. These are the kind of "big" stories that likely don't happen each year. When they do occur, an editor needs to decide where to place them in the book (Fig. 11.7).

A traditional section can be expanded to accommodate the special story, or a new, usually smaller section can be created. The new section, since it is unexpected and not found in last year's book, will get more attention and will be considered by many to be important. Its placement within the book is another consideration. Placed near the opening, its importance is stressed. However, a story on a major event that occurs without much advance warning—hurricane or tornado destruction—will have to be placed, depending upon the publishing deadline, wherever it will fit since much of the book may have already been completed.

Some special sections are published every year. Reporting local, state, national and international news and sports and entertainment highlights as a series of stories gathered into one section is a popular option. Some preprinted inserts of this kind are available from yearbook publishers. Often, this section takes on a newsmagazine look, with art and photos accompanying the stories. Nonlocal photos can be purchased from photo service bureaus such as Worldwide Photos of the Associated Press in New York City. A local newspaper may allow the yearbook staff to print some of its pictures; credit should be given to outside photo sources in the form of a credit line next to each photo. As much as possible, these stories should be localized with student

By Reggie Powell

DATING 'BLOOPERS'

Are you just too cool to

make mistakes or do you

make Steve Urkel look

like some kind of a stud?

It's not always the most popular guy or the most popular girl who gets all the dates. When it comes to dating, some are smooth as butter, and others can hardly put one foot in front of the other. Dating is a part of high school that everyone experiences in one way or another. Most find that the key to dating is to relax. When the time to date comes for you, just remember to take a deep breath, and be yourself.

Senior sweethearts Mike Dewey and April Trenary do a little relaxing on Senior Lawn. The two dated during the majority of high school. "We survived because we love each other", said Dewey (99).
photo by: Reneè Pickheim

Mickey Mahlmeister

Keyon Cornejo

Mona Fely

Tony Obr

Scott Walrath

on dating...

Tell us the funniest thing that ever happened on a date.

I was playing football on the beach and as I began to run into the ocean, I fell straight into the ocean.
- Mickey Mahlmeister

My mom showed my boyfriend naked baby photos of me.
- Amanda Strack

I was trying to get this girl's number and I accidentally sneezed right in her face.
- Keyon Cornejo

My blind date was only 5'1" and I'm 5'10".
- Anessa York

One time when I was talking to a girl, my cousin depanted me right in front of her.
- Mona Fely

I fell down the stairs at my boyfriend's house on Prom night and his whole family saw it.
- Gina Baldenegro

I went out to dinner and the waiter gave me a kids menu.
- Rachel Taylor

I was on a date at the movies and my date spilled his skittles all over the place.
- Corina Rodriquez

On a MORP date we were eating dinner and I blew a big "snot rocket" out of my nose due to a cold.
- Scott Walrath

Amanda Strack

Anessa York

Gina Baldenegro

Rachel Taylor

Corina Rodriquez

Fig. 11.6. Most student portrait sections include human interest features and candid photos. Often, the features are "Q&A," including this one: "Tell us the funniest thing that ever happened on a date." *Historian*, McClintock High School, Tempe, Ariz.

Lois Lindstrom:
HERO 12, Yearbook 11
Veronica Lopez
Matthew Lulling
Matthew Lunsford:
Orchestra 9-12, NHS 11-12, Tennis 9-10,
JCL 11-12, Environmental Club
Brooke Lustig

Micheal Ly: Band 9-12, FBLA 9-12,
Business Internship 12, NHS 11-12
Nathaniel Magnusson:
X-Country 11-12, Track 11-12
Christopher Mahlmeister:
Football 9-12, Wrestling 9-12, Track 9-12
Travis Maiden
Sabrina Malan: Softball 9, Choir 9,
Drama 10-12, Photo 10-11, Newspaper
11-12, Yearbook 9-10,12, Orchestra 9-11

Ramiro Maldonado
Sara Marianella: Softball 9-10,
Student Council 11-12, Band 9-12
Jenice Martin
Lisa Martinez
Maria Martinez

Mildred Martinez:
Photo 10-11, Yearbook 10-12,
Student Life Editor 11,
Peer Tutor 11-12
Kyle Matthew:
V Swimming 9-10,12, V Soccer 10-12
Nicole Mayo: Spiritline 9-12
Cassandra McCaughey:
Dance 11-12
Elizabeth McCollum: Drama 10,
Guidon 9-12, Editor-in-Chief 11-12

Ryan McCracken
Leah McFarland: Spiritline 9-12,
Dance 9-12, SADD 11, Band 9
Rebecca McGirr: Basketball 9-12,
Softball 9-12, German Club 11-12
Nick McIntosh: Wrestling 10-12,
Track 9-11, Football 9
Kara McMahon: Drama 10,
HERO 12, Yearbook 11

Melissa McSherry:
Choir 9-10, Dance 12,
A Cappella 11-12, Drama 11-12,
Sonia Mead: V Soccer 9-12,
X-Country 9-10, V Track 9-10,12,
Yearbook 12, Spirit Club 9,
Student Council 11
John Medlin: VICA 9-12, ICE 12
April Melheim:
Choir 10-12, Yearbook 10-12, AFS 10-11
Alison Mello: Band 9-12

20th Century

The Senior Class of 1999 was the last class before the turn of the century. The 20th century would soon be history, and these pages are dedicated to reflect the moments that will always be remembered.

Movements throughout the 20th century included the Industrial Revolution, the Great Depression, two World Wars, the Civil Rights movement, the Cultural Revolution and the end of the threat of communism. Throughout all of these movements, we managed to put a man on the moon and to see the birth of the automobile, airplane and the Internet. The 20th century marked the beginning of the communications revolution and no one could imagine what would lie ahead.

"One small step for man, one gaint step for mankind."
-Neil Armstrong, (1930 -   )

"I did not have sexual relations with that woman, Monica Lewinsky."
-Bill Clinton, (1946 -   )

Bill Clinton

The long awaited goal of landing a man on the moon was achieved in 1969. The historic flight of Apollo 11 was launched on July 16.

One of the most memorable moments caught on film during World War II was the flag-raising on the island of Iwo Jima in the Pacific.

Reelected by a landslide in 197 Richard Nixon w brought down b revelations of his administration's misdeeds known "Watergate."

Fig. 11.7. Some space in the yearbook needs to be set aside for unexpected events and special commemorations. This book recorded the passing of the 20th century with photos, a feature story and some memorable quotes. *Clan,* McLean High School, McLean, Va.

k not what your
ntry can do for you,
what you can
for your
untry."
n F. Kennedy,
17 - 1963)

"No one can make you
feel inferior without
your consent."
-Eleanor Roosevelt,
(1884 - 1962)

"If a man hasn't
discovered
something he will
die for, he isn't fit to
live."
-Martin Luther King Jr.,
(1929 - 1968)

"If you want to
succeed you should
strike out on new paths
rather than travel the
worn paths of accepted
success."
-John D. Rockefeller,
(1839 -1937)

The Sixties were an exciting, revolutionary and turbulent time of great social and technological change. The hippies brought flower power, counterculture and psychedelic light shows. The music of musicians such as Jimi Hendrix were products and symbols of this era.

Most products used today by people in industrialized nations are made through the process of mass production, by people working on assembly lines using power-driven machines. In 1913 Henry Ford introduced the assembly line in the manufacture of his model T Ford.

In November, 1960, at the age of 43, John F. Kennedy became the youngest man ever elected president of the United States. He was also the first Roman Catholic president and the first president to be born in the 20th Century. President Kennedy was assassinated in Dallas, Texas on November 22, 1963.

Feature Story Ideas for the Yearbook

• Popular destinations for spring break
• College visits
• Names students give their cars
• Sports heroes
• Unusual study places
• Preparing for SAT/ACT tests
• Buying a prom dress
• Favorite Internet web sites
• First dates, first kiss
• Extracurricular activities of your teachers when they were in high school
• How many Jessicas, how many Michaels? How many students in your school share the same first (or last) name?
• One book students would bring with them to a deserted island
• Favorite music to study by
• Caffeine addicts
• A day in the life of a straight "A" student
• Athletes on the sidelines due to injuries
• In 10 years, what job will you have?
• Banned book week
• Diversity of languages spoken by students
• Home schooling
• Buying your first car
• Students as community volunteers
• The body-obsessed teen
• Legal rights of 18-year-old students
• Violence in America—students' views
• What Sesame Street taught seniors
• Catalog and Internet shopping for clothes

and community tie-ins.

Although yearbooks rarely publish long, in-depth reports, some books break with this tradition. In addition to their traditional coverage, they focus on one topic, often a teen or community concern, and report it on several consecutive spreads. Usually with more text than photos or graphics, these multisourced stories are often placed in the student life section. If they extend beyond three or so spreads, they could be a distinct section. For example, racial, ethnic or religious prejudice or dating and sexuality could be the subject.

Multispread stories are not restricted to coverage of controversial or sensitive topics. Lighter topics—teen fashion trends, cultural festivals, homecomings—can be developed into longer stories that extend for two, three or more spreads. Occasionally extending a story beyond the norm (one spread) creates an unexpected and usually pleasing surprise for the reader.

Yearbooks can also showcase student creative writing and reproduce student artwork. A section with poems, essays, short stories and other literary forms and reproductions of paintings, drawings and other fine art can add the visual spark to the text. The result is a literary magazine within the context of the yearbook.

A humor section and an occasional humorous story in other sections are also options. A humor story requires special editing to remove any libel or offensive content. Light, human interest topics are best suited for humorous treatment. Some are the best Halloween ghost stories, April Fools' Day jokes, embarrassing things that happened on dates and the best student excuses to teachers for late assignments. Instead of humor presented in prose form, a comic strip could be created just for the yearbook and run as a mini comic book.

Student and faculty deaths can also be covered in the yearbook. The preferred form is the brief, newspaper-style obituary. The obituary should give the basic facts—birth and death dates, full name, survivors, major life achievements—and can also include comments from those closest to the deceased, such as friends, teachers and parents. The cause of death is desirable but not required. A photo should accompany the text. An obituary in this form is appropriate and dignifies the person's life and death. It is preferred to a tribute; a tribute could accompany the obituary as a separate story. The appropriate place to put an obituary is at the close of the portrait section.

Another option for marking the death of a student or faculty member is to print his or her name and dates of birth and death under a heading "Died This Year." This would be printed following the portraits for the relevant class or the faculty section, adjacent to the list of those not pictured. A yearbook staff should adopt a policy for reporting deaths so when one happens it is easier to respond to student, faculty and parent requests.

FACT GATHERING AND REPORTING

To effectively capture and summarize an event in pictures and words requires advance planning by a team of yearbook journalists, including editors, reporters, photographers and artists. Working at times together and other times independently, each of these students contributes visual and verbal pieces for what will eventually become a complete story.

At the beginning of the school year, the editor plans a ladder diagram, a page-by-page delineation of the book's contents. Some pages may be set aside for unanticipated stories or "breaking news." The creation of the ladder is the first step in reporting the year's stories. Almost every story gets a name, one or a few words to identify the page's or spread's contents.

After the ladder is completed, individual story assignments are made by the editor. With a team approach, the editor discusses the assignment and the possible photo, text, art and graphics for the story with the adviser and with the reporter, photographer and layout designer who will work on the story. This prereporting stage suggests coverage angles for the reporter and photographer to pursue. Some flexibility should be allowed, for the reporter and photographer may find other newsworthy angles equally or more important during the fact-gathering and photo-shooting stages of the story development. The editor and adviser can also suggest specific interview sources and other resources, which may be especially important for inexperienced reporters and photographers.

As the story is developed by the reporter and photographer, a layout designer and artist can do preliminary design work for the story spread. Usually, the design coordinates with other stories within the same section of the book. Completed graphics and other art, and the final layout or complete pagination of the spread's contents, is not done until all the visual and word page elements are completed, including the final editing. This two-stage layout design process allows for some possible changes in content between the time the story is assigned and when it is fully completed.

The team approach is collapsible if the staff is small or organized in a different way with one person completely responsible for the reporting, writing, photography, graphics, layout design and pagination. In that case, a team may still be formed with the addition of the editor and the adviser as consultants and, in the case of the editor, the person who checks the story before it is published.

Ideally, the story is developed in advance of the event, is reported and photographed as the event occurs and is finished within a week or so after the event. This allows for easy fact checking, identifying persons in photos and soliciting comments from those involved in the event while it is still fresh in their minds. Reporting done long after an event will likely suffer from lack of specific and colorful commentary and possibly no candid photos.

Reporters can conduct interviews in person, over the telephone or through computer e-mail. Questions should be prepared in advance, but there should be some flexibility to pursue unexpected angles that arise during the interview or for spontaneous follow-up questions.

Background information and other facts previously published can be gotten from the school's newspaper; previous yearbooks; statistics available in the school's athletic, activities and administrative offices; and the school's library. A key word search on the Internet may also yield some useful information. For nonschool stories, the fact gathering may expand to community resource centers. For example, for a student life story on teen volunteer work in the community, potential sources for interviews and records are local hospitals, churches, senior citizen centers, hospices, the United Way and various charities.

The photographer should plan how the story will be told in pictures before the event or photo shoot takes place. The reporter needs to convey to the photographer what kind of pictures are desired, including specific content, sizes (verticals and horizontals) and angles (close-up to long distance or wide angle). Who is involved in the event and what is occurring should be fully understood in advance so the most

- Favorite electronics
- Time crunches: study, work, recreation
- Backpacking, hiking getaways
- Discovering your family tree
- Olympic dreams of your school's athletes
- Local bands, local music scene
- Classes then and now, what was taught at your school 50 years ago compared with what is taught today
- Extreme sports
- Origins of your school's name
- Most often broken school rules
- Training as a distance runner
- Shoe, footwear trends
- Most influential person in students' lives
- Defining popularity
- On the job, students at work
- What do students fear?
- Teacher of the year: Who would you name?
- The book that changed your life
- Five characteristics of highly successful students
- Dinner from a vending machine
- Dating dos and don'ts
- What you can do (and can't) during the short break between classes

relevant action and persons are shot.

For most photo stories, a range of close-up to long distance shots and vertical and horizontal shapes should be taken. The long distance shot sets the stage and provides an overview of the scene; a medium shot focuses on the action and identifies those involved; a close-up shows the emotional impact on one or more participants. Then the reporter and layout designer will have a good variety of pictures to consider as they build the layout during the editing and pagination stages. Being able to select from this variety will likely create a photo-word story with more visual impact than one with more limited photo images, such as all horizontal close-ups.

Photographers are also helped by seeing a preliminary layout for the story so they have some idea as to how their photos will be used.

A staff artist or visual reporter may join the story team at either the prereporting stage or as the story is edited and the layout is being drawn. The story may be enhanced with the addition of an information graphic—a chart, graph, diagram, map or fact box—which is another way to report the story. These are called "information graphics" or, abbreviated, "infographics" or "infographs." In some ways, they are like other special effects, and they should be used infrequently.

Since the yearbook is more permanent than a newspaper or magazine, and is published only once a year, fact checking, verification of spelling, especially of names, and editing for libel or unsuitable content is vital at all stages, including the final proof from the printer.

WRITING THE WORD STORY

Once the facts and comments have been gathered and the reporter has the photos that were taken of the events, the word story can be written. Seeing the photos that will be used for the story will help the reporter write a story that links directly at least one or more of the photos with the word story. For example, on the same spread, a photo of the winning goal in the state soccer championship match can be linked directly to the main word story that leads with a replay of the scoring of that goal. Not all photos on the spread have to be directly linked or referred to in the text; stand-alone photos with fully developed captions are acceptable.

Upon examination of the information and opinions recorded during the fact-gathering stage, the reporter decides if a news or a feature method of story and lead development will be used. Sometimes this decision is made by an editor who wants a particular style used for all stories within a section.

If a news approach is taken, the writer evaluates the information and ranks it from most important to least important—in other words, the inverted pyramid form of story development is used. Opinions, both direct and indirect quotes, are used to qualify facts. Often, the news summary lead is selected to begin the story, with some or all of the *what, who, where, when, why* and *how* answered in the opening paragraph. The writer may also choose a news-feature lead for a news-style story. The news-feature lead often focuses on the most unusual of the *what, who, where, when, why* and *how* in the first sentence and opening paragraph.

The *when* element, the timeliness aspect, is not as significant in a yearbook as it is in a news story in a newspaper. There rarely are advance stories in a yearbook, and it is assumed by the readers that the events covered in the book happened this year (although beginning a story with "This year ..." is considered a weak and avoidable opener).

The *what, who, why* and *how* answers usually make much better lead paragraphs and opening sentences. They are more consequential and have more human interest value.

All opinion in the story is attributed to someone. Direct quotes are included only if the comments or facts are unusual or colorful. Indirect quotes (paraphrases with no quotation marks) are used frequently. The writer's opinions are left out of the story. For example, if a reporter wrote, "The homecoming game win was the biggest victory of the season," it would be bad journalism because the adjective "biggest" expresses an opinion. To use "biggest" properly in the sentence, it has to be attributed to someone other than the reporter. As a direct quote with attribution, it would be better to write: "The homecoming game win was the biggest victory of the season," said football captain Jeff Stone. Or as an indirect quote: According to football captain Jeff Stone, the homecoming win was the biggest victory of the season.

Even if the inverted pyramid style is used, which allows for deleting the final paragraph if space is tight, the last paragraph in a yearbook story deserves as much creative attention as the opening one. If the yearbook story needs to be shorter, it should be trimmed in other ways or places.

If a feature story or infographic is the style used, the reporter examines the information and opinions for human interest appeal (Fig. 11.8). What potential emotional impact could any of the facts or opinions have on readers? The facts or opinions with the strongest potential to raise the curiosity of the reader and elicit a response—happiness, sadness, humor, shock, amazement, disbelief—could become the story's lead. A clever play on words; allusions to commonly known literary or artistic works, films or songs; and other devices used in storytelling can be effective openings for a yearbook feature. Storytelling is somewhat the opposite of the inverted pyramid; the highest point of interest—the climax—is not in the opening or, usually, the immediate follow-up paragraph of the storytelling form of writing.

Space limitations in a yearbook and the form itself usually mean the feature story will be narrowly focused on one or a few facts and opinions. Feature writers sometimes report only what some have called a "slice of life," a limited but interesting or newsworthy piece of someone's life. The scope of the yearbook feature is smaller than that of the yearbook news story or news-feature. For example, a feature story about a teacher who is retiring could focus on her recollections of her favorite or most troublesome former students. A feature for a homecoming story could be a behind-the-scenes look at the building of one parade float.

Leads for features are often more creative or unusual than ones for yearbook news stories, which often use a summary opener. All the lead variations found in Chapters 3–7 in this book will be useful for yearbook feature writers.

Since the yearbook largely focuses on people and their activities, the feature form is especially suitable for personality sketches and descriptions of the sights, sounds, smells and human emotional responses of an event. Also popular is the "you are there" story, with the writer putting the reader into the situation through the mind and body of one actual participant. A story about a driver's education, behind-the-wheel class, focusing on one student driver, is an example of this form.

Following the opening paragraph, the feature is developed with more facts and often many direct and indirect quotes from the person profiled or from a small number of persons whose opinions add color and interest to the story.

The closing paragraph deserves almost as much creative attention as the opening. The reporter may save an especially interesting quote, fact or statistic to use here, one that may help sum up the main focus of the story or refer back to the lead.

Students like to see themselves and their friends in photos, and they like to read what their friends and others had to say about an event or issue reported in the yearbook. To satisfy this natural reader curiosity and to report a story with more depth and accuracy, the reporter should include student sources and quote students directly and indirectly in most feature, news and news-feature stories. Readers are curious about what others think and have done. If they see names in a story, they are more likely to read it.

In addition to citing names and including comments from those interviewed, the story will likely be more interesting if as many specific details are included as possible. Include exact statistics and facts, rather than generalities and vague estimates. For example, a homecoming football game story could open: "A chilly north wind and a kick-off temperature of 45 degrees didn't stop nearly 2,000 Central fans from giving their undefeated Cardinals a standing ovation as they entered Brown Stadium for the 40th homecoming football game." The same lead, without most of the details, could read: "A sell-out crowd gave the football team a standing ovation as it entered the stadium for the homecoming game." The former has more color, has more details and would likely be more interesting to readers; the latter is acceptable, but not as good as the former.

To achieve uniformity, consistency and professionalism, yearbook reporters use accepted journalism style when they write. The Associated Press publishes a style manual that is commonly used and is applicable for most high school writing. This textbook has a style chapter that will be useful for yearbook writers too.

Some of the common style concerns for yearbook reporters include dates and numbers, abbreviations for school group names, courtesy titles and class identifiers for students and the capitalization of courses, classes and events. If the Associated Press style manual is adopted, a supplement could be created to address some school-only needs.

Paragraphs, especially the lead or opening, are short, often one to three sentences long. However, this recommendation should not create an obvious pattern. A variety of paragraph lengths is usually desirable. Sentence lengths should also vary; the reader should not be aware of any patterns unless, for example, a staccato is created for an intentional effect. Short paragraphs and simple sentences encourage readership.

The Horches...

With a family of five, mother Genevieve, father Phillip, senior, Stephanie, freshman, Philip, and ten year old Gen, it was hard to keep everyone's busy schedule intact and still spend time together.

"We try to eat together every day. We like to go to Santa Cruz every summer, and we go camping together," Genevieve said.

But while this family tried to keep things together, a hardship came upon them. Seven years ago, Phillip fell off a roof and broke his back while working in construction.

"My dad was home a lot more, and my mom had to get three jobs to support us. I tried to help more around the house, and I took care of my younger brother and sister a lot," Stephanie said.

Although their father's injury put much stress on the family, they pulled through, and grew stronger from the difficulties.

"I think we're closer now. We have a lot of family parties with our whole family there," Stephanie said.

The Davises...

The lives of the Davis family were forever changed when Konnor Jean was born three weeks pre-mature, on July 9, 1996 at Mercy San Juan Hospital. Konnor was released eight days after his birth to his mother Lorri; father and Del Campo teacher Tom; Del Campo senior, brother Kyle; and sister Kelli, class of '96 Del Campo graduate.

"It was a very tough time for us, but we got through it as a family. We try to keep a sense of humor during tough times," Lorri said.

With a new member of the family the Davises became a great deal closer, despite the 15 year difference in age from the closest sibling, Kyle.

"Having Konnor has taught both Kelli and Kyle about the responsiblities that are involved in having a child," Tom said.

Although changes arrived with Konnor, many of the Davis family traditions remained the same. Every summer they visit their relatives in South Carolina for their family vacation.

familiar

Fig. 11.8. Feature writing, with a human interest angle introduced in the lead and developed with direct and indirect quotes throughout the story—even for short stories—is the most popular form of writing in yearbooks. *Decamhian,* Del Campo High School, Fair Oaks, Calif.

The Molinis. . .

When their mother moved to San Diego two years ago, junior Sara Molini, and sophomore Theresa Molini started living full time with only their father, Greg Molini.

"The hardest part to adjust to was getting used to not having my mom around," Sara said.

It was hard at first for the girls to adjust to just living with their dad, but they soon adapted to a new lifestyle, and even found some benefits.

"I don't get in trouble as much and I get more of what I want because my dad can't tell me to go ask my mom anymore," Theresa said.

After becoming accustomed to a new way of life, the three found interests in the same things.

"We like going to old, classic car shows, and baseball and basketball games," Sara said.

Without their mother living with them, the sisters found that they grew closer.

"My sister and I are a lot closer. Because my mom isn't around so we have to talk to each other about 'the girl stuff'," Theresa said.

The Nelsons. . .

After living in Australia with his parents for nine months, junior Andy Nelson decided to move back to California, where he felt more comfortable in school and church.

"I'd lived here since I was one or two and this is my home. I came back for my friends, family, and church," Andy said.

Moving away from his parents in August, Andy lived with family friends. But when that fell through, Andy's brother, 26 year old Bryce, offered to let Andy live with him.

"I've been living with him since January. We have a lot in common, we're interested in a lot of the same things," Andy said.

Although the two get along and have many of the same interests, it was still a difficult transition to make.

"It's been an adventure. The hardest part is keeping schedules together between school, work, and church group," Bryce said.

support

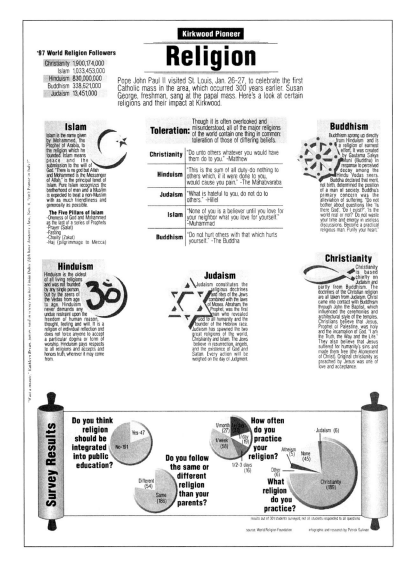

Fig. 11.9. The word story in a yearbook often takes a form other than prose. Here's an example of a large amount of information delivered efficiently to readers through a full-page information graphic. *Pioneer,* Kirkwood High School, Kirkwood, Mo.

Word choices are important if writers want readers to start and finish their writing. Reporters should select specific nouns and lively, active verbs when writing the story. Generally, for news, news-feature and feature stories, the use of adverbs and adjectives is usually restricted to the indirect and direct quotes from sources cited in the copy. However, other writing forms—storytelling or first-person accounts, for example—are less restrictive.

Reporters should verify the spelling of all names. The permanency of the yearbook and its status as likely the only published history of one year in the life of a school and its students and staff make the need to be accurate one of the most important concerns for all reporters and editors. Spell checkers in software programs should not be relied upon as the only verification for accurate spelling. Unless the spell checker has a customized dictionary, it can't verify most proper nouns. Checking the accuracy of dates, statistics and any unusual information is also important. A yearbook is a record, and all facts and figures should be correct. A reporter can double-check notes as the first draft is written. An editor should also verify important statistics and facts during the editing process.

Careful editing will also include an evaluation of the flow or development of the story. The transitions from paragraph to paragraph should be smooth. With the exception of the question and answer, or Q&A, format story form, the reporter's questions should not be included as transitions. The interviewees' responses and simple transitional words such as "according to" and simple attributions such as "said" are preferred; writers should avoid the awkward and space-wasting use of phrases such as, "When asked what she thought of …"

OTHER WAYS TO WRITE THE STORY

Text copy, whether it is the only story on the spread or is made up of two or more stories, including sidebars, can take forms other than the prose form of news, news-features and features. Deviations from these traditional and popular journalistic forms may be desirable occasionally to break what could be a monotonous flow or to fit information that could be better reported in another form (Fig. 11.9)

The short story or storytelling form may be appropriate for certain topics.

Similar to children's stories or short stories read in literature classes, the opening of this journalistic writing form includes some set-the-scene description, the presentation of the principal persons and the introduction of some conflict that needs to be resolved. The body of the story tells the reader how the persons involved in the situation go about resolving the conflict. The story's ending is the solution to the conflict and how it affects the persons involved. With this form, the suspense builds to a high point of interest near the end of the story.

Many think the storytelling form of writing is how persons naturally relate incidents to each other. This form could be effective for reporting an especially significant athletic contest or relating a specific science class experiment and its results, among other possibilities.

The question and answer interview format, or Q&A, with a brief lead that introduces the interviewee and summarizes the reason why the person is being interviewed, is another alternate text form. It can be used for long interviews with newsmakers such as the school's principal or a star athlete who holds several school records in a particular sport. The long, full-story Q&A should be used only sparingly so it doesn't lose its uniqueness. The short-form Q&A, made up of (1) one to only a handful of questions and responses from one person or (2) one question and responses from several persons, can be a useful and frequently used sidebar in any section of the book. For example, in the sports section, the short-form Q&A sidebar could be an interview with a team's captain or senior athletes who lettered in the sport. The shorter Q&A can even be used on every spread.

Dialogue or a playlike dramatization could be a suitable way to present a word story on a variety of topics in any section of the book, especially a section on student life. The dialogue could be fictitious for a story about dating, with the story labeled as fiction. Or a real situation, such as a report on the first day of school, could be dramatized with real dialogue and real "stage" directions.

In theme copy and sidebars in any section, the first-person diary or journal story form can be an effective form for many topics. This form can be an appealing contrast to the third-person, objective form of the news, news-feature or feature story. A participant in an event can provide a compelling, personal and often emotional "insider" account that can reveal more than an interview with a reporter.

Though rare, information presented as a poem, song (complete with music), crossword puzzle, cryptogram, essay or form more commonly associated with other print media can provide a unique and successful surprise element to the yearbook. These forms may not be suitable for news with a serious edge.

Although more commonly found in newspapers, the information graphic is another alternate way to present a story in a stand-alone or supporting way in a yearbook The information graphic, or infographic, the shortened term, is the incorporation of one or more illustrations, photos, graphics or some other form of art with words and/or figures to report specific, often narrowly focused, information. These elements are tightly organized to form a self-contained message. This process—creating the information graphic—is often called "visual reporting" and is the product of reporters and artists working together.

Information graphics can take many forms. Some are bar graphs, pie charts, timelines, summary boxes, diagrams and lists. Some of these are more appropriate for newspapers than yearbooks. Scoreboards in the sports section are the most common information graphic in yearbooks. In addition to a listing of the results of a season's contests, they can also include small photos, art, brief quotes and a list of record holders for the season. All of these elements are organized into a "box" or self-defined rectangle. The scoreboard serves as a quick reference for the reader.

Another popular information graphic is the list. The results of student surveys, such as most popular movies or television shows of the year, are organized into a list. The list can be graphically enhanced with art and display type to create an attractive page element. Diagrams, such as an architect's blueprint of the school, and timelines, such as one that traces the history of the school for an anniversary book, are also appropriate for the yearbook. Bar graphs and pie charts, without any art, are not recommended for yearbooks since they lack visual interest.

Schools with large populations of students who speak a language in addition to English may want to publish some copy in other languages. This could be especially suitable for stories and events involving a large number of English as a second language students. For example, coverage of students celebrating Mexican

Independence Day could be printed in Spanish and, if space permits, with an accompanying English translation. Publishing an entire yearbook as a split run, each edition of the same volume in a different language, though ambitious, could positively affect sales and the status of the yearbook, especially among communities without the yearbook as a tradition.

As is true with visual special effects, overuse of any nonprose way of writing the word stories of the year can greatly diminish their appeal. An occasional first-person account or Q&A will likely add the variety that readers enjoy.

CHECKLIST FOR THE YEARBOOK REPORTER

- Brainstorm for story development ideas with other staff members.

- To coordinate and exploit all possible visual and verbal elements of all major stories, work as a team with a photographer, page designer and, possibly, an artist.

- Working with a photographer, plan each photo shoot to get a full range of shots, from close-ups to long shots, verticals to horizontals.

- Interview more people for a story than you think you'll need; select the best responses for the word story.

- Tell some aspect of the story with a brief sidebar, an information graphic or an alternate story form. Readers may prefer several short word stories on a spread rather than one long story.

- Choose the best journalistic story form for the content—news, news-feature, or feature. Or use the storytelling method of development.

- Write a lead that grabs the readers' attention; develop the story to hold their attention; end the story with some sparkle, something memorable.

- Link the main word story with at least one photo on the spread, preferably the dominant photo (the largest photo).

- Double-check the spellings of all names and proper nouns.

- Review your word story and accompanying photos for positive multiculturalism. Be an inclusive yearbook so all the school's population groups are represented.

EXERCISES

1. Find out the racial, ethnic and, if possible, religious composition of your school. List each group as a separate heading. Now list events and issues important to each group, such as special celebrations. Finally, prepare a list of yearbook stories that report some or all of these events and issues. Some events and issues could be combined into composite stories representing all or several groups.

2. List five events, such as the school's musical, that your yearbook covers every year. Under each, list five new angles to report that don't duplicate reporting done in the most recent yearbook.

3. Develop a five or more point checklist for photographers who will cover a sports event for your yearbook. What should they shoot? Should they shoot the spectators?

4. Select one aspect about teens and driving such as moving violations, arrests for intoxication, insurance rates or motor vehicle deaths and find some statistics about it. How can you use this information in a story in your yearbook?

5. Write a first-person journal account as a student focusing on one of these events: class picture day, any Friday, the opening day of the school year, the day of a final exam, or the day when classes were canceled due to bad weather.

Using Journalism Style

When writing a story for your school newspaper, yearbook or magazine, would you write *Nov. 22, Nov. 22nd, November twenty-second* or *November 22? Number 10* or *number ten? Twenty-fifth* or *25th? Marathon County, Marathon county* or *Marathon Co.? Well known* or *well-known? U.S. Army, United States Army, Army of the United States* or *army of the United States? Atlanta, Georgia, Atlanta, Ga.,* or *Atlanta, GA?*

The English language permits so many variations that a stylebook, or manual, is necessary to provide consistency. Otherwise, for example, one story might have *Jan. 13, 2001,* and another *January 13, 2001.*

Either AP (Associated Press) or The New York Times style is appropriate for student publications, although some adjustments may be made. Students will then, as career preparation, learn style that is practiced in the professional workplace. Many commercial newspapers depart occasionally from AP style to suit local readers' preferences. The style sheet in this chapter offers some variations on AP style suitable for student publications.

Some suggested primary style considerations follow.

NAMES AND IDENTIFICATION

The first time a person is named in a story, his or her complete first and last name along with some identifier should be used.

Faculty members are identified by position or subject taught, whichever is appropriate for the particular story. Titles can also indicate job, rank or profession (for example, coach, principal, superintendent, nurse, counselor, athletic director, English teacher). Short titles precede names: "English teacher Laura Pearson" or "basketball coach James Rogers." Longer titles usually follow: "Mrs. Wendy Smith, chair of the Language Department," or "Marci Rosmarin, School Centered Education committee chairperson."

Students are identified by class, year of graduation or some other method appropriate to the school (senior Sarah Kagan; Lucy Meed-Sygrove, '01; David Choe, 4).

In some stories students may be identified in other ways. For example, an editor-in-chief of the paper may be identified by that title if it is appropriate to the story. In sports stories players are identified by the positions they play or hold (Colin Allred, linebacker; Captain Morgan White). Do not make up titles by mere description, such as "harpsichordist Becky Lucas." Alumni are identified by year of graduation (Margie Pak, '90). Only one identifier is needed on first reference. Do not overdo identifiers, such as "senior forward and team captain Karen Greening." The other relevant identifiers can be used in subsequent references.

A student publication may choose to make no distinction between name references for adults and students, or it may choose to differentiate. Today, major newspapers differ on the use of courtesy titles for women and men (Mr., Mrs., Miss and Ms.). Some papers use no courtesy titles, some only for women and some to indicate a married couple. These titles are rarely used in sports coverage. If courtesy titles are used for adult women in your publication, request from each adult woman her preference for *Ms., Miss* or *Mrs.* and abide by it. If no preference is sought, use only *Ms.* or *Mrs.* For adult men, use *Mr.* Whether courtesy titles are used is not as important as is a consistent plan for all stories, all year. When courtesy titles are used, they typically appear on second and subsequent references.

The second and every other time the adult is mentioned in the story, use the courtesy title and the last name, or just the last name. For example, the first reference would be "math instructor Jennifer Dusenberry," and the second reference would be "Ms. Dusenberry," or "Dusenberry." If there would be no confusion, the proper name can be alternated with the job title to give more variety. For example, for second and further references, the story could read, "the math instructor said" and then, later, "Ms. Dusenberry said." The job title with the last name may also be used for the second and further references.

A choice exists for the second and any further times the person is mentioned in the story. Some student publications use only the last name in these succeeding references; others just the first name. The former follows most professional style manuals. Either is acceptable, as long as a consistent plan is adopted and followed for every story, all year. If a story mentions many persons, it may be less confusing to follow a policy of using only last names in second and further references.

Accuracy of name spellings should be a priority. Remember, what you think is spelled "John" could be spelled "Jon," "Jonn" or "Jean." If the adult uses only a first initial and a full middle name, then respect that preference. Do not use only a first name initial and a last name. Husbands and wives should be referred to by name (Mr. and Mrs. Jeff Mays or Jeff and Shonda Mays, *not* Mr. Jeff Mays and wife).

CAPITALIZATION

Capitalization rules are pretty standard among publication style guides.

Always capitalize the following:

- All proper nouns and proper adjectives (Joyce, Shakespearean, Antarctica)

- All titles when they precede names (Principal Vickie Richie, Queen Elizabeth)

- First and all words in titles of books, periodicals, speeches, plays, songs, except for articles, prepositions and conjunctions (*A Tale of Two Cities, Sports Illustrated,* "Free Speech, Its Problems," *Friends,* "Rudolph, the Red-Nosed Reindeer," *Man against the Sea)*

- Holidays and special school events (Thanksgiving, New Year's Day, Homecoming, Senior Day, Spring Swing)

- Sections of the country (the West, the Atlantic States)

- Names of nationalities and races (Indian, German, Ethiopian—also see later discussion for identification of minority groups)

- College degrees when abbreviated (B.A., M.A., Ph.D.)

- Names of clubs, buildings, departments, schools, colleges (Spanish Club, Beardsley Gymnasium [or Gym], English Department, Ferris High School, Cornell College)

- Names of streets (Fifth Street, Oak Avenue, Park Boulevard)

- Geographical names (Hudson River, Lake Tanganyika, Rock of Gibraltar)

- Names of classes only when the term *class* is used and the reference is to a particular class in the school (Freshman Class, Sophomore Class, *but* freshmen, seniors)

- Names of specific courses (American Literature I, *but* the field of American literature; History II, *but* the study of history; Journalism III, *but* journalism as a career)

- Names of languages (English, French, Korean)

- Names of athletic teams (Yellowjackets, Bullfrogs, Green Wave, Blue Blazers)

- Words or abbreviations, such as *No., Fig.* and *Chapter,* when followed by a number, title or name (No. 10, Fig. 4, Chapter 6)

- All other words traditionally capitalized, such as noun references to the deity of all monotheistic religions (God, the Father, Allah), political parties and the like. Consult an English handbook when in doubt.

Do not capitalize the following:

- Titles when they follow names (Seth Levy, assistant principal; Ryan McGlothlin, director of athletics; Daniel Villarreal, chairperson of the Social Studies Department; Angela Yeung, editor-in-chief of the *Evanstonian*)

- Names of school subjects, unless they are languages or specific courses (He is taking Spanish, American History I, Physics M. and Art IV. He hopes to study chemistry and journalism next year.)

- Directions, unless they mean a geographic place (He lives on the south side of the street. She moved to the South.)

- Parts of time (a.m., p.m., o'clock)

- Seasons of the year, except when personified (fall, winter, but Old Man Winter)

- Names of rooms, offices, buildings, unless they have an official proper name (room 159, the journalism room, the guidance office, the fieldhouse, the library, but Ragland Reading Room, Beardsley Gym)

- The subject of a debate, except the first word (Resolved: That free enterprise is basic to this American way of life)

- Committees (entertainment committee, refreshment committee)

- Descriptive or occupational words used as "titles" (pitcher Nolan Ryan, actress Winona Ryder)

- Title modifiers such as *former* and *the late* (the late John Lennon, former President Clinton)

- College degrees when spelled out (bachelor of arts, master of science, doctor of philosophy)

ABBREVIATIONS

Normally most publications avoid all but standard, commonly understood abbreviations of accepted titles,

but here are the usual "rules."
Abbreviate

- Names that are well-known as abbreviations (YMCA, PTA, AIDS, UN, NASA, NATO). Note: Write such abbreviations without periods and without spaces.

- Titles when they precede last names (Dr. Garcia; Rev. Kelly, *but* the Reverend Lynn Kelly; Mr. and Mrs.; all military titles, such as Pvt. and Lt.)

- Names of states when they follow the name of a city, except very short or one-syllable names, such as *Iowa, Ohio, Utah, Maine* (Madison, Wis.; Buffalo, N.Y.; *but* Des Moines, Iowa)

- Names of months when followed by a date, except very short months, such as *April, May, June, July* (Nov. 19, 2001; Oct. 7, 2003; *but* June 14, 2000)

- College degrees (B.A., M.A., Ph.D., Ed.D., D.D., LL.D.)

Do not abbreviate

- Names of streets (Eastwood Avenue, Central Street)

- Titles following a name (Susan Ginsburg, professor of history)

- Days of the week

- States when used without a city

- *Percent* (the symbol % should be used only in tabular material or in headlines when used with a figure)

- Positions when not used as titles (secretary, treasurer, president)

- *Department* (English Department)

- *Christmas* (not Xmas)

- The year, except when used to identify students or alumni (1992; Susan Meyercord, '90)

- *United States* as a noun; it can be abbreviated as an adjective (in the United States, but U.S. history)

NUMBERS

Spell out all approximate numbers and numerals up to and including *nine* except for dates, scores, addresses, ages, time and money (about 2,000 are expected; Sept. 4, 1996; Ames, 14, West Des Moines, 7; 7 Wilson Avenue; 4 o'clock; 5 cents; 3 years old).

Do not begin a sentence with a number in figures; if a sentence must start with a number, it should be spelled out. (Twenty-five students will ...; or About 25 students will ...; *not* 25 students will ...)

Spell out ordinal numbers (sixty-sixth).

Do not use *d, rd, st* or *th* in writing dates (May 19, 1997; *not* May 19th, 1997).

When two numbers are used together, avoid confusion by spelling out the first, whether the number is above or below *nine* (fourteen 4-year-old children, *not* 14 4-year-old children).

In a list containing numbers below and above *nine*, use figures for all. (Those on the committee include 5 from GAA, 11 from the Student Council, 3 from the French Club and 14 from the hall monitors.)

For sums of money less than one dollar, use figures and the word *cents* (10 cents, *not* $.10; 5 cents, *not* 5 cts.).

Do not use ciphers when giving the exact hour or an even number of dollars (4 p.m., *not* 4:00 p.m.; $5, *not* $5.00).

Do not use the date when an event occurs within or close to the week of publication (Friday, next Friday, last Tuesday, tonight, yesterday).

For numbers of four or more digits, except serial numbers—house, telephone, pages, years—use a comma (4,945; 469,958,000).

PUNCTUATION

No style manual includes all the rules for the use of all punctuation marks. Any good English text will do that. A style manual should, however, include any deviations from standard English style. A few special uses are common in newswriting, and they should be included in a style sheet.

THE COMMA AND THE SEMICOLON

Do not include a comma before the *and* in a simple series. (Those on the committee are Susan Clarke, Paul Block and Dale Jackson.)

Do not use a comma between a man's name and *Jr.* or *Sr.* (Fred Black Jr.).

Use commas and semicolons in lists of names and identifying terms. (The committee consists of Gerry Brown, chairman; Shawn Jourdain, vice-chairman; and Cam Carhart, secretary-treasurer.)

Use a semicolon between the main items in a series when commas occur within the series.

Use a comma in a compound sentence before the conjunction. (The Key Club led the school in the aluminum can drive, and the Chess Club nearly tied.) When the coordinating conjunction is not present, use a semicolon. (The Key Club won; the Chess Club came in second.) When the coordinating conjunction is present, use a semicolon if there is extensive punctuation in one or more of the clauses. (The Key Club, with 27 juniors and seniors, led the school in the aluminum recycling drive; but the Chess Club, with five sophomore members, nearly tied.) If the clauses are both short, either the comma or the conjunction might be dropped. (The Key Club won and the Chess Club lost. The Key Club won, the Chess Club lost.)

THE COLON

Omit the colon in a list following a *be* verb, such as *are* or *were*. (Those elected were Stefanie Boyar, Suresh Vasan and Bryan Parker.)

Use the colon to cite time in a track event (3:05.2).

QUOTATION MARKS

A period or a comma at the end of a quotation is always put inside the quotes. (We have just read "The Lottery.")

A question mark or an exclamation mark goes inside the quotation marks only if it belongs to the material quoted. (Have you read "The Lottery"? She asked, "Have you finished the story?")

A semicolon or a colon always goes outside the quotation marks. (Incomplete homework assignments may be a symptom of academic "burn-out"; it is a sign of more serious problems.)

Use quotation marks around the titles of one-act plays, speeches, poems, short stories, songs and articles within publications ("The Telephone Only Rings Twice," "Birches," "The Outcasts of Poker Flat," "Tenderly").

Do not put quotation marks around familiar nicknames; ordinarily only use nicknames in sports stories (Babe Ruth, Magic Johnson). But unfamiliar nicknames should be quoted, (Don "Duffer" Stevens).

Do not put quotation marks around slang expressions (to do so implies an apology for using them).

Do not put quotation marks around names of animals or characters in books or plays.

THE APOSTROPHE

Ordinarily form the possessive of all singular nouns by adding the apostrophe and *s* (the boy's book, the fox's den). If the singular noun ends in *s,* add the apostrophe and *s* (hostess's address) unless the next word begins with *s* (hostess' seat). Because stylebooks vary, it is correct to have only the apostrophe after a singular proper noun ending in *s* or to add an apostrophe and *s* (Charles' hat, Charles's hat). Consistency requires you choose a stylebook and follow it every time.

Form the possessive of a plural word ending in *s* by adding only an apostrophe (the boys' books, the girls' uniforms).

Form the possessive of a plural word not ending in *s* by adding an apostrophe and *s* (men's league, children's party).

Use an apostrophe in abbreviations of classes or years (Sarah Bass, '01; Class of '98).

Use an apostrophe followed by *s* to form the plurals of single letters and numbers and of symbols (A's and B's, size 7's, How many *c*'s in recommend?). The apostrophe is not, however, used for plurals of numbers or multiletter combinations (1990s, ABCs). Stylebooks vary on the use of the apostrophe for plurals when there is internal punctuation in a multiletter combination. Note: The plural *s* added to italic letters (or titles) is in roman type (three *Newsweek*s).

Use the apostrophe, not opening single quotation marks, to indicate omission of letters (wash 'n' wear, *not* wash 'n wear or wash n' wear).

Omit the apostrophe in names of organizations when the possessive case is implied and in certain geographic designations (Citizens League, Actors Equity Association, Pikes Peak).

THE HYPHEN

Use a hyphen in compound numbers and fractions (forty-eight, three-fourths). Remember a hyphen joins, so no spaces are used before and after a hyphen.

Use a hyphen with compound adjectives of two or more words (note-taking skills, grade-point average, front-page story, out-of-state student, all-state diver). Note: A hyphen is not used after an adverb ending in *ly* (tightly laced shoes). The hyphen is frequently omitted when two words are joined to function as a noun; see a dictionary for current spellings, since form changes (makeup *not* make-up; layout *not* lay-out).

Use a hyphen when combining numbers and measurements to make an adjective (Jones is a 210-pound tackle; Johnson is the 6-foot-8-inch center).

The dash is used to separate or create a longer pause when a comma will not suffice. A dash is visually longer than a hyphen. A space is used before and after the dash.

ITALICS

Italicize

- Names of newspapers, books, magazines, long musical selections, works of art, boats or ships, plays and record albums (*The New York Times, Moby Dick, Rolling Stone, The Phantom of the Opera, Mona Lisa*)

- Words from other languages that have not become an accepted part of English (The meal was prepared *à la francaise;* Geoffrey's goal is to graduate *cum laude.*)

- A letter of the alphabet or a word used specifically as a word (The word letter has two *t*'s in it.)

- An editor's note to a story

- A word to be emphasized (He repeated he had *never* been a candidate.)

Use italics for emphasis with caution. A reader ignores overused italics.

SPELLING

Since a number of words have several correct spellings, a style manual should include the preferred forms of those appearing most frequently in news stories. For other words, consult a standard dictionary to determine the preferred form, which should be used consistently.

Following is a list of words that frequently appear in school news stories and are often misspelled. Make your own additional list.

EXAMPLE 12.1

absence
a cappella
adviser
advisory
algebra
all right
alumna (f.s.)
alumnae (f.pl.)
alumni (m.pl.)
alumnus (m.s.)
apparatus
arithmetic
assembly
association
attendance
athlete
athletics
audience
auditorium

backfield
baseball
baseman
basketball
believe
biology
bookkeeping
business

cafeteria
calendar
captain
chaperon
cheerleader
chemistry
choir
chorus
classmate
college
commencement
commercial
committee
council (student)
counselor
criticism

curriculum
custodian

defense
drama

eligible
embarrass
emphasize
English
existence
experiment

faculty
familiar
February
field house
finally
football
foreign
forty (but fourth)
forward (on a team)
foreword (in a book)
fullback

geometry
German
government
graduation
grammar
guard
guidance
gymnasium

halfback
handball
heavyweight
high jump
hockey
homecoming
homeroom
homerun

incidentally
initiation
intramural
its (possessive), it's (it is)

laboratory
league
lettermen
library
lightweight
lineup (noun), line up (verb)
literature
long jump
lose vs. loose
lunchroom

mathematics
misspell

necessary (but unnecessary)

occasion
occurred
occurrence
offense
opponent

permissible
planning
phase
physics
poll vs. pole
practice
preparation

principal (of your school)
privilege
professor
psychology

quarterback
quartet
questionnaire

receive
recommend
referee
registrar
rhythm
role vs. roll
runner-up

schedule
secretary
semester
semifinal
senior
separate
sergeant
shining
shortstop
shot put (but shot-putter)
similar
society
sophomore
Spanish
speech
sponsor
stopping
studying
superintendent

tackle
teenager
textbook
theater
their vs. there
thorough
tomorrow
tonight
touchdown
treasurer
tryout (noun), try out (verb)
typewriting

unanimous
university
until
upperclassman

volleyball

weather
Wednesday
weekend
weird
whether vs. weather
writing
written

SCREENING SEXIST EXPRESSIONS

What we say and write about men and women often reveals attitudes toward sex roles that many persons find objectionable. Language does affect values, especially when we are speaking of persons who belong to groups other than our own. In general, our goal should be to avoid the use of words and phrases that directly or indirectly suggest limited opportunity for members of any group, whether by sex, race, ethnic description or religion.

Gender-free terms should replace sex-designating terms. Change

- *Mailman* to *mail carrier*

- *Fireman* to *fire fighter*

- *Policeman* or *policewoman* to *law enforcement official* or *police officer*

- *Newsman* or *newswoman* to *reporter*

- *Actor* and *actress* to (only) *actor*

- *Chairman* to *chairperson* or *chair*

Job designations by gender should not be mentioned unless pertinent to the story. They imply that the occupations are inappropriate for the individual holding them. Change

- *Male nurse* to *nurse*

- *Woman* or *lady lawyer* to *lawyer*

MARITAL STATUS, APPEARANCE, SEXUAL STEREOTYPES

The appearance of a woman (or man) should not be described unless the description is essential for the story. A girl-watching or male-watching tone—using words or phrases such as *buxom, blonde* or *big hunk*—should be avoided. Clichés and jokes at women's or men's expense such as *woman driver* or *dumb jock* should also be deleted.

PROBLEM WORDS

For greater accuracy and less damage to sensitive value systems, find substitutes for problem words. Change

- *A member of the Christian right* to *religious conservative* or *religious activist*

- *Forefathers* to *ancestors, forerunners* or *forebears*

- *Man-hours* to *work hours, staff time*

- *Common man* to *the average person, the ordinary citizen*

- *Lady* (unless that connotation is appropriate) to *woman*

- *Man-made* to *manufactured, produced*

- *Coed* (as a noun) to *student* (Logically, the term *coed* refers to any student at a coeducational college or university.)

- *A reference to a man or a woman* to *feminist* only if he or she identifies himself or herself as one

- *Muslim terrorist* to a more specific political group if the person(s) is a member of a group that is involved in terrorism

RACE OR ETHNIC LANGUAGE

Identifying someone as a member of a minority group is done only when it is essential to the reader's full understanding of the story. The decision to use racial, ethnic, religious or sexual orientation labels should be made only after careful consideration for their news value.

Minority groups of all kinds deserve to be identified, if there is a need to use such identification in the story, with labels acceptable to them and conforming to what is advocated by official groups representative of these minorities.

Racial, ethnic, religious or sexual orientation stereotypes, like male-female ones, should be eliminated from all writing, art and photography. Some of this bias is subtle and unintentional. For example, if you are doing a story about unmarried teenage mothers, it would be wrong to cover, in words and photos, only those of certain racial or ethnic groups, since being unmarried and pregnant crosses all racial, ethnic and economic boundaries.

A good reporter needs to understand that some words are used within the community, but once someone outside the community uses the words, they carry derogatory meanings. Other words such as *barrio* started as neutral descriptions but over time have suggested derogatory stereotypes and should be avoided.

Labels popular and acceptable in the past may not be acceptable today. For example, the term *Negro* was acceptable for media use in the 1960s, but today *black* is used, and *African-American* is now preferred by many. If a reporter has doubts, a comprehensive, up-to-date style manual should be consulted. When race or ethnicity is relevant, a good reporter may ask what label is preferable.

Acceptable labels for some of the major minority groups in the United States include

- *Asian-American*

- *African-American* or *black*

- *Native American* or *American Indian*

- *Hispanic, Latino/Latina, Chicano/Chicana*—although any one of these is considered derogatory in certain regions of the United States

- *Native Alaskan*

- *Pacific Islander*

- *Gay* (male), *lesbian* (female), *homosexual*

Some of the subgroups within a large minority group prefer to be identified by more specific labels such as *Chinese-American, Cuban-American* or an exact Indian tribal name (which may not be the commonly accepted tribal name imposed by traders and settlers). The best advice is to be current and specific.

Some minority groups have media membership organizations, such as the following. Students and teachers can write to these organizations to request information on programs, learning materials or scholarships.

Asian American Journalists Association, 1765 Sutter Street, Suite 1000, San Francisco, CA 94115. Tel: (415) 346-2051; e-mail: national@aaja.org.

National Association of Black Journalists, 8701 Adelphi Road, Adelphi, MD 20783-1716. Tel: (301) 445-7100; e-mail: nabj@nabj.org.

National Association of Hispanic Journalists, 1193 National Press Building, Washington, DC 20045-2100. Tel: (202) 662-7145; e-mail: nahj@nahj.org.

National Lesbian and Gay Journalists Association, 2120 L Street NW, suite 840, Washington, DC 20037. Tel: (202) 588-9888; e-mail: nlgja@aol.com.

Native American Journalists Association, 3359 36th Avenue S, Minneapolis, MN 55406. Tel: (612) 729-9244; e-mail: info@naja.com.

The San Francisco State University website called NEWSWATCH.sfsu.edu can be helpful in dealing with racial and ethnic language.

Editing Copy: Coaching Writers

Publication writing, at its best, is a story torn and pasted inside a locker door, a dog-eared page of a yearbook, the topic of a cafeteria conversation over pizza and corn.

Writing is putting words on a page that people use, quote and remember. A writer and a copy editor working together can make that happen. To produce stories that readers want and need to read, the copy editor must discuss the story with the writer at many stages of the writing process. The copy editor works with the writer to improve writing. A good copy editor may not be the best writer on a staff but is someone who understands what makes good writing.

Copyediting used to mean capitalizing "Dallas Cowboys" and taking a comma out of "lions, tigers, and bears." Oh my, how copyediting has changed. Copyediting now encompasses a practice called *coaching writing*, which means discussing the story during the writing process. Correcting spelling, grammar and style errors is still a very important part of copyediting. Today a copy editor also coaches writers by asking the right questions and discussing the content, structure and flow of a story.

THE COACHING WRITING PROCESS

Understanding the coaching part of copyediting will give the copy editor something to say to a first-year staff writer or an experienced sports editor asking for writing advice. Discussion can happen just outside the lockers during a passing period. The copy editor can ask the questions in a five-minute phone conversation. And the intense writing discussions can come in a secluded area of the hallway outside the staff room during class. Taking copyediting beyond proofing for spelling and punctuation errors is critical to improving writing.

One of the keys to good copyediting is to know what questions to ask the writer. Coaching questions should come from the editor who sees the story from the reader's perspective. The questioning process should help the writer develop a sense of the story's purpose and focus.

"What did you learn about this story?"

"What part of the interview or observation did you have a reaction to?"

Questions such as these should be aimed to help the writer talk out the story. By answering these questions, the writer can discover what is new or interesting.

The questions can be organized so that the copy editor asks them in three basic stages: the planning stage, the collecting stage and the writing stage.

PLANNING STAGE

"So what's the reader going to want to know?"

"What are you, the reporter, going to need to know before you interview? What will help you make sure you understand what's being said in the interview?"

"What do you think the reader is going to find interesting in this story?"

The purpose of coaching questions in the planning stage is to help the writer hone the questions or focus before the interview. The questions also ask the writer to think about what sort of background he or she needs to do before starting to collect the information through interviews. When talking through the planning stage, the reporter should develop an outline of the information needed.

COLLECTING STAGE

"What did you see when you went to play practice?"

"What details do you remember from the ballerina's room? What do those details say about her?"

"What do you think your best quote is?"

Questions in the collection stage should help the writer sort through the images and information gathered from interviews and observation. The copy editor will also help the writer see what information is needed through reinterviewing or reobservation. During this stage, the copy editor may help the writer find a lead or the first quote.

WRITING STAGE

"So what do you think this story is about?"

"What do you think is going to be complicated about this story? What do you think is going to be hard for the reader to understand?"

"What were you surprised people said when you interviewed them?"

The questions in the writing stage should be aimed to help the writer sort through the research and interviews. The writer should be trying to decide which are the best quotes to use verbatim or word-for-word. The questions can help the writer to decide what parts are complicated enough to require careful wording or step-by-step treatment.

In any of the three stages, the copy editor's role is also to give the reporter something to build on and to get the writer excited about the story.

"I liked that quote that you had from Coach Dupree. That could go high in the story."

"I think the teacher who survived her bout with cancer and then wanted to tutor Josh, who was facing brain cancer, is a great anecdote that could be your lead."

Identifying the strongest parts of their research is crucial to helping writers improve each draft.

But now the deadline is approaching. The copy editor has talked the writer through the eighth draft. Time is a factor, and final changes have to be made. As the deadline approaches, the role of the copy editor starts to evolve from that of writing coach to fixer.

RESOURCES NEEDED TO COPYEDIT

A good copy editor will want to have quick access to the numerous resources.

• A journalism stylebook, such as the one from the Associated Press or *The New York Times,* as well as a school style sheet

• A dictionary and thesaurus, even though both may be built into the word-processing program. A complete, unabridged dictionary on CD-ROM will be useful for those staffs that have a CD-ROM reader on their computer. Some word-processing programs have dictionaries and thesauri as well as spelling checkers. The checker should be customized to include style points, frequently used names and other words common to high school events and teen issues.

• A school directory that lists all students, faculty and staff so the reporter and editor can verify the spelling of names and, for faculty and staff, titles. This information may be available electronically in some schools through the registrar or data clerk.

• Local business and residential telephone books to verify the spelling of names and to check addresses

• An almanac and biographical dictionary, useful for verifying facts and the names and accomplishments of well-known persons who may be cited in stories

• A grammar handbook with a quick reference section, helpful for both reporters and editors. The copy editor may want to prepare a list of the most common grammatical errors to post for all reporters.

• Back issues of the school newspaper and recent school

yearbooks and magazines to verify information in story updates and for ongoing coverage

Hunkered down in the middle of these resources, the copy editor can begin the final edit. To evaluate the story, the copy editor breaks it down into parts.

THE LEAD

- In a straight news lead, is the most important and timely information there?

- Could the lead be shortened and remain clear?

- In a feature lead, does the anecdote, image or statement fit the tone and focus of the story?

- Are all the facts correct?

The lead makes a difference in whether students actually read the stories. The lead is that crucial to the story and therefore something very precious and personal to writers. If the writer's lead is saved, he or she will promise to clean the copy editor's room for 20 years. If the lead is shredded, it may be another year before the copy editor reviews the same person's writing again.

In some professional publications, a copy editor on deadline is asked to discuss the lead with the writer before making any changes, while edits later in the story can be made without consulting the writer.

BODY ORGANIZATION AND FLOW

While most beginning writers would like a formula here, there isn't one.

But a copy editor can certainly start with these questions:

- Are there unanswered questions?

- Did you organize the parts of the story so that they make sense?

- Did you read the story aloud to make sure the story flows?

In their book *Coaching Writers*, Roy Peter Clark and Don Fry list these among their tips for copy editors to give writers:

- Ask what the reader needs to know and in what order.
- Arrange the material into a narrative with a beginning, a middle and an end.
- Write a series of subheads for the sections by visualizing what the story will look like.
- List the players and their motives.
- Type two screensful quickly without worrying about sentences or sense, then print it, underline important things and rearrange them into an outline. Then kill the two screensful.
- Arrange materials into scenes, chapters or both.

REPORTING

FACT CHECK

The copy editor should be a master of detail and, if necessary, challenge every fact, every name and every word.

- Eliminate doubtful facts.

- Check facts against each other to ensure consistency.

- Confirm facts and verify names.

- Check figures, especially to see that totals tally.

- Be especially careful of dates and times. Check every date, month and day, with the calendar.

The copy editor should read to see whether all important information is given. If not, he or she should insert the needed facts or return the story to the reporter. The copy editor should not guess at facts or information but should double-check facts before automatically changing them.

The copy editor should make sure the writer has used the right source for the right information. If a science teacher says three teachers are retiring, the copy editor should have the writer double-check the information by interviewing the principal.

Journalists should typically avoid encyclopedias, weekly newsmagazines, books and newspapers as firsthand research. The writer should use these sources as background, then go straight to people for interviews.

For depth in the story, the copy editor should ask

the reporter to consider these as possible sources:

- Students
- Student polls
- Teachers
- Parents
- Alumni
- District statistics
- Doctors/psychologists
- Regional education administrations
- Municipal/county statistics
- Professional sources
- Building or local administrators
- Area college professors
- Teens at other schools
- School organizations or clubs
- Book authors
- Advocate organizations, such as Mothers Against Drunk Driving or the National Rifle Association

CLARITY AND CONCISENESS

Once the copy has been corrected for reporting errors, the copy editor makes sure each sentence and paragraph is clear, active and strong. If the copy editor has to stop to say, "Huh? I don't get that" or "Wait, I need to reread that sentence," the writing may not be clear. If the copy editor says, "I really want to stop reading now," then the writing may not be concise. Odds are that the writer needs help reorganizing paragraphs or recasting sentences.

The copy editor can put the following list next to the piece to be copyedited and go to work.

- If any paragraphs need to be rearranged, do so.
- If paragraphs are repetitive, combine them or delete one.
- If paragraphs are too long, divide them.
- If the copy has long lists of names, put them into a

sidebar or replace them by summarizing the contents.

- Emphasize an important idea by placing it at the beginning of a sentence.
- Tighten the writing by eliminating unnecessary words, phrases and clauses and by combining related expressions.
- Simplify complicated sentences.
- Energize sentences by changing passive voice verbs to active voice (occasionally, of course, the passive voice may be desirable). In the following sentence an active-voice verb is better.

> **The Wampus Cats played a strong defensive game. (*Not:* A strong defensive game was played by the Wampus Cats.)**

In the next sentence a passive-voice verb is better because it features the subject.

> **Ryan Coleman was reelected Student Council president. (*Not:* The student body reelected Ryan Coleman Student Council president.)**

- Eliminate trite expressions.
- Strive for sentence variety.
- Improve diction by using specific and exact words: *quibble* is different from *argue* or *debate*; *nice* is general for *affable, kind, pleasant* or *desirable*; *candid* is a synonym for *frank, impartial, open, sincere, straightforward, truthful* and *unprejudiced*, but with its own special meaning; *tree* is general, while *pine, oak* and *elm* are specific.
- Eliminate editorial comment unless the story is the type in which it is permitted, that is, a column, an editorial or a review.

DETAILS

While a copy editor may correct spelling, style and grammar mistakes along the way, the possibility is always there that those errors will be made again in the correction process. One last read to polish the story is necessary. The credibility of the writer and the publication depend on it. The reader who sees three spelling errors in one paragraph will doubt the accuracy of the re-

	HOW THEY ARE USED	WHAT THEY MEAN	HOW TYPE IS SET
TYPE SIZE and STYLE	Lansing, mich.--	Capitalize.	LANSING, Mich.—
	College Herald	Small caps.	COLLEGE HERALD
	the Senator from Ohio	Change to lower case.	the senator from Ohio
	By Alvin Jones	Bold face.	**By Alvin Jones**
	Saturday Evening Post	Italicize.	*Saturday Evening Post*
PUNCTUATION and SPELLING	"The Spy"	Emphasize quotes.	"The Spy"
	Northwestern U.	Emphasize periods.	Northwestern U.
	said, "I must . . .	Emphasize comma.	said, "I must …
	Johnsons'	Emphasize apostrophe.	Johnsons'
	picnicing	Insert letter or word.	picnicking
	theatre	Transpose letters.	theater
	Henry Cook, principal	Transpose words.	Principal Henry Cook
	days	Delete letter.	day
	judgement	Delete letter and bridge over.	judgment
	allright	Insert space.	all right
	those	Close up space.	those
	Geo. Brown	Spell out.	George Brown
	100 or more	Spell out.	one hundred or more
	Doctor S. E. Smith	Abbreviate.	Dr. S. E. Smith
	Six North Street	Use numerals.	6 North Street
	Marion Smythe	Spell as written.	Marion Smythe
POSITION	Madison, Wis.--	Indent for paragraph.	Madison, Wis.—
	today. Tomorrow he	New paragraph.	today. Tomorrow he
	considered serious. Visitors are not	No paragraph. Run in with preceding matter.	considered serious. Visitors are not
	But he called last night and said that he	No paragraph.	But he called last night and said that he
	]Jones To Conduct[or ⟨Jones To Conduct⟩	Center subheads.	**Jones To Conduct**
MISCELLANEOUS	He was not unmindful	Bridge over material omitted.	He was mindful
	one student came	Kill corrections.	one student came
	or more	Story unfinished.	
	30 or #	End of story.	————

Fig. 13.1.

Copy-editing symbols

Skills of a Copy Editor

• Have a broad knowledge; stories in all fields will pass the copydesk.

1. Be acquainted with all important events and trends.
2. Know your own publication and its policies.
3. Be alert to the times.
4. Know books, plays, magazines and reviews, legal and governmental structure and procedures.
5. Know names, localities, political and other social relationships.
6. Know geography, history and human nature.
7. Know your own school and community.

• Be able to write standard English and to edit it into poorly written stories.

1. Be skillful in handling sentences and paragraphs.
2. Have a strong command of words.
3. Be able to make all writing concise.
4. Be able to edit copy consistently according to the stylebook.

• Be able to distinguish editorializing from a sound inference based on fact. Edit out all editorializing. The following is not editorializing since the first phrase is followed by fact:

"Maine will meet its toughest opponent of the season Tuesday when the undefeated Arlington Heights

porting in the rest of the story.

In the last read-through of a story, the copy editor should

• Correct misspellings. Use but don't depend on a spell checker. For example, the computer still doesn't suggest "they're" when the writer incorrectly used "there."

• Correct errors in grammar and usage.

• Correct errors in style.

• Adjust stories to prescribed length:

1. Cut paragraphs.

2. Eliminate unimportant sentences or paragraphs.

3. Combine two sentences, making one sentence a subordinate clause or phrase in the other.

4. Change clauses to phrases and phrases to well-chosen words.

5. Use a single vivid verb or noun in place of a less specific verb or noun plus modifiers.

COACHING WRITING CONTINUES

The copy editor's job should not end even after spelling errors are corrected and the story is published. Set aside a few minutes to discuss the story with the writer without the pressures of a deadline.

"How did you feel about the story?"

"What, if given time, would you have done to improve the piece?"

"What other interviews did you still need?"

An after-publication discussion should be aimed to evaluate the story and to learn lessons from the process. The copy editor can commend a strong lead, correct habitual problems or reinforce some practices that the writer can use to improve the next story.

Making the point that the writer has a good eye for details, needs to do more interviews or needs to double-check facts can only improve the quality of the publication and the writer as the year goes on.

While a younger writer must be open to this discussion or criticism, both writer and copy editor must set aside egos and focus on improving the product. Writing tends to be a very personal endeavor, so any critical analysis of that work may make the writer want to do a Jackie Chan move on the copy editor.

Remembering that both the writer and copy editor are there to give the reader a clear, interesting story should help to eliminate any tension or any need for a trip to the emergency room.

Maintaining a civil tone eases the pain of critical analysis. The copy editor who barks out, "this stinks" or "what nose-pickin' moron wrote this," will not get the writer's respect or attention. The copy editor could easily begin with, "How can I help you on that story?" or "I think that's a great story you have this deadline. Let's talk about it."

While a copy editor's name may not appear at the top of the story, the lack of such recognition does not reduce the copy editor's worth.

A good copy editor understands that his or her goal is not only to improve the piece on the computer but also to improve the writer's skills.

A dedicated copy editor takes pride in the basketball player who actually stops in the gym to read this month's issue. He or she enjoys the progress of the entertainment writer who can now understand how to organize feature stories.

COPYEDITING ON A COMPUTER

On-screen story editing is practiced by most collegiate and professional publications and is becoming increasingly popular among high school publication staffs. For those staffs who find copyediting on paper to be a more thorough process for catching errors, Figure 13.1 presents a set of copy-editing symbols to use. Copy editors who do all copyediting on screen should develop a set way to differentiate between editing comments and actual text. Publication staffs use all caps, outline text, underlined text, strikethrough letters or italics to identify all copy-editing comments. Some word-processing programs have nonprinting text commands to use.

Management of edited story drafts must be handled carefully. A disorganized staff might find an early draft full of spelling errors and copy-editing comments published in the newspaper or yearbook. The organization system that the publication staff chooses may depend on the copy-editing system and computer system in place.

At Carmel High School, the *HiLite* staff, advised by Tony Willis, submits all copy electronically, preferably by e-mail. The reporter saves the copy under his or her name, a slug and the issue date, such as Willis/farmingclub/8-17. The copy goes to the copy editor who edits it and adds his or her title to the file name so it becomes Willis/farmingclub/8-17/copyed. From there, the story goes to the assigning editor and then to the editor-in-chief, with each person making edits and adding to the file name. The final version then gets saved to the server in the "copy to place" folder. Page designers use only the final draft in that file to design the page.

COMMON EDITING MISTAKES

- Using synonyms for *said*. Don't worry about the overuse of the word *said*. The word is neutral enough not to cause problems. Don't force words such as "he smiled" or "she chuckled" as attributions when it is physically hard to chuckle a quote.

- Using the school initials. Most students do not have to run back to the lobby to check the seal on the floor to remind themselves where they go to school. Initials in a school publication are a redundancy unless the story is making a comparison with other high schools.

- Inconsistent use of style rules. Do not use *May 29* in one story and *May 29th* in another. Know the publication style rules and stick to them.

- Improper use of *it's*. *It's* should be used where the word *it is* will work. *Its* is used to show possession.

- Including "when asked" to set up quotes. The reader assumes that direct quotes

Yellowjackets invade Memorial Stadium."

- Have what may be called a "bifocal" mind, one that shifts instantly from meticulous examination of details to the overall story.
- Recognize effective, even dramatic writing.
- Have a creative imagination; be able to see a good story in a poor one and to shape it by good editing.
- Exercise great care and patience.
- Understand reference sources and be able to consult them quickly and easily.

are results of questions from a reporter, so omit the phrase. "When asked" can be correctly used if there's a need for clarity. One case may be in a speech story where the reporter is including quotes from a post-speech interview.

- Combining several quotes in the same paragraph. When the speaker changes topics, a new paragraph is recommended. The new paragraph helps the reader understand the change in focus. Shorter paragraphs make readability easier from a design standpoint.

- Misuse of the word *stated*. The word should be used only when the quote is from a written or prepared text. The word *stated* should not be used to attribute spoken words.

- Name misspellings. Never assume you know how to spell a person's name. *John Smith* could be spelled *Jon Smithe* or *Jonn Smythe*. Do not even assume the name in the school records is correct. The reporter should ask the person to spell his or her name.

EXERCISES

1. One of the first steps in learning how to edit copy is to study and learn the most common principles of the style manual. Consistency in style is often the difference between an excellent and a potentially excellent newspaper.

   Study your style manual, or if you do not have one, use Chapter 12 as your guide. Rewrite each of the following exercises on a separate sheet of paper. Some of the cases may not be covered in your style manual. They are included here to promote class discussion and an eventual consensus. If your newspaper does not have an official style manual, these exercises may be used as the basis for forming one. You may occasionally need to consult your dictionary or other style manuals to settle a problem.

   (Note: Consider the first time you see a name to be the first reference. If the same person appears in later sentences, copyedit as though the references are the second and subsequent references.)

   Names and Capitalization

   1. Ferris high school basketball players worked out for three hours Friday.

   2. The Itasca Wampus Cats defeated the Bonham purple warriors 10-1 at Friday's baseball game.

   3. The freshman service club is collecting toys for families who lost their homes in the floods.

   4. Senior Seth Levy did not want to take a History class, even though it was required.

   5. Jeannie Elliott scored two goals in her first soccer game.

   6. Mrs. Whitney Bodine started her lesson by singing the National Anthem.

   7. The children loved Mrs. Whitney Bodine because her teaching style was a little unorthodox.

   8. The birds often nest in the roof of the gym during the Fall.

   9. First baseman Jason King hit two home runs off Starting Pitcher Johnny Seale.

   10. King spent the next three games on the bench of tovar memorial ballpark.

   11. Amanda Webb '02 is recovering from a broken leg suffered during a rodeo accident.

   12. More than 200 students showed up for the class party at bardwell lake.

   13. New students are expected to enroll in at least one class of german or spanish.

   Abbreviations

   14. Teachers received a 1% pay raise even though they asked for a 10 percent increase.

   15. The play is scheduled for February 15.

   16. Academic Decathlon members will travel to Okla. for their retreat.

   17. Dallas Cowboys running back Tony Dorsett holds the National Football League record for the longest run.

18. Wed. was the first day students were allowed to return to school after the accident.

19. The district added eight more portables along Lampier St.

20. The SCE ruled that teachers would have to remove all tatoos.

21. Speech teacher Rebecca Bennett is in her fourth year as the head of the Fine Arts Dept.

22. Two 15-year-old hunters rescued a baby deer in the hills of Asheville, North Carolina.

23. Six members of the state championship team signed letters with N.C.A.A. Division I schools.

24. Monday was the last time the boy was late to Doctor Olivia Belsher's class.

25. The Downhill Ski Club will meet at 5 p.m., November 23, in the library.

Numbers

26. Calculus teacher Gregg Fleisher started class at 7:00 a.m.

27. The gymnast fell off the balance beam in her 1st attempt.

28. The next game is May 29th.

29. The boy's father sold the car to his youngest son for one hundred dollars.

30. The Panthers won the area soccer championship two–one.

31. Senior goalie Susan Killough made 4 saves in the 6–1 bidistrict win.

32. The drill team will meet at freshman Tricia Hughes' home at fourteen Churchill Road.

33. Pianist Pam Murdock, seventeen, will perform a medley of Peter Frampton songs at 6 p.m., Monday, in the concert hall.

34. Wide receiver Colin Fitzgibbons caught touchdown passes of five, 10, fifty-five and 33 yards.

35. Admission to the concert is fifteen dollars.

36. The boy moved to Boston from a town with a population of one thousand five hundred people.

37. More than twenty-five students were home with food poisoning.

38. Junior Caryn Statman couldn't stand another day with 20 5-year-olds.

Punctuation and Italics

39. Freshman Adrienne Lee could not believe that her mom packed her bananas, apples, and oranges for lunch.

40. In Friday's choir concert, soprano Amy Cunningham sang I Love a Parade.

41. "Why do I have to go to the Hanson concert with you", Cunningham said.

42. Leon Solimani, a 224 – pound linebacker, joined the team after the second game.

43. Sophomore Sarah Strauss' goal is to appear on the cover of Rolling Stone.

44. Senior class president Bryan Parker admitted to getting five Cs and two Bs on his report card.

45. The workshop's steering committee included: Mike McLean, secretary, Mary Pulliam, president, Chris Modrow, historian, and Randy Vonderheid, treasurer.

46. The Class of 82 will have their 20-year reunion this year.

47. Sophomore Duane Yee played the lead role in the school's presentation of Hamlet Tuesday night.

48. I absolutely love the dog "Astro" in the cartoon The Jetsons.

49. President Tanner Bodine, Jr. will speak to the Sketch Comedy Club on Jan. 15.

50. Freshman James The Real Deal Ragland will start at center in the opening game of the playoffs.

2. We learn to recognize printed words in much the same way that we learn to recognize persons we know. Their overall appearances seem to be enough to give us quick identification.

Psychologists call the total appearance of an object its configuration or the sum of its parts. We can hardly take the time to spell out every word we see in reading copy. We learn to depend on configuration or total form in examining for correctness. We therefore should challenge any word form that raises the slightest suspicion that it is mispelled.

Did you catch it? "Mispelled" is misspelled! This is a troublesome word that should always be examined. Other spelling demons are listed below.

Number a paper from 1 to 50. Let your hunches guide you and rewrite those words you believe are misspelled. Mark OK if the word is spelled correctly. (If a space is left blank, you are charged with an error.) If you sense a word is incorrectly spelled, you may add one-half point to your total score, even though you haven't spelled it correctly.

Hint: More than half the words are misspelled.

1. recieve
2. alright
3. sophomore
4. berserk
5. habatat
6. misjudgement
7. lieutenant
8. restraunt
9. accomodate
10. fourty
11. repremand
12. sabotage
13. seperate
14. protocol
15. larceny
16. ilegal
17. occured
18. sponsor
19. elegible

20. corupt
21. corparate
22. excell
23. succeding
24. commit
25. facsimile
26. penicillin
27. paralel
28. elipse
29. embezzlement
30. incidious
31. patronage
32. athlete
33. decathlon
34. potpurri
35. nourish
36. concensus
37. liason
38. libary
39. Febuary
40. lisence
41. municipal
42. legistlature
43. indictment
44. peeve
45. hary-kary
46. fallible
47. questionnaire
48. misspell
49. oponent
50. integral

3. An Associated Press Managing Editors committee created a list of the 50 most common errors in newspaper writing. Examples of these errors appear in the following sentences. Correct the following errors in word usage, spelling and grammar.

1. The parents served refreshment afterwards.

2. The funeral service was held in the First United Methodist Church.

3. Even though the senior had less errors on the test, he made a better grade than his brother.

4. More than half of the town went to church on Easter Sunday.

5. The game will start at 8 p.m. tonight.

6. The principal agreed to drop the policy prohibiting people from wearing hats in the building and the increase of the number of minutes between class periods.

7. In the summer months, more than half of the senior class was employed.

8. I'll never be able to tell who's dog this is without an identification tag.

9. The sprinter won the race after alluding the former state champion.

10. The committee, composed of three juniors, five seniors and five teachers ...

11. Junior Hili Banjo headed up the fashion show.

12. I implied that the speaker was talking about the principal when saying "He was wrong."

13. The team must improve it's rebounding to win this year.

14. Freshman Aaron Ofseyer decided to become a meteorologist rather than a Jewish rabbi.

15. Economics teacher Suresh Vasan closed down his car business to become a teacher.

4. Cut unnecessary words. *Dallas Morning News* writing coach and assistant managing editor Paula LaRocque lists the following phrases as examples of wordiness in newswriting. Your job is to make them more concise. Cut the extra words or replace the phrase with one word that's more precise.

1. make use of

2. true fact

3. personal friendship

4. conduct an investigation into

5. on the occasion that

6. large in size

7. 12 noon

8. set a new record

9. a distance of 35 miles

10. in the vicinity of

11. crisis situation

12. in the event that

13. a number of

14. the reason is because

15. consensus of opinion

5. Edit the following story written for a daily newspaper. Using all you've learned in this chapter and Chapter 12, correct all errors.

Sweet Water, Tex – National guard troops patroled yesterday against looter after-tornados carved a 2-mile long, half-mile-wide swath through this east Texas town, killing 1 person, injuring some one-hundred others; and leaving 1500 persons homeless.

Ranging up to $20 million, dollars, officials said the destruction toll could have been worse. They marvelled at the fact that only one person was a fataality.

"After i saw the extent of the damage, I thought we'd have many more inujries and certainly more deaths," said Sweetwater mayor David Maddox. "It was luck. It was a miracle."

As national guardsman patroled the streets to watch for looting, volunteers and salvation army workers served over 2,000 meals to person left homeless by the disaster, said Mitchell Anderson,

Public Relations Director for the Salvation Armys' Texas division.

"Sweetwater is still in a mess. People are cleaning up but it will be a long time", said Mitchell. "People are sifting through the debris by hand. Thats all that is left from some of these trailur homes".

The U. Weather Bureau said 2 tornadoes smashed into the sothern part of the city of 12,00 early Saturday after merging in the air.

Mayor Rick Rhodes estimated property damages at between $15 and $20 million and sid that about 100 persons were injured and some 1500 left homeless.

Police Chief Jim Kelley said clean up efforts were progresing. "We're getting a lot of volunteer types," he said. Their swooping in there, and they're helping."

Governor George Bush visited the city yesterday and talked with residents's of the Sun Village Housing Project, a Federally subsidized development for senior citizens which was hard hit. The storms only fatallity ws a 87-year-old man who lived there.

One resident, Gadys lane, stood looking through what used to be a side wall of her house asd Bush spoke.

"It was just like I was in a vacum," said Mrs. Lane. I was down on my knees begging the lord to take care of me. I didn't care about the house.

"The only thing I can say is tough times never last, but though people do, and we've got a lot off toughj people around here," said Bush.

6. The following sentences contain errors in fact, structure and style. Using copyediting symbols, correct spelling, grammar, punctuation, redundancies and sexist expressions.

1. Mary has studyied filing, bookeeping, and word processing.

2. Exhausted after the days work, it was difficult for Joan to enjoy the concert.

3. Bridgetown's 46 policemen in January, February and March, in 27,647 man-hours of work drove 117,786 miles – more than four trips around the earth, or 22,000 miles farther than the maximum distance from the earth to the sun.

4. The students were given the basic fundamentals of the course.

5. The sponsers were elated over the finantial outcome which netted a little over one hundred and fifty dollars.

6. Cattle graze on ranges in the district, and farmers grow cotton, vegetables and citrus fruits, including grapes.

7. 15 girls from each school will be at the Central high school which will make 150 girls.

8. After working day and night for the past monthes the 82 piece Central band, under the direction of L.Irving Cradley are ready to do their best to win the district title at Dacon tomorrow night.

9. My turn finally came to bowl.

10. She had neither completed her English nor her Spanish.

11. Plagiarism is where you take the work of another and pass it off as your own.

12. He was a member of the committee in charge of the making of the student directory.

13. He hoped to get the true facts of the problem.

14. Coach Joe Voegle, of Spalding Institute, is the director of the clinic and hopes to have a prominent referee to be appointed by the local refferee's association, appear at one of the sessons to explain the new rules and their affect on the game.

15. In describing his earliest beginnings he said he had grown up as a child.

16. Arriving late at night, all the lights in the house were out.

17. The teacher asked for a brief synopsis of the book.

18. Housewives are feeling the pinch of inflation.

19. Jim is a person of strong will and who always gets his own way.

20. The team had won two straight in a row.

21. Those elected were Jack Swanson, President, Mary Clements, vice President, and Dale Cook, Secretary treasuer.

22. The cleaning women were already in the building when we left.

23. After his death he received the award posthumously.

24. A rattlesnake bite, followed by a series of homemade anecdotes, sent an Almont man to the hospital yesterday.

7. The next two stories are rough drafts turned into you, the copy editor. Using the coaching writing tips in this chapter, write out a number of questions to ask the writer to help improve the story. What points would you make to the writer to improve the story for the next draft? What good information does the writer have here? What information does the writer need to go back and get before writing a second draft?

Story 1

Marcus Goree isn't your average basketball player. He's 6-8. And he's one of the best in the area.

Many other players on the team have been playing since they were little. Goree's only been playing for four years.

Originally, Goree wanted to play football.

It wasn't until coach Gail Dupree asked him to play basketball that he decided to play.

Dupree said that Goree didn't look a basketball player. Besides being tall, he said he was skinny and pretty clumsy at first.

"Goree was like the Scarecrow in the Wizard of Oz," Coach Dupree said. "He had a great work ethic, but he had no self-esteem. The only thing I did that year was fix his self-esteem. Even his teammates would tell him he was sorry. All I did was tell he was the man."

But Dupree worked very hard with Gorree for the next two years.

"Marcus is a coach's dream," Coach Dupree said. "Some players come in and think they know everything so you can't coach them. Goree knew nothing so all he wanted to do was to be coached."

Goree improved and was a leader on the team his junior year. His scoring has improved as well. Enough now that colleges are recruiting him. He attended all the camps he could this last summer. He goes to scouting combines where scouts have been impressed by his ability to dunk.

He's being recruited hard by a lot of schools including University of Southern California, Texas, Baylor and New Mexico. Some scouts have even come to his house. But Goree still has to improve on his SAT score before he can be eligible for a scholarship. He says he's not worried.

Neither is coach Dupree.

"I feel real happy for Marcus," Coach Dupree said. "He came so far in four years. It makes me feel good to watch him play. He overcame a lot to get where his is now. In four more years, who knows where he'll be."

Story 2

Sophomore Warren Oakes thinks he's tough. Every time he walks in the gym for P.E. class, he flexes his arm at Coach Duff, and that's why she calls him Muscles. But today when he flexed his arm, she did not give him her usual reply.

"You forgot to say 'Hi Muscles.' Remember that's my name Coach Duff," sophomore Warren Oakes says as he flexes his arm and gives her a tough look. "Are our friends coming today?" he asks, referring to the three students from the E.D. Walker unit who join them to form the seven-person adaptive P.E. class.

As he continues to tell a joke about Bill Clinton, the gym door opens and in comes the trio wearing sneakers, shorts and smiles—the usual attire for this P.E. class.

The adaptive P.E. class was designed to provide special education students, especially the three who transferred from E.D. Walker special education high school, with a sheltered class to develop their skills and coordination. But unlike the other P.E. classes, they do not run long distances or do any strenuous exercises. Instead they play simple games and warm up with easy exercises.

"There's no hostility, no meanness, no rudeness," P.E. coach Kathleen Duff said. "In here it is such a warm and loving environment. The kids are so sweet."

When Coach Duff agreed to teach the new class, she had no idea how many would be in the class or what disabilities they would have. When only two showed up on the first day, she worried she wasn't going to have enough for a game of four-square. But a few more showed up in the next week, so she didn't have to throw the towel in. Now her dilemma lies in creating games that everyone can understand and enjoy.

"I just try to incorporate activities where everyone feels success at their own level, while still feeling comfortable, and also at a level where everyone feels challenged," Coach Duff said.

These activities include modified versions of softball and bowling, which are both sports that can appeal to a wide range of disabilities. A special ramp was also transferred from E.D. Walker so that 20-year-old Kelly Newsom, who is autistic, can push the ball from waist-level and knock down pins like everyone else.

Even though dart-throwing and bowling are geared toward the individual level, they are seldom done alone. Someone is always there shouting "Way to go" to someone else.

During a routine 15-minute walk last week, Newsom lost interest and started walking towards the side of the gym. Just as she was about to sit down on the gym floor, Oakes turned around and said something motivational to her to get her back into the group. Newsom smiled, grabbed his hand and restarted her laps.

When freshman Rosa Lopez refused to participate in darts, Oakes told her to wake up and get up there and take her turn. When she did, she ended up with the highest score and a high five from Coach Duff and Oakes.

But sometimes it takes longer to get it right. Senior Jose Garcia swung at the plastic softball a whole lot more than once before smacking a home run into the back wall. It took Oakes three or four tries before he could get a dart to stick in the board. But they never give up and Coach Duff never stops prodding them. As soon as she said, "Come on Muscles, let's see what you can do," he stuck one on the outside of the dart board.

"A lot of coaches say if we don't do very well then they don't like it," Oakes said. "But if we mess up in class then Coach Duff always say at least we try. I think she's got a real heart for helping people."

Last year Oakes felt left out in his P.E. class because it was so big. He felt neglected by his coach and often refused to dress out. The reason for this was never clear, but now he suits out everyday, so he is obviously more comfortable.

During the last half of fourth period, the P.E. class moves to room 131 to watch TV or spend time talking to Coach Duff. Oakes tells her about his life and about his activities outside of school.

"We talk about anything from his interests to our shared interest of jazz music to daily happenings and concerns about school," Coach Duff said.

Writing Headlines

Next time the school newspaper goes out, sit and watch your readers. It's not quite MTV entertainment, but you will learn something. The majority of readers are scanners. Watch as their eyes dart from side to side, from headline to headline or photo to photo as if they were watching a tennis match. Readers will scan the page looking for that one key word or phrase that touches a part of their lives or that's clever enough to make them laugh. Then they'll stop and begin to read.

This observation exercise will reveal how important headline writing is. The headline, or the large type on top of a story, is what catches the readers' attention. A vague, poorly written headline sends readers off to the horoscopes, and the writer's hard work is dismissed. A well-written headline entices readers to read the lead, and you are one step closer to the goal of getting people to read a story.

The headline is important because

- It names or summarizes the important facts of the story. The headline makes it simple for readers to glance quickly through the newspaper, yearbook or magazine to select which stories to read.

- It communicates the mood of the story. The headline gives readers a sense of the story's tone. A feature story's light tone can be conveyed through a play on words. A news or a news-feature story would have a headline with a straight-forward informative voice.

- It signals the relative importance of the story. The headline's role in helping readers decide which story is more important is discussed in Chapter 16. The general rule is that the larger the type, the more important the story.

TEASER AND TELLER HEADLINES

Copy editors refer to headline content as either a "teaser" or "teller." The teller headline gains the reader's attention by clearly and concisely summarizing the story. The voice of the teller is typically straight-forward. Teller headlines are most often designed using one or two standard typefaces.

The teaser headline attracts by arousing curiosity or by entertaining readers. A play on words such as "Try-athlete" may intrigue readers enough to pause at the story. But to make sure readers take the next step to read the lead, the teaser should always be accompanied with a teller headline as a secondary headline. In this case, the teller "Sophomore hopes to finish first triathlon after five attempts" helps to clarify the story. The teaser headline is typically connected to a feature story or any story that is not a straight news story.

In many magazines, newspaper feature packages and yearbooks, designers make creative use of type on the teaser headline. The typefaces often mirror the content of the story in an attempt to entertain visually. Designer headlines are discussed later in this chapter and in Chapter 16, the design chapter.

GETTING THE WORDS TO FIT ON THE PAGE

Headlines have to fit into a specific space on the page. That's one of the greatest challenges in headline writing. The larger the typeface size, the fewer the words that can fit into the space. How to determine the number of letters or words that can fit has changed over the years.

Computers with page design, word-processing or paint and draw software allow the headline writer to see instantly if the headline fits. In any system, if the headline doesn't fit, the editor adds or subtracts information or looks for shorter or longer words to say the same thing. The rewriting process is the same when manually counting headlines; however, the process can be slower.

Computers have allowed the writer to change the type size or the letter spacing in small amounts to make the headline fit. But that doesn't mean headline writers should scrunch their cherished words so that they are unreadable or shrink the size so they are hardly bigger than body type. The minimum and maximum sizes of headlines are discussed later in the design chapters.

For the purpose of explaining how to make headlines fit, the count assigned to each letter, space and punctuation mark will be one unit. Note below how the system works. Also notice how each line is counted separately and there are no spaces counted at the end of the lines.[1]

111111111111111111111111 = 26 count

Senior gains new identity,

111111111111111111111111111111 = 30 count

access to liquor in 45 minutes

KINDS OF HEADLINES

While teller/teaser labels for headlines refer to content, headlines are also identified by appearance—certain kinds of headlines have certain content qualities.

A one-line headline is basically a single, unbroken sentence. Typically, the one-line headline is a teller.[2]

FBI mounts manhunt for '72 grad

A two-line headline is one sentence broken into two lines.[3] Each line is counted separately. A gap of white space is unsightly at the end of one line of a two-line headline.

Halloween flooding devastates residents

A three-line headline is one sentence broken into three lines. Typically these are teller headlines. Remember that each line counts separately.[4]

Irish dancers win first place at talent show

A deck is a secondary headline that is positioned under the main headline and is typically a teller.[5] The deck can go under another teller headline. The deck always adds information and is helpful in explaining complicated stories.

Cancelled permit foils annual parade

■ Tailgate party to replace Homecoming tradition

The hammer is a short phrase or even a single word that is set in a point size much larger than the headline underneath.[6]

STUCK

Juniors denied off-campus; lunch lines longer than ever

A tripod is a combination of a large word or phrase followed by a two-line headline set in type half the size.

Both lines of the second part nearly equal the height of the larger, opening words, as in this headline.[7]

Meriting recognition: 12 seniors selected as high achievers on PSAT test

The jump headline accompanies the part of a story that continues on a different page.[8] Many jump headlines may be written as another headline for the story—usually as a one-line headline. However, some publications opt for using only key words, such as in the following jump headline for a story about a foundation's evaluation of a school.

REPORT CARD   Continued from front page

Designer headlines, used primarily for newspaper features and in yearbooks and magazines, establish the mood through choice of type. They are also created by adding graphics or manipulating type size. Readability of type should still be a consideration in creating a designer headline. Well-written designer headlines that use type to match the content or message can be extremely effective (Figs. 14.1–14.5).

WRITING A TELLER

Even though the headline has the fewest words of any element in a newspaper or yearbook, it often requires as much thought and care as the story and other elements on a page. While headlines typically are created on deadline, the writer should put maximum effort into creating good ones. If the story was written by someone else, read through the entire story to understand the content. Mentally, or on the computer screen or paper, summarize the most important information in the story in one brief sentence. Try it again, this time trimming even more words. Rewrite, using synonyms or reconstructing the sentence, until the headline fits the space, tone and content of the story.

The headline should follow these guidelines:

- Be accurate, above all. Specific facts in the headline should be completely supported in the story.

- Be informative. Try to answer as many questions as a news lead does.

- Be fair. If the story covers two sides of an issue, try to reflect the differences in the headline. Do not editorialize directly or indirectly unless the headline is for an opinion story such as a review or editorial. The headline should give the same impression as the body of the story.

- Do not put anything in the headline that is not in the story.

Fig. 14.1. *Update,* Herbert Henry Dow High School, Midland, Mich.

Rollin' dough

District to gain
funds from ads
on buses

Fig. 14.2. *Panther Prints,* Duncanville High School, Duncanville, Texas

HEADLINE CONSTRUCTION RULES

Headline-writing rules are continually changing among professional newspapers and magazines. *The New York Times,* for example, now uses articles such as *a, and* and *the* more often than it used to. The use of past tense verbs is more accepted to make sure the headline is clear. Still most publications adhere to the following guidelines:

- Avoid padding. *A, and, the, their, his* or *her* should not be used in hard news headlines. Notice the deletion of the word in brackets in the following headline.

Director calls [the] possibility of drug testing athletes 'highly unlikely'

However, use of *the* in the following headline is necessary to keep the headline from sounding awkward.[9]

All in the family

Students suffer when mothers battle disease

- Use active verbs in tellers.

Sick and tired

Rare disease drains senior's energy, health

- Omit forms of the verb *to be,* if possible. Notice the correct deletions of the words in brackets.

Senior party preparations [are] underway as graduation nears[10]

Flu bug attacks students; many absences [are] reported[11]

- Opt for the active voice over the passive voice whenever possible. The first headline shows the correct use of the active voice; the second the correct use of the passive voice.

Debate team ranks first in district, state contests

Five '97 graduates given top awards at commencement

- Use the present tense to describe past events. This use is known as the historical present.

Council approves $1 million renovation project

- The past tense is showing up in more publications, especially when it enhances clarity. In the following

DYING
to be heard
Recent teen suicides provokes reactions among students, survivors

Fig. 14.3. *Stinger*, Irmo High School, Columbia, S.C.

Dallas Morning News headline, past tense is used because the killers were dead by the time the story ran.

Pair made video before Littleton killings

- Use the infinitive form of the verb for future events. Any other tense would only confuse the reader.

Crawl-space renovation to begin within month

- Do not separate the following items from one line to the next. Avoid these breaks:

  1. Preposition and its object

  AP Art students pressured to finish portfolios, pass exam

  2. Parts of the same verb

  Science club president to promote plastic recycling

  3. Parts of names that belong together

  Senior waits 10 hours for Star Wars premiere in pouring rain

  4. Abbreviations

  Alum wins NC AA top honor

  5. Noun and its adjacent adjective

  HHS Band involves feeder-school bands to boost future participation

Pat Garrison's game is getting better and better all because he has **a head for golf**

Garrison shoots for the Green!!!

Fig. 14.4. *Green Raider,* Ridley High School, Folsom, Pa.

6. Compound words

Nat Chambers elected vice-president of Creative Club

- Don't repeat words in the headline.

Test scores fall

Students' test results fall for third consecutive year

- Generally use numerals, although numbers through nine may be spelled out.

Tennis team dominates: Eight head to leagues after an almost flawless season[12]

Senior class collects 123 pints in blood drive[13]

- "Down style," or capitalizing only the first word of a headline and all proper nouns, has become the preferred style of most publications.[14]

Irmo experiences two fires in two days

- Instead of general words, as in the first headline, opt for specific words that fit the same space. The second headline has been written with stronger, more precise language.[15]

VIOLENCE: coming closer to home

Abuse leaves terror in path of destruction

Fig. 14.5. *Peninsula Outlook,*
Peninsula High School, Gig
Harbor, Wash.

New bill requires increased language requirement

State may require two years of high school Spanish

- Punctuate headlines correctly; omit periods.

    1. Commas are often used to replace *and*. In all other cases, standard English usage rules that apply for commas apply in headlines.[16]

Yellow Ribbon Week reminds friends, family to listen

    2. Use the semicolon to attach two related thoughts.

Tornado destroys field house; clean-up to take three weeks

    3. Use single quotation marks rather than double.

**Putting 'the boot' down
Delinquent parking tickets prompt school officials to purchase new tool**

- Do not use obscure or unnecessary abbreviations.

    Wrong: **New FHS principal changes discipline plan**
    Right: **New principal changes discipline plan**

- Never abbreviate a day of the week.

- Never use a day of the week and date together.

- Do not abbreviate months except when a numeral follows (Jan. 27).

- Write nothing in the headline that isn't in the story. If you know something interesting or important has been omitted, insert it in the story.

- Do not use names unless the persons are commonly known. Use a synonym that would be more meaningful.

- Avoid placing headlines and nonrelated pictures near each other, especially when an unexpected connection may be perceived.

FEATURE HEADLINES

Entertainment is the goal when writing the teaser headline. *Dallas Morning News* editor/writer Nancy Kruh discusses the process for writing a feature headline and offers tips.

> With feature journalism now a staple in every section of the daily newspaper, copy editors are being called upon increasingly to write headlines that sell a story with word play, as well as information.

> Crafting a feature headline that's entertaining, compelling and sophisticated requires all of a copy editor's creative skills. The best editors tend to look upon the challenge almost as a word game: How can you make a headline fun—and make it fit the space? The

deftest headlines are a delight with or without the story: "She stole his heart, so the police had to write her a ticket," "If all goes as planned, it's an accident," "Hundreds of mouses flock to cat's Web page," "It's picture day at school, so make it a snap."

Becoming an accomplished feature-headline writer takes practice but also requires an avid attentiveness to language and popular culture. You simply can't write wonderfully inventive headlines such as "Nobody troubles the nose I've seen"—as *Dallas Morning News* copy editor Steve Steinberg did for a column about the perils of an oversized nose—without knowing the old expression "Nobody knows the trouble I've seen." Imagine trying to write a feature headline about, say, "Star Wars" without knowing about The Force or R2D2.

Besides wracking your brain for idioms associated with the main themes of your story, you also can rely on a dictionary, which often includes common expressions in its definitions. (For example, here's some of what Webster's New World Dictionary offers for "heart": "eat one's heart out," "after one's own heart," "break one's heart," "take to heart," "do one's heart good." There also are all these related words: "heartache," "heart attack," "heartbeat" and "heartburn.") Many other reference works besides the dictionary have compiled slang expressions and idioms; check your local library or bookstore for those.

Once you've gathered a few catch phrases, it's time to get your wheels turning. Here, for example, is how Carolyn Poh, another accomplished *Dallas News* copy editor, brainstormed a headline for a feature about the coffee-table books on sale for Christmas. First, she gathered words associated with "books" and "coffee," such as "tome," "binder," "pages," "chapter," "slick,"

"cream," "sugar," "beans," "grind" and "stir." Then she free-associated her way to these four clever headlines: "Best of tomes, worst of tomes" (a play off Charles Dickens' "best of times, worst of times"), "Binders keepers," "In the slick of things" and "Cream of the coffee table." The latter was the one ultimately selected for publication.

Here are a few guidelines that can help you get inspired when you're assigned to write a feature headline (examples have all been written by *Dallas News* copy editors):

1. Freshen a cliché by exploiting its literal meaning. For instance, "A chip off the old block," is a flat and trite headline if the accompanying story is about sons who have taken up their fathers' professions. But the same headline is fun and inventive if the fathers happen to be carpenters. Here are other examples: "Kids' tastes get a bit hard to swallow," "Women's soccer team has the world at its feet," "Bartending couple endured two rounds of love on the rocks," "Toilet-seat debate has ups and downs."

2. Turn an idiomatic expression into a catchy headline by switching words: "Sculptor has stones of heart," "You've lain in your bed—now make it."

3. Alter spelling, but not pronunciation: "Cat gives paws to writing career."

4. Alter (very slightly) spelling and pronunciation: "The musician with sax appeal," "Mooch obliged: Author relies on fans' hospitality for national book tour," "Fame thrower."

5. Use a word with two meanings (but only if both meanings are appropriate): "He has few reservations about hotels," "The business of having a baby is all in the delivery," "She has never been hooked by the lure of fishing."

6. Use rhyming words or alliterations: "Saucy Aussie," "Noodling with doodling," "Star-studded dud," "Roughneck romance," "Intricate intrigue hits home."

7. Change a word in a well-known phrase: "Self-adhesive stamps: If you can't lick 'em, buy 'em," "They're only young twice."

8. Employ evocative and subject-appropriate language: "Tale of American West shoots for suspense," "The forceful return: 'Star Wars' blasts into theaters again."

9. Use opposites, such as "up, down" or "rich, poor": "Hard times bring out a light touch," "Novel makes short work of long life."

10. Have your own say. A direct comment to the story or its subject, particularly in the upper line of a deck, can be quite an eye-catcher: "Beat it, kid: Not everyone likes 'Little Drummer Boy,'" "Give 'em yell, mom: Dallas Cowboys cheerleader is 37, married and has four kids," "It's Ms. Cinderella to you, bub: New play toughens a traditional heroine."

A few final thoughts: Word-play headlines have become so popular, editors occasionally stretch puns beyond the bounds of reasonable taste, inviting groans from readers. You'll have to decide for yourself where you draw the line, but here are a few excesses you can use as benchmarks: "Allergies must have a wheezin'," "There's a lot of finny business going on here," "She's Hillary-ous," "With cows, it's always one thing or an udder."

It's also wise to avoid certain idioms and headline tricks that have become hackneyed over the years. These include playing off the subject's name, "Tom is Cruising to another hit movie"; using

parentheses, "Naughty but (n)ice cream"; and employing any of these clichés: "Yes, Virginia, there is a Santa Claus," "A sign of the times," and "Tis the season." Relying on these crutches is not just unimaginative. It's lazy.

Some examples of quality feature headlines from high school publications include

• A sports story about two girls trying out for the school's wrestling team[17]

Wrestling with change

• An entertainment story about the drama club's twisted production of "Alice in Wonderland," where Alice is in an insane asylum[18]

Alice in ... La La Land

• A sports story about a St. Louis Cardinals record-setting home run season

One dinger with extra distance, please ... Big mac super sizes the homer record

• A health story about the increased uses and effects of caffeine[19]

**Buzzing about caffeine
Wonder drug helps
many students make it
through school day**

• A story about an alumni Trey Dyson, who had an extraordinary college freshman season

Slicin' & Dyson

SV alumnus tears through opposition, named Rookie of the Fall at USC

• A news-feature about the campaign of a mother whose son was killed in a drunk-driving accident

A drunk driver shattered the lives of a local family. Now in memory of her son, Sue Anderson gives Lakota students ... A crash course

- A movie review of *Lost and Found,* comedian David Spade's 1999 movie[20]

  Not an Ace of Spade's

- A story about the problems homeowners in the community have had with students' reckless behavior[21]

  Neighbor Hoods
  U-Highers' reputation in community could use some holiday giftwrap

NOTES

1. *Lowell,* Lowell High School, San Francisco, Calif.

2. *Redwood Bark,* Redwood High School, Larkspur, Calif.

3. *Paladin,* Kapaun Mt. Carmel High School, Wichita, Kan.

4. *Lance,* Robert E. Lee High School, Springfield, Va.

5. *Edition,* Anderson High School, Austin, Texas.

6. *Maroon,* Stephen F. Austin High School, Austin, Texas.

7. *Panther Prints,* Duncanville High School, Duncanville, Texas.

8. *Axe,* South Eugene High School, Eugene, Ore.

9. *Central Times,* Naperville Central High School, Naperville, Ill.

10. *Apple Leaf,* Wenatchee High School, Wenatchee, Wash.

11. *Apple Leaf,* Wenatchee High School, Wenatchee, Wash.

12. *Trapeze,* Oak Park and River Forest High School, Oak Park, Ill.

13. *Peninsula Outlook,* Peninsula High School, Gig Harbor, Wash.

14. *Stinger,* Irmo High School, Columbia, S.C.

15. *Stampede,* Burges High School, El Paso, Texas.

16. *Panther Prints,* Duncanville High School, Duncanville, Texas.

17. *Hy News,* Belleville Township High School, Belleville, Ill.

18. *Academy Times,* Charles Wright Academy, Tacoma, Wash.

19. *Tide Lines,* Pottsville Area High School, Pottsville, Pa.

20. *Viking Shield,* Spring Valley High School, Columbia, S.C.

21. *U-High Midway,* University High School, Chicago, Ill.

22. *Hillcrest Hurricane,* Hillcrest High School, Dallas, Texas.

23. *Hillcrest Hurricane,* Hillcrest High School, Dallas, Texas.

EXERCISES

1. Clip and mount five tellers and five teasers from your area daily newspaper. Explain the difference.

2. Clip and mount five headlines from your area daily newspaper and rank them for quality. Explain why each grabbed your attention and why.

3. On a separate sheet of paper grade each of the following headlines (A, B, C, D or F) on how well it exemplifies the principles of good headline writing. Justify your grade.

   a. A news-feature about what people can do when they turn 18[22]

As the YEARS go by

Opportunities increase as students reach 18

b. An informative feature story about how to pack for holiday trips[23]

SCRUNCHED UP
Packing tips for perfectly wrinkle-free holiday vacations

c. A story about protesting an assembly film

**Commotion
is caused
by picture**

d. A straight news story about a faculty retirement

**Murdock leaves
Central faculty;
successor named**

e. A football game story

Team excells in 42–7 win

f. A new story about a new musical

"Leader of the pack" is named musical

g. A news-feature on a new program requiring truants to clean up the school

**Cleaning up their acts
New custodian enforces community
service**

h. A feature story about keeping New Year's resolutions

Resolving problems

i. A feature story about a special education physical education class

Something special in the air

**P.E. class encourages students to learn
skills in positive atmosphere**

j. A news story about an upcoming state poetry contest

Roper to compete for first state title

4. For the following story write a two-line headline with each line counting no fewer than 17 and no more than 23.

A Lakota freshman school student has been charged with illegal possession of a deadly weapon after the student was allegedly found with a BB gun in his locker on April 22.

Along with the legal charges, the student has also received a ten-day suspension and a recommendation for expulsion for his illicit activities.

The weapon was found after a school administrator received an anonymous tip that there was a student at the school who claimed to have a gun.

According to Assistant Principal Lee Corder, after the administration called the police a brief investigation of the student was held and the BB gun was found.

Corder feels that the situation was dealt with efficiently.

"I think that it (the investigation) created very little disturbance in the building," said Corder. "It was handled quickly and responsibly without incident."

Lakota freshman Andrea Piri said she was amazed that something like this could happen.

"I was surprised that anybody would bring a BB gun to school. It's obvious that they'd be caught," said Piri.

Lee Delaveris
Lakota Spark
Lakota East High School
Liberty Township, Ohio

5. Write a one-line main headline counting between 16 and 22 and a one-line secondary headline counting between 26 and 32.

"To bee or not to bee." That is the question concerning maintenance personnel who have to deal with the campus bee problem.

The typical lunch has been drastically changed for those students who eat outside, because of the bee swarms around trash cans. Lunch-goers move from table to table and girls scream at the top of their lungs, when pestered by a bee swarm.

"I just sit there and hope the bees leave me alone," senior Bruce Nguyen said.

"We are doing as much as humanly possible to get rid of the bees at this point," plant manager Connie White said. "You're messing with the forces of nature when you leave out food. Students can help by putting trash in its proper place."

Assistant principal Quinn Kellis also emphasized the need for a clean campus. "The problem we have is we can't spray insecticides while students are on campus. So we've been using traps and mild soap that's diluted to kill the bees," Kellis said. "The best solution is to keep the area clean."

Though the hive has been located, everyone still needs to do their part, White said. Once a month the kitchen cafeteria area is sprayed by an exterminating firm, but that doesn't stop them from coming back.

Patty Barney
Ridge Review
Mountain Ridge High School
Glendale, Ariz.

6. Write a one-line main headline counting between 13 and 20 and a two-line headline with each line counting between 22 and 29.

After two years of discussion, the banning of book bags will become a school policy effective at the beginning of the school year.

There are several reasons that the administration thinks this is a good idea.

"They block hallways, doors and classroom aisles. If we needed to evacuate the school properly, the book bags would be in the way. Fire prevention officer (Dean E. Spitler) did an inspection and recommended that we get rid of them. To continue having book bags would be going against a professional opinion," Principal Dr. Kathleen Crates said.

Another reason backpacks are a problem is that they enable students to bring unnecessary items into the building.

"They allow students to carry in things that aren't healthy in the learning environment. From pop bottles to weapons, they can carry it in without anyone knowing that they have it. They add to the congestion in the halls and are also clinically proven to be bad for students' backs," Crates said.

Hidden objects in book bags are also a concern to Junior Principal Patrick Hickey.

"From the standpoint of security, book bags give students a way to bring contraband into the school. There are hundreds of book bags laying around unattended, and no one questions whose book bags they are. Students could easily leave a book bag that is dangerous laying around in the cafeteria or music wing.

"When purses are left laying around, people bring them down to the office right away. No one would think twice about taking a book bag down to the office," Hickey said.

While administrators think eliminating book bags will increase security, some students are opposed to the whole idea.

"Book bags are supposedly a fire hazard, but I don't understand how a pile of books that could get scattered on the floor is any better than books inside of something. We could find an alternate solution to the problem, like using book bag racks in the classrooms," Junior Amy Chester said.

Yet there are also students who don't really care about the new book bag policy.

"It's not like people are going to have to go to their lockers every period, you take two books and go to your classes and switch books later. There is a big enough place to put them under your desk where they won't be in the way. There are ways to get around without a book bag, but no one wants to work with the system," Sophomore Mike LaRocco said.

Kristin Cramer
Blue and Gold
Findlay High School
Findlay, Ohio

7. Write a one-line headline counting between 26 and 32.

With a high voltage smile, Kevin Dixon, Summit's junior and high school science teacher, carefully places 12 ocean blue marbles on the wooden game board.

"Blue marbles represent the electrons, red marbles represent the protons, and the yellow ones represent the neutrons," he says.

Instead of drawing how the atomic structure of the carbon atom looks on the chalkboard, Mr. Dixon uses a new game to give a better feel of how atoms are made.

He also uses the other new "toys" he received this past summer, including plas-

tics maps of the human body and frog.

A grant of $7,500 approved by operations manager Fred Dallas and general manager Larry Lenzi of Multifoods Distribution Systems of Dallas, paid for the Summit's new dry laboratory.

"No water, no specimens, or no chemicals. Everything is a model," said Mr. Dixon in describing a dry lab.

In addition of the new game, Mr. Dixon received CD ROMs that have computerized versions of earth worms, frogs, fetal pigs and even the human body; new National Geographic videos; and plastic maps of the human body.

"The kids up here learn better from tactile styles, meaning they work better with their hands," explains Randy Cothran, the alternative school's principal.

The new dry science laboratory was designed specifically for this purpose. The CD ROMs that use computer animated versions of the frog will help the students see how the insides of the frog, or whatever model being used, looks like instead of using live frogs.

"Anything on computer is tactile; anything you can touch is tactile. It helps the students learn better," Mr. Dixon said.

When students use the new program, an animated scalpel appears on the computer screen and a student can start to dissect the computerized specimen with a click of a mouse.

Although the students have not been introduced to the science laboratory yet, Mr. Dixon anticipates it to be a successful learning tool, and most of all, fun for the students.

"The lab will be open to any students at the Summit," he said.

Mr. Dixon and Mr. Cothran stress that the students learn much better with their hands, rather than reading it out of a textbook.

Trisha Nemec
Panther Prints
Duncanville High School
Duncanville, Texas

8. Write a one-line headline counting between 26 and 32.

Vandals, allegedly TPHS students, broke into Del Mar Pines Elementary School damaging or stealing $7,000–8,000 worth of equipment Nov. 5th.

There is a $1,000 reward for information about the break-in, which is technically considered a "commercial burglary." The incident occurred between 8 p.m. and 1:25 a.m. The vandals stole two TVs, three VCRs, three boom boxes and one laptop computer. They also destroyed one computer and one boom box. Three windows were broken in the process and several doors were forced open. All four buildings of the school were broken into, with damage being done to the majority of the rooms.

"Everything seems to be pointing to students of TPHS. The police say this because there was a pep rally at a high school Thursday night and the elementary school is located very close to it. It was obviously done by high school age kids," Marci McCord, administrator at Del Mar Pines, said.

No school was held on Friday due to the destructive vandalism. This caused some problems for busy parents who had to deal with their children not being in school for a day. A school-wide security system is going to be installed at the approximate cost of $5,000 to prevent further problems involving burglary.

"Most kids at TPHS are really good. They help us out a lot here. A few bad apples ruin it for everybody. We shouldn't be too judgmental about these," McCord said.

Detective Lew Johns is in charge of the case. Police suspect multiple vandals who were of high school age based on the kind of damage done. Fingerprints were collected at the scene of the crime, and have been analyzed although information from the fingerprints has not been released. There is at least one suspect at current.

Del Mar Pines officials ask that anyone who has information regarding the break in call either Del Mar Pines at 481-5615. Detective Johns at 552-1700, or 235-TIPS.

Brett Howell
Falconer
Torrey Pines High School
San Diego, Calif.

9. Choose a feature story from a newspaper or magazine. Write six different teasers for the story. Keep them short. Be creative.

Understanding Typography and Production

Helvetica, Fenice, Times Roman, Hobo, Zapf Chancery, New Baskerville, Stone. New names for school mascots?

Students who learn to love typography instantly recognize these names as particular styles of typeface design, and those that get hooked by the type bug can even point out the distinctions of the individual letter forms. Typeaholics learn to love and appreciate the eccentricities and quirks of letter forms and exploit their principles in well-designed type displays.

Because the page designer can be the best friend or worst enemy of the writer, good designers understand and appreciate the value of carefully chosen type. They understand how the space between the letters—kerning—and the space between the lines of type—leading—can add to that readability.

With the advent of desktop-publishing software, student designers literally have at their fingertips the power to transport their readers through visual/verbal displays of their word content. They can add to the feeling a reader has for a page design or topic.

Although the vast majority of schools are now using computers and desktop-publishing programs for production of pages in a process known as *computer pagination*, other schools with limited access to computers rely on traditional methods of type preparation, primarily on services that provide desktop publishing.

With the proliferation of desktop-publishing software, many companies have begun selling typefaces. Type CDs can be ordered through numerous vendors, and typefaces can be bought and downloaded to the computer directly off the CD by simply calling in a credit card number. Many typefaces are offered for free over the Internet. Some of these typefaces will display correctly on a computer screen display but will not print correctly. It's best to buy typefaces from companies that specialize in selling type.

TYPE TERMS

Defining terms that relate to typography will help the designer in choosing and understanding type.

- *Typeface or font:* a range of type in all the characters in one size and weight.

* *Type family:* a range of text in weights (i.e., light, bold, heavy, extra bold) and postures (i.e., italic, bold italic) for a particular typeface. Some typefaces are versatile, offering as many as 10 or 11 variations of structure within the same type family. Other typefaces might offer only one variation of the face.

* *Leading:* the space between the lines of type. Body text is traditionally set with 2 points of leading (the size of the type plus 2 extra points of leading; i.e., 9 point type/11 point leading). Solid leading means the type size is equal to the leading value (i.e., 9 point type/9 point leading), which could cause ascender and descender letters to merge if they align in the text.

* *Body text:* generally between 9 and 12 picas, the size in which traditional text stories appear on the page.

* *Bullets:* typographic or graphic devices used to mark entry into paragraphs or text passages. Bullets can be dots, squares, checks or symbols and can be used in color to create repetition.

* *Display type:* type sizes 14 points and above used to display information such as headlines, secondary or deck headlines and other graphic information.

* *Drop caps:* letters set in larger sizes at the beginning of text or throughout the text, directing the reader's eye to the beginning of stories. These letters usually "drop" into the first few lines of text.

Fig. 15.1. *Blue and Gold* newspaper of Findlay High School uses a strong combination of traditional serif type for its body text and bold and roman weight, condensed sans serifs for its headlines. The combination is a strong one in that the headlines serve as strong visual entry points for the readers' eyes while the traditional serif

Hence, the name. In addition to drop caps, letters can "rise above" the other lines of text, can be set to the side of the text or can be printed beneath the text in a color or shade of color.

* *Agate type:* the smallest point size type a publication uses. Agate type is traditionally used for setting sports scores and classified ads in newspapers. The size might range between 5 and 6 points.

* *Alignment:* the method used for starting and ending lines of type. Left aligned means the type starts on a common left margin but features uneven arrangement on the right. Right-aligned features type with a common right arrangement, but a ragged left alignment. Centered type is type set to the middle of an alignment.

Justified type lines up on both the left and right edges. Force justified is a computer alignment that will add space between letters or words of type to cause them to fill up a line of space. This pattern creates awkward "rivers of white space," which inhibit readability.

- *Points:* a unit of measurement in type. There are 12 points in 1 pica. Type that is 1 inch in height is 72 points tall.

- *Pica:* a unit of measurement in type. There are 6 picas in an inch.

- *Baseline:* the line upon which all the letters sit.

- *Ascenders:* letters that fall below the baseline and include the letters *g, j, p, q* and *y*.

- *Descenders:* letters that rise above the baseline and include the letters *b, d, f, h, k, l* and *t*.

- *C/lc:* refers to the use of capitals and lowercase letters in design.

- *Down style:* the practice of capitalizing only the first letter of a headline and proper nouns that occur after the first letter. The style is easily read because it mimics sentence style.

- *Small caps:* refers to the use of letters that are the height of lowercase letters but have the posture of capital letters.

- *X-height:* refers to the height of the lowercase letters in proportion to the capital letters. Typefaces with large x-heights are more visible on the printed page, especially in small sizes.

CATEGORIES, OR RACES, OF TYPE

Although type could be classified in numerous categories according to its historical origin, placing type in six simpler categories makes it easier to use and reference.

SERIFS

Serif types, by tradition the easiest typefaces to read, are marked by the finishing strokes or touches on the ends of the stems. These finishing touches were indicative of particular styles as designed by their original designers. Serif typefaces have been the preferred choice for text for centuries. Because of this tradition of readability, serif typefaces remain popular for text type. The serifs often help the reader connect the letters visually (Fig. 15.1).

Most designers place serif types into subcategories based on the time period in which they were designed. For example, old style serifs, among the first serif typefaces, are noted for consistent contrast, sloped or rounded strokes and slanted and curved serifs. The rounded letters will also exhibit an angled tilt in the swelling. The tops of the ascenders will have a distinctly oblique serif. The serifs angle out from the stem and end in a bracketed serif.

The transitional serifs exhibit more contrast between thick and thin strokes, show almost no tilting in the angle of the swells of the rounded letters, are slightly less oblique at the tops of the ascenders and often have squared off serifs rather

type is easy to read. Additionally, *Blue and Gold* creates contrast for sidebars ("Zero Tolerance") by using sans serif type to create contrast with the text so the reader understands the differences between the content of the sidebar list and the story. Sans serif types are also used in the grid along the left side of the page where the paper places quotes, a list, a couple of current event factoids and a simple contents list. Captions on pictures begin with bold, sans serif lead-ins. Captions are in italic serif to contrast with text type. *Blue and Gold,* Findlay High School, Findlay, Ohio

Fig. 15.2. Square or slab serif type-faces work particularly well in headlines where a strong visual voice is needed. The square serifs on "wrong" in this head-line lend emphasis to this word, as well as the size and weight of the type. The small cracks showing up at the bottoms of the letters indicate the connection to mishaps in student performances. Square serif typefaces are hard to work with beyond their use in headlines and other forms of display information. *Axe,* South Eugene High School, Eugene, Ore.

than rounded ones.

The modern serifs have a pronounced difference between the thickest and thinnest strokes, have completely vertical stress, feature serifs that are squared off and have unbracketed serifs.

SANS SERIFS

Sans, a word originating from French for *without,* indicates typefaces whose stokes do not end in serifs. Known as being geometric, precise and monotonal, sans serif typefaces are great for creating contrast between body type and other kinds of information, and in organizing information. Many typeface designers rely on sans serif typefaces for headlines, secondary headlines and text heads (small heads within the text). Additionally, sans serif typefaces are great choices for information used in alternative story displays. They create contrast with the main story and are easy to read in smaller amounts of information.

SQUARE OR SLAB SERIFS

Square or slab serif typefaces end in precise, blocky or straight-line serifs. Although difficult to use in text type because of the wide nature of the letters, slab serifs suggest a certain ruggedness and stability. They can work for display type and for contrast between different kinds of information displayed (Fig. 15.2).

SCRIPTS OR CURSIVES

Typefaces that resemble connected or disconnected handwriting, scripts or cursives suggest a certain informality and can work effectively in certain kinds of advertising or in displaying specific kinds of information (Fig. 15.3). Their low readability and low contrast make them difficult to work with for headlines or other strong visual hierarchy displays.

BLACK LETTER

Most commonly referred to as Old English, black letter types are often associated with the nameplates of newspapers such as *The New York Times.* Of Germanic origin, these typefaces have extremely low readability, especially when used in all-cap lettering. Black letter typefaces are often used for engraved invitations and to invoke certain moods at Halloween and other holidays. Few scholastic publications have use for any black letter typefaces.

NOVELTY

Types that can't be simply categorized into these other classifications often are labeled as novelty or miscellaneous typefaces. Exhibiting some "extra" quality, they are designed to display characteristics of their names or quirky characteristics that cause them to attract attention (Fig. 15.4). Novelty typefaces should not be used for text display and should be limited to display type. Too often, designers rely on novelty typefaces to do the job of good design. A well-written and clever headline in a standard typeface can be far more effective than a poorly written one displayed in a novelty typeface.

CHOOSING TYPE

Page designers are better off choosing serif and sans serif for most of their type design. Within these categories, bolder variations of serifs and sans serifs work best for display type such as in headline displays. Book or roman weights work best for copy display. An occasional use of a script or novelty typeface for a logo or for the theme statement might be effective in conveying the content of the message and in creating contrast with the other type choices.

With the advent of desktop publishing, a vast array of typefaces has been made commercially available. Some of these typefaces are quite visually effective, with smoothed edges that will print and read well. Others are produced by cheaper methods and could cause problems for printers when they use digital file format or when they download fonts to their systems. It's best to check with your printer when making typeface choices. Remember, too, that if your printer does not own the typeface choices you use in your designs, you will need to provide a downloadable file of that type to the printer in order for the type to print correctly in the finished design.

Designers need to consider several factors of type selection that affect readability and legibility (Fig. 15.5).

- The x-height of the type. Typefaces with large x-heights often have large, open counters in their letters and will print visibly and easily on the page. These type-

Fig. 15.3. Script typefaces, often resembling someone's personal handwriting, are friendly and personal. In this question and answer story format with an English teacher, the use signals to the reader that this content is different from a traditional story, delving into her personal life and religious background. The contrast between the bold serif type on the questions and the roman weight on the answers also helps the readers jump into each question and answer. The white space separating the individual questions and answers also provides good readability for this package. Finally, the informal picture adds to the package of information that invites the reader in for a closer look. *Crossfire,* Crossroads School, Santa Monica, Calif.

Fig. 15.4. Double trucks—subjects receiving two pages of coverage in the center of the newspaper—often present subjects that may lend themselves to the use of novelty typefaces. In this double-truck coverage of the current trend toward adult-oriented cartoons, the staff of the *Stampede* wisely chose a novelty typeface for the emphasis words "Tooning in" in the primary headline. The use of one spot color screened to different percentages adds to the headline's appeal. The color repetition in the drop cap letters on each story makes a strong connection to the primary headline and helps the reader establish entry points into each story's opening. Wisely, the staff chose to reserve the use of the novelty headline for the primary headline on the package, rather than to repeat the headline style on each individual story on the subject. By maintaining the strong sans serif headline style used throughout the paper for each of the truck's individual stories, the newspaper focuses the reader's entry into the topic and ensures a readable headline on each story. Overusing novelty typefaces weakens their appeal and creates confusing readability. *Stampede*, Burges High School, El Paso, Texas

faces are known as "big on the body." Some old style serifs have smaller x-heights, have smaller counters and eyes (the inside of the lowercase letter e) and need increased size on the page to encourage readability.

- The width of the text line. Very narrow lines of text and very wide lines create difficult reading patterns. When designers set type in widths as narrow as 5 picas, they should choose typefaces that are slightly condensed and should avoid justified lines of type. Type set in wide lines, generally wider than 20 picas, will be more difficult for the reader's eye to follow.

- The alignment pattern. While it's generally accepted that justified type alignment and left-aligned type are the easiest reading patterns, some designers choose centered type for headline display and right-aligned for captions placed to the left of a picture.

- The typeface itself. Novelty typefaces are often difficult to read and to discern in print. The characteristics that give them novelty classification can make them hard to read. They should be avoided for long text displays.

- The posture of the type. Italic type and type set in bold weights generally create slower, denser reading patterns for the reader's eye. Use these postures in moderation.

- The color of the type. Type in color can also slow readability. Color works best when used in limited amounts of type, such as headline displays, bullets, drop caps, headers and pull quotes.

- The leading. A current typographic trend shows designers using increased leading measures. On a computer, auto leading is usually activated. Auto leading will add a percentage of the point size of the active font's character to the leading value. Setting your own leading values gives you control over how far apart the lines of your text appear. For instance, type set in all caps is harder and slower to read. A designer can counteract that readability by setting the leading value at a higher percentage so the lines appear to be farther apart. The extra white space will "air out" the type, making it less dense.

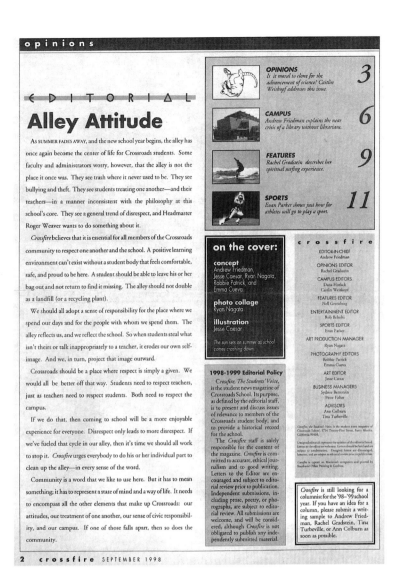

Designers should become accustomed to setting pure leading values rather than letting desktop-publishing programs make leading choices for them. Most desktop-publishing software programs also allow designers to change the auto leading value in a preferences file.

- The kerning. The space between letters and numbers can aid readability. In setting headlines in display type sizes, desktop-publishing programs' preset leading values will create typographic spacing problems. Numbers, for instance, will usually print too far apart. Other letter combinations can be tightened to eliminate uneven white space. Setting kerning values should be done individually between letter pairs in combination with the kerning control in the program. Kerning is difficult to see correctly on the computer screen. It isn't until the designer prints out a copy of the page that he or she can see typographic gaps in kerning. The object of correct kerning is to make it invisible and consistent.

Some layout software programs offer predetermined "tracking" values that can be used in place of individually kerning letters. These values often range from loose

Fig. 15.5. The editorial page of the newspaper is one in which a distinctive look should be achieved. Readers need to differentiate the persuasive content of this page from the more objective content offered in other sections of the paper. *Crossfire's* editorial page makes use of a larger type size and a wider grid format to distinguish the newspaper's editorial. Because the line length of the editorial is 26.5 picas wide, the staff wisely chose a more generous leading to allow the type to maintain an airiness that maintains strong readability. *Crossfire,* Crossroads School, Santa Monica, Calif.

Fig. 15.6. Many techniques can be used to maintain contrast and creative approaches to type display. The overlapping of type and screening of the letters *o* and *t* in the "Worth mentioning" headline add interest to this "standing headline," one that appears on news briefs in every issue of the paper. In addition, the designer has created a focal point through the large and backward *R*. Note that "mentioning" appears in sans serif, condensed type while "worth" appears in serif. The headline unit is held together by a hairline rule. Other contrasting headlines appear on "At the meeting place," a standing headline used for calendar listings, and on "Counselor's corner." In all cases, the headlines are designed as strong units of type that create interest for their consistent content. *Stampede*, Burges High School, El Paso, Texas

to very tight. Unfortunately, they don't take into consideration individual kerning problems and should not be used to replace good individual letter kerning.

TYPE CONTRAST AND CREATIVITY

One of the most interesting and rewarding areas of type design is choosing and designing type for visual creativity. Many combinations of type can be created that display a sense of the spirit of the design.

A headline should serve as a unit of information on a page. Designers can create contrast through combinations of type categories, by emphasizing words in the type display, by using color and by changing the positioning of the type display (Fig. 15.6).

Creating emphasis words in headlines can be done through size, through type posture and through color. Emphasis words should be carefully chosen so they work effectively with the story's content. In emphasis headlines, subordinate words such as articles and prepositional phrases can be lightened through weight, posture and size.

Color can bring the reader to a particular part of a headline. Repeating that color for text heads or story subheads can exploit the principle of grouping. Our eye tends to group things by shape and color (Fig. 15.7).

Headlines can be woven together in interesting arrangements and patterns. Headlines whose baselines have been rotated 90 degrees will effectively display information in bolder typefaces and when only a limited number of words is rotated. Desktop-publishing software makes it easy for designers to set type on skews, to baseline shift selected letters of type and to set type into shapes (Fig. 15.8).

In using any of these methods of contrast, the designer must consider readability as the most important factor.

Type wraps or run-arounds are created when the designer interjects a visual, a logo

Fig. 15.7. Colors selected for color temperature work well on this double-truck display. Red, a hot color, works to display the words "sweating" and "heat" in the headline. The cool blue subordinates the less important "the" in the headline. Designers have carefully echoed the colors by screening them down to lighter percentages and using them to help separate the individual stories in this package of information. Red and blue continue to be effectively used in the information graphics on the right and left sides of the page. Wisely, the staff confined its use of color to display type and did not use it on text, where its use would have slowed down the readability. *Hillcrest Hurricane,* Hillcrest High School, Dallas, Texas

or an illustration into the type display and causes the type to contour to the shape of the visual. Often, the pictures are used as cutouts, where their backgrounds have been removed leaving only a shaped image. Because these shaped images are "active" visually, designers should limit their use. Designers seeking type run-arounds should make sure the lines of type created by the run-around are readable, that hyphenation isn't excessive and that the reader isn't being asked to make awkward jumps around the visual. Using justified alignment on the text display will usually be more effective when type runs around an image, particularly one with four sides (Fig. 15.9).

Desktop-publishing software also makes it easy for designers to create type picture boxes in which the letters can be filled with color or pictures. Doing so requires pretty bold type displays and recognizable images or effective use of color.

TYPE CONSISTENCY

Creating style templates for the various type patterns in a publication will create consistency and ensure that the publication doesn't have a scattered, eclectic look on every page. It will ultimately save the designers a lot of time when importing text from word-processing software programs used by different staff members.

In a desktop-publishing software program, style sheets can be defined for each individual type area on the page. These could include the text type, headline type, secondary headline type, caption type, folio type and any other design styles being used by a particular page or section of the publication. Style sheets offer designers the opportunity to choose typeface styles, sizes, leading values, kerning values, indents, colors, drop caps, rule lines and many other type specifications. The style can

America is a melting pot of cultures, but what about Hinsdale Central...

are our courses

Culturally
diverse

[enough?]

Written by Elizabeth Ogren

Art by Alix Feinkind

16   FEATURE THE DEVILS' ADVOCATE

Fig. 15.8. Skewing the baselines, the lines upon which type normally sit, creates a typographic headline that again visualizes the verbal message, diversity. Mixing capitals and lowercase letters reinforces the effect. *Devils' Advocate*, Hinsdale Central High School, Hinsdale, Ill.

also be defined by clicking in a type display and setting that up as a style sheet. Once set and saved in a template mode, the styles will open when a designer opens the template and begins designing a page for that template. Style sheets save designers enormous amounts of time checking consistency from page to page.

Elements that should be consistent throughout a publication include the body text, the folios, standing heads, the nameplate, section headers, pull quote designs, captions and secondary or deck heads. The use of special, stylized headlines set in typefaces that are not consistently used throughout the publication will often be by designer choice. These heads, referred to as "art heads," shouldn't overwhelm page content or interfere with readability.

Observe good professional newspapers such as the *Boston Globe, Chicago Tribune, Minneapolis Star-Tribune* or any good local newspaper to see how creative and attractive headlines can be designed using a limited number of typefaces consistently throughout the newspaper. These publications create attention-getting headline display on feature pages through creative headline content and strong, creative arrangements of type.

When placing text type on a page, designers should ensure that baselines align in columns of type that fall beside each other. Most desktop-publishing software programs enable designers to control the baseline alignment within a text box. Text shapes tend to appear in modules, or four-sided design shapes, although other patterns can be used.

Captions should be placed next to pictures, preferably in a point size or two smaller than the text size used on the page. Using bolder weights and condensed type variations often allows writers to pack more information into a caption and create contrast with the body type.

Visual hierarchy in design ensures that a reader processes information in a logical and coherent way. Designers should choose sizes, weights and postures of type to draw the reader into the largest type display first and should then subordinate the type sizes and weights for information in a logical way. Text heads, pull quotes and secondary or deck headlines should appear in type sizes that are larger than text size but smaller than headline size, and in a typeface whose weight provides contrast to the body text.

Large passages of body text should not appear in italic or bold. Designers should seek to use the "book" or roman (text) weight versions of the type for ease of readability.

Captions and page folios should be smaller in the visual hierarchy. The smallest size type used on the page might very well be for picture credits giving credit to the photographers who shot the images. These picture credits often appear in type as small as 6 or 7 points.

Placement of elements on a page or spread is another factor in hierarchy. Elements placed in prominent page positions, known as the visual entry points, should be larger and more prominent. As the reader's eye moves toward the bottom of the page, typographic display (usually headlines) will become smaller. This story placement is also determined by the news value of the content (Fig. 15.10). See Chapter 1 for more on news values.

PRODUCTION

With the advent of desktop-publishing software, most designers have taken over primary responsibility for the prepress production of their publications. Files are given to printers in digital format, in camera-ready copy for converting into film for plating or in film format ready for plating. Staffs with low-resolution printers (anything under 600 dpi) should probably consider the use of a service bureau or prepress bureau to output pages to film or paper before providing those pages to the printer.

Schools using laser printers will find improved reproduction of type and image. Laser printers create characters and images by drawing them through a computer language, such as PostScript or TrueType, on a metal drum with a laser beam. The image becomes visible by electrostatically attracting dry ink powder—toner—to the image. The toner binds to the paper by heat and pressure. Laser printing is similar to photocopying.

Some schools use ink jet or dot matrix printers for output. These methods are lower quality than PostScript and are generally not acceptable for student publications.

Fig. 15.9. A collage illustration provides a strong visual entry point into this package of stories about teen image. Since the visual is holding the package together, the designer has placed it so that the type on both the left and right stories touch it or "wrap around" it. Since the type contours to the image, it interrupts the normal reading pattern. However, the designer has wisely chosen to maintain a pica of white space between the edge of the illustration and the text and has maintained readable line widths. Since the illustration wraps into less than half the column width, the designer has also avoided excessive hyphenation of words or holes of white space that would have been distracting to read. *Peninsula Outlook*, Peninsula High School, Gig Harbor, Wash.

Fig. 15.10. An excellent illustration of an effectively designed front page using page hierarchy that is utilitarian to the reader. The news value of stories is indicated by the size of the headlines used. Internally, the page is consistently spaced so that no awkward white space holes appear. Baselines of type in stories align across the page, creating clear story boundaries. A column of short news briefs runs down the left side of the page, offering visual relief from the longer stories on the rest of the page. A strong photograph anchors the page with a caption and lead-in in a contrasting type. The strong sans serif headline style provides good reader entry points into the stories. A consistent style has been used for each story's byline. Additionally, the long front-page story text is broken up by a pull quote in a distinctive typographic style utilizing strong left alignment. The page is balanced and graphically appealing. *Update,* Herbert Henry Dow High School, Midland, Mich.

When taking electronic files to a printer or service bureau, the designer must make sure to include all file formats, scans and typefaces that will be used in the production of the pages. Most desktop-publishing software programs have the capability to "collect for output," so they can gather the files they will need to ensure correct printing or will warn the designers of missing file information. Designers can often access utility checks to see if any files are missing that would cause the information to print incorrectly.

Service bureaus output pages or film on high-resolution image-setters, usually front-ended to computers so the files can read PostScript and other computer formats. Many schools purchase tabloid printers capable of outputting pages up to 11 × 17 inches and that offer higher-resolution output, eliminating the need for production through a service bureau or printer.

PRINTING

Most printing today is done by the offset lithography method, based on the principle that oil and water do not mix. The offset method is printing from a smooth plate surface onto which the image has been "burned," or exposed through a large camera. The areas to be printed are treated so ink (oil-based) from the printing rollers adheres to them, while the remaining surface is treated with water rollers that reject the oily ink. The inked image is then transferred—offset—to a rubber roller surface, called a "blanket," that prints the image on the paper.

In order for photographs to be reproduced through offset printing, either they must be scanned directly into the desktop-publishing program and produced as output or the originals must be screened by the printer and stripped into the pages where holes created by black or red windows on the layouts will provide clear areas on the negatives.

Offset lithography for newspaper printing is primarily done by web presses,

presses that print from continuously fed rolls of paper. Presses are also being perfected that print both sides of the paper at the same time, making the printing process fast. Most web presses are limited in the kinds of paper they are able to print, so papers with higher pulp content, such as newsprint, are ideally suited for web presses. With improved presses, printers can use higher grades of paper, allowing many publications to be printed on paper that is "whiter" and heavier than newsprint.

A popular variation of offset printing is a flexographic press used primarily in newspaper and paperback book publishing. An inexpensive and simple method of printing on a web-fed press, flexographic printing uses rubber plates and water- or solvent-based inks in a two-roller system. The process is considered more environmentally friendly since soy-based or vegetable inks can be used in combination with recycled paper stocks.

Yearbooks and magazines are also printed primarily through the offset method, but often on sheet-fed rather than web presses. Sheet-fed presses take single sheets of paper into the press at a time and can print both sides at once. The single sheets are large, allowing for the printing of several pages on each side of the form. Each side of the paper is known as a flat and might consist of four or eight pages. The two sides are called "signatures." A signature is then folded and trimmed to allow for normal reading. A printer determines how many forms are required to produce the book's or magazine's total page run.

Because the pages on a signature must be arranged in what is known as "printer spreads," pages that will print across from each other, printers often use "imposition software" on the electronic files provided by the school. Designers find it easier to design in "reader spreads," the configurations of pages that face each other when reading.

Books and magazines require binding, a method of holding together the printed pages. Magazines are usually bound by saddle-stitching, a method of placing staples in the center of the magazine directly in the gutter. Magazines can also be "perfect bound," where strips of glue applied along a flat gut-

Fig. 15.11. Spot color, the use of a single color in design, is effectively used in this newspaper's front page. A screened version of the color has been used in the nameplate area. The primary headline in the front-page story's package has been highlighted by using a darker shade of the same color. This color is then used for reverse header bars in quick-read information appearing in the left column of the front page. Note the use of text heads in the story to provide visual relief in long story forms. *Lion*, Lyons Township High School, LaGrange, Ill.

Best-selling and Favorite Typefaces

According to the Adobe Company, the best-selling Adobe typefaces in the world are

- Minion multiple master
- Helvetica condensed
- Optima
- Univers
- Futura 2
- Tekton multiple master
- Futura 1
- Helvetica light and black
- Univers condensed
- Myriad multiple master

Favorite and recommended typefaces for publication use include

- Caslon 540
- Century/Century Expanded/Century Old Style/Century Schoolbook
- Charter
- Corona
- Gulliver/Gulliver Compact
- Bodoni
- Cheltenham
- Times Roman
- Bauer Bodoni
- Franklin Gothic
- Nimrod
- Ionic

ter hold pages together. "Side-stitching" is used to refer to staples placed not in the gutter but slightly away from the gutter.

These binding methods have a definite effect on page margins and gutter margins. Magazines printed and saddle-stitched will open completely flat, allowing designers to take information closer to or across the gutter without a problem. Other binding methods, including mechanical or wire binding, side-stitching and perfect binding require larger gutter margins because the pages don't lay completely flat. In newspaper printing, only the middle pages of the paper will actually be printed on the same sheet of paper. This "double truck," as it's referred to in newspaper design, offers an excellent opportunity for staffs to design areas that go across the page.

Yearbooks are bound by collecting and sewing together the various forms or signatures by a process known as "Smythe-sewing." Binders use big machines that look like sewing machines to stitch a heavy-weight thread across the forms. Then a wide gauze strip is glued to the sewn pages and attached to a hard-back cover that has been rounded and backed to allow the book's multiple pages to lay open for reading. The gauze is covered on the inside by end sheets or end papers, often incorporating a design or color. Small, decorative "headbands" are finishing touches at the top and bottom of the sewn forms that cover up the binding.

Before offset became the primary printing form, other methods were more popular and are still used by some printers. These forms include letterpress and gravure printing.

Letterpress, the standard before offset, is printing from a raised surface. Type characters are cut into metal. Before metal type was invented in 1450 by Johann Gutenberg, they were cut into wood.

Gravure printing uses a raised or sunken surface into which the image has been etched. Gravure printing is excellent for high-quality reproduction, especially of photographic images, and is used in book publishing, in textile printing and by magazines such as *National Geographic.*

With improvements in desktop publishing and laser printing, many schools produce their pages directly from laser printer output, either photocopied or mimeographed, often in school print shops. Improvements in photocopiers now allow for quality photoreproduction and can be used effectively in small schools without incurring printing charges for short runs where a limited number of final copies is needed.

The use of color in printing is referred to as either "spot color," the use of a single color, or "four-color," the use of full-color. Color adds significantly to the overall cost of the printing. The use of very specific color shades or tones can be chosen from patented inking processes manufactured by companies such as the Pantone Matching System, the most common method used in printing in the United States. These colors could actually incur "five-color printing," adding to the color cost. Four-color printing simply means the paper has to pass through four, individual color inking presses that contain cyan (blue), magenta (red), yellow and black inks in order to reproduce as full color. Five-color requires the page to pass through an additional color press to apply a special colored ink (Fig. 15.11).

With color becoming more of a standard in printing, fully digital presses are being developed that allow for faster and less expensive use of color. Already, many yearbook staffs have produced full-color volumes. It's also common to see color throughout a high school newspaper. In order to reproduce color photographs in a newspaper, magazine or yearbook, the pictures must be "separated" into the four-color negatives needed to produce the color image. This can add significant costs to the printing job. With digital submission, the cost is minimized since the images print out digitally. Many yearbook publishers require four-color photos be submitted in the actual size they will appear in the book. If they are not, the staff could incur additional costs.

In high-quality printing, especially in which color is used, designers will be able to check proofs of their color before the job is actually printed. Low-end proofs, often "bluelines" or brownlines because of the color they appear in proof form, allow staffs to check photographic and type positioning and to check for errors in the copy. High-end color proofs are provided by different processes when required for color proofing and matching. Making corrections to either proof form will incur additional charges. Proofreading should be done as completely as possible before proofing occurs.

Printing is one area of technology that will continue to evolve. Already, printing press manufacturers are developing four-color, high-speed presses that will enable a digital file to go directly from the printer's front end, connected directly to a PostScript computer, immediately to the plating process, the last step before actual printing. Low-end printing processes, such as photocopying, also continue to evolve, making short-run printing possible from the local photocopying facility for almost immediate distribution.

EXERCISES

1. Find examples of each of the six main categories or races of type, including serif, sans serif, square or slab serif, scripts or cursives, novelty and black letter. Cut out an example of each from a newspaper or magazine and label it. Discuss the use of the typeface within the context of the publication.

2. Using newspapers from out of town or from another state, find five examples of logos used in advertising for local businesses, products and services. Try to find an example of a logo for a local restaurant, a service, a children's store, a clothing store and a motel/hotel. Cut out each logo and paste it on a sheet of paper. In groups of three, exchange your lists and discuss your impressions of the businesses or services based on the logos. How would you dress to go to the restaurant? Is the children's store exclusive or mainstream? Who would the consumers be for the clothing store?

3. From newspapers or magazines clip five examples of type that fits the criteria for being readable and legible. List the factors that make the type examples readable and legible.

4. Visit this web site where typefaces are sold commercially: http://www.philsfonts.com. At the site, click on the great links button, then at the next window "type links." Visit several of the commercial-type foundries listed here. Look through some of the available typeface choices, observing the cost of the typeface, versatility (number of variations), usefulness and readability. Make a list of typefaces you would like to buy and own.

5. Find examples of type that use the following techniques for creating contrast: a headline in which a word or two is emphasized through size variation; a headline in which color has been used to create contrast; a headline with an interesting arrangement and positioning of words; type that has been set on a skew or where the baseline is shifted from a normal position; and a type run-around or wrap-around. If you have access to a computer and design software, using these samples create your own headlines in the same styles.

6. Using a local newspaper, examine the front page and an inside page and discuss the paper's use of visual hierarchy. If you have access to a pica ruler, measure the point size of the headlines on the front page and write the size next to each headline. Discuss the newspaper's consistency in use of body text, secondary or deck heads, bylines, headlines and captions. Next, look at the way in which the stories appear on the page. Draw boxes around each story unit (it may include a related picture) and see how many fall into modules of four sides. Look for consistency with the placement of text baselines in related columns of text.

7. If you have a local print shop or newspaper in your town, arrange a visit to the print shop or invite a printer to talk to the class, bringing examples of the different printing steps. Observe the printing method being used by the printer and have the technicians explain the different printing steps from start to finish. Ask questions about any process or procedure you don't understand.

8. Get copies of a newsmagazine such as *Time*, *Newsweek* or *U.S. News and World Report.* Open the cover and find the staples used in the binding. This process is called "saddle-stitching." Open to the center of the publication and see how easily the pages lie open. Look at pages facing each other at the back of the magazine where elements are printed across the two pages. Observe whether they line up correctly. Next, get a copy of *National Geographic,* a magazine that is side-stitched. Open the cover and find the staples. Open to the center of the publication and see how flat the pages lie open. Look at two pages printed across from each other at the back of the magazine where the elements have been printed across the two pages. Do they line up? Get a copy of the school's yearbook. Look at the end sheets at the front and back of the publication. Notice how the end sheets are holding the printed pages into the cover. Examine the spine and see how flexible it is in allowing the book to lie open. Look into the spine at the top or bottom of the book and see if the binding is finished with headbands.

Newspaper Design and Layout

Just as drivers need a road map when going on a long trip, readers need guidance in making sense of the information presented to them in a newspaper. Without any attention to the way the newspaper is visually presented to the reader, few would be interested in reading the content of a typical edition. Layout designers are integral partners to writers, editors and photographers. Good writing deserves to be read. Good photographs should be viewed. It's the job of the designer, sometimes referred to as the "presentation director" at professional newspapers, to make sure the reader stays interested despite distractions and shortened attention spans.

Typically, high school newspapers appear in one of three sizes: newsmagazines, traditionally 8.5 × 11 inches; tabloid size, traditionally 11 × 17 inches; and broadsheets, traditionally 14 × 21 inches. Access to laser printers that can produce finished pages in these sizes or in portions of these sizes will give designers easier access to pagination, laying out the publication completely in the computer before printing out the finished pages.

The layout designer can employ the principles of good design to maintain effective visual hierarchy and attractively designed pages (Figs. 16.1–16.3).

ELEMENTS OF DESIGN

Designers begin by considering the elements they will work with on the page. Text, including headlines, captions and stories, will create gray masses of weight on the page. Because text can "gray out" in long columns, creating long masses of text that can discourage readability, designers should pay attention to visual devices that will help break up the text and offer options for readability. Elements such as drop cap letters—large initial cap letters starting paragraphs—or text heads—small headlines placed within the story that help to create transitions at natural junctures—work well as visual breaks (Fig. 16.4).

Pictures, both black-and-white and color, as well as visual illustrations and drawings will create the weight of black on the page and in design. These denser visual areas need to be balanced with both the text weight and the space not used on the page, known as "white space."

White space, which makes up about 50 percent of all pages, creates the weight of white on the page and in the design. White space refers to both the space not used by the designer to create separations and alleys between text, as well as spaces left horizontally between the lines of the text, between the decks of the headlines and between the various elements of design. White space is an effective device for moving the reader from one element to another on the page. Surrounding a larger story with a bit of extra white space will dually serve to draw the reader to that el-

Fig. 16.1. The small size of the newsmagazine facilitates production since facing pages and spreads can be printed on single sheets of tabloid paper directly from the laser printer. Newsmagazines can vary their front pages to emphasize their strongest story, whether visual or verbal in content. Even with a visual approach, newsmagazines can vary the number of pictures shown on the front page. *Devils' Advocate,* Hinsdale Central High School, Hinsdale, Ill.

Fig. 16.2. In a tabloid format, visual hierarchy and page architecture become important components. A primary story package features a large picture to accompany the text. A second story runs beneath the story, but without a picture. Along the right side of the page, the column "Minutenews" provides a strong summary of capsulized information that is a quick read. Note also the use of the simplified index information across the bottom of the page in reverse type. *Academy Times,* Charles Wright Academy, Tacoma, Wash.

ement while creating separation between it and other page elements (Fig. 16.5).

Learning to balance the three elements and weights of design will ultimately allow the designer to create interesting, reader-friendly pages that will effectively showcase both text and visuals and create clear reading patterns for the reader.

PRINCIPLES OF GOOD DESIGN

Balance: Balance in design simply means that the page is visually and evenly weighted. It doesn't mean that everything appears the same size, but it does refer to creating design that prevents the look of any design elements becoming distracting. If all the pictures are placed at the top of the page, the page will look top-heavy. The same problem will occur if all the pictures

Fig. 16.3. In a broadsheet newspaper, designers have the opportunity to really "package" information, including visuals and verbals in interesting ways. High school newspapers should also take advantage of the opportunity to define the space in interesting ways without worrying about having a set number of static stories begin on the front page. In this edition of the *Update*, the staff presented short bios of leaders in the school. The use of color helped to group the students by grade classification, although the stories from the different grade levels are not necessarily placed adjacent to each other. The dominant visual cutout is used to grab the reader and pull attention into the package. The name headlines and identifying pictures help establish the profiles. Notice how readers can enter and exit through any one of the profiles. Providing many points of entry on a page is important in grabbing reader interest. The page design also offers short "Quick Takes," briefly summarized stories, along the left side of the page, all with pictures; a concise index at the top of the page; and an information graphic anchoring the bottom left corner. *Update*, Herbert Henry Dow High School, Midland, Mich.

consistently throughout the newspaper, often referred to as "standing heads," is a good way to create unity. Using the same size and typeface for most stories or using the same type family for headlines will also give the publication a unified look. The need for unity doesn't mean the designer can't deviate from the newspaper's typeface styles for a feature story or for an in-depth piece. Doing so helps to draw the reader's attention to something of special content in the newspaper. However, using different typefaces for every story in the newspaper will confuse unity, creating disparate and confusing messages for readers (Fig. 16.6).

Scale: Depending on the size of the publication, the designer must start with a series of vertical spaces dividing the page. These vertical spaces, called "columns" or "grids," help guide the reader in placing stories in the design. In addition to vertical columns, some designers will use an intricate series of horizontal columns to maintain alignment across pages and spreads so that lines of type within stories will also align. The grid or column method should create an appropriate and readable width for lines of type and layout of stories.

Proportion: Proportion must be considered by the designer. Maintaining proportional differences of 1:3

appear on the left or right side of the page. A large visual at the top of the page (creating a dense black weight on the page) needs to be balanced with something visual at the bottom.

Rhythm: Rhythm often refers to the visual flow of the page: good typography that coordinates well together, for instance, or a range of headline sizes that work well together for the size of the page being designed.

Unity: The pages must create unity throughout the publication so there's a sense of repetition in the use of elements that the reader grows familiar with during the reading process. Using a particular style of type and design for the nameplate and for elements that appear

Fig. 16.4. Even without a dominant photographic element on its front page, the *Central Times* manages to provide an interesting package of information for its readers. The blue color repeated only in display areas helps guide the reader through the front-page content. The newspaper provides many visual entry points into front-page content through a "nut graph" headline appearing above the front-page feature package, through the blue, all-cap headlines on the index information and through the alternative copy information packaged with the front-page feature. This two-part story series, which finished in the next month's paper, also features a story logo that connects to the promo at the bottom of the package. In addition, designers have used all-cap text heads, again in blue, to break up the text in the package, providing yet additional reader entry points. *Central Times,* Naperville Central High School, Naperville, Ill.

Fig. 16.5. A package of information on the school's sports radio program provides a good opportunity to use white space to package a variety of different text forms and to draw the reader to this special content in the sports section. Generous leading between the story's beginning text lines helps to create interest in the information. Narrow measures of white space, often referred to as "rails" in newspaper design, help to create contrast with the other story on the page and help to focus the reader's attention on the alternative ways in which the information is presented. *HiLite,* Carmel High School, Carmel, Ind.

Fig. 16.6. This newspaper does an effective job of showcasing content using the design principles of balance, rhythm and unity. Even though its sections are contained within the paper rather than published separately, the repetition of the nameplate design, including its type, helps the readers make the transitions between sections and content. The newspaper effectively showcases content through the use of bold type in its headlines. The primary story on each page uses headline type in a bold, sans serif face to draw in the reader through a strong visual hierarchy. A consistent internal and external margin provides a clean separation for each story. Column widths, narrower on the front page than on inside section fronts, help to create distinction for the front page. The sans serif type used on the front page's news briefs column, "NewsCenter," also creates contrast; these shorter items contrast with the other front-page stories. Throughout the paper, the repeating and consistent use of type and design elements connects the pages visually but provides individual attention for distinctive content. *Blue and Gold*, Center High School, Antelope, Calif.

creates asymmetrical designs that are far more visually interesting than symmetrical ones. For instance, when using a visual in design, the proportion of the largest visual on the page should often be two to three times larger than any other visual. Similarly, larger, more important stories should take up more space on the page than smaller, less important stories (Fig. 16.7).

Visual hierarchy: One of the designer's most important considerations, visual hierarchy is used to help the reader understand the significance of the information's importance. Stories with greater news values should appear at the top of the page with larger headlines. As the reader's eyes progress from the top of the page to the bottom, the headlines will be smaller in size to indicate a less important news value. This pattern of visual hierarchy is maintained on every page to help readers process information and edit the content they will read (Fig. 16.8).

INFORMATION PACKAGING

Another important consideration for designers is "packaging" the available information for the reader.

ten — The Central Times — sports — April 30, 1999

ALAN LIU — *I Was Just Thinking...*

The end of sportsmanship?

STRETCH

Crazy for Pong

▶ As ping-pong becomes increasingly popular in various parts of the country, Central students are catching 'pong fever.'

DEFENSE

Boys' track paves way to placing third at conference

UFO?

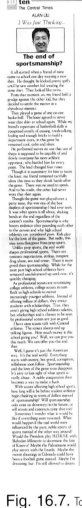

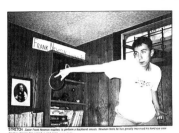

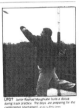

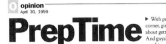

Fig. 16.7. Taking up about two-thirds of this page, the feature story on Ping-Pong features a large, dominant picture that provides for a 1:3 ratio in relation to the next largest picture on the page, the discus thrower picture anchoring the bottom right corner of the page. The Ping-Pong feature uses narrow rails of white space along the edges of the design to both bring the reader into the story and to visually separate it from other content. The pictures are effectively placed on the page to provide strong balance in the design. *Central Times,* Naperville Central High School, Naperville, Ill.

opinion — April 30, 1999 — three — The Central Times

PrepTime

▶ With prom just around the corner, girls are starting to fret about getting ready in time. And guys? They're sitting back watching their girls freak out.

GIRLY prom-day plans

9:30	Wake - up
9:45	Pre-dance work out
10:15	Leave for tanning
10:30	Tan ($9)
11:15	Lunch time
11:45	Shower
12:00	After shower stuff (lotion, moisturizer, comb out hair, etc...)
12:10	Facial mask
12:30	Blow-dry hair
12:40	Snack time
12:50	Leave for pedicure
1:00	Pedicure / Manicure ($68)
2:30	Hair Styling ($40)
3:45	Snack time
4:00	Make-up ($15)
4:20	Get dressed (Dress $240, shoes $40, purse $20, jewelry $15, nylons, underwear, bra $30, boutonniere $10)
4:45	date arrives, pictures with date
5:00	group pictures
5:45	leave for dance

Guy 'spends youth' shopping with sister

ADAM PAGE — *Just Throwin' it Around*

The man behind the disease

Ants' second-floor invasion prompts life questions

ANTZ

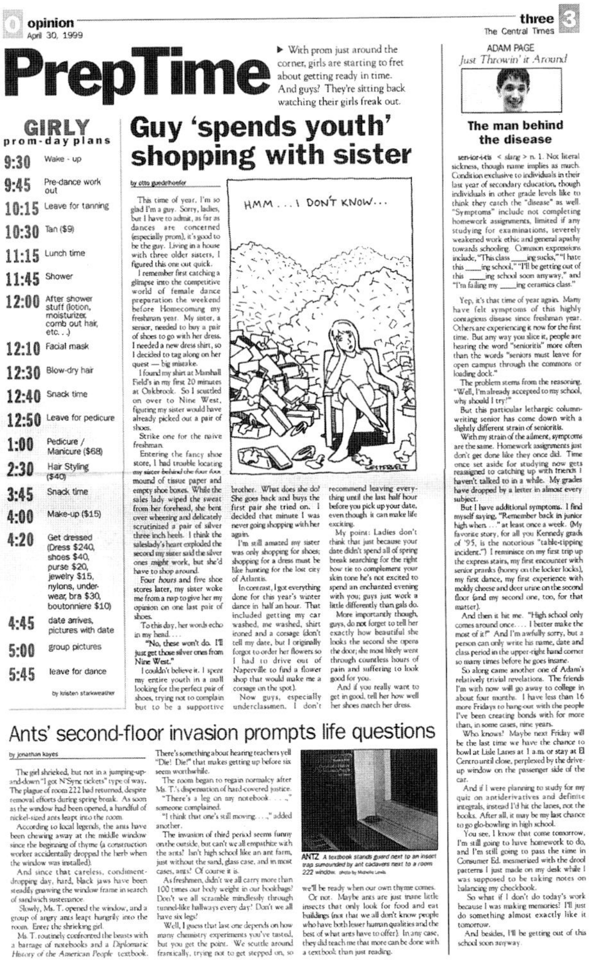

Fig. 16.8. The most important content on this opinion page is effectively showcased by the sans serif bold typeface used for the headline of the prom prep time story. Two other headline layers, including a "nut graph" summary, provide the reader with facts and details before entering the text. The sidebar summarizing the timeline of prom day plans is a strong second read and, possibly, a first read for many readers who might initially be less interested in the text. The second-most-important story appears beneath the prom prep time story and has a lighter sans serif type for the single-deck headline. A regularly written column appears on the right side of the page where it effectively anchors the outside of the page. *Central Times,* Naperville Central High School, Naperville, Ill.

Fig. 16.9. Although sports content usually does not appear on the front page, this unusual domination of the league in fall sports led the staff of the *Axe* to make an exception. Utilizing the entire front page, the staff created a package that includes a story summarizing the season, a graphic cutout connected to the "Domination" headline and individual pictures from three of the sports teams. A summary box at the bottom anchors the page visually and provides a "quick read" for any reader who chooses not to read the story text. *Axe*, South Eugene High School, Eugene, Ore.

Sometimes, a designer only has a single story without visuals. Working with an editor, a designer might be able to extract some of the information from the story and present it in a separate story placed adjacent to the primary story. Or, working with a photographer or an illustrator, the designer might be able to have a combination of photographic and text elements in which to present a single story. This combination might give the readers greater interest in the information. A reader might look at the shorter story presentation, find something of interest and begin reading the primary story. Or something in the visual or in the caption for the visual might give the reader a reason to read the primary story (Fig. 16.9).

Because of readers' splintered interests and attention spans, information packaging is becoming a more important consideration in layout and design. Packaged stories generally are given prominent page display and visual hierarchy, often focusing the reader's attention to that content first when looking at the page. Because of this, designers often surround a package with a bit more white space to further draw the reader to the content.

Packaging information requires the designer consider various approaches to layout. These include visual through photographs or illustrations or typographic through dominant headline displays. Working with photographers and illustrators, designers can come up with effective ways of displaying visual content. (Also see Chap. 20.)

GRIDS AND COLUMNS

As mentioned before, designers begin working on pages by dividing the space into a number of vertical and/or horizontal spaces depending on the size of the publication. Traditionally, newsmagazines often work with fewer vertical grids or columns, while larger formats such as broadsheets offer more options for dividing the page space (Fig. 16.10). In recent years, professional newspaper designers have begun using 12-column grids for broadsheets. Smaller publications, such as the newsmagazine, will rarely divide space into more than five to seven grids or columns. To do so would create awkward column widths.

Multiple-grid formats offer designers wide choices in creating layouts for stories. Readability of column widths must be considered when deciding how wide to make columns of type, but combining these columns

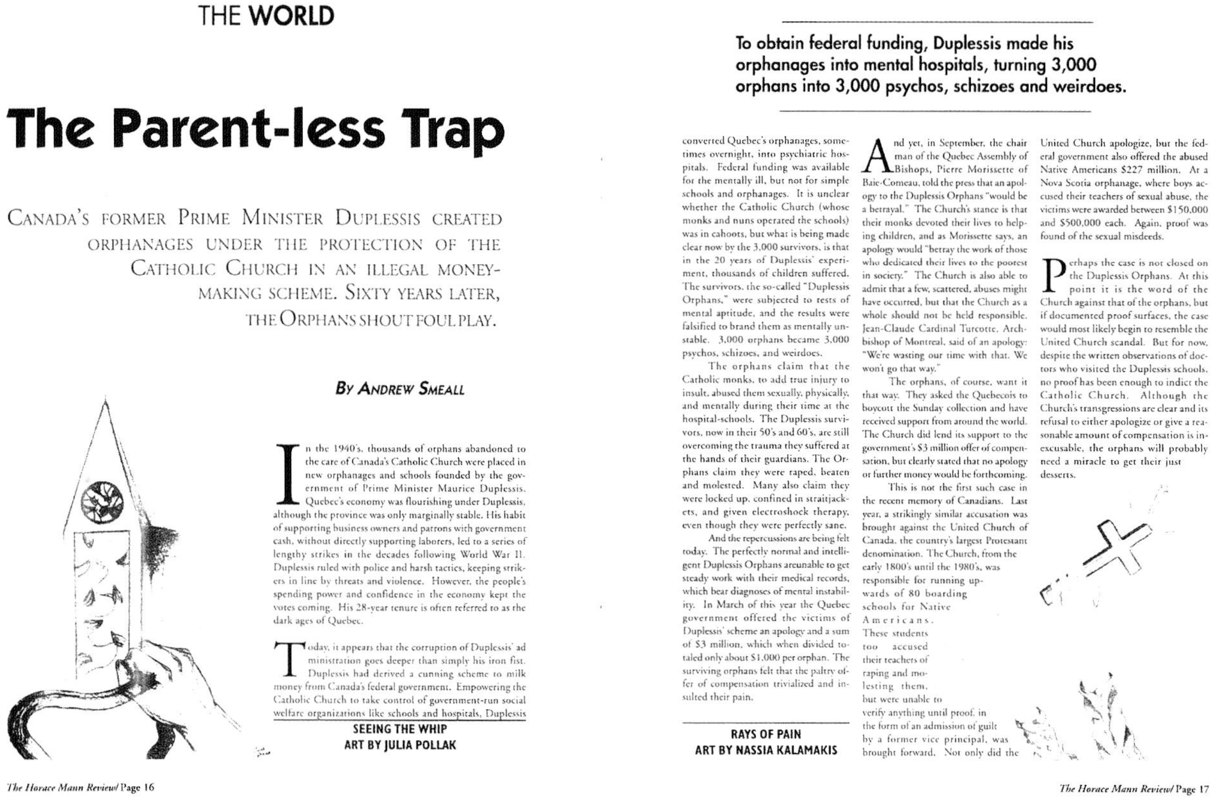

THE **WORLD**

The Parent-less Trap

CANADA'S FORMER PRIME MINISTER DUPLESSIS CREATED
ORPHANAGES UNDER THE PROTECTION OF THE
CATHOLIC CHURCH IN AN ILLEGAL MONEY-
MAKING SCHEME. SIXTY YEARS LATER,
THE ORPHANS SHOUT FOUL PLAY.

BY ANDREW SMEALL

In the 1940's, thousands of orphans abandoned to the care of Canada's Catholic Church were placed in new orphanages and schools founded by the government of Prime Minister Maurice Duplessis. Quebec's economy was flourishing under Duplessis, although the province was only marginally stable. His habit of supporting business owners and patrons with government cash, without directly supporting laborers, led to a series of lengthy strikes in the decades following World War II. Duplessis ruled with police and harsh tactics, keeping strikers in line by threats and violence. However, the people's spending power and confidence in the economy kept the votes coming. His 28-year tenure is often referred to as the dark ages of Quebec.

Today, it appears that the corruption of Duplessis' administration goes deeper than simply his iron fist. Duplessis had derived a cunning scheme to milk money from Canada's federal government. Empowering the Catholic Church to take control of government-run social welfare organizations like schools and hospitals, Duplessis

SEEING THE WHIP
ART BY JULIA POLLAK

The Horace Mann Review/ Page 16

> To obtain federal funding, Duplessis made his orphanages into mental hospitals, turning 3,000 orphans into 3,000 psychos, schizoes and weirdoes.

converted Quebec's orphanages, sometimes overnight, into psychiatric hospitals. Federal funding was available for the mentally ill, but not for simple schools and orphanages. It is unclear whether the Catholic Church (whose monks and nuns operated the schools) was in cahoots, but what is being made clear now by the 3,000 survivors, is that in the 20 years of Duplessis' experiment, thousands of children suffered. The survivors, the so-called "Duplessis Orphans," were subjected to tests of mental aptitude, and the results were falsified to brand them as mentally unstable. 3,000 orphans became 3,000 psychos, schizoes and weirdoes.

The orphans claim that the Catholic monks, to add true injury to insult, abused them sexually, physically, and mentally during their time at the hospital-schools. The Duplessis survivors, now in their 50's and 60's, are still overcoming the trauma they suffered at the hands of their guardians. The Orphans claim they were raped, beaten and molested. Many also claim they were locked up, confined in straitjackets, and given electroshock therapy, even though they were perfectly sane.

And the repercussions are being felt today. The perfectly normal and intelligent Duplessis Orphans areunable to get steady work with their medical records, which bear diagnoses of mental instability. In March of this year the Quebec government offered the victims of Duplessis' scheme an apology and a sum of $3 million, which when divided totaled only about $1,000 per orphan. The surviving orphans felt that the paltry offer of compensation trivialized and insulted their pain.

RAYS OF PAIN
ART BY NASSIA KALAMAKIS

And yet, in September, the chairman of the Quebec Assembly of Bishops, Pierre Morissette of Baie-Comeau, told the press that an apology to the Duplessis Orphans "would be a betrayal." The Church's stance is that their monks devoted their lives to helping children, and as Morissette says, an apology would "betray the work of those who dedicated their lives to the poorest in society." The Church is also able to admit that a few, scattered, abuses might have occurred, but that the Church as a whole should not be held responsible. Jean-Claude Cardinal Turcotte, Archbishop of Montreal, said of an apology: "We're wasting our time with that. We won't go that way."

The orphans, of course, want it that way. They asked the Quebecois to boycott the Sunday collection and have received support from around the world. The Church did lend its support to the government's $3 million offer of compensation, but clearly stated that no apology or further money would be forthcoming.

This is not the first such case in the recent memory of Canadians. Last year, a strikingly similar accusation was brought against the United Church of Canada, the country's largest Protestant denomination. The Church, from the early 1800's until the 1980's, was responsible for running upwards of 80 boarding schools for Native Americans. These students too accused their teachers of raping and molesting them, but were unable to verify anything until proof, in the form of an admission of guilt by a former vice principal, was brought forward. Not only did the

United Church apologize, but the federal government also offered the abused Native Americans $227 million. At a Nova Scotia orphanage, where boys accused their teachers of sexual abuse, the victims were awarded between $150,000 and $500,000 each. Again, proof was found of the sexual misdeeds.

Perhaps the case is not closed on the Duplessis Orphans. At this point it is the word of the Church against that of the orphans, but if documented proof surfaces, the case would most likely begin to resemble the United Church scandal. But for now, despite the written observations of doctors who visited the Duplessis schools, no proof has been enough to indict the Catholic Church. Although the Church's transgressions are clear and its refusal to either apologize or give a reasonable amount of compensation is inexcusable, the orphans will probably need a miracle to get their just desserts.

The Horace Mann Review/ Page 17

Fig. 16.10. In a newsmagazine, columns or grids are often configured in standard three- or four-column widths to facilitate text readability. Even with standard widths, designers can take text across a column and a half or can further divide the page into two columns to create contrast for story beginnings or special content. *Horace Mann Review,* Horace Mann School, Riverdale, N.Y.

and creating wider columns generally makes for ease of readability. The more narrow grids can be used for detail elements such as captions, drop cap letters or nut graph deck heads. Placing text in narrow grids, as narrow as 5 to 7 picas, generally produces low readability. When using narrow columns for text, designers should consider using condensed typefaces and unjustified alignment patterns so the text doesn't appear with frequent hyphens or large holes of white space between words (Fig. 16.11). (See Chap. 15 for more information.)

MARGINS AND SPACE

External margins are white space borders surrounding the page on all four sides. Necessary in newspaper printing because the presses cannot print to the edge of the page, margins also provide balance to the page and create alignments for the text, causing the readers' eyes to return to natural points on the page. Generally, margins can be as narrow as a quarter of an inch or can be a bit wider depending on the publication's page size.

Internal margins, the spaces between the columns vertically and horizontally, should be consistent and even for pages to look balanced and well proportioned. Although exceptions are sometimes made, vertical internal margins tend to be about 1 pica wide. This space allows designers to place text columns beside each other without the lines of text becoming confused with those appearing next to them. Horizontally, the designer should also maintain a consistency in space sepa-

Fig. 16.11. As text wraps around logos, pull quotes or illustrations and photographs, the widths of the columns left wrapping is an important consideration in readability. Both primary stories at the top of this tabloid page place information wrapped into the text columns. The columns of the left story are one and a half of the standard four columns, which still allows the wrapped text width to be 12 picas wide, preventing awkward gaps between words. The justified text also creates a clean wrap around both design elements. The right story's pull quote wraps into the standard five-column width. Although the text widths wrapping the pull quote are only 7 picas wide, the staff has done a good job of preventing awkward white space holes by controlling the line kerning and line breaks. Note that each text element on this page appears in a different column width, but all are based on a standard four- or five-column configuration. *Peninsula Outlook*, Peninsula High School, Gig Harbor, Wash.

Fig. 16.12. Consistent internal margins, both horizontal and vertical, give this page a clean architecture and an easy-to-follow format. Note that 1 pica of white space is used consistently to separate elements vertically. Headlines and text are placed consistently apart so no awkward white space holes are left on the page. Stories end on common baselines across the page, also creating clean patterns of readability. *Little Hawk*, City High School, Iowa City, Iowa

Fig. 16.13. On a page with many visual entry points for the reader, content is maintained in consistent four-sided modules throughout the design. Some modules, such as the column running along the right side of the page, are more vertical, allowing contrast and separation for the more horizontal modular elements in the first three columns of the page. *Blue and Gold,* Center High School, Antelope, Calif.

ration. To help the reader differentiate between unrelated content, 2 picas of horizontal separation are suggested. When a publication's layout creates large areas of unplanned white space the layout can distract the reader's eyes from the content and concentrate his or her "eyeflow" in these large white holes. Therefore, the designer must plan carefully to ensure that separations, both vertical and horizontal, are consistent throughout the publication (Fig. 16.12).

MODULAR DESIGN

If you were to go back and study design from the 1950s and earlier, you would find designers creating story layouts that generally weren't easy to follow. Columns of type might extend vertically down a page several inches and in the next column extend down the page by a greater or lesser number of inches. This design pattern, often referred to as "dog leg design," for its resemblance to a dog's leg, has been abandoned in recent years in favor of easier readability patterns.

Today, designers primarily use modular design. Modular design involves placing information in vertical or horizontal shapes of four sides. Although designers can't always make design modular, especially on pages where ads of different sizes are placed, the fewer deviations from even text columns, the easier it will be for the reader to follow the flow of the story. Packages of content can also follow modular design principles, with all elements lined up within four sides (Fig. 16.13).

PREPARING FOR DESIGN

The process of designing first involves sketching a preliminary plan for the page, often referred to as a "page dummy." These page dummies, usually drawn in reduced size, allow the designer to consider the options for placing elements on the page before actually sitting down at the computer to formally arrange the elements. Dummies should reflect the external page margins and the grid or column method and should show the internal margins. Along the page horizontally, inches will be scaled down to reflect the depth that stories will take on the page. Preparing pencil dummies allows the designer to experiment with placement of elements and to determine whether designs will reflect solid design principles in completed layouts. Moving elements around on the dummies will offer designers options for story placement as well as visual size and placement.

Because dummies are a designer's sketch pad, a common method of indicating elements is used. Headlines might be represented by a series of X's on the design with a suggestion indicated for the actual size and typeface. Stories will be indicated by arrows drawn vertically down columns indicating both the width and the length of the assigned story. Pictures and visuals will be represented by large boxes with an X drawn in them. Designers can write in a short description of the picture assigned to that spot.

Dummies are often drawn well in advance of the completion of stories and the completion of photographic assignments. When stories are edited and visuals are complete, designers should re-evaluate the dummies to make sure the designs reflect the edited stories and the strength of the visuals. If story length or picture quality has changed, designers should reflect these changes by drawing new dummies. For instance, if a photographer's best image is a vertical, but the dummy predicted a horizontal dominant image, the designer should redraw a new dummy utilizing the strength of the actual photograph rather than the planned photo.

Although editors often give writers suggested story lengths when making story assignments, story lengths can change during the reporting process. If a story becomes longer or shorter than the assigned length, designers will also need to make changes to their dummies.

Good designers will become adept at designing pages. Page dummies should be easily changeable to reflect the importance of stories and the value of visual strengths. Throughout the process, the designer must remain flexible and sensitive to changing news value and story-telling potential. Never should visuals be forced into positions that compromise their potential. Never should a story be edited just to fit a space on a dummy. Rather, designers should work from the strength of the reporting, editing and photography when laying out the pages. This process will guarantee the most successful method of bringing information to the reader.

After page dummies have been adjusted and re-drawn, designers should take them to the computer for completion of the pages. Templates reflecting the margins and column grids of the page can be stored in the computer with style sheets, computerized type information that will facilitate consistency throughout the publication. Stories written by individual writers and edited on-screen can be imported through word-processing programs into the templates and flowed into the design. Staffs using page layout and design software will find endless opportunities for creating interesting designs. Large initial letters dropped into the text, text heads breaking up the text and other graphic devices for text relief are easily created through layout and design programs.

Photographs taken with digital cameras can be

Fig. 16.14. With a clean, readable nameplate encompassing space for story references to interesting inside content, the *Edition* establishes a professional look immediately on its front page. Other story references appear at the bottom of the page, anchoring that space. Using a front-page package on technology allows the staff to treat the package differently from a traditional front-page design with more stories. Note the extra white space on the outsides of the story used for additional content including a computer jargon factoid box. Front-page design should not appear static with elements in the same positions each issue. Allowing the best front-page content to determine how the page will look will always provide stronger use of that content. *Edition*, Anderson High School, Austin, Texas

Fig. 16.15. Inside pages of this publication carry consistent folio lines at the top of the page and repeat the name of the newspaper as it appears on the front page. Note the use of oval, reversed-type standing heads used on the summary boxes for new shows and wish list. In addition, a timeline appears throughout the newspaper, anchoring the bottoms of the pages. A consistent byline style is used for each writer, which also creates unity through the newspaper's pages. *Blue and Gold,* Findlay High School, Findlay, Ohio

downloaded directly into the computer and imported into picture spots on layouts. Or pictures taken with cameras using film can be scanned on flatbed or negative scanners and imported into picture spaces on layouts. Importing the pictures directly onto the layouts helps designers see how the pictures will be cropped and helps them evaluate the page's balance by seeing the actual density of the text, visuals and white space.

SPECIAL CONSIDERATIONS FOR DESIGN

FRONT PAGE

A front page is the window to the publication. It is the reader's first impression of that issue, and it should look different each issue (Fig. 16.14). Some elements should maintain consistency, including the design of the newspaper's nameplate and the design of other elements such as teasers that attract readers to inside content and index information that points readers to the rest of the publication. Many newspapers have begun using color on their front pages, either in the nameplate information or more extensively in color photographs.

Front-page content should offer information that readers will find interesting and relevant. Old news, or news that readers will already be aware of, will rarely provide interesting front-page content for readers with access to multiple forms of information. Many publications package a front-page "feature" story rather than trying to print news. Because many publications publish infrequently, a feature story, in-depth story or similar content will give the designer many options.

Front pages can often contrast longer stories with shorter news briefs to provide more visual entry for readers. Visual entry points result when readers have multiple starting points on a page. Optional starting points attract different kinds of readers—those who are scanners as well as traditional readers.

Something of visual interest should appear high on the page, preferably above the fold. In newsmagazines, a photograph with a cover teaser to inside content might be the only content on the front page. Regardless of the visual used, designers should vary its size and placement in subsequent issues to avoid predictable layout patterns.

Typography used in nameplates should be functional, clean and simple rather than heavily ornamental or overdesigned. The nameplate should establish the newspaper's identity without competing with the content of the front page. The typeface should be readable and distinctive. Because the typeface in the nameplate should be repeated for section headers and standing headlines elsewhere in the publication, it should work well in smaller sizes. The nameplate should also include the date of issue, the volume and issue number in Arabic, rather than in roman, numerals and the name of the school.

As the reader turns the pages, each page should include a page folio—information placed at the top or bottom of the page that includes the page number on the outside of the page, the name of the publication and the date of the publication.

Fig. 16.16. Special feature sections allow designers to create diversity in the look of the design to draw readers to the special content, while maintaining a sense of connectedness to the primary publication. In this special 14-page senior section, the staff of the *Crossfire* used its traditional logo at the bottom of the front page but used specialty type for the name of the section above the illustration. The use of magenta spot color throughout the section also helps to separate its special content from that of the traditional publication. *Crossfire*, Crossroads School, Santa Monica, Calif.

Fig. 16.17. Giving prominent page position to the staff editorial, the *Trojan Talk* editorial page displays the editorial in a sans serif type in a larger size to contrast with the smaller, serif type used for other editorial page material. The wider columns of type in the editorial further serve to spotlight it. Note the staff masthead appears appropriately in a narrow column on the left side of the page. *Trojan Talk,* Lincoln High School, Tallahassee, Fla.

INSIDE PAGES

Items such as columns, news briefs, section heads and other content that appears in each issue can be visually designed to repeat the typeface in the nameplate, as well as the style or arrangement of type in the nameplate. Inside pages can repeat the name of the newspaper as it appears on the front page. This repetition gives the publication a unified appearance (Fig. 16.15).

Designers can employ different grids or column methods in different sections of the paper. Using varying column widths offers visual variety and creates distinctive content areas for the reader. Sections of the paper can start on single right pages to create reader awareness of content change when it isn't possible to print separate sections.

Throughout the newspaper, designers will need to deal with placement of ads. Ad space should be designed so it leaves modules of space for content rather than awkward, uneven spaces. Some publications, especially newsmagazines, place several ads on single pages, allowing ad content to be separated from editorial content (Chap. 21). The only pages on which ads shouldn't appear are the editorial or opinion pages. In most newspapers, ads traditionally don't appear on the front page or section fronts inside the paper. Many European professional newspapers are now placing advertising on their front pages, primarily in narrow horizontal banners across the bottoms of the pages.

Designers should also design facing pages as single visual units to prevent problems in the design. Placing banner headlines across the tops of two facing pages will create off-balanced designs and could confuse the reader. Visuals shouldn't appear directly across from each other in the design, or facing pages will appear off-balanced.

FEATURE PAGES

Feature page design is the heart and soul of the designer's work. Creating strong visual/verbal connections through well-designed illustrations or excellent photographs combined with strong, detail-oriented headlines gives designers endless opportunities for creating interesting visual units. Surrounding these feature packages with a bit of extra white space brings the reader to the story content and helps separate it from the rest of the page's content. Designers should seize the opportunity to be creative, clever and fun when the content dictates. When serious or complex content is being used, the designer needs to make sure the design reflects the more serious tone of the content. Color should also be used appropriately on feature pages.

Feature pages offer designers the opportunity to be a bit more experimental with typeface choices. Many newspapers change typefaces for feature presentations to help the reader understand the change in content (Fig. 16.16). Typefaces with vi-

sual connections to the story content can be effective, or the newspaper can choose a different but consistent typeface for feature content throughout the publication. For instance, many professional newspapers switch to strong sans serif typefaces for feature stories despite using a serif type for headlines on other news stories. The arrangement of type and the positioning of the type in relationship to the story can also be more creative. White space can be more generously used on feature pages to isolate and separate the content of the stories from other page content. The leading of the type in the story might be expanded to indicate its special content.

EDITORIAL PAGES

Because editorial pages should reflect the opinions of the newspaper's staff as well as other contributors, and

Fig. 16.18. The strong use of the visual illustration brings the reader's interest and attention immediately into this double-truck design. The illustration also contains the spread's primary headline but further serves to include detailed information about the change in the appearance of the printing of money. Note how the staff took the topic of money and broke it down into several different content areas. One story covers investing, the left sidebar lists inventive ways to make money and the infographic provides summarized factoids about money. One of the more interesting areas of content is the "Cash Crazed" sidebar in which the staff provided incentives for students interested in earning a dollar. This kind of interactive coverage is being increasingly used by publications, largely influenced by popular TV shows on MTV. *Peninsula Outlook,* Peninsula High School, Gig Harbor, Wash.

Fig. 16.19. Interesting sports coverage can include in-depth stories about issues in the world of sports. Creatine, a controversial chemical supplement used by some high school athletes, is an appropriate topic for full-page coverage. The long legs of the text have been broken up by text heads, providing various entry points into the story. The factoid at the bottom of the page provides additional information and shows the product to the reader. *HiLite,* Carmel High School, Carmel, Ind.

therefore should mark the change in voice that editorial pages represent in the newspaper, the staff should design these pages distinctively. Editorials should be clearly labeled as such. The headline should clearly state the staff's editorial position. Using a different column grid will also help differentiate the editorial content. Many staff editorials appear in consistent positions and wider column grids on the editorial page (Fig. 16.17).

Editorial pages will make extensive use of standing heads in a consistent design for the newspaper's columnists. Columns often feature small face shots of the writers.

Visuals on the editorial pages will be primarily editorial cartoons. Cartoons should be used to help break up the text. Other options include photo polls where several people are asked the same question and their responses are edited to reflect the most interesting comments. Photo polls can picture small, tightly edited head shots of people whose responses are printed. The backgrounds and head sizes in these pictures should also be consistent.

Letters to the editor or to the newspaper's web site from readers will often appear on these pages.

The newspaper's masthead and its staff listing should also appear on the editorial page. The listing may include only the major editors of the paper or everyone on the staff. The masthead should appear in a consistent place on the page. Many staffs also choose to include their editorial and advertising policy in agate-size type as part of the masthead.

The primary concern on the editorial page is preventing the pages from appearing too dense with text or from "graying out." Designers should seek to keep the pages interesting and visually appealing.

DOUBLE TRUCKS/CENTER SPREADS

The middle two pages of the paper are printed on one sheet of paper, offering the designer endless possibilities for treating the space as one design unit. Large headlines can be placed across the gutter, the fold between the two pages, and visuals can be used in even larger sizes.

Double-truck coverage should be built around large and significant visual display. Visual/verbal connections should be strong and should attract the reader to the information presented in the design. A strong visual used significantly large in the design will usually be more effective than a variety of smaller visuals. Using a flexible grid or column method offers possibilities for changing the width of text in different parts of the double-truck presentation to create contrast and relieve the reader's eyes. Each part of the package should add to the overall presentation of information. Visual forms should provide contrast with strictly verbal forms in offering information to the reader. White space should also be a consideration. Filling up all corners of the page from top to bottom, left to right, will result in pages that look static and cluttered. Using extra white space around the visual or around the headline display will help provide balance on the page (Fig. 16.18).

SPORTS PAGES

Sports page designs will often utilize larger, action-packed pictures of teams in competitive situations on the field or court. Sports pages can also utilize sports briefs columns providing capsulized summaries of teams' seasons as they progress. Features focusing on sports personalities, issues or controversies can enliven the sports pages, providing interesting and diverse coverage (Figs. 16.19).

PICTURE USE

Pictures are strong reader entry points, and because they are important in design, photographs deserve special attention. Pictures in strong vertical or horizontal shapes are far more interesting than square shapes. People in photographs should be large enough so their heads are at least the size of a nickel. Static pictures of people posing for the camera are not as interesting as pictures showing people in natural situations (Fig. 16.20). (Also see Chap. 20.)

Pictures shouldn't be an afterthought in design, confined to small spaces in the corners of pages or layouts. Rather, designers should seek to design from the strength of good photographs, using them in significant sizes and in interesting positions. Careful attention to cropping will make strong pictures even stronger and more visually interesting.

Well-written, detailed captions will add to the appeal of good pictures. Some readers will only read the picture caption without ever reading the story that accompanies it. Thin, hairline or 1 point rule lines placed around pictures in the design will help give them definition on the pages.

SPECIAL CONSIDERATIONS FOR USING COLOR

SPOT COLOR

Just as in professional newspapers, color is becoming more common in school newspapers. Spot color—the use of a single color in design—is a less expensive way of using color than four-color. Four-color, called that because it is made from the four process colors, magenta or red, cyan or blue, yellow and black, requires the page to be run through four different presses, each applying one of the colors (Fig. 16.21).

Newspaper printers may offer the staff spot color called "run of the press" (ROP) at an even cheaper price. ROP color simply means the printer will use color already on the press, with the staff taking advantage of that color. Unfortunately,

Fig. 16.20. A picture package featuring three candid pictures from the school's talent show offers the reader a chance to see three different performances. The package features a dominant image and two smaller, supporting pictures, all of which are cropped effectively. Note that the pictures were taken during the actual show, providing stronger visual interest for the reader. *Stampede*, Burges High School, El Paso, Texas

Fig. 16.21. Four-color is used as a standard in this broadsheet newspaper, but only on the front and back, which require only one run through the press since both pages are printed on the same side of the same sheet of newsprint. With the use of four-color, the staff used a spot color—green, in this case—for the shadow for the type in the nameplate and for the information graphic anchoring the bottom left of the page. "Isolated color" is used in the top photograph, in which the staff has selected parts of the image to appear in black-and-white. Using computer software imaging programs, designers can get very creative in manipulating photographs. Here, the picture's isolated color helps point out the controversial confederate flag and the boys who hoisted it during a senior picture. The story details the fight over First Amendment rights of free expression in school. *Update,* Dow High School, Midland, Mich.

the color used will not be the staff's decision, often resulting in weak, less effective use of color. For instance, if the printer is already printing a publication with yellow spot color ink and uses it in your publication for the nameplate or for display type, the weak color may not be strong enough to lead the reader's eyes to the type displays that you've designated as color in your design.

When used effectively, spot color can create unity through the publication. Warm, strong colors such as red are better spot color choices for visual signals such as headlines and standing headlines. Cool colors, such as green and blue, will be less active and weaker as visual signals. Lighter percentages of warm colors work well to display content in "screened boxes," when the designer is seeking to separate the content and draw the reader's eyes to it.

Designers should be careful to avoid overusing color, particularly spot color, by using it for every headline in the publication, page or spread. Inappropriate use of color in headlines can affect the reader's perception of the story's content and news value. Body text in color will slow the reader down in processing the information and could discourage readability.

Some colors simply do not work well for color use. Colors such as yellow are difficult to read and will create weaker, less visible content. The most agreeable combination for text is black on white. Reverse type, white on black, slows down the reader and creates dense type areas in the newspaper.

FOUR-COLOR

Four-color is expensive to produce and, because of the way a newspaper is printed, can only be used on certain pages without incurring additional costs. Color photographs must be separated into the four process colors before they can be reproduced in the newspaper unless they are submitted as digital files electronically. Separating traditional color prints into the four process colors is expensive and time-consuming. The cheap quality of newsprint results in high color saturation, and the off-white color of the newsprint results in colors that won't reproduce as vividly or accurately. But with almost all professional publications using color consistently, many high school publications are using color in every issue, even if just for color photographs. Advertisers requesting color for ads can sometimes help bear the cost of color used elsewhere in the newspaper, but news content and value should always be appropriate when designing with color.

PACING THE PUBLICATION

When decisions are made about content, designers should work closely with reporters and editors to make suggestions for effective visual presentation. Teams of writers, editors, photographers and designers working together can improve the story-telling process for the reader.

Deciding on the most effective way of telling stories means the publication will vary its content and create flexible and varied story-telling forms. When reporting events that have already occurred, teams should look for ways to make the information fresh and interesting. A picture page with a succinctly written story and detailed captions may provide all the information necessary and be far more interesting than a traditional prose presentation reporting primarily old news. Or, in a story about the costs of athletic programs, a good infographic showing how much money is spent on an athletic uniform from jerseys to shoes might be a more interesting way of telling that story without any traditional text accompanying the infographic.

Creating teams in the student newsroom will improve discussions of content and storytelling and will ensure that pages don't slip into predictable story counts or layout designs from issue to issue or page to page within the same issue. Involving different kinds of storytellers, from writers and editors to photographers and illustrators, in decision making will ensure that all options are considered. Individuals will feel more empowered in the process, and no one's strength will become an afterthought in reporting. (Also see Chap. 20.)

KEEP IN MIND

- Mixing alignments can create visual contrast and draw the reader's attention to particular stories. A primary story in left-aligned type will create contrast and comparison for that story in relation to others on the page or spread.

- Headlines need a strong visual voice. Using bold, sans serif typefaces will help organize the headline information and create strong reader entry points into story beginnings.

- Reverse type and screened type can slow down the readability of stories. Such devices should be used in limited amounts.

- Boxing elements should be done only when the content dictates its use. Boxing an element brings the reader's attention to the story's content in a stronger way. Try to avoid boxing more than one story on a page, or the reader will see a conflicting and confused visual hierarchy.

- Generally, column widths of 10 to 20 picas are preferred for ease of readability.

- Captions are most effective when placed underneath the pictures they describe. Using a contrasting typeface for the caption helps to create contrast with body type.

- Packaging summary stories such as news briefs and clubs' briefs into well-written, tightly edited reports will result in higher readability than a series of stories separately placed on a page.

- Every page needs a dominant visual entry point placed prominently on the page, preferably near the top.

- Using screens of color or black for placement behind text slows down the reader's eyes and should be used sparingly. Screens should be kept to lighter percentages, such as 20 to 30 percent. Coarse screens with visible dots per inch will also create reading static. Designers using laser printers should increase the dots or lines per inch in the printing command to keep dot patterns light and less distracting.

- After completing designs, print them and hang them on a wall. View them at arm's length, as readers will do. Evaluate their effectiveness using the design principles. Make sure the design creates clear and logical reading patterns and makes best use of available design elements.

EXERCISES

1. Take an issue of the local or community newspaper and evaluate its use of the design principles, including balance, rhythm, unity, scale, proportion and visual hierarchy.

2. Using a local or community newspaper, find an example of packaged content, including a single picture and story; two or more pictures and story; and two or more story forms and illustration. Examine each package and notice how the reader's eyes are

brought into the package. Notice what visual design devices were used by the designer in creating separation between the packaged content and the rest of the page's content.

3. Using a copy of a local newspaper, indicate the front page's margins by drawing lines around them. Using a different color pen, indicate the width of the paper's grids or columns. Measure the widths using a pica ruler and mark the width of the columns on the page. Measure the width of the internal margins and mark it on the page. Measure between unrelated content areas and note the width of the newspaper's horizontal internal margins by marking it between each story. Draw boxes around each individual story package and note whether the design is laid out in modular design units. Do the same with an inside page with ads placed on the page.

4. Using a copy of your school's newspaper and a dummy sheet, draw a pencil dummy for one of the paper's pages. Make sure to indicate accurately the length of stories and the height of headline displays. In each picture space indicate the width and height of the picture and include a one- or two-word "slug," or summary, of what the picture will be. Compare your dummy to the actual page, checking for accuracy.

5. Using a dummy sheet, draw a design for a sports or news page for the next issue of your school newspaper. Begin by deciding what content should be on the page. Then indicate in the dummy the amount of space each content area should have. If you have access to a computer and to a layout software program, transfer your design onto a page template.

6. Look through several copies of exchange newspapers from other schools. Find examples of pages that are well designed. Write a short paragraph explaining what makes the pages successful and attractive. Find examples of pages that are poorly designed. Write a short paragraph explaining what makes these pages less successful in design.

7. Find examples of pages in professional or school newspapers that use strong vertical and horizontal photographs. Analyze each picture's use in the paper: How is the picture's size and content used in the design? Does the picture's caption add to the information obtained from reading the story? Is the picture strong enough to serve as a visual entry point for the reader?

8. Using a copy of your school newspaper, circle every entry point on the page.

9. Find an example of a double truck in your school newspaper or in an exchange newspaper from another school. Answer these questions: Is there a central visual entry point? Is it typographic, illustrative, photographic or a combination? Is the page well balanced? Is the text material sufficiently divided so it maintains interest without "graying out"? Is the content deserving of the space and effort needed to tell the story?

10. Find a page in a newspaper or in your school newspaper that uses only spot color. Is the color used effectively? Does it make visual connections in its repeated use? Is the color distracting from the content of the page?

Next, find a page in a newspaper or in your school newspaper that uses four-color. Is the color used effectively? Is the color used in more than just photographs on the page? Where else has it been used? Is the color creating distractions or adding to the appeal of the design?

Next, compare both color pages to a black-and-white page. Which do you prefer? Why?

11. Find a page in a newspaper that uses stories laid out in varied column widths. Measure the widths of the columns with a pica ruler and write their widths on the page. Are the narrowest and widest widths between the recommended 10 to 20 picas? Are the widths readable and attractive in the design? Do they help provide contrast in the content?

Yearbook Page Layout

Small groups of students gather together in hallways and outside areas around the school carefully turning each page of a freshly printed book. Stopping to admire themselves or their friends, they erupt in spontaneous laughter as they relive memories of the school year. It must be yearbook delivery day, that special day in the late spring, summer or fall when yearbook staffs deliver their much anticipated and prized volumes.

A historical record of the year, a yearbook seeks to capture coherently the sights, sounds and memories of the school year in a volume that fairly represents the students in the school and their diverse interests.

Yearbook design has undergone revolutionary change in the last decade, primarily due to the integration of desktop publishing. The changes have occurred in every area of design, from the way yearbooks tell stories to the integration of visuals on spreads. Gone are many of the rules that made yearbook design formulaic and static (Fig. 17.1).

Even with relaxed rules, the principles of good design remain intact: quality photographs that capture the moments involved in high school activities, well-written copy that serves the historic function for its student readers, complete caption information and informative and well-designed headline displays.

Even the organization of the book has been an area for experimentation by yearbook staffs. Many have moved away from clichéd, catch-phrase themes to graphic or single-word unifiers. Staffs have experimented with the traditional section organization to organizing and reorganizing content in as few as three sections. In response to yearbook innovation, many state and national judging associations have relaxed rules to allow for experimentation.

Using the theme "Three Times Over," the *Deka* staff of Huntington North High School divided the book into three sections: "Pleasure," "Power" and "Prosperity." Each of the three sections accommodated two of the book's traditional sections. Other sections have experimented with dividing the book by senses: sight, smell, touch.

No matter how the yearbook is organized or unified by its designers, it's important to understand the elements that lead to successful and attractive page designs.

SPEAKING THE LANGUAGE

Defining terms yearbook designers need to know will help you understand how to get started with page design (Fig. 17.2).

- *Body copy:* the text that verbally tells the story on the page. Stories can also appear in alternative forms that could include sidebars, infographics, question and answer formats, first-person accounts, bio boxes, charts and diagrams, pull quotes

Fig. 17.1. In order to appeal to more student readers and show more people in the book, many yearbook staffs have begun using pictures in smaller sizes, but increasing the number of pictures on the spread. By traditional definition, this book's dominant image is still dominant, appearing twice as large as any other image on the spread. The spread's contemporary design also frees it from the static design often associated with yearbooks. *American,* Independence High School, San Jose, Calif.

and factoids. Often, alternative forms of copy are used to supplement traditional text stories. Several forms can appear on a single spread to amplify the overall story being told.

- *Bleeds:* photographs that cover page gutters or that cover external margins and align with page edges.

- *Captions,* or *cutlines:* the information describing picture content that should be included for most pictures. Complete captions identify the principal people pictured (full name and grade in school), state what they are doing (in present tense) and can add detail, background or results (can be written in past tense). Captions often use quotes from the key pictured people as second or third sentences.

- *Divider pages:* a single page or spread that uses a distinctive design and introduces the beginning of another part of the book. Traditionally, sections of a yearbook include theme, student life or activities, academics, sports, ads, index, clubs and organizations and the people section.

- *Drop caps:* oversized introductory initial letters that drop into the first few lines of the story to visually mark and lead readers into the beginning of the text. The typography in the drop cap can match the largest or boldest type in the headline unit for strong repetition.

Fig. 17.2. Page elements found in yearbook spreads are identified in this example: (**A**) graphics, (**B**) bleed, (**C**) headline, (**D**) body copy, (**E**) gutter margin, (**F**) folio, (**G**) internal margin, (**H**) caption, (**I**) external margin. *Highlander*, Highland Park High School, Highland Park, Texas.

- *External margins:* the white space on all four sides of a layout used to showcase the content.

- *Folios* and *page numbers:* page numbers should go to the outside edges of the pages, but folios can be expanded to include information such as specific page content and section content.

- *Graphics:* the use of lines, borders, screens, colors, textures, illustrations or particular styles that create visual continuity when used consistently in design.

- *Grids* or *columns:* a series of equal or unequal design spaces created between the margins to guide placement of content.

- *Gutter margin:* the area of space between the pages. Gutter space should be taken into consideration when a photo bleeds or goes across the gutter.

- *Headlines:* Each introductory page needs a headline to draw the reader into the page content. Headlines are often combinations of primary headlines, those that are largest in the design and often created as a design unit, and secondary headlines. Secondary headlines should amplify and expand the reader's knowledge of the page content by adding details through specific nouns.

- *Internal margins:* margins between columns or grids that separate content.

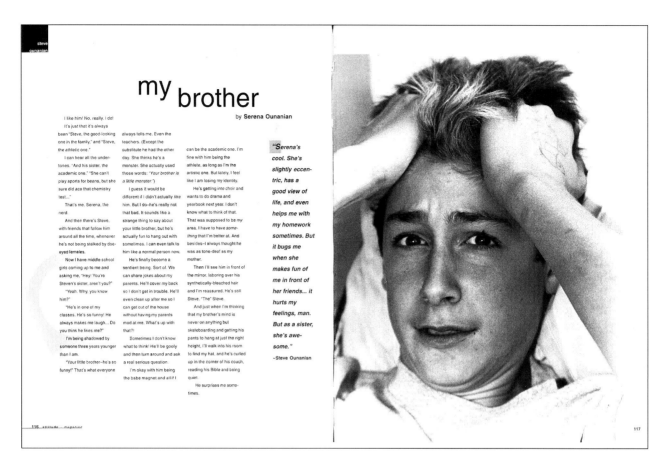

my brother
by Serena Ounanian

I like him! No, really. I do! It's just that it's always been "Steve, the good-looking one in the family," and "Steve, the athletic one."

I can hear all the undertones. "And his sister, the academic one." "She can't play sports for beans, but she sure did ace that chemistry test..."

That's me. Serena, the nerd.

And then there's Steve, with friends that follow him around all the time, whenever he's not being stalked by doe-eyed females.

Now I have middle school girls coming up to me and asking me, "Hey! You're Steven's sister, aren't you?"

"Yeah. Why, you know him?"

"He's in one of my classes. He's so funny! He always makes me laugh... Do you think he likes me?"

I'm being shadowed by someone three years younger than I am.

"Your little brother—he's so funny!" That's what everyone always tells me. Even the teachers. (Except the substitute he had the other day. She thinks he's a monster. She actually used those words: *Your brother is a little monster*.")

I guess it would be different if I didn't actually *like* him. But I do—he's really not that bad. It sounds like a strange thing to say about your little brother, but he's actually fun to hang out with sometimes. I can even talk to him like a normal person now.

He's finally become a sentient being. Sort of. We can share jokes about my parents. He'll cover my back so I don't get in trouble. He'll even clean up after me so I can get out of the house without having my parents mad at me. What's up with that?!

Sometimes I don't know what to think! He'll be goofy and then turn around and ask a real serious question.

I'm okay with him being the babe magnet and all if I can be the academic one. I'm fine with him being the athlete, as long as I'm the artistic one. But lately, I feel like I am losing my identity.

He's getting into choir and wants to do drama and yearbook next year. I don't know what to think of that. That was supposed to be *my* area. I have to have some-*thing* that I'm better at. And besides—I always thought he was as tone-deaf as my mother.

Then I'll see him in front of the mirror, laboring over his synthetically-bleached hair and I'm reassured. He's still Steve. "The" Steve.

And just when I'm thinking that my brother's mind is never on anything but skateboarding and getting his pants to hang at just the right height, I'll walk into his room to find my hat, and he's curled up in the corner of his couch, reading his Bible and being quiet.

He surprises me sometimes.

"**Serena's cool. She's slightly eccentric, has a good view of life, and even helps me with my homework sometimes. But it bugs me when she makes fun of me in front of her friends... it hurts my feelings, man. But as a sister, she's awesome.**"
–Steve Ounanian

Fig. 17.3. Generous margins around the page offer the designer a balanced layout, particularly when a large, dominant image is used. The wide horizontal margin across the top of the page provides ample space for a reverse-type header bar containing the name of the student profiled in this story. Ample bottom margins are needed to balance the visual center and to allow the staff to include complete folio information. Bleeding the close-up portrait off the bottom of the page makes it larger and more dramatic. *Wings,* Arrowhead Christian Academy, Redlands, Calif.

- *Spread:* two facing pages. Yearbook designers usually design spreads instead of individual pages.

- *Spread unity:* elements that connect two facing pages so they are visually perceived as one design unit. These can include pictures bleeding across the gutter, graphic devices such as lines or background textures, or headlines that span the pages.

- *Theme:* a verbal statement that is used and repeated in key elements of the book to unify its design. Often called a "catchphrase," it is chosen by the staff because it relates to something about the school or about the year. The traditional areas in which themes appear include the cover, the endsheets (front and back), the opening pages, the divider pages and the closing. Theme design can also be integrated into sections of the book through special features or through "minithemes" that play off the theme phrase.

In recent years, many staffs have experimented with using devices other than traditional catchphrases to unify the book. These devices can include graphics, colors, logos or combinations of these.

- *Visual hierarchy:* a clear sense of size, proportion, scale and content that leads the reader through the design in a coherent way. Readers' eyes should be moved through the content, often following a Z reading pattern.

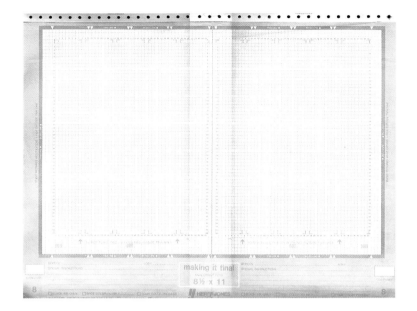

Fig. 17.4. Layout sheets available in tablets printed to the trim size of the yearbook allow designers to draw their pages before placing the elements on pages online or transferring the design to a triplicate form for the publishing company. This layout sheet from Herff Jones Yearbooks shows a designer a 10-column design using the blue brackets, a six-column design using the blue squares and an eight-column design using the white triangles along the top edge. Layout templates online also allow students to select the number of columns or grids they want to design with.

- *Visual continuity:* design factors that keep a section of the book coherent and unified. These factors can include graphics, particular typefaces and grid or column structures.

GETTING READY TO DESIGN

A yearbook designer begins with a page area set to the size of the finished book. This size ranges from 7.75 × 10.5 inches to 8.5 × 11 inches to 9 × 12 inches. While it's traditional for the yearbook to be printed as a vertical book, some staffs have even experimented with the standard sizes by turning the books horizontally and having the books bound on the narrow side.

Once the designer knows the book's trim size, margins are created on the page. Progressive margins—those narrowest at the gutter and widest on the bottom margin—are traditional in magazine and yearbook design. Margins allow pages to maintain white space to frame content in a consistent manner throughout the book and allow for placement of page folios. Folios traditionally appear in the bottom margin but could appear in other locations (Fig. 17.3).

The designer then decides on a grid or column structure to provide a skeletal structure for placing content. Generally, a designer should stop an element on every margin at least one time on a spread to define it or make it visible in the skeletal page structure. Stopping content between the margin and the outside edge of the page will be confusing to the reader because it will blur the margin's structure. In this case, the designer should bleed the content, but primarily if it's pictorial. Bleeding copy can be a problem for the printer and for the reader, since some of the verbal content could be compromised when the book is bound. Layout sheets provided by the publishing companies producing the final book will indicate a variety of grid structures that can be used (Fig. 17.4).

Not all designers use strict column grids or structures in design. Some choose to create free-form designs in which pictures and other page elements are placed without regard to staying within grids or columns. While this can be a successful design strategy when used by experienced designers, most beginning designers find it easier to design within a grid page structure (Fig. 17.5).

Many magazines use three- or four-column designs as standard structures throughout their publications. Yearbook designers often find greater freedom by experimenting with a series of narrower grids, often as narrow as 4 or 5 picas wide. Using a more narrow grid pattern allows a yearbook designer to combine columns and internal margins to create a variety of content widths. Options for using narrower column grids appear primarily in elements used for display and could include

- *Visual/verbal separators:* use of a column as an isolation element

Fig. 17.5. Breaking away from traditional grids or column structures allows designers to be more experimental in their approach to design. This spread on how students spend their time alone is designed to be less structured than a traditional design. The contrast in structure helps the student reader perceive its different content. *Epic,* Center High School, Antelope, Calif.

• *Display space:* use of a column to create stronger display area for a typographic element or a picture element

• *Alternative copy space:* use of a column for a different form of content for contrast (Fig. 17.6)

In recent years, student designers have created section templates for yearbook design. A section template is essentially like creating a style sheet for the design of an individual section of the book and can include a basic column structure, a headline style, an alternative copy style and a format for the layout. The styles can be saved as templates in a desktop-publishing program and can be opened by individual designers.

In addition to saving the skeletal page structure, a designer can create a type template so text brought in from a word-processing program can be "styled" to the typeface choices, sizes and alignments for that section for uniformity.

Section templates can save a lot of time for individual designers but can also result in a heavily stylized section that compromises picture quality and creates visual redundancy, or visual uniformity, when the reader looks at the book. Therefore, designers should be careful to keep the templates flexible. Designers should be able to base their picture placement decisions on the content of the pictures to be used on the spreads, rather than making those decisions by conforming to a predetermined picture size or shape.

An additional consideration for yearbook designers should be content in design. Yearbook staffs have to sit down and decide how they want to tell stories to their readers in terms of page allocation and story-telling forms. Pacing is an important consideration in design because it allows the designer flexibility when designing content. For instance, big events during the school year might need more than one spread in the book. An example might be homecoming, the prom, a big school celebration or a winning sports season. In those cases, the best way to tell the story might be on two to three carefully planned layouts that continue the cov-

erage just as a magazine might do. This coverage is often referred to as "jump" coverage since the coverage jumps from spread to spread (Fig. 17.7).

Other topics, such as modes of transportation, might be better covered through a single page of coverage or through a traditional double-page spread. Many schools give clubs single pages of coverage. Tackling a serious issue that is relevant to the school or a big celebration such as an anniversary might call for a special section of coverage of many spreads. Designers need flexibility in covering topics so the stories can be fully covered.

Content can also be organized around general topics such as stress. Individual stories on a spread could include different methods for dealing with stress, what causes stress, relaxation techniques or a poll indicating most stressful times of the day or year (Fig. 17.8).

Yearbook designers also have to be aware of story-telling forms. Let's take the modes of transportation idea. Having photographers take pictures of cars in the parking lot is not the way to tell this story. Good pictures need people in them. Doing a series of individual vignettes of student drivers and their unusual cars with bio boxes of relevant questions (such as where the student got the car, how much it costs to maintain and the most unusual element of the car) might make that topic one worth covering. Having the photographers shoot the pictures in interesting set-

Fig. 17.6. Narrow grids or columns—as narrow as 3 to 4 picas wide—offer the designer many options for column multiples for pictures and verbal content. Because of the narrow width of the columns, designers must use column multiples for copy to keep the line lengths readable. The variety of options available in these narrow formats allows content to vary in width to separate it from other parts of the design. Note the width of the upside-down and sideways feature here, an alternative copy on this spread. Its width, wider than the copy blocks, as well as the spot color blue, help the reader understand the difference between it and the other copy on the spread. *Highlander,* Highland Park High School, Highland Park, Texas

We trudge off to the halls of Casa Roble every day, driven by some mysterious force. Our parents want to see the 4.0 GPA. Our administration demands a next generation of thinkers. Our teachers think we need to know where the graph crosses the X-axis. Those are their reasons. Reasons that are valid, but not ours. We come in search of something else, something unique, something we can only find here. We care little for the computer applications, verb conjugations, and senior projects of their school. We seek the hidden communities and inner-workings that beat in harmony with our hearts. In the following section, *Rampages* offers a series of stories that detail the everyday lives and events that illustrate the essence of high school life. The following pieces are meant to look into emotions in a manner that any student can relate to, and paint portraits of our school that anyone can recognize. It is important to note that all of the photos in this section are completely independent of the stories, so as you read this section (or just look at the pictures), don't go thinking Billy Bob from the picture in the upper right is "guy with spiky hair" in the story below. Now, that said, the question we want to ask here isn't "Am I just a school?" but, "Am I just school?"

by Michael Catinari
UNDER THE SURFACE
OBSERVING THE WORLDS OF STUDENT LIFE

Although most see high school as a place of learning, it is also a place of feeling. We not only sharpen our minds but shape our souls as well.

44 student life

Fig. 17.7. Using the concept of a special magazine inside the yearbook that relates to the book's theme "Influences," this special jump section continues on for several spreads. The section is held together visually through similar design styles. The section offers well-written commentary on a variety of lifestyle issues, most of which are written in the first person. The use of the nouns across the top of each spread, with one word in black and the others in gray, indicates the focus of that spread's attention. *Rampages,* Casa Roble High School, Orangevale, Calif.

tings where simple backgrounds could be used to display the cars would also make the pictures more interesting than those shot in crowded, busy school parking lots.

Every event that happens during the year should be considered for its storytelling potential before any attempt is made to design a spread. Content in the book should also evolve from year to year. Cultural trends mark change. Several years ago, yearbook staffs started covering trends such as students using ATM machines and students surfing the Internet. Now both of those topics are rather dated. A careful evaluation of the book's content needs should be made by the entire staff at the beginning of the year. Flexibility should also be built into this system so the staff can appropriately cover unforeseen events as they occur during the year.

DESIGNING THE PAGES

A designer needs to have all the component parts before beginning design. Carefully edited pictures that show varied content, different people, strong compositional styles and combinations of both vertical and horizontal forms will help the designer in creating an appealing design. The designer could work from the section template with the typographic styles also defined and saved as part of the template.

Once the page content has been decided, the photographs taken for that content should be gathered, and decisions should be made about their use. These decisions should include

* Choose the dominant image. The dominant image should be the most compelling photographic choice. Close-ups, emotion-filled shots, strong angles and interesting content will always draw a reader's attention. Isolate the picture from among your choices that does this best (Fig. 17.9). The editing process is one that works best when done in partnership with a photographer. See Chapter 20 for more information on choosing and editing pictures.

* Edit your supporting images. Eliminate pictures that show the same or similar content, pictures that show the same person more than once and pictures with weak quality such as those that are out of focus or that have backgrounds that interfere with the subject matter. Decide how many images you want to place on the spread, that is, how many you need to tell the story. Additional editing considerations are using pictures with the same number of people in them or with only one person in them and using too many pictures shot from the same camera angle or with the same lens. A good story needs close-ups, detail shots, wide angles, medium shots and a variety of telephotos.

* Look for strong horizontals and verticals. Horizontals and verticals are the most interesting visual forms. Avoid square-shaped pictures.

* On the computer open the section template and begin designing by first placing the picture that has been chosen as the dominant image. In traditional design, a dominant would be used on the page that would be two to three times larger than any other supporting picture. Recent trends indicate that staffs are using dominant pictures in smaller size ratios to allow for the integration of more images on the page.

Preferably the picture's focus should face toward the gutter rather than off the page, keeping "eyeflow" on the page. Some designers are allowed to ask the photographer or the publisher to merely "flop" or "flip" the negative if the picture isn't facing into the page. Doing so is an ethical compromise. It's better

Fig. 17.8. Avoiding redundant clubs coverage, the staff of the *Arvadan* found common topics between various clubs in the school and used those common topics to generate various kinds of scatter story coverage on the spreads. DECA and FCCLA copy is focused on their competitions but includes a sidebar rating their field trips, a profile of each club and a collection of candid pictures with complete captions. Note no traditional copy appears on the spread, although the information on the spread is packed with content and detail. *Arvadan*, Arvada High School, Arvada, Colo.

DE

DECA Members: J. Ackley, A. Adkins, N. Ammari, T. Antonio, J. Arreola, M. Batch, M. Beer, E. Blakley, J. Blalock, J. Blay, J. Bogner, B. Bretches, A. Brewster, P. Brickner, A. Buena, J. Buesser, N. Burke, D. Byrd, B. Carelli, S. Carpenter, D. Carroll, J. Carter, R. Chan, K. Chanssoorath, J. Chanthavong, S. Chin, J. Clark, A. Cleland, A. Clevenger, C. Cliver, C. Coates, F. Cobos, T. Cox, D. Crow, R. Crowder, F. Cundari, C. Cushing, K. Daiker, M. Degtyat, T. Deberrera, R. Denket, H. Dietz, N. Dominguez, E. Duffus, K. Duffy, A. Duran, J. Evans, J. Fahrenholtz, J. Feeley, C. Felton, K. Findley, J. Foltz, C. Ford, J. Fraser, S. Fuchs, S. Gadlin, L. Genaro, W. Gerber, M. Gharibyar, G. Gonzales, N. Graham, M. Griffin, A. Grody, A. Grubb, L. Grzebieniarz, M. Grzebiennarz, A. Golley, B. Haack, J. Hammerli, K. Harrand, J. Hart, J. Harris, D. Heer, J. Hiffer, A. Huff, J. Hunt, S. Hunter, C. Jentzsch, K. Jessen, B. Johnson, H. Kelly, K. Kennison, K. Kerodoneray, J. Kerner, O. Khrestowa, J. Kimball, M. Knight, K. Kosowapki, P. Kosowapki, J. Kruckenberg, J. Kurtz, J. Layton, H. Leitch, D. Lopez, N. Luenckenholl, A. Luft, D. Ly, D. Ma, U. Mai, J. Malecha, G. Manzo, M. Martinelli, K. Matthes, J. Mayeda, B. Mazoti, B. McCaffery, T. McHenney, B. McManus, M. Mejia, S. Mewaldt, B. Meyer, D. Miller, C. Minton, M. Moffet, A. Monaco, B. Montano, S. Moon, S. Moravec, S. Mondovin, J. Morning, R. Morris, H. Nguyen, T. Nguyen, R. Mikkel, T. OConnel, M. Oetting, B. Ohlin, A. Oliver, A. Olson, S. Ortez, D. Patterson, J. Perato, G. Pergola, B. Pettit, P. Phommachith, B. Pocewicz, R. Powell, T. Ramos, S. Rana, B. Reed, N. Rhoades, S. Riedesel, R. Risner, V. Rivera, M. Rodriguez, R. Rumbaugh, S. Santos, A. Sasek, R. Scardina, J. Schenck, J. Schrock, N. Sexton, K. Shade, S. Shoemate, J. Smousansa, J. Smousansa, S. Smidih, M. Smith, S. Solomon, S. Speer, K. Speight, P. Springston, L. Stanislao, J. Markeweather, M. Stevenson, H. Stuckey, S. Murychenko, N. Talamantez, B. Thatcher, T. Nguyen, C. Vang, M. Vang, M. Vigil, G. Vitale, B. Walker, T. Wall, K. Walter, J. Warren, K. Wazny, S. Wells, L. Wentworth, D. Wester, R. Witte, M. Wright, D. Yang

- **President:**
  Gina Pergola
- **Vice president:**
  Kathleen Wazny
- **Secretary:**
  Nick Burk
- **Treasurer:**
  Pat Springton
- **Publicity Director:**
  Stacy Hunter

- **Sponsors:**
  Jeff Wasinger, John Bucci
- **Number of members:** 184
- **Purpose:**
  A program designed to get students started in, or advance in marketing related occupations
- **Activities:**
  District, State, National Conferences
  Sales Lab Project: $45,950
  Blood drive
  Poinsetta Fundraiser

FC

Front Row: Autumn Moser, Brittany Huizing, Diana Hughes **Back Row:** Ms. Derbin, Amanda Bishop, Debra Hughes, Ms. Calhoun

- **President:**
  Amanda Bishop
- **Vice president:**
  Debra Hughes
- **Secretary:**
  Autumn Moser
- **Treasurer:**
  Diane Hughes
- **Sponsors:**
  Peggy Calhoun

- **Number of members:** 6
- **Purpose:**
  To provide service to the community and give members an opportunity to develop the skills, requires to succeed in the real world
- **Activities:**
  District Championship
  State Championship
  Volunteering at homeless shelters

Travel

Rate the competition trips...

- ● Rather be dead
- ● ● Still alive
- ● ● ● Loving it
- ● ● ● ● It's heaven

● ● "Driving was okay at the beginning because you get to talk with your friends, but you run out of things to talk about and it gets boring."
Amanda Bishop, FCCLA

● "Driving to state was terrible! There wasn't anything to do. There was

nothing to look at. Everywhere you looked there was grass, grass, grass!"
Debra Hughes, FCCLA

● ● "I don't like it very much, because you feel so nervous right before competition. Tensions are worse when you are able to see the place where the competition takes place."
Bernadette Montano, DECA

● ● "Although the trip to competition can be pretty boring, it does however,

give me a chance to talk to my friends. I try to take advantage of that free time as much as possible since I am usually so busy."
MelissaWright, DECA

● ● ● "I like the trip a lot, mainly because I'm not in school. Another reason is that it gives me the chance to meet other people with my same interest."
Daniel Byrd, DECA

Drooling with hunger, Jennifer Schaefer and Gina Pergola eagerly scoop up delicious Mexican food. The food was part of the DECA District Election.

First

Giving their best to take take first

Q: What motivates you to do well at competition and how does it motivate you?

"Everything is up to yourself and you are the one who has to face the rewards or consequences. This allows us to grow and learn a lot by making us take responsibility for our own actions."

-Kacey Chansisek, DECA

"My motivation for DECA competitions is the thought of knowing where I would stand in the real business world. Also, I like to know that I am a winner."

-Sinet Chin, DECA

"The thing that motivates me to do well in DECA competitions is the thought that I could be the person on the stage receiving that 1st place trophy for a job well done."

-Nick Burke, DECA

"My motivation to do well at FCCLA competition is knowing that I have achieved something good in high school."

-Brittany Huizing, FCCLA

"What motivates me at competitions is getting the chances to acquire the skills I need to succeed in the future. Another motivation is the need to kick butt!"

-Autumn Moser, FCCLA

"My motivation is so that I can laugh at all of those who tried and failed. Last year I received a first place trophy and felt good about it."

-Ryan Witte, DECA

"My motivation is knowing that anyone can move up to the next level of competition. I try to think positive."

-John Sinouansai, DECA

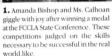

1. Amanda Bishop and Ms. Calhoan giggle with joy after winning a medal at the FCCLA State Conference. These competitions judged on the skills necessary to be successful in the real world.like.

2. Stopping for a playful pose Sara Carpenter, Katy Wazny, Stacy Hunter, and Dana Crow enjoyed a night in Glenwood. DECCA members got the chance to compete.

3. Splish Splash, John Sinoueinsai, Uyen Mai, and Nick Burke take a dip at the DECA Glenwood Conference. The conference was to prepare the DECA members for the upcoming District Conference on December 8th.

4. Freezing to death, Jacquelyn Bogner and Crichelle Jentz wait for their ride to the DECA District Election. Bogner was a voting delegate. Her job was to pick the DECA district 14 officers who would go on to run for the state officers.

5. Sinet Chin studies feverishly for the state candidate test. Chin had to pass the candidate test with a seventy percent in order for her to go on to run for vice president at the DECA District Elections.

6. Autumn Moser counts the lollipop money from the FCCLA fundraiser. Money earned was used to to give members the oppurtunity to participate the state competition.

Mixed emotions
Feeling the joy of their win but pain of their loss, the Varsity Cheerleaders celebrate second place at the NCA National competition. The finals were held at the Dallas Convention Center Monday, Dec. 29.

"Compared to other schools, we are so lucky to be able to go to a school where we don't have to fear for our lives, our teachers actually do care, and we have the resources to be able to learn things."
—Sonya Cole, 12

Curtis Gintin

Fig. 17.9. Dominant images should be chosen for their potential story-telling content and their ability to stop and focus the reader's attention on the spread's content. Emotion, such as that showing on the faces of these cheerleaders who just won second place in a competition, holds the reader's attention and freezes the moment for the yearbook reader. *Panther,* Duncanville High School, Duncanville, Texas

for the designer to use the natural direction of the image. Another content consideration should be whether the picture bleeds across the gutter. The designer must be sure that important content, such as faces, won't be printed in the gutter, where they will be trapped in the binding and impossible to see.

• As each picture is positioned in the layout, the designer should plan for the placement of the caption for the picture. Readers prefer captions placed adjacent to the pictures they describe. Move 1 pica (the internal gutter) away from the picture and indicate where the caption will be, type the caption in on the computer or import it from the word-processing file.

Two captions can be stacked 1 pica apart, but when three captions are stacked together, the reader will have a harder time figuring out the coordination of the captions with the pictures. Designers should also avoid placing captions directly on top of pictures. Unless there is a consistent, even tonal area for placement, the type could become unreadable. Also, the content of the picture can be compromised when the caption is placed on top of it.

Captions should conform to column widths and should be consistent in column widths on the spread. An exception might be a caption appearing in a single column on a narrow column structure.

In yearbook design, another device a designer can use to create section style is a caption lead-in, a specifically designed style of typography that provides information for the caption and helps direct the reader visually to each of the captions (Fig. 17.10).

Yearbook designers should also keep in mind that type spanning across the gutter will be a problem due to the book's binding. Words could become trapped in the gutter and become unreadable. Designers who want a headline to move across the gutter should probably design the headline so the words stop at the gutter margin on the left page and start again at the gutter margin on the right page. Using heads bleeding across the gutter requires careful attention to writing. Text and captions should never be placed in the gutter.

• When placing the next image, the designer should make sure it is placed apart from the dominant image by only 1 pica, generally the size of the internal margins. Stay on the column guides and use a combination of columns that allows the photograph to be showcased effectively without compromising its content. Continue to use strong vertical and horizontal crops.

• Continue to place the pictures in the layout until a pleasing arrangement has been

created. The designer should also place the body text from the word-processing program and make sure that the line lengths are readable and that the story is laid out in a module, a shape with only four sides. Copy in multicolumn grid formats should use a combination of columns that allows for ease of readability, generally widths between 10 and 20 picas.

Positioning the headline in the layout will be an important decision. While it is traditional for headlines to be placed adjacent to their stories, a headline can appear next to the text, underneath it, jutting into it or dropping into it in a "well" arrangement. If a nontraditional headline placement is chosen, the designer should take advantage of a typographic device such as a strong drop cap in the dominant headline style to focus the reader's attention to the beginning of the story.

As the designer works, attention should be given to placing white space so it appears toward the outside edges of the layout, rather than trapped between page elements. Grouping pictures together and placing captions in outlying areas creates strong page eyeflow.

Many schools are now producing pictures on digital cameras or scanning their images after film is developed. The value is that the images can be viewed on the computer screen in their actual locations and sizes. Designers can make sure faces are not trapped in the gutter, that pictures are cropped effectively and that content works well together on the spread.

Fig. 17.10. Each caption has been placed in this layout so it is in the space adjacent to the picture it identifies. Each caption is consistent in width and style, using a very distinctive caption lead-in to focus the reader's attention on the entry point of the caption. Note that the caption style also relates visually to the headline style chosen for this section. Changing the styles of captions and headlines in each section of the book helps create separation between the sections. *Citadel,* Overfelt High School, San Jose, Calif.

Fig. 17.11. Portrait pages are best arranged when the panels of pictures appear in rectangular shapes across the spreads. Head sizes and backgrounds should be consistent. Name blocks are placed to the outside edges of the panels aligned next to each panel in normal first name/last name arrangement. Adding features and sidebars to panel pages adds interest. Also note the position of the feature at the bottom of the page. Moving the features around will help break visual redundancy in the design of the people section. *American,* Independence High School, San Jose, Calif.

SPECIAL CONSIDERATIONS

- Portrait pages require designers to work with large blocks of student portraits, usually shot by a studio photographer hired by the school district. These pictures are generally arranged as a single vertical or horizontal block on each page, with narrow rule lines placed between the photos for separation. Place name blocks to the outside edges of the pictures in first name/last name arrangement (Fig. 17.11).

Even if these portraits are shot by different photographers in the school's community, it is important for the yearbook staff to work with the photographers to keep the head sizes in the pictures a consistent size. Differing head sizes on the pages will create distracting images.

- In sports and clubs sections, group shots should be laid out as horizontals and should be cropped tightly so no extraneous visual information appears with the group. Careful coordination between the group shot photographer and the page designers is required to ensure the group shot shapes will work on the layouts. If the photographer arranges the group in a strong vertical design, the designer will have to accommodate that shape on the layout, which could pose problems. In an attempt to make the pictures larger to show the individual faces of the club or sport members, many staffs have moved the group shots to separate sections of nothing but group shots. Published in special inserts or sections at the ends of sports and club sections, these allow readers to thumb through "albums" of images looking for their friends. Regardless of where in the book they are placed, the heads of the people in group shots need to be at least the size of a dime so they will be visible.

- The design of theme pages, section dividers and other thematic elements will need special attention. Readers need to know they are looking at special content. Designers should pay attention to consistencies in graphics that will help the readers visually "group" or connect these elements when they come to them in the book. Creating a strong graphic style in the opening and closing section, and adapting elements of that style to the dividers, will reinforce this design for readers. The use of color, larger pictures, logos and specially designed text will help readers connect these elements. Designers also might use wider text displays, increased leading or similar typographic devices (Fig. 17.12).

  Copy in theme pages needs to be unique, specific and interesting.

  Many schools using catchphrase themes will break the theme down into "minithemes" and incorporate these phrases into copy or special features in individual sections of the book. This helps reinforce the theme idea through the entire book.

- Designers who use photos cut into shapes that follow the contour of the actual photo content should keep in mind that those shapes are strong attention-getters since they are active shapes. They usually will provide visual entry and dominant attention on the page. Designers should simplify the rest of the design to prevent competing visual elements. Also, photo cutouts need to be anchored on the page or attached to something visually. One way to anchor these pictures is to add shadows in a picture-altering program.

- Pay attention to the design of the ad section. Display ads from local businesses need to be visually different. Avoid using the same typeface in each ad. Make sure each ad has a

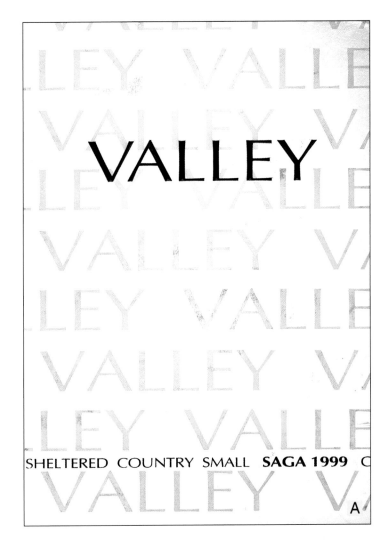

Fig. 17.12. (**A**) Using the theme "Valley," the name by which its school is commonly known, the staff of the *Saga* chose words that were representative of the community to complement the valley theme and ran those across the lower third of the cover. (**B**) On the front endsheet, the staff complemented the words with a row of connected pictures showing students from the school throughout the book. (**C**) The opening section continues to use strong descriptive words indicative of the students. The staff made sure to name each person pictured on every spread, even in the small shots. It also made sure each picture showed someone different in the school. Through the use of the small portraits, the staff greatly increased the number of pictures published. *Saga,* Loudoun Valley High School, Purcellville, Va.

You said you were fun, you said you were unique, you said you were clean. But you were not trying to sell your school, you were just telling it how you saw it. You chose to describe it with the words any students would have used to describe high school. But they were not just words, they were perspectives that connected individual faces, ideas and dreams to each other and to yourselves. Each connection brought you closer to realizing the community you called Valley.

COOL EXCITING WORK FREEDOM CROWDED PRISON FRIENDLY PRIDE WILD UNIQUE HARD GARDENS   COMFORTABLE LOYAL SPIRIT FAMILY BORING CHALLENGING SOCIAL MONOTONOUS UNITY

B

strong visual or a strong type message. Column methods may be used for the ads that correspond to the ad's price. For instance, many staffs now sell their ad sections by dividing page space into a series of blocks. Many books offer as many as 9 to 12 blocks of space on a page. Advertisers can then purchase a multiple of blocks for their ads. Some schools offer discounts for full-page ads (Fig. 17.13).

The use of senior ads, friend ads and club ads has enabled many staffs to eliminate the outside sale of ad space. These ads can be sold in standard sizes by dividing pages into module shapes and selling blocks or combinations of blocks. In the smaller block sizes, the yearbook staff might want to create a standard design style, enabling the parent to add an individualized message or picture.

Ad sections are excellent places to include features that help students remember the cost of different items during their school year or for community-related features. In all cases, careful attention should be given to designing interesting ad sections.

• Another section that can be used to amplify the book's theme development is the index. Every person pictured in the book should be listed in one complete alphabetical index. The index is also an excellent place to list the book's advertisers, clubs, sports and activities as they appear throughout the book. The index should be designed with a column structure in place. Typographic devices such as dot leaders can be used between the name and the page numbers to lead the reader's eye across the listings.

Many schools enliven these pages by including can-

Valley has made me the person that I am today. The friends that I have made and the opportunities given to me by this school have shaped the way I think, act and live my life. - Seth Morris

I have been affected positively; the teachers, students and facilities provide a homelike environment. Valley has helped prepare me to be a strong, independent person in the future. -Amy Paschall

Valley has helped me grow. I have developed new relationships, become involved and learned more responsibility. For me, Valley means friends, fun, work and responsibility. -Richie Ketterman

Valley makes me want to come to school. I feel privileged to go to such a top quality school and to hang out with my friends. -J.R. Creamer

Work
Friends
Active
Pride
Fun

did pictures with captions or by including an alphabetical section of club and sport group shots throughout the index. Making the group shots large enough for each individual face to be the approximate size of a dime is a good rule of thumb for group shot size.

- Schools whose yearbooks publish in the spring encounter early spring deadlines preventing coverage of the complete school year. Many of these schools choose to publish a small special insert, usually given to a printer in the local community who can produce the work in a short amount of time. These special inserts cover the activities of the school that occur after the book has been sent to the yearbook publisher. In addition to giving the staff continued design work throughout the semester, the special spring magazines make the yearbook a more complete book. Many staffs continue using their section design

templates and theme styles in these inserts. Incorporation of the section can be accomplished through a special glue strip on the insert. The student can then decide where in the book to place the insert.

Many yearbook publishers also sell special entertainment and news event sections that can be purchased and placed in each book to add to the coverage of the year.

CD AND INTERACTIVE COVERAGE

With the growing increase in home computers, many schools expand the coverage of the yearbook by producing CD-ROM additions to the printed book. The value of these productions comes in their ability to include motion and sound as natural adjuncts to the

Fig. 17.13. With the increase of senior ads in yearbooks, many schools have reduced the number of outside ads they now publish. For schools still publishing both kinds of ads, integrating the ads throughout the section will be more visually interesting to the student reader and will prevent visual redundancy. Business advertisers will also appreciate the extra attention they get from being mixed with the popular senior ads. The appeal of business ads can be increased if they picture students from the school. *Clamo*, Clayton High School, Clayton, Mo.

printed content of the book. Eventually, staffs can be creative in designing content for these sections, which could include the entire portrait section of the book, for instance. Rollovers could include students' names, participation in school activities or awards won during the year, or where they're headed after high school.

Senior ads could eventually include the parent's voice actually congratulating or reading a message to the senior student.

Club and sports group shots would be another natural fit for the CD-ROM. Students too often complain about the small size of the pictures used in the printed book. Displaying the pictures on a computer screen would enable a student to see the pictures in larger size and to see the individual faces in the groups.

CD-ROMs can also include more audiovisually oriented events of the school year—the sounds of the homecoming royalty being announced at the game, the school fight song played by the band or selections from a talent show or assembly—offering many choices that would add value to the printed book and add to its historical value to the students.

THE USE OF COLOR

Color is becoming a standard in yearbooks as it is in many other facets of design. Most yearbook publishers already are planning for full-color book production in the near future on a wide-scale basis. Already, many schools' photographers are

shooting color negative film and converting it to black-and-white when the pages aren't being printed in color. This enables them to take all the film to a local color finisher, often at a discount store, where finished prints can be quickly and cheaply returned to the school.

Color can add significantly to the impact of the book, displaying the beautiful blue skies, fall colors, winter snows and spring flowers that students experience during the year.

Using color effectively in design requires attention to detail. Display type used for headlines and secondary headlines works well in color, but smaller type displays such as copy and captions rarely read effectively in color. Colored text type tends to slow down the reader, discouraging readability.

Warm colors always come forward in design. Designers looking for color connections through photographs can often pull color, or repeat strong color, from a dominant image and create a strong connection between the photograph and the page content. This color repetition will often create a connection visually for the reader of the page (Fig. 17.14).

Too much color, or overuse of color, can also create confusion in design. When color is overused, the reader is overwhelmed by the color and distracted from the content. Color used effectively can create connections. Pull warm colors—red, oranges, yellows—to the forefront and let cool colors—greens, blues—recede.

Attention should be paid to color values when choosing colors. Some colors are

Fig. 17.14. Taking color cues from the dominant photographic image's blue water, the staff of the *Arvadan* used the color to visually connect the spread. Because readers visually connect color, the reader is led logically through the content of this spread. *Arvadan*, Arvada High School, Arvada, Colo.

hard to work with on white backgrounds, particularly some shades of red, yellow and green. Color contrasts need to be strong and effective. Textured backgrounds with color can also add clutter to the page and distract from the content.

EXERCISES

1. Using standard layout sheets provided by the school's yearbook publisher, design a layout in both three- and four-column design formats. Begin by cutting out pictures from magazines. Try to find pictures that are the right size for the space you want them to be on the layout. Then, using the magazine, cut out blocks of copy and trim them down to fit the spaces on the layout where you want them to appear. Don't worry about the readability of the text. Find an example of a headline in display-size type (above 14 points) to place where you would want a headline to go. Exchange layouts with a classmate and critique each other's designs:

   a. Did you maintain consistent internal margins with only 1 pica of space separating content?

   b. Are there white space holes that distract the eye?

   c. Is the dominant image large enough to serve as a central entry point to the design?

   d. Are the supporting pictures of varied shape, size and content?

   e. Is the design visually attractive?

2. Brainstorm for at least five different techniques that could be used to create a theme or graphic device that would work for your school's yearbook for this year. Begin by making a list of interesting facts about the year at your school. From that list, generate ideas for each fact. Share the list with classmates and get their opinions on visual and verbal ways in which your ideas could be expressed.

3. Using the yearbook from your school or exchange copies of yearbooks, look at the theme or graphic unity of the book. In small discussion groups, critique it using these questions:

   a. Is the theme or graphic unity clearly understandable to the reader?

   b. Is it presented in a contemporary and interesting way on the cover?

   c. Is the theme or graphic unity included on the endsheets (unless they are white)?

   d. Is the theme or graphic unity clearly developed in both the opening and closing pages of the book?

   e. How do the divider pages continue the theme or graphic unity?

   f. Do you think the staff was successful in developing the theme or unity throughout the book? In what other ways was the staff able to reinforce the theme or graphic unity?

4. Get a copy of your state's judging standards for the yearbook. Evaluate your school's most recent yearbook using the judging standards. How well do you think your school's yearbook fulfilled the standards? What are its strengths; its weaknesses? How could these weaknesses be improved?

5. Create a graphics file by cutting up magazines or newspapers and looking for 10 examples of the following visual treatments:

   a. Headlines with secondary or deck headlines

   b. Use of color in design

   c. Caption starters

   d. Graphics such as use of color, lines, screens and textures

   e. Sidebars or supplementary copy treatments

   Cut out each example, paste it on paper and write a short explanation of why you think the example works successfully and how it could be adapted for a section of a yearbook.

6. Choose a section of the yearbook and develop a design strategy for the section using the graphics file

you created in exercise 5. Create both a visual and a verbal strategy for the section. Make a list of the typefaces you would choose for the body text, captions, folios and other verbal treatments you have designed. Specify point sizes, leading values and typefaces for each verbal area on the spread. Using your design strategy, paste up a sample of your design using material from magazines. Evaluate the spread's design strategy by presenting it to your classmates and having them critique its strengths and weaknesses.

7. Using picture magazines such as *Sports Illustrated* or *National Geographic,* cut out three layouts that you think are successful and write a critique of the strengths by answering these questions:

a. Does the use of pictures tell a complete story?

b. How does each picture contribute to the strengths of the visual presentation?

c. Does the verbal content complement the visual content?

8. Divide into teams of three to five students with each team taking a different section of the yearbook. Evaluate the content in the section in the last three copies of the school's yearbook. Has the content evolved or has it remained consistent? What evidence of cultural trend coverage is in the section? Does the section tell stories in different ways? Is any special section coverage included? Could any special content have been included? Is the design different in each of the three volumes?

9. Look through a collection of magazines and newspapers and compile a list of catchphrases that appear in ads, in headlines or in other content areas. Without choosing a particular product's advertising slogan or using material that would be too closely identified with a product, which phrases could be used as themes? Would any of these catchphrases be workable in your school's yearbook? Next, look through a book of idioms, or commonly used expressions. Write down expressions that would be relevant to your school this year.

10. Look through exchange copies of yearbooks in the school's publication room or library or through past issues of your school's yearbook. Choose a book that did a good job of developing a theme idea. Present it to the class. Show specific pages in which the theme appears and explain how the theme creates unity. Read selections of copy that provide specific details that reinforce the theme. If the book uses "minithemes" in the sections, present and explain those to the class.

Newsmagazines, Special Sections, Inserts and Supplements

NEWSMAGAZINES

A student dies in a drunk-driving accident, three weeks before the next newspaper comes out. The student's death, the fourth such death in this community in the last two years, resulted from an alcohol-related incident. Clearly it is a story that warrants coverage. A lack of timeliness doesn't allow for the standard straight news story. An 8 1/2 × 11 or letter-size newsmagazine won't allow for the page 1 in-depth story most broadsheet newspapers run.

The student newsmagazine was born of a situation like this one. The student newsmagazine, a print hybrid of a newspaper and a feature magazine, began and grew in popularity in the 1970s. It has maintained its position, second to traditional school newspapers, throughout succeeding decades. In the introductory situation, a newsmagazine could cover a wide range of stories. The impact the student's death had on the parents and friends could be one news-feature. The publication could report on the community meetings to solve the problem of underage drinking. The alternatives to drinking could be an informative sidebar.

Professional weekly newsmagazines such as *Time* and *Newsweek* obviously cannot compete with the timeliness of the radio, TV or even daily newspapers, so they found a niche market in providing the public with more depth and even analysis of the week's news. Student newsmagazines have not moved as much into the area of news analysis. In fact, high school newspapers and newsmagazines have more similarities than differences. The cover, design and coverage are the three primary aspects that distinguish the newsmagazine.

COVER

One of the most distinctive characteristics of the newsmagazine is its cover or page 1. In contrast to newspapers, which usually display three or more stories on page 1, a newsmagazine will display one story as its primary or only focal point. The publication's size, which is typically tabloid or an 8 1/2 × 11, dictates such treatment

Fig. 18.1. Cover from the newsmagazine *Westlake Featherduster,* Westlake High School, Austin, Texas

Fig. 18.2. Cover from the newsmagazine *Ahlahasa,* Albert Lea High School, Albert Lea, Minn.

because three or more stories would give the cover a crammed appearance. The cover may be a photograph or some art or the start of a story. The cover space may be shared with brief teaser headlines about other stories inside the publication. Often, the cover story jumps inside for continued special display, sometimes in the centerfold. This introduction and development of the cover story and the focus of the story as a news-feature are two of the most significant distinguishing characteristics of a newsmagazine.

The story that's featured on the cover should have substantial reader appeal, one that has facts that may not be known to most readers. It should be carefully and accurately reported and well-written and edited. It should contain much original source reporting and be worthwhile. The *Westlake Featherduster* cover highlights 12 pages of coverage on the causes, impact and solutions for drunk driving (Fig. 18.1). Not every cover

story has to be a serious, earth-shaking investigative piece. However, most should report either a significant academic-related concern, such as the impact of the school budget or changes in class scheduling, or a school tie-in to a topic of interest to high school students, such as physical fitness or diets. Traditional school activity stories, such as homecoming or the school play, can be featured on the cover, but a special effort should be made to provide a fresh angle to these stories.

With only the nameplate and teasers occupying space, the cover is a blank canvas for the designer. Start a story there, use a strong photo or piece of art alone with a headline or package any combination. Make sure all the pieces are good. After all, the cover is the reader's first impression.

The photo or art should have a strong center of interest that appeals to students. Visuals should be cropped to maximize the impact of the center of interest and should be technically flawless with proper contrast (Fig. 18.2). If artwork is used, it should reproduce with sufficient contrast and tonal quality. Whether you use art or a photo, you'll need a teaser and a teller headline to go with it. An action photo with people will also require a caption, which can appear on page 1 or inside the cover page. The story that starts on the cover can jump inside to the centerfold or to another prominent inside-page position (Fig. 18.3).

Many newsmagazines split their cover space between a cover story or stand-alone photo/art and a series of teaser headlines or refers (referring to inside content). These brief headlines can be lively, startling and captivating, noting a story or other element and enticing the reader to look inside the publication. Artwork, small photos and graphics can be used in conjunction with these headlines to heighten interest.

The nameplate and accompanying essential information—the name of the school, the city and state, the date of issue, and the volume and issue numbers—should be included on the cover, usually at the top or the top half of the page. The typeface and design should be readable, professional-looking, contemporary and suitable for the contents. Inside section folios and other design elements can be designed in the same style and with the same typeface as that used on the nameplate.

Fig. 18.3. The page 1 story of this newsmagazine jumps to an inside page. *Edition,* Anderson High School, Austin, Texas

DESIGN

The size of the newsmagazine often dictates the inside page design and organization. Much of the publication is organized into departments or sections and displayed as a unit. For example, all the news summaries are placed on one page or into one designated portion of a page, collected under a standing head. The departments and sections are labeled with content headings, such as sports, news, in-depth and entertainment. The smaller-size page doesn't often allow for more than one package of briefs or a story and sidebars. But the smaller page size doesn't mean that art can't be used large, as in Figure 18.4. This tabloid's two-page spread uses white space to maintain a clean innovative look.

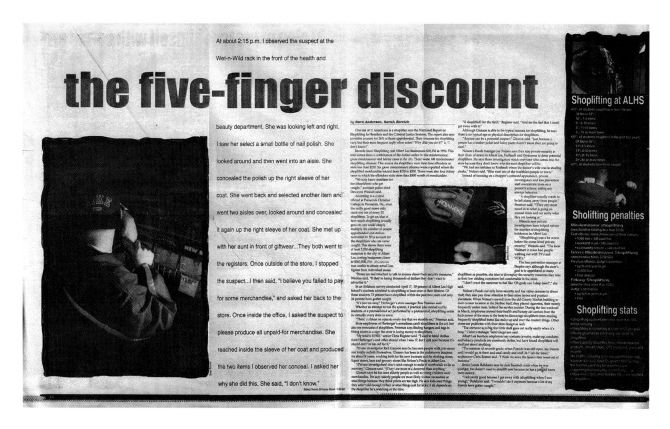

Fig. 18.4. Centerspread from a tabloid-size newsmagazine. *Ahlahasa*, Albert Lea High School, Albert Lea, Minn.

Fig. 18.5. Contents page from the newsmagazine *Spark*, Lakota East High School, Liberty Township, Ohio

The general appearance takes on a magazine look once the cover story and the departmentalized inside content is placed (Fig. 18.5). Design unity is achieved in some basic ways through selection and careful use of text and display type; through use of grid and columns; through similar design for page, section and regular column headings; and through special art and graphics that embellish everything from page folios to text initial letters and backgrounds. Much like a well-designed newspaper, the successful newsmagazine is designed as a package.

Ads are placed at the bottom of inside pages, excluding the cover, centerfold and editorial and op-ed pages. Occasionally, ads are grouped on one page and given a department heading and graphics to conform to the other sections and departments. It is unwise to have two facing pages with only ads because readers are more likely to skip over them.

Design continuity is usually maintained in regularly published sections, such as sports or features, through uniform grid and column structure; text and display type size and face variations; and the design of standing heads, folios and graphics. The front page of these inside sections often carries a version of the newsmagazine's nameplate, customized to indicate the specific content within the section.

COVERAGE

Infrequent publication of a newspaper due to budgetary, time or staffing constraints has led some schools to adopt the newsmagazine in place of a regular newspaper. However, factors other than frequency of publication may cause a staff to change its format from a newspaper to a newsmagazine. One is the desire for a change. If a change is made, editors should draw up a plan to ensure that the readers are still given all the information they need as students. For example, an investigative cov-

er story on teenage alcohol abuse is fine, as long as the results of the debate tournament are also printed somewhere in the newsmagazine.

Monthly newsmagazines, or those published less frequently, have to focus substantially on the advance story to retain the credibility, vitality and timeliness necessary for a news medium. By "featurizing" most news and focusing on angles other than immediacy, the newsmagazine that is typically published monthly has minimized the timeliness dilemma.

The primary focus of a newsmagazine is on feature material or news-features that de-emphasize immediacy or timeliness—the *when* angle—in favor of such other news elements as consequence, proximity, human interest and the *why* and *how* of an event. News is largely featurized. However, a news peg is often essential to this featurization.

Newsmagazine content is similar to a newspaper's and includes news-features, news summaries, editorials, opinion columns, in-depth and investigative reports, sports and a variety of human interest and informational features. Visuals, such as

Fig. 18.6. Special section from the *Tom Tom*, Bellevue East High School, Bellevue, Neb.

Fig. 18.7. Special section from the *Rockwood Summit Talon,* Rockwood Summit High School, Fenton, Mo.

photographs, illustrations, cartoons and information graphics, complete the editorial plan.

Outside of the staple of the newsmagazine—the feature—newsmagazine sections and their contents break down like this:

- The centerfold, if not used for the jump of the cover story, gets special attention. It can contain an in-depth feature with related sidebars and visuals or a photo essay. It is second only to the cover in prominence and for readership. It can showcase the best writing, photography, art and graphics.

- Editorial page and op-ed page (opposite the editorial page) content includes traditional newspaper elements: a staff editorial; opinion columns; letters to the editor; an editorial cartoon; reviews of films, theater, live and recorded music, television, books and other events; guest columns; interpretive and analysis pieces; and the staff masthead. Occasionally, random reader opinion on topical issues is included in a photo poll or similar device.

- News stories, including capsule summaries, gathered into a briefs column are placed on one page or more within the same section. They are not scattered throughout the publication as is sometimes done in a newspaper. Some newsmagazines will do a newspaper-style front page without the nameplate on page 3 of the newsmagazine. Thus, the newsmagazine has a magazine-style cover and a newspaper-style front page inside.

- Sports reporting is handled in much the same way as news. Results of competitions are summarized in sports packaged briefs. Advance contests are highlighted as major stories, and opinion columns and features on recreation and personal fitness are included in the overall sports budget.

- The newsmagazine can include some specialty reporting on student lifestyle interests, such as health and personal grooming, personal finance and money management, employment and continuing education opportunities, legal concerns and entertainment previews. Reporting of local crime, with student or school tie-ins, and deaths of students and faculty and staff are also common in both student newsmagazines and newspapers.

SPECIAL SECTIONS AND INSERTS

The impact of a multimillion dollar bond issue or the statistics and emotions of a basketball team's state championship run can make for special coverage through an insert, a special section or a special edition.

For sections devoted exclusively to one-time project reporting—such as an in-depth story and sidebars on summer jobs or an investigative piece and sidebars on the funding of sports in the school—the layout and overall design can differ from the design of the other sections. Some elements, such as the body text, will remain constant, but a different type may be used for headlines, and different graphics and photo treatments may be included. The number of columns may also differ from that of the main publication.

Special sections can be used as seasonal or special events advertising shoppers. For example, the December holidays, prom, spring vacation travel or a new fashion season can be the focus of a four-page ad section. All ad copy could relate to the central theme or event. Related consumer stories could tie into the ads to complete the promotional package.

Major news events are often the subject of special sections. Staffs can decide to give readers more depth to major events but should be sure the coverage is warranted. In Figure 18.6, the *Tom Tom* staff used a four-page special section to look closer at its school's own security and solutions to violence after a shooting in Columbine High School where 13 students and teachers were killed.

Other opportunities for special sections or inserts include major sports accomplishments, student and other elections, significant academic program changes, senior graduation and all-school events such as homecoming. These one-time extras can give more students opportunities to serve as editors, as well as provide more display space for writing, photography and art. Often, these extras are keepsakes because of the event they commemorate.

Special sections or inserts may be done as stand-alone extras published outside of the regular newspaper or newsmagazine schedule. An unexpected event, such as a school sports championship, may even lead to a special, stand-alone edition (Fig. 18.7).

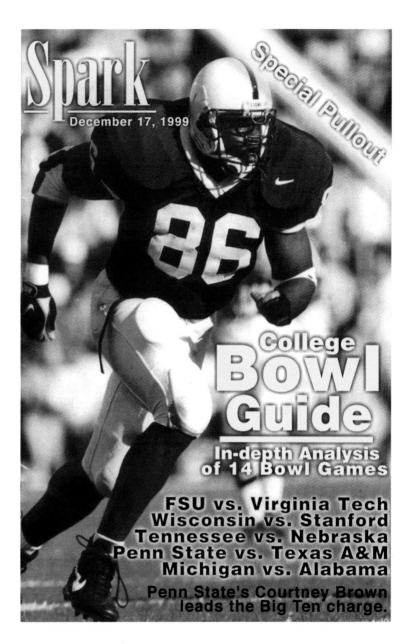

Fig. 18.8. Supplement from the *Spark,* Lakota East High School, Liberty Township, Ohio

Planning a Newsmagazine, Special Section, Insert or Supplement?

Answer these questions to create a statement of purpose for the publication.

• Why are we publishing it?
• Who will want to read it?
• Why will they want to read it?
• What will they read and see?
• What will make it unique?

Your publication planning checklist should include the following:

• Statement of goals
• Target audience
• Frequency of publication
• Content plan
• Promotion plan
• Format and design plan
• Type and printing specifications
• Content submission plan
• Staff organization plan and duties list
• Production schedule
• Budget
• Reader evaluation tool

SUPPLEMENTS

Ambitious staffs from around the country have added magazine supplements to their newspaper. These supplements are distinct in content, design and sometimes size from the host news publication.

Supplement content varies, but it is different from the traditional mix of news, features and opinion in the host newspaper or newsmagazine. Some examples of supplements are collections of students' creative writing, personality interviews, entertainment guides and sports features. Some are produced as class projects, largely independent of the regular newspaper production staff.

Supplements are usually smaller in size than the host news publication. For example, a broadsheet newspaper may have a tabloid-size supplement, and a tabloid-size publication may have an $8^{1/2} \times 11$-inch supplement. In Figure 18.8, the *Spark,* an $8^{1/2} \times 11$-inch publication, produces a 5×7-inch College Bowl preview supplement.

Size is not the only way to distinguish a supplement from its host. The design varies. A supplement is designed as a magazine or a newsmagazine, with special cover treatment and other visual signs dictated by its unique content.

Photo manipulation computer programs and computer art programs have put professional-looking design within range of many more high school publications. Design and coverage ideas come from many sources. A variety of newsstand magazines can provide both design and reporting inspiration. No design or story should be copied or plagiarized, of course, but these ideas can be altered and localized, or they may suggest new interpretations. A clip file or bulletin board for random ideas should be kept in the staff workroom. All staffers should be encouraged to bring in file ideas—a headline, a photo, an ad, a story—to build a resource center. Since newsmagazines and newspaper supplements draw on both magazines and newspapers for their format and style, clips from both are helpful.

Magazine-style newspaper supplements broaden the publishing experiences of students. Students learn both newspaper and magazine production.

Planning is critical when selecting management of the supplement or insert. The editor or top editors of the supplement or insert should be someone other than the editor of the host publication to avoid work overload. However, the editors should communicate regularly to match production schedules and to avoid duplication.

Students can get a head start on advertising supplements or inserts by planning all of them at the start of the school year. Ads may be sold in the fall and related consumer stories written during lulls in the production schedule of the host publication.

Special project reporting usually requires more time than most other reporting assignments. A reporting team, including a graphic designer to provide the supporting information graphics, might work one issue ahead to ensure thorough and accurate work.

EXERCISES

1. Examine copies of one or more of these national newsmagazines: *Time, Newsweek* and *U.S. News and World Report.* What sections or departments does each have? How is the cover story presented on the cover and then jumped inside? What news is summarized? What evidence do you see of design continuity in each publication?

2. Choose a topic or event from the last year that could have been a focus of a supplement for your publication. Plan the supplement. Develop at least five story ideas and three sidebars for the supplement. What photos or illustrations could you have for the supplement? What information graphics could you include?

3. Take a broadsheet publication or a tabloid currently designed in standard newspaper layout form and redesign the front page. Decide on the primary story and then sketch your design.

4. Prepare a list of topics that could be reported in depth in either a supplement or a newsmagazine cover story. List five that are school related and five that are local, state or national stories with student tie-ins.

5. Plan a supplement for your present news publication. Sell advertising to finance its production costs. Review the publication planning guidelines in this chapter as you begin your work.

Online Journalism

As computers and online services grow faster, the information superhighway has become like the German Autobahn—more of a super highway where speed and access are almost unlimited. Students cruise through information resources at school in their classrooms and at home through personal computers. Tapping the potential of this resource, student journalists can do research and interviewing for their own reporting and can offer their student readers supplemental information and additional contact with their publication outside its normal publishing schedule.

Students tapping into the potential of the Internet will find unlimited information resources. Not only can students research and gather information, they can read information that has appeared in print on similar topics. They can even interview and communicate with people, organizations and governmental agencies that might have been unreachable through traditional methods such as the telephone. Using powerful search engines and limited search requests, students can conduct efficient online research to gather information on topics ranging from entertainment to serious in-depth reporting. In the professional press, computer-assisted reporting, as this process is known, has enabled stories to be written more accurately and thoroughly on a variety of subjects. Tapping into resources previously unavailable or inaccessible is now possible due to the wealth of information available through online sites.

Learning to conduct efficient online searches in computer-assisted reporting may be enhanced by consulting with librarians or media specialists, who can help student journalists to navigate complex sites and information. Consulting with economics teachers and those who teach statistics can aid students trying to make sense of complex numbers and information they have gathered from online sites.

From time to time, students may also have access to entertainment figures, political candidates, media figures and others through online services that make these personalities available to those using their services. Students can view actual scenes in places as remote as outer space, can tour museums in locations around the world and can access the resources of libraries and news-gathering organizations. Students can participate in online forums with other student journalists or can conduct online forums to gather information for future stories.

Student publications can independently or through Web providers create web sites where students can access information and up-to-date reports and where students can view video and still photographs and hear audio clips. Waiting for the next issue of the school newspaper to publish a late-breaking story or announcement is a thing of the past for student journalists with online publications (Fig. 19.1).

The availability of such instantaneous and exciting resources introduces new, unique problems and situations for student journalists. Companion Web publications can and should be more than mere repeats of the printed publication, but managing and updating the information may require additional resources, both in

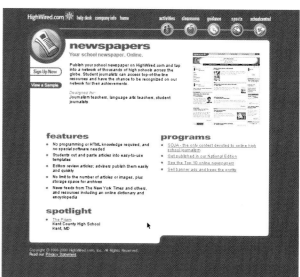

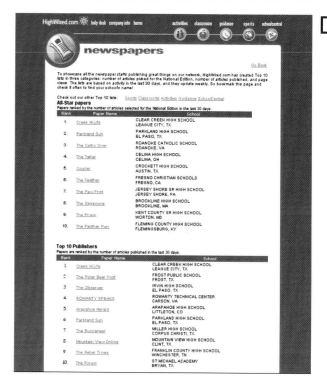

Fig. 19.1. One good use of the newspaper's web site is to provide information beyond the publishing schedule of the school's print newspaper. The school's graduation ceremony is a perfect use of the web site. Not only did the staff provide a gallery of graduation pictures, it provided the pictures in color, something it probably could not have done in a print version. Also, an extensive selection of graduation pictures was available to scroll through. *Patriot Press Online,* Northern High School, Owings, Md.

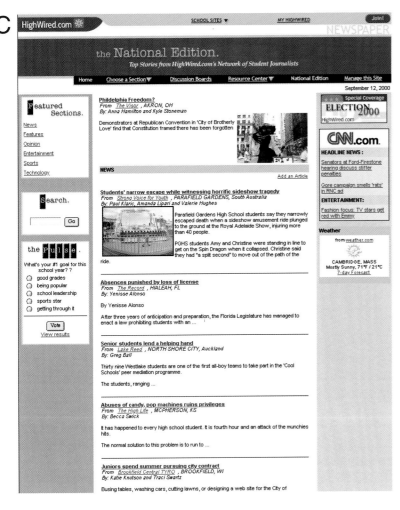

C

the National Edition.
Top Stories from HighWired.com's Network of Student Journalists

Home   Choose a Section ▾   Discussion Boards   Resource Center ▾   National Edition   Manage this Site

September 12, 2000

Featured Sections.

News
Features
Opinion
Entertainment
Sports
Technology

Search.

[   ] Go

the **Pulse**.

What's your #1 goal for this school year? ?
○ good grades
○ being popular
○ school leadership
○ sports star
○ getting through it

[Vote]
View results

Phildelphia Freedom?
From *The Visor* , AKRON, OH
By: Anna Hamilton and Kyle Stoneman

Demonstrators at Republican Convention in 'City of Brotherly Love' find that Constitution framed there has been forgotten

NEWS
Add an Article

Students' narrow escape while witnessing horrific sideshow tragedy
From *Strong Voice for Youth* , PARAFIELD GARDENS, South Australia
By: Paul Klaric, Amanda Lipari and Valerie Hughes

Parafield Gardens High School students say they narrowly escaped death when a sideshow amusement ride plunged to the ground at the Royal Adelaide Show, injuring more than 40 people.

PGHS students Amy and Christine were standing in line to get on the Spin Dragon when it collapsed. Christine said they had "a split second" to move out of the path of the ride.

Absences punished by loss of license
From *The Record* , HIALEAH, FL
By: Yenisse Alonso

By Yenisse Alonso

After three years of anticipation and preparation, the Florida Legislature has managed to enact a law prohibiting students with an ...

Senior students lend a helping hand
From *Lake Reed* , NORTH SHORE CITY, Auckland
By: Greg Ball

Thirty nine Westlake students are one of the first all-boy teams to take part in the 'Cool Schools' peer mediation programme.

The students, ranging ...

Abuses of candy, pop machines ruins privileges
From *The High Life* , MCPHERSON, KS
By: Becca Swick

It has happened to every high school student. It is fourth hour and an attack of the munchies hits.

The normal solution to this problem is to run to ...

Juniors spend summer pursuing city contract
From *Brookfield Central TYRO* , BROOKFIELD, WI
By: Katie Knutson and Traci Swartz

Busing tables, washing cars, cutting lawns, or designing a web site for the City of

Special Coverage

ELECTION 2000
HighWired.com

CNN.com
HEADLINE NEWS:
Senators at Ford-Firestone hearing discuss stiffer penalties

Gore campaign smells 'rats' in RNC ad

ENTERTAINMENT:
Fashion focus: TV stars get red with Emmy

Weather
from weather.com

CAMBRIDGE, MASS
Mostly Sunny, 71°F / 21°C
7-day Forecast

Fig. 19.2. In just a few years of hosting web sites for school publications, HighWired.com has become a popular provider for high schools across the country. The site features HTML templates enabling easy staff management of newspaper content. (**A**) On its initial splash page, HighWired.com makes it easy for visitors to find the newspaper or school location they are seeking. (**B**) Once clicked into the newspaper site (note the simple newspaper icon in the top left corner that corresponds to the icon on the initial page), visitors can sign up, view a sample or try a demo. (**C**) HighWired also updates news from member newspapers across the country in a national digest page that is regularly updated. Note other features of this page include an online survey of student goals and a searchable database for articles on specific topics from member sites. (**D**) In addition, HighWired also features a page showing the top 10 school newspaper sites based on selections from those sites for the HighWired national edition. This page is updated weekly and also enables viewers to see other top 10 lists. Finally, HighWired regularly interacts with its member newspapers by sponsoring online contests and providing publishing and reporting opportunities for student journalists.
Courtesy of HighWired.com

people and equipment, in order to do a good job. Publications may need to recruit additional staff members to manage the online publications. Those with knowledge of online software skills will be particularly valuable. Or student journalists can collaborate with students in broadcast classes to provide their readers and viewers with fresh, updated information. Publications should have a definite plan for providing content online before even beginning to experiment with such efforts. Creating an online site that is never updated or changed, especially after advertising its coming, ensures its failure.

CREATING WEB PUBLICATIONS

Many schools and school districts have already created online sites to keep parents updated and to provide information to those in their communities, particularly taxpayers. School publications can become links from these already existing school sites with the permission of the school or district. Using commercial online Web providers such as HighWired.Com also provides student publications with opportunities for online publishing. Using existing web site providers can help student publications get their sites up and running without worrying about designing the space. Some providers create templated sites where staffs must only be concerned about entering content rather than also designing the content (Fig. 19.2). School sites may have censorship policies or may require information be submitted to their Web masters before being placed online. Publications' staffs may find those restrictions too limiting in what they are able to do with their sites.

Because Internet sites are accessible to virtually anyone with a computer, some schools have created strict rules about content that can appear. For instance, some schools have prohibited pictures of students from being published online or have disal-

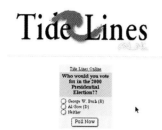

Fig. 19.3. A simple survey with specific responses can generate survey results, but they are not scientific or necessarily reliable, limited as they are to those students who have access to the web site and who are interested enough to participate in the poll. Even given these limitations, however, survey results can form the basis of a story, an infographic or additional reporting. *Tidelines Online,* Pottsville Area High School, Pottsville, Pa.

lowed publishing the names of the students in pictures on the online site. Other schools require permission forms, known as "photo releases," be signed by individuals and sometimes parents of the individuals in pictures before their pictures can be placed on a web site. Online publications often must protect their First Amendment rights, just as they do in printed publications. (See Chap. 23 for more information.)

During the interviewing process, reporters may want to mention to their sources that the information they are providing may be used on a web site, just as they mention to sources that they are being interviewed for a story for the newspaper, yearbook or other publication. If the interview is being conducted online, or if information is being gathered in publication e-mails or polls, students should be informed of the publication's intent to use the responses in print. Student journalists should be sensitive to the way in which information obtained from online interviewing or polling can be skewed by repeated contributions from single sources. Some students may make frivolous comments or may not take the interview seriously, particularly if they can reply anonymously to the questions (Fig. 19.3).

Using information obtained from web sites requires the attribution of those sources in the story. Information used in a story appearing in a Web publication should be used primarily for research and backgrounding, just as it would be if a reporter was reading a story in a printed publication. Original research is always preferred. Interviewing local sources provides information of greater value to the publication's readers. Reporters can provide Web resources for readers so those seeking additional information can easily access it.

A Web master, an online editor, needs skills similar to those of the student editor. The person chosen should understand news values, bring an understanding of good news judgment, be organized and exhibit leadership skills. The Web master can work almost as an equal to the print publication's editor in determining how stories will appear on the web site and how the information will be different from that of the printed publication. The Web master will possibly need the resources of a different group of reporters who can update printed stories and edit content that doesn't make it into the printed publication. Web writers can develop their own stories, either ones that occur between publishing deadlines or original ideas that are more appropriately presented on the Web rather than through the printed publication. Reporters can work with the Web staff to gather information through e-mail forums or through responses gathered by including the publication's e-mail address or writers' individual e-mail addresses at the ends of stories.

Students can be encouraged to respond to information they have read in the printed publication. That response can be printed through traditional letters to the editor or can be placed on the Web as a forum for discussion and dialogue. These discussions can prove valuable to the printed publication in gauging reader opinion and interest in information that could form the basis of future content.

The process of picture editing ensures that some good photographs won't be used in the printed publication. A good Web photo editor will cull through the edited film, looking for additional good quality pictures to place on the web site. Many professional sites, such as that of the *Dallas Morning News*, use clickable slide shows where additional photos appear in still form for readers who want to see more visuals from an event. Creating similar slide shows would be a perfect opportunity for providing a greater number of pictures of students at events such as the prom or homecoming where the printed publication is limited in how many pictures will be shown. Just as in editing for print, the photo editor should make sure the content in the pictures is varied and interesting. An effort should be made to picture a diverse group of students. Technical quality must also be considered (Fig. 19.4).

Working with videographers, reporters can obtain sights and sounds reporting that can be edited and digitized into short film clips on the Web to supplement the printed information and provide additional information in ways that the printed publication cannot provide. Or the student publication can make arrangements to actually broadcast events on the web site. Recently, editors for the Carmel, Ind., *HiLite Online* simultaneously broadcast one of their school's football games on their web site.

INVOLVING THE READERS

Newspaper staffs can offer their readers access to additional content on their web sites. For instance, a student who wants to review an entertainment form may be interested in writing about it on the Web, particularly if it is timely. Many students will be interested in reading a Web report about a concert that happened the previous night or a CD that was just released. Linking the reader to the band or entertainer's web site, as well as other web sites of interest to those readers, will generate more interest. This same concert review printed in a publication two to three weeks later will be old, outdated and uninteresting to student readers who are thinking ahead to the next upcoming concert.

Online publications should cause printed publications to evaluate how they tell stories and how they present information to their readers. No longer limited by long lapses between publishings, newspapers must keep content fresh and lively in both the print and online publications to maintain interest. The flexibility of using writers in different ways may give online and print publications more opportunities for feature-oriented or in-depth writing requiring longer reporting periods.

Publications can sponsor photo contests or literary writing contests in which students can submit poetry, short stories, art or photographs and have the works published periodically on the web site. If the school has a published literary magazine, this project might be sponsored cooperatively with that staff. Or teachers of creative writing classes, art and photography classes and other hands-on classes could choose student work

Fig. 19.4. This award-winning web site provides space for photojournalists to extend the range of their photo shoots through a photo essay. Editing pictures to the one or two of the photographer's best images for the print edition is limiting. Editing to include other good pictures, with complete captions on the web site, creates interest and encourages readers to visit the site. *North Star: Online Edition,* John W. North High School, Riverside, Calif.

to appear on the web site during the semester. Students whose work appears on the site could be tapped as potential staff members for either the web site or the printed publication.

ENHANCED YEARBOOK CONTENT

Yearbook staffs have endless possibilities for Web content. Maintaining interest in the publication as it is created, a yearbook Web master can edit content and publish it on the web site to provide previews of the printed

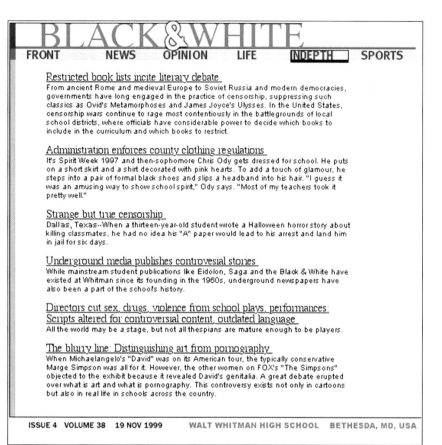

Fig. 19.5. A directory of index tabs at the top of the screen placed horizontally underneath the newspaper's nameplate helps take readers to the section of the newspaper they are looking for. Once in that section, a digest directory provides a capsulized version of the content with a brief summary of the story. Readers who want the entire story can click on the headline to get to additional information. *Black and White*, Walt Whitman High School, Bethesda, Md.

book or to supplement its content. Showing students' pictures that have been shot from various events will make the students excited about the printed publication. The book's sales campaign can be advertised on the web site. Forms for purchasing the printed volume can be provided on the site, and options for paying for the book can be provided.

Once the yearbook staff has decided on a theme for the book, it can be shown on the web site to get the students excited about the book. If the staff doesn't keep the design of the cover a secret until the end of the year, the cover could be posted on the site. Or the staff could conduct an online vote on possible cover ideas if staff members are having a hard time deciding between several designs. Giving readers a personal stake in the outcome of the book will make them more connected to the publication throughout the year.

Yearbook staffs can provide supplemental coverage that is impossible to include in the limited space of the printed book. The possibilities here are endless but could include audio/video clips from club events and special school activities. Club group shots could be enlarged on the screen so faces could be seen more easily than in the printed book. Polls and surveys could be conducted online for inclusion in information graphics or in other reporting. Again, reporters should be sensitive to the comments made through online reporting. Minor sports and different level sports could receive expanded coverage.

On the yearbook web site, as on the newspaper web site, content could be interactive. Students could submit photographs, first-person writing or artwork that the yearbook staff could edit and use.

DESIGN OF THE WEB SITE

Most publications will want to make the web site's design similar to the printed publication's. Using the printed nameplate will create a connection to the printed publication. The web site can use a series of connections to sections of the yearbook such as student life or academics. The newspaper can categorize the Web stories according to news, feature, sports or other sections (Fig. 19.5). Content unique to the web site should be highlighted.

Type chosen for the web site should be easily read. Readability should be a primary concern. Type in standard typefaces will process more easily and will appear more consistent regardless of the kind of computer the student reader uses. Type should be large enough in size to be visible on the screen. Designers should be aware of the need to keep line lengths short, between 10 and 20 picas for easiest readability, and attention should be given to devices such as leading, the space between the lines of type. Double-spacing between paragraphs and other design devices such as text heads within the text will aid in readability. Stories on the Web may need to be edited more tightly but certainly should contain content different from that in the printed publication. The stories can provide updated information, supplemental information or reaction. Links to additional information can be created in the text.

Rather than the entire stories, headlines with summaries of stories can be provided. Interested readers can then click in to read entire text presentations. This digest service benefits readers scanning content for something of interest.

Color is another important consideration for Web designers. Just as certain colors are difficult to read on the printed page, color can complicate readability on web sites. Black type on white screens remains the clearest and least tiring color choice. Designers should be very careful about combining black on red or on other bright colors because the type will appear to resonate or move on the screen. Many readers will be discouraged by low readability and will stop reading. Just as the designer is the best friend to the written word in print, the same applies in online publications. Design should be secondary to readability.

Photographs should be scanned at resolutions and in compression formats that will enable easy viewing but will keep the files compact enough to open easily and quickly for the viewers. Photographs already scanned for the printed edition at higher resolutions should be reduced to the 72 dots per inch resolution needed for faster Web viewing.

Links to content should be easily accessed and clearly located. Placing links in consistent typographical designs in one location on the site will help readers find them. Navigation of the site should be user-friendly. Including e-mail addresses of the online staff and making it easy to contact the online staff will ensure reader contact. When possible, links to additional information about stories and topics can be placed at the ends of stories for readers who are interested in obtaining more information. Providing an online search engine by topic will eliminate some of the frustration of readers looking for specific content.

Video and audio clips should open easily and should be digitized in standard compression software so interested viewers will have easy access to the information. Careful attention to editing will make best use of the space and memory necessary to include these clips on the site.

Occasional reader surprises such as contests, forums, special events and dialogues will keep readers coming back to the sites for fresh content. Contest giveaways such as free yearbooks or free newspaper subscriptions would be appropriate prizes.

COOPERATIVE EFFORTS

As more schools develop web sites and online content, publications can create cooperative efforts with publications in their regions and states. Some states such as Texas have already established statewide efforts to share information and news reports. Linking to other publications' sites can provide student readers with other perspectives and points of view about issues of concern in their own schools. Linking to state and national press associations gives readers opportunities to compare news in their schools to that of other schools. Student writers can also access information about other schools in their state and in the nation when doing research for stories. Many newspapers include summary reports of news from other schools to keep readers informed of happenings in schools around the state and region.

Students can also arrange for joint interviews through Internet providers. The subjects can respond to questions in real time. Interviewers can follow up with questions in response to comments from other interviewers or from the subject being interviewed.

A different form of cooperative interviewing is video conferencing. Through school or district video-conferencing facilities, students can interview people in distant locations and can actually see and talk to them through video hook-ups on both ends of the conference. Pursuing this possibility broadens the resources available to student journalists. Video conferencing can either be one-way or two-way communication.

With all the communications possibilities available to student publications, and with more sure to come in the future, student journalists can take advantage of better research and reporting opportunities to improve their ability to tell stories, both visually and verbally.

EXERCISES

1. Visit the web site of your local newspaper, if it has one, or of a larger, regional newspaper. Analyze its effectiveness by answering these questions:

   a. Is the site visually interesting and easy to read?

   b. Is color used effectively?

   c. Is the site easy to navigate; is it easy to find specific information on the site?

   d. Is it easy to contact staff members for comments or questions?

   e. Is the content different from that of the printed publication? Is it fresh and updated frequently?

   f. Are pictures used effectively on the web site?

2. Visit the Student Press web site at http://student-press.journ.umn.edu/. Once at the site, click on "NSPA," the National Scholastic Press Association web site. Then click on "The Best of the High School Press Online." The site maintains links to winners of the national press association's annual contest for newspaper web sites. You'll also find links to online publications through the site's "Members Online" section. Visit several newspaper web sites and analyze their effectiveness in design and content. Which sites are your favorites? Why?

3. Using college financial aid as a search topic, compile a list of resources that you might want to visit online to do research on this topic. Then visit some of these sources online. What sources are most valuable to you? What links did you find from your online search that proved even more valuable? How could this information be used in research for a possible story in your school newspaper? From information you obtained in your online search, compile a list of questions you might ask of a local source.

4. Using online resources, find answers to the following questions and note the web sites from which you obtained the information:

   a. How many people live in your state according to the most recent statistics?

   b. How many people live in your county?

   c. How many people live in your metropolitan area?

   d. What's the average income in your state?

   e. What's the major industry in your state?

   f. What's the per capita growth in your state?

   g. What's the average rainfall in your city each year?

5. If your school or student publications have an online site, evaluate its effectiveness using the criteria in exercise 1. In class, discuss the site's strengths and weaknesses.

6. On paper, outline and sketch an online site for yourself. Choose a name and design for the site. What colors would you use? How would you divide your site's content?

7. Visit the web site of a metropolitan city newspaper and view an online photographic display. Are the photographs easily viewed? Do they load correctly? Do the photographs offer interesting content and information?

8. Visit the web sites of three metropolitan city dailies on one day and compare their coverage of national news. What additional links are provided to the stories? What photographic coverage is included?

9. Invite the school's media specialist or a local media specialist to discuss online search engines and efficient online searches. Prepare a list of five general topics from five different sections of the newspaper to use as sample search topics.

Visual Storytelling: Pictures, Art and Graphics

Close your eyes. Think about a picture that has significant personal meaning to you. Recall the smallest details of its content from the expressions on the faces in the picture to the clothes the people are wearing.

Keep your eyes closed. Concentrate on a famous picture you've seen or studied but didn't witness in person. Recall the significant details of the picture's content.

Amazing, isn't it? Almost everyone can recall the content of a favorite personal image and a famous historical image just from memory. Such is the power of visual images. Details as minute as facial expressions, clothing and other circumstances of the pictures can be vividly recalled by people with such information stored deeply in the hippocampus of the brain, the brain's permanent storage area.

Just as images are important and powerful in everyday life, they are important in student publications. Readers with distracted attention spans or bombarded with information resources will edit the information they choose to read and see. Images with stopping power, those that readers find interesting and meaningful, will be viewed and often remembered.

In a student publication, images can be used for a variety of reasons: to identify, to report, to entertain, to inform and to amuse. But most importantly, pictures are an important part of the story-telling process. They shouldn't be used to fill space, to decorate pages or for other extraneous reasons. Rather, pictures and other visuals should be used because they add to the verbal reporting. They provide a different kind of interest and information to the publication, and they appeal to and attract the interest of readers in different ways.

For the yearbook and newspaper, photographers should constantly be shooting pictures in the school, in classrooms, in hallways, before school, after school, at sports events, at club meetings and at other special events. Photographers should carry cameras to class with them so the students in the school become accustomed to having their pictures taken and will react with natural expressions instead of reacting to the presence of the camera.

Experienced photographers will help younger, less-experienced photographers by mentoring them through the process of shooting, especially in large gatherings where they may be intimidated by the size of the crowd or during sports events when they need guidance to cover all the parameters, from the crowds in the stands to the action on the court or field. Shooting as partners will enable the photographers to feel more comfortable and less conspicuous and will result in the photographers moving around, getting close to the subject matter.

Fig. 20.1. A good black-and-white photograph has a wide range of tones from black to white. Highlight areas, such as the sky in this picture, which often wash out in high-speed black-and-white films, should show detail and should not disappear into the page. Midtones should show range from lighter gray to darker gray. Shadows should be black. The photographer covering this cross-country event exposed her film correctly and rendered a print that will reproduce well in a student publication. Alexandra Fuller, Park City High School, Park City, Utah

Photographs aren't the only form of visuals available to designers. Cartoons, illustrations and infographics can also provide visual interest to stories and enliven page layouts. Staffs should look beyond their own members in seeking illustrators and cartoonists to add variety to layouts.

The use of effective graphics in design also adds to attractive layouts. The use of rule lines, screens, colors and text details gives the layout designer many tools for effective design.

PHOTOGRAPHS

Photographs should be used in design both for their content—what they add to the verbal information—and for their technical strengths. Technically, a picture's strengths must be solid. Good publications staffs create acceptable parameters for technical strength and adhere to the standards throughout the publication. Selecting content, on the other hand, is more subjective. A student trained as a good picture editor can prove valuable in working with photographers and editors to select the pictures for publication that do the best job of providing meaningful content.

TECHNICAL PARAMETERS

A good photograph has several qualities. First, it's always in focus so the important content can be seen and understood by the viewer. Second, the picture should have a range of good exposure. Areas of the picture known as the shadows are rendered in darker shades of black in the print. Midtones show as shades of gray. Highlights are the lightest areas of the print, but not necessarily white. Generally, the highlight areas should retain some detail (Fig. 20.1). When using more than one picture on a page, it's important that the tones in the pictures are consistent. A washed out print will lose all appeal next to a picture with good tonal control.

When taking the picture, good photographers are careful to correctly expose film using the camera's light-metering system. In a traditional darkroom good photographers use printing filters that will help them reproduce all tones of good exposure. In the darkroom, photographers learn to use advanced printing skills that will enable them to "burn in," or darken, areas that would reproduce without tone in the publication or will "dodge" areas that would reproduce too dark and with all solid tones.

Good photographers must take the publication's printing method into consideration when preparing the print for publication. Many newspaper and yearbook printers have a difficult time reproducing black-and-white photographs in which the contrast—the range of tones—is too extreme. Prints with a little less contrast will often reproduce more effectively. Photographers must then adjust the contrast in their finished prints to ensure the tones will be reproducible.

Another important quality of a good photograph is one free from technical flaws, such as fingerprints and scratches that may have occurred during the film development or printing stages. When these scratches show up on the final print, good photographers will take time to use spot-toning fluid and fine brushes to correct these flaws. Good filing systems for negatives and clean darkroom practices will help eliminate these preventable flaws from occurring.

CONTENT AND COMPOSITION

Good photographs have strong content. While evaluation of content is subjective, certain qualities are universally agreed upon.

A good picture uses good compositional techniques. Photographers can take advantage of many techniques when placing the content in their images. Using some of the traditional rules of composition will improve the content.

- *Center of interest.* The reason why the photograph was taken should be obvious to the viewer. The content should be immediately visible and strategically placed in the frame (Fig. 20.2). Beginning photographers who stand too far away from their subjects may create images in which the viewer is left to search for the photograph's meaning. Photographers who fill the frame with meaningful content will produce images of higher visual interest. With standard lenses, photographers may need to be as close as 5 to 7 feet away from their subjects in order to fill the frame with meaningful content. Those who have longer lenses, called "telephotos" or "zooms," can bring content into their frames from a distance farther away from the subject.

- *Rule of thirds.* Photographing a subject by placing it directly in the middle of the frame usually results in a less interesting and static picture. Long a rule in art and architecture, the "golden mean points" dictate that meaningful content be placed in areas of the frame other than in the center. When looking through the viewfinder of the camera, the window that enables the photographer to see the content, the photographer can visually divide the space into thirds both vertically and horizontally. The intersections of these thirds result in the golden mean points. These points are more powerful areas for placing primary visual information in the frame. When using the rule of thirds, photographers should make sure that what is next to the subject is adding to the visual context of the photograph (Fig. 20.3).

Fig. 20.2. The emotion of this picture makes it one that is immediately attractive to readers. The photographer used a fast shutter speed to stop the action of this teacher during a homecoming pep rally. The clean background and repeating pom-poms add to the photo's appeal. In addition, the subject is large in the photograph, which further adds to the appeal. *Aurora*, Lee's Summit North High School, Lee's Summit, Mo.

Fig. 20.3. Photographers can add to a photograph's dynamic appeal by placing the subject matter at the intersection of the rule of thirds—two vertical and horizontal intersections that occur when looking through the viewfinder and dividing it into thirds. Here, the photographer had his camera held vertically and he used the bottom right intersection to place his subject matter. Note the strong balance of the Frisbee in the top left corner providing a natural frame for the subject. *Devils' Advocate,* Hinsdale Central High School, Hinsdale, Ill.

- *Leading lines.* Lines in photographs can lead the viewer directly to the primary subject matter. These lines can be obvious, such as a road or path someone is walking on, or can be subtle, such as geometric lines repeated in a stairwell or in an architectural detail (Fig. 20.4).

- *Framing.* Framing in a picture takes advantage of foreground or background detail to provide a partial border or frame around the subject matter (Fig. 20.5). Portrait photographers often use parts of flowers or tree branches to subtly frame the faces of their subjects to provide textural interest. Photographers shooting scenic images often place nearby trees in the foreground in the image to show distance and scale.

- *Grounds.* Though photographs compress three dimensions into two, they can still show depth and indicate spatial differences. Placing meaningful content in the foreground, the middle ground and the background of the image will take advantage of this principle (Fig. 20.6). If the information in any of the areas is not contributing to the contextual information, the photographer can often use a technique known as shallow "depth of field" to improve it.

Depth of field refers to the range of focus from the foreground to the background in the image. Photographers control the depth of field through three factors when taking the picture: the lens used, the size of the aperture or lens opening and the distance they are from their subjects. A good photographer seeking to eliminate a distracting background could change camera position to effectively clean up the information behind the subject, preventing it from being distracting. But if changing position isn't possible to completely eliminate the distracting elements, the photographer could use shallow depth of field to make the background information less focused

Fig. 20.4. Especially in sports, arms and legs can serve as visual leading lines that take the viewer into the action of the moment. Note how your eyes are led by the strong direction of the vertical arms and fingers in this volleyball shot. The horizontal lines of the flag in the background provide strong framework, but the shallow depth of field keeps them from becoming distracting to the action. Rob Mattson, Lamar High School, Arlington, Texas

Fig. 20.5. In this picture story on a junior ROTC unit at the school, the photographer used the strong shape and uniform detail of the color guard members to frame the sergeant's face as he inspects the unit. The photographer used his depth of field sharply on the sergeant and allowed the color guard members to be slightly soft in focus to take the reader more strongly to the sergeant, the subject of this picture. *Hurricane*, Hillcrest High School, Dallas, Texas

Fig. 20.6. In this package of pictures from the spring performance of the school's arts department, the depth of field in the dominant picture is extremely long, providing good detail for both subjects close to the camera and those farther away. Sometimes, being able to show depth is important to the meaning of a photograph. *Stampede,* Burges High School, El Paso, Texas

and less distracting. Viewers will concentrate visually on areas of sharp focus rather than areas that are out of focus in the image. When using shallow depth of field, the information in the frame isn't blurry, indicating camera movement when the picture was taken. Rather, it's soft in focus.

- *Lighting.* Interesting lighting can make a picture more appealing (Fig. 20.7). Silhouettes—images that show shape against a light background—are one example of interesting lighting. Dramatically lighted skies or interesting sunsets after storms can also create lighting that adds to a picture's appeal. Pictures shot with light coming into the camera from side angles will result in interesting "side light" that emphasizes texture and form. Outline light, strong light from behind the subject, can provide a "halo effect" in the picture, particularly effective when shooting people since the sun will be away from their faces. Pictures of people shot in bright sunlight with the sun behind the photographer will result in "flat light," or light that flattens the shadows and eliminates any detail. The photographer will also have problems with squinting subjects whose eyes may be almost shut. Shooting outdoors on overcast days will also result in flat light where no shadows or texture detail will be present.

- *Impact.* As mentioned earlier, impact is the photograph's stopping power. A viewer may be attracted to an image because of its dramatic content. Pictures of conflict often fall into this category. Dramatic images of peak action in sports have strong impact because they show viewers action that is often impossible to see on the field when the event is being viewed. Or pictures shot at peak moments may show players' bodies at diagonals to the ground, indicating the intensity of the moment. This diagonal motion is also visually interesting because it's dramatic.

Impact can result when strong emotion or reaction is present in a picture. High school is a ripe ground for emotion. Competitions are held for clubs and organizations. When someone is named a winner or a loser of such a competition, emotion is bound to occur. Sporting events are full of emotion, with players, fans, cheerleaders and parents all interested in the outcome. Even classrooms in the

Fig. 20.7. Interesting light can make an otherwise ordinary situation more interesting to look at. Schools are often built with rows of windows providing strong backlight in both classroom and hallway areas. Taking advantage of the strong backlight in this hallway, the photographer let the lighting add to the graphic appeal of the photograph through the shadows cast by the windows and by the light appearing on the students' faces. Aiming cameras at windows or into light requires special attention to exposure. Eric Diamond, Essex Junction High School, Essex Junction, Vt.

Fig. 20.8. School events often provide great opportunities for school photographers looking for good emotion and reaction shots. At a dance honoring seniors, students dancing and having fun are immediately obvious from these two images. The photographer showed the good times from this event. Shooting in gyms, cafeterias and auditoriums at night requires the use of a flash. Controlling the flash intensity is vital in making pictures that aren't washed out or overlit by the flash. *Cardinal Voice,* Laguna Creek High School, Elk Grove, Calif.

Fig. 20.9. Stand-alone photographs are those used because of their appealing qualities or strong news or timeliness factors. This photograph of students watching a professional basketball game during a school dance shows the intensity of the moment. When photographs are used without accompanying stories, they can feature small headlines in distinctive styles in addition to the caption. Also, note the rule line box placed around the photograph, which helps separate it from the rest of the page content. *Cardinal Voice,* Laguna Creek High School, Elk Grove, Calif.

school can be arenas for emotion or reaction when a student is asked to perform a dissection in biology, present a speech or act out a literary classic with classmates (Fig. 20.8).

Impact can also result from humorous incidents. A group of cheerleaders practicing a pyramid who tumble into disarray with arms flailing and intense laughter will cause the viewer to feel the fun of the moment. A student holding a baby for the first time in a child development class will elicit viewer response if the interaction between the student and the baby is interesting. Meaningful relationships will create interesting content with impact. Schools are full of potential relationships including those of older and younger students, peers, friends, boyfriend/girlfriends, teachers and students, and athletes and coaches, to name just a few.

TELLING STORIES THROUGH PHOTOGRAPHS

Often, a well-chosen, single image will be effective in presenting information to a viewer. The single image can be used by itself as a "stand-alone" photograph, or it can accompany a story. A stand-alone image requires a complete caption to give the reader the necessary information and detail and to provide identification for the people pictured. Many newspapers use stand-alone images in a particular design style, with a small headline, or catchline, above the image and a complete caption underneath. These stand-alone photos are often set off in the design by rule lines or boxes to indicate their singular story-telling function. Stand-alone pictures can be news pictures, pictures of events or activities, or feature-oriented pictures used because of their interesting content (Fig. 20.9).

Single pictures used to accompany text should be carefully chosen. The content should amplify that of the verbal text. Designers should vary their size and placement in the design so they don't become predictable and static. The images should be cropped to strengthen content and eliminate distracting elements. The picture's size and shape should be determined by its strengths and should not be dropped into predetermined holes in the layout or compromised in content because of a predetermined picture shape on the layout.

PICTURE PACKAGES OR GROUPS

When more than a single image is needed to tell a story, a picture package or group can be used. Usually two or three images, a picture package is edited to make sure each image in the package adds to the reader's understanding of an event. Therefore, photos should contribute different information. For instance, one picture might be an overall or wide shot giving the reader a feel for the event. Another shot might be a close-up where the photographer has used a longer lens to isolate a few individuals participating in the event. An additional shot might show the outcome or result of the event or activity (Fig. 20.10).

Another type of picture group is a picture sequence. Sequences are used to show a series. A speaker with an interesting visual speaking pattern could be shown in two or three shots with different expressions and gestures. A sports sequence is appropriate to show a pivotal play or series in a game. Or a sequence could show how to do something such as how to paint a mascot on a face before a big game. How-to sequences sometimes use numbers in the captions (Fig. 20.11).

PICTURE STORIES

Picture stories are just like verbal stories except told with images rather than just with words. A picture story should have a beginning, middle and end. Subjects for picture stories are abundant in schools. Subjects should be broad enough to offer a range of picture possibilities, but narrow enough to be able to tell the story in about five to seven well-chosen pictures. Picture stories can be used on single pages or on double trucks (Fig. 20.12).

A photographer working on a picture story needs an adequate amount of time to be able to develop the story. The time commitment involves observation and could also involve a bit of research before the photo shoot even begins. A photographer might work in conjunction with a reporter so that a verbal story can appear with the picture story to complete the presentation. Good, detailed captions should also be a part of the presentation. In a picture story, a dominant picture, at least two to three times larger than any other, should establish the event for the reader. The dominant image should be the largest in size in the layout, but it should also be the most compelling image. It doesn't necessarily have to be the beginning picture in the story.

The other pictures accompanying the dominant image should be carefully edited to make sure that each is contributing new information to the reader's under-

Fig. 20.10. In a three-picture package on a winter dance and pep assembly, the designer edited the pictures to show three different aspects of the events, each featuring different people and different situations. Complete captions identify all the participants. Each picture's different shape adds to the design. Axe, South Eugene High School, Eugene, Ore.

Fig. 20.11. A picture sequence is a carefully edited series of pictures that tells how to do something. Here, a story on carving a Halloween pumpkin provides a sequence of pictures showing a suggested procedure. *Northwest Passage*, Shawnee Mission Northwest High School, Shawnee, Kan.

standing of the event. Careful attention should also be paid to making sure each picture is a different size and shape in the layout, with emphasis on strong verticals and horizontals. Pictures in stories should be edited so the people in the images are different sizes. The number of people pictured in each photograph should also vary (Fig. 20.13).

Picture stories should not be "how-to" edits in which the reader is shown how to do something sequentially. That is a picture sequence, not a picture story.

TRADITIONAL AND DIGITAL SHOOTING

When photographers are learning to use equipment, they may find it easier to work with simple 35 mm cameras, long a staple of the publications' world. Simple 35 mm cameras have working light meters that require the photographer to take light meter readings and change both f-stop settings and shutter speeds. Learning how to use these settings will help the photographers learn to control depth of field to eliminate a distracting background or to use a fast shutter speed to stop moving action.

More advanced photographers will feel comfortable with more advanced cameras, those with sophisticated, multimode exposure systems and automatic focusing systems. These cameras often use dedicated flashes, those that determine and set correct exposure with flash systems made for the camera. Beginning photographers using sophisticated automatic cameras may be intimidated by the equipment until they learn to work all the bells and whistles on the camera.

Simple and advanced 35 mm cameras enable the staff to purchase a range of lenses for shooting. In addition to traditional 50 mm lenses, which reproduce subject matter in normal view, a staff needs additional lenses so the content of photographs can vary, avoiding visual redundancy in lens use and selection.

A wide-angle lens, starting somewhere in the range of 35 mm and encompassing lenses as wide as 24 mm, will enable the photographer to shoot "wide shots," those that show a greater range of subject matter horizontally in the frame.

Extremely wide lenses, sometimes called "fisheye lenses," will be novelty lenses that are too limited for normal shooting. More extreme fisheye lenses produce pictures that show a 360 degree range and produce images that are completely round.

Beyond the 50 mm standard lens, photographers can benefit from a range of short telephoto and zoom lenses. Short telephotos, beginning at about 70 mm, will enable photographers to shoot portraits, for instance, without being right in the subject's face. In a classroom, a short telephoto will enable a photographer to bring action into the camera lens when he or she can't move in close to the subjects. Short telephoto lenses work well in some court shooting, such as volleyball or basketball, from certain angles on the field.

Zoom lenses incorporate a range of focal lengths in one lens. Popular with many publications' staffs, zooms have some limitations. They aren't as "fast" as fixed focal length lenses, because they incorporate a range of focal lengths in one lens. A fast lens is one with a large maximum f-stop or lens aperture such as F:2 or F:2.8. Fast lenses are often important in high school shooting because the light situations in the school are often dim. Lenses with larger maximum f-stops will enable the photographer to shoot without resorting to flash or artificial light. Zoom lenses are usually heavier to hold because of the range of focal lengths incorporated into their design. This heaviness can result in camera "blur" or movement that will be visible in the picture. A staff considering a zoom lens should shop carefully for one with a minimum of limitations.

Medium telephotos provide a focal length of between 100 and 200 mm. These lenses are useful in classrooms and in many sports shooting situations, especially for court sports such as tennis, volleyball and basketball.

Long telephotos range from 300 mm lenses and longer in focal length. Few schools can afford to buy really long, "fast" telephoto lenses because they will often cost thousands of dollars. Instead, many schools opt to purchase slower lenses, those with maximum f-stops in the range of F:3.5 or

Fig. 20.12. A picture story is a story told in pictures, but with accompanying text. A good picture story avoids visual redundancy through careful editing that ensures each picture contributes new information to the story being told. In this picture story on the band placing third at the state competition, an excellent set of pictures provides a beginning, middle and end to this event. Note how each picture provides not only different aspects of the story but features different picture sizes and shapes, and each is shot from a different perspective and angle. *Panther Prints*, Duncanville High School, Duncanville, Texas

Feb. 26, 1999 PANTHER PRINTS

Most beautiful & handsome, favorites, royalty honored at

Coronation

Proud winners
Wrapped in a bear hug, seniors Jennifer Ames and Chris Ashy celebrate their wins as Most Beautiful and Most Handsome. Having never been nominated for Coronation in the past, Ames was especially surprised about her win. All winners received pewter keychains engraved with their category.

Most Beautiful and Handsome
Freshmen Jessica Hildreth and Danny Johnson, Sophomores April Plummer and J-Bob Thomas, Juniors Jamie Garcia and Mori Hernandez, Seniors Jennifer Ames and Chris Ashy
Class Favorites
Freshmen Jodi Reynolds and Chris Johnson, Sophomores Haley Miller and Ricky Smith, Juniors Ken Stapleton and Tyler Breckington, Seniors Morgan Malone, Jenny Ronai, Andy Harrington and Sommy Hurd
Royalty
Freshmen Derrica Pigsee and Stephen Lefresse, Sophomores Zanpaila Morrel and Anthony Grant, Juniors Stephoni Crabtree, Ryan Lee, and Michael Crewe, Seniors Michelle Lennu and David Sykes
Mr. and Miss DHS — Brooks Larr and Kyle Yamaguchi

Tears of shock
Senior Brooks Larr is unable to control her tears after being named 1999's Miss DHS. "I have never had a greater honor or a greater shock," Larr said. "God has truly blessed me in immeasurable ways." Senior Kyle Yamaguchi was named Mr. DHS. They both received plaques in order to remember the event. Both students have dedicated time to clubs, office positions, and Student Council to better the name and reputation of Duncanville High School.

Excited
Walking under the balloon archway, seniors Jeremy Hurd and Jada Burrows listen as their accomplishments are read. Other nominees for Mr. and Miss DHS were winners Kyle Yamaguchi and Brooks Larr, David Sykes, Terrance Dean, Brice Tidwell, Leigh Atkins, Jaclynne Blake, Morgan Malone, and Kathleen Coate.

Talent
Performing between announcements, Janelle Lankford sings "Slow Jam." Other performers included Brooks Larr, Jenny Christin and Ian Dishon, Stephen Toepenty and Emily Nelson, a dance group, and the High Hats.

Photos by Matt Slocum

Surprise
Upon hearing her name called, sophomore April Plummer gasps at being named Sophomore Most Beautiful. Classmate J-Bob Thomas (not pictured) was named Most Handsome. Voting was done through English classes.

Class favorites
Sophomores Haley Miller and Ricky Smith celebrate their selection as Favorites of the Class of 2001. The Coronation was held Feb. 11 in Alexander Auditorium.

Fig. 20.13. A special event at the school makes an excellent choice for a picture story. The dominant image's close crop and large size used in the layout add to its appeal. Each of the other pictures is also carefully edited for content. Good picture stories show a variety of people. *Panther Prints*, Duncanville High School, Duncanville, Texas

F:4. These slower lenses may be adequate for the school's shooting needs when used with very fast films, such as Kodak's 3200-speed black-and-white film. Poorly lit football stadiums will render these lenses mostly inadequate even with fast films if the maximum shutter speed isn't fast enough to stop the action on the field. A sports photographer will usually need to shoot at shutter speeds as fast as 1/500 of a second to stop sports action. With sophisticated cameras offering even faster shutter speeds, faster lenses become even more of an important factor in stopping action.

A better option might be for the school to occasionally rent or borrow a long telephoto lens. Many large camera stores rent equipment. Renting such a lens a couple of times during a season might be adequate. However, using a long telephoto lens for the first time will prove difficult for most photographers without any previous experience. The lenses are heavy, difficult to use and difficult to stabilize. Long telephoto lenses must also be used with a monopod, a single-legged support system that screws into a thread in the lens and provides support for it during use.

Many schools begin mentoring programs with local professional newspaper photographers and others in their communities. These professionals often shoot the school's athletic events. The mentor might be willing to occasionally let the school's photographers use the lens and might provide instruction on its use during a few minutes of a game. Many local newspaper photographers started out as high school shooters and remember the limitations of sports shooting without the right equipment.

Some photographers will buy lens doublers that will double the range of the lens. For instance, a 75 mm lens will now shoot 150 mm. Lens doublers may be a good choice, but they will reduce the maximum f-stop of the lens, and they may lead to images that aren't sharp if they aren't good optical investments.

Other options for obtaining lenses are pawnshops, garage sales or Internet buying sites such as eBay.

Another necessary accessory is a flash to shoot in low-light situations. Photographers shooting with fast film in low-light situations can avoid shooting with direct flash, flash aimed directly at their subjects from camera position. Photographs shot with direct flash will have harsh, dark shadows and will often re-

SHARING SENTIMENTS
Junior Julie Arnold discusses her IB experience with her freshman buddy in the new IB buddy program.
photo by Lindsay Barclay

produce with washed out or faded highlight or bright image areas. Even with good printing in the darkroom, photographers will have a hard time eliminating these artificial effects that will be distracting when reproduced in the yearbook or newspaper.

Newer camera models often sell companion flashes called "dedicated flash systems." These sophisticated flash systems provide automatic exposure for pictures when using flash.

Flash use will be more natural when it is "bounced" off a low white ceiling or wall. Photographers using flashes with pivoting heads can aim the head at an angle so the light will hit the wall or ceiling and bounce light back to the subject. This technique requires the flash be used at a stronger intensity setting. The photographer must set the distance for the flash, adding the flash to ceiling and ceiling to subject distance to get a correct exposure. The technique also requires a ceiling no more than about 10 feet away. The bounce flash technique provides a shower of light on the subject that is very pleasing, rather than harsh. The photographer can combine bounce flash with a small white card placed on the flash head. This card will kick light back into the subject's face and eyes.

Flash can also be used off-camera in what is called "indirect flash." The photographer can throw the shadows behind the subject or out of camera range by aiming the flash out of the picture range but still illuminating the subject.

Flash may also be used outdoors in what is called the "synchro-sun" technique. This technique will help even the shadows provided by natural light or can provide stronger, more interesting light outdoors on overcast days.

Many schools have already begun buying digital cameras, which record images electronically inside the camera. These images are then downloaded directly into the computer to be placed in layouts. The advantage of digital cameras is the instantaneous image capture allowed by the cameras. They are very useful for dead-

Fig. 20.14. Overlines, or catchlines, in reverse type on gray bars help provide visual entry points into the content areas. They also take advantage of the fact that most students will enter the content through the picture areas. Complete captions on each picture further draw the reader's eyes through bold identifiers prefacing the caption information. Note that the photographer's picture credits are placed at the end of the captions in a contrasting, condensed typeface. *Edition*, Anderson High School, Austin, Texas

The Thrill of Victory

A 19 year record falls as Amy Manson -13- and Kati Daly -19- celebrate inside Beyer's goal box. This goal was the game winner putting the ladies on top 2-1. An estimated crowd of 800 students and parents stood in the rain to watch our first win over Beyer. Remarkably there were no complaints about the weather. When the season ended, Beyer and Downey reigned as the CCC Co-Champions.

Fig. 20.15. A complete caption written in five sentences provides many details and facts for its reader. This picture and caption were used on the front endsheet of the school's yearbook. *Shield*, Thomas Downey High School, Modesto, Calif.

line shooting, when the time required to process and print the traditional way in a darkroom would be prohibitive.

Even though many digital camera models are now competitively priced, good digital cameras offering a range of options and sophisticated shooting settings are still beyond the affordability of many schools. Many schools settle for simple digital cameras with lower resolutions and limited options. These will work effectively for the occasional deadline picture but will need to be supplemented by cameras shooting traditional film, especially for difficult shooting situations such as sports.

Simple, inexpensive Polaroid cameras are preferred by some staffs waiting for digital cameras to become more affordable. Polaroids enable the staff to quickly produce images, such as mug shots or simple event shots, for deadline needs. However, the film is expensive and will result in wasted money in the hands of an inexperienced shooter. Polaroids also have little use other than shooting head or mug shots.

Point and shoot cameras, with simple operation, will enable almost anyone on the staff to produce usable images. But the limitations in lens use will prevent these cameras from working in all shooting situations. They are excellent choices for loaning to clubs and organizations whose members may be attending a field trip or competition in a distant location that staff photographers would not be able to attend. Loaning them to chaperones or club sponsors accompanying the groups will also be a good way to get pictures that otherwise might not be available to the staff. Encouraging this cooperative camera arrangement is a good way for staffs to expand their coverage.

Similarly, a supply of single-use cameras provided to underrepresented school populations, club members attending distant events or staffers who need to shoot pictures for stories for deadline will be helpful in fulfilling the photographic needs of the newspaper or yearbook. Many schools without the benefit of separate photography staffs will find a need to supply writers with training and cameras in order to provide their own photographs.

Staffs should make sure to keep a log of where the film or cameras have been placed and to follow up with the contributors to make sure the pictures are returned to the staff. Some yearbook staffs offer training sessions for contributing photographers to teach them basic compositional skills before passing out the film or cameras. Giving printed photo credits for the contributors in the yearbook or newspaper will be an appropriate way of providing recognition for these outside staff contributors.

Occasionally, pictures can be obtained from local media outlets including community newspapers. Yearbook staffs often get a certain amount of professionally shot film as part of their yearbook portrait contract. In all cases, it is better if students take their own pictures for their own publications, but seeking the help of outsiders is sometimes necessary to ensure good coverage.

CAPTIONS AND CUTLINES

Every picture, with few exceptions, will need a caption. Captions are complete sentences that provide information and details about pictures for the reader. Complete names should always be provided. People in pictures should be named from left to right, but it isn't necessary to include "left to right" since that's a normal reading pattern. When pictures are being named in some other arrangement, such as clockwise, it might be necessary to state the naming pattern. Staffs should make sure the names in captions are spelled correctly by double-checking the names against an official list of students provided by the school's registrar or through a staff resource file. Many schools with computerized records may be willing to give the publication staff a computerized list of student names. Each year, the staff can delete the graduating seniors and add freshman and new students to the list without starting completely over. Staffs may also want to further identify students by using their year of graduation or traditional grade in school (freshman, sophomore, etc.) after their names.

Captions can start with small-sized overlines, brief summaries that provide visual entry into the caption information. These overlines, or "catchlines" as they are sometimes called, should be printed in a contrasting typeface, possibly a bold or a bold italic, in a point size one or two sizes larger than the caption type. In yearbooks, sections will often be designed to coordinate the graphics in the page headlines to the design of the overlines. Overlines are commonly used in newspapers with stand-alone photos. Often, the overline appears above the picture (Fig. 20.14).

Captions can begin with different parts of speech to avoid a redundancy in their grammatical construction. For instance, on a yearbook spread with seven pictures, if all captions begin with names or with prepositional phrases, readers will become bored with the construction. Details and specific nouns should be used to add to the reader's understanding of the story. Captions can be more than one sentence in length. Often, a second sentence is used in yearbook captions to add outcomes or results to the first sentence's description of the pictured information (Fig. 20.15).

Because captions describe what is going on when the picture was taken, the information should be in present tense, especially in the first sentence. Follow-up information may be written in past tense to indicate the passage of time.

Good captions require good reporting. If photographers don't provide basic caption information for the designers, reporters should talk to the people in the pictures to find out what was going on and possibly to obtain quotes. Making up information about what was going on will usually result in inaccurate information, threatening the credibility of the staff. On the other hand, caption information should not be obvious nor should it merely repeat what the viewer can tell from looking at the picture.

In naming people pictured in group shots, the rows should be designated as "front," "second," "third" and so on until the back row. Using "first," "second," "third" without "front" and "back" is confusing. In group shots, complete names should be used in the captions. Again, it isn't necessary to tell the naming pattern unless it isn't left to right.

To add dimension to captions, quotes are often included. Reporters can ask questions of the people pictured to get their reactions to the pictured information. Quotes will often add rich texture and personal understanding to the captions.

Captions should be placed adjacent to the pictures they describe, either under the pictures or next to them. If the picture bleeds across the gutter, the caption should not bleed unless the picture is on a double truck or centerspread. In that case, the caption should be placed under the picture on the widest side, beginning on the margin of that page. In placing long captions under wide, horizontal pictures, the designer may want to break the captions into columns to keep the line lengths from being wider than comfortable reading patterns allow.

Some publications include the photo credit (for the person who took the picture) at the end of the caption.

Fig. 20.16. Tight cropping adds to the impact of this reaction shot of a student involved in a pudding-eating contest at school. The crop also results in a strong vertical shape. Consulting with photographers on the best crops for photographs is crucial in good publications' photography. Michael LoBue, Golden West High School, Visalia, Calif.

Others place this information at the bottom right edge or on the right side of the photograph. No matter where it appears, a picture credit is needed for each photograph. The picture credit can appear in a type size a point size or two smaller than the caption information, and it can be in a contrasting typeface, such as a condensed type.

CROPPING PHOTOGRAPHS

Cropping is both a visual and a physical process. Visually, cropping seeks to improve the content of the photograph by eliminating distracting elements or those not needed to tell the picture's story. Good cropping makes the image have more impact in the design and can correct certain photographic flaws such as scratches or the subject being too small in the picture because the photographer was too far away (Fig. 20.16).

In sports shooting, cropping can make pictures more dramatic by removing parts of the photograph not essential to the action. For instance, in upper-body sports such as volleyball and basketball, cropping out the legs of an athlete using primarily her arms can make the interaction of the arms and the ball more dramatic. In cropping sports shots, designers must also be aware that cropping out the ball or eliminating the opponents removes the visual context of the pictured action and weakens its meaning. In sports action shots, the ball should definitely be part of the image.

If pictures are submitted digitally, the images can be scanned or downloaded directly into the computer and produced or submitted electronically. These photographs will already be placed in picture positions on the pages. Designers will be able to see the effects of their cropping and picture use. Pictures imported into layout and design programs should not be stretched vertically or horizontally from their original proportions. Designers should carefully check the measurements palette when the pictures are imported to make sure the x

and *y* coordinates remain consistent.

Pictures produced and submitted to the printer as prints will often require cropping by the printer before the pictures are stripped into the layout windows. Pictures printed through traditional printing will be halftoned, reshot through a halftone camera through a fine screen, in order to allow the continuous tones of the image to be rendered through dots and reproduced in ink. Before submitting the image to the printer, the designer will need to indicate cropping on the print to allow the proportions of the image to be correctly reproduced in the desired size.

In yearbook publishing, printers often provide the staffs with cropping devices, often a pair of large **L**-shapes connected by a diagonal bar. The designer sets the cropper to the desired shape, positioning the square along the outer edges of the desired space on the layout and tightening the diagonal bar to hold the proportions of the space. Then the cropper is applied to the picture. As long as the bar stays in place, the two **L**s can be moved to allow the proportions to stay consistent. Cropping devices have small indentations in the corners to allow the staff to place cropping marks with grease pencils without placing them directly on image areas.

Newspaper cropping is done with cropping wheels, two attached rotating circles. Or cropping can be done through the use of a calculator or slide rule. The newspaper designer is seeking a proportion that will tell the printer how much the picture should be reduced or enlarged to fit the layout. To crop a picture, the designer must know the dimensions of the picture space and one of the desired dimensions of the actual print. Lining up the actual vertical next to the desired vertical on the wheel, the designer simply looks at the actual horizontal dimension, which will give the designer the unknown horizontal shape and the proportion of enlargement or reduction needed by the printer. This can also be done using the horizontal dimension if that is the more important dimension.

Designers indicate desired cropping dimensions on the border of the actual image by drawing small black lines on the print. Pictures used in newspapers will require photo tags attached to them that tell the printer on which pages and in what positions the pictures are being used. Yearbook staffs will also tag their pictures, usually with preprinted labels from the yearbook publisher that are attached to the backs of the prints in areas that will be cropped into the printed book. The label also provides a place for the staff to write in the page number and position in which the picture appears on the layout. The label should be filled out with a soft leaded marker so the picture's surface won't be damaged, and the picture information should be allowed to dry before prints are stacked so it won't transfer onto the front of other pictures. Stacking pictures back-to-back is always a good idea.

Some schools avoid cropping problems altogether by simply having photographers print pictures to their desired size. When this is done, photographers should remember that the printer needs at least an additional eighth to quarter of an inch of extra space around the image to prepare the image for print.

PHOTO EDITING

Visual redundancy results when the same information is repeated in photographs, just as verbal redundancy results when information is repeated in print. A good picture editor working carefully with the other photographers and designers can make a big difference on a publication.

Unfortunately, many staffs give someone the title of photo editor without training that person to do the job or explaining what a photo editor does on a publication.

Photo editors should be present at all staff and planning meetings and contribute to the discussion of story development and advance planning. They should help writers make photo assignments that will both contribute to the story development and be possible for the photographers to shoot. They should make assignments to the photographers, taking into consideration their individual strengths. They should discuss the assignments with the photographers and suggest possible picture angles and images and should make sure the photographers have the right equipment and supplies to adequately shoot the assignments. Photo editors should make sure photographers are provided with detailed information about the events or activities they will shoot, including the time and place they will occur and the possible use of the pictures in the publication.

Photo editors should make sure darkroom and camera supplies are frequently inventoried and should be responsible for making lists of needed supplies well in advance of the supplies running out.

After photographers shoot and process film, photo editors should individually sit down with the photographers over a light table using a loupe magnifier, a small

Fig. 20.17. Cutout photographs with no backgrounds are best when created that way in a studio shot against a white background that can easily be removed electronically on a computer. This photo cutout works well with the story format. *Informer,* Laingsburg High School, Laingsburg, Mich.

viewing device that enlarges the negative and shows the detail. Photo editors can offer photographers advice on cropping, on improving their shooting and on technical problems such as proper exposure. As mentors, photo editors can help younger photographers improve their photographic vision and improve their abilities to contribute to the story-telling function of the publication. Occasionally, inviting in local professional photographers, perhaps those who have graduated from the school in previous years, will also help mentor and develop the vision of young photographers. These photographers can help students by explaining how to do something, such as how to correctly use a flash, or they can look at the pictures the photographers have shot and offer advice on improving the composition and content.

Using a grease pencil, a soft-leaded pencil that writes on photographic paper, the photo editor, photographer and page designer can decide which images should be enlarged from the overall shoot for use in layouts by individual staff members. The grease pencil can also indicate the proper cropping for the image as it's enlarged by the photographer.

After enlarging the images, photographers should make sure to provide complete caption information for each image. Photographers are journalists, too. During assignments, they should carry reporter's notebooks, small notebooks that slip into camera bags or pockets, in which they can record the names of the people they photograph as well as other details. When covering a game, the photographer should get a copy of rosters or programs so names can be easily matched to numbers on uniforms. Also during sporting events, photographers can occasionally shoot a frame of the scoreboard so the progression of important plays during the event can be referenced.

Last, photographers should do any retouching to correct any visual flaws in the final print. Spot toning fluids in a variety of warm and cool shades can be used with a range of fine brushes to touch up flaws in prints. A print-finishing area where an enlarging lamp is provided will help the photographers when spot toning.

Prints should be stored in files or envelopes labeled with appropriate subject matter such as "varsity football," "homecoming" or "fall play" and stored for later use by staff members when drawing layouts.

This constant processing and editing of film during the year will ensure that photographers become more competent and will help organize the photographic process so photographers don't have unrealistic amounts of work to do just at deadline time. It also ensures that good quality prints can be produced when photographers have ample time to improve print quality.

For the yearbook staff, this collection of edited prints shot during the year and stored in clear files should be used when designing layouts. Taking out the possible pictures and choosing the best ones will provide the strongest edit for the yearbook spreads. The editing should be a collaborative process by both designers and photographers or the photo editor. When choosing pictures for spreads, designers should make sure each picture is chosen because it contributes different information to the spread, shows different action and people and offers different sizes and shapes of images to use in the layout.

For staffs using digital cameras or scanning negatives or prints, photo editors should make sure photographers are trained to complete the digital work. A consistent, clear and easily understood method of filing the images for the layouts should be used. Consistent scanning will make a big difference in overall picture quality. Photographers should use picture-editing software to complete basic picture alterations such as burning, dodging and cropping. Backing up computer files is always a good idea, especially during deadline time. Also, original images should be carefully stored for retrieval in case images are lost or missing in the computer files or layouts. An organized system of storage and retrieval will prove invaluable in meeting deadlines and in maintaining historical files for future use. It will also ensure that negatives are properly taken care of and easy to find.

ABUSE OF IMAGES

Because photographs are so important in the design process, designers should be careful not to abuse them in their layouts. Following are some of the abusive design decisions that can weaken the impact of photographs.

- *Creating cutout shapes.* Removing the background of the photo in image alteration programs is quite quick and easy (Fig. 20.17). However, unless the picture was shot in a photo studio or planned as a cutout, re-

moving the background by cutting it out can result in a loss of contextual information that distorts meaning. Cutout shapes are visually active and need to be grounded in design by being placed next to lines or borders or by creating a soft shadow of the image to appear with it.

- *Creating cookie-cutter shapes.* Applying shapes such as circles, triangles or ovals on pictures compromises their content in the same way as cutting out the images. Contextual information is removed or cropped. Readers have a hard time understanding the meaning of incomplete information. Pictures designed to be placed in shapes should be carefully shot by photographers in studios where the backgrounds can be controlled.

- *Mortising pictures.* Placing pictures so they overlap or touch each other can also compromise content. If the pictures have areas of dead space where they can overlap, it's generally a good indication that they need tighter cropping. Overlapping the images also creates connections between pictures where there may be no real connection.

- *Duotoning images.* Duotoned images are those in which a single color has been applied to a black-and-white image. Duotones are often effective. For instance, duotoning black-and-white images with brown ink will give them the effect of sepia-toned prints, a classic brown-toned bath applied to pictures to give them the look of antiquity. However, using garish or inappropriately bright colors on images of people will make the pictures distracting. Rather than viewing the content, viewers will try to find meaning in the colors.

- *Tilting photos.* Photos turned so they are slightly off a straight horizontal baseline will result in pictures that seem slightly playful and off-kilter. Tilting should only be applied if it's appropriate to the content of the image. A tilt of less than 12 degrees will also maintain stronger readability for the image.

- *Creating photo patterns.* A recent trend in using pictures is positioning them in patterns with similar-sized shapes and with the images touching or separated only by thin hairline rules. A pattern needs visual contrast in tones and in content or it will be viewed as one large, continuous image.

- *Creating collages.* Blurring images together through

image manipulation software can be effective if it is done for a specific purpose and its use is limited.

- *Creating postage stamp–sized images.* Especially trendy in year-book design, the use of multiple images in small sizes needs careful attention. Pictures need to be carefully cropped and edited to make sure they will still be "readable" in such small sizes. Maintaining quality in multiple images may be difficult for some staffs.

- *Flipping or flopping images.* When photographers print pictures in the darkroom, they place the negative in the enlarger so it will reproduce as it was seen in the camera. Designers sometimes create layouts in which the "eyeflow" in the picture might be facing off a page, leading the reader off the page with the eyeflow. In these cases, designers sometimes resort to flipping the image, by having the photographer or printer reverse the image's eyeflow. Doing so is considered ethically dishonest.

  If writing or numbers appear in the picture, they will be backward, immediately alerting the viewer to the picture's changed orientation. Even without numbers or words, people in the pictures will be aware of a change in details, such as a part in their hair or jewelry or watches appearing on the wrong arm or hand. Rather than flipping images, designers should work to arrange pictures so the eyeflow faces naturally toward the gutter. This is another reason for a need in flexibility when drawing dummies or layouts, particularly if it's done before the pictures have been taken and edited.

- *Creating visual clichés.* A good photographer avoids visual clichés, pictures that are common and often overused. In sports, clichés result when photographers shoot predictable images. For instance, in basketball the cliché shot is the one of the player shooting the ball in the basket. Because high school photographers rarely have the restrictions on shooting positions that college and professional sports enforce, they should move around the court and field when shooting. Moving out of the end zone when shooting basketball will enable photographers to try different shots such as defensive moves rather than always shooting the offensive action.

  Taking pictures of teachers standing at the blackboard or administrators talking on the phone results in clichés that are often posed because the person being shot thinks the photographer wants the photograph to appear that way.

- *Creating highly stylized images.* Particularly on yearbook staffs, designers draw layouts before the pictures have been taken. Planning for a highly stylized form of picture use, such as over-lapping large image areas, extreme shapes or sizes or other stylized devices, can create compromises in image quality and

Code of Ethics, National Press Photographers Association

The National Press Photographers Association, a professional society dedicated to the advancement of photojournalism, acknowledges concern and respect for the public's natural-law right to freedom in searching for the truth and the right to be informed truthfully and completely about public events and the world in which we live.

We believe that no report can be complete if it is not possible to enhance and clarify the meaning of words. We believe that pictures, whether used to depict news events as they actually happen, illustrate news that has happened or to help explain anything of public interest, are an indispensable means of keeping people accurately informed; that they help all people, young and old, to better understand any subject in the public domain.

Believing the foregoing, we recognize and acknowledge that photojournalists should at all times maintain the highest standards of ethical conduct in serving the public interest. To that end, the National Press Photographers Association sets forth the following Code of Ethics, which is subscribed to by all of its members:

1. The practice of photojournalism, both as a science and art, is worthy of the very best thought and effort of those who enter into it as a profession.

2. Photojournalism affords an opportunity to serve the public that is equaled by few other vocations, and all members of the profession should strive by example and influence to maintain high standards of ethical conduct free of mercenary considerations of any kind.

3. It is the individual responsibility of every photojournalist at all times to strive for pictures that report truthfully, honestly and objectively.

4. As journalists, we believe that credibility is our greatest asset. In documentary photojournalism, it is wrong to alter the

Football players brave scorching heat for the chance to play.

Making the Cut

by Evan Parker

It's 110 DEGREES OUTSIDE at Pacific University in Stockton, California. Here, the San Francisco Forty-niners are running drills. It's summer training, tryouts, hell month, whatever you want to call it.

The players use every bit of energy to show the coaches that they can play good football, that they can play Forty-niners football. Some players want to play for the Forty-niners so badly that they run themselves into the ground. Some players get so dehydrated that they are on IVs in between plays; some just give up and go home. Some run 'til they puke, and a few 'til they end up in the hospital.

Defensive Linebacker Curtis Easson says, "People only see the stuff on Sunday, the games. What they don't know is how hard we work outside of the games. Sometimes we can work 12 hour days during the week. You have to work extremely hard to get to this point, but it is worth it."

"...The level of competition in sports is so high today that it seems like nothing less than perfect performance is acceptable..."

At the end of the day, the Forty-niners sit in their air-conditioned dorm rooms, but they can't move; they can't even think. They don't want to think because the only thing on their mind is the heat, the running, the sweating, and tomorrow's practice. They want to go home to their pools, their margarita machines, and their toddlers.

Some players go home with serious injuries. Some ailments are due to hot weather and some result from athletes pushing beyond what their bodies can handle to play pro football.

But these injuries aren't just limited to professional sports; this August two high school football players in the Midwest died from the heat at their training camp. For what? "Even though it is really hot, I love playing the game so much that it doesn't bother me. I am willing to take that risk to play this game," said Harvard-Westlake football player Andrew Beckett, who has been practicing in temperatures in the 100's.

In the past few years, we have lost many young athletes to drugs, ailments, injuries, and now the weather. But in order to keep sports exciting, the athletes have to be so much better, faster, and stronger than the average human. The level of athleticism and competition in sports is so high today that it seems like nothing less than perfect performance is acceptable.

To succeed at any level, athletes have to pay a price. That price can be paid by giving up their afternoons for practice or by putting on pads and gear and running around under the blazing sun. Some pay the price with hard work and dedication, and sadly, some end up paying the price with their lives. The irony is, without that kind of dedication and desire, sports wouldn't be half as exciting.

Fig. 20.18. This photo illustration, electronically manipulated to make it look like the football player is on fire, works well with the story about what it takes to be a professional athlete. The photo credit indicates that the picture is a collage rather than an actual image. *Crossfire, Crossroads School, Santa Monica, Calif.*

content of a photograph in any way (electronically or in the darkroom) that deceives the public. We believe the guidelines for fair and accurate reporting should be the criteria for judging what may be done electronically to a photograph.

5. Business promotion in its many forms is essential, but untrue statements of any nature are not worthy of a professional photojournalist and we severely condemn any such practice.

6. It is our duty to encourage and assist all members of our profession, individually and collectively, so that the quality of photojournalism may constantly be raised to higher standards.

7. It is the duty of every photojournalist to work to preserve all freedom-of-the-press rights recognized by law and to work to protect and expand freedom of access to all sources of news and visual information.

8. Our standards of business dealings, ambitions and relations shall have in them a note of sympathy for our common humanity and shall always require us to take into consideration our highest duties as members of society. In every situation in our business life, in every responsibility that comes before us, our chief thought shall be to fulfill that responsibility and discharge that duty so that, when each of us is finished, we shall have endeavored to lift the level of human ideals and achievement higher than we found it.

9. No Code of Ethics can prejudge every situation; thus common sense and good judgment are required in applying ethical principles.

Statement on manipulation of photographs:

As journalists we believe the guiding principle of our profession is accuracy; therefore, we believe it is wrong to alter the content of a photograph in any way that deceives the public.

As photojournalists, we have the responsibility to document society and to preserve its images as a matter of historical record. It is clear that the emerging electronic technologies provide new challenges to the integrity of photographic images. This technology enables the manipulation of the content of an image in such a way that the change is virtually undetectable. In light of this, we, the National Press Photographers Association, reaffirm the basis of our ethics: Accurate representation is the benchmark of our profession.

We believe photojournalistic guidelines for fair and accurate reporting should be the criteria for judging what may be done electronically to a photograph. Altering the editorial content of a photograph, in any degree, is a breach of the ethical standards recognized by the NPPA.

Fig. 20.19. Taking advantage of artistically talented students in the school, publications' staffs can add to their visual variety by occasionally using good artwork. This story's focus on Cuban leader Che Guevara features an excellent color drawing of the leader that adds visual appeal to this story. When it isn't possible to get photographs with content, art is always a good alternative. *Lowell,* Lowell High School, San Francisco, Calif.

Visual Storytelling

Decide on a visual strategy:

• *Photographic.* Use photo(s) large and dominant if photo(s) is good and would attract the reader's attention; ask the question: What photos would help tell the story? Avoid set-up, posed or clichéd shots.

• *Illustrative.* Use if the story lends itself to illustration rather than photographic treatment; keep in mind that

illustrations should be really strong visually and dominant in size. Give your text to an artist so the artist can connect visually with the words in the story.

• *Typographic.* If you don't have strong photographic or illustrative material to choose from, consider using a typographic treatment, including large primary heads with detail-oriented deck heads; varied headline positions; typography that matches the mood or tone of the story; emphasis type; large initial caps; and other type-as-illustration techniques.

Decide on a verbal strategy:

• *Factoids/summary boxes.* Use if the story contains policy changes or suggests a strategic approach. Can also use to summarize the major points made by speakers. Consider small bullets to draw in the reader's eye.

• *Profile box.* Is the story primarily about an individual or a group? If so, consider a profile box with relevant information headers in bold type. Set the profile in a typeface contrasting in weight and stroke to the primary story.

• *Harper's Index/Q&A.* Use if the story is full of facts and figures that could use simplification. Also use for elections.

• *Timelines.* Use for stories that are sequential in organization of information, that trace historical significance or that show change over a period of time.

• *Sidebars.* Use if there is an angle or dimension to the story that is particularly interesting or could use more detail. Sidebars can be written in first person to amplify a particular detail of the main story.

• *Infographics/locator maps.* Use if the story has a complex set of numerical sequencing or data that can be better understood through visual presentation. An infographic should be based on visual icons. Avoid straight pie charts and encyclopedic charts. Look to *USA Today, Time, Newsweek* and other popular publications for interesting ways to clarify information through visual means.

• *Story or paragraph captions with a picture package.* Telling part of the story through a package of two or more pictures that show different aspects of the story can be valuable. Make sure the captions add to the presentation by adding information through a few sentences or a couple of graphs of information.

• Always possible:

Callouts. Callouts are pull quotes in which interesting, relevant or colorful quotes or information is displayed in a point size larger than the body text but smaller than the headline text (preferably about 14 to 18 points), with a distinctive design strategy that the reader recognizes. If the person is particularly colorful, or the story controversial, consider a box of quoted material. This can also be used as a pro/con box to present conflicting viewpoints.

Logos. Develop a visual strategy based upon icons that immediately relate to a story, lend it a graphic strategy and visually tie together a series of stories, particularly over a course of time or in different parts of the newspaper.

Text Heads. Break up the story by inserting subheads at natural junctures in the story to help create reader "eyeflow."

Always keep in mind:

• Combining two or more of these forms may help the reader understand the story more clearly. If so, determine which are appropriate and avoid duplication of information.

• To avoid reader confusion, make sure information presented in alternative story forms looks different from the main story. Consider using a sans serif font if the story is in a serif font. Consider using a different weight of text if fonts are limited. Consider varying the line widths of alternative copy. All of these techniques will help indicate to the reader that the information is separate from the primary story.

• Make sure your visual/verbal forms are helping the reader clarify and process the information being presented. Keep your reader in mind at all times. Don't add visual/verbal forms unless they do clarify information.

• Make sure the visual/verbal storytelling forms are helping to attract the reader to the story. Remember that offering the reader a variety of visual/verbal forms may cause the reader to enter the story in a different way. Make sure the reader is getting valuable information regardless of whether he or she enters the story through the main story.

• Remember your time frame. What can realistically be produced in the amount of

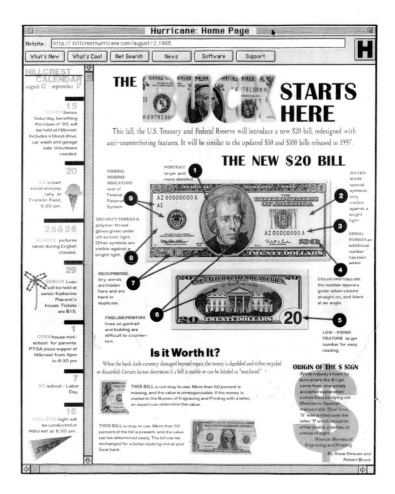

Fig. 20.20. Instead of a traditional prose story on the new design of the $20 bill, the staff of the *Hillcrest Hurricane* created an information graphic in which it presented information in a visual, rather than a verbal, way. Note the numbered pullout points illustrating new features of the bill. The bottom of the information graphic adds two additional pieces of information to the reader's understanding of the topic. *Hillcrest Hurricane,* Hillcrest High School, Dallas, Texas

time you have before publication? Consider your resources. Do you have someone with the ability to produce complicated or stylistic art? Do you have time to work with a photographer to produce top quality photographs that add to the reader's understanding of the story?

• Keep the writer's angles, situations or focus in mind at all times. Connecting visuals with verbals reinforces the story and makes it more vivid for the reader. Make sure every person working with the story understands where the story is going. If it changes, or if team members discover new or interesting angles along the way, rethink the visual/verbal. Add to or adjust as necessary. Don't repeat information.

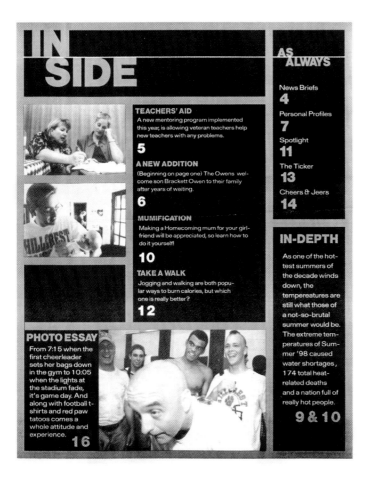

Fig. 20.21. In this newspaper's contents listing, shades of gray and black are effectively used to separate content areas for the reader. Reverse type and gray type in appropriate sizes provide good contrast. The leading and point size of the type lead to readability even though the type is used in non-traditional color. Screens of black are perceived as color tones by readers. *Hillcrest Hurricane,* Hillcrest High School, Dallas, Texas

content. Designers intent on creating such styles should consult carefully with photographers and photo editors to see if these styles will be possible and to make sure the photographers are looking for images that will accommodate the designers' needs, if possible.

IMAGE ALTERATION

With the growth in image-altering software programs, it is now easier than ever to manipulate images by combining parts of them, by moving objects around in the images or by editing out parts of the images and replacing them with other images. To do so may be unethical and could cause legal problems for the staff.

Photographers must protect the truth and accuracy of their images, just as writers must check the accuracy of their reporting. In news and feature pictures, readers expect the content to be accurately represented. Altering news and feature images should not be allowed in a publication. Allowances are made for alterations that could be made in a traditional darkroom: burning, dodging, adjusting contrast and cropping.

However, in the last few years, artistic uses of altered images have been extensively used for illustrative purposes. As long as the photographer is altering only his or her own images, and not combining them with others without permission, these illustrative uses of photo manipulation could be considered like any other illustration. They should be labeled as photo illustrations or photo enhancements, rather than with traditional photo credits, to help the reader understand that they are illustrative, not accurate portrayals of news or feature events (Fig. 20.18).

Not all readers will understand the differences between the labeling of pictures as traditional photo credits or as photo illustrations and photo enhancements. It is important for students to understand the need to protect the readers' belief that what they see in a picture really happened.

The National Press Photographers Association, the association to which most professional photojournalists belong, adopted a code of ethics when image manipulation software problems were emerging in the professional world. This code of ethics is one that student photojournalists should seek to understand and use. (See related sidebar.)

ART AND ILLUSTRATIONS

In addition to pictures, illustrations can be effective visuals in publications. Illustrations should be used when designers are seeking to show something different from what a photograph will show or when a photograph is inappropriate or impossible to get. Using a variety of illustrative forms will also provide reader surprise and keep the visual content fresh and interesting. Illustrations in a range of styles—from cartoons to artistic renderings—can effectively coordinate with story content (Fig. 20.19).

Illustrations don't have to be created solely by staff members. Just as professional publications do, staffs can seek outside artists of different talents and styles to add dimension to visual presentations. Allowing the illustrator to read the story or text will result in illustrations that tell stronger visual stories. Combined with strong headline presentations, these illustrations can be refreshing and fun.

Illustrative style possibilities are endless. Creative photographers with access to studio lighting and supplies can create interesting photo illustrations. Collages, three-dimensional art, watercolors, pen and ink drawings, caricatures—all could effectively showcase verbal content. Communicating needs with art teachers and outstanding art students with interesting styles will provide other opportunities for visual presentation.

Good artwork should be detailed and provide dimension. Single-dimension artwork is often flat and uninteresting. Artists should make sure to be inclusive in representing school populations.

INFORMATION GRAPHICS

An additional form of visual presentation is information graphics, information presented in visual ways. Information graphics utilize visuals as ways of breaking down complex information and making it understandable to readers. Information graphics can appear in a variety of forms, including pie charts, graphs, bar charts, locator maps, diagrams and sequence maps (Fig. 20.20). Good information graphics can be designed with the help of statistical charting software programs for better accuracy in representing the information. Sources of information used in the graphics should be provided to help the reader understand the accuracy of the information presented. Or, if using the results of a student poll, the size of the sample providing the information should be presented at the end of the information graphic.

Information graphics should be used to help readers process and understand complex information, especially numbers, trends and statistics. They can also help readers understand how something happens or where it happened and who the key players were.

Staff artists are logical resources for information graphics, or if the school offers a class in computer graphics, students can be recruited to help create information graphics.

Accuracy is crucial in presenting information visually just as it is in presenting information verbally. Numbers, representations of numbers and comparisons should be checked for understandability, accuracy and clarity.

OTHER GRAPHIC FORMS

In addition to creating visual interest through photographs and illustrations, designers have other graphic tools to create visual interest. These include the use of rule lines, boxes, screens of color, isolation elements and text display elements.

Rule lines can be used singly or in several variations of widths combined together. Rule lines can separate, connect, frame or box content. Rule lines are sometimes used to create visual connections between separate pages when they are designed as a single visual unit.

Designers can use screens, shades of solid color, to isolate and separate content, to connect visual elements and to bring the reader's eyes to a particular area of the page (Fig. 20.21).

Isolation elements, primarily created through increased white space, can isolate and separate visual from verbal or move the reader's eyes from one page area to another.

Designers have a wealth of text display choices for creating interesting graphic areas on pages. Headline designs, arranged as strong visual units on the page, can utilize size and shade changes as well as changes in typography to create interesting displays. (See Chaps. 14 and 15.)

The use of drop caps, large initial letters beginning paragraphs, or text heads throughout the story will add contrast and break up large passages of gray text. Pull quotes can be lifted from the text and placed in display-size type to draw interest to the text. Designers can use other devices such as white space between story transitions or between natural junctures in the story to vary the density of the text.

Graphics work best when they work somewhat invisibly. Overdone graphics that draw attention to the graphics and distract the reader from the overall page content should be avoided. The ultimate goal of good visual communications is to contribute to the story-telling process.

EXERCISES

1. Using magazines or newspapers, cut out examples of photographs that exhibit these rules of composition: impact, center of interest, shallow depth of field, rule of thirds, interesting lighting, action and emotion. Label each photograph and tell what its compositional appeals are.

2. Develop a set of parameters for the quality of images that should be used in a publication. Consider these factors: Will or should the staff use pictures that are out of focus; that show the backs or tops or people's heads; that are scratched or marred by poor practices; that are of the same people; that are flipped or flopped; that are of staff members' friends? Justify your reason for each decision.

3. Using a supply of old pictures from the yearbook or newspaper staff, find a picture that would be a good stand-alone shot. Design a style for how the picture could be used in the newspaper. Write a catchline and caption for the picture.

4. Using the yearbook's cropping method or the newspaper's cropping wheel, practice cropping pictures to improve their content.

5. Import a picture into a layout on a school computer using the publication's layout program and scanning equipment. Practice cropping the picture electronically.

6. Cut out five examples of information graphics from professional publications. Find examples of a pie chart, a bar chart, a diagram, a locator map and a chart. Examine the content and determine whether the forms have been used effectively.

7. Find examples of these abusive picture techniques: a cutout image, an image cut into a cookie-cutter shape, a mortice, a photo pattern, a photo cliché and a collage. Paste each example to a sheet of paper and write an explanation of how each was used in print. Was it effective in its presentation?

8. Using these five topics visualize picture stories that could be developed for each of the topics: the prom, graduation, homecoming, a field trip and a debate tournament. Make lists of possible pictures that could be taken and indicate what kind of lens might be appropriate for each picture. Go through your list and add compositional qualities that would improve the pictures.

9. Using a point and shoot camera or a single-use camera, take a roll of pictures of students participating in an activity or event at your school. Have your film processed and edit your pictures to two. Write captions for each of the images and design a picture package using the two images.

10. Cut out five different pages from professional publications in which artwork or illustrations have been used instead of pictures. Paste each to a sheet of paper and explain its effectiveness in visualizing the story it illustrates. Underline passages in the story that relate directly to elements of the art or illustration. Explain how it utilizes detail and color. What style is used in the art?

11. Cut out examples of layouts that have rule lines; color used to separate and isolate content; headline units using color, contrast or visual detail; white space used for visual or verbal separation; and pull quotes and text heads in a story. Paste each example to a sheet of paper and label each with its graphic use. Evaluate the effectiveness of each graphic use.

Advertising in Newspapers and Yearbooks

It's a favorite American teen pastime—spending money—someone's, anyone's.

There's Heidi, who just *had* to spend her $320 check from flipping burgers at the Dairy Mart. Then there's Ryan, who would whine until his mother bought "the right brand" of cereal. Teens are spending more money today than ever before. Teenage Research Unlimited Inc. found that teens represented a buying power of $141 billion in 1998. The increase in teen buying power in the late 1990s makes student publications a viable advertising medium for businesses.

Look around and take notice of all the ways businesses focus their advertising on teens. Soft drink companies vie for exclusive school vending contracts. Broadcasting companies provide televisions in exchange for showing advertising along with newscasts in classrooms. Companies buy advertising space on school buses. School newspapers and yearbooks offer advertisers a direct link to America's 30 million–plus teenagers.

The communication link creates a beneficial relationship for everyone involved. The four major roles advertising plays for publications, businesses and readers are

1. *To provide income for the publication.*

   Nearly all media—newspapers, magazines, Internet, radio and television—derive most of their income from advertising. School publications with little school funding find advertising a necessity. Even those publications with school district funding may find advertising a great way to raise money for buying additional computer or camera equipment.

2. *To perform a service for businesses.*

   Because the school newspaper and yearbook communicate with teens in a limited geographic area, businesses can reach a specific audience with focused messages about products and services. Clearly, as shown in the introduction, teens provide a market that businesses want to reach. With daily newspaper readership shrinking among teens, the school's newspapers, yearbooks and web sites are effective ways for businesses to reach a younger audience. Advertising can create brand or business name recognition, sell products or services or help hire employees.

3. *To perform a service for readers by making them aware of products and services.*

Students are always searching for new restaurants, weekend jobs or the latest sales on athletic shoes. Advertising can make students aware of all of these things. Advertising can help students earn money and then help them spend it wisely. Informing students about services such as an SAT prep class or a driving school will help meet student needs.

4. *To build a bond between the business community and the student body.*

Even though scholastic publication advertising is not a donation, ads in a high school newspaper or yearbook are still signs of local support. Building a bond and respect between the student body and businesses strengthens the sense of community. When a pharmacy buys a full-page yearbook ad, parents and students shop there, in part, to show their appreciation for the business's investment in the student endeavor. The community, as a whole, is stronger for such an exchange.

CREATING AN ADVERTISING PROGRAM

Advertising can be a vibrant, fun part of the scholastic journalism program. From the preparation stages to the sales visits to the design and placement, each stage of creating an advertisement is creative and interactive. The many possible career choices in the field of advertising are explored in Chapter 24.

PREPARATION

An informed salesperson is a successful salesperson. The advertising salesperson must fully understand information about the school, the publication and the business. The advertising director should collect and organize such information to arm and train advertising salespeople so they can bring the three together.

One of the first steps is understanding the market or, in this case, the student audience. The best salesperson knows who makes up the audience, their buying power and their habits. Students spend large amounts of money. Sometimes it's their money. Sometimes it's their parents' money. The TRU study found that teens spent $94 billion of their own funds and $47 billion of

their families' money. Conduct your own market survey, and you may be surprised by how much students spend, what they spend it on and where they spend it. Lakota East High School found that seniors spend an average of more than $130 a month. Multiply the individual spending profiles times the more than 1,500 students at Lakota East, and you will see that the *Spark* reaches an audience with sizable spending power.

A few questions you can include in your own student survey are

- How much do you have to spend in one week?

- How much do you spend for clothes each school year?

- In what stores do you buy these clothes?

- What do you do for entertainment each week?

- How much do you spend on this entertainment each week? How much for movies? Concerts? Video games? Videos? Other activities?

- How much do you spend per week on food? Outside the school cafeteria, where do you buy this food?

- How much do you spend on school supplies each week? Where do you buy them?

- How much do you spend on transportation? Do you own a car?

- Which stores do you buy from the most? Why?

- Which stores do you buy from the least? Why?

Keep the survey short to encourage students to complete the form. A one-page questionnaire with ranges of answers to circle may help. In addition to knowing the buying power and habits of the readers, a good salesperson needs to know how many people are in the school and where they are from.

The advertising staff should take all this information and incorporate it into a set of professional-looking sales aids. The sales aids can include a rate card, a flyer and sales charts or graphs.

Although it can be many sizes or shapes, the rate card, typically, is a small brochure containing all the basic information about advertising in the publication, the publication itself and the market. The rate card should be a well-designed brochure that answers most of the advertiser's questions (Fig. 21.1).

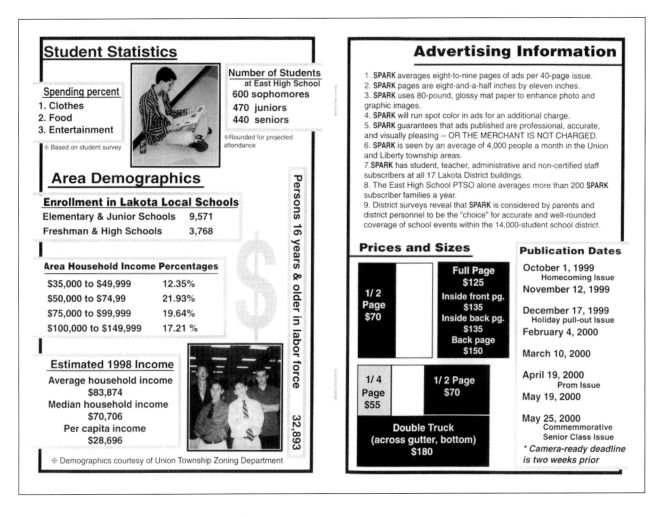

Student Statistics

Spending percent
1. Clothes
2. Food
3. Entertainment

✢ Based on student survey

Number of Students
at East High School
600 sophomores
470 juniors
440 seniors

✲Rounded for projected attendance

Area Demographics

Enrollment in Lakota Local Schools

Elementary & Junior Schools   9,571
Freshman & High Schools   3,768

Area Household Income Percentages

$35,000 to $49,999   12.35%
$50,000 to $74,99   21.93%
$75,000 to $99,999   19.64%
$100,000 to $149,999   17.21 %

Estimated 1998 Income
Average household income
$83,874
Median household income
$70,706
Per capita income
$28,696

✢ Demographics courtesy of Union Township Zoning Department

Persons 16 years & older in labor force   32,893

Advertising Information

1. **SPARK** averages eight-to-nine pages of ads per 40-page issue.
2. **SPARK** pages are eight-and-a-half inches by eleven inches.
3. **SPARK** uses 80-pound, glossy mat paper to enhance photo and graphic images.
4. **SPARK** will run spot color in ads for an additional charge.
5. **SPARK** guarantees that ads published are professional, accurate, and visually pleasing -- OR THE MERCHANT IS NOT CHARGED.
6. **SPARK** is seen by an average of 4,000 people a month in the Union and Liberty township areas.
7. **SPARK** has student, teacher, administrative and non-certified staff subscribers at all 17 Lakota District buildings.
8. The East High School PTSO alone averages more than 200 **SPARK** subscriber families a year.
9. District surveys reveal that **SPARK** is considered by parents and district personnel to be the "choice" for accurate and well-rounded coverage of school events within the 14,000-student school district.

Prices and Sizes

1/2 Page $70

Full Page $125
Inside front pg. $135
Inside back pg. $135
Back page $150

1/4 Page $55

1/2 Page $70

Double Truck (across gutter, bottom) $180

Publication Dates

October 1, 1999
Homecoming Issue
November 12, 1999

December 17, 1999
Holiday pull-out Issue
February 4, 2000

March 10, 2000

April 19, 2000
Prom Issue
May 19, 2000

May 25, 2000
Commemmorative
Senior Class Issue
* Camera-ready deadline
is two weeks prior

The card could include some of the following information:

- Publication dates

- Deadline dates for space reservation and copy

- Basic publication information such as address, phone number, fax number and e-mail address

- Reasons to buy an ad in the publication

- Readership information, such as number of readers, buying power and habits

- Policies on what ads you will and won't accept

- Billing and payment policies, such as discounts, acceptance of checks and billing dates

- Design information, such as a requirement that logos must be on a white background

- Additional costs, such as charging for taking photographs for the ad

Fig. 21.1. Rate card. *Spark,* Lakota East High School, Liberty Township, Ohio

CARMEL HIGH SCHOOL HILITE AD SALES STAFF	Art Bortolini · 506-1030 · abortolini@hilite.org
	Jon Campbell · 575-9276 · jcampbell@hilite.org
	Stacie Feldwisch · 848-2821 · sfeldwisch@hiite.org
	Nichole Freije · 848-1789 · nfreije@hilite.org
520 East Main Street Carmel, Indiana 46032-2299	Chase Graverson · 844-3240 · cgraverson@hilite.org
	Dave Hoffman · 843-1980 · dhoffman@hilite.org
(317) 846-7721, Ext. 1143 Fax: (317) 571-4066	Quinn Shepherd · 844-2408 · qshepherd@hilite.org
	Jon Titus · 571-9744 · jtitus@hilite.org
Web: www.hilite.org	Jake Wilson · 844-5437 · jwilson@hilite.org

Fig. 21.2. Advertising staff business card. *HiLite,* Carmel High School, Carmel, Ind.

Don't overwhelm the advertiser with information. Make the rate card easy to read and use.

The sales graphs and charts can be as varied as the publication's sales needs. For example, compare the percentage of students who read your publication with the percentage who read the closest major daily. Display all the tuxedo rental businesses that have advertised in your publication as a way to encourage other formal wear businesses to do the same. List the dates of upcoming dances and special events along with survey information about the amount of money students spend getting ready for the big occasions. These flyers can be quick reference material for a salesperson.

Every salesperson should also be armed with staff business cards and contracts. The Carmel High School *HiLite* staff is able to get all of the advertising staff on one card (Fig. 21.2).

A professional packet of material, typically uniform in design, serves several purposes. The packet gives the salesperson something to work from during a sales call. If the businessperson is busy or uninterested, the salesperson can leave the packet for later reference. The business owner may come back to the packet and will have the prices and phone number handy when he's ready to call and purchase an ad. In any case, a professional packet can help refute what has been the age-old adult opinion that all teens are lazy or unprofessional.

The salesperson may also have billing forms, proofing forms and an assortment of sales and thank you let-

ters (Fig. 21.3). The additional forms can help establish a trust and bond between the business and the salesperson, increasing the likelihood that the business owner will buy again.

PUBLICATION KNOWLEDGE

A good salesperson should not have to refer to the packet for basic information such as advertising rates and deadline dates. The numbers should be as familiar to the salesperson as his or her birthdate. The salesperson needs to know the number of subscribers to the newspaper or the number of yearbooks sold, the number of students in each class (freshman to senior) and the percentage of boys and girls.

A basic understanding of the publication can dispel the myth that you are some kid out begging for money and enhance your image as a professional.

ADVERTISING POLICY

A written advertising policy will help salespeople deal with questions that arise.

The policy may deal with ad sales for political campaigns, health centers where pregnancy tests or abortions are performed or businesses that get a majority of their income from liquor sales. In one case, a pizza place that students frequent has a logo with the words "Friends of wine and beer." Does your policy prohibit the running of the ad? Do you ask for a different logo? Ask to crop that portion out?

Does the ad have to sell a product or service? What happens if a person buying space in the newspaper of a high school with a large Jewish population wants to run an ad claiming the Holocaust never happened? Do you accept congratulations ads? Do you accept political ads?

What about sex-related advertising? Does your yearbook run an ad for a store that sells condoms? Do you advertise R-rated movies? What about a tanning salon ad with a photo of a woman in a revealing swimsuit?

The advertising policy may also deal with minimum advertising sizes. Often a 1 × 1-inch or a 1 × 2-inch ad is not large enough to adequately advertise a product or service.

Some schools also have policies on what can be included in senior yearbook ads. Senior wills-type messages with inside jokes are a libel and ethics concern for some publications.

BUSINESS KNOWLEDGE

The salesperson must observe and understand the business he or she is trying to sell an ad to. Know that a sporting goods store has new school team T-shirts to sell. Know that students are into buying crushed fruit drinks. Information such as what products or services students buy from the area clothing stores, movie theaters and video stores will make you a valuable ally for the business owner.

Discover answers to questions about each business:

- Who is the store manager?

- Who is the person who handles the business's advertising?

- What products or services does this business have of interest to your readers?

- What medium does the owner prefer advertising in? What sizes of ads does this business buy regularly? What is the business trying the hardest to sell?

- What upcoming events are there that the business would be interested in advertising for?

PUTTING THE SALESPERSON AT EASE

Knowing who to talk to and what to talk to them about will put the advertising salesperson at ease.

Taking all this information and combining it into a smooth sales approach can still be difficult. Practice helps. Organize an ad meeting in the summer. Invite a professional salesperson to discuss tips for selling ads. Role-play typical ad sales calls to practice the approach. The more times a person talks through a sales approach the more at ease he or she will feel.

The role-playing should be realistic. More experienced salespeople will know the scenarios that you may face in the sales call. Some examples are

- The business owner who doesn't have time

- The owner who doesn't advertise in high school publications

CARMEL HIGH SCHOOL FAX COVER SHEET

520 East Main Street • Carmel, Indiana 46032-2299
Phone (317) 846-7721, Extension 1143 • Fax (317) 571-4066
Jake Wilson, HiLite advertising manager • jwilson@hilite.org or hilite@ccs.k12.in.us

Page 1 of _____-page fax to 571-4066

To: **Jake Wilson** (c/o Tony Willis)
Carmel High School HiLite

Fr: _____(name)

_____(business advertised)

Re: Ad proof response

Da: _____

I have reviewed my ad which will run in the _____ issue of the Carmel High School student newspaper, the HiLite and I am returning it with this cover sheet as follows:

❑   It has no corrections or changes and may be printed as is.

❑   I have described below any changes, deletions or additions that need to be made:

_____

_____

_____

_____

❑   On the ad that accompanies this cover sheet, I have clearly marked changes, deletions or additions that need to be made.

Signature: _____

I wish to receive a second proof after these corrections are made: ❑ YES   ❑ NO

THANK YOU FOR YOUR ASSISTANCE. WE APPRECIATE YOUR BUSINESS.

Fig. 21.3. Proofing form. *HiLite*, Carmel High School, Carmel, Ind.

Ad Script -- A typical day on the job

*(The setting is Papa John's Pizza. Phil is a **SPARK** ad salesman. His job is to make money. This could be the middle, end or beginning of the year. Regardless, Phil does not return without a filled out ad contract for fear of bodily harm from the hands of Amy Silver or Catherine Matacic. The time is 4 p.m. The salesman is dressed professionally. He is calm, cool, and collected. He has some background on the business: their competitors, previous advertisements with SPARK, their competitors advertisements in SPARK, and their prime target audience. Phil is just being himself and flashing them a handsome smile. Advertisers like to be secure with and trust the people they send their checks to. That trust and security hinges on the moment he walks in their store. Phil must make a good first impression.)*

Phil: Hi! May I speak with the manager?

Papa John's Delivery Boy: He isn't in right now.

Phil: Well, may I speak with the assistant manager?

Papa John's Delivery Boy: Hold on one second. *(Delivery boy goes and fetches the assistant manager, who is on the telephone. Phil has to wait a couple of minutes. John Deluca approaches the counter.)*

John: Hi! How may I help you?

Phil: My name is Phil Tork, and I'm from Lakota East High School's nationally acclaimed student newsmagazine **SPARK**. I've come here to tell you about a great opportunity your company has been missing out on. That opportunity is the local teenage, pizza hungry market. The easiest way to hit them and their parents is through their school. **SPARK** distributes to over 1,000 students, parents, teachers, and community members. We are one of the largest high school publications in the state and have been in operation for over five years. We would like you to consider advertising with our paper. Here is a copy of our ad information, publication dates, ad sizes and also a placement sheet. We do inserts and would gladly print out coupons with your ad. Coupons are a really good idea because those indicate to you whether the ad is working and whether you are satisfied with the job we are doing. Here is a list of other companies in the area who have advertised with us. I'm pretty sure Pizza Hut and Dominoes are on the list. Our space fills up pretty quick. So are you interested?

John: Do I have to give you the money now? *(Looks unsure about what he is getting into.)*

Phil: You can but you don't have to. After each publication is distributed, we will send you a bill through the mail. If we make any mistakes on your ad, we will gladly give you a free ad in our next issue. If you buy more than one ad a year, we can easily change the ad to say something else, but you would need to send us the new information.

John: Okay. I'll purchase a quarter page for the October, December and May issues. *(Phil fills out the required spaces on the placement sheet, informs John of the total price and writes down the company's name, address, and telephone number.)*

Phil: We have the technology to do camera-ready ads. Do you have any material that you would like to see placed in the ad, such as your logo or coupons? *(John hands him what he wants on the ad.)* Would you like us to design the coupons for you?

John: Sure.

Phil: What would you like them to say? How about ... *(The lights and sound fade out on the scene. Phil has just received a lot of stringbook points toward his quarter grade and a lot of gratitude from the business department. And all it took was to become a salesman for a day.)*

NOTE: NOT ALL ASSISTANT MANAGERS OR MANAGERS ARE AUTHORIZED TO PURCHASE ADS. IF THEY CAN'T, ASK WHO TO TALK TO, OR WHEN THE OWNER WILL BE IN, THEN STOP BACK ON THAT DATE. DON'T GET FRUSTRATED IF YOU DON'T SUCCEED IN EVERY STORE YOU WALK INTO. JOANN TIEMANN TWO YEARS AGO WENT TO OVER 12 STORES IN ONE DAY AND ONLY TWO STORES BOUGHT ADS.

Fig. 21.4. Ad script. *Spark,* Lakota East High School, Liberty Township, Ohio

- The manager who uses the "I already donated money to the band" excuse

Then be creative. Will the owner question the image of your school? Will the owner be abrupt and angry because she had to fire an employee that morning? Will the owner agree to buy an ad only if you also pass out flyers for him? The more situations you face in role-playing, the more comfortable you'll be in dealing with situations as they arise in real sales calls.

Before going out to sell, salespeople should have a specific territory to cover. The territories can be organized regionally. A salesperson may feel more at ease if covering an area in his or her neighborhood with businesses he or she frequents. Establishing a rapport between the salesperson and the business is important in a successful sales call. Another way to learn the sales call is to go with a more experienced salesperson.

The Sales Call

There's one sure way to fail in a sales call. Walk into a business and mumble, "Do you want to buy an ad?" You'll get the easy response. "No." You do not need to fail. Give the business owner a reason to buy. A salesperson should know that because businesses differ, the reasons they would want to purchase ads vary. The salesperson must communicate the information that fits the needs of the particular customer and the special type of store. An advertiser convinced of the value of advertising in the school publication can be spoken to differently from one who is skeptical. A new business owner may need information about your school's location and size as well as the total buying power of your readers. A previous advertiser may need a reminder that prom is only four weeks away.

A salesperson may have made contact with the business owner before making the sales call. Some publication staffs call and make appointments to come by. If you are not comfortable with the business to begin with, a face-to-face call to set up an appointment may be better. While the visit could be time-consuming, considering many managers or business owners may not be in or available, making the appointment face-to-face will go further in establishing a rapport with the business owner. A long-time Dallas newspaper advertising salesperson said that the business owner must like you as much as the publication to want to buy an ad.

A salesperson armed with all the knowledge and sales aids mentioned earlier will be more at ease in the presentation. Remember that the salesperson is a skilled individual who helps the business owners communicate better with students through a school publication. As discussed in the opening, the creation and sale of advertising is a professional service.

Some considerations in making the sales call:

- Dress in appropriate clothing.

- Begin with a reason the business owner would want to advertise.

- Know all the reasons why a business owner should advertise in the school yearbook or newspaper.

- Try to determine all possible objections a business owner might raise and plan valid rebuttals.

- Remind advertisers that the most effective ads are not one-time propositions. A salesperson should emphasize that regular advertising builds an image in the minds of readers that brings product and store recognition. A store running an ad only once has a poor chance of leaving a lasting impression. After all, consider the number of McDonald's ads you've seen since you were born.

- Go armed with a predesigned ad for the business. The time you take to develop a concept and design an ad will show the business owner that you care about his or her business. Even if the sales call does not end in a sale, the salesperson has been successful in building the respect of the business owner.

- Keep notes to analyze the results of successful or unsuccessful sales presentations with businesses. A file on a business will help the salesperson keep up with the account. For example, too often a business owner may say, "I really want to advertise before prom." A good note taker will write down the owner's comment and return six weeks before prom.

- Understand that many chain businesses look to corporate offices to purchase advertising. Some publication salespeople have been successful by persistently calling corporate offices to make the sale. A publication can join certain agencies that sell advertising to corporations on behalf of a large group of school publications, primarily newspapers. In other cases, salespeople have encouraged local managers of

A

Fig. 21.5. (**A**) Ad designs often begin as quick, rough sketches. (**B**) To develop a quality design, brainstorm a lot of possibilities. Notice here how many different logo designs the agency developed for this lively Pizza Hut campaign. (**C**) After settling on a look, the ad designer can still make subtle changes to it. (**D–F**) The finished product is a varied display of media and conceptual development. Notice in **E** and **F** the clever play of the idea of a "personal" pizza. *Pizza Hut, the Pizza Hut logo and Personal Pan Pizza are trademarks of Pizza Hut, Inc., and are used with permission.*

chain businesses to use community relations funds to buy advertising for their products or services or for hiring purposes.

- Tactful persistence pays off. Most sales are made after at least five calls. Rapport and respect take time. Coming back to the business owner to show new designs or to see if he or she needs anything will often pay off eventually. Patience and persistence are key.

TELEPHONE SALES

In some schools where administrations are concerned with the liability of allowing students to leave campus to sell ads, a phone campaign may be a necessity. A good written phone script may help. However, the script should not sound as if it is being read. The sales tips above typically apply. A face-to-face meeting after school or on a weekend prior to a cold call is preferable and will help establish a rapport with the business owner. A telephone call may also suffice on a follow-up call when the salesperson has already made the sale and is trying to extend it for another issue.

CREATING AN ADVERTISEMENT

Research estimates in the late 1990s show people will see an average of more than 1,600 advertising images a day. Incredible, isn't it. Faced with advertising images on billboards, book covers, web sites and T-shirts, among many others, the reader will not give much notice to a business card thrown onto the page. The quality of the ad concept and design is critical.

Advertising must have a message that sells name recognition, connects a feeling to the product or informs the reader about benefits of the product or service. One ad sells the cool, go-all-out image of a brand athletic shoe. Another ad convinces a student that if he wants to impress his date, he'll buy roses from the

B

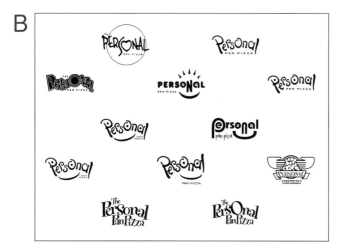

C

florist at the corner. A third ad sells the 15 percent discount on burger and fries students will get when they show their school ID at the neighborhood burger restaurant.

DEFINE THE MESSAGE

Often the advertiser knows what aspect of the business he or she wants to advertise. Whether the advertiser suggests some copy or the advertising salesperson develops the message, make sure the point is simple. The message can be as specific as "Rent your tux for homecoming from us" or as abstract as "the Pizza Shack sells fun." Both are simple, clear messages that must be visually and verbally communicated in an interesting way. The message should clearly define what makes the particular business advertising different from all other businesses of the same type.

In the book *Hey Whipple, Squeeze This: A Guide to Creating Great Ads*, Luke Sullivan explains what a good ad must accomplish:[1]

> It's as if you're riding down an elevator with your customer. You're going down only 15 floors. So you have only a few seconds to tell him one thing about your product. One thing. And you have to tell it to him in such an interesting way that he thinks about the promise you've made as he leaves the building, waits for the light, and crosses the street. You have to come up with some little thing that sticks in the customer's mind.

Sullivan provides a wealth of suggestions for delivering the message creatively through a print ad. Here are a few of his suggestions:

• Find the central truth about your whole product category. The central *human* truth. Hair coloring isn't about looking younger. It's about self-esteem. Cameras aren't about pictures. They're about stopping time and holding life as the sands run out.

---

1. *Hey Mr. Whipple, Squeeze This: A Guide to Creating Great Ads*, Luke Sullivan, Copyright © (1998 John Wiley & Sons, Inc., New York, N.Y.). Reprinted by permission of John Wiley & Sons, Inc.

D

E

F

Fig. 21.6. Advertisement. Drake University, Des Moines, Iowa

- Focus first on the substance of what you want to say. Remember styles change; typefaces and design and art directions, they all change. Fads come and go. But people are always people. They want to look better, to make more money; they want to feel better, to be healthy. They want security, attention and achievement.

- Ask yourself what would make you want to buy the product.

- Get to know your client's business as well as you can.

- First, say it straight. Then say it great. To get the words flowing, sometimes it helps to simply write out what you want to say. Make it memorable, different or new later. First just say it.

    Try this. Begin your headline with: "This is an ad about ..." And then keep writing.

    Whatever you do, just start writing.

- Remember notebook paper is not made solely for recording gems of transcendent perfection. A sheet of paper costs about one squillionth of a cent. It isn't a museum frame. It's a workbench. Write. Keep writing. Don't stop.

- Think of the strategy statement as a lump of clay. You've got to sculpt it into something interesting to look at. So begin by taking the strategy and saying it some other way, any way. Say it faster. Say it in English. Then in slang. Shorten it. Punch it up. Try anything that will change the strategy statement from something you'd overhear in an elevator at a sales convention to a message you'd see spray painted on an alley wall.

- Try writing down words from the product's category. You're selling outboard engines? Start a list on the side of the page: Fish, Water, Pelicans, Flotsam, Jetsam. Atlantic. Titanic. Ishmael.

What do these words make you think of? Pick up two of them and put them together like Tinkertoys. You have to start somewhere. Sure it sounds stupid. The whole creative process is stupid.

- Allow your partner to come up with terrible ideas; just say "that's interesting," scribble it down and move on.

- Don't look for what's wrong with a new idea; look for what's right.

- Stare at a picture that has the emotion of the ad you want to do.

- Cover the wall with ideas. Don't settle on the first passable idea that comes along.

- Quick sketches of your ideas are all you need during the creative process. Just put the concept on the paper and continue moving forward.

- Get it on paper quickly and furiously. Be hot. Let it pour out. Don't edit when you're coming up with ads.

    Then later, be ruthless. Cut everything that is not A-plus work.

THE STEPS IN CREATING THE ADVERTISEMENT

Taking the ideas from the brainstorming process to the computer screen is the next step. The design breaks down into four elements: illustration, headline, body copy and logo. Each of the elements should work together to communicate the clear message that was developed in the steps above. In Figure 21.6, the Drake University ad creates the simple idea of "make your mark at Drake." That mark visually is a fingerprint. Look closer to see that the mark Drake wants you to make is by writing a play, designing homes and helping find a cure for a disease. All the elements work together to deliver their message that Drake University will help you be somebody.

Fig. 21.7. Advertisement. *HiLite,* Carmel High School, Carmel, Ind.

The illustration, a photo or artwork, is usually the dominant feature of the ad. In the visual hierarchy, discussed in Chapter 15, the illustration is typically more prominent than the other elements. The advertising art director wants to demonstrate the product, service or business, the feeling or the benefit. People are visual. Good dominant visuals, placed in the optical center, grab the reader's attention. In Figure 21.7, good-looking flowers for homecoming is the important message. The illustration makes that message clear with a tightly cropped strong visual of tulips.

The headline is rarely used as the dominant visual element in an ad. However, the headline is still critical in whether the advertisement effectively communicates

Two Types of Advertising

Display Advertising

Display advertising is exactly what its name suggests—advertising that displays, through type and illustrations, the product or service a merchant wants to sell. Well-designed display ads have type appropriate to the product or service and effective illustrations and borders. Such ads help to make news pages attractive and direct readers' attention to the ads.

Classified Advertising

Classified advertising is also exactly what its name suggests—advertising in the section of a paper that classifies products and services under appropriate headings: "Jobs Wanted," "Used Books" and services available primarily for teenagers. Few school papers have classified ad columns, yet a classified ad column is just as appropriate as it is for a large city daily. Such a column could be a source of revenue and perform a real service to readers. Personal ads in newspapers are discouraged because they can create ethical and in some cases legal problems. Make sure all ads sell a legal service.

Fig. 21.8. Advertisement for the first ever broadcast of a high school football game from a high school website. *HiLite,* Carmel High School, Carmel, Ind.

its message. The ad's headline should give the benefit of the product or business and complement the illustration. In Figure 21.7 the headline targets the teen market with the store's primary sales message that it will make sure your flowers will look good for homecoming. In this ad's case, as it should be in all well-designed ads, the type selection helps create a feeling for the business or product. The script type adds to the elegant feeling the art director wanted to create. Type contrast or art, as discussed in Chapter 15, can also be considered. A well-written headline, created in a clean and easy to read serif or sans serif type, is preferable to illegible novelty type. Ad headlines should also be short and punchy. A secondary headline in many retail ads, or ads that advertise a specific store, may be the store name. Often, however, an advertiser has a logo that you will use. But once again, rarely is the name of the store the dominant headline. In Figure 21.8, an in-house ad run by the Carmel High School *HiLite,* the headline and white space effectively communicate the message. An in-house ad is an advertisement that promotes the publication itself. Here, the use of the date and the subhead "the revolution begins" creates suspense for the coming of something big. In this case, the *HiLite* was advertising the live webcast of the high school football game, the first such broadcast from a high school website.

The copy is the written text of the ad. The copy reinforces the message communicated in the headline and illustration. The text should be specific and vivid, helping to sell the product or service by personalizing the benefits of the product. In the Drake University ad (Fig. 21.6), the headline states you can make your mark at Drake. The copy lists the specific ways this can be achieved (for example, by being part of a community where you can use what you learn and by having the personal attention of professors).

If the ad is a retail ad, which advertises a specific business, the copy will usually include the basic information of address, phone number and store hours. The local retail ad is also more likely to include prices for specific products. Try to limit the copy. Keep it short and snappy. In the visual hierarchy of the design, the body copy typically is secondary. The designer should choose much smaller type sizes and weights. Clean, easy to read serif and sans serif types are preferable.

The logo is the trademark of the company. Typically company provided, the logo is given larger display than the body copy, but not usually larger than the headline and illustration, which are being used to sell the product or the service.

Make sure that the logo is on a white or light background if you have to scan or reproduce it. A logo on dark-colored paper will muddy and become unreadable in the reproduction.

As already mentioned, the illustration is usually the dominant element in the design. The reader's eyes are attracted by the illustration, and from there the eyes must make a clear and logical movement through the ad. The eye movement is called "gaze motion." The reader's eyes move left to right, but a dominant football player on the right side of the ad looking to his left into the headline will surely take the reader's eyes to the headline. Use visual hierarchy to move the reader's eyes through each element of an ad. A larger headline under a dominant illustration will be a logical gaze motion. The last thing the reader should see is the logo. The concept works like hearing a song the moment before you get out of your car in the morning. The last song you hear sticks in your mind throughout the day. The art director hopes the same thing happens with the last visual element you see—the logo. Then advertising works like going to a party where you do not know anyone but one person. In a crowded room, you seek out the person you know to talk to. You're comfortable with the person you're familiar with. Logo or name recognition creates such familiarity. An advertiser wants a reader zipping along a row of restaurants to stop at the one the reader recognizes from an ad.

White space is also a consideration in ad design. White space can help to frame and give emphasis to elements. Figure 21.8 shows how white space adds to the design. Elements should not be crammed into a space. Avoid the use of decorative dingbats and big, overwhelming borders. A simple 1 point rule often suffices. Let the four elements defined earlier—illustration, headline, body copy and logo—attract the reader's attention.

SOME OTHER CONSIDERATIONS IN AD DESIGN

- Do not put coupons on back to back pages in the newspaper.

Fig. 21.9. Advertisement. *U-High Midway,* University High School, Chicago, Ill.

Fig. 21.10. Advertisement. *U-High Midway,* University High School, Chicago, Ill.

Fig. 21.11. *Hillcrest Hurricane,* Hillcrest High School, Dallas, Texas

Fig. 21.12. *Hillcrest Hurricane,* Hillcrest High School, Dallas, Texas

- Once you've completed an ad design, try it out on some friends. Let them look at the ad and see if they get the desired message. Ask them what message they got from the ad to see if it matches the desired one. If an ad takes explanation, it fails.

- After the ad is designed, the process is not over. Providing the business owner with an ad to proof or proofing the ad yourself is critical to doing good business. Make sure the ad contains an updated coupon date, correct address, fax and phone information and a cleanly reproduced logo.

- Once the advertisement runs, the advertising salesperson should deliver a copy of the newspaper or the yearbook page to first-time advertisers to encourage repeat business. A tear sheet or copy of the reproduced ad serves as proof of the business's purchase.

- Make sure all billing is prompt.

- A satisfied advertiser is a repeat advertiser.

EXERCISES

1. Evaluate the ads in Figures 21.11–21.13. Do they really sell a service or a product? Is the concept creative? Are they effectively designed? If not, how might they have been improved? Is the copy effective? If not, why not? In your discussion use all the principles you studied in this chapter.

2. Write a carefully composed critique of an ad from a recent issue of your school publication. Discuss the kind of advertising it represents, the layout, the copy and the placement on the page. Is the advertising professional? Is the business getting its money's worth? Redesign the ad, if necessary.

3. Choose three of your favorite TV commercials. Explain what product benefit each ad is trying to communicate and how the ad communicates the

Fig. 21.13. *Hillcrest Hurricane,* Hillcrest High School, Dallas, Texas

message. Decide which ad is the most creative and explain why.

4. Conduct a market survey of the purchasing power and buying power of your student body. In small groups, discuss what areas you need to survey in order to collect information that would help an advertising salesperson. Distribute the poll through homeroom classes or during an activity period.

5. Make a list of possible advertisers for your school publication.

6. Select a product or service that you know well and believe would be appropriate for an ad in your school publication. In small groups, discuss what the possible message or benefit for the product or service would be. What makes it better than other products or services similar to it? Design an ad for it with the message you selected in mind.

7. From daily newspapers or magazines, clip, mount and label three ads that you think are especially ef-

fective in layout. Beneath each discuss the reasons for its effectiveness. If you have an overhead projector, plan to show the class your best ad.

8. Select five area businesses and decide what information an advertising salesperson would need to know about the businesses to sell them an ad. Vary the business types.

9. Label the prices of 10 ads in your yearbook and newspaper to prepare for a sales call. Use removable self-adhesive notes if necessary. Are there extra costs for photography? Are there discounts?

10. Prepare a sales pitch for the following businesses. Role-play in front of the class with another class member playing the business owner. Have the class discuss the demonstration.

a. A flower shop that you hope will buy an ad in the issue before homecoming

b. A new sporting goods store

c. A new multiscreen theater that is trying to hire employees

d. A restaurant that specializes in 20 types of burgers

Ethics for Student Journalists

Whether their work is published on paper, published online on the Web or broadcast on radio or television, journalists are legally restricted and morally guided by some specific laws and guidelines and some general underlying principles. Some of these rules and principles are called "ethics." Laws and ethics are what a journalist calls upon to help answer sometimes troublesome questions (can a reporter tape a phone conversation? accept a free concert ticket?) about news gathering, reporting, writing and editing.

WHAT ARE ETHICS?

Learning the difference between good and bad conduct is a measure of maturity in a society. As children mature into adolescence and then adulthood, they ideally acquire standards or codes of conduct that are based on moral judgments. These are called personal ethics.

Personal ethics, the standards one lives by to do the right thing in everyday life, are often derived from the examples set by the home, school, church, peers and government and are desirable if one is to live happily in a morally good society.

Personal ethics tell someone that murder is generally bad and wrong and that sharing food with someone who is poor and hungry is generally good and right.

In addition to personal ethics, many professions, including medicine, law and journalism, have special ethics for members of those professions to follow. For journalists, these ethics guide them in the pursuit of truth in the news-gathering process. Organized into a code or set of guidelines, journalism ethics reflect journalism's mission in society, personal morality and some media laws.

THE FIRST AMENDMENT, MEDIA LAW AND ETHICS

The First Amendment to the U.S. Constitution is the basis for the laws and codes that guide journalists in the United States in their work. It provides the freedom journalists need to gather information (including from the government) that may be newsworthy.

Although the free press part of the First Amendment is one of the most important safeguards in the Bill of Rights, it is a general statement. Since the Bill of Rights was ratified in 1791, federal courts, the U.S. Supreme Court, Congress and state governments and courts have elaborated on what a free press means, including at the high school level.

Through the years, these court decisions and laws have created legal guidelines for journalists to follow as they gather and report news. Some of these laws tell journalists if how they get information is illegal—for example, tape recording a tele-

365

phone conversation without the other person's knowledge is illegal in certain states. Other laws, such as those on libel, deal with the publication of information that is not true.

However, laws are not enough to guide a journalist on the job. Personal and professional ethics answer many of the questions regarding news gathering that laws don't answer. Journalism membership associations, such as the Society of Professional Journalists, and individual media companies, such as the *Washington Post* newspaper, have written codes of ethics for their members and employees. The codes are revised occasionally to meet the ever-changing job of gathering the news for publication.

School media—newspapers, yearbooks, magazines, broadcasts and online web sites—are affected by many of the same laws that guide the nonstudent media; the U.S. Supreme Court further limited the First Amendment press rights of public school students in 1988. (See Chap. 23.)

Like their nonstudent counterparts, school news media often supplement legal guidelines with additional standards of practice. Whether compliance is voluntary or mandatory, codes of ethics for journalists have these additional benefits:

- They help establish a sense of professionalism among all who work for one news organization or belong to the same association, and among journalists at large.

- Adherence to codes helps establish credibility with readers and viewers; the public is confident it can believe what it reads, hears and sees.

- Codes provide a uniform measure for dealing with news-gathering problems. Journalists bring diverse training and personal values to their work. Codes alleviate the potential for problems that could be caused by uneven training and different values.

JOURNALISM NEEDS AN ETHICS CODE

Although the American public hasn't always held journalism and journalists in high esteem, journalism is a reputable and respected profession and is the only one specifically mentioned for protection in the First Amendment. Because of its importance in an open society with a freely elected democratic form of government, journalism needs to be governed by a code of ethics.

Journalism serves many useful and vital functions in a democratic society:

- Journalism informs the public about facts and events that are important to it.

- Journalism ensures the free flow of information that is important to the birth and continuation of a democracy.

- Journalism provides a forum for diverse viewpoints.

- Journalism serves as a watchdog of government and other institutions to alert the public about wrongdoing.

- Journalism advocates changes in the public's interest.

- Journalism pursues the truth with unwavering commitment.

To meet these responsibilities and fulfill its mission, journalism needs an ethics code that allows for self-evaluation and results in public confidence in the accuracy and fairness of the work being done.

INDIVIDUAL JOURNALISTS NEED AN ETHICS CODE

An ethics code will only be effective if the journalists who work at the newspaper or other medium that has a code know it and use it to do their work. Each journalist, no matter the significance of the job being done, has a stake in the credibility of the publication with the public.

To meet the demands of the job and to live up to the standards society and journalism itself have set for those who work in the profession, these goals are important to achieve:

- A journalist can be trusted to be accurate, honest and independent and to keep promises.

- A journalist is respectful and is sensitive to community standards and taste.

- A journalist has a high regard for personal privacy.

- A journalist treats persons with courtesy and compassion.

- A journalist is fair and impartial.

- A journalist is concerned about completeness and the context of facts and opinions used in stories.

- A journalist acknowledges and corrects errors.

- A journalist listens to the questions and complaints from the public.

- A journalist strives for excellence in all aspects of work.

- A journalist considers the public interest in decision making.

If a journalist follows these guidelines, then the highest ethical standards are being observed and the credibility of the work will be unquestioned.

ETHICS IN ACTION: NEWS GATHERING

Few would argue with the merits of these lofty ideals, but how they apply to real, on-the-job reporting and editing, including in a high school newsroom, is sometimes confusing or overlooked.

Journalism ethics govern the process of reporting and publishing, from the first inkling or idea, through the information-gathering stage, to the writing and editing steps and, finally, to the finished, published work. This is valid for print, broadcast and Internet-based publishing.

The reasons why a story is reported and how the information for that story is obtained are often as important to a journalist as what the story finally becomes once it is published. Ethics enter into these stages of the reporting process.

In the planning or prereporting stage of a story, the reporter—sometimes with the guidance of an editor or, in a school newsroom, a faculty adviser—analyzes the potential for the story. Questions such as these come to mind: How newsworthy is the story? What does the public need to know? Who will the story affect? What will the effect be? Some of these questions aren't answered until after all the information is gathered. One or more angles of the story are selected to investigate, and sources are considered for the necessary information to develop the story. At this stage, the reporter considers the fairness and relevance of the angle or angles chosen and the qualifications and reliability of the sources selected for the interviews and other fact-finding.

Also at this stage, the reporter's own stake in the story is considered. The reporter removes him- or herself from the story if he or she is personally involved in it in a way that could lead to a conflict of interest accusation from readers or if the reporter has some significant bias regarding the topic. For example, a student reporter who is a member of a student government body and a reporter for the school paper should not report on student government activities in which he actively participates. If he did, readers might think the story was not objective.

If the story lacks news or human interest values, its publication may be considered an example of distortion of the subject's importance, bias toward a special interest group or propaganda. If the sources aren't seen as reliable by the public or they aren't the most knowledgeable, the credibility of the story, the reporter and the publication will suffer.

Conflict stories with differing opinions are often troublesome for reporters. With these often complex, multisource, conflicting opinion stories, the reporter should carefully present all of the information, double-check facts for accuracy and include the opinions of those involved, especially those who have a minority or opposing view. The result will then likely be a story that is considered by most readers or viewers to be fair. For example, gun control is a controversial issue in many places, and proponents and opponents have strong opinions. A reporter who covers this topic should accurately report the positions on both sides of the issue. However, not all topics deserve equal coverage of opposing views. Some stories, such as the Holocaust, don't usually need the kind of opposing viewpoint balance that is required in other stories.

During the fact-finding or reporting stage of the story, the reporter also calls upon personal and professional ethics for guidance. The reporter asks several questions: Has enough information been gathered for the reader to clearly and fully understand the story? Depending upon the complexity and depth of the story, do the points of view represent different ages, races, sexes or ethnic or other groups? And, as was done in the reporting stage, the reporter again assesses the quality and validity of the sources: Are the "expert" persons and records the best and most reliable available?

Whether in person or on the phone, during interviews the reporter clearly informs the interviewee that the information being sought may be published. If the reporter is seeking off-the-record information for background and not for publication or quoting directly or indirectly in a story, that is also made clear to the interviewee.

Quoting a source accurately is vital to a reporter's and the publication's credibility. Use of a recorder or good notetaking is important for all interviews. As a matter of good ethics, the interviewee should be told that a recording is being made. It is also illegal to tape-record phone conversations in some states. The appropriate time to clarify information or check the completeness of a quote from a source is during the interview or during a follow-up phone call or second in-person interview. Beginning reporters, especially, will want to verify quotes and facts before ending an interview. It is unprofessional and it hurts the credibility of the paper for a reporter to give a source a completed copy of the story before it is published.

It is unethical and likely illegal for a reporter to steal or knowingly receive stolen information for a story. Although there may be some exceptions to this with consideration for the life or death importance to the public of the story, it is rarely justifiable. Within a school, taking records from the school's office without permission is stealing.

Use of the Internet by reporters to gather information raises some ethical concerns. Because of the ease of creating and widely disseminating information on the Internet, the accuracy of some of it could be doubted. Internet sources may not be as reliable as other sources. The person or agency sponsoring the web site may be a factor regarding its reliability. The accuracy of information obtained on the Internet should be verified through other sources if possible. Reporters who gather information from Internet bulletin boards or chat rooms should identify themselves as reporters and tell those involved that what they are writing may be published. A reporter who monitors chat rooms and bulletin boards or subscribes to listservs only for background information and not to quote someone as a source for a specific story does not have to identify himself or herself as a reporter. Persons who participate in an Internet chat room, bulletin board or listserv don't automatically think they may be the source for a published story, so reporters should respect this privacy.

ETHICS IN ACTION: WRITING AND EDITING

During the writing stage, ethics again play a role as the reporter turns recordings, notes and drafts into a polished story ready for publication.

The reporter writes a lead that doesn't distort any information or slant the story in a deceptive way. If a narrative or story-telling lead and method of story development is used, the reporter should avoid embellishing the facts just to tell a more exciting story. If the inverted pyramid form is used, the reporter should consider the order in which the facts are presented, from most important to least important with regard to what the reader needs to know rather than what the reporter personally thinks is interesting. Overemphasizing or overwriting any one of the *what, who, where, when, why* and *how* of a story can distort the facts.

All facts and statistics and the spelling of names are verified. This complies with one of the reporter's most important goals, accuracy. Incorrect information and errors in spelling, especially in a person's name or other proper nouns, negatively affect the publication's credibility with its audience.

Direct and indirect quotes are reviewed for accuracy too. Are the quotes fair and used in the context of the questions asked during the interview? The reporter takes great care to accurately and fairly represent the words of the person being quoted.

As the story is developed, the reporter is mindful of the divergent viewpoints encountered in the fact-finding stage and incorporates them into the story. If a divergent view is not newsworthy—it may be old, too bigoted, false—then balance just for the sake of balance may be unnecessary. The reporter and editor judge each story individually for balance.

Upon examining a final draft or during the editing stage, if there is any question that some readers may think the story unfair because of a perceived lack of balance or a missing fact, the reporter may want to reopen the fact-finding stage and interview one more person or search for information in one more source. This may be especially important if the topic is somehow controversial. The reporter may be unaware of the need to revise the story until after it is written and given to someone else for editing.

Finally, and most important, the reporter examines those who have a stake in the publication of the story. Will anyone be hurt or helped by the story? If someone will be hurt, can the reporter defend the harm as justifiable or deserving? Does the good outweigh the harm? Sometimes it is wise for the reporter to put him- or herself in the place of the person who may be harmed to resolve any questions as to whether or not publication is justifiable.

The reporter also realizes that sometimes doing the

right thing will not please everyone and someone may be harmed. The result of this kind of prepublication analysis may mean that the story will be changed to maximize the good effects and minimize the harmful ones. The final test is: "Are the reporter's personal ethics satisfied?"

QUESTIONS AFTER PUBLICATION

After a story is published, the reporter or editor may be called upon by readers to explain some aspect of it or defend its publication entirely. In advance of this potential questioning, the reporter should be able to stand by his or her story as true and newsworthy.

Depending upon the importance of the story, a follow-up may be planned to report the criticism or explore new angles suggested by a reader.

If an error is found in the story, a correction should be published in the next edition. If a clearer explanation of some facts in the original story is warranted, even though no errors were found, then a clarification should be published. Both corrections and clarifications should be published in a prominent but appropriate place, though usually not on page 1. Often they are published on the editorial page.

To possibly improve a publication's credibility with the public and to provide readers with a regular outlet to air their complaints about the publication, a reader advocate can be appointed. The advocate would be a student who is knowledgeable about how a news medium functions but is not on the editorial or business staff. The reader advocate is a neutral party who investigates reader complaints and issues brief reports that will be published in a subsequent edition.

An alternative to a reader advocate is a publications advisory board composed of students and nonstudents (teachers, parents) who convene only to mediate staff disputes or to review reader complaints and issue explanations or make recommendations for change. An advisory board does not serve as a censor for any prior review function.

A MODEL ETHICS CODE FOR HIGH SCHOOL JOURNALISTS

In addition to the personal ethics and obligation to fairness and accuracy a reporter brings to a story, other, very specific rules and guidelines have been created by news mediums and professional journalism groups for journalists to follow. Most nonstudent news mediums adopt a formal code of ethics. Student journalists may do the same, including acceptance of codes by such groups as the Society of Professional Journalists. However, students are likely to need some guidelines and rules specific to student media as well.

Student journalists may want to incorporate some or all of these rules and guidelines, organized alphabetically here, into their own code of ethics:

Acceptance of free tickets, gifts, meals, transportation and other amenities is questionable. Generally, gifts from news sources and vendors should not be accepted. However, token gifts such as pens, notepads, T-shirts and the like may be accepted if there is no indication that the gifts are being offered in return for some influence regarding the content or operations of the publication. Some say the dollar value of acceptable gifts shouldn't exceed $5. If money is available for tickets, a sports reporter or arts critic should not accept free tickets to an event he or she is assigned to cover. The same is true for transportation to an event and free meals. From a practical standpoint, most school publications don't have budgets to cover these expenses. In that case, acceptance of free admission is okay, but the reporter should be reminded that there is no obligation to do a more positive story because of the free admission.

Advertisers should not receive special treatment or undue favorable comment with regard to editorial content.

Anonymous sources should be used sparingly if at all. The credibility of a story suffers if information is not attributed directly to someone. However, anonymous sources may be used if the editor considers the information to be important enough. If possible, the information offered by an anonymous source should be verified with another source, even if the second one is also anonymous. In the published story, the unnamed source will be more credible if he or she is linked even generally to some agency or institution; the need for anonymity should be carefully preserved by not being too specific. If the editor is unsure about the reliability of the information or source, it is wise to hold or kill the story. (See *Confidentiality*.)

Clarifications—further explanation or additional facts that may make some information clearer to the reader—may be published if the story is significant. They can be placed adjacent to *corrections*.

Confidentiality should not be promised to a source by a reporter without the permission of the editor and after consultation with the publication's adviser. Granting and preserving the confidentiality of a source is often difficult for a nonstudent journalist and nearly impossible for a student journalist. Generally, confidentiality should only be promised to a source if there is real danger that serious physical, emotional or financial harm will come to the source if his or her name is revealed. Some states legally honor the confidentiality bond between a source and a journalist. In some cases reporters who refuse to reveal a source's name can be jailed or fined. Most likely, secondary school student journalists are not covered by any state shield laws, which may protect nonstudent journalists. Consequently, students could be compelled to reveal a source's identity.

Conflict of interest can negatively affect the credibility of the reporter and the publication. To avoid a conflict of interest, a reporter should not be assigned to cover a story in which he or she has any substantial involvement. An editor should decide what degree of involvement would disqualify a reporter from a story. A reporter is obligated to tell the editor about any memberships or participation in any activities that may be a reason to disqualify him or her from a story. For example, a reporter who is a student government member should not report student government activities. This policy helps ensure a certain amount of objectivity that is important to the publication's independence.

Corrections are published in the next edition of the publication in a prominent and consistent position. Errors are never knowingly published. Corrections for yearbook errors can be published as an insert and distributed separately.

Crime news gets special care from reporters and editors. Care should be taken to protect the rights of those charged with but not convicted of a crime. The person charged is the "suspect" or the "alleged ..." The reporter must know the state laws regarding the identification of those persons under 18 years who are charged or convicted of a crime. Criminal cases are a matter of public record, and the records, unless otherwise dictated by a court, are open to student reporters.

Crime victims usually receive special care from journalists. Reporting the names and addresses of crime victims may be governed by state laws. Students who write crime beat stories need to know the laws that affect coverage of sexual abuse crimes such as rape and incest. Generally, victims of sexual abuse are not identified. However, some journalists and legal officials now advocate the identification of these victims. If law permits, this may be negotiated between the victim and the editor. Also, the victim of nonsexual crime may be identified; the publication has some responsibility to give some protection to the victim, such as publishing an inexact address. A question the reporter asks him- or herself is "What harm will result if the victim is identified?" With the exception of major crimes, an arrested person is not named until charges are filed.

Electronically altered photos (using a scanner, software and a computer to change the content of photos in any way other than improving contrast or removing flaws such as dust or scratches) are prohibited in most instances, and always for news or news-feature photos. Readers, including those for news-oriented web sites, expect the photo they see published to be the exact image of what existed when the photo was shot. Slight cosmetic changes, whether done on a computer or in a traditional darkroom, are acceptable. Photos for certain kinds of human interest feature stories, such as fashion coverage, can be altered electronically—objects can be added, removed or reshaped, for example. Highly fanciful photo images, clearly done with the assistance of a computer, can also be published since the reader will easily detect that reality has been tampered with. Photos for all hard news stories, including sports, which are nonfeatures, should not be given a fanciful, computer-altered interpretation.

Fabrication (creating a person, a situation, a dialogue, statistics or any pivotal or incidental information and passing it as real) is prohibited in most instances and almost always in news stories. If anything fictitious is included in a story, it should be clearly stated that the person, situation or whatever is fiction. Generally, columnists have more freedom to create characters and situations, and readers usually realize the intent.

False identity, concealed recording devices, stolen documents and eavesdropping are methods of gathering news that are ethically questionable or illegal for all journalists. In the normal course of gathering news, no journalists should misrepresent him- or herself. In extraordinary circumstances when information can not be gotten any other way and the nature of the information is seen as extremely important to the well-being of readers, an editor, upon consultation with an adviser, may give permission for a student journalist to go undercover and to misrepresent him- or herself. Care should be taken to avoid harmful situations. A journalist should not steal or knowingly accept stolen materials. Only under extraordinary circumstances should a reporter record an interview or speech without the permission of the speaker or interviewee. However, permission is unnecessary when the interview or speech is routine and frequent and the recording is openly done. Permission is assumed. For example, a reporter may record the weekly press briefing by the mayor without requesting permission each time. Tape-recording a telephone conversation without the agreement of the other party is illegal in at least 10 states. The obvious placement of a tape or other voice recorder in full view of the interviewee may be sufficient, but a polite request will usually lead to permission granted. Committing an illegal act such as entering a locked, private building without permission to record a source is prohibited. Entering a person's computer e-mail files without permission is also prohibited. Eavesdropping to gather news is often unethical, even if legal entry is made, because it presumes that the reporter has not properly identified him- or herself.

Identification of a person as a member of any group (racial, ethnic, religious, sexual-orientation, economic, social or other) should be limited to those instances when that membership is essential to the reader's complete understanding of the story. Labels of any kind should be used carefully to avoid negative stereotyping. If a group label is used, the reporter should use the one accepted by journalists and acceptable to the person being so identified. For more information on this, refer to Chapter 12.

Journalists should neither directly assist nor hamper *law enforcement* officials with their work. Traditionally, the press is a watchdog of government and law enforcement, and it must remain independent to preserve this function. Some states provide better protection for journalists than others, and sometimes journalists are jailed for refusing to cooperate with police investigations and court proceedings for not submitting notes and photographs to the police or the courts. Laws protecting journalists and their materials are called "Shield Laws." However, law enforcement agencies and government have an obligation to give public information to the press.

Membership on multiple staffs may be a problem for student journalists. If a journalist is on the staff of more than one medium, that journalist should not cover the same beats if the two or more mediums are competitive and have a similar frequency of publication. Print and online publications are often competitive. The school newspaper and yearbook would not generally be competing mediums in this case. This prevents the dilemma as to which medium gets the story first.

Negative stereotyping (generalizations in stories and photos that may unjustly and negatively stereotype a population group) should be a factor for consideration as stories are edited and photos selected for publication. All aspects of reporting, from the selection of interviewees and research statistics to the content of photos, should be examined for fairness. Population groups subject to this problem are often racial, religious, sexual-orientation or ethnic minorities. For example, a story about unwed, school-age mothers should not be limited to one race or economic group, and a story about openly gay teens should not automatically include comments from nongays who disagree with homosexuality on religious grounds. In these two instances, negative stereotypes could be that only minority girls have children outside of marriage and that being gay is immoral.

News and commentary should be easily distinguishable. News and news-feature stories that include analysis should be labeled as "analysis." Opinion columns, including reviews, should be identified as opinion or commentary in some consistent way.

Ownership of work produced belongs to the publication regardless of whether the staff member is paid or not. An editor or adviser may authorize reproduction of the work in a form other than its originally intended form. The act of voluntarily joining a staff indicates acceptance of this policy.

Reporting personal details about a public person's life is an ethics consideration for a reporter and editor when the public person is associated with a newsworthy event or issue. For the sake of high school media, public persons include the school's administrators, teachers, school board members and those students who are acknowledged leaders such as a class president or the star of the school's basketball team. (See Chap. 23 for a more thorough presentation of public figures and privacy.) Public figures, including those private persons suddenly thrust into the public spotlight by an unexpected event, are open to more media scrutiny of their private lives than a private person. The journalist takes great care to report only those facts about a public person's private life that are newsworthy and relevant to the reasons why the person is a public figure. Although public figures, especially elected officials and those who are employed by public institutions, have an obligation to talk with the press, a journalist should not overly badger a public figure for an interview or photo. Repeated polite requests and reminders of the public's right to know will usually be successful.

Photo illustration and posed photos are acceptable; group poses don't need any special notice, but if action is recreated for the sake of a photo, the accompanying caption should mention that the scene was recreated.

Photos of victims of accidents, crimes and natural disasters should be monitored carefully by the editor. They have a tremendous impact on the reader. The victim's privacy may conflict with the public's right to know. It's not always easy to draw a line between sensationalism and reality and good and bad taste. Care should be taken to maintain the dignity of the persons in the photo. Why the reader should see the photo should be considered carefully before it is published.

Plagiarism (taking someone's words, art and other original work and passing it off as one's own) is prohibited and may be illegal if the source of the work is copyrighted or otherwise legally protected. For the purpose of journalism, plagiarism is further defined as word-for-word duplication of another's writing, whether it is printed on paper or electronically on the Internet. It also refers to duplication of broadcasts on radio or television. Facts taken from a published source should be attributed to the source and independently verified if possible. Paraphrasing published information is acceptable, but copying the original writer's unique phrases is unacceptable. For a story, a direct quote from a live person is preferable and may have more credibility than a direct or indirect quote from another newspaper, magazine, book, web site or other published source.

Profane or vulgar words are a part of everyday conversation, right or wrong, but generally they are not used in student news media. Profane or vulgar words are not in themselves legally obscene. Use of them in student media is rare and is limited to those cases when they are judged by an editor to be essential to the full understanding of a key aspect of a story or central to a person's style of speech. The age range of the readers is a factor to be considered; use should be prohibited for publications serving readers under 14 years. Profane and vulgar words should not be used to sensationalize a story or to shock readers. For example, a story about the sale of illegal drugs, to be authentic, could include conversation and words that may be profane or vulgar if the reporter and editor consider these words to be pivotal in the recreation of the drug sale. A story about someone saying profane or vulgar words and then being reprimanded in some way for doing so may also be a case when the words themselves are pivotal to the story. Sometimes using ellipses in place of the words draws more attention than the word itself; however, this may be an acceptable compromise. Community standards also are a factor to consider.

Sexist labels and descriptions should be eliminated from writing and replaced with neutral words. For example, the use of "ladies" to distinguish a boy's sport from a girl's should be reviewed for possible sexism and lack of parallelism; if "ladies' basketball," then it follows that "gentlemen's basketball" would be parallel. If "boys" is used, then "girls" is the preferred opposite.

Sexually explicit words that refer to body parts and functions, not vulgar or profane, should be used for accuracy and understanding in all stories about health and sexuality. Vulgar street language should not be used in place of medically acceptable terms. For example, a story about AIDS may need to include terms that have sexual overtones to make the story factually accurate and truthful.

EXERCISES

1. As a reporter for the school paper, you are assigned to cover the Student Council. You are not an elected or appointed member of the council. Should you vote in the all-school Student Council elections?

2. You are a reporter for the school newspaper. Later, you also join the school's drama club and the Young Republicans. You do not cover the activities of either of these two groups for the paper. You are asked to act in the school play and to be the vice president of the Young Republicans. Should you accept these offers and still remain on the newspaper staff?

3. The principal of your school is arrested for driving while intoxicated. Should you report the arrest in your school newspaper? The Student Council president of your school, an 18-year-old, is arrested for driving while intoxicated. Should you report the arrest in the school newspaper?

4. Two of your faculty members die in a two-week period. One dies of a heart attack and the other dies of AIDS. Should you report the causes of death in your paper?

5. As the movie reviewer for your paper, you are invited to a free screening of a new film. At the screening, the film's distributor is giving everyone a complimentary T-shirt and the soundtrack compact disk. Should you accept the invitation to the film and the accompanying promotional merchandise?

6. Planned Parenthood asks to buy ad space in your newspaper. Should you accept the ad?

7. You are the editor of your school yearbook. During the school year there is a shooting on school grounds, and three students are killed. Your student photographer has pictures of the bodies, each covered with a blanket, lying where they were shot. You report the shooting in your yearbook. Do you publish the pictures of the bodies?

8. As the newspaper editor, you hear that students under the legal drinking age are buying alcohol regularly at a local liquor store. Should you assign an underage reporter to attempt to buy liquor at the store and then write about the results of your "sting"?

9. As a reporter for the student life section of your yearbook, you decide to interview several lesbian and gay students at your school for a story about sexual orientation. You promise these students that their real names will not be used. Should you have made that promise?

10. For a story about unmarried teen mothers, you photograph a group of five teen mothers, three black and two Mexican Americans, with their babies. The mothers agree to be photographed and identified in your story and the photo caption. Your school has a minority population of 5 percent black and 25 percent Mexican American. Are there any ethical concerns for you, the reporter-photographer, regarding this story?

Student Press Law

When the authors of the U.S. Constitution and Bill of Rights were pondering the protection of individual freedoms, were free expression rights for young students debated? Did they think the student press should be uncensored? No opinions on this were recorded; it is unlikely that the subject was ever considered, although the first student newspaper in the United States, *Student Gazette,* was published in 1777 at the William Penn Charter School in Philadelphia.

Nonetheless, student journalists in the United States have some of the same free expression rights given to other journalists in the First Amendment to the U.S. Constitution. Through the years since the final ratification of the Bill of Rights, which includes the First Amendment, on Dec. 15, 1791, legislators, judges and others have defined this right in more detail. They have created laws that now govern all journalists.

What students publish in their print newspapers, yearbooks and magazines, broadcast on radio and television and post online on the Internet is guided by state and federal court decisions and state and federal laws adopted since the First Amendment was accepted. These court decisions and laws affect official, school-sponsored student media. In some cases, they also affect personal media, communication that is published off campus and not sponsored or sanctioned by a school.

However, not all student media are subject to all or the same laws. Whether the student media are published in a public or private school and where that school is located can affect the application of these laws. Media published by students off-campus and with no school support are not usually affected by some of the laws that govern media published in a public or private school.

WHERE YOU PUBLISH MAKES A DIFFERENCE

How a public school differs from a private school in some basic ways is an essential consideration for the study of the First Amendment and its application to student journalists who attend these schools and publish their student media.

- A public school is funded primarily with money from local, state and federal governments.

- A private school is funded primarily with money from individuals and nongovernmental bodies.

- Public schools must conform to government laws because they are funded with money from governments that enact these laws.

- Private schools must conform to only some government laws because they are funded mostly or wholly with nongovernmental money.

- One law that private schools do not have to enforce is to allow free expression to those who attend a private school.

375

- In public schools in all states and in the District of Columbia, students have limited free expression rights.

- By enrolling in a private school in all states, except California, and in the District of Columbia, students voluntarily relinquish their constitutionally protected but limited right to free expression.

- In California, students enrolled in private schools have had limited free expression rights since 1992. In that year, California passed what is known as the Leonard Law, Education Code section 94367, named after the law's primary sponsor, Senator Bill Leonard. The law prohibits private schools in California from punishing students because of "speech or other communication" that would be protected by the First Amendment if engaged in outside the high school or college campus.

- Private schools in other states and the District of Columbia may voluntarily allow free expression.

Since some private schools allow their students the same limited free expression rights as public schools, regardless of their location, the information in this chapter will be relevant and useful to all student journalists. Some laws, such as those on copyright and libel, do not distinguish between public and private school media and are applicable to both.

Some laws regarding free expression rights apply only to student journalists in specific states. So where you publish may be a factor too.

WHAT THE FIRST AMENDMENT SAYS

Constitutional scholars say that free expression rights were so important to those who founded the United States that these rights were listed for protection in the opening statement of the Bill of Rights. The denial of free expression was one reason the colonists rebelled against British rule.

This statement of free expression, the First Amendment, states: "Congress shall make no law respecting an establishment of religion, or prohibiting the free exercise thereof; or abridging the freedom of speech, or of the press, or the right of the people peaceably to assemble, and to petition the government for a redress of grievances."

Freedom to publish information and opinion was considered so important by James Madison, and others who wrote the Constitution, and George Mason, whose writing in Virginia help inspire the Bill of Rights, that the press was named as the only specific occupation receiving this special, protected status.

But this status enjoyed by the press was not to remain unlimited for long. During the more than 210 years since the adoption of the First Amendment, courts and legislative bodies have curbed press freedom. Despite these limits, even extending to high school media, the essence of the right granted in the First Amendment to the press remains a guiding principle in our society.

THE COURT SYSTEM DEFINES FREE EXPRESSION FOR JOURNALISTS

Those who granted the press in the United States its freedom also provided a constitutional mechanism for those who disagreed with the press to challenge its information-gathering methods and what it published. That mechanism is the federal court system. A state court system exists for each state and functions in a somewhat similar way to the federal court system.

If someone thinks what is published in the press is unlawful, or if someone thinks there is unlawful interference with the publication of something, that person may petition the court system to find out if the action is constitutional and legal. Public school media and public school officials, as agents of the government, must abide by the Constitution and the decisions of the courts.

The federal court system, which has decided most of the important cases in student press law, is organized in this way:

- The federal courts are divided into trial and appeals courts.

- Federal trial courts are called "district courts."

- Appeals from district courts are taken to one of 13 circuit courts (such as the U.S. Court of Appeals for the First Circuit).

- Appeals from the circuit courts are taken to the U.S. Supreme Court.

- Rulings (decisions) from one circuit court do not apply to other geographic circuit court jurisdictions.

- Rulings (decisions) by a circuit court do apply to all the district courts under its geographic jurisdiction. When lower courts must abide by rulings of a higher court, the lower courts are *following precedent;* the higher courts have *set precedent.*

A hypothetical censorship situation involving a high school student can illustrate how the federal court system works.

A public high school student in Illinois was suspended from school for distributing an alternative student newspaper, one not sanctioned by the school, on campus before the school day began. The suspended student sued the school in federal trial court for denial of his First Amendment rights. The court found that the student was denied his First Amendment rights. The school then appealed the decision to the U.S. Court of Appeals for the Seventh District (Illinois is in the seventh district). The appeals court reversed the lower court's decision and said that the school had not violated the student's First Amendment rights. The student then appealed the appeals court decision to the U.S. Supreme Court. The U.S. Supreme Court agreed to hear the appeal and decided in favor of the student. The Supreme Court's decision then became the law for all the states, setting aside the decision made by the appeals court.

If, in this hypothetical case, the U.S. Court of Appeals for the Seventh District had affirmed or agreed with the first court's decision and no further appeals were made, then this decision would become the law for those states within the seventh district, including Indiana, Wisconsin and Illinois.

Laws and actions by government, including public schools, can be challenged through the federal courts. These court decisions help interpret and form the ever-evolving body of law in the United States.

SUPREME COURT DECISIONS AND STUDENT MEDIA

With the growth and maturity of student media in the 20th century, disputes over content, editorial control and circulation have led some student journalists, teacher-advisers and school officials and the public into federal courts to air a grievance. Federal courts at all levels—district, circuit and the highest court, the Supreme Court—have decided cases pertaining to free expression for public school students. Many of the precedent-setting decisions have been made by the circuit court.

The U.S. Supreme Court has decided three cases directly relating to high school student expression, verbal (written and oral) and symbolic: *Tinker,* 1969; *Bethel,* 1986; and *Hazelwood,* 1988. The *Hazelwood* case was the first one directly regarding student media, but the majority opinion by the justices mentioned other forms of student expression. Two of these three cases, *Tinker* and *Hazelwood,* have affected student media more directly than the *Bethel* case.

In deciding the *Hazelwood* (Missouri) *School District v. Kuhlmeier* case in 1988, the Supreme Court, in a majority opinion, said public school officials could censor student expression in a nonforum, school-sponsored activity, such as a student newspaper, yearbook, magazine or broadcast. To censor, the school official must present a reasonable educational justification. The Hazelwood East high school principal censored stories on teenage pregnancy and the effects of family divorce on children.

In the *Bethel* (Texas) *School District v. Fraser* case in 1986, the Supreme Court said that the First Amendment does not prohibit school officials from determining what speech in the classroom or in school assembly is inappropriate and allows school officials to discipline students for vulgar or otherwise offensive speech. The case was the result of the punishment of a student by school officials for using vulgar references and innuendoes during a school assembly.

In 1969 the Supreme Court acknowledged that high school students have First Amendment rights in its *Tinker v. Des Moines* (Iowa) *Independent Community School District* decision. The court said a student's free speech rights are protected as long as that speech does not disrupt the work of the school or the rights of other students. The school officials had punished students for wearing black armbands during school to protest the Vietnam War.

Along with some decisions made by lower courts, the *Tinker* and *Hazelwood* cases now form the basis of student press law and guidelines for public, and in some cases private, high school media.

The 1988 *Hazelwood* decision did not overrule the 1969 *Tinker* decision, but it did narrow its application in significant ways.

TINKER AND ITS LEGACY

For almost 20 years, the *Tinker* decision and some other significant lower-court cases helped high school student journalism develop a legal framework to operate under and encouraged professional standards. In 1988 the Supreme Court's *Hazelwood* ruling significantly altered that legal framework. Though its impact is diminished, *Tinker* remains a basis for much of the student press law followed today, and many legal experts consider it to be the most important First Amendment case for students.

The *Tinker* case, however, didn't begin as a student media confrontation. It began when three students, one in junior high and two in high school, despite a ban by school officials, wore black armbands to school to protest the Vietnam War. Suspended from school for this action, they sued the school district, claiming a violation of their free expression rights under the First Amendment. They lost in the lower courts but won in the Supreme Court. The decision expanded free expression rights.

- The justices said that students and teachers do not lose their rights of free expression once they enter the schoolhouse door.

- Free speech by students in school is protected as long as it does not cause a "substantial disruption or a material interference with school activities."

- Students have a right to voice unpopular opinions.

- The decision applies to both junior and senior high schools.

Although *Tinker* was about symbolic speech (wearing an armband), it soon was applied to other forms of speech, including student media. The sweeping statements made by the justices in the majority opinion became the basis for a series of lower-court decisions that favored free expression for students. These lower-court decisions had limited application because of the courts' geographic structure.

LOWER COURTS APPLY *TINKER* STANDARD

One of the first lower-court applications of *Tinker* to student media was made in 1970 in *Scoville v. Joliet* (Illinois) *Township High School District Board of Education*. The Seventh Circuit Court of Appeals said that two students could not be punished for distributing an underground (alternative) paper on school grounds despite content in the paper "urging students not to accept, for delivery to parents, any propaganda issued by the school and to destroy it if accepted."

The school claimed that this statement could bring about disruption of the school. The court said that no disruption actually occurred, so the students could not be punished. The threat of disruption was not sufficient reason to deny free expression; in this case, the expression was in the form of distribution of a non–school-sponsored student newspaper.

In another post-*Tinker*, pre-*Hazelwood* decision that expanded student free expression rights— *Fujishima v. Chicago* (Illinois) *Board of Education*, 1972—the Seventh Circuit Court of Appeals said that a principal may not review a publication prior to distribution. A school rule requiring prior approval by the principal was ruled as unconstitutional. The publication was non–school-sponsored.

Another important lower-court decision before *Hazelwood* affirmed the concept of a student publication being a public forum. In *Gambino v. Fairfax County* (Virginia) *School Board*, 1977, the Circuit Court of Appeals for the Fourth District said that once a school newspaper is established as a "public forum," it cannot be censored even though the school financially supports it and the students receive academic credit. The court defined "public forum" as a publication that (1) consists of published news, student editorials and letters to the editor and (2) is distributed outside the journalism classroom.

Building upon the *Tinker* and these and other lower-court decisions, many student publications and school districts adopted three guidelines that included the central *Tinker* provision on disruption and two other areas of unprotected speech.

- Students will not publish any material that could substantially disrupt the school routine.

- Students will not publish anything that is obscene.

- Students will not publish anything that is libelous.

Under the protective blanket of the *Tinker* decision, student media at many schools have freely reported a range of topics, including school budgets, teacher contract disputes, teenage sexuality and child abuse, without prior review or censorship of any kind.

THE *HAZELWOOD* DECISION AND ITS IMPLICATIONS

Unlike *Tinker,* which was broadly about free expression and the expansion of First Amendment rights to students, the *Hazelwood* decision directly targeted school media and who controlled their content, and it limited the First Amendment rights of students.

Student journalists at Hazelwood East high school in suburban St. Louis, Mo., had written articles about a variety of topics of concern to teenagers for publication in their school newspaper. When the paper was returned from the printer, one page was missing, which included an article on teenage pregnancy and one on the effect of divorce on families. Exercising prior review, the school's principal ordered the two stories to be removed before publication. It was customary at the school for the adviser to submit the paper before publication to the principal for his approval.

The three Hazelwood East students who wrote the censored articles decided to sue the school for violating their First Amendment right of free expression. The school's principal said he censored the articles because he thought the topics were inappropriate for a high school publication and that the students interviewed in the story about teenage pregnancy, who were not named, could be identified by the readers. This happened in the spring of 1983.

In 1985, a federal district court in Missouri agreed with the principal and said that the censorship was acceptable. The court said that the newspaper was a part of the school's curriculum and not a forum. This was a significant reversal of a trend, since *Tinker*, of federal court decisions generally extending free expression rights to student journalists. But the three students appealed the decision to the next highest court.

More than three years since the censorship occurred, the Circuit Court of Appeals for the Eighth District, in July 1986, reversed the lower court's decision and found that the students' First Amendment rights had been violated by the school. The court said that although the newspaper was produced by a class, it was a forum for student expression and could not be censored.

Yet the saga was not over. Unhappy with the decision, the school district had one appeal left, to the U.S.

Supreme Court. In October 1987, the Supreme Court justices heard arguments from the lawyers representing the students and the school. About three months later, Jan. 13, 1988, the Supreme Court issued its decision.

By a five to three vote, the justices found in favor of the Hazelwood school district. This far-reaching decision brought these changes:

- The Supreme Court gave school officials the right to censor student media under certain circumstances.

- Although the *Hazelwood* case was especially about a student newspaper, the decision affects all high school media, including yearbooks, magazines, radio and television broadcasts and video.

- There are two crucial aspects to the decision: (1) the definition of a school newspaper as a public forum and (2) the justification for the censorship by the school official.

- The Supreme Court decided that the Hazelwood East paper was not a public forum and therefore not protected by the *Tinker* decision.

- In calling the Hazelwood paper school sponsored and not a public forum, the court gave three criteria to determine if a school publication is school sponsored: (1) Is the work supervised by a faculty member? (2) Is the publication designed to impart particular skills or knowledge to student participants or audiences? (3) Does the publication use the school's name or resources?

- If the answer is yes to any of these questions, then the publication is considered school sponsored and may not be protected under the First Amendment and *Tinker* guidelines. Clearly, the public forum notion was narrowly defined, if not severely impeded, by the Supreme Court.

- Whether a school publication is produced as a credit-bearing class, or an extracurricular activity, does not matter in the public forum consideration under *Hazelwood*.

- The Supreme Court said that the Hazelwood East High School adviser acted as the final authority in almost every aspect of the production, including content. There was no written policy stating that the paper was a forum. These two points led the court to decide that the Hazelwood paper was not a public forum.

- Censorship may not be allowed under the *Hazelwood* guidelines if the student publication is a public forum. One of the strongest determining factors is an official policy statement by the school designating the publication as a public forum and giving student editors final authority on content. In these cases the broader *Tinker* guidelines apply.

- Although censorship by school officials was permitted by the court with the *Hazelwood* decision, it is not required. School officials may choose not to exercise this right.

- Although prior review of a school-sponsored publication by the school administration is permitted without written guidelines under the *Hazelwood* decision, it undermines the authority of the editor and publication adviser. Prior review threatens a publication's credibility as a reliable news source, its ability to serve as a watchdog of those in charge of the school and its overall independence. Even though it is permitted, authorities such as the Student Press Law Center say it is unwise to exercise it.

- If a school official decides to censor student media, the official must be able to prove that the censorship "reasonably relates to legitimate pedagogical (educational) concerns."

- The school official who censors student media has the burden of demonstrating that the standards set by the Supreme Court under *Hazelwood* have been met.

- The Supreme Court gave some examples of content that could be censored: (1) material that is ungrammatical, poorly written, inadequately researched, biased or prejudiced, vulgar or profane, or unsuitable for immature audiences; (2) topics such as "the existence of Santa Claus in an elementary school setting, the particulars of teenage sexual activity in a high school setting, speech that might reasonably be perceived to advocate drug or alcohol use, irresponsible sex, or conduct otherwise inconsistent with the shared values of a civilized social order"; and (3) material that would "associate the school with anything other than the neutrality on matters of political controversy."

- The Supreme Court also said that a school official may review nonforum, school-sponsored publications before they are printed.

Although the *Hazelwood* decision substantially limited the free expression rights of student journalists at many public high schools and narrowed the application of *Tinker*, the *Tinker* decision is still law for those student publications that are officially designated by school officials as public forums and those alternative, nonschool student publications, print and online.

POST-*HAZELWOOD* COURT DECISIONS

Since the Supreme Court's *Hazelwood* decision in 1988, several lower federal courts and state courts have decided cases that affect high school media in certain states and, to some extent, curbed the reach of the 1988 landmark case.

The first post-*Hazelwood* decision came quickly. In the same year as the Supreme Court's decision, the Ninth Circuit Court ruled, in *Burch v. Barker,* that a school policy requiring students to submit a non–school-sponsored publication to school officials for review prior to distribution was unconstitutional.

Although this decision was made in 1988, it originated in 1983. Five students from Lindbergh High School (Renton, Wash.) were reprimanded by school officials for distributing an alternative publication at a class picnic. The students sued, claiming the school violated their First Amendment rights. Nearly four years later, in 1987, a federal district court in Washington ruled in favor of the school officials.

The students appealed the decision, and the higher court reversed the lower court's decision and found in favor of the students.

The *Burch v. Barker* decision, a victory for independent, non–school-sponsored media, applies to all public schools within the Ninth District, including Alaska, Arizona, California, Hawaii, Montana, Nevada, Oregon and Washington.

In 1989, two federal courts told two high schools to what extent they could apply the *Hazelwood* decision. A Connecticut court ruled, in *Lodestar v. Board of Education,* that a school could not censor a student literary magazine because the magazine had a history of independence and was not primarily a school activity designed by school officials. In neighboring New York state, another court said, in *Romano v. Harrington,* that a paper produced after school hours and not in a credit-bearing class had more freedom to comment editorially than a paper produced during school hours in a credit-bearing class. The New York school had fired its newspaper adviser after the paper published an editorial disapproving of the then-proposed national holiday commemorating the birth of the Rev. Martin Luther King Jr. The adviser sued, claiming a violation of First Amendment rights.

In a case that originated in 1989 but wasn't decided finally until 1994, *Desilets v. Clearview Regional Board of Education,* the New Jersey Supreme Court affirmed a junior high school reporter's right to publish a review of two R-rated movies.

Reporter Drien Desilets wrote reviews of *Mississippi Burning* and *Rainman* for his junior high paper, *Pioneer Press.* In his articles, he recommended the movies, but he didn't include any dialogue or profanities from the movies. The school's principal, exercising prior review before publication, deleted the reviews from the paper and said he objected to the subject matter of the films, not the content of the reviews. Later, a lawyer arguing in court for the school district said the reviews violated the district's policies against material "believed to constitute a danger to student health."

In ruling in favor of the student, the highest state court in New Jersey said, "the R-rated movie reviews in this case do not appear to raise educational concerns that call for the kinds of editorial control exemplified by the (U.S.) Supreme Court in Hazelwood."

While Drien Desilets was fighting for his free expression rights, students at a public school in Massachusetts became involved with a would-be advertiser in a content dispute that would lead to a Supreme Court ruling four years later.

In 1994, Douglas Yeo, a community activist in Lexington, sued the Lexington School Board after student editors of the Lexington High School newspaper and yearbook refused to publish his paid advertisement encouraging sexual abstinence. The school had enacted a condom distribution policy in 1992, and Yeo had tried to place the ad since then. The students said it was their policy to not run ads of a political nature. The school allowed the students to make content decisions regarding their publications, including the placement of paid advertising.

Yeo said his First Amendment right of free expression and his Fourteenth Amendment right to equal protection had been violated by the refusal to run the ad. Yeo claimed that the paper and yearbook are government publications because they are published at a government-supported public school.

The school and students won the first round in the district court, which said that not the school but the students, who are not considered agents of the state, were responsible for the paper's content and could refuse to publish an ad. Yeo appealed the decision to the First District Court of Appeals.

The First District Court reversed the lower court's decision and found that the two student publications were government publications and the student journalists were state actors. It based its decision, in part, on the fact that both publications carried the name of the school. Yeo won this time, but his victory proved to be temporary.

Backed by support from the National School Board Association, the Student Press Law Center and others, the school's attorneys asked for and were granted a rehearing of the case by the appeals court. The court also withdrew its decision. Following the rehearing, the appeals court justices said that students were not agents of the state after all because decisions made by the students are not attributable to the school. "As a matter of law," said the justices, "we see no legal duty here on the part of school administrators to control the content of the editorial judgments of student editors of publications."

Yeo then asked the U.S. Supreme Court to review the First District's decision. In fall 1998, the Supreme Court declined this request. The decision by the First District justices stands as law. Student journalists at Lexington High School and at public schools in the First District now have the freedom to establish their own advertising policies, refusing those they find objectionable.

PUBLISHING ON THE INTERNET

Law governing what is published on the Internet is evolving almost as rapidly as the technology used in this form of communication. Publishing on the Internet is, in some ways, no different than publishing through more long-established means, especially print. Generally, laws that apply to student journalists who publish print newspapers, yearbooks and magazines apply to those who publish online versions of these same publications or new ones that don't exist first in print. As is the case with print media, where and when an online "publication" is produced does make a difference regarding the application of some of these laws. Even the reporting and information-gathering process, if the Internet is involved, may also be governed by certain laws.

If the online publication is produced at a public school during school hours with the school's computers, and it is entered onto the school's server as its host web site, then it is generally governed by the *Hazelwood* standards and subsequent lower-court decisions. The question regarding whether the online web site is a public forum may be a determining factor in the extent of the application of *Hazelwood* standards. If a site is established as an open forum through a written policy by school officials, then content is controlled by the students. If there is no history of the web site being an open forum, then it is subject to potential prior review and censorship by school officials.

Regardless of the status of the web site as an open forum, libel, privacy, obscenity and copyright laws apply to the work that is posted online. Regarding these four areas of press law, online writing, art, photography, sound and video should be treated as if they were printed. For now, libel laws that apply to publishing something in print will apply to something that is published on the Internet on a web site or posted as a public e-mail message. Students should be aware that the act of publishing on the Internet can be as simple as clicking the "send" button on a computer monitor screen. Even though the school may be the Internet provider, it is the students who are legally responsible for the published Internet work if the school does not involve itself in the editorial process.

Web sites and e-mail may or may not be a reliable, accurate source of information for a story. A second online or "human," in-person contact may be necessary to check facts. Letters to the editor arriving by e-mail should be verified with a follow-up phone call because the paper is legally responsible for whatever it publishes, even a non–staff person's writing.

Reporters who seek opinions and information for stories from others in Internet chat rooms and through e-mail should identify themselves as journalists and tell those whom they talk with that their responses may be published. This is good ethics and protects the sources' right to privacy.

Some schools have restricted school-sponsored online publications in various ways that are different from restrictions placed on print media at the same school. These restrictions have included the removal of last names from persons mentioned in all stories and the prohibition of photos of students who could be identified. The most common reason given for these restrictions is to protect the students from nonschool preda-

tors; the distribution of print publications is more restricted. Opponents of these restrictions say that the elimination of last names and photos strips the online publication of much of its news value.

Using the Internet at school to gather information for print and online stories is also subject to emerging legal restrictions. In an attempt to limit access to web sites that contain material that some find objectionable, some schools have placed filtering software on their computers to block a student from reaching the objectionable sites. Critics of this say that the filtering often blocks students from legitimate educational sites that may contain some of the same words or phrases used in the objectionable sites but the words are used in a much different context. A student reporter, for example, who may be researching on the Internet a story about breast cancer may be blocked by a filtering system from access to all sites that contain the word "breast."

Federal, state and local governments have also dealt with Internet content and access. The federal government enacted laws that attempted to control access to web sites, particularly in public schools and libraries, considered objectionable to minors due to the sites' explicit sexual nature. It also enacted laws that punish those who knowingly provide objectionable material to minors over the Internet. Opponents of these laws claim that the Internet is protected by the First Amendment and that its global scope makes it difficult to control. So far, courts have said governments must not restrict the content on the Internet, but that could change.

Since laws that govern media differ from country to country, which country's laws apply when the information is on the global Internet? That question remains to be answered. There are troublesome issues, such as who can be sued for libel if someone from one country claims she was defamed by someone from another country in an online chat room? Is the Internet provider, the host of the chat room, liable and the "publisher" in this case? Do the libel laws of the country where the libelous remark was read apply, or where the libelous remark was typed on a keyboard and sent out onto the Internet? Courts around the world will likely wrestle with these problems for years.

OTHER WAYS TO EXTEND FREE EXPRESSION RIGHTS TO STUDENTS

Even though the *Hazelwood* decision hampered the free expression of public school students, there are ways other than the federal court system to protect student First Amendment rights. Laws and educational codes at the state level can lessen or nullify the effects of *Hazelwood.*

California's Education Code Section 48907 is an example of state-level legal protection for students. It reads:

> Students of the public schools shall have the right to exercise freedom of speech and of the press including, but not limited to, the use of bulletin boards, the distribution of printed material or petitions, the wearing of buttons, badges, and other insignia, and the right of expression in official publications, whether or not such publications or other means of expression are supported financially by the school or by the use of school facilities, except that expression shall be prohibited which is obscene, libelous, or slanderous. Also prohibited shall be material which so incites students as to create a clear and present danger of the commission of unlawful acts on school premises or the violation of lawful school regulations or the substantial disruption of the orderly operation of the school.

Passed in 1976, the California code is similar to the standards of student press conduct following the *Tinker* Supreme Court decision. Despite the subsequent *Hazelwood* decision in 1988, the code remains in effect.

Massachusetts became the first state since *Hazelwood* to pass a law protecting "the rights of students to freedom of expression in the public schools as long as it does not cause any disruption or disorder." The law also protects school officials from civil or criminal action for any statement made or published by students. The law, Sections 82 and 86 of Chapter 71 of the General Laws of Massachusetts, was enacted in 1988.

In the Massachusetts law, it is important to note the protection given to school officials. Some school officials in other states support editorial control of student media by a school official as protection against libel and other claims made against the publication or the school. However, legal experts, including those at the Student Press Law Center, say that if school officials do not con-

trol the editorial content of the student publication, then it is unlikely they or the school could be sued successfully for libel or other illegal content.

Since 1989, Arkansas, Colorado, Iowa and Kansas have passed laws protecting student expression similar to the ones in California and Massachusetts. First Amendment advocates in other states have attempted to get their state governments to follow suit, but so far they haven't been successful.

Some school districts have adopted policy guidelines giving First Amendment rights to students under their jurisdiction. In Dade County, Fla., the public schools have a policy that follows the *Tinker* guidelines. It prohibits three unprotected areas of speech: (1) libel, (2) obscenity and (3) expression that causes substantial disruption. Despite some challenges, the Dade officials have reaffirmed these guidelines since the 1988 *Hazelwood* decision.

The Student Press Law Center has written standard policy guidelines and model legislation. Student journalists and advisers in school districts with no student media policy guidelines may want to work with their school administrators to adopt the Student Press Law Center's guidelines for student media.

UNPROTECTED EXPRESSION: LIBEL AND OBSCENITY

Even if there had never been the *Tinker* and *Hazelwood* Supreme Court decisions, there are some things all journalists, including students, can not publish. These fall into the broad category of unprotected speech and include libel and obscenity. A third, as defined by the *Tinker* decision and pertaining to public school students, is any expression that substantially disrupts the order of the school.

Libel is printed communication—words, photographs or artwork—that exposes a person to shame, public hatred, ridicule or disgrace, damaging a person's reputation in the community or injuring the person's livelihood. For libel to occur, four conditions must exist:

- The communication was published, in that it was given to at least a third party.

- The person(s) supposedly libeled can be identified.

- Injury or damage to reputation has occurred.

How to Protect Yourself From a Potential Libel Claim

• Know your sources. Are they trustworthy?

• Don't publish information from a source who won't reveal his or her name even to you, the reporter.

• If you think the information from the source is controversial or may be doubted by others, ask the source if the information is true.

• Carefully separate fact from opinion. Don't report allegations as facts and attribute all opinion.

• Take good notes. Don't rely on memory.

• If the source has documents regarding the subject, ask to see them and then compare them to what the source said in the interview.

• Review complex and potentially troublesome stories with editors.

• Verify information with a second source (or more) for complex stories.

• If you have any doubts about the truthfulness of a statement, particularly one that may be derogatory about another person, don't publish it.

• Avoid personal "attack" stories. Deal with criticism of someone's performance as part of a story that deals with the underlying issue.

• Publish corrections and retractions if you find out after publication that something you wrote is not true.

• Once a story is published, answer all complaints politely and as soon as possible.

• The publisher (editor, writer, photographer, artist) knew the communication was erroneous and was negligent.

Provable truth is the best and only absolute defense against libel. Even if damage has occurred, if the communication is provably true, no libel would exist. Believing something is true without evidence is insufficient.

A publication, print or online, is legally responsible for any libelous communication it publishes, even in third-party letters to the editor, advertisements and quotes from sources.

Privilege is a second defense against libel. Reporters can publish fair and accurate accounts of official proceedings, such as school board meetings and court proceedings, and reports, such as court records, without being overly concerned about libel. Although accuracy is always expected, the reporter does not have to verify the accuracy in such proceedings and reports.

For example, if at a school board meeting that is open to the public a teacher is accused of falsifying credentials, the accusation can be published even if later the accusation is proved incorrect. For fairness and as a matter of good journalism ethics, the publication would be obliged to print the correction or an updated story.

A third defense against libel is the *public official, public figure* rule. If a person is designated as a public official or public figure, actual malice in publishing a story would have to be proved. The person bringing the legal action against a reporter, for example, would have to prove that the false and damaging statement was published with knowledge that the statement was false or with reckless disregard as to whether it was false or not.

Distinguishing between public and private officials and figures is an important factor in determining a defense against a libel claim. A *public official* is a person who has or appears to have a substantial responsibility for or control over the conduct of government affairs. Public school principals, superintendents and school board members are public officials. In some jurisdictions, teachers are public officials.

Public figures are those persons who voluntarily thrust themselves into the public limelight due to personal achievement or who have attempted to influence the resolution of a public controversy. A public figure is, for example, a student who voluntarily runs for student government office or a student's parent who circulates a petition to ban certain books from the school library.

It is not easy to determine the status of a person as a public figure. Likewise, it is difficult for the plaintiff (the complaining party) in a libel case to prove actual malice by the reporter.

A fourth defense against a libel suit is the *fair comment* rule. A reporter and others in journalism are allowed to express an opinion about a matter of public interest. Some examples of this are reviews of movies, television, music, plays, concerts, restaurants, athletic contests and the performance in office of elected officials. For a journalist to successfully use fair comment as a defense, there must be real public interest in the matter, and it must be an opinion, not an allegation of fact. Also, the opinion must be based on certain facts that must be stated. Satire generally is not libelous providing it is clear to the audience that it is a satire and should not be understood as serious fact.

Although no cases have been fully prosecuted in the courts in the United States, students under the age of 18 may be sued for libel. The reporter, photographer or artist may be sued, as well as the editor for approving the work. The school may or may not be held accountable, depending on state laws.

Essentially, obscenity is hardcore pornography, and it arouses sexual feelings through its explicit and graphic depiction of sexual activity. However, the courts have said that vulgarities, four-letter profanities and material that is offensive or in poor taste are not legally obscene. The Supreme Court also said that material that is not obscene for adults could be obscene for those under 18 years old, but it still must meet the 1973 standards (content must not be libelous or obscene or cause significant disruption in the school).

As defined by the Supreme Court's *Tinker* decision, the third area of unprotected speech for high school students is any material that would substantially disrupt regular school activities. The Supreme Courts said a threat or potential disruption is not a sufficient reason to censor a publication. The burden is on the school official to prove substantial disruption.

For high school journalists, the material in question should be considered within the context of the story. For example, a story about sexually transmitted diseases may need to include description and words of a sexual nature. This type of story requires explicit, clinically acceptable language that some may consider offensive or inappropriate for a teenage audience. However, these words and descriptions would not be considered obscene by the Supreme Court's standards.

Although vulgarities and profanities are not obscene, most journalists refrain from using them in their work unless they are intrinsic to the accuracy and completeness of the story. Although these words may be a part of everyday conversation, they are seldom used in published journalism.

COPYRIGHT AND STUDENT JOURNALISM

Journalists, including those who work in art and design, can look at copyright law in two ways: It protects their original work from unauthorized use by others, and it reminds them as they are creating their work that they cannot use work done by someone else without permission from the creator. Although this is simply stated, in practice it may not seem this obvious or easy to follow.

All material is automatically copyrighted once it is produced, even without a formal registration of the copyright. A copyright can be indicated in these ways: ©, *copr.* or the complete word *copyright* plus the name of the copyright holder and the year the work was first published.

Almost all creative works can be copyrighted, including newspapers, yearbooks, magazines, photographs, ads, plays, CD-ROMs and sound recordings. News or facts cannot be copyrighted, but the collection of those facts into a news story can be copyrighted.

To register a copyright in the United States, a form can be requested from Information and Publications Section LM-455, Copyright Office, Library of Congress, Washington, D.C. 20599. Or a copyright can be registered online at http://lcweb.loc.gov/copyright/. The cost to register a copyright in 2000 was $30.

No copyrighted material may be reprinted or republished in a nonprint form without the approval of the copyright holder unless it is done under the "fair use" exception granted by law. Part of a copyrighted work may be reproduced without permission under the "fair use" law if

- Know the law.
- Ask your publication's adviser for advice.

How to Protect Yourself From a Potential Obscenity Claim

Obscenity is another type of unprotected speech in the United States. Obscenity was defined by the U.S. Supreme Court in *Miller v. State of California* in 1973. To be legally obscene, material must meet all three of these criteria:

- Whether the average person applying contemporary community standards would find that the work, taken as a whole, appeals to the prurient interest
- Whether the work depicts or describes in a potentially offensive way sexual conduct as defined by state law
- Whether the work, taken as a whole, lacks serious literary, artistic, political or scientific value

- The use is for a nonprofit, educational purpose.

- It doesn't affect the potential sales market of the original work.

- It doesn't reproduce a substantial portion of the work (regardless of the length of the work).

Writers can use excerpts from books, magazines, plays, music or similar works to review the works or to use as supporting material in an opinion column, editorial or story. As a matter of ethics, the author or creator should be cited.

Work found on Internet web sites is protected by copyright laws. Art, video, photographs and music have the same copyright protection as stories, and journalists should respect the creator's ownership. Artwork and photographs shouldn't be copied from other published sources and used in yearbooks or other student media without the permission of the copyright holder.

Unless a specific contract exists between the creator of the work and an employer, and unless the creator is a paid employee, the employer owns the copyright for the work. In some circumstances, especially in a freelance or school setting, the creator gives the employer one-time use of the work but retains ownership.

PRIVACY RIGHTS AND JOURNALISTS

Journalists are sometime torn between what they see as the public's right to know and an individual's right to protect his or her privacy. This conflict isn't inherent in every news story, but when it does become a problem, there are some ethical standards and laws that guide journalists and those under scrutiny.

States have laws respecting the right of privacy for all persons. The right to be left alone is not, however, absolute. Public figures—a president, film actor, musician, superintendent of schools, school principal—have a limited right to privacy. A private person who is thrust into the spotlight because of involvement in a newsworthy event may also lose the right to privacy.

One form of invasion of privacy is intrusion into a person's solitude or into his or her private area activities. Intrusion can be the use of sound recorders, cameras and other physical news-gathering devices.

A second form of invasion of privacy is the publication of private facts about a person that would be offensive to a reasonable person and of no legitimate con-

cern of the public. Publishing private and sensational information about a person's health, sexual activity or economic condition is an example of this form of invasion.

Reporting news events that occur in public is not an invasion of privacy. Information from public records, such as birth and death certificates, police reports and judicial proceedings, may be used by reporters. However, the newsworthiness of facts about a private person should be judged in these ways:

- The social value of the information.

- How deeply the facts intrude into the person's private activities.

- The extent to which the person voluntarily assumed a position of public notice.

The passage of time may also affect the newsworthiness of a fact. If private and sensational facts about a formerly public figure who is now a private person are reported, an invasion of privacy claim may be justifiable.

The third type of invasion of privacy is the publication of information about a person that is false or places the person in a *false light* (the person would be regarded incorrectly by the public). The information must be highly offensive to a reasonable person and published with knowledge or a reckless disregard of whether the facts are false or would put the person in a false light. An example of this type of invasion of privacy would be the inclusion of such information in a photo caption that accompanies a photo of a person, thus making something untrue appear to be true.

The last type of invasion of privacy is *misappropriation*, which is the use of a person's name, likeness or endorsement without the person's consent—often to sell a product. Student journalists are encouraged to get the written consent of any person whose name or likeness appears in an ad. If the person is a minor, parental consent may be necessary, depending on state law.

ACCESS TO PUBLIC MEETINGS AND PUBLIC RECORDS

Records of official government proceedings on the local, state and federal levels are important information sources for reporters. Every state, the District of

Columbia and the federal government have *freedom of information laws*, allowing all citizens access to a vast amount of information. Individual state laws vary, and there are some restrictions on just exactly what information can be made public.

Information in all sorts of forms—paper, computer files and video- and audiotape—is accessible according to these state and federal laws. Access to these records may not be automatic and instantaneous, due to variations in the laws. In many cases, a reporter has to apply to the agency in writing to receive the information.

Unfortunately for reporters, the states and the federal government do not maintain a central location or one controlling agency for all government records. Each agency maintains its own, so a reporter must learn what agency has what kinds of information. On the local level, the location of records is fairly obvious. Minutes of a school board meeting are kept at the school board office. Records of police arrests are kept at the police department or county courthouse.

The process is more complicated on the state and federal levels. Beginning reporters must learn how the state and federal governments operate in order to submit requests for information to the correct agency.

Reporters usually have to pay for copies of these records. Some states and the federal government may waive these fees if the reporter's work will benefit the public. The reporter has to request the fee waivers.

Governments at all levels place some restrictions on the kinds of information that can be made public. These restrictions are exemptions in the freedom of information laws. Restricted information includes some medical, personnel and law enforcement files; student school records; and library circulation records. On the federal level, exemptions for national security reasons are noteworthy. Exemptions vary by state.

Reporters must learn the freedom of information laws in each state in which they work, as well as those of the federal government.

Student reporters should ask their state's attorney general's office for clarification on the use of state freedom of information laws by those under 18 years of age.

If a reporter has difficulty obtaining information despite the freedom of information laws, other legal and more direct means sometimes are available, including in-person and telephone interviews with those involved in the government proceeding.

Open meetings laws (sometimes called *sunshine laws*) are related to freedom of information laws. All states, the District of Columbia and the federal government have these laws. In general, open meetings laws require certain government agencies to open their meetings to the public. Reporters who cover government proceedings in person rely on these open meetings laws to allow them to gather information.

States and the federal government place some restrictions on public access to meetings, but a closed meeting that excludes reporters is the exception. The underlying idea is that government should operate in the sunshine (thus the term *sunshine laws*).

Some examples of *closed* or *secret meetings* (also called *executive sessions*) include personnel actions, such as hiring and firing employees; legal discussions with attorneys about impending actions; and labor union negotiations. For example, a reporter may not be allowed to be present when a teacher union negotiates with the school board for a new contract. Government agencies are usually required to announce meetings and agendas in advance, even for emergency sessions. Thus a reporter can anticipate news coverage.

Student reporters should consider school board, city council and other local government meetings as good opportunities to cover news events firsthand. The open meetings laws give them access to these proceedings. If possible, student reporters covering government groups for the first time should call officials of the groups in advance to introduce themselves and to get any agendas and other instructions available to the media. Press credentials may also be required.

WHERE TO GET LEGAL ADVICE

For legal advice, often at no cost, student journalists and advisers can turn to various local, state and national organizations. One of these groups, the Student Press Law Center (SPLC), is the only national organization serving exclusively as an advocate of student First Amendment, free expression rights.

The SPLC answers questions about the laws governing student media, ethics and concerns about publication policies. With its staff lawyers or through its legal referral network of lawyers who donate their time to students and teachers throughout the United States, the SPLC also gives legal advice on censorship and other First Amendment issues. (The address for the SPLC is included in this book's "Directory of Journalism Associations and Related Organizations.")

State civil liberties unions may be contacted for support in First Amendment controversies. Their local addresses can be found in the phone book or with the help of a librarian in smaller cities or rural areas. These state groups and their national parent group, the American Civil Liberties Union, also have sites on the Internet's World Wide Web.

Many large commercial newspapers maintain legal counsel who specialize in press law. A reporter or editor of such a paper may be contacted for help.

Colleges and universities with journalism programs often have a professor who specializes in press law. That person could be a source of help with media-related law questions and First Amendment issues.

CASES CITED IN THIS CHAPTER

Bethel School District v. Fraser, U.S. Supreme Court, 1986.

Burch v. Barker, U.S. Court of Appeals for the Ninth Circuit, 1988.

Desilets v. Clearview Regional Board of Education, New Jersey Supreme Court, 647, A.2d. 150 (NJ, 1994).

Fujishima v. Chicago Board of Education, U.S. Court of Appeals for the Seventh Circuit, 1972.

Gambino v. Fairfax County School Board, U.S. Court of Appeals for the Fourth Circuit, 1977.

Hazelwood School District v. Kuhlmeier, U.S. Supreme Court, 1988.

Lodestar v. Board of Education, U.S. District Court, Conn. 1989.

Romano v. Harrington, ED-NY, 1989.

Scoville v. Joliet Township High School District Board of Education, U.S. Court of Appeals for the Seventh District, 1970.

Tinker v. Des Moines Independent Community School District, U.S. Supreme Court, 1969.

Yeo v. Town of Lexington, U.S. Court of Appeals for the First Circuit, 1997.

EXERCISES

1. What are the Freedom of Information (FOI) laws in your state? Consult your librarian or do an Internet search. There may be a Freedom of Information Commission in your state. Your state attorney general's office may also help. The Society of Professional Journalists also maintains a database on all state FOI laws. How would you use the law to help you get information about someone arrested in your city for a drunk-driving accident or to find out all the bidders and their bids for the purchase of new school vans for your school district?

2. Has anyone in your state within the last 10 years filed a libel suit against the media? Report the specifics and the resolution of up to three instances. Consult your librarian or a lawyer or do an Internet search. Briefly discuss if your student publication could be sued for libel and what you would do to resolve the conflict.

3. Name the justices on the U.S. Supreme Court. Did any members of the present court vote on the *Hazelwood* case in 1988? If any did, how did they vote? Who selects the justices, and how long do they serve on the court?

4. As a class, discuss this question: Under what circumstances could a private person become a public figure with regard to libel laws and privacy concerns? Is the daughter of a U.S. president a public figure? Is your school's football coach a public figure? Is a person who is wounded in a robbery a public figure?

5. If a juvenile in your school is charged with a crime, can your student newspaper print the name of that student? Discuss the legal and ethical issues involved.

6. Can you reprint in your yearbook or newspaper a Jim Davis "Garfield" comic strip? Can you use the "Garfield" character as a stand-alone figure?

7. As a class project, conduct a First Amendment petition drive. Reprint the First Amendment with the heading "Ballot Initiative" on it and ask a random mix of persons in a public area, such as in front of a shopping mall, if they support the statement and would sign your petition to get it on the ballot in the next general election. Keep track of those who read it but decline to sign the petition or say they don't support it. Discuss the implications of your findings.

Careers in Media

Few high school athletes will ever play professional sports. Few high school band members will ever appear on stage at Carnegie Hall later in life. Few high school drama students will ever appear on Broadway stages. But student journalists can not only earn money for their work in high school and in college but can pursue many opportunities for careers after high school.

In addition to learning tangible skills that can be used later in life, high school journalists also develop strong skills in critical thinking, logic and organization and interviewing. According to research that appeared in a 1994 study of high school journalists entitled *Journalism Kids Do Better*, authors Jack Dvorak, Larry Lain and Tom Dickson found proof that journalism skills pay off for students. Among the study's findings: Journalism kids do better in 10 of 12 major academic areas; journalism kids write better in 17 of 20 comparisons of collegiate writing; journalism kids value high school journalism more highly than required English courses in fulfilling major language arts competencies; and finally, journalism kids are "doers" in schools. They are more involved in cocurricular and community activities.

Students who become editors and managers of their publications develop critical leadership and people skills that will definitely help them later in life. High school publications provide a strong sense of accomplishment for the individuals working on them since they are seen by a large community of people in and outside the school. With the growth of online publications, that audience continues to grow. Student journalists can win individual and staff awards for their work and can even earn college scholarships. Once in college, former high school journalists can use their portfolios of work to get paid positions on college publications even if they aren't pursuing journalism as a career.

The skills learned on high school publications will prove valuable in other ways. Desktop-publishing skills will help students produce more polished presentations for class work. Photographic skills will improve even family snapshots. Advertising skills will arm students with persuasive arguments and marketing skills. Writers will be able to research, write coherent and well-organized papers and quickly compose their thoughts. Designers will be desirable volunteers for school or community organizations in need of brochures or flyers for projects.

In addition to working for school publications, many students seize opportunities to expand their portfolios by contributing to community newspapers, teen sections and school public relations offices.

In the last few years, many professional newspapers have started teen sections and have begun training programs or internship programs for students who are interested in journalism careers (Fig. 24.1). Although few pay the student writers who become correspondents for these sections, student journalists can improve their skills and build their portfolios with contributions to these sections. The sections are published frequently, often weekly. Students can usually find time to work on both the teen sections and their own student publications if they have good organizational skills.

Fig. 24.1. Cover of *hj* magazine. The growth in newspaper teen sections offers student journalists opportunities to build their portfolios through practical experience. Working with professional editors also provides valuable contacts for future internship and work experience. *The Herald Co., Syracuse, N.Y. ©2000 The Syracuse Newspapers. All rights reserved. Reprinted with permission.*

Teen section reporting often gives students opportunities to report and photograph events of broad interest. The newspaper may even send the student reporters and photographers to professional events, giving them opportunities to write stories and use photographs in both the teen section and their own publication. Another advantage of working on community publications is they allow students to interact with professionals. Not only will students improve their journalism skills by working with professionals but they will also get the chance to ask questions about careers in media and find out the paths these professionals took to get their media jobs.

Small- or medium-size community newspapers often hire students as "stringers," particularly in sports departments. Stringers are writers or photographers who periodically contribute stories or photographs to a publication. Stringing for a newspaper during high school can result in forming relationships that could lead to paid internships during summers away from college or during holiday periods or to permanent positions after college.

Many students choose to work for more than one student publication during high school to expand their skills. Writing for both the yearbook and the newspaper, or photographing for both publications, gives students the chance to have more of their work published and to hone their skills. Or students may prefer to contribute different skills to separate publications, broadening their abilities and giving them an opportunity to see where their interests develop.

Almost all school districts have public relations offices and other publications' offices. For instance, the athletic director's office may be in charge of publishing a football program or other sports publications. The school's public relations director may publish a newsletter mailed to parents or may maintain a web site for the school district. Or each high school's principal may publish periodic information sent to parents. These publications provide opportunities for students who can often earn internship or local credit. If credit isn't possible, students can still gain published examples for their portfolios.

AFTER HIGH SCHOOL

Countless opportunities abound for working on college publications. Yearbooks, magazines, newspapers, online publications, college and department publications' offices—all will provide students with opportunities to pursue their interests in media careers. Many college publications offer paid positions on their staffs or provide a certain amount of money per article or photograph used in the publications. Working on college publications offers opportunities to cover interesting speakers, well-known entertainers, competitive sporting events and breaking news.

Majoring in journalism or media-related careers will provide students with the training they need to prepare for professional jobs. Large colleges of communications or journalism schools will enable students to choose between different areas of communications as majors. Within these majors, specific career skills are available. For instance, in some schools advertising majors can choose between tracks in creative advertising or advertising management. Advertising management jobs prepare students for careers as account managers or media buyers. Creative advertising skills will prepare students for jobs as creative directors or art directors.

Working on college publications is rarely required, even when a student is majoring in communications. Students who choose to supplement their classroom education with hands-on work on college publications will find more opportunities for summer internships and job positions after college. College publications also provide leadership training in staff management. Membership in college press associations provides opportunities for winning awards and recognition and sometimes cash prizes. These associations also host annual national conventions where students can expand their knowledge and create liaisons with professionals.

Student chapters of professional press associations create connections with professionals and offer interesting discussions of topics journalists face in the real world such as ethics and job hunting. They can also offer opportunities for internships and awards. The National Press Photographers Association offers a student competition called Student Photographer of the Year. The winner of the competition receives an internship and prizes. The William Randolph Hearst student competition offers students in journalism schools a wide range of contests that provide cash prizes and recognition for winners. The Society of Professional Journalists recognizes outstanding student chapters and college publications.

Students preparing for careers in media need good portfolios of published work to show prospective employers for internships and jobs after college. The portfolio can be compiled of work published in college publications, as well as work published during internships or other professional opportunities. Almost all media organizations offer formalized internship programs in various areas from advertising and editing to photography. Competitive internship programs have early deadlines, usually near the end of the fall semester, for students to complete the application process. College students often do two or more internships during college, some for college credit or for pay. Colleges often require students to obtain junior standing in school before completing an internship for credit. This ensures the students will have taken the basic courses in their field of study so they will be prepared for the work they will be asked to do in the internship. Starting out at smaller media organizations is a good way to get an initial internship. Many students complete a second internship at medium- to large-sized media organizations.

As newsrooms seek to diversify their staffs and do a better job of representing the voices of their diverse communities, they provide many opportunities for minority students interested in media careers. The Poynter Institute for Media Studies in St. Petersburg, Fla., offers several competitive minority programs, including one in design. Syracuse University in conjunction with the Newhouse Foundation offers a minority fellowship for graduate study in newspapers for students interested in journalism careers who haven't majored in communications in undergraduate programs. The fellowship includes a full-tuition scholarship, an internship at the Syracuse newspapers, a stipend and the possibility of a job at a Newhouse newspaper after graduation. The Dow Jones Newspaper Fund offers a summer internship program for minority students. Minority students have their own professional organizations and national conventions where recruiting is a primary concern.

Students can also obtain yearly updated internship information from professional organizations such as the Society for News Design and the National Press Photographers Association.

AFTER COLLEGE

Students who have had a good internship and have built competitive portfolios during college will find endless opportunities for entry-level jobs after college graduation. Even without an undergraduate communications degree, a competitive portfolio and internship experience will help students obtain jobs in media. With the growth of media forms, students can look in many areas of communications to find job opportunities.

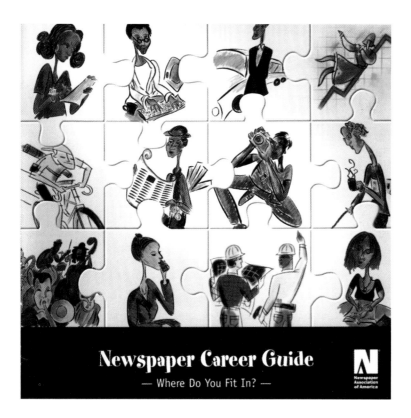

ADVERTISING

Jobs in advertising range from sales and account management to media buying. They also include creative areas such as art direction and copy writing. Media buyers, account managers and ad salespeople work with the advertising accounts. Creative jobs involve creating concepts and campaigns for advertising clients and may encompass both print and broadcast work. Many advertising agencies employ people in related agency endeavors such as public relations and logo design.

Those interested in advertising can also find opportunities within media organizations such as newspapers and magazines and within the parent companies of media operations. Many newspapers and magazines are owned by large media conglomerates, companies that could own a variety of media forms.

PUBLIC RELATIONS

Fig. 24.2. Cover of *Newspaper Career Guide*. The Newspaper Association of America publishes a yearly guide to newspaper careers. It can be obtained for free from the association. The guide contains information that helps students sort their skills and interests into career areas available in newspaper. *Reprinted with permission of the Newspaper Association of America.*

A growth area in communications, public relations departments are a part of almost every corporate agency, including health care systems, professional sports teams and major entertainment businesses. Smaller companies may hire public relations agencies, often called "full-service agencies," for their capability at handling everything from crisis communications to public relations campaigns.

Public relations agencies hire designers to create logos, brochures, flyers, pamphlets, annual reports, campaigns and any other communication such as a corporate newsletter distributed to company employees or customers. Public relations departments and agencies hire good writers capable of writing press releases that will be sent to media outlets to inform them about developments within a company. Freelance photographers are often employed to shoot photographs for annual reports or to produce photographs of personnel who have been hired or promoted. Basic photographic skills can be quite helpful to people working in public relations departments within companies. Often, the company will not be able to hire a freelance photographer to shoot pictures of every corporate event that the office may want to include in company newsletters. Digital cameras can prove quite helpful in giving public relations professionals access to photographs for various needs.

NEWSPAPERS

Of course, newspapers need good writers and editors. But newspapers hire people with many other skills. Newspapers need people with wide-ranging visual skills—those who can create interesting page layouts, coherent and useful information graphics and compelling photographs and those who can do so under deadline pressure (Fig. 24.2).

Newspapers hire good designers who can create interesting page designs on a daily basis. Presentation directors are often the managers or overseers of newspaper design departments. They work with illustrators, graphic artists and other designers.

With the growth in newspaper Web pages, entire areas of newspaper newsrooms have expanded to encompass people who keep the newspapers' web sites updated throughout the day and night. Web sites often employ their own staffs of writers, photographers, designers and producers. Individuals with multiple skills will be valuable assets to web site managers.

Many newspapers are members of larger media organizations, offering opportunities for journalists to produce work that is seen by a larger audience.

Small newspapers often hire students who have some photographic knowledge. With limited photographic personnel, small newspapers need writers who can occasionally take their own photographs. Knowledge of basic camera operation and compositional skills will prove helpful to young journalists seeking entry-level jobs.

Writers or students trained in information-gathering and researching skills can find interesting jobs in newspaper research libraries. With the growth in computer-assisted reporting, newspapers need people who can conduct information research and who can make sense of the information they find. They often work hand-in-hand with reporters as stories are developed.

WEB AND MULTIMEDIA DESIGN

The growth in the Internet has created an entirely new area of communications growth. Companies specializing in creating and maintaining web sites for corporate clients hire people with media skills. Some of these same companies are involved in other multimedia forms such as producing CD-ROMs.

Web design companies often create web sites for corporate clients and may continue to maintain the sites by periodically updating the information on them. Or they create the web sites and turn them over to the companies, often providing training to the site producers.

Web designers are also involved in creating Web advertising or can work for advertising agencies in creating Web advertising.

Multimedia designers work on projects such as books, magazines, catalogs and promotions. They can work for multimedia production companies, be employed by individual media companies or freelance for a variety of clients.

MAGAZINES

Although many magazines hire freelance writers with established reputations for feature-length articles, a staff of writers, designers and managers is in place to handle the day-to-day operations of the magazine's production. Magazines hire good editors and fact checkers, those whose responsibility it is to check the accuracy of the information in the stories before they go to print.

Magazine designers are often known as art directors. They are responsible for the design of the feature-length articles, as well as the overall design of the publication. From time to time, the publication's design might need to be updated, a process known as a redesign. Redesigns are often done by staff designers, although occasionally outside design consultants are hired to work with the magazine's staff.

PHOTOGRAPHY

In addition to photojournalism, a career practiced by photographers who work for newspapers and some magazines, photographers can study advertising or illustration photography. Advertising photographers are hired by companies who need product advertising or by advertising agencies in producing ads or campaigns for clients. The creative vision and skills of advertising photographers help them secure clients. Illustration photographers are hired primarily to illustrate feature-length articles.

Many photographers prefer documentary photography, a form of storytelling used by magazines such as *National Geographic*. Documentary photographers are concerned with in-depth photography, and their vision can take them all over the world to document conflict, people, strife and accomplishment. These photographers work primarily as freelancers and can spend many years building their reputations before being hired by top professional magazines. Many photojournalists grow interested in working on long-range projects and initiate or accept documentary projects either as freelance work or for the publications for which they photograph.

Most publications also hire picture editors, those whose responsibility it is to manage the operation of the photographic operations on their publications. Picture editors rarely shoot. They spend their time making assignments, editing film with photographers and advising the publications about how the photographs should be used. Most picture editors are former photographers who have worked their way into management positions. Beyond picture editing, newspapers hire managers for picture departments and to oversee the newspaper's visual direction. These editors are often given the titles of assistant managing editor or managing editor.

WIRE SERVICES

Wire services are agencies that provide information to various publications from across the world. Set up in bureaus in assorted locations, wire services provide stories, photographs and sometimes graphics to member publications. The Associated Press, Agence France-Presse and Reuters are among the largest of the world's wire services. Publications must subscribe to or pay for the service to utilize its information services.

Just as on a newspaper staff, the agencies hire writers, editors, photographers and managers to service each bureau and to provide coverage of events happening in their locations.

Because many publications are now owned by large media companies, these conglomerates offer their own network services of reporters, designers, photographers and artists who produce material that can be used by member publications.

BROADCASTING

In addition to hiring staffers who can write, produce, photograph, edit and anchor, radio and TV operations need designers for producing on-air graphics. Students with good design skills and knowledge of standard software packages can transfer their skills to broadcast editing equipment to produce graphics for story content and to produce story promotions graphics for use during ratings periods.

Some TV networks have their own web site staffs, as well as staffs who produce CD-ROMs for promotion of fall and special programming throughout the year. These promotions require writers, producers, photographers and editors.

FREELANCING

Freelancers can work for several publications and can be hired by different companies and organizations. Because they work for themselves, rather than for an organization, they have to be good financial managers, schedulers and promoters, or they have to hire people to do these jobs for them. They can pick and choose from among the jobs they are offered. Freelancers rely on their reputations to get work, or they hire reps to show their portfolios and help them get hired for various jobs.

Freelancers must maintain their own equipment, such as computers and cameras, and be responsible for their own transportation. They often have to plan for retirement, maintain health plans and pay taxes throughout the year.

Freelancing work for multimedia companies and Web production companies is in demand, with designers often moving from project to project, working for different companies for various periods of time.

OTHER OPPORTUNITIES

In addition to the growth in multimedia and traditional media forms, other career opportunities are abundant for people with media experience. Book publishers, most primarily located in New York City, hire copy editors and designers to work in their publishing operations.

Companies who publish catalogs need people who photograph, write copy and design the publications. Many catalogs are also now available on web sites.

Beyond the professional world, students who have journalism experience may want to use their skills in public service opportunities. Journalists can perform public service work that helps special interest groups or philanthropic causes.

Journalism skills will be even more valuable as communications tools evolve and change. Wireless communications, which will lead to new forms of delivering messages, are on the horizon. Computer technology will continue to dramatically change, as it has about every five years. Media forms will converge, and students with broad skills and knowledge will be highly competitive in the job market.

Another media buzzword, "convergence," means many traditional media forms will evolve and blend, requiring employees with wide-ranging skills in a variety of different media areas.

Regardless of the form messages take, individuals with media skills will find they are valued in a job market where information is instantaneously reported and received.

EXERCISES

1. Plan a journalism career day or week for your class. Divide the class into various groups based on media forms. Have each group contact professional organizations to obtain speakers. Each group should plan and coordinate the speaker's appearance in the class. Groups should prepare the class for the visits by providing brief biographical information about the speakers in advance. This information can be obtained from each speaker. Students should be encouraged to generate questions for each speaker. If possible, videotape the speakers for later use.

2. Look through the *Newspaper Career Guide* for ideas for careers. Make a list of your interests and strengths in journalism. How could these interests be tailored to specific media careers?

3. If your local newspaper publishes a teen section, contact that section's editor and invite the editor to come speak to your class. Find out how students from your school can get their work published or how they can become contributing editors for the section. Discuss story planning and ideas. Where do the newspaper's stories originate? How could these ideas be used by your newspaper or yearbook staff?

4. Invite a group of staff members from a local college newspaper, Web publication or yearbook to speak to the class about getting jobs on college publications. If possible, arrange a follow-up visit to the college publication's offices for a tour. If your community does not have a college, invite a group of the school's alumni now working on college publications to the school during a college vacation or break period. Ask them to bring copies of their published work to discuss with the class.

5. In groups of three to four students, plan newsletters for various community or volunteer groups such as the local zoo or the Humane Society or for your school if the school doesn't already publish a newsletter. Identify a need to be served by this publication in advance of planning it by contacting the organization about its communications needs. In each group, discuss the needed content and draw a sketch showing a possible design for the newsletter, including a nameplate. Discuss and present each newsletter in the class.

PROFESSIONAL AND STUDENT ORGANIZATIONS

American Copy Editors Society
John McIntyre, copydesk chief
Baltimore Sun
501 N. Calvert Street
Baltimore, MD 21278-0001
ph (800) 829-8000 x6160
e-mail: johnemcintyre@hotmail.com

American Society of Magazine Editors
919 3rd Avenue, 22nd Floor
New York, NY 10022
ph (212) 872-3700
fax (212) 906-0128
e-mail: asme@magazine.org

American Society of Newspaper Editors
11690B Sunrise Valley Drive
Reston, VA 20191-1409
ph (703) 453-1122
fax (703) 453-1133
e-mail: asne@asne.org

Asian American Journalists Association
1765 Sutter Street, Suite 1000
San Francisco, CA 94115
ph (415) 346-2051
fax (415) 346-6343
e-mail: national@aaja.org

Associated Collegiate Press
National Scholastic Press Association
2221 University Avenue SE, Suite 121
Minneapolis, MN 55414
ph (612) 625-8335
fax (612) 626-0720
e-mail: info@studentpress.org

Associated Press Managing Editors Association
50 Rockefeller Plaza
New York, NY 10020
ph (212) 621-1552

Association for Education in Journalism and Mass Communication
121 LeConte College
University of South Carolina
Columbia, SC 29208-0251
ph (803) 777-2005
fax (803) 777-4728
e-mail: aejmc@sc.edu

Association for Women in Communications
1244 Ritchie Hwy., Suite 6
Arnold, MD 21012-1887
ph (410) 544-7442
fax (410) 544-4640
e-mail: pat@womcom.org

Brechner Center for Freedom of Information
PO Box 118400
3208 Weimer Hall
Gainesville, FL 32611
ph (352) 392-2273
fax (352) 392-3919
e-mail: schance@jou.ufl.edu

Columbia Scholastic Press Association
2960 Broadway-CMR 5711
Columbia University
New York, NY 10027-6902
ph (212) 854-9400
fax (212) 854-9401
e-mail: cspa@columbia.edu

Dow Jones Newspaper Fund
PO Box 300
Princeton, NJ 08543-0300
ph (609) 452-2820
fax (609) 520-5804
e-mail: newsfund@wsj.dowjones.com

The Freedom Forum
  1101 Wilson Boulevard
  Arlington, VA 22209
  ph (703) 528-0800
  fax (703) 522-4831
  e-mail: news@freedomforum.org

Freedom Forum First Amendment Center
  1207 18th Avenue S
  Nashville, TN 37212
  ph (615) 321-9588
  fax (615) 321-9599
  e-mail: info@fac.org

Freedom of Information Center
  University of Missouri
  127 Neff Annex
  Columbia, MO 65211
  ph (573) 882-4856
  fax (573) 884-4963 (attn: FOI Center)
  e-mail: kathleen_edwards@ jmail.jour.
  missouri.edu

Great Lakes Interscholastic Press Association
  302 West Hall
  Bowling Green State University
  Bowling Green, OH 43403-0237
  ph (419) 372-8725
  e-mail: lglomsk@bgnet.bgsu.edu

Journalism Education Association
  103 Kedzie Hall
  Kansas State University
  Manhattan, KS 66506-1505
  ph (785) 532-5532
  fax (785) 532-5563
  e-mail: jea@spub.ksu.edu

National Association for Journalists with
Disabilities
  614 51st Street
  Oakland, CA 94609
  ph (510) 658-2193
  fax same as phone
  e-mail: najd@batnet.com

National Association of Black Journalists
  8701A Adelphi Road
  Adelphi, MD 20783-1716
  ph (301) 445-7100
  fax (301) 445-7101
  e-mail: nabj@nabj.org

National Association of Hispanic Journalists
  1193 National Press Building
  Washington, DC 20045-2100
  ph (202) 662-7145
  fax (202) 662-7144
  e-mail: nahj@nahj.org

National Association of Science Writers
  P.O. Box 294
  Greenlawn, NY 11740-0294
  ph (516) 757-5664
  fax (516) 757-0069
  e-mail: diane@nasw.org

National Federation of Press Women
  P.O. Box 5556
  Arlington, VA 22205
  ph (800) 780-2715
  fax (703) 534-5751
  e-mail: presswomen@aol.com

National Institute for Computer-Assisted
Reporting
  138 Neff Annex
  Missouri School of Journalism
  Columbia, MO 65211
  ph (573) 882-0684
  fax (573) 884-5544
  e-mail: info@nicar.org

National Lesbian and Gay Journalists
Association
  2120 L Street NW, Suite 840
  Washington, DC 20037
  ph (202) 588-9888
  fax (202) 588-1818
  e-mail: nlgja@aol.com

National Newspaper Association
1010 North Glebe Road, Suite 450
Arlington, VA 22201
ph (703) 907-7900
fax (703) 907-7901
e-mail: info@nna.org

National Press Photographers Association
3200 Croasdaile Drive, Suite 306
Durham, NC 27705
ph (800) 289-6772/(919) 383-7246
fax (919) 383-7261
e-mail: nppa@mindspring.com

Native American Journalists Association
3359 36th Avenue S
Minneapolis, MN 55406
ph (612) 729-9244
fax (612) 729-9373
e-mail: info@naja.com

Newspaper Association of America
1921 Gallows Road, Suite 600
Vienna, VA 22182-3900
ph (703) 902-1600
fax (703) 917-0636
e-mail: naainfo@naa.org

Northwest Scholastic Press Association
210 Memorial
Union East
Oregon State University
Corvallis, OR 97331-1618
ph (541) 737-5409/(888) 893-2191

Poynter Institute for Media Studies
801 Third Street S
St. Petersburg, FL 33701
ph (727) 821-9494
fax (727) 821-0583
e-mail : info@poynter.org

Quill and Scroll Society
School of Journalism and Mass
Communications
University of Iowa
Iowa City, IA 52242-1528
ph (319) 335-5795
fax (319) 335-5210
e-mail: quill-scroll@uiowa.edu

Society for News Design
129 Dyer Street
Providence, RI 02903-3904
ph (401) 276-2100
fax (401) 276-2105
e-mail: snd@snd.org

Society of Professional Journalists
16 S Jackson Street
Greencastle, IN 46135
ph (765) 653-3333
fax (765) 653-4631
e-mail: spj@spjhq.org

Student Press Law Center
1815 N Fort Myer Drive, Suite 900
Arlington, VA 22209
ph (703) 807-1904
e-mail: splc@splc.org

GLOSSARY

A

Academics section—the part of the yearbook covering classroom and learning activities both at school and outside of school

Advance story—announcement-type story for coming event

Advertising policy—a written policy that details the publication's policies concerning ad sales and use in the publications

Advocacy editorial—editorial that interprets, explains or persuades

Agate type—the smallest point size in type a publication uses; traditionally used for sports scores and classified ads

Air—white space ("fresh air") around type and illustrations

Align—instruction to bring type into straight line

Alley—see **internal margin**.

Alteration—change made in copy after type has been set

Ampersand—symbol for *and* (&)

Anchorperson—principal person in charge of newscast

Angle—point of view from which something is written

Anonymous source—source whose name is changed or omitted in story to avoid embarrassment or because the story's subject is sensitive or controversial

Aperture—the size of the opening on a camera lens

Art—illustration(s) to accompany stories or ads

Art head—specially designed headline that may break away from consistent typefaces or styles used in the rest of the publication

Ascender—stem or loop that extends above x-height of letters

Assignment book (sheet)—record of reporters' assignments kept by editor

Associated Press—cooperative wire news service owned by its member newspapers and radio and television stations. See **wire service**.

Attribution—statement fixing source of information in story

B

Backgrounder—a story or part of a story that provides information that explains events or reasons for news

Backgrounding—the process of reading and doing research in preparation for asking questions and interviewing sources for a story

Background lead—see **descriptive lead**.

Bad break—use of hyphenated line as first line of page or column. See **widow**.

Balance—in writing, refers to facts in stories being given proper emphasis, putting each fact into its proper relationship to every other fact and establishing its relative importance to the main idea or focus of the story; in design, refers to the weight of the page appearing even

Banner (streamer)—one-line head that extends across top of page

Bar—thick rule used for decoration or to reverse a line of text

Baseline—the imaginary line upon which all type letters sit

Beat (run)—reporter's specified area for regular news coverage; scoop or story obtained before other media can print or air it

Beat system—a plan to cover routinely all potential news sources in a specific area

Big on the body—typefaces with large x-height proportions to capital letters

Biweekly—publication that appears once every two weeks, as distinguished from semiweekly (twice a week)

Black letter type—commonly known as Old

English typefaces, these types are of Germanic origin and are used primarily in newspaper nameplates or flags

Bleed—illustrations and type extended beyond regular page margins to outside page edges

Bluelines—inexpensive proofing method for printing in which the inked areas will appear blue

Blur—in a photograph, indicates movement by the photographer during the exposure

Body type—type used for main text, as distinguished from headlines

Boldface (bf)—heavier, blacker version of type style

Book—in magazine terminology may mean magazine (as in "back of the book")

Book weight—the preferred stroke weight for text type. See **roman**.

Border—line or frame that surrounds element in design

Bounce flash—diffused flash softened by aiming the direction of the flash at a low, light ceiling or wall and allowing the flash to shower the subject with light

Box—printed rule around story or headline or instruction to create it

Brite—short feature, usually humorous

Broadsheet—full-size newspaper, often measuring 14 by 21 inches

Budget—list of content for newshole (nonadvertising space) of newspaper

Bullet—visual or typographic device, usually at beginning of paragraphs or before items in list

Burning in—in a traditional darkroom or through computer imaging software, adding tone to an area of a print that would print without detail

Byline–author's credit printed with the story

C

Callout—see **pull quote**.

C and lc—capital and lowercase letters

Canned material—filler material, usually not local, used as time copy

Caps (uppercase)—capital letters

Caption—lines of text describing illustrations and photographs

Caption lead-in—see **catchline**.

Catchline—headline for cutline, usually used between photo and cutline. Also known as *caption lead-in*

CD-ROM—compact disc, read-only memory

Center of interest—a photographic compositional quality that makes it obvious why a photograph was taken

Center spread—two facing pages at centerfold of publication that are made up as one page

Chronological story form—a time sequence story form

Clarification—a follow-up item published after a story has been printed that needs a clearer explanation of facts

Classified ad—advertising in the section of a publication that classifies products and services under appropriate headings

Cliché—overused, trite expression that weakens the overall content of a story

Closed-end question—question that should be avoided in interviewing because it can be answered with a yes or no response

Clubs section—the section of a yearbook in which school organizations and their activities are covered

Coaching writing—a discussion and working relationship between a writer and editor to improve the writing process

Cold type—type set by direct-impression method or on typewriter composing machines, as distinguished from hot metal from typesetting machines

Collage—art produced by pasting up a variety of elements into a single composition

Collect for output—a preflight check made by a computer software program to make sure it has all needed files for correct output

Color separation—process of separating color originals into process printing colors

Column—see **grid**.

Column inch—unit of space 1 inch deep and one column wide, used primarily in measuring advertising space

Column rule—thin line separating columns of type

Commendation editorial—an editorial that praises the actions of a person or group of people

Community feature—a feature story that relates the school to parts of the community with ties to students

Comparison lead—a lead that compares time, size or culture, for example. See **contrast lead.**

Computer-assisted reporting (CAR)—the process of using computerized database research to supplement traditional reporting methods

Condensed type—narrow or slender typeface taller than its width

Confidentiality—protecting the identity of a source because of real danger that serious physical, emotional or financial harm will come to the source if his or her name is revealed

Conflict of interest—a reason to disqualify a reporter or a photographer from covering an event in which he or she has substantial involvement

Contact sheet—photographic print made from negative or positive in contact with sensitized paper

Continuous tone—photo image that contains gradient tones from black to white without use of screening

Contrast—the range of tones from white to black with all gray tones in between in a photograph

Contrast lead—a lead that contrasts time, size or culture, for example. See **comparison lead.**

Convergence—the evolution and blending of traditional media forms with emerging technology

Copyediting—the process of tightening and improving writing, checking for accuracy and style

Copy fitting—counting words or letters to determine amount of copy that can fit into a certain area

Copyreader—person who corrects or generally improves material intended for publication

Copyright—a legal protection for original work that prohibits its use by someone other than the creator without permission

Correction—a revision published in the next edition of a publication after a story containing an error in fact has been printed

Courtesy title—the use of *Mr., Ms., Mrs.* or *Miss* along with the name of a person

Coverage—the range of pictures and verbal stories throughout a publication

Credit line—line giving source of picture or story

Crop—to eliminate areas of a photograph. See **crop marks.**

Crop mark—mark on margin of photo indicating area to appear in a publication

Cropper's L—cardboard or plastic L placed on photo to show how cropping will affect content

Cursive—type resembling handwriting but with letters not connected

Cut—in letterpress terminology, photoengraving of any kind

Cutline—see **caption.**

Cutoff rule—line across column separating text and advertising or between stories

D

Datebook—a master calendar of all school activities

Dateline—line at beginning of news story telling the point of origin (date is seldom included)

Deadline—time at which copy must be presented in order to be printed

Deck—see **secondary headline.**

Dedicated flash—a flash that coordinates with an automatic or program camera to determine correct flash settings electronically

Delete—to remove text (letter, word, sentence, paragraph or story)

Departmentalization—grouping contents of publication by subject matter

Depth of field—the range of focus from the foreground to the background present in a photograph

Depth reporting—see **in-depth reporting.**

Descender—part of letter that descends below x-height

Descriptive lead—a lead that describes the story's setting or gives details leading up to the story itself. Also known as *background lead*

Desktop publishing (DTP)—use of microcomputer; word-processing, page design and other software; an image scanner; and a laser printer to produce a publication. Theoretically, this all fits on a desktop.

Direct address lead—a lead that temporarily speaks directly to the reader by using the second-person pronouns *you* and *your*

Direct flash—flash aimed directly at the subject from camera position

Direct quote—information from sources used in quotation marks because it contains their exact words

Display ad—an ad that displays, through type and illustrations, the product or service a merchant wants to sell. See **retail ad.**

Display type—type larger than body type used in headlines and ads; usually 14 point and above

Divider page—in a yearbook, a page or spread that introduces a new section of the book to the reader

Dodging—in a traditional darkroom or through computer imaging software, holding back light from an area of a print that would have blocked detail

Dogleg—column of type extending down page, not squared off under multicolumn headline

Dominant element—the largest element with the most impact on a page; a minimum ratio of 2:1 should be maintained in size to command dominant reader interest

Double spread (truck)—two facing pages made up as single unit

Down style—newspaper form of capitalization using minimum capital letters, primarily for the first letter and only for proper nouns following the first letter

DPI—dots per inch

Drop cap—large initial letter set in larger size than rest of text; appears at the beginning of text or at junctures throughout text

Dry offset—use of raised-image plate for direct printing on offset press without water dampening

Dummy—usually scaled-down layout showing format and general appearance of publication

Duotone—two-color halftone reproduction from a one-color photograph

E

Ear—space devoted to information at either side of nameplate

Editorial—the opinion of the newspaper as it appears on the editorial page; it appears without a byline and represents the views of the editorial board

Editorial board—on a high school publication, an editorial board is usually made up of editors of the publication who meet to make decisions about the publication's editorial policies

Editorial cartoon—distinctive art combined with a few words or a sentence or two that commends, criticizes, interprets, persuades or entertains as other editorial page content

Editorializing—inserting a reporter's or editor's opinion in a news story

Editorial of criticism—see **problem-solution editorial.**

Editorial short—a brief editorial of from one word to one or a few sentences usually grouped with other editorial shorts under a standing column heading

Em—unit of space equal in size to a square of any type size, approximately a cap M

En—one-half em

Endsheet—decorative and functional heavy paper that holds pages into book binding and that can be used for design elements such as yearbook themes or contents listings; end paper

Engraving—metal or plastic plate on which image (cut) is etched

Ethics—codes of conduct that guide journalists in the pursuit of truth and the news-gathering process

Expanded type—typeface wider than standard type of the same design (extended)

External margin—margin framing the page

F

Fabrication—creating a person, a situation, a dialogue, statistics or any pivotal or incidental information and passing it as real

Facsimile transmission—scanning of graphic material to convert image into electric signals to be transmitted through the air or by land wire

Factoid—list or summary of facts

Fair comment—a defense against libel that allows a reporter and others in journalism to express an opinion about a matter of public interest

Fast lens—a lens with a large maximum f:stop, usually in the range of F:2.8 or larger; this lens allows more light to reach the film during exposure

Feature—story that goes beyond factual news reporting with emphasis on human interest appeal; element in story highlighted in lead; item in newspaper such as cartoon and syndicated material supplied by "feature" services

Feature fact—the most important fact and the one that makes the best beginning for the lead of the story

Featurize—to write a news story with characteristics of a feature story

Filler—item, usually short, used to fill holes around stories and ads

Film speed—a number on a roll of film (also called ASA) that determines its sensitivity to light

Filtering system—a restriction placed on Internet access

First Amendment—the part of the Constitution that guarantees Freedom of the Press

Fisheye lens—an extremely wide-angle lens that produces a photograph of 360 degrees

Fixed focal length lens—a camera lens with only one focal length as opposed to a zoom, which encompasses a range of focal lengths

Flag—nameplate (or logo) of newspaper. See **masthead.**

Flat—single side of a printed signature containing half the pages of the signature

Flat light—light shining directly on subjects from in front that tends to flatten out the dimensions and details of the subject

Flexographic printing—a type of offset web press that uses rubber plates and water- or solvent-based inks in a two-inking system

Flopping/flipping—in photography, printing the picture opposite from its natural orientation usually so it faces into the page gutter rather than off. This process should be avoided.

Flush left or right—instructions to set type even with margins, left or right

Folio—page number

Folio line—type on each page giving name, date and page number

Follow-up story—a story that reports on an event after it has taken place

Folo (follow) copy—instructions to set exactly as copy reads, even in error

Font—see **typeface.**

Force justify—an alignment pattern that causes type to spread across a line width and leave awkward white spaces between letters or words

Format—size, shape and general physical characteristics of publication

Four-color process—three primary colors plus black, which reproduce full-color spectrum

Fourth estate—term for journalism or journalists, attributed to Edmund Burke and first used in the House of Commons (The three original estates were nobles, clergy and commons.)

Framing—using objects in the foreground or background to provide a natural frame around subjects in photographs

Freedom of information (FOI) laws—federal and state laws that allow all citizens access to a vast array of information

Future (book)—editor's calendar of upcoming events

G

Galley—three-sided metal tray for ads and body type, used in makeup and proofing; also short for *galley proof*

Galley proof—proof of typeset matter, usually one column, before paging

Game story—a sports story in which the significant details, game summary and highlights, and player and coach analyses are presented on a timely basis

Gathering—assembling folded signatures in proper order. See **signature**.

Gaze motion—a clear and logical pattern of eye movement through a design

Glossy—photograph with glossy finish

Golden mean points—the intersections created when a composition is divided into the rule of thirds. See **rule of thirds**.

Graf/Graph—paragraph

Graphic—visual design device such as line, screen or art that enhances text and overall page appearance

Gravure—see **rotogravure**.

Grid—geometric pattern that divides page into vertical and horizontal divisions and provides underlying layout/design structure. Also known as *column*

Grounding—anchoring visual or verbal content on the page so it isn't floating

Grounds—the three dimensions present and seen through the eyes that are compressed into two dimensions in photographs

Gutter—space between columns

Gutter margin—the space between two facing pages

H

Hairline—fine line stroke of type character (modern roman) or thinnest printing rule used for borders

Halftone—printing plate made by exposing negative through screen converting image into dots

Hammer headline—a short phrase or single-word headline with an accompanying, smaller headline underneath it

Hard news—important factual information about current happenings

Hardware—equipment that makes up computer system, as distinguished from programming for system (software)

Headbands—colored strips of fabric attached to the top and bottom of book binding to finish it

Headline schedule—collection of headlines with unit counts, sizes and the like, available for publication

Highlights—the lightest areas of a photograph

Historical feature—a feature story that brings the past to life through coverage of a timely event

Historical present—use of the present tense in a headline to describe past events

Hold—instruction not to set into type or print in paper

Horizontal makeup—makeup emphasis on multicolumn headlines over stories displayed in rectangular forms

Hot type—refers to composition by linecasting machines employing molten metal

Human interest—emphasis (usually) on persons that seeks emotional identification with reader

I

Illustration—drawing, art, map or other form of nonphotographic material used in a publication

Impact—a photograph's power to stop viewers and engage them in its content

Imposition software—software that places page forms in order to be printed on single sheet to form signature with numbered pages

Indent—copy mark to set type certain distance from margin

In-depth reporting—single story, group of related stories or series resulting from detailed investigation of background information and multisource interviewing

Index—a complete, alphabetical listing of each person, club, event, advertiser and subject in the yearbook

Indirect flash—flash used off camera and aimed off subject so shadows fall outside the subject area

Indirect quote—a paraphrase of information from a source. It does not require quotation marks.

Infographic/infograph—short for *information graphic;* any chart, map, diagram, timeline, etc., used to analyze an object, event or place in the news

Informative feature story—a feature story in which readers are given information about ordinary topics that they may deal with each day, in and outside of school

Initial—large first letter of paragraph measured by multiple of number of lines that run around it (e.g., 36 point equals three lines of 12 point body). See **stickup.**

Ink jet printer—printer that sprays ink onto a printed page

Insert—material to be placed in story already written or set

Inset—picture or design carried within natural boundary of another reproduction

Internal margin—space also known as *alley* that appears between columns of type and in the gutter

Internet—system of computer networks all over the world that are linked together through telecommunications systems

Internship—working relationship in which student is hired for short period of time to perform professional responsibilities for publication or other media organization

Interpretative article—see **news analysis.**

Inverted pyramid—form of news story with most important facts first and remainder in order of descending importance; form of certain headline decks

Isolation elements—visual or verbal elements that are separated or surrounded by white space as a way to attract the reader's eye

Italic—variation of roman letters that slant to right

J

Jet printing—ink sprayed under pressure and droplets charged electrically and deflected by computer to form image

Jim dash—short, centered, thin-line rule used between headline decks and short related items

Jump—to continue story in another column or page

Jump head—headline for portion of story from another page

Justification—adjustment of spacing between words and word divisions so that all lines of type are of equal length and align on both the left and right sides

K

Kerning—adjusting the space between letter pairs, primarily in display (headline) type

Keyword—use of specific words in electronic searches that will yield necessary information

Kicker—short line above larger headline

Kill—delete (remove) paragraph, story or advertisement

L

Ladder diagram—a chart showing a page-by-page delineation of a yearbook's content

Laser printer—a printer that uses a computer language to render type and images on paper

Layout—drawing or sketch for piece of printing

lc—lowercase letters

Lead (leed)—opening elements of story, usually summary statement of fewer than 40 words

Lead (led)—thin strips of metal used for spacing between lines; space between lines of type

Leading line—real or suggested line present in a photograph that leads the viewer's eye to the center of interest. See **center of interest.**

Legibility—extent to which line of type may be read in brief exposure. Important for headings. Compare with **readability.**

Letterpress—form of printing in which ink surface of type or plate is pressed on paper

Letterspacing—placing of space between letters of word

Libel—malicious defamation of person made public by any printing, writing, sign, picture reproduction or effigy tending to provoke him or her to wrath or expose him or her to public hatred, contempt or ridicule

Ligature—two or more letters cast together (e.g., ffi)

Light meter—a meter usually built into a camera that determines correct exposure based on available light and the sensitivity of the film

Line cut—photoengraving of (line) drawing without surface screening, as in cartoon

Line gauge (pica rule)—measuring strip of wood or metal marked in pica increments, 6 to an inch

Lithography plate—plate with metal or stone surface carrying image. Water or acid separates the nonprinting (see **offset**) areas from inked surface.

Locator map—graphic map that helps readers identify the location of a place or event mentioned in a story

Logo—a visual brand or identifier

LPI—lines per inch

M

Makeup—assembling of type, cuts and/or ads on page

Market survey—a poll conducted by a publication's advertising staff to determine the buying habits of its readers

Masthead—identification statement of newspaper's vital statistics, usually on editorial page

Measure—width of line of type or page, usually expressed in picas

Microcomputer—small desktop computer that contains a tiny electronic chip capable of interpreting, storing and processing information

Modified news lead—a soft or indirect lead that can be more creative and less "formulaic" than traditional news leads

Modular—layout/design style that uses vertical and horizontal four-sided shapes, balanced informally, for all page elements. See **module.**

Module—unit or component of page set off by box rules or white space on all sides

Mondrian—page utilizing rectangles of harmonious shapes and sizes

Monopod—a single leg support used for stabilizing cameras when photographing with extremely long lenses

Montage—composite of several pictures, or parts of pictures, blended together

Morgue—newspaper reference library

Mortise—placing pictures so they overlap or touch

Mug shot—a small identifying picture usually cropped to show only the face or head and shoulders of a writer or person identified in a story

N

Nameplate—the name of the newspaper or publication as it appears on the front page or cover

Negative—negative image on transparent material used for printing positive picture

New journalism—fictional techniques applied to news events

News analysis—effort to explain "news behind the news." It approaches editorial form but does not involve deliberate value judgments. Also known as *interpretative article*

News brief—a story limited to one or a few paragraphs that may appear with other briefs

News elements—values that give news importance including timeliness or immediacy, proximity or nearness, consequence or impact, prominence, drama, oddity or unusualness, conflict, sex, emotions and instincts, and progress

Newsgroup—site on the Internet where persons with similar interests can gather electronically and enter messages about related topics

Newshole—space left for news after ads have been positioned

Newsmagazine—a publication traditionally 8.5 × 11 inches in size

Newsprint—paper made from wood pulp and used by newspapers

News summary lead—hard news lead that gets readers immediately to the main point of an article

Novelty lead—see **oddity lead.**

Novelty type—typefaces whose appearance is visually augmented or quirky. The appearance may connect to the typeface's name.

Nut graph/graf—summary paragraph located near the beginning of a story, usually identifies subject; also known as *focus graph/graf*

O

Obit—abbreviation for *obituary*

Objectivity—goal in newswriting of converting news event into precise, unbiased description

OCR—optical character recognition; process in which machine reads typewritten page and produces paper tape or other form of input

Oddity lead—a creative lead that succeeds in attracting readers because it is different, often using humor, a startling statement or an allusion. Also known as *novelty lead*

Offset—lithography; process in which image on plane-surface plate is transferred to rubber blanket roll from which impression is made on paper. See **lithography plate.**

Op-ed—opinion-editorial; refers to page opposite editorial page, usually devoted to analyses, opinion columns, reviews and special features

Open-ended question—question preferred during an interview because it elicits detailed answer and provides information for quotes

Open meeting laws (sunshine laws)—laws that require certain government agencies to open their meetings to the public

Opinion column—a column written to express the views of one writer. Opinion columns appear on editorial or opinion pages and appear under a column title.

Optical center—point about 10 percent of page height above mathematical center, fulcrum for page balance

Outline light—light coming from behind a subject in a photograph that can provide a "halo effect"

Overlay—sheet of transparent paper placed over illustration, text, headline, photo or page background, giving printer special instructions on color application, screening and similar work

Overline—headline over illustration

Overrun—copies printed in excess of distribution needs

P

Pace—the rhythm in writing created by word choice, sentence length and construction, and paragraph lengths

Packaging—an arrangement of information on a

page that may include visuals and alternative story forms accompanying a main story

Page proof—proof of entire page for checking before printing

Pagination—electronic design and eventual production of newspaper pages by newsroom editors

Panchromatic—film sensitive to all visible colors

Pantone Matching System—a patented color process allowing the selection of very specific shades and tones of color

Pasteup—composite page of proofs, artwork and the like, ready to be photographed for offset reproduction

Perfect bound—a binding method in which strips of glue are applied along a flat gutter to hold the pages together

Photo credit—photographer's byline appearing with photograph

Photo cutout—cutting a photograph into the shape of some of its content and removing the background; also known as COB, cutout background

Photoengraving—process of making printing plates by action of light on film

Photojournalist—reporter who covers news and features with camera

Photo release—form for obtaining signed approval from person appearing in commercial picture or for picture possibly not privileged as news

Phototypesetting—preparing printing surface for offset reproduction by photographing letter images on film or paper, usually electronically, at great speed

Pica—printer's unit of measure, 6 picas to 1 inch

Pica rule (pica pole)—see **line gauge**.

Pick up—instruction to printer to use material from earlier setting or issue

Picture editing—the process of selecting pictures for use in a publication

Picture package—a combination of two or three images from a single event or situation used with a caption to show different aspects of the event or situation

Picture sequence—a series of pictures of a singular subject or action

Picture story—a story told primarily through pictures with a short amount of text, full captions and a complete headline

Plagiarism—taking someone's words, art and other original work and passing it off as one's own

Plate—piece of metal or plastic carrying printing image on its surface

Point—unit of measure used principally in measuring type sizes in which 72 points equal 1 inch; printer's terminology for any punctuation mark

Point and shoot camera—camera with mostly automated functions that is simple to use and produces consistent exposures

Portrait section—a yearbook section featuring mug shots of individuals and school faculty and staff

PostScript—computer language invented by Adobe Systems

Presentation director—the designer in charge of the overall publication's design and look

Press release—stories prepared by individuals and organizations seeking publicity

Primary colors—in light: red, green and blue

Primary source—an eyewitnesses to an event or the creator of an original work—a physical or intellectual property

Print—a photograph

Printer spread—an arrangement of pages as they will be printed on a flat or signature

Prior restraint/review—reference by court of law prohibiting any future news or comment to case

Privilege—a second defense against libel that allows reporters to publish fair and accurate accounts of official proceedings, such as school board meetings and court proceedings, and reports, such as court records, without being overly concerned about libel

Problem-solution editorial—an editorial used when the publication's staff wants to call attention to a problem or wants to criticize someone's actions. Also known as *editorial of criticism*

Process colors—the four ink colors needed to reproduce color in a publication; includes cyan (process blue), magenta (process red), yellow and black

Profile/profile box—a type of feature story in which the writer captures a central focus of someone's life that others might find interesting or entertaining

Progressive margins—margins that are most narrow at the gutter and increase in size at the top, sides and bottom of the page

Proofreading—the process of checking for accuracy and necessary corrections in finished copy or pages before they are printed

Provable truth—the best and only absolute defense against libel

Public official/public figure rule—a defense against libel that allows reporters to publish stories about public officials or public figures in which actual malice would have to be proven by the persons bringing legal action against the reporters

Puffing—making reference to commercial interests in news or features

Pull quote—quote or short amount of text taken from the body of a story and reinserted, often in a contrasting way, to break large areas of text or to simply highlight it. Also known as *callout*

Put to bed—completing work of putting paper on (bed of) press for printing

Pyramid—ad arrangement on page, with wider ads at bottom and with peak of pyramid usually on the right

Q

Q and A—copy that features questions and answers in a dialogue format

Question lead—a lead that asks a question, often hypothetically

R

Rate card (schedule)—list of prices for ads of various sizes and length of run in a newspaper used as an aid by an ad salesperson

Readability—quality of type that determines ease with which it can be read in quantity; how well written something is, how easily read. Compare with **legibility.**

Reader advocate—a neutral party who investigates reader complaints and issues brief reports that will be published in a subsequent edition of the publication

Readership—measure of number of readers attracted to story or publication

Reader spreads—the natural flow of pages in a publication as viewed by a reader

Refer—cover or front page easer that refers readers to inside content

Retail ad—an ad for a specific business. See **display ad.**

Retraction—printed statement correcting error made in earlier story (in libel case can help establish absence of malice)

Reverse—photo turned wrong face up in engraving process so that left side appears as right; type that prints white with background in black

Reviews—student critiques of entertainment in which writers offer their opinions about events that have already occurred or about new releases or issues

Revise—second proof of galley in which errors made in first proof have been corrected. See **galley proof.**

Rhythm—in design, refers to the visual flow of a page

Rivers of white space—holes of white space inserted between text in poorly typeset copy

Robot—used by a search engine to locate web sites on the Internet that fit a specific criteria and are then added to the search engine site database or list. See **search engine.**

Roman—type style of book weight upright letters characterized by serifs. Compare with **italic**.

Rotogravure—intaglio printing in which ink fills minute wells in plate and is forced out under pressure

Rule of thirds—a photographic compositional framing technique in which the photographer divides the viewfinder into thirds both vertically and horizontally and places the subject along the intersection of one of the thirds

Running quote—multiple paragraphs of quoted material in succession with closing quotation marks omitted until the end of the quote

Run of the press (ROP)—color printing using whatever color the printer happens to have on the press, providing a less expensive color use

S

Saddle-stitching—a binding method in which staples are applied through the gutter of the publication

Sales call—a meeting between the publication's ad salesperson and a potential advertiser

Sans serif—type style without serifs

Scale—in design, the use of grids or columns that guide the designer in placing text and visuals

Scaling—determining new size of enlargement or reduction of original art

Scanner—input device for a computer that turns pictures and art into digitized images for editing and pagination on the computer

Scoop (beat)—important story released in advance of other media coverage

Scoreboard—a complete listing of a team's season including the opponents and outcomes of the games or competitions

Screen—pattern available on software or as an acetate transfer sheet that is used as background or is placed over type or another page element; glass plate or film with etched crosslines placed between negative and plate when making halftone; number indicating number of lines per inch in halftone (e.g., 65-line screen, 150-line screen)

Screened color—a percentage of color ranging between 10 and 100 percent used to lighten or darken the color

Script—typeface that resembles handwriting. See **cursive**.

Search engine—used on the Internet to find information electronically through key words

Secondary headline—a headline unit in a smaller type size than the main headline that provides details and amplifies the main headline for the reader. Also known as *deck*

Secondary source—a person with some knowledge of information but not from personal involvement; a published work that cites the words of others, work that has already been published in a primary source

Series reporting—stories broken into parts and presented over the course of several issues

Serif—type with small finishing strokes at the ends of main strokes of letters

Service bureau—a prepress finishing company that produces high resolution output of digital files on paper or film for printing

Set solid—body text set with leading equal to the point size of the type; can result in letters touching

Shadows—the darkest areas of a photograph

Shallow depth of field—a photographic technique that allows one area of a photograph to be in focus while other areas are not, bringing the viewer's eye to the content

Sheet-fed press—a press that prints a single sheet of paper at a time

Shopper—publication with newspaper format devoted to advertising with very little news

Sidebar—a companion story to a main story; usually provides specific information about a narrowly defined topic related to the main story and is placed in a layout adjacent to the main story

Side light—light that illuminates the subject from the side and provides good texture and form

Side-stitching—a method of binding in which staples are placed in the sides of the pages, but not in the gutter of the publication

Signature—large sheet of paper printed with (usually) 4, 8 or 16 pages on either side and folded to form one unit of a book or other publication

Single-use camera—inexpensive camera with fully automated operation that is recycled by manufacturer after development

Slug—metal spacing unit 6 points thick; metal line from linecasting machine; words to identify piece of copy (guideline)

Small cap—a letter set to the posture of an uppercase letter, but to the height of a lowercase letter

Smythe-sewing—a book-binding method in which signatures of pages are connected by a heavy thread sewn across the forms and then glued to a gauze strip

Soft news—news in which the primary importance is entertainment, although it may also inform, and is often less timely than hard news

Source—information obtained from an interview with a person

Special edition/section—a published report of from one to several pages usually reserved for late-breaking news or special kinds of content

Sports section—the section of a yearbook in which organized or individual in-school and out-of-school athletic events are covered

Spot—short commercial or public service announcement over radio or television

Spot color—the use of a single color in addition to black on a printed page

Spot news—timely, important news

Spread—two facing pages

Spread unity—elements that visually connect two facing pages

Square serif types—typefaces with wide, blocky serifs attached to the stems of letters

Stand-alone photograph—a photograph that appears with caption information, but not necessarily with a story

Standard lens—a lens in the 50 mm range that reproduces a subject exactly as seen through the camera

Standing head—head that appears consistently in publications issue to issue and identifies content such as briefs and columns

Stickup—first letter of paragraph that rises above base of first line

String book—reporter's collection of his or her printed stories

Stringer—person who works casually or freelances for publications rather than working as a paid staff member

Stripping—in offset terminology, positioning of negatives on flat prior to platemaking

Student life section—often the first main section of the yearbook following the opening section. Coverage is provided of social activities and the discussion of issues of concern to teenagers.

Style manual—a list of writing conventions including abbreviations, punctuation and word selection that guides writers and maintains consistency in writing style throughout the publication

Style sheet—definition of type styles set for various information in a publication and applied consistently to type through a computer layout and design software program

Subscription database—an information source providing data for a price

Symposium interview—a feature story in which panels of students discuss timely topics of interest to readers

Synchro-sun flash—flash used as a fill light to balance shadows cast by natural light outdoors

Syndicate—company that provides nonlocal feature material

T

Tabloid—newspaper format that is about 11 by 17 inches

Tear sheet—sample of newspaper page, proof of publication to an advertiser

Teaser—graphic that often appears above the paper's nameplate on page 1 that promotes inside stories. Usually it is made up of a headline that teases the reader and some simple art or a photo.

Teen section—special interest newspaper section targeted toward student readers, often with contributions from student reporters and photographers

Telephoto lens—a camera lens that brings content distant from the photographer into the camera's range of view

Template—a skeletal page structure stored electronically in a page layout program allowing the designer to structure the page; can include type style sheets

Ten-second editorial—brief editorial comment presented in as few as two paragraphs

Text head—short, summary headline of from two to five words dropped into natural junctures in longer stories to help break up the text

Theme—a visual or verbal unifier that creates continuity throughout a yearbook

Theme development—the development of specific pages of the yearbook in which a word or visual theme appears in some repetitive form to link the designs

Thirty (30 dash)—symbol for end of story or almost anything else in journalism, including reference to journalists' obituaries

Thumbnail—miniature rough sketch of layout

Thumbnail cut—one-half column cut

Time copy—copy that may be run at any time

Time sequence—a chronological story form

Tint block—background of color for type or picture

Tombstoning—use of similar headlines side by side

Tracking—uniform kerning in a range of text

Transition—word or phrase that ties together paragraphs and develops story continuity

Transpose (tr)—to exchange the position of two letters, words or lines

Trend sports story—a sports story in which the writer covers a highlighted trend of a team since the time of the last publication

Trim—to shorten copy considerably by deleting unnecessary words

Tripod headline—a headline combining a large word or phrase followed by a two-line headline set in type half its size; both lines of the second part equal the height of the larger, opening words

Typeface—a range of type used for all the characters in one size and weight. Also known as *font*

Type family—a range of text in weights and postures for a particular typeface

Type wrap—type that contours to the shape of a picture; also known as *type runaround*

Typo—typographical error

U

UHF—ultrahigh frequency; TV channels 14 to 83 with limited range

Unity—in design, refers to a sense of continuity in use of type and column grids throughout a publication for consistency

Universal copy desk—central desk that edits all copy

Up style—copy for heads and body type set with maximum possible capitals

V

Videotext (teletext)—text without audio capacity, displayed continuously on TV screen as full page or as "scroll" with lines of stories rolling up from bottom of page

Vignette—cut in which background screen gradually fades away

Vignette lead—an anecdotal lead that relies upon a form of the storytelling method of story development

Visual continuity—design factors that keep a section of a publication coherent and unified

Visual entry points—a series of visual devices used by readers to enter content or pages

Visual hierarchy—an organized method of displaying information on a page, allowing a reader to understand the importance of the information by the size and weight of its headline(s) and its placement on the page

Visual redundancy—weak picture editing in which two pictures provide the reader with the same content or meaning

W

Washed out—a photographic print in which no pure black areas have been produced

Web—paper on roll for rotary press

Web master—the editor of an online publication

Well—U-shaped advertising area formed by running ads up both sides of page, or headline display area formed by running legs of type on either side of the headline

White space—the area of a page not filled with content; needed for balance in page design

Wide-angle lens—a camera lens in the range of 35 mm to 24 mm that gives a wider angle of view of a subject

Widow—partly filled line at top of column of type

Wirephoto—picture received electronically from distant point, usually by telephone line

Wire service—agency that provides information to member publications from across the world

Word processing—computerized method of typing and editing

Word theme—yearbook theme or unifier that is verbal and chosen because it is tied to specific events or issues related to the school community or to teenagers in general

Wrap—to continue type from one column to the next, as in "wrap around pix"

Wrong font (wf)—type of different style or size from that specified

W's and H—the what, who, where, when, why and how information that forms the basis for all stories

X

X-height—type dimension from top to bottom without descenders and ascenders

Z

Zoom lens—a camera lens that allows a photographer to use the lens between a minimum and maximum focal length range built into the lens

Z pattern—the pattern a reader's eyes follow as they move through a page entering at the top left, moving across, diagonally down and to the right of the page

OTHER RESOURCES

For continued in-depth study of some of the topics covered in this edition, here's a list of books, videotapes and magazines. The list is just a sampling, not a comprehensive compilation, of journalism resources.

ADVERTISING

Conrad, Michael. *The 100 Best TV Commercials: And Why They Worked.* Times Books, 1999.

Sullivan, Luke. *Hey Mr. Whipple, Squeeze This: A Guide to Creating Great Ads.* New York, N.Y.: John Wiley and Sons, Inc., 1998.

ADVISING

Culpepper, Alyce. *Broward Teen News Television Production Guide and Staff Manual.* Manhattan, Kan.: Journalism Education Association, 1998.

Dvorak, Jack, et al. *Journalism Kids Do Better: What Research Tells Us about High School Journalism in the 1990s.* Bloomington, Ind.: ERIC, 1994.

Greenman, Robert. *The Adviser's Companion.* New York, N.Y.: Columbia Scholastic Press Association, 1993.

Osborn, Patricia. *School Newspaper Adviser's Survival Guide.* West Nyack, N.Y.: The Center for Applied Research in Education, 1998.

BROADCASTING/TELEVISION/VIDEO

Carroll, Victoria McCullough. *Writing News for Television.* Ames: Iowa State University Press, 1997.

Kalbfield, Brad. *Associated Press Broadcast News Handbook.* New York, N.Y.: The Associated Press, 1998.

Silvia, Tony and Nancy F. Kaplan. *Student Television in America: Channels of Change.* Ames: Iowa State University Press, 1998.

Tribute to Charles Kuralt, video, Twentieth Century Fox, 1997.

Wulfemeyer, K. Tim. *Radio-TV Newswriting: A Workbook.* Ames: Iowa State University Press, 1995.

COACHING WRITING AND EDITING

Clark, Roy Peter and Don Fry. *Coaching Writers: Editors and Reporters Working Together.* New York, N.Y.: St. Martin's Press, 1992.

Clark, Roy Peter and Don Fry, *Coaching Writers: The Human Side of Editing,* 30-minute video, St. Petersburg, Fla., 1993.

Fellow, Anthony R. and Thomas N. Clanin. *Copy Editors Handbook for Newspapers.* Englewood, Colo.: Morton Publishing Company, 1998.

Goldstein, Norm, ed., and Louis D. Boccardi. *The Associated Press Stylebook and Briefing on Media Law.* New York, N.Y.: Perseus Books, 2000.

Kessler, Lauren and Duncan McDonald. *When Words Collide: A Media Writer's Guide to Grammar and Style,* 5th edition. Belmont, Calif.: Wadsworth Publishing, 2000.

O'Conner, Patricia T. *Woe Is I: The Grammarphobe's Guide to Better English in Plain English.* New York, N.Y.: Riverhead Books, 1996.

The Oxford Dictionary and Usage Guide to the English Language. Oxford, Great Britain: Oxford University Press, 1996.

Smith, Helen F., ed. *The Official CSPA Stylebook,* 20th edition. New York, N.Y., 1996.

DESKTOP PUBLISHING

Adobe Creative Team. *Classroom in a Book* series. Berkeley, Calif.: Peachpit Press, 1999.

EDITORIAL WRITING

Fink, Conrad C. *Writing Opinion for Impact.* Ames: Iowa State University Press, 1998.

Sloan, William David, Cheryl S. Wray and C. Joanne Sloan. *Great Editorials,* 2nd edition. Northport, Ala.: Vision Press, 1997.

FEATURE WRITING

Bragg, Rick. *Somebody Told Me: The Newspaper Stories of Rick Bragg.* Tuscaloosa: University of Alabama Press, 2000.

Bugeja, Michael J. *Guide to Writing Magazine Non-fiction.* Needham Heights, Mass.: Allyn and Bacon, 1998.

Garlock, David, ed. *Pulitzer Prize Feature Stories.* Ames: Iowa State Press University Press, 1998.

Jay, Edward, Jay Friedlander and John Lee. *Feature Writing for Newspapers and Magazines: The Pursuit of Excellence,* 4th edition. Addison-Wesley Educational Publishers, Inc., 1999.

Stewart, James B. *Follow the Story: How to Write Successful Nonfiction.* New York, N.Y.: Simon and Schuster, 1998.

HIGH SCHOOL JOURNALISM

Ferguson, Donald L., Jim Patten and Bradley Wilson. *Journalism Today,* 6th edition. Lincolnwood, Ill.: National Textbook Company, 2001.

Hall, H.L., *High School Journalism,* 3rd edition. New York, N.Y.: Rosen Publishing Group, 1998.

Harkrider, Jack. *Getting Started in Journalism,* 3rd edition. Lincolnwood, Ill.: National Textbook, 1997.

Hawthorne, Bobby. *The Radical Write: A Fresh Approach to Journalistic Writing for Students.* Dallas, Texas: Taylor Publishing, 1994.

INTERNET

Harmack, Andrew and Eugene Kleppinger. *Online! A Reference Guide to Using Internet Sources.* Boston, Mass.: Bedford/St. Martin's, 2000.

Houston, Brant. *Computer-Assisted Reporting: A Practical Guide.* Boston, Mass.: St. Martin's Press, 1999.

Paul, Nora M. *Computer-Assisted Research: A Guide to Tapping Online Information,* 4th edition. Chicago, Ill.: Bonus Books, 1999.

INTERVIEWING

Barone, Jeanne Tessier and Jo Young Switzer. *Interviewing Art and Skill.* Needham Heights, Mass.: Allyn and Bacon, 1995.

Metler, Ken. *Creative Interviewing,* 3rd edition. Needham Heights, Mass.: Allyn and Bacon, 1997.

JOURNALISM HISTORY

Newton, Eric, ed. *Crusaders, Scoundrels, Journalists: The Newseum's Most Intriguing Newspeople.* Arlington, Va.: The Freedom Forum, 1999.

Stephens, Mitchell. *A History of News.* Fort Worth, Texas: Harcourt Brace College Publishers, 1998.

Ward, Hiley H. *Mainstream of American Media History*. Needham Heights, Mass.: Allyn and Bacon, 1996.

MULTICULTURAL VIEWPOINTS

Arnold, Mary, ed. *Full Palette Diversity Guide.* Iowa City: University of Iowa, 1996.

Campbell, Christopher. *Race, Myth and the News*. Thousand Oaks, Calif.: Sage Publications, 1995.

Covarrubias, Jorge. *Manual de Técnicas de Redaccion Periodistica*. New York, N.Y.: The Associated Press, 1996.

Wilson, Clint C., II and Felix Gutierrez. *Race, Multiculturalism and the Media: From Mass to Class Communication*, 2nd edition. Thousand Oaks, Calif.: Sage Publications, 1995.

NEWSPAPER DESIGN

The Best of Newspaper Design, Society of News Design. Gloucester, Mass.: Rockport Publishers, annual.

Harrower, Tim. *The Newspaper Designer's Handbook*, 4th edition. Black Lick, Ohio: McGraw-Hill, 1998.

Stovall, James Glen. *Infographics: A Journalist's Guide*. Needham Heights, Mass.: Allyn and Bacon, 1997.

PHOTOGRAPHY

National Press Photographers Association. *The Best of Photojournalism, Newspaper and Magazine Pictures of the Year*. Durham, N.C.: National Press Photographers Association, annual.

Parrish, Fred S. *Photojournalism: An Introduction*. Belmont, Calif.: Wadsworth Publishing, 2001.

PRESS LAW AND ETHICS

Keene, Martin. *Practical Photojournalism: A Professional Guide,* 2nd edition. Woburn, Mass.: Butterworth-Heinemann, 1997.

Law of the Student Press, 2nd edition. Arlington, Va.: Student Press Law Center, 1994.

Steele, Bob. *Doing Ethics in Journalism,* 30-minute video. St. Petersburg, Fla.: Poynter Institute, 1994.

REPORTING AND WRITING

The Annenberg/CPB Multimedia Collection. News Writing Video Series. South Burlington, Vt.: Annenberg, 1993.

Knight, Robert M. *The Craft of Clarity: A Journalistic Approach to Good Writing*. Ames: Iowa State University Press, 1998.

Rich, Carole. *Writing and Reporting News: A Coaching Method*. Belmont, Calif.: Wadsworth Publishing, 2000.

Scanlan, Christopher, ed. *Best Newspaper Writing*. Chicago, Ill.: Bonus Books/The Poynter Institute, annual.

SPECIALTY WRITING

Blum, Deborah and Mary Knudson, eds. *A Field Guide for Science Writers*. New York, N.Y.: Oxford University Press, 1997.

Gastel, Barbara, M.D. *Health Writer's Handbook*. Ames: Iowa State University Press, 1998.

Jungblut, Joseph A., ed. *How to Conduct a High School Poll*. Iowa City, Iowa: Quill and Scroll Society, 1997.

SPORTSWRITING

Anderson, Douglas. *Contemporary Sports Reporting,* 2nd edition. Belmont, Calif.: Wadsworth Publishing, 1993.

Fensch, Thomas. *The Sports Writing Handbook,* 2nd edition. Hillsdale, N.J.: Lawrence Erlbaum and Associates, 1995.

Mulligan, Joseph F., and Kevin T. Mulligan. *The Mulligan Guide to Sports Journalism Careers.* Lincolnwood, Ill.: VGM Career Horizons, 1999.

Index

Page references given in *italics* refer to illustrations.